The Disinherited

HENRY KAMEN

The Disinherited

Exile and the Making of Spanish Culture,
1492–1975

HARPER

An Imprint of HarperCollins*Publishers*
www.harpercollins.com

HarperCollins books may be purchased for educational,
business, or sales promotional use. For information, please
write: Special Markets Department, HarperCollins Publishers, 10 East 53rd Street, New York, NY 10022.

First published in Great Britain in 2007 by Allen Lane, an
imprint of Penguin Books.

FIRST U.S. EDITION

Library of Congress Cataloging-in-Publication Data is available upon request.

ISBN: 978-0-06-073086-4
ISBN-10: 0-06-073086-2

07 08 09 10 11 OFF/RRD 10 9 8 7 6 5 4 3 2 1

Contents

List of Illustrations

Photographic acknowledgements are given in parentheses.

1. Decree stipulating the expulsion of the Jews in 1492 (Archivo Historico Provincial, Avila)

2. Juan Luis Vives (Hulton Archive/Getty Images)

3. *Judgement in the Alhambra of Granada*, Mariano Fortuny, 1871 (Museo Dalí, Figueres/Index/The Bridgeman Art Library)

4. Miguel Servet, in an eighteenth-century print (Michael Servetus Institute (Instituto de Estudios Sijenenses 'Miguel Servet'), Villanueva de Sijena, Huesca, Aragón)

5. Title page of the first Protestant bible in Spanish, 1569 (Michael Servetus Institute (Instituto de Estudios Sijenenses 'Miguel Servet'), Villanueva de Sijena, Huesca, Aragón)

6. The expulsion from Spain of members of the Society of Jesus, 1767 (British Library Board. All rights reserved [T*.19 (6), 1473 dd.4 (3)])

7. *The Second of May*, Francisco de Goya, 1814 (Archivo Iconografico/Corbis)

8. *Odalisque*, Mariano Fortuny, 1861 (Scala archive, Florence)

9. Juan Antonio Llorente, lithograph, 1823 (Mary Evans Picture Library)

10. José María Blanco White, 1812 (National Portrait Gallery, London)

Preface

The experience of mass exile has marked almost all European nations in modern times, from Ireland in the sixteenth century and Bohemia in the seventeenth to Russia, Poland and Germany in the nineteenth. Individuals, groups and entire communities have been forced out of their homeland and obliged to take their families and their scant possessions to live, often permanently, on foreign soil. The movement of refugees has been exacerbated in our own generation by a rising tide of social conflict and confrontation that has extended through all the continents of the globe. It is not easy to categorize or classify uprooted people. All who flee from havoc are usually classified as refugees. When they are so many that they amount to a real uprooting of ethnic or religious communities, they are sometimes referred to as a diaspora.[1] The term 'exiles', as used in this book, usually refers to refugees whose experiences, being those of literate persons from a privileged social and intellectual background, are accessible to study because they left written evidence. The exile is a disinherited person, but uses his deprivation to reclaim his identity and his distinctive culture. It has been claimed recently by a writer that 'modern western culture is in large part the work of exiles, émigrés, refugees'.[2] This book addresses that issue, through the example of Spain, on the same writer's premise that exile is 'a potent, even enriching, motif of modern culture'.

The brightest prospect for an exile is the hope of being received instead of being rejected. Some western nations, notably England and the United States, have built their greatness in good measure on the practice of generously sheltering thousands of dispossessed persons.[3] The Spanish experience has been profoundly different. Spain is the only European country to have attempted to consolidate itself over the centuries not through offering shelter but through a policy of exclusion. One of the most significant, and also most neglected,[4] factors in the formation of modern Spanish culture has been the reality of exile. A historian has observed recently that 'from way back, Spain has been a country of departures'.[5] The phrase conjures up an image of thousands of Spaniards waiting patiently in the seaports for vessels to take them to unknown destinations, an image that happens to be valid not simply for the twentieth century but also for the four hundred years that preceded it. In other nations, the people arrive, in Spain they depart.

How did that situation come about, and what happened to the exiles? When this book first began to take shape, it soon became obvious that Spain was (like Russia) a special case in European civilization. In other nations, such as Bohemia, Ireland and Poland, foreign aggressors were far and away the most compelling cause of the damage brought about by expulsion and exile. In Spain it was the Spaniards who damaged themselves, time and time again. By driving out key cultural minorities and important sections of its own elite, Spain may have been reaching out to one solution but ended up by achieving another, undermining its own identity as a nation and ensuring that it would always have a defective elite culture. The phenomenon was by no means an accidental or marginal one, for the fate of exiles should rather be seen as one of the crucial characteristics of Spanish history. The matter may best be summarized by an exile, the physician Gregorio Marañón, in a lecture that he delivered in Paris in 1942. Recently arrived as a refugee in the French capital, he identified exile as one of the great determining features of his country's history.

One can say that there has been no stop in emigrations since Spain first became a state with the union of Castile and Aragon,[6] and when in 1492 the last Muslim king lost Granada. In the space of just over four centuries since then, there have been fourteen great exoduses, without mentioning innumerable expulsions. From the end of the eighteenth century above all, the Spanish frontiers, particularly those it shares with France, have been constantly deluged by émigrés. It is no exaggeration to say that very few Spanish men of state have not known this great sadness. This is tantamount to saying that the history of Spain has been a continuous civil war. That is the unfortunate truth, and in it we can find the principal cause of the ill fortunes of our country.[7]

Marañón had particularly in mind the elite exiles, of whom he was one, and above all the political figures who tend to be the first victims of internal conflict. People of ordinary condition, however, were at all times always the majority. In many European countries, the elites tend to leave because their life becomes difficult, whereas by contrast the ordinary people tend to remain because they have nowhere to go. This was never the case with Spain, where the movement of people embraced all social classes. Between 1492 and 1975, the terminal dates of the present narrative, it is possible that around three million Spaniards left their native land under political or economic pressure, without counting the very many others who formed part of a regular process of emigration. The dimensions of the exile impacted upon Spanish consciousness profoundly, and had an undeniable impact on the history of the western world, including the Americas.

In order to make up for the damage, the country had to come to terms with the influence of the absent (the exiles) in the formation of a character, a culture and an identity. This was never a successful procedure, because the exiles developed their own, often very different, perspectives. Those who returned attempted to create a modern character by appealing to alien principles, drawn from other cultures such as those of France, Germany and England (and, in the case of Hispanics in the New World, the Anglo influence of the United States). From an early period, Spaniards and Hispanics in their home countries were faced by an uncomfortable choice between what was considered indigenous and what had been brought in from outside. Continuing expulsions, moreover, produced a constant turnover of native elites, political leaders and even monarchs, making it impossible to establish continuity in the formation of an acceptable cultural tradition. In its turn, this encouraged a certain disdain for imported elite culture and reform, and a reversion to principles of traditional culture, such as the cult of *casticismo* in Spain and of *jibarismo* in Puerto Rico.

Perhaps the most astonishing aspect of Spain's exiles and expatriates, and therefore logically the central theme of this book, is that (as happened also in the case of Russia)[8] they represented a major thrust of their country's culture during five centuries. Some of the most memorable masterworks of Spanish culture, the *Christian Woman* of Juan Luis Vives, the *Bible* of Casiodoro de Reina, the treatises of Fadrique Furió Ceriol, the liturgical music of Cristóbal de Morales and Tomás de Victoria, the *Spiritual Guide* of Molinos, the *Iberia* suite of Albéniz, the *Bulls of Bordeaux* of Goya, the *Nights in the Gardens of Spain* of Falla, the canvases of Miró, Buñuel's *Chien andalou*, the *Guernica* of Picasso, Marañón's *Antonio Pérez*, Américo Castro's *Structure of Spanish History* and Rodrigo's *Aranjuez Concerto*, were produced on foreign soil and in a foreign environment, often and inevitably drawing on the memory of the motherland to give further meaning to the act of creation. When assessing the work of cultural figures across time, it would make little sense to omit the consideration that they not only produced much of their work outside their country, but that in many cases the work they created in exile was prohibited or else wilfully forgotten within their homeland. The thinker Miguel Servet, the essayist Blanco White, the explorer Malaspina, were among the many who were deliberately forgotten and had to wait between two and four centuries for recognition within Spain. This was never the fault of that convenient scapegoat of all ills, the Inquisition. In nearly all cases, the spokesmen of the prevailing culture, of whatever political colour, were those who refused to accept outside intruders. Probably no other country in Europe – except possibly Ireland – has owed so much of its real cultural achievement to figures who could not work fruitfully within its borders.

Though exiles are at the centre of this book, they are by no means its only theme. The mere fact that they left a significant gap in their society of origin had enormous consequences both for themselves and for their homeland. The notion of exile becomes real only when contrasted with its apparent opposite: the homeland. The problem is that all too often the homeland lacks any overall definition, and this book therefore looks briefly at key aspects of national culture that evoked a reaction from Spaniards who had contact with the outside world. What remain in the exile's memory are the smells and sounds of the village, the fields, the marketplace, and the taste of home-cooking, sensations without which there can be little idea of loss, and therefore no immediate sense of deprivation. During his absence, however, an exile begins to create a vision of the world he came from, and out of this imagined memory a new picture of the homeland is born. The problem in the Hispanic world was that this process had another counterpart. Those who remained behind were also concerned to give substance to their homeland, and usually came up with quite a different vision of it. In Spain this took the form of a rejection of outside culture. A persistent tradition that can still be found in the Spanish mind and has its origins in a folk memory stretching back nearly five centuries firmly rejects all that is associated with foreign civilization as tainted. It follows that all those exiles who went abroad and allowed themselves to be influenced by alien culture are also tainted and, by definition, are enemies of the Hispanic way of life.[9] It is a theme that recurs in every chapter of this book, each time with differing overtones. The division of opinion is by no means a political one, but can be found at both ends of the political spectrum.

At the same time, these pages explore not simply the question of exile but also the debates that arose in the homeland and were taken abroad wherever the exiles went. Within these debates crucial importance has to be given to the problem of identity. Who are more authentic: those who leave or those who remain? Is the United States more Irish than Ireland? Is New York more Puerto Rican than San Juan? And do the exiles carry away with them a truth of which the others are deprived? Time and again in Hispanic history the exiles have, with special arrogance, claimed for themselves a unique quality that entitles them to be regarded as the preservers of the Golden Fleece. They distorted their own vision of the world, and their views often seem convincing because they set their ideas down in print. The problem of identity is always a vexed one, more so when seen across a perspective of centuries when the problem takes on features that blur reality and produce little more than an illusion of truth. The distortion becomes all the greater when a misplaced chauvinism tries to present the exiles as non-exiles, when, for example, a restless spirit such as Miguel Servet, who divested himself of his Spanishness in his teens, is presented as a faithful son of Spain.

Compulsory exile is almost always a political phenomenon, but since this book is not about politics it expressly avoids the two major and well-studied themes of political émigrés and economic migration. Rather, it is concerned with the reasons that made exile not only an obligatory but also a desirable option both for cultural minorities as well as for writers, poets, composers and artists who felt uneasy in their own country and of their own accord opted to live in another environment. I have consequently dedicated some space to examining the background conditions that determined why Jews in 1492, Protestants in 1559, Muslims in 1609, liberals in 1813, or writers in 1936 and 1939, felt the need to leave their homes and country. It is evident that in all these cases the threat of violence was a paramount factor, and I have consequently touched briefly on the nature of that violence. The backdrop explanations (about anti-Semitism, anti-Arab feeling and anticlericalism, for example) serve to answer the question 'What made exile necessary?', since exile is seldom a voluntary choice.

My account, therefore, touches on aspects of the Spanish condition that profoundly affected the lives of the creative minority and turned exile into a way of life that persisted over centuries. But it also touches on other persons who felt the need to become 'expatriates' and 'internal exiles', who seldom suffered any obstacles over living in or returning to their country. As happened also in Russia and Ireland, some who were deeply concerned for their country felt unable to live in it, but, ironically, used their absence as a method of bringing to life the reality that eluded them in the homeland. Exile, clearly, was not always a question of expulsion, but also very often of alienation. It was an experience, an attitude, an orientation, and sometimes even a dimension of the imagination. Many exiles never left, but remained within the country. Internal exile is also a powerful dimension of deprivation. Since this is not a literary study, however, but a historical survey, my narrative does not explore a theme that many others, including for example the writer Juan Goytisolo, have examined with greater profundity.

Because my narrative could have been developed in many different directions that I have not taken, it seemed sensible to ignore some threads of the argument and pursue others in order to 'map territories of experience beyond those mapped by the literature itself'.[10] This book is not, of course, a simple survey of Spanish culture. It considers, rather, how the phenomenon of exile affected and influenced creativity *outside* the homeland over a period of five centuries. I have preferred to touch only on figures whose exile found an echo among the international public and whose names are both recognizable by the informed reader and relevant to the limits of the narrative presented here. My omissions are intentionally substantial. I have specifically left out many persons whose significance was local to Hispanic contexts rather than universal, or political rather than cultural (the political exiles from the year 1800 down to 1939, for example, are notably absent from these pages). But I have also drawn briefly into the picture other persons, even from other nations, who are relevant to the story.

Themes and controversies have been presented mainly through the perspective of exiles, and the role of non-exiles, however important and crucial for understanding the internal history of Spain, has had to be left to one side. By the same token I have been obliged to bypass many women exiles, who played an undeniably relevant part both in events and in culture, but tended to be mainly political figures (like La Pasionaria or Federica Montseny in the 1930s) or had only a local cultural role (like the accomplished Catalan writer Mercè Rodoreda). The bibliography for the period covered by the book could clearly have been immense. Though I have restricted the references given, with few exceptions I have personally consulted all the books, articles, music and works of art to which I refer. I regularly employ the word 'Hispanic' for broad contexts where the word 'Spanish' is inadequate, and where there is little risk of confusion with the limited meaning given to it within the United States today. I also use the term 'Castilian' where the context is Castile rather than the whole of Spain. Where there is no ambiguity I use the word 'America' to apply to the United States. Book titles are usually given in English, even if no translated version exists. Unless otherwise noted, all translations, from all languages and including all poems, are my own; I am responsible for renderings that may seem too free.

I am grateful to Professor Stanley G. Payne, of the University of Wisconsin-Madison, and to Professor Luce López-Baralt, of the

University of Puerto Rico, Río Piedras, for looking over a few chapters, and for valuable comments and help with references. My publisher at Penguin Books, Simon Winder, has given invaluable help and advice, ironed out wrinkles in the text, and saved me from more than a handful of errors. By way of explaining the perspectives I have adopted, it may help the reader to know that this is a book written by an expatriate who has lived all his life within cultures that have sheltered him but were not his. I have benefited from the riches of many lands and languages, but even within that richness, for which I have never ceased to be grateful, there has always persisted an inescapable feeling – which many readers will know only too well – of being somehow disinherited.

Lake Oconee, Georgia, 2006

Prelude: 1492 – A Cultural Legacy

The attempted assassination was carefully planned. In the streets of Barcelona it was a crisp, clear December in the year 1492, the seventh day of the month and bright with Mediterranean sunshine. Excited groups of people gathered in the small Plaza del Rey to welcome their king, Ferdinand of Aragon, who was in the palace of the Diputació attending a meeting about judicial matters. He had been in the city since 18 October, with his wife Queen Isabella of Castile, but was attending the court meeting alone. At the end of the session, the officials left the courtroom and began to move down the staircase. As Ferdinand descended with them, the assassin darted out from hiding and aimed a knife blow at the back of his neck. Fortunately, a gold collar chain deflected the point of the blade, which, however, plunged deep between the king's shoulder blades. Ferdinand fell to the ground, crying, 'Santa Maria! Treason, treason!' His attendants leapt on the assassin and used their weapons to stab him in three places, but Ferdinand had enough presence of mind to prevent them killing him. Half conscious, the king was lifted up and borne carefully to the royal palace.[1]

News of the murder attempt spread rapidly through the city. Queen Isabella heard of it a short while before they brought her husband back, and fainted away at the news. When she recovered, she reacted with her customary composure. Fearing that the attack on Ferdinand was part of a more serious conspiracy, she ordered that a ship be made ready in the port to sail away if necessary with her children. Since their marriage in 1469, Princess Isabella of Castile and Prince Ferdinand of Aragon had faced a long uphill struggle to consolidate their authority. By the 1470s they were effective rulers, though their respective realms,

'Castile' and 'Aragon', remained wholly independent units within a broader territory called 'Spain'. Within the realm of Aragon, the province of Catalonia together with its capital Barcelona had recently been the scene of two major rebellions, of the nobility against the king, and of the peasants against their lords. Isabella could not be sure whether the present incident was a continuation of one or other of the troubles. The king's condition turned out to be more serious than first thought. The wound was small, but the blade had penetrated to the bone and fractured it, so that surgeons had to remove the broken bit of bone. Ferdinand became feverish. Seven days after the attempt his condition deteriorated and it was feared he would die. The queen helped to attend to his needs day and night. Two weeks later, he was over the worst and gave signs of recovery. A few more weeks, and he was able to sit up and show himself to his subjects at the window.

The would-be assassin turned out to be a sixty-year-old Catalan, of the class of peasants known as 'remença', who had recently been in rebellion against landowners in Catalonia. The attempt was related explicitly to the uneasy social situation in the province, and was thankfully not part of a political conspiracy. In the first worrying moments, however, speculation related the attempt to major issues that had dominated the political scene over the preceding months. The year 1492 had been a turbulent one for Spain. In January the army of the king and queen had marched into the southern city of Granada and brought an end to seven centuries of Muslim power in the Iberian peninsula. Thousands of Muslims died in the conflict, further thousands were enslaved, and tens of thousands were driven out. There were still up to half a million practising Muslims who remained in the territories of the monarchy. Had the assassin been a disgruntled co-religionist who thought to avenge the defeat of his people in Granada? The year had also been memorable for the expulsion of tens of thousands of Jews from Spain. People in Catalonia would long remember how the vessels filled with refugees made their way in spring down the River Ebro to the sea, and from there across to Italy. Had the assassin been a vengeful Jew determined to punish Ferdinand for his very prominent part in the expulsion? It seemed less likely that he would be one of those former Jews who, several years before, had assassinated a royal official, the

Inquisitor Arbués, in the neighbouring kingdom of Aragon. The Inquisition, fortunately, was now firmly established and opposition to it was very muted. Most troubling of all, had the assassin been recruited and paid by members of the Catalan elite who had fought against the king's father and resented Ferdinand's long absences from Catalonia and his neglect of their interests? It was undoubtedly a relief when the would-be assassin, who was tortured and then barbarically executed, turned out to be only a half-mad peasant who had acted alone.

As the queen waited in the small hours by Ferdinand's bedside, she would have had occasion to pass over in her mind the tumultuous events of the year, and her own presence now in a realm which was not hers[2] and whose language she did not understand. She was never quite at home in Catalonia. As she waited, did her mind go back to one of her more impetuous decisions in April, at the military camp of Santa Fe near Granada, when she had pressured her husband to give support to an unknown Italian navigator named Columbus, who had promised to find a new way to Asia that would give Spain access to untold riches? Months had passed since he sailed from the southern coast with three small vessels, and she had heard nothing from him. When the king was well again, Isabella and Ferdinand brought to a successful conclusion, in January 1493, another significant achievement: a treaty by which the king of France returned to Catalonia the frontier counties of Roussillon and Cerdagne. It was not until March that a letter from Columbus (then in Lisbon) arrived in Barcelona for the king and queen, announcing a successful return from his voyage. And it was only in mid-April of 1493 that the navigator, proud of his achievement, was received by the rulers in the city. He was not sparing in his glowing description of the marvels he had discovered, and they in turn bestowed on him unstintingly the honours he had been promised.

When the rulers left Catalonia in November 1493 and headed back to Castile, they could look back on a series of events that were in every sense decisive for their nations. By that time, Columbus had set out again across the Atlantic on a second voyage. Hundreds of Spaniards of all professions set out with him enthusiastically. Ferdinand and Isabella, for their part, were pleased that they had achieved external peace with their great enemy, France, and internal peace with the occupation of Muslim Granada and the removal of the troublesome Jews. The nightmare of the assassination attempt faded into the background. Their realms, known by the collective name 'Spain', were poised to embark on an unprecedented and complex journey into what appeared to be a future full of promise. But there was no intention of sharing that promise with all Spaniards. A multitude of Jewish Spaniards had already been denied any part in the good times to come. Already there were advisers of the queen who were preparing to mete out the same treatment to Muslim Spaniards, who would shortly be forced to choose between converting to Christianity or leaving the country. Spain was about to become a land of perpetual leave-taking, a nation that in order to enhance its own feeling of cohesion was prepared to drive into exile hundreds of thousands of its own native sons and daughters. For another four hundred years and more, to a degree that was unique in western civilization, exile became the spectre that haunted Spain's cultural destiny.

I

The Survival of the Jew

If any infirmity can be said to be most specifically Jewish, it is melancholy, because of the sadness and fear contracted from the injuries and oppressions of exile.

Isaac Cardoso, *Excellences of the Jews* (1679)[1]

No sooner had Ferdinand and Isabella managed to secure their power as rulers of Spain, than they were absorbed by an issue that was disrupting political life in the towns of southern Castile. Members of the clergy came with complaints that Jews who had allegedly converted to Christianity were still practising their old faith in secret. It was a problem with a very long history.

Jews had been in the peninsula from at least the third century, and in medieval Spain – which came to be known in their tradition as 'Sepharad' – they constituted the single largest Jewish community in the world. Their presence created, at least in Christian minds, a stereotype of rich town-dwellers, though by the fifteenth century most lived in the small villages that were typical of the medieval countryside. There they farmed, bred sheep, kept vineyards and orchards, and usually lived peacefully with their Christian neighbours. In the towns they often occupied professions that involved daily contact with Christians: shopkeepers, grocers, dyers and weavers. Sometimes they became identified with a particular profession: in the small town of Murcia in the year 1407, for instance, there were thirty Jewish tailors. The regular contact between Spaniards of different religions, called '*convivencia*' or coexistence by historians, was typical of the medieval period. As in multicultural communities in the world of today,

5

Christians, Jews and Muslims in late medieval Spain were able to work together even while they experienced regular tensions, frequent misunderstandings and occasional acute conflicts.

The richer Jews enjoyed noble rank in their own communities and collaborated with Christian and Muslim kings in the performance of specific tasks. Jewish society, however, had its own separate life and was not integrated into the lifestyle of the two main religions. Like any other unprivileged minority they were excluded from jobs and professions exercising authority (for example, in town government or in the army), but served in a broad range of middle and lesser callings.[2] They managed, for example, to play a significant role in public life in the areas of medicine and financial administration. Many rulers (including Ferdinand) had Jewish doctors, and many (like Isabella) employed Jews as financiers. The number of Jewish tax officials, however, was always very small. Occasionally, Jews were able to play a significant cultural role as translators from Arabic, a tongue the Christians had difficulty in learning, but their overall impact on Spanish society was inevitably limited. As a small minority they could not flaunt great buildings and palaces, and the only outstanding remains of their period of splendour are the elegant but discreet synagogues they managed to construct, notably in Toledo. In the thirteenth century their community formed just under 2 per cent of Spain's population, totalling maybe some 100,000 persons. Subsequently their conditions of life worsened, and in many towns they were obliged to live in segregated areas or ghettos, known as 'aljamas'. Their numbers shrank dramatically, as intermittent persecution forced many to abandon their traditional religion.

In 1391 there was a fierce outbreak of anti-Jewish riots all over Spain, and in order to escape a worse fate most Jews accepted conversion to Christianity. It was a dramatic change. From then on, Jews were no longer a significant minority and their numbers shrank almost to vanishing point. In Barcelona, where visitors can still see the part of the city to which Jews had been restricted, the authorities in 1412 closed the ghetto (or 'Call') because there were no Jews left. By contrast, the converted 'New Christians' (they were also termed 'conversos' or 'Marranos') were now far more numerous than those Jews who had refused to change their faith. When the epoch of troubles passed, many of the converts drifted back into the practice of Judaism, and no attempt was made to discipline them for not being true Christians. In any case, what was a 'true Christian'? In late medieval Europe, there were no strict rules, nor any firm statement of belief, to define what it meant to be a Christian. The overwhelming majority of the population was ignorant of the basic elements of belief, and took part only sporadically in the rites of the Church. Converso religion, usually Christian on the outside but with many elements of Jewish practice mixed in, fitted into this ambience of undefined and uncertain Christianity. Had the problem only been one of confused religious practice, the situation of the conversos might have gone unnoticed.

The perennial issue of political rivalry, however, clouded the waters of social coexistence. In many large towns of southern Spain, such as Toledo, Seville and Cordoba, conversos were numerous enough to carry political weight, and even to control the city council. Enmities and rivalries picked on the issue of 'race' as a sticking point, and the ambiguous religious practice of the conversos sparked off a vigorous controversy. Some members of the clergy, backed up by others who were motivated by political or social rivalry, accused conversos of being 'false' Christians who aimed to gain control of the country. Disputes over the matter went on for over a generation, until in 1478 Ferdinand and Isabella set up, with the pope's help, a new judicial tribunal, the Inquisition, whose principal task was to investigate whether the conversos were indeed 'heretics', as many alleged, or 'true' Christians. The tribunal in its first years acted with unprecedented severity (usually – as we shall have occasion to comment later – through arrests and punishments, accompanied by a few executions), but failed to solve the matter adequately. Eventually the inquisitors came to the opinion that it was the continued presence of the small Jewish population that encouraged the conversos to cling to their 'heresy'. They accordingly persuaded the crown that the right step was to expel all Jews from Spain. Ferdinand and Isabella issued a decree to this effect on 31 March 1492, while they were in the city of Granada, newly conquered from the Muslims of the south of Spain. There were substantial variations in the texts sent to different parts of the country, but the basic message was the same:

We order to be expelled and do expel from all our realms and lordships both west and east all Jewish males and females, both adults and children, that dwell in the said realms and lordships.

The order gave the Jews until the end of July to leave the country, and decreed death and confiscation of goods for those who returned. The move was not unexpected, for there had been small local expulsions since at least 1480, when some towns in the south of Spain made Jews move out and live somewhere else. Anti-Jewish pressure in Spain was by no means exceptional, and fitted into a pattern common to the rest of Europe. In late medieval times, Jews had been expelled by England and by France. Towards the end of the fifteenth century other Mediterranean states such as Provence, Parma and Milan also resorted, like Spain, to expulsion. It seemed as though the history of Jews was forever involved with problems of departure. Continual social pressures had in any case turned them into 'internal exiles', victims of discrimination who had consciously adjusted their lifestyle to the often hostile society in which they lived.

The 1492 decree was not, for all that, one of strict 'expulsion', for in practice the authorities throughout Spain offered Jews a firm choice between conversion and emigration. Some Jewish communities actually received official invitations, which survive in manuscript, that 'those who become Christians will be given aid and be well treated'.[3] The decree, in principle, was not racist or anti-Semitic, since it permitted Jews to stay as long as they became Christians. The number of those who opted to change their religion was impressive indeed. 'Many remained in Spain who had not the strength to emigrate and whose hearts were not filled with God', complained a Jewish chronicler resident in Italy. Equally explicit was the account written by the Cretan Jew Elijah Capsali on the basis of evidence he had received directly from exiles. 'In those terrible days, thousands and tens of thousands of Jews converted.'[4] Their motives were comprehensible. 'Those who stayed here,' a converso woman testified at the time, 'did so in order not to lose their property.'[5] As a consequence, a relatively small number were affected by the decree. The total of Jews living in Castile in 1492 probably did not exceed 80,000,[6] and less than half left permanently. From the eastern realms

8

of the peninsula, in the provinces known jointly as the Crown of Aragon, the exiles may have been around 10,000 (out of a total Jewish population of 18,000).[7] The permanent exiles therefore did not total more than around 50,000 persons, a figure that is barely a third or a quarter of what scholars used to suggest before modern research changed the picture.

Many emigrants had to sell up and leave, others left their property in the keeping of Christian relatives. The roads were filled with carts loaded with belongings that made their way across the frontiers, mainly to Portugal, or down to the seaports. Exiles had to put up with terrible hardship: an Italian diplomat who saw them arriving in Genoa commented that 'no one could witness the sufferings of the Jews without being moved'. And it was precisely the sufferings that persuaded many to give up the attempt and return to their homeland. A rabbi reported that among those who made it to Africa, 'many could not take it any more and returned to Castile. Likewise this occurred to those who went to Portugal and the kingdom of Fez [in Morocco]. And it was the same everywhere else.'[8]

The expulsion inevitably bred many myths, among them the misapprehension that it was an attempt by the government to achieve a Spain united in religion. No such intention was ever expressed by Ferdinand and Isabella,[9] who ruled over realms where the resident Islamic population (which, for the moment, they made no move to expel) was five times greater than that of the Jews. Some of their advisers even opposed the expulsion decision. The king's own sixteenth-century biographer (who happened to be an inquisitor) states: 'many were of the opinion that the king was making a mistake'.[10] One fact was indubitable: the expulsion ended public acceptance of the Jewish religion, which disappeared for over four centuries from Spanish soil. It was the first great emigration of Spanish citizens from their native territory, and the biggest ethnic cleansing to take place up till then in any European country. But the Semitic presence remained, in the form of the tens of thousands who had decided to remake their lives within a Christian society, just as others had been doing in previous generations, preserving their lifestyle and contributing almost invisibly to the enrichment of Hispanic civilization.

The expulsions of 1492 had no negative economic consequences.

Jews, especially after 1391, had played only a small part in the country's economy, and their disappearance after 1492 had a similarly small impact.[11] In some towns there was for a time a shortage of doctors, a profession in which Jews had been prominent, but the lack was soon remedied. In many cases, the exiles left their property with converso relatives who carried on family businesses. Though their presence was immediately obliterated, however, their culture was not. The tens of thousands of conversos in the peninsula continued the traditional way of life even though there was little chance of preserving their old religion. Mass conversion, indeed, made it possible for ex-Jews to merge easily into the majority Christian community, bringing with them the old Jewish forms of speech, social behaviour, food and thought. The almost impalpable Jewish presence became a permanent feature of Hispanic culture. Religious zealots in the Christian community were aware of this, and through them the Inquisition continued to harass suspected judaizers among the conversos for generations.

Of the 50,000 or so who left the peninsula, it is likely that the majority, from central and southern Spain, went initially to Portugal and North Africa. There were very few Jews living in the east of Spain, where they had easier access to the Mediterranean coast and logically took ship from the ports of Valencia in order to make their way to Italy, some to Genoa and Livorno but the majority to Naples. There is no evidence that any went to Turkey or the Middle East, for they had no ships to transport them, and no reliable documents attest their presence there. It may have been over half a century before the first refugees reached Turkey, for they went first to other lands that were easier to reach and where their religion was tolerated. Christian travellers around the year 1550 reported meeting peninsular Jews in Egypt, in Palestine and even further east, in Goa in India, but there is little to identify them with the exiles of 1492. Asia had its own Jews, of remote and undocumented origin. Overall, it is impossible to trace the movements of the exiles.

They had known their homeland as 'Sepharad', but now they retained only a memory of it, as they wandered through the world.[12] The majority of them, with no other alternative available, made for Portugal, where they were soon absorbed into the numerically small population. Though the king of Portugal subsequently, in 1497, ordered the Jews in his realm to convert to Christianity and treated them brutally, most of the exiles remained there, converted, and became a useful and integral part of their host country. Their problems as a rejected minority did not cease, however, and they suffered periodic riots against them during the next half century. A few, particularly in 1497, took a risk and crossed over to the North African territory of Fez, where they did not receive a friendly welcome. In time, they formed part of the North African community of Jews, scattered through the various towns of that coastline. They were safe from Spanish or Portuguese interference, and developed their own complex culture while still preserving, for centuries, a few remnants of their Hispanic roots in language, customs, food and music. Shem Tov ben Jamil, a refugee from the kingdom of Navarre who finally found shelter in Fez, at the end of his life looked back on the terrible events he had experienced. 'I have decided, with a broken heart,' he declared, 'to write about' what transpired during the exile.[13] Everywhere, the refugees clung on to the memory of where they came from. One hundred years after the expulsion, the Jews who had ended up in Tunis were still called 'the community of the exile', and in the eighteenth century their insistence on their origins made them set up their own synagogue and cemetery, separate from that of the other Jews.[14]

The impact of the Sephardic diaspora (which was extended when the Jews in Naples, who by now included many émigrés from Spain, were ordered to convert or leave that territory in 1508) has, like the numbers of those expelled, usually been measured by emotional involvement. It has been traditional for Jews to lament the events of 1492 as a great disaster, a reference point for all other subsequent disasters. Chroniclers did not hesitate to present what happened as a repeat of the Babylonish captivity. The finest of them, Rabbi Elijah Capsali of Crete, a contemporary of these events, described how the Christians made the Jews suffer, 'killing them by the sword, by starvation and by plague, selling them into captivity and forcing them to convert'.[15] Historians vied with each other to magnify the numbers of the expelled. In a study written in 1992 to commemorate the five-hundredth anniversary of the expulsion, a leading Jewish scholar maintained – with a blind eye to the impossibility of the figure – that 200,000 Jews had been driven out of the peninsula.[16] No attempt was spared to depict the misery of the diaspora, and down to our day many Jews cultivate a romantic yearning for Spain as their lost homeland, and look on the scattering of 1492 as a prefiguring of the Holocaust of the twentieth century.

Not all exiles, however, were interested in conserving the role of being victims. One of the incredible characteristics of the people of Israel has been its ability to rise above the ashes of disaster. The exiles were thrown into strange lands, but they often turned defeat into success. As Rabbi Capsali prophesied, 'the exile which appears so terrible to the eye will be the cause of the growth of our salvation'. The end of Iberian Jewry represented the closing of one chapter in history, but it also ushered in an age of success for the Jews in western Europe, as those from Spain went to other parts of the continent and contributed with their knowledge and skills to the development of civilization. The expulsion in reality helped to underline the degree to which many Jews, and above all their intellectuals, had long been internal exiles in Sepharad and were able to turn to their own advantage the absence from home, which far from being a chastisement became a channel that opened out possibilities of liberation, free expression and dissidence of ideas.

The diaspora could not fail to leave its mark on the Christian nations of Europe. Jews had always lived in the strange social situation of not having a culture of their own in a society of their own. They lived within other cultures. As the British medievalist Christopher Dawson once said:

The Jews are always there, but they are never wholly there. I mean that at no time has a completely Jewish culture dominated its social environment, as Arab or Persian or Chinese cultures have done. There has been a discontinuous series of Jewish cultures, each of which has produced a rich intellectual harvest, but none of which has been an independent sociological and political whole.[17]

The Jews of Spain therefore picked up their culture and took it with them.

After Portugal, the area that received most exiles was Italy, where many princes, and the papacy itself, were happy to accept them. The favoured destination was Naples, soon to become part of the Spanish empire and with the biggest Jewish population in Italy, many of Spanish origin. In the generation after the expulsion, in effect, Italy became the big centre of Spanish Jewry, and the chief Spanish families, notably the Abravanels, settled there. Though far from home, Spanish Jews in Italy continued their intellectual production. One of the curious products of this period was the publication in Venice in 1528 of a work, *The Andalusian Wench* (*La lozana andaluza*), written by a converso cleric in Rome, Francisco Delicado, narrating the memoirs of a Spanish prostitute of converso origin, and her life in the city of the popes. One of the persistent themes of the work, which is explicitly erotic as well as amoral, is the sense of exile, a memory of the homeland from which the Jews had been driven. Delicado also published at Venice an edition of the *Celestina*, a work to which we shall return.

Venice was the city where the great figure among the first exiles, Isaac Abravanel (1437–1508), settled and wrote (in Hebrew) his chief philosophical works. Abravanel's family came originally from Spain, but he was born in and spent half his adult life in Portugal, moving in 1483 to Castile, where he became one of the chief financiers of Ferdinand and Isabella. 'I served them for eight years,' he testified later, 'I also acquired great wealth and honour.' But as a result he found little time for what chiefly concerned him, reflecting on the scriptures. 'In order to work for a non-Jewish king, I abandoned my inheritance.' When the expulsion was decreed he refused to convert (unlike his distinguished colleague, eighty-year-old Abraham Senior), and left with all his family for Naples. In recognition of his outstanding services to the crown the king allowed him to emigrate with his gold and valuables, but his remembrance years later was only of 'the bitter and hasty exile and forced conversions when we were exiled from Spain'.[18] After some uneasy years in Naples, he moved to Sicily and Corfu, then to the Adriatic coast, settling finally in Venice in 1503.

During his last years he devoted himself to messianic reflections (in a trilogy written from 1496 onwards) on the historic destiny of the persecuted Jews. In daily contact with exiled Jews, 'young and old, their spirit broken', who had fallen into an outlook of pure defeatism and were lamenting that 'the sun of justice and healing will never rise', Abravanel asserted forcefully that his people still had a God-given destiny. Even those who had 'betrayed our religion' by embracing Christianity and attaining wealth and honour among the nations would not be able to escape the same destiny, 'for God will separate them and keep them distinct and apart'.[19] His published writings, infused by a profound rejection of the violence of his time, looked forward to an eventual liberation and may have helped to nurture the messianic tendencies that had already been present among Jews before 1492 but became more pronounced among the leaders of the Sephardic dispersion.[20] He felt that the Jews' current wanderings among 'the wilderness of the peoples' would shortly come to an end with the arrival of the Messiah.[21]

For over a century, the presence of active Jewish communities in Italy gave life and hope to those who remained behind in Spain yet continued to nurture the hope of living freely once again as Jews. Very many drifted over from one peninsula to the other. Abravanel's son Yehudah, who was known to the Italians as Leone Ebreo or 'Leo the Jew', was also a distinguished writer and became physician to the Spanish viceroy of Naples.[22] He was author of a notable Renaissance work called *Dialoghi d'amore* (*Dialogues of Love*), which he may have written in Hebrew but was eventually published in Italian in 1535, some years after his death. It achieved considerable success, with subsequent translations into Spanish (1590, done by the Castilian-American writer the Inca Garcilaso de la Vega), French, Latin and Hebrew. The work fell thereafter into obscurity, and had to wait for recognition until the nineteenth century, when it was rediscovered by scholars in Germany and Spain and republished only in the 1920s.[23] He also composed in 1503 a striking *Complaint against Fate*, in Hebrew, which lamented the sorrows of the expulsion, the destruction of his family (his infant son had been left behind in the peninsula), the tears of his wife and the ashes of his hopes.[24]

The 1492 expulsion must have had a profound influence on Hispanic Jews, but it produced few writings of importance apart from the work of the Abravanels and of chroniclers. It was some time before the impact of the exile spread to other countries in Europe. The first Hispanic settlements in the Netherlands are not reported until the early sixteenth century, and the first in France a few years after that.[25] Many chronicles written at that time claimed, in an evident attempt to establish continuity with the Sephardic tradition, that Hispanic Jews arrived much earlier, but there is little evidence to support them. One undoubted fact is that by around the year 1600 the town of Amsterdam had become the most important centre of Iberian Jews in Europe. There were few of them, and the majority came from Portugal rather than from Spain, but both countries in fact shared a common heritage, for many 'Portuguese' Jews were descended from those who fled Spain in 1492, and continued to use both the Portuguese and Spanish languages in their speech. The Jewish presence in the Netherlands therefore had significant consequences for Hispanic culture, since the exiles set up the first independent Jewish presses in western Europe, where writers of Portuguese origin such as Menasseh ben Israel and Orobio de Castro published books in the Castilian language.

Meanwhile the Jews who had chosen conversion in 1492 or who returned to Spain after having at first chosen exile settled down to form a fundamental element in the Spanish way of life. Converts or their descendants had been known as 'conversos' or 'Marranos' since the fourteenth century, when widespread riots in 1391 had forced tens of thousands of Jews to become Christians. They retained many of their traditional customs regarding family life, sociability and diet, and continued by preference to mix among themselves rather than with 'Old Christians' of non-Jewish origin. In a previous age this might have been overlooked as harmless. However, the times in the 1490s were different and there were always neighbours or clergy who objected to quasi-Jewish customs as 'heresy'. The tendency of conversos to stick together (especially for marriage) also aroused social and political enmity. As a consequence, though Jews and Judaism had disappeared from Spanish soil, the phenomenon of anti-Semitism was very much alive, for conversos were perceived as crypto-Jews even though little evidence may have justified it.[26]

A factor that undoubtedly contributed to tension was their claim to have a separate identity.[27] Already a powerful minority in southern Castile by the mid-fifteenth century, they were secure of their social position and proud to be both Christian and of Jewish descent. As many of their own writers affirmed clearly, they were a *nation*. They had their own individuality, and took pride in it. The chronicler Andrés Bernáldez reported that 'they entertained the arrogant claim that there was no better people in the world than they'. The writer Alonso de Palencia reported complaints by Old Christians that the conversos acted 'as a nation apart, and nowhere would they agree to act together with the Old Christians; indeed, as though they were a people of totally opposed ideas, they openly and brazenly favoured whatever was contrary to the Old Christians.'[28] Implicit in the attitude was the claim that they were even *better* than Old Christians, because together with Christian faith they combined direct descent from the lineage (*linaje*) of Christ.

Converso separateness had a certain logic. The large number of converts after 1391 could not be easily fitted into existing social structures. In Barcelona and Valencia in the 1390s they were given their own churches, in each case a former synagogue. They also set up their own converso confraternities or church guilds. In the Crown of Aragon they called themselves proudly 'Christians of Israel'.[29] They had their own social life and intermarried among themselves. These converso attitudes were probably created by self-defensiveness rather than arrogance, but they contributed to the wall of distrust between Old and New Christians. In particular, the idea of a converso *nation*, which rooted itself irrevocably in the mind of Jewish Christians, made them appear as a separate, alien and hostile entity. This had fateful consequences. The problem continued to haunt Hispanic society for the next five centuries.

The principal instrument of anti-Semitism in Spain was the Inquisition, founded in 1478.[30] Throughout the four centuries of its existence the tribunal directed the major part of its attention to rooting out the Jewish elements in peninsular society. A persistent opinion about its activities is that it was a fearful instrument of terror that oppressed the people, restricted their liberties, censored their reading, and tortured and condemned thousands of people to death. That was the image assiduously fostered by opponents of Spain – both Catholic and Protestant – in the great imperial centuries, and repeated tirelessly thereafter by many who preferred to see the past in those terms. In reality, the impact of the Inquisition on Catholics and Protestants was much less than often imagined. The principal victims were, time and again, conversos of Jewish origin, not the population as a whole. In the later sixteenth century Spaniards of Muslim origin were also repeatedly harassed by the tribunal, which they came to hate fiercely. Over the same period, though with much less vigour, Spaniards who were neither of Jewish nor of Muslim origin were disciplined for heretical beliefs and for moral turpitude. But the brunt of persecution, in the great age of Spain, fell principally on the conversos.

Conversos had suffered the cruelty of exile long before Jews were affected. A dozen years prior to the expulsion, the simple threat of bringing in the Inquisition had precipitated the flight from Spain of thousands of conversos, who preferred the safety of absence to what they viewed as the risk of trumped-up charges and unjustified arrest. In Catalonia alone, some six hundred of them left in 1486 when the Inquisition was about to be introduced. The city of Barcelona warned King Ferdinand that it would be 'totally depopulated and ruined if the Inquisition were introduced'. However, the tribunal was eventually brought in, and the conversos continued to flee. In subsequent years there was no doubt about who constituted the chief victims of the new institution. Over 99 per cent of the people cited for prosecution by the Inquisition of Barcelona between 1488 and 1505, and nearly 92 per cent of those cited by that of Valencia between 1484 and 1530, were Christian conversos of Jewish origin. In practice, few of the people named in the documents ever came to trial; they had all fled. The total number of exiles is impossible to guess, for the process of emigration went on for years. There were tens of thousands of people of Jewish origin in Spain, and a substantial number must have decided not to risk living there any longer. The fact of flight was in no way a presumption of guilt, even though the Inquisition seems to have thought so. In reality, there is no systematic evidence that conversos as a group were secret Jews. Nor is it possible to build on this fragile evidence any picture of a converso consciousness whose principal feature was the secret practice of Judaism.

It was no surprise that converso and Jewish writers should have an abiding image of the Inquisition as a terrible and fearful institution. In the sixteenth century the exile Samuel Usque, who had a Spanish background but wrote in Portuguese, presented in his work *Consolations for the Tribulations of Israel* an image of the Inquisition as a wild beast in the form of an eagle:

a wild monster of such strange form and horrible appearance that all Europe trembles at the mere mention of its name. Its body, an amalgam of hard iron and deadly poison, has an adamant shell made of steel and covered with enormous scales. It rises in the air on a thousand wings with black and poisonous pinions, and it moves on the ground with a thousand pernicious and destructive feet. Its flight is swifter than the eagle's, but wherever it passes its shadow spreads a pall of gloom over the brightest sun. It desolates the entire countryside with its poison until it is like the Syrian deserts and sands where no plant takes root and no grass grows.[31]

Long after 1492, and generations after anyone had ever seen one in the streets of Spain, the 'Jew' continued to be an object of fear and opprobrium. People of converso origin were identified by gossip and rumour as Jews, and in some spheres suffered serious discrimination. Whenever anything went seriously wrong, in problems of daily life or in the elevated domains of politics and foreign policy, it was blamed on Jews. It became common to claim that the Dutch, at that time in rebellion against the Spanish monarchy, were Jews. Disputes based on the pre-1492 heritage continued in full vigour during the entire four centuries when there were no Jews in Spain. Rejection of the 'Jew' found notable expression in an anxiety to be free, or 'pure', of Jewish taint. The concern could be dated back to the days in the fifteenth century when conversos were powerful in political life, and public bodies that wished to discriminate against them would stipulate that candidates (for jobs, or for political office) had to have 'purity of blood' (*limpieza de sangre*), that is, be free of Jewish ancestry. The concern for 'purity', however, was – contrary to what is often affirmed – always very limited, and anti-Semitism along these lines was never officially backed, never given any support by the laws, practised in very few areas and virtually unknown in most of Spain outside Andalusia. When a move was made in 1547 by the archbishop of Toledo to impose a purity law in his cathedral, Philip II (then regent of Spain) suspended it and the royal council denounced it. In 1562 the administration of the University of Salamanca likewise rejected any idea of imposing such laws. In various crucial fields, such as among the nobility, in administration, universities and the Church, indeed in virtually all aspects of public life, people of converso origin were – with few exceptions – accepted without problems. It seemed as though Spaniards wished to forget about Jews as a problem, even while they kept up many anti-Semitic prejudices.

One of the most interesting aspects of the generations that followed the conversions of 1391 and the expulsion of 1492 was the significant part played by people of converso origin in the intellectual and religious life of Spain. The literary scholar Américo Castro was later to argue that their place on the margins of society made people of Jewish origin particularly active in intellectual life. It is incontestable that some of the best-known figures of Hispanic culture in the reign of Ferdinand and Isabella, and later in the so-called 'Golden Age' during the reign of Philip II, were of Jewish origin. They were by no means physically exiles, and appeared to be fully integrated into Spanish society. The best known of them among religious figures were the religious reformer St Teresa of Avila and the poet St John of the Cross. Diligent researchers have been able to draw up a list of many other significant names for the fifteenth to the eighteenth century, all of them occupying a central place in Hispanic culture as clergy, poets, preachers, nuns, writers and scholars.[32] Those who watched over public orthodoxy carefully ignored the phenomenon, and indeed one of the most typical consequences of the 1492 expulsion was the way in which Spaniards pretended that it had never happened. Anti-Semitism undoubtedly existed, but it was kept under covers. The violent persecution of conversos by the Inquisition came to an end around 1530, just over a generation after the expulsions. After that Spanish society tried to draw a veil over the whole affair. However, there was no way of entirely eliminating the deep-rooted hostility to Jews. Spain of the Golden Age became permeated with a subtle and corrosive anti-Semitism that turned into one of the most typical components of Hispanic culture, long after Jews ceased to play any part in peninsular life. At the same time, ironically, Jewish and converso attitudes remained deeply ingrained in Hispanic culture.

The invisible Jewish presence penetrated into Spanish folklore, literature, music and even into daily food. It was so pervasive and profound that literary scholars and historians have often run the risk of exaggerating it. The best-known example of this is the dramatic work known as the *Celestina*. This work, written as a dialogue and divided into acts, emerged in print in 1499 in Burgos with the title *The Comedy of Calisto and Melibea*. Another, slightly longer version was published in 1502 in Seville as the *Tragicomedy of Calisto and Melibea*. The plot, similar in respects to that of Shakespeare's play *Romeo and Juliet*, centres round a young nobleman, Calisto, who falls in love with a girl, Melibea, but cannot gain access to her so calls on the services of a mature lady of pleasure, Celestina, to act as go-between. Celestina carries out her mission successfully, and persuades Melibea to meet Calisto by night in her garden. The lovers also have a subsequent secret meeting, when the alarm is given and in his haste to escape Calisto falls off a ladder and dies. The despairing Melibea then kills herself by jumping off a tower. It is the old, universal story of the tragedy of young love. The real force of the drama, however, lies less in the two lovers than in the person, character and role of the worldly and experienced Celestina, truly one of the great figures of world literature. Some scholars have linked the drama with Jewish culture on the assumption that its likely author, Fernando de Rojas, was of Jewish origin and was presenting a converso vision of society in his work. Arguments in favour of this view were put forward by the Princeton professor Américo Castro, whose intuitive interpretation came to dominate Hispanic literary studies in the United States.[33] Unfortunately, no indisputable evidence has emerged that Rojas was indeed of Jewish origin. Nor does the text of *Celestina* indicate convincingly that its themes are Jewish, or that the society of that time was obsessed by the Jewish question.[34] This has not prevented scholars of literature entertaining themselves with the rich possibilities of the theme.

In the traumatic year 1492, laden with terrible consequences for the children of Israel, a boy child, Juan Luis Vives (1492–1540), was born to a converso family in the city of Valencia. His parents, who had four more children in subsequent years, brought him up as a believing Christian. They themselves, witnesses of the expulsion, retained along with their Christianity a strong affinity for their Jewish past. Juan was sent to study abroad in Paris at the age of sixteen, a year after the death of his mother in an epidemic. After his studies in Paris he moved in 1514 to various cities in the Netherlands, settling finally in Bruges, where in 1524 he married a Valencian girl of Hispano-Jewish origin. He acquired an international reputation for learning and in 1517 was appointed tutor to the teenage noble Guillaume de Croÿ, whom the new king of Spain, Charles V, had just appointed archbishop of Toledo. It was also the year when Vives first met the scholar Erasmus, destined to become one of his closest friends. In 1520, when King Henry VIII of England was the guest of Charles V at an official banquet in the Netherlands, Vives first met the king's close friend and Chancellor of England, the humanist Thomas More.

Vives was a prime example of possibly the most constant and recurring phenomenon of Hispanic culture: the exiled intellectual. He retained a lifelong affection for his homeland, though in practice he accepted that his real home was Bruges, to which 'I feel as attached as I was to my own Valencia, and the only name I can give it is "my *patria*", because [he wrote in 1526] I have been living in it fourteen years and I always come back to it as my home.'[35] In 1522 – a year after de Croÿ died in a riding accident and so deprived him of a good income as private tutor – he took the momentous decision to try to return home to Spain, but one after another a series of circumstances frustrated him. Early in the year he heard (too late to be able to profit from it) that the duke of Alba had invited him to return to Spain as tutor to his eldest son.[36] The duke and duchess of Alba were perfectly serious about the invitation. Even though they may have known of Vives' Jewish origins, they certainly harboured no anti-Semitic prejudices, and were active patrons of Teresa of Avila. Indeed, the duchess's favourite spiritual adviser, who continued in that role throughout the lives of his patrons, was yet another person of Jewish origin, the friar Luis de Granada.

Vives had barely recovered from this disappointment over the Alba invitation, when the University of Alcalá in Spain invited him to occupy the chair of Latin that had fallen vacant with the death of the humanist Nebrija. Shortly afterwards he received the news that his father, who had been arrested by the Inquisition in 1520 on charges of practising Judaism, was gravely ill. The invitation and the family news may have sufficed to draw him back to Spain, but he had serious reservations. In March 1523 he wrote to his friend Francis van Cranevelt, 'I am deeply distressed because I do not know what to decide. I hate to go back home, but to stay here is not possible. Now they [his sisters] are calling me; recently I had another letter. The expenses of the journey are intolerable; the danger terrifies me.' Two days later he wrote again, explaining that he was wandering 'from here to there, trying desperately to stick to something, still unwilling to accept the fact that yesterday's safety and stability are gone for ever'.

Finally he decided that before returning to Spain he would go to England, where he knew More and had received letters of invitation from the king himself. He went there in 1523 (returning to Bruges briefly in 1524 to get married). He took up a post at Oxford and became tutor to the daughter of Catherine of Aragon and Henry VIII, the Princess Mary (who later became queen and wife of Philip II of Spain). On one occasion the king and queen came to Oxford to listen to one of his lectures. Vives continued to have doubts about going to Spain, where 'everything is darkness and night, no less in what is happening than in what I feel'. Concern for his father and for his family, whose goods had been seized by the Inquisition, was uppermost in his mind. However, he was also worried that the lack of adequate libraries in Spain would be an obstacle: 'they tell me that I shall not find facilities for study'. He soon regretted having chosen to go to England. He was treated very well personally, but he detested both the food and the climate, which combined together to worsen his digestion and his gout. His departure five years later in 1528 (one motive for leaving was that he did not wish to give his opinion on the thorny question of the king's divorce, which shortly became the cause of the English Reformation) was none too soon. By then he had heard the worst of the news concerning his family: how his imprisoned father was eventually burnt at the stake as a heretic in 1524, and the bones of the mother he had adored were subsequently disinterred and burnt.[37] Not long before, he had commented of his mother, 'my memory of her is the most sacred of memories, and whenever I think of her I embrace and kiss her in spirit'. After these terrible events, Vives remained a permanent exile from Spain, though references to Valencia recur throughout his writings. His marriage, his friendships and his humanist contacts convinced him in the end that his real homeland was Bruges.

Though there were never any doubts about Vives' Catholic faith, his culture continued to retain traces of its Hispanic and Jewish origins. His wife, Margarida Valldaura – to whom he was happily married for the sixteen years up to his untimely death from gout in 1540 – was of converso origin, and his chief Spanish contacts – the humanist Juan de Vergara in Valladolid, the theologian Pedro Maluenda in Louvain – were also conversos by origin. Vives continued to be remembered in Spain as a scholar of Renaissance humanism, and some of his Latin works were published there, but no word was ever uttered about his Jewish origins, though those in authority must have known of them. His standing, of course, was as a European scholar, not a Spaniard, for he moved outside the narrow intellectual world of the peninsula. His best-known scholarly works were fundamental essays on education (*De Disciplinis*, 1531) and on rhetoric. His *Instruction of a Christian Woman*, written in 1523 and dedicated to Henry VIII's wife Catherine of Aragon, but meant as a guide for the upbringing of the Princess Mary, was widely appreciated. Translated into English (1529) and six other languages, it was his only work to be rendered into Castilian during his lifetime. Published first in Valencia in 1528, it was brought out in an improved translation the year after at Alcalá. The first section of the book dealt with unmarried girls, the second with married women, and the third with widows. A certain austerity of temperament can be noted in his view that marriage was meant 'not so much for the procreation of children as for the good relation and understanding that a man and woman need to have', an opinion that reduced the sexual element to a secondary plane. The study that achieved most practical success was his pioneering *On the Relief of the Poor* (1526), which he began in Oxford and published in Bruges. While approving the traditional Christian view that the poor have a right to succour, he opposed public begging and called for the establishment of hospitals to take the indigent off the streets. Many towns in north Germany and the Netherlands were at that time looking for new ways to care for the homeless poor, and Vives' tract became a seminal document they consulted, with translations over the next five years into French, Spanish and Italian.[38]

The silence over his family background was a sign that Spaniards wished to conceal a problem. Indeed, his Jewish origins were hidden so effectively that scholars only learnt about them in the twentieth century. For his part Vives lost hope of ever achieving recognition in his homeland. Shortly before his death he stated that 'Spaniards are indifferent to study. I shall be read there by few, and understood by even fewer.'[39] His words were only too true. The *Christian Woman* featured in few libraries in Spain. His small handbook of *Latin Exercises* (*Exercitatio linguae latinae*) was usually published without even his name on the cover. He was better known among the European educated classes, and became the only best-selling Spanish author of his time in Europe, where by the seventeenth century publishers had issued forty-nine editions of the *Linguae latinae* and thirty-two of the *Christian Woman*. In Spain, by contrast, he had to wait two centuries before a fitting edition of his works was published (in Latin, edited by the Valencian scholar Mayans i Ciscar in 1782–90). England and the Netherlands were the only countries to give due credit to his ideas and philosophy.

Few writers of that time were more conscious than Vives of what it was to be an exile. In his firm decision that Bruges was his real abode, he drew a contrast between the suffering that emanated from his original home, and the repose in what otherwise seemed to be a place of exile. People, he wrote, prefer to live:

in a place where life passes quietly and peacefully, either because of its customs and government, or because of the amiable sweetness of the character of its inhabitants. Such a place they regard as their homeland, there where justice, peace, and concord are revered. And they regard as the place of their exile the place where one citizen harasses another or a newcomer; where one curious or trouble-making neighbour annoys another; where one's spirit is disturbed by a relative, a friend, a slight acquaintance, or an utter stranger, and one is torn from his repose. It is not only impossible to endure this; to see it is so revolting that *many prefer to abandon their houses and their homeland*, which have also been those of their forefathers, and to go away to distant lands.[40]

On this view, and clearly in Vives' own memory of his childhood, the real place of exile was his native Spain. However much he may have preserved the desire to return once more to his roots, he knew that by all his criteria he was no longer a part of Spain but belonged outside it.

Though Hispanic Jews no longer lived in Sepharad, many continued to feel it was their home. The early exiles never ceased to lament their absence from their native land, and took with them some of the cultural heritage of language, music, food and clothing, but these elements tended to be specifically Jewish rather than 'Hispanic'. They had lived as Jews above all, and it was the culture of their faith that endured. The principal language they had spoken was Castilian, which consequently became an important element in books they published outside Spain, as well as in everyday social discourse. Exiles and their descendants continued to speak Castilian in many communities in Italy and the Middle East. A Spanish traveller in Salonika in 1600 reported that Jews he met there spoke a language as fine as that spoken in Toledo. At the same time the rabbis who ministered to the exiles tried to close the gates on the past by consigning Sepharad to oblivion. The country was treated by them officially as accursed, 'a land of idolatry', and Jews were discouraged from going back to it.

Despite the prohibitions, many continued to feel a profound kinship with the land that had rejected them, and held it their chief pride to have come from Spain. As with the hundreds of thousands who would be driven from the peninsula over the next four and a half centuries, deprivation compelled them to redefine their attitude to their origins. It was not merely a question of looking backwards. In a sense, the land they had lost was also the promised land of the future. In a telling phrase, some of the chronicles refer to 'Jerusalem which is in Sepharad', meaning that Jerusalem was the real home and Spain simply a manifestation of that home. Spain, or at least an imagined Spain, continued to be a focus of attention. At the same time that their rabbis forbade them to return, therefore, some Jews made an effort to do so.[41] A feeling for Sepharad permeated the memory of exiles and helped to stimulate developments in thought and literature. Jews and conversos living outside Spain felt that they were different from others, and different even from other Jews, precisely because they were from Sepharad. The cultivation of specific Hispanic cultural habits, which meant combining features of both Spain and Portugal, became a distinguishing feature of the exile communities.[42] Peninsular Jews came to play a part in the European intellectual world. Amsterdam, for example, was home to the young philosopher Spinoza, whose family had come from Sepharad.

From time to time in subsequent generations there were exiles who returned home. Among them was Antonio Enríquez Gómez, born in 1600 in the town of Cuenca in central Castile. His parents were Portuguese who had been tried by the Inquisition for Judaism. Brought up as a Christian, he worked as a trader in Madrid and wrote drama in his spare time. Drawn towards his Jewish origins, he decided to emigrate in 1635 and went to live in France, first in Bordeaux and then in Rouen, where he became a practising Jew. In the 1640s he published in Rouen a number of poetical works, among them one that sharply attacked the Inquisition. However, he felt deeply frustrated by the lack of a public for the Castilian language in which he wrote, and finally returned to Spain in 1650, and lived and wrote for thirteen years in Seville under the pseudonym Fernando de Zárate. While in Seville he had the unusual opportunity to see himself, in his identity as the refugee Enríquez Gómez, burned in effigy (the form of punishment reserved by the Holy Office for absent heretics) in an *auto de fe* there in April 1660. The inquisitors eventually caught up with him in his new identity. He was arrested in September 1661, but before he could be brought to trial he died of a heart attack in the cells in March 1663. In July that year he was once again condemned in effigy in an *auto*.[43] Another returnee of that period was Cristóbal Méndez, who lived in Amsterdam as a full member of the Jewish community throughout the 1650s, after a peripatetic life as a merchant in other communities in Venice, Livorno, Bordeaux and Bayonne. In 1660 he returned to live in Seville and Madrid, unable to resist the pull of his ancestral roots, and very soon fell into the hands of the Inquisition.[44] His trial lasted three years, until 1665, when he was sentenced to life imprisonment but released after three years. Apart from a mention of his name in 1671, he disappears thereafter from the record.

Long after the expulsion, the Hispanic Jews continued to make a significant contribution to western culture. Indeed, of all the groups of émigrés who left the peninsula in the subsequent four hundred years, the Jews were the only ones to make any substantial impact on the philosophical ideas of the world outside. The fact gives them a unique importance in Hispanic history. One of the interesting aspects was the dissemination of the philosophical tradition known as the Kabbalah,[45] which had a long and significant role in European thought. The Kabbalah was a mystical approach to religion that had been influential among learned Jewish circles in medieval Spain, based in part on the thirteenth-century biblical commentary called the Zohar. It was a form of thought, contemplation and belief that could only be transmitted from teacher to pupil, and by its nature was not accessible to the general body of believers. When the Jewish teachers were expelled in 1492, they took their lore with them, and Hispanic kabbalism, which had already become known in parts of the Jewish world, established itself in some areas as the dominant form of mystical thinking, notably among the Jewish community in the small town of Safed in Palestine. As a consequence of the expulsion, indeed, kabbalism ceased to be the preserve of a select group of erudite teachers, and entered into the mainstream of popular Jewish practice in select communities in the eastern Mediterranean. Some of the exiled kabbalists applied their thinking to the circumstances of the expulsion, and directed their ideas towards apocalyptic and messianic expectations. One of them was Abraham ben Eliezer ha-Levi (died c.1528), an exile who spent his last years in Jerusalem. Like other exiles, notably Abravanel, he fixed his hopes on a speedy coming of the Messiah. The messianic movement, greatly fuelled by the expulsions that had taken place in western Europe, lived under the awesome feeling that the world had reached the end of time, and that the people of Israel would soon achieve the awaited salvation.[46]

Exiled Jews also helped to spread the printing press, which had only just begun to function in Spain. When they published in exile, their first books tended to be in the typeface of the Spanish language. The first Hebrew book printed in Constantinople bears the date 1494, and was issued by members of a Jewish family from Toledo[47] who left Sepharad before the expulsion. The printers subsequently, in 1505, brought out a Bible (that is, the Old Testament), with a preface which stated that:

From the day that God had confounded the whole earth through bitter exile, the exile from Sepharad, all good things abandoned us. The survivors were compelled to wander from country to country. Suddenly God provided a remedy. A few survivors found their way to Constantinople, among them two brothers, David and Samuel Nechamias, who were blessed by God to be great experts in the art of printing.[48]

The most significant converso figure of the seventeenth century was Fernando Cardoso (1604–80). His parents were Spanish conversos who lived in Portugal until 1610, when they returned to settle in Medina de Rioseco. Shortly after this move to Spain, as Fernando's younger brother recalled later, 'my parents told me that I am a Jew'.[49] This suggests that Fernando, as elder son, had by then been informed that his family felt themselves to be in some sense Jews, though not necessarily in terms of religious belief or practice. The young Cardoso shone as a student, won a teaching post in philosophy at the University of Valladolid, and obtained the sponsorship of the influential duke of Medina de Rioseco, which stood him in good stead when he moved on to Madrid. In 1631 he wrote for the duke's benefit a discourse on one of the remarkable natural phenomena of that year, the eruption of the volcano Vesuvius in Italy. As a resident of Madrid he was also a direct witness to a disagreeable affair in 1632, the arrest and execution by the Inquisition of a number of Portuguese converso immigrants who were accused of having flogged the image of Christ on a crucifix.[50] Cardoso was by now a practitioner of medicine, obtaining in 1640 the coveted post of court physician to King Philip IV. He became an active member of cultural groups in the Spanish capital, and a friend of the leading playwright Lope de Vega. It chanced that he was a direct witness to the circumstances of Lope's death in 1635. Cardoso informs us that Lope was attending one of his lectures in the Scottish seminary in Madrid:

He came, an illustrious listener, to honour me, when either because of the odours in the church or the density of the crowd, the famous man fainted and, taken to his house, died on the third day. [Lope's presence at the lecture] is a debt which I shall always owe to his memory.[51]

At court Cardoso benefited from the patronage of the chief minister of the time, the count duke of Olivares, but when Olivares fell from power in 1643 life became difficult for the Portuguese in Madrid, especially for those who were (like Cardoso) of Jewish origin. The Iberian peninsula did not provide congenial ground for Jewish speculative thought, a fact that certainly prompted Cardoso to make the surprising decision he took in 1648. He put together his savings, packed his large collection of books, and accompanied by his younger brother Miguel set sail for Italy. They landed at Rome but then moved to Venice, which became their home for five years. As many Spaniards, whether Jewish or not, were to do time and again over the next three centuries, Cardoso sought through a discreet and voluntary exile a way to fulfil his beliefs and creativity.

The stay in Venice was a brief prelude to his final destination, the nearby city of Verona, where he went with his wife in 1653, formally became a Jew and changed his first name to Isaac (his brother took the name Abraham). Apart from what can be gleaned from his writings, nothing is known of the nearly thirty years that he lived there, a period in which he wrote perhaps the most important intellectual works to be produced by any Spanish Jew in the two centuries that followed the exile of 1492. During his stay in Verona the only matter to disturb his tranquillity seems to have been the notorious case of Sabbatai Zvi. Sabbatai was an east European Jew from the city of Smyrna who in 1665, under the influence of his own confused mind and the ministrations of a friend called Nathan of Gaza, proclaimed himself to be the long-awaited Messiah and managed to convince a great many Jews (including Abraham Cardoso) of his claims. The case excited an unprecedented degree of messianic fervour among Jews throughout the Mediterranean and in eastern Europe. Barely a year later, however, Sabbatai scandalized all his followers by turning Muslim.[52] Even though Abraham, now resident in Tripoli as physician to the ruler there, was an impassioned supporter of Sabbatai, Isaac took up his pen to attack the pseudo-Messiah and, in consequence, broke off relations with his brother.

As with the Sabbatai case, Isaac's publications were responses to philosophic movements in the outside world, and are clear proof that he had felt himself shut in by the parochial interests of his friends in Madrid. In 1673 he published at Venice in Latin his *A Free Philosophy (Philosophia libera)*, a substantial exposition, 750 folio pages in length, of atomist philosophy[53] similar to the ideas of the French philosopher Gassendi, with passing references in his text to Jewish culture.[54] In those same years he had further reason for indignation when the Amsterdam Jew Baruch Spinoza (who had been expelled from the community by his fellow Jews) published in 1670 his best-known work, the *Tractatus Theologico-Politicus*. Cardoso saw Spinoza's work as a challenge not only to the Jewish faith but to the honour of Sephardic Jews (Spinoza's family were originally from Spain). In consequence, he published at Amsterdam in 1679 his *Excellences of the Jews*, written in Spanish in order to reach directly the hearts and minds of the exiled Sephardi community. The *Excellences* takes its title directly from the fashion at that time in Spain among certain writers who claimed that the Spaniards were the chosen people of God, supreme above all peoples for their excellence.[55] Cardoso set out to demonstrate that, on the contrary, it was the Jews, condemned to a life of permanent exile, who were the elect of God:

> It elicits no little admiration to see a people dispersed and scattered among the nations, and exiled for so many centuries, guarding its rites and cere- monies, being like a republic apart, governing itself by the law that God gave it.[56]

Cardoso's story was just one among many, for throughout those generations there was a constant movement of conversos between Portugal and Spain, as well as a regular migration of the exiles in Europe from one Jewish community to another. It was a virtually endless history of restlessness. Despite the shadow of the Inquisition, Iberia gave to Jewish and converso exiles a common bond that made them all 'men of the nation'. Even those who were no longer practising Jews felt a profound kinship, based less on religion than on cultural origin, with the converso world from which they had emerged. Return to the ancestral homeland became for some a perfectly normal option, one that helped them to define their identity both as Spaniards and as Jews.[57] The way back chosen was usually through the world of trade, because of the personal and family links they had with conversos resident in Madrid or in Seville, Spain's two principal economic centres. However, the expulsion had given Jews the possibility also of identifying with the European environment, and they by no means looked back only to Sepharad or to ancestral tradition. Jews had been educated within a Christian environment, and much of it rubbed off on them. Isaac Abravanel, despite his close links to traditional Jewish thinking, read writings of the Italian Renaissance, and recognized the relevance of Renaissance writings on politics and magic. The often confused intellectual development of the Iberian exiles had a certain relevance for the history of European thought. Some Iberian Jews seemed to lose their bearings once they found themselves in the open sea of western European ideas. A few of those who contributed to the new brand of converso consciousness in Europe went so far as to break off links with orthodox Judaism. Exile became a liberating force, though it sometimes had tragic consequences, as in the case of Uriel da Costa, who ended up in Amsterdam but was expelled by the Jewish community there and eventually committed suicide.

Perhaps the most outstanding international figure to return to his ancestral faith was Orobio de Castro (1617–87), who was born in Portugal and moved with his parents around the mid-century to Málaga in Spain.[58] He studied medicine at the University of Osuna. In 1654 he and his family were arrested by the Inquisition of Seville on a charge of secretly practising the Jewish faith. They appeared in an *auto de fe* but were lightly punished and eventually, in 1658, released. A couple of years later they left Spain. Orobio went over the French frontier to Toulouse, where he taught for a while, then arrived in 1662 in Amsterdam, where he participated in the rich intellectual world of the Jews and became a leading defender of traditional Judaism. When in Amsterdam he described the path that had taken him where he was:

In Spain I presented a Christian appearance, since life is sweet; but I was never very good at it, and so it emerged that I was really a Jew. While I was there, confronted with the risk to my freedom, status, property and even life, I was in reality a Jew and a Christian merely in outward appearance.[59]

Long after the expulsions of 1492 there continued to be a small but not insignificant drift into exile of people of Jewish origin. Conversos who felt out of place in their homeland, or who ran the risk of coming into conflict with the Inquisition, made the decision to live abroad. An anonymous document by a Toledo converso, dated to the year 1538 and written it seems to influence members of the Cortes (parliament) meeting in the city, complained that 'bit by bit many rich persons leave the country and go to foreign parts, so as not to live all their lives in fear', a specific reference to the fear of being denounced to the Inquisition. The trend to voluntary exile was, however, of small proportions. Most conversos, if indeed they were at all conscious of being conversos a century or more after the expulsion, enjoyed all the privileges of Christian society and lived in Spain tranquilly.

Some made their way to the New World, but the little information available about them has all too frequently been romanticized. All the so-called 'Jews' in early America were Christians, not Jews, and all were of Portuguese rather than Spanish origin.[60] There is no documentary evidence for the emigration of Hispanic Jews to the New World, or for the survival of Jewish practices among a significant number of people in America, or across any length of time.[61] They were all, of course, voluntary exiles, for their future in the peninsula was at best uncertain, but they seem to have made a success of the trades they chose to follow. Some Semitic Christians fell foul of the Inquisition in America, and were punished as they would have been in Europe. They remained few in number, hardly enough to be called a community, and their specifically Jewish cultural contribution to America was insignificant before the nineteenth century.

By contrast, one voluntary exile who went to the New World (for still unexplained and mysterious reasons) was beyond all doubt one of the stars of Hispanic culture. This was the writer Mateo Alemán. Of Jewish origin through at least one of his parents, he was born in 1547 in Seville.[62] His father was a doctor, later employed in the royal prison in Seville, and Mateo was destined for the same profession, which he studied at the universities of Salamanca and Alcalá. He later changed his mind about his career, got married, and idled his time away while he amassed debts, which got him thrown into debtors' prison (for two months) in 1580. At a loss over what to do, he planned to go to America (where a cousin had gone nine years before). The laws prohibited people of Jewish origin going there, and this may have proved an obstacle when, in 1582, he applied for permission to emigrate. However, two witnesses testified that he really had no Jewish blood, and the required consent was granted. For some reason, he did not leave. After further troubles, which landed him in prison again, he moved to Madrid and took it into his head to write. The end product was a volume called *Guzmán de Alfarache*, in which the hero of the title dedicates himself (not unlike Alemán) to a life of roguery. It was published anonymously in 1599 and was an immediate hit.

No other literary work published in Spanish ever achieved such instant success. It not only caught the attention of the few in Spain who could read, but stimulated the imagination of readers in other countries as well. There were five printings of the book in 1599, and eleven the year after (including publication in Antwerp, Lisbon and Paris). By the time Alemán managed to capitalize on his success and publish a Second Part to the novel in 1604, the book had gone through twenty-six printings. During his lifetime three foreign translations came out: in French (1600), Italian (1606) and German (1615). He became the most widely read and best known of all the writers of Golden-Age Spain, to the extent that half a century later the writer Gracián considered him to be the most accomplished of Spain's authors, better even than Cervantes. What was it about the *Guzmán* that excited contemporaries? The novel, which relates the adventures of a vagabond boy who runs away from his home in Seville and goes to the capital, Madrid, followed in the footsteps of a similar work that had been published in 1554, the *Lazarillo de Tormes*. The *Lazarillo* was a slim work, a witty and ironic commentary on a young boy's escapades. By contrast the *Guzmán* is a substantial work of sixty chapters, lacking irony but full of illuminating anecdotes about the reprehensible aspects of life in the Mediterranean world. It takes the reader through the boy's misadventures in the capital, his vagrant life in Italy, and his return to Spain where he once again takes up his life of mishaps and petty crime. At the end he is condemned to the galleys for his life of roguery, and suitably repents of his follies. The work aims less to entertain than to criticize and point a moral, and it was no doubt because of its moral stance, adopted firmly throughout the novel even in the midst of descriptions of crime, profligacy, sexual misdemeanour and worldly corruption, that made educated readers feel they were deriving profit from reading it. The combination of profligacy and moralizing began a literary vogue that soon caught on not only in Spain but among writers elsewhere in the continent. The life of the *pícaro* (rogue) depicted by Alemán, gave rise to similar picaresque novels by German, Italian, French and English writers on the theme of low life and the moral redemption that could be acquired even after a lifetime of crime. For the first time, a Spanish work pioneered a vogue in literary creativity throughout western Europe.

Success brought no happiness to Alemán, who was obviously a troubled and unstable person. His debts and reckless living landed him in prison again in 1602. By now his fame had reached the New World, where many copies of his work were distributed and enjoyed better fortune even than the subsequent writings of Cervantes. However, in Spain the success was counterproductive, with printers running off pirate editions of his work. Worst of all, a fellow writer, a converso and author of a piece called La pícara Justina (1605), attacked him covertly for his scandalous private life.[63] Fearing that he might be denounced to the Inquisition, in 1607 Alemán decided to abandon everything and go to America, after taking care to secure permission by bribing an official. The voyage across the Atlantic in 1608 lasted two months, during which he managed to make friends with a fellow passenger, the new archbishop of Mexico who was going to take up his post as archbishop and viceroy but died less than four years after his arrival. When Alemán stepped ashore, vigilant agents of the Inquisition confiscated one of the books he had brought with him. Ironically, it happened to be a copy of the first (1605) edition of the Quixote, one of the earliest to arrive in the New World. Thanks to the influence of the archbishop, the book was later returned to him. Mexico delighted Alemán, who called it a 'noble city' and referred to himself as a 'happy and fortunate exile'. The exile probably lasted no more than seven years, and he is thought to have died in 1615.

By seeking refuge across the ocean, Alemán was putting into practice what the rogue novels advocated, a life of rootlessness. It was the essence of the pícaro to be always on the move,[64] escaping from his own society into that of others, from his own traditional set of values into the different values encountered in the world outside. From this point of view, exile was not a deprivation. It was an enrichment and a liberation. The rogue Guzmán in Alemán's novel goes so far as to laugh at the problem: 'exile can be a serious matter for "good" people, but for "bad" people, to whom the entire world is home, it is a joke.'[65] Nothing better suited a delinquent than to be on the move, forever wandering in search of some way to turn the odds, by fair means or foul, against an unfair and unpitying universe.

At about the time that Alemán was writing about a wandering vagabond, an anonymous writer published in 1602 at Leiden in the Netherlands a short, four-leaf pamphlet describing the career of the Wandering Jew. According to an old Christian legend, one of the Jews present at the trial of Jesus before Pontius Pilate had pushed him and told him to 'Get on!', whereupon Jesus replied, 'I go, but you will wait until I return!' Since then that Jew had been fated to wander the earth, and had been seen by various people in different places. The 1602 pamphlet relates that the previous bishop of Schleswig had, when he was young, met at Hamburg in 1542 a man named Ahasuerus, who declared that he was the ill-fated Jew. The pamphlet goes on to report other sightings of the Jew, including an incident at Madrid in 1575 when two German diplomats had seen him. The exotic story excited interest, especially in the Germanic lands, and the pamphlet was repeatedly printed, and translated into several languages. Though seemingly innocuous, it encouraged an attitude to Jews that was fundamentally anti-Semitic. For the next three centuries and down to today, there have continued to be reports of sightings of the mysterious wanderer. Curiously enough, at no time was the legend of the man ever tied to the real history of the expulsion of Jews from the Mediterranean, and Spain remains prominently absent from the list of countries where the Wandering Jew figured in popular mythology. In the Twenty-Fifth of his *Erudite Letters*, the learned Benedictine monk Feijóo in the eighteenth century explored and dismissed the significance of the story.

Rejection of the Jewish past continued in the peninsula among Spaniards until well into the twentieth century. The cultural legacy was almost intangible, for there were no great buildings to sustain the memory of Jews, only ruins. One example may serve for all others. In the fourteenth century the Jews of Toledo, who already had other places of worship, constructed a new and elegant synagogue, one of the architectural prides of Spain, integrating strong influences from

Mudéjar (that is, Islamic) art. When the community disappeared in 1492 the synagogue was given to the military Order of the Knights of Calatrava, and the great hall of the building was converted into a church, dedicated to Our Lady of El Tránsito, under whose floor the leading members of the order were buried. By the eighteenth century the order was in decay. The church fell into disuse and was tended by a hermit. Years later it was used for a while as a military barracks. Not until the twentieth century was what remained of the Synagogue of El Tránsito restored as the inspiring but modest museum it is today.

When the Englishman George Borrow went through Spain in the years between 1835 and 1840, in an attempt to bring the Bible to a people living not only in Romish darkness but in the travails of a brutal civil war, he encountered little more than ghosts of the Jewish presence, fragments of folk memory that could barely be described as concrete survivals. His memoirs of those years, which he published in 1842 as *The Bible in Spain*, became a classic of its kind. Borrow's principal contact was with gypsies, whose language he learned to speak, but 'Jews' also feature frequently in his pages, always as clandestine figures hiding constantly from official Catholic Spain. Not much, admittedly, remained of the Jewish heritage in that period. Even today there is little for the tourist to identify. The city of Toledo features the Sephardic Museum, the nearby Church of Santa Maria La Blanca (an ancient synagogue) and the former Jewish quarter. The synagogue of Maimonides can be visited in Córdoba, and ancient synagogues can be seen in towns such as Avila, Cáceres, Estella and Seville, though most have long since been used as churches. Streets to which Jews were restricted in medieval times, notably in Seville and Girona, have been methodically restored to give them tourist appeal. Overall, little remains of the everyday environment in which Jews used to live.

The absence of the Jews for close on four centuries gave rise to highly imaginative myths of what did and did not happen in 1492. From the seventeenth century onwards, various public figures of a liberal tendency attempted to explain their country's backward state by suggesting that in 1492 the forces of fanaticism had driven out of the country hundreds of thousands of Spain's wealthiest and most gifted citizens. The thesis was that Spain had been a flourishing place in medieval times but had gone downhill since 1492, and the return of Jews would restore the economy. This was the legend of 'decline' to which – for centuries and for a wide variety of motives – ideologues, politicians and scholars clung. There was another corollary to this tale. Since Jews were supposed to have been rich and astute, once in exile they were blamed for using their money to conspire against the interests of the country that had expelled them. It was an attitude calculated to boost anti-Semitism, in a country that ironically had no Jews. From the sixteenth century onwards, public spokesmen openly and insistently blamed the nefarious Jews for the Protestant Reformation, the revolt of the Dutch, the rise of atheism, the loss of the overseas empire, the revolt of Portugal, the rise of anticlericalism, and the spread of communism.

Dissemination of the legend about their unique genius for finance fortunately had some favourable consequences for peninsular Jews. In the 1630s Spain's chief minister, Olivares, made extensive use of the services of Portuguese financiers of Jewish origin. The special utility of these 'New Christians' was that they maintained business links with their family members in other countries, and were able to transfer money easily to European cities where the crown had to pay its bills. The international character of the Jewish dispersion could therefore be used to profit by the country that had dispersed them. The arrangement worked very well indeed. A Jesuit in Madrid even reported that the government was planning to allow Jews back into the country, and the king's chamberlain confirmed that there were plans to permit a Jewish quarter in the capital. The idea continued to receive support. In the 1690s a Castilian diplomat serving in Holland, Manuel de Lira, who was friendly with Spanish Jews in Amsterdam, favoured Jews being allowed back into Spain. A government minister made a similar proposal to King Charles IV in 1797, but nothing happened.

In fact, the link with Hispanic Jews had never been entirely broken, and they could be found residing with official permission throughout Spanish territories long after the 1492 decree. They were officially tolerated in Naples until the early sixteenth century, in Milan until the late sixteenth and in the North African colony of Orán until the end of the seventeenth century. They also returned (mostly from Morocco) to live in the peninsula when the town of Gibraltar became British territory by the terms of the Treaty of Utrecht in 1713. The Treaty expressly prohibited the British extending any sort of toleration to the two condemned minorities of Spain's imperial age, the Jews and the Muslims. However, the British government had no intention of discriminating over beliefs, and welcomed immigrants of all religions into both Gibraltar and Minorca, the two territories they controlled. A century later, a good part of the population of Gibraltar was Jewish, and since then Jews have played an important role in the life of the Rock. In contrast to the pro-Jewish outlook among a few Spaniards, however, the predominant attitude throughout Spanish society continued to be one of unmitigated hostility towards the real or imagined Semitic past. The most notable example was the profound racial discrimination practised in the island of Mallorca against the so-called Chuetas, a minority that had been persecuted by the natives of the island (and by the Inquisition) and lived in a state of virtual marginality until the twentieth century.

Ironically, the first radical political reformer of the nineteenth century may have been of Jewish origin and was also, to boot, an exile. Juan de Dios Alvarez y Méndez, known by his adopted surname of Mendizábal, was born in 1790 of humble origins in Andalusia, and began his upward career as a contractor of supplies to the patriotic forces fighting the French army which had invaded the peninsula. He became associated with Liberal politicians, and joined them in an enforced absence of twelve years in London. When the Liberals returned to Spain he was appointed minister of finance, and became prime minister in 1835. He attempted to save a bankrupt Spanish government by two revolutionary measures: a new system of state credit, and the confiscation of Church property. The latter measure – known as the 'desamortización' (or 'disentail', a measure comparable to the dissolution of the monasteries in Reformation England) – represented the biggest transfer of land ever to take place in Spain's history, and literally changed the face of the country as monasteries and churches were suppressed. 'In Madrid alone forty-four churches and monasteries vanished. Nine were sold as building sites, one was converted into a ministry, another into the Senate house, others became a riding school, a prison, a theatre and barracks.'[66] Logically, Mendizábal was bitterly criticized by conservatives, who exploited to the full the rumour that he was a Jew. Caricaturists of the time depicted him as having a tail (many Spaniards of the day seem to have believed that Jews had tails). It was a symptomatic reaction. Both then and since, it has been commonplace in Spain to hint that prominent figures of the opposite political colour are Jews or of Jewish origin.

The theme of the Jewish past drifted inexorably into focus, after three centuries of deliberate neglect during which official Spain attempted by various means to conceal it or to repress the fact that Jews had once been a vital part of society. In the mid-nineteenth century a handful of Spanish intellectuals began to pay attention to the question. It was not a spontaneous urge, and arose almost exclusively because of the significant role that Jewish personalities, finance and culture were playing in the political life of England and France. Nearly four hundred years after the expulsion, the literary scholar Adolfo de Castro published (in 1847) the first short history of the forbidden subject, his *History of the Jews of Spain* (he took care to note in the preface that he himself was not a Jew). The following year the historian José Amador de los Ríos published a path-breaking volume on the theme, and much later, in 1876, brought out three volumes of a *Social, Political and Religious History of the Jews*.[67] The historian Rafael Altamira, an active member of the Institución Libre de Enseñanza (see Chapter 6), also began to pay attention to the subject. One of the most prominent literary men of the day, Juan de Valera, contributed the preface to Amador's book. When Valera wrote an essay on the Inquisition a few years later, he emphasized the key role of the Jews. In his discourse of reception into the Academy of Language in 1876, he developed one of his favourite themes, on the special role of Jews and Muslims in the formation of western culture. 'Not only the Arabs, but the Jews as well, shone out among our people, producing sages, poets, and philosophers who had an immense influence on the development of man in Europe.'[68]

The new concern for Jewish history was evidently trying to make up for four centuries of neglect and prejudice, but behind the interest there was an unmistakable political agenda, supported principally by romantic Liberals: to emphasize that Spain had contributed to the making of Europe through a unique medium almost no other country could boast, its exotic past. The history of Hispanic Jews was therefore presented primarily through Spanish eyes, as an extension of Castilian achievement. Attention was focused on the contribution made by Jews to the emergence of Spain, and even to the discovery of America, an achievement seen by Spaniards as uniquely their own. Studies began to emerge on the theme of whether Columbus had been a Jew. The idea, first broached in 1894 in *Christopher Columbus and the Participation of the Jews in the Spanish and Portuguese Discoveries* by the German writer Meyer Kayserling, was taken up enthusiastically by writers for whom a Jewish origin would convert Columbus into being a Spaniard rather than (what he was for others) an Italian. The best presentation of this idea was the work of the diplomat Salvador de Madariaga, whose *Christopher Columbus* (1939) argued that although born in Genoa, Columbus came from a family of émigré Catalan Jews. Madariaga's fascinating book put together an abundance of circumstantial indications (they were hardly solid enough to be called 'evidence'), and it proved easy for professional scholars like the American historian Samuel Eliot Morison, author of the standard life of the mariner, to rebut his claims. Once set in motion, however, the legend of Columbus as a Jew has been difficult to eliminate. Outside Spain, Jewish scholars were evidently grateful for the unexpected attention to Jewish themes. But they were also worried whether the focus was wrong. They criticized Amador de los Ríos for approaching his theme without any knowledge of Hebrew, and treating the Hebrew language as if it were irrelevant to Jewish culture. In effect, the medieval Jews were being approached by Spanish writers more as Spaniards than as Jews.[69]

During the nineteenth century a few Jews had visited Spain and lived there without problems, despite being officially prohibited. The Cortes in 1855 sanctioned their presence by voting that no Spaniard or foreigner be harassed for religious beliefs. This affected only private belief. In 1868 the government of General Prim went a step further, abrogating the 1492 expulsion decree and allowing the return of Jews (as well as of Protestants). The ban on the public exercise of other religions was eventually removed by Article 21 of the Constitution of 1869, which established religious freedom for the first time.

The enthusiasm of ministers for the measure was obvious, but also betrayed a curious naivety about the historical context. The presence in Madrid of a handful of rich foreign Jewish bankers, whose activity contrasted with the poor condition of Spain's economy, served to reinforce the view that Jews were the secret to success. Emilio Castelar, prime minister and a university professor of history, declared confidently in the Cortes debates in 1869 that but for the lamentable expulsion of 1492 Spain might have been able to produce its own Spinoza and its own Disraeli. Like Castelar, progressive and Liberal intellectuals of the mid-nineteenth century followed the fashion of declaring themselves to be pro-Jewish. They took this position because it accorded with a myth that they themselves had created, namely that the Semitic heritage offered a way out of economic problems and an escape from conservative Catholic ideology. But they had no effective knowledge of Judaic culture, nor any informed views about the role that Jews had played in the distant past of Spain. In the same years, writers of the Romantic school (see Chapter 5) timidly dared to put Jewish characters into the texts of their novels, in conscious imitation of the way that Sir Walter Scott had introduced them in the pages of his novel *Ivanhoe*. Their efforts, however, were half-hearted and they never managed to shake off the prevailing unfavourable image of Jews that reigned in the popular mind.

Spanish culture therefore retained, down to our day, an unusually strong anti-Semitic flavour. A recent opinion survey (2005) carried out in twelve European countries showed that the highest level of hostility to Jews could be found in Spain.[70] The ethnologist Julio Caro Baroja has called attention to the way in which, generation after generation, strange ideas about Jews continued to permeate the folklore of the Spanish countryside. Specific towns and streets were said to be the traditional abode of Jews, and specific families and family names were associated with Judaism. Very frequently, the word 'Jew', which as in other countries remained a standard term of abuse, was used to mean little more than 'a bad Christian', in the way that it has universally been used to mean simply a miser. At best, the 'Jew' remained a mysterious, wholly unknown figure, part of the mythology of the past and wholly unconnected with the real world of the present. The relevant clauses in the 1869 Constitution were the first timid step towards re-establishing the cultural links broken in 1492. Most Spaniards had never seen a Jew, nor knew what one looked like.

When the Spanish army captured the North African town of Tetuán in 1860, the Liberal General O'Donnell reported to his superiors how the town's Jews came out to welcome his men, 'whom they embraced as liberators, greeting them in Spanish with cries of "Welcome! Long live the Queen of Spain!"' It was a historic moment, but also a bewildering one, for Spaniards were not quite sure what to make of it. A newspaper correspondent who was present at Tetuán was fascinated at having seen his first 'Jew': 'the Jewish race looked just as I had thought and imagined, and as I had read in Shakespeare and other poets'.[71] The new Spanish consul in the town expressed satisfaction that to his knowledge the Jews there were no longer committing the crime of infanticide (which Spaniards for centuries had accused them of). Spanish clergy arrived, intent (as though it were still the fifteenth century!) on converting them to the true faith. The novelist Galdós, who devoted several ironic pages of his series of novels, *National Episodes*, to the futile war in Morocco, could not decide whether the newly recovered Jews still formed part of the Spain they had come from four centuries before. 'The Jews either have no home or they have two, their present one and their traditional one. The latter one is Spain.' Galdós introduced Jewish characters into his novels,[72] even indirectly into his work *Fortunata y Jacinta* (1886), but they remained straw figures rather than a convincing part of the Spanish landscape. Since few Jews took advantage of the new tolerant legislation of 1869 (by 1877 there were less than four hundred in Spain) the government in 1881 offered to accept Jews expelled by Russia back into 'what was their original home', blissfully unaware that the Jews of Russia were not Sephardim.[73] From this period there were no significant obstacles to Jews who might wish to immigrate. Few did so, since Spain had little to offer them.

The pro-Semitic views of the Liberals of the mid-nineteenth century never bore fruit in any significant political or cultural consequences. The great Castilian writers of the final decade of the century therefore had little to say about Jews. Many were notably anti-Semitic, in part as a result of ideas that came from France and Germany, where the events associated with the Dreyfus case on the one hand, and the teachings of idealist philosophers on the other, could not fail to leave their mark. Essayists who examined the medieval period somehow managed not to see any Jews in it. José Ortega y Gasset put together the sixteen essays that form his *Invertebrate Spain* (1921) without once mentioning either the Jews or the Arabs. Writers of fiction were rarely conscious of Semitic survivals in Spanish society. The works of the novelist Pio Baroja (see Chapter 7) offer typical evidence of the fundamental indifference of thinking Spaniards on the matter. Some of the Jewish personages in his novels tend to be depicted unfavourably, though the author's prejudices merely coincided with those of the society he was describing. On the one hand he was capable of expressing the most rabid anti-Semitic sentiments, on the other he had good personal relations with Jews in Madrid, and in his later years expressed outrage at the excesses of German anti-Semitism in the 1930s.[74]

The early decades of the twentieth century changed matters considerably for the Jewish community. In 1905, during a state visit to England, King Alfonso XIII received a deputation of England's Sephardic Jews. In 1910 the first Jew was elected to the national parliament, the Cortes. Then in 1915, over four hundred years after Hebrew had disappeared from the Spanish university curriculum, the government created a chair of Hebrew Literature at the University of Madrid, and brought in a British Jew from Berlin to occupy it.[75] The first synagogue in Madrid was opened in 1917. During these years, the interest of politicians in the Jewish question was based less on idealism or altruism than on a persistent nationalist and imperialist vision of Spain. The failure of Spanish military efforts in North Africa and, above all, in Cuba, where the United States eventually wiped out Spanish power in 1898 and took over what remained of the old empire (see Chapter 6), encouraged Castilians to succour their wounded pride by looking elsewhere for comfort. They found it, among other places, in the Jewish question.

A handful of alert public figures, anxious to strengthen the crumbling fabric of their culture, looked to the absent Jews as a means of extending Spain's authority. Their view was that the Sephardic dispersion was an extension of Spain's personality, and that the exiles of five centuries before should consider Spain their true home. They did not, of course, want all those Jews to come back to the peninsula. Rather, they wanted them to recognize that they were products of Spain's culture. The writer and diplomat Juan Valera pointed out in 1897 that there were tens of thousands of 'Spanish Jews' in the eastern Mediterranean who were 'almost fellow citizens', who had extensive incomes, and who, above all, 'attempt to preserve in all purity the language of Cervantes'.[76] A common language, in the opinion of many like Valera, became a historic link that confirmed Spain's claims to cultural hegemony. Among those who shared this outlook was Dr Angel Pulido, a physician, senator and prominent Liberal, who spent most of his spare time in an extensive correspondence with Jewish communities everywhere. After a journey down the Danube when he encountered fellow passengers who conversed with him in his tongue, he wrote excitedly in 1903 that 'from Vienna to Constantinople there live scattered at least two million Jews whose language is old Castilian'. In an attempt to gain political clout for the language, Pulido attempted to persuade Jewish leaders from the Balkans that their real cultural home was in the peninsula. His last published work, *Hispano-Jewish Reconciliation* (1920), indicates his goal. Pulido passed over the obvious fact that Sephardic culture had long since lost its Hispanic roots, and that in the nineteenth-century Balkans, for instance, it was the French way of life (projected from Paris by the highly influential Alliance Israélite Universelle) that most influenced Jews.[77] Through its system of education, adopted by the Sephardi communities as a way of gaining access to west European culture, the Alliance encouraged the use of French and Italian as active languages rather than Spanish.[78]

There were, evidently, political undertones to the promotion of interest in the exiles of four hundred years before. Pulido's sights were set on France. He explicitly opposed the Jews returning to Spain, and felt they should stay where they were. But they should recognize the Castilian cultural heritage, and become hosts to the new wave of emigrants that Spain was sending out in those days into territories that were nominally within the French area of influence. By around 1920 the stream of Spanish workers pouring into French Algeria totalled some 200,000, according to official figures, and a similar number had gone to France itself. The new attempt at cultural hegemony (that is to say, the diffusion of 'Spanish speakers') would be reinforced if the number of Sephardim could be added to those of Spaniards, and both groups together would extend the language into zones controlled by France.[79] The Madrid government took the highly unusual step in 1924 of issuing a decree which extended Spanish citizenship to 'persons of Spanish origin' (meaning the Sephardim) in the Mediterranean, but the decree was indignantly repudiated by other countries, which were aware of Spain's motives. Pulido's campaign stimulated considerable interest among scholars who were delving into the Semitic past of the peninsula. The leading medievalist Ramón Menéndez Pidal, for example, promoted interest in Judaeo-Spanish ballads that might still survive among descendants of the exiles in North Africa. Between 1896 and 1956 he managed to collect around 2,500 texts of old ballads, sometimes with a clear indication of the original melody. Preserved in Spain, the texts constitute the world's largest collection of traditional Sephardic poetry.[80] Research into and practical renderings of traditional Sephardic ballads constitute an important part of the effort to maintain alive the historical culture of peninsular Jews as transmitted to the Mediterranean.[81]

The survival of the Castilian language among Jews was an interesting cultural phenomenon, but it raises problems that have still not been adequately resolved. Most scholarly commentators agree that the language referred to as 'ladino' ('Latin') never existed as a spoken but only as a written medium,[82] and the more correct term for the spoken language is 'judeoespañol',[83] which accompanied exiled Jews into the Mediterranean and eastern Europe from the fourteenth century onwards, and was spoken in North Africa, Italy and the Balkans. Others, however, have presented good reasons for maintaining that there was, and is, no clear division between the spoken and written forms of the language.[84] In each area it had its own name and vocabulary, since loanwords came from the other regional languages, such as Arab, Greek and Turkish. It was habitually written in Hebrew characters until the eighteenth century, but thereafter the continued dispersion, emigration and assimilation of Jewish communities in various countries reduced the language to being virtually only a spoken one, and when it was written it was set out in the dominant

European script, the Latin alphabet. By the nineteenth century, the language was no longer pure Spanish (if indeed it had ever been Spanish), for it had evolved and created its own forms. However, because it still retained some medieval archaisms (such as, for example, the word '*vos*' for polite 'you') those who came into contact with it were excited by the idea that the pure language of the past was still preserved and spoken in distant corners of the continent.

The number of people who spoke the language was at all times impressive. Around the year 1900, over 12 per cent of the population of Sofia (Bulgaria) spoke *judeoespañol*, and nearly 50 per cent of the population of Salonika (Turkey). Thanks to ethnic cleansing[85] and population changes after the two world wars, these figures are of course no longer valid. In Israel today, up to 100,000 Jews come from the *judeoespañol* tradition and continue to speak and use the language. In Turkey, some 20,000 people still use it. Its existence has continued to provide a focus for Spanish political initiatives. Like others who were anxious to recover dignity for their battered country, the writer Unamuno considered the tongue to be a romantic projection of Spain itself. In a work of 1928 he referred to

> Ladino, the noble tongue
> In which we sigh for Zion
> And weep for lost Spain,
> Land of our hopes.

In the conviction that it is not really a historically autonomous language but simply an extension of old Castilian, the Spanish state since that period has attempted to control its evolution. It has subsidized the *judeoespañol* newspapers and radio stations in Israel, and through pressure from the Academy of Language encourages standardization of its vocabulary and grammar according to the norms of official Castilian.

Meanwhile, the theme of the Semitic past became a battleground among Hispanic historians. Castilian writers of the late nineteenth century were deeply concerned, as we shall see (Chapter 6 below), by the cultural backwardness of Spain. Many of them looked outside Spain and towards Europe for the solution to the problem. In preferring Europe, they not only pushed out of their vision of Spain anything that did not seem European, like Muslims or Jews, but also downplayed the contribution of these cultures to Spain's past. Serious writers, like Amador de los Ríos, attempted to correct the balance but their research was often superficial. Professional historians lacked the perspective, methods and languages necessary to look into the subject. One of the first scholars to accept that Jews had played a role in Spain did so in order to reject them immediately, with a disdain that bore all the marks of classical anti-Semitism.

Claudio Sánchez-Albornoz was a respectable professor of medieval history (see Chapter 2), who left Spain in the 1930s at the outset of the Civil War. In a massive two-volume study titled *Spain, a Historical Enigma* (1956), he roundly denied that the Jews had done anything useful for the Hispanic world. 'What is Jewish and what is Hispanic are in sharp opposition,' he claimed; and hoped that his study 'will help to dissipate the image – welcome to Jewish scholars and many other enemies of my Hispanic *patria* – of innocent, suffering Jews.' The Jews, who had generously been sheltered by the Christian people when fleeing from persecution, spent their time in Spain, according to him, 'sucking up its riches and increasing the general poverty. It is important not to forget this, if we wish to understand the history of Spain.' For centuries they continued to exploit the poor Christians through their usury and greed for wealth, which brought a logical retribution. The situation became worse when Jews allegedly converted to Christianity but continued their role as usurers (since Sánchez-Albornoz was a progressive republican he was less worried by the theme of converted Jews as heretics). The expulsions of 1492 would have benefited the country if they had been carried out a century or more earlier, for the Jews had made themselves so hated that 'if the expulsion had not been decreed there would have been a massacre'. Had they been driven out of Spain at the same period that England had driven out its Jews (1290), Spain would now be rich like England. In sum, he claimed, 'the involvement of Spanish Jews in the foundation of Spain was always negative, provoking hostility instead of contributing good qualities.'[86] The Jews had distorted the true course of Spain's history, and had incidentally inspired the establishment of the Inquisition and were therefore directly responsible for it.

These views were not peculiar to the author only, but shared by an extensive sector of the intellectual class. When another scholarly colleague, Américo Castro, came up with a radically different view of the role of the Jews, Sánchez-Albornoz decided that he had to write his *Spain* as a decisive rebuttal. 'I shall stand up, as I have stood up,' he proclaimed, 'against this outrageousness!'

In this way one of the best known of the controversies among Spain's historians took shape. Like Sánchez-Albornoz, Castro (1885–1972) also became an exile from Spain in the 1930s, when many educated men from the upper-class elite left the country during the chaos provoked by revolutionary violence and a military rebellion. Born to Spanish parents in Brazil, Castro returned with them to Spain when he was five, graduated eventually from the University of Granada in 1904, and went on to Paris for three years of study. He took his doctorate in 1911 at the University of Madrid, where four years later he secured a chair in the history of the Spanish language and began writing articles for the press. In 1925 he published *The Thought of Cervantes*, a path-breaking study of the author of *Don Quixote* and one that he later wished to disown, on the grounds that his ideas had moved on radically since then. In the 1920s he travelled extensively in the New World, including a year in the United States as a visiting professor at Columbia. He was in Germany on a visiting post when the Spanish Republic was established in 1931, and the new government made use of his presence there to appoint him as ambassador. Subsequently he served in government bodies in Madrid, but on the outbreak of the Civil War in 1936 he left and went to live in Buenos Aires.

After spending periods at the universities of Wisconsin-Madison (1937) and Texas, he accepted a call to Princeton in 1940 and settled down to teach there for twenty-two years. Castro was regarded as one of the world's most distinguished Hispanists. His field was linguistic studies but he gradually found himself being pulled into the challenge of interpreting Spain's historical character through its cultural past. His *magnum opus*, titled in Spanish *Spain in its History. Christians, Muslims and Jews* (1948), was written in Princeton but published in Buenos Aires. Over the years, he brought out three different versions of the same work. The edition best known to English-language readers was *The Structure of Spanish History*, published in Princeton in 1954.

It was a notable landmark in modern Spanish historiography. Castro wrote always in Spanish, but his work was translated into English, Italian, German, French and Japanese. He also earned international recognition as a teacher, serving as visiting professor at universities in Argentina, Chile, Mexico, Cuba, Puerto Rico, Germany and throughout the United States.

Castro's unique achievement, based on years of study and reflection at Princeton, lay in altering completely the way we understand Spain's past. His target was, as he put it, the prevailing way of writing history, 'with its determination to include a past that does not belong to it, and to exclude the most characteristic elements of its reality'. Previous scholars had depicted 'Spain' (a word applied loosely by the Romans to the geographic area of the Iberian peninsula) as having an uninterrupted existence since well before Roman times. In their search for evidence of a continuous 'Spanish' culture in the peninsula, writers had been happy to claim that pre-Romans, such as the famed defenders of Numancia, were 'Spaniards'. The essayist Ortega y Gasset presented the Roman emperor Trajan as a 'Spaniard' from Seville, and the medievalist Menéndez Pidal presented the Roman philosopher Seneca as a 'Spaniard' from Córdoba. 'Spain', even though it did not speak Spanish or have any political identity, thus joined the ranks of western culture. What came afterwards was, for these scholars, almost irrelevant. The Jews barely existed in this landscape, and the Arabs were invaders who were quickly absorbed and Hispanized. The 'most characteristic elements' of Spain were in this way defined out of existence. Castro, by contrast, felt that the Jews and Arabs had played a vital and positive role in the formation of the cultural mixture that would later become Spain. The central proposition of his thesis, put forward in 1948 and further developed in 1962, was that the relationship between Arabs, Jews and Christians (for him, the three 'castes') produced a society that created the basic elements of the language and culture of the Hispanic peoples.[87] A special role was allotted to the Jews, whose literature, customs and language penetrated medieval Christian society and influenced it profoundly. All the great geniuses of the sixteenth-century Golden Age, he claimed (with an uncanny intuition that often turned out to be correct), were of Jewish origin. Economic progress also was due to the Jews. 'The history of Spain,' he claimed, 'was built on the base of a Jewish economy.' Major features of the Hispanic experience were thus explained in terms of a positive Jewish contribution.

After a century of arid traditionalism and anti-Semitic prejudice, the ideas of Castro came as a breath of fresh air in the Hispanic world. The writer Juan Goytisolo recalls how in 1948 in Spain, 'I had just entered university and like others of my age I took to the reading of authors who were considered acceptable by the establishment', and how 'my disappointment was total'. Shortly after, he came across the work of Castro, which affected him profoundly. 'It broke with the prejudices of our way of writing history. Castro tackled with audacity, originality and vigour the old question that we had approached since we were young: "How did Spain's special national character come about, and when?"'[88]

Castro's influence was felt on both sides of the Atlantic. Though he was teaching within the down-to-earth, pragmatic environment of the Anglo-Saxon world at Princeton, Castro put forward his theses in the visionary style of the Hispanic prophets. His students, many of whom went on to become major scholars in the universities of the United States, eagerly devoured his brilliant arguments.[89] Other scholars reacted swiftly to his sweeping affirmations, and in Spain, which was little disposed to concede any particular role to the Jews, his ideas fell on stony, and indeed hostile, ground. Rumours circulated that Castro was of Jewish origin himself. The antagonism of Sánchez-Albornoz was not only professional but became personal, as often happens among university professors. In the 1940s Sánchez-Albornoz was invited by a Princeton department to spend a year at the university, and accepted the offer, despite advice from Menéndez Pidal that he should not do so. An oft-repeated anecdote tells us that one day in the University library the two embattled scholars unintentionally coincided, but continued to move among the books without once recognizing the presence of the other. In the same way, Castro failed to receive recognition in Spain, for ideological rather than academic reasons. Spanish scholars wedded to the idea that Spain was essentially a European and not a Semitic country rejected his vision as an unacceptable 'oriental interpretation' of the past.[90]

*

In the early twentieth century new forms of anti-Semitism filtered into Spain, mainly as a backwash from the Dreyfus era in France. When right-wing political movements began to develop they adopted the vocabulary of anti-Semitism, and the forces that backed Franco's rebellion in 1936 had no doubt that Jews (together with Communists and Freemasons) were subverting their country. 'Our fight is not a Spanish civil war,' the notorious radio-general Queipo de Llano ranted, 'but a war for western civilization against world Jewry!' Though many Jews served in the International Brigades that fought for the Republic against Franco in the Civil War, the Left during those war years was equally committed to anti-Semitism, in part because that was the line decreed by the Soviet dictator Stalin, busy at the time eliminating all Jewish colleagues and intellectuals. Franco, however, made a surprisingly original departure from these attitudes, when he agreed to accept into Spain after 1940 a large number of refugees from the Nazi regime's racial extermination policy. It appears that during the second half of the Second World War, Spain acted to save an estimated 11,535 Jews, most of them refugees who had managed to reach the Spanish border.[91]

The return of Sephardic families to their ancestral homeland was numerically insignificant, and had little impact on public opinion. Presumed differences between right-wing and left-wing attitudes, however, faded when it came to an issue that continued to unite Spain's leaders for a good part of the century: hostility to the state of Israel. After the Second World War the Franco regime, which had always maintained close links with Germany but never went so far as to ally with it militarily, was given the cold shoulder by the democratic states that had won the struggle against Hitler. When Franco attempted to come out of the cold by offering to recognize the new state of Israel, he was rebuffed by the latter, whose leaders were well aware of the general's links with the country that had been responsible for the Holocaust. From that time, both the Right and the Left in Spain were united in their ideological hostility to Israel. It mattered little that in 1952 the Israeli delegate to the UN, Moshe Tov, supported the adoption of Spanish as one of the official languages of the UN, because of the importance of Latin America but also because of 'our love for and identification with Spain'. In 1955 Israel, attempting to counter the hostility of the Soviet Union and the Socialists, decided to seek the support of Spain, but Franco had just succeeded in securing an alliance with the United States, and no longer needed an ally that his own supporters rejected. It was not until 1986, eleven long years after the restoration of democracy in Spain, that a Socialist government reluctantly stepped into line with the rest of the non-Arab world and recognized that Israel existed. It took a long time for traditionally pro-Arab Spaniards to come to terms with the existence of Jews. The change in attitude came about in part because of the need to attract American money in order to restore the wholly dilapidated monuments associated with Jewish Spain. At the same time a myth, designed to uplift the cultural image presented to the outside world, began to be cultivated about Spain as the happy and historic home of three religions, in which logically the Jewish religion was included. The centuries of exile were over, but the task of understanding the Jewish heritage of the peninsula still remained to be done.

2

The Persistence of the Moor

Violins are weeping over the Arabs leaving al-Andalus,
Violins are weeping over lost time which will never come back.
Palestinian poet Mahmud Darwish[1]

Of all European countries, Spain was the most profoundly Islamic and had the longest experience of Muslim rule. In the year 711 an Arab-Berber army crossed over from North Africa in order to intervene in quarrels among the Christian rulers of Spain, and decided to stay. The Muslim intervention turned into a domination of the Iberian peninsula that lasted for nearly eight hundred years. Resistance from Christians continued in the mountainous northwest, where a chieftain called Pelayo led the opposition. Later the resistance came to centre on Galicia, where in the ninth century people took comfort from the discovery of a tomb that was proclaimed to be of St James the Apostle, who was speedily adopted as patron of the struggle against the Muslims. Meanwhile the Arabs had consolidated themselves under the rule of the powerful emirate of Córdoba, whose authority stopped short only at the mountain barrier of the Pyrenees, where the forces of the ruler of the Franks, Charlemagne, managed to hold them at bay. In the three centuries that followed the first Berber invasions, Islamic civilization made an indelible impact on Hispanic culture.

By the tenth century the territory called al-Andalus – it covered four-fifths of modern Spain – was a country under firm Muslim control and had become the most powerful and cultured state in western Europe. The Christian population, as well as the small minority of Jews, were left undisturbed in their faith but became in some measure Arabized in both culture and language. Under the rule of Abd-ar-Rahman III (912–61) the emirate of Córdoba reached what is commonly regarded as the peak of its splendour. Perhaps the last great figure of the Córdoban empire was al-Mansur, chief minister and virtual ruler from 981 to 1002. He undertook aggressive campaigns against the Christian north, sacking Barcelona, attacking León and Coimbra, and destroying the church of St James at Compostela. But after him al-Andalus fell into decay and confusion, as discordant rivalries broke up the unity of the realm. Christian rulers took advantage of the situation, beginning a slow occupation of Muslim lands in a process that historians have called 'the Reconquest'. A decisive battle against Muslim armies at Las Navas de Tolosa (1212) confirmed the end of their hegemony. Only one large territory remained under their rule: the emirate of Granada. Substantial Muslim communities, however, continued to exist throughout the rest of Spain, particularly in the kingdom of Valencia. Nearly three centuries went by before the Christian rulers were in a position to resume the wars.

The second phase of the historic struggle, which began with the capture of a frontier town of al-Andalus by the Christians in 1482, was slow and piecemeal. Ten years later the capital Granada capitulated after being besieged for a year and a half. In January 1492 the rulers of Spain, Ferdinand and Isabella, entered the Alhambra, last and most beautiful of the Muslim palaces in the peninsula. When the last Muslim king in the Hispanic realms, Abdallah (known to the Spaniards as Boabdil), abandoned his capital to the Christian forces and set off into exile with his followers, he reined back his horse to take a final look at the city he had lost, and could not restrain his tears. An oral tradition records that his mother, who accompanied the small group, scolded him: 'You do well to weep like a woman for what you could not defend as a man!' To this day the place where Abdallah stopped to lament his misfortune is known as 'the last sigh of the Moor'.[2] His departure marked the end of Islamic power but also the beginning of the slow disappearance of a culture that, over the centuries, had played a major role in creating Hispanic civilization. The 'last sigh', more than being merely the lament of a defeated king, became a symbol of the lost glory of a civilization and stimulated subsequent generations to examine and analyse the roots of cultural exile.[3]

The conditions for the peaceful handover agreed upon by both sides included a guarantee of tolerance for the Islamic faith. But it was not respected by the victors. The aggressive conversion methods of some clergy, who were strongly supported by the queen's confessor, Cardinal Cisneros, ended in the closure of Granada's principal mosque, located in the Albaicín quarter. There were riots in the streets, and eventually a major uprising throughout the province. When the revolt was suppressed the government decided to impose a harsh policy. Over the next few months the Muslims of Granada were systematically converted by force; others were expelled or allowed to emigrate. By 1501 it was officially assumed that the kingdom had become one of Christianized Moors, known thereafter as 'Moriscos' (a term used only by Christians, for the so-called Moriscos referred to themselves as 'Moors' or 'Muslims'). They were granted legal equality with Christians, but were forbidden to carry arms and subjected to growing pressure to abandon their racial culture. A huge bonfire of Arabic books, ordered by a royal decree of October 1501, was held in Granada. It was the end of the capitulations and of Muslim al-Andalus. 'If the king of the conquest does not keep faith,' lamented the former imam of the mosque at Granada, 'what can we expect from his successors?'

With Granada apparently converted, Isabella was not inclined to tolerate Muslims elsewhere in her realms. In February 1502 all Muslims in Castile were offered the choice between baptism and exile. The majority in the interior had little option but baptism, since emigration was rendered almost impossible by stringent conditions. In coastal Granada, departure was somewhat easier. They emigrated in such numbers that soon the territory was left with possibly only 40 per cent of its pre-1492 population.[4] With the obligatory conversions, Islam vanished from Castilian territory, and continued to be tolerated only in the eastern half of the peninsula, in the provinces known collectively as the Crown of Aragon. By repeating a step that had already been taken against the Jews, Isabella abolished plurality of faiths in her dominions but also created within the body of Christian society the wholly new problem of the Moriscos. The new converts thought that by accepting baptism they would be left in peace. From about 1511, however, various decrees deliberately attacked their cultural identity in an effort to make them abandon Muslim ways. Rigorous measures were taken at Granada in 1526, when all the distinctive characteristics of Morisco civilization – the use of Arabic, their clothes, their jewellery, ritual slaughter of animals, circumcision – were expressly forbidden, and the local tribunal of the Inquisition was transferred from Jaén to Granada in order to take judicial measures against backsliders.

The religious repression that affected most Spanish Muslims after the fall of Granada appears at first sight not to have been as terrible as the events, which will shortly be our concern, of a century later. However, for Muslims they created a wholly new perception of their place in the peninsula. Their homeland had been al-Andalus, they knew no other. The expulsions and conversions succeeded in transforming their homeland, and of course the parts of Spain or Africa to which they went, into a place of permanent exile. From now on, they might be physically resident within the peninsula, but it was no longer entirely their home. The sentiment is clearly expressed in the moving document that a group of Granada's leaders sent to the Sultan of Turkey, Bayezid II, in 1501, written in the Arabic script called *aljamiado*[5] and cast in the form of a *qasida* poem. The letter commences with the greeting:

> Peace be with you in the name of the slaves who remain
> in al-Andalus, in the West, the land of exile,
> who are bordered by the shimmering Mediterranean
> and the bottomless, deep, and tenebrous Ocean.

It goes on to explain how the reality of defeat and exile had entered into the hearts of Spanish Muslims:

> May God prolong your reign and your life
> and preserve you from every evil and misfortune!
> May he aid you with victory and triumph over your enemy
> and keep you in His favour and care!
> We complain before you, my Lord,
> of the injuries, shame, and enormous calamity which befell us!
> We have been betrayed and converted to Christianity,
> breaking with our own religion; we have been oppressed and
> dishonoured![6]

The Jews had been driven out into a foreign exile, but for Muslims the exile was *inside* al-Andalus, the land they had known as home. In the century after 1502 the Islamic population of Spain was systematically harassed and marginalized. In the 1520s the Muslims of the Crown of Aragon were also ordered to convert to Christianity. The new converts did not find the change of any benefit. Religious confrontation was common.[7] In the everyday contact with Old Christians there was periodic irritation and conflict over dress, speech, customs and, above all, food. Moriscos slaughtered their animal meat ritually, did not touch pork (the meat most commonly eaten in Spain) or wine, and cooked only with olive oil, whereas Christians cooked with butter or lard. They tended also to live apart in separate communities, which could lead to antagonism. Above all, the Inquisition from time to time prosecuted those who were notoriously not observing the Catholic faith. Throughout Spain there was ample evidence that most Moriscos were proud of their Islamic religion and fought to preserve their culture. The Morisco María de Lara, prosecuted by the Inquisition of Granada in 1572, admitted: 'at home we were Muslims, outside home we were Christians'. She and her family ate their meals virtually in secret within their own houses, so as not to betray the fact that the meat they consumed came from an animal that had been ritually killed. Oppression only strengthened Morisco separateness. 'They marry among themselves and do not mix with Old Christians, none of them enters religion nor joins the army nor enters domestic service nor begs alms; they live separately from Old Christians, take part in trade and are rich', runs a report of 1589 made to Philip II on the Moriscos of Toledo.[8] By contrast, for Moriscos the inquisitors were 'thieving wolves whose trade is arrogance and greed, sodomy and lust, tyranny, robbery and injustice'. The Inquisition was 'a tribunal of the devil, attended by deceit and blindness'.[9]

In Granada the discontented population responded in 1568 with a massive uprising that took over a year to put down. Some of the Morisco leaders saw no sense in the rebellion, and actively helped the Spanish authorities to repress it, contributing to the task with their own men and resources. For the rebels, there was no mercy. As punishment over 80,000 of them, including men, women and children, were forcibly expelled from Granada to the interior of Spain.

Approximately one in every four of the exiles died through sufferings and destitution. The aristocrat and historian Diego Hurtado de Mendoza, who was an eyewitness to the entire campaign, described how 'it was immensely sad for those of us who had seen them when they lived comfortably and well-off in their homes. Many died by the wayside, of travail, weariness, grief, hunger and wounds. They were robbed and sold into captivity by those very persons who were meant to be protecting them.'[10] The general who directed the operation, Don Juan of Austria, could not repress his pity at what he described as 'the saddest sight in the world, for at the time they set out there was so much rain, wind and snow that mothers had to abandon their children by the wayside and wives their husbands . . . It cannot be denied that the most distressing sight one can imagine is to see the depopulation of a kingdom.'[11] Even this did not seem an adequate solution. There were serious international dimensions, for the Turkish navy was at that time threatening Spain, and had sent troops to help the rebels in 1570. A decision to expel the entire Morisco population was reached in the 1580s in the final years of the reign of Philip II, but nothing was done because Spain was deeply involved in war in the Netherlands. When peace treaties in 1609 brought the conflict to an end, ministers turned again to the issue. In 1609 the government put into effect its decision to expel the Moriscos, a total of some 300,000 persons.

The move had been delayed for so many years that there was time for dissent to be expressed on the question. When the mass ejection was first being mooted, an official of the Inquisition spoke up and opposed the move, 'because after all *they are Spaniards like ourselves*'. Time and again, officials and intellectuals spoke up for the Islamic minority, defended them and opposed any extreme measure such as expulsion. A well-known theologian of the time, Pedro de Valencia, condemned the proposed move as 'unjust'; a government official, Fernández de Navarrete, stated that it was 'a mistaken policy decision'. Even Philip III's chief minister, the duke of Lerma, who eventually directed the measures of 1609, admitted that it was 'terrible to drive baptized people into Africa'. Yet over the five years 1609–14 the expulsions went ahead.

The country had few naval resources and would not have been able on its own to accomplish the operation, which was made possible only through the help of hundreds of English, French and Italian merchants, who agreed to charter their trading vessels.[12] The first act of expulsion took place at nightfall on 2 October 1609, when seventeen galleys from Naples and a dozen foreign merchant ships sailed out from the port of Denia in Valencia, with five thousand Moriscos on board, destined for the Spanish colony of Oran in North Africa. For the next five years, in all the villages where they lived, the soldiers systematically rounded up and escorted to points of embarkation tens of thousands of Spaniards of Arab origin. Some villages rebelled and were duly castigated; in Valencia alone over five thousand Moriscos died as a result. Hundreds took flight and lived in the mountains as outlaws, but they were slowly rooted out. Thousands of children 'under the age of reason' (that is, less than twelve or fourteen years old) were retained in Spain against the wishes of their distraught parents. The inhabitants of the totally Morisco village of Hornachos in Extremadura, agreed in 1610 to accept expulsion to Africa on one condition: that they could take their children with them.

After centuries living in Spain, many communities of Arab origin were wholly Christian. They accepted expulsion with resignation, but many chose to go to Christian France rather than to Muslim Africa. Some went by ship, others were officially allowed to enter France by a 1610 decree of King Henry IV. Fearing that the refugees would ally with the French, Spain's traditional enemies, the Spanish government soon closed the frontier. In any case, by 1611 the ports of other Christian states in the Mediterranean were refusing to accept any Morisco refugees. It was a different problem with the group of fifteen villages in Murcia, where the Arab population had been Christian since the thirteenth century. The king's own confessor, together with the local Inquisition, agreed in 1614 that the people there were Christian. They were expelled regardless. Many refugees successfully made it back to their old homes and survived illicitly in a changed and hostile Spain. In effect, however, the Muslim presence in Spain was totally wiped out in one blow. It was until the twentieth century the biggest ethnic cleansing to have been carried out in western history.

Many exceptions, amounting to several thousand, were made, and allowed to remain in the country because of special circumstances.

They included the thousands of children who were put into care to be brought up as Christians. Also included were adults who had married non-Moriscos, or could demonstrate that their parents were non-Moriscos, or had a certificate from the local bishop saying they were authentic Christians.[13] It was inevitable that many who were expelled simply made their way back and tried to carry on their lives as before. For decades afterwards, Moriscos could be found throughout the peninsula. A typical returnee was Diego Díaz, a butcher by profession, who explained how in 1609 'they put us on a ship to take us out of Spain. We put into port in Algiers, where I was for six months. After that, I got into another boat, a fishing boat. When I saw the Spanish coastline I jumped into the water and swam ashore at Tortosa. From there I went to Valencia, where I learnt my trade.'[14] He managed to carry on his life without incident, quite publicly, for over twenty years, until quarrels with his neighbours got him into trouble with the authorities. For him and thousands of others, Spain – despite the suffering – had always been home. As he explained, with an impressive feeling for the history of his people, 'We came here three hundred years ago to serve the monarchs of Castile.'

The vast majority of expelled Spaniards had to settle for a new life in the Muslim territories of North Africa.[15] Others managed to negotiate with the Ottoman authorities of eastern Europe, in order to migrate to the Balkans. A decade later an agent of the English government in Morocco reported that he found Moriscos there who 'complain bitterly of their cruel exile, and desire deeply to return under Christian rule'.[16] The émigrés from Hornachos settled in what had been the deserted town of Rabat in Morocco, and gave it new life; others settled in Salé, just across the river from Rabat. Through the centuries these émigrés have managed to retain a certain nostalgic and imagined folk memory of the land from which they came. Their houses, their vocabulary, even their music, retain vestiges of the Andalusia that had been their home, and the guitar their music-players strum in the street at night is the guitar that sings of lost Granada.[17] The memory survives.[18] A whole quarter of the city of Tunis is still called Zuqaq al-Andalus, recalling the exiles who once lived there. In the port of Bizerta there is still a quarter called Hawmat al-Andalus, or the Andalusian quarter. Other exiles moved beyond the capital of Tunisia, to towns like Testour and Sloughia in the valley of the River Medjerda, or Soliman, Menzel Bou Zelfa and Grombalia in the Cap Bon region. They preferred to marry among themselves, a practice that helped them preserve their cultural traditions, the style of the houses they built, and the songs they sang. Traditional Andalusian music, called *ma'louf*, still survives in the region. A traditional ballad in Tunisia goes:

> May rain lavishly sprinkle you as it showers!
> Oh, my time of love in Andalusia:
> our time together was just a sleeper's dream
> or a secretly grasped moment.[19]

Miguel de Cervantes, who published his *Don Quixote* in the epoch of the expulsions, was typical of many Spaniards who greeted the campaign against the Moriscos with a certain ambiguity.[20] Though he applauded the government for 'expelling poisonous fruit from Spain', he also presented the fate of the exiles with some sympathy and compassion. 'Wherever we are we weep for Spain,' says Ricote, a Morisco character in the novel, 'for we were born there and it is our native land.' The testimony of some exiles, by contrast, shows that they were happy to escape from their misery: 'day and night we were pleading with God to take us out of so much tribulation, for we wished to be in the lands of Islam'.[21] The mass ejection from the peninsula of Spaniards whose ancestors had lived there for untold generations was a policy that would eventually have a fundamental impact on Hispanic culture.

Fortunately, the exiles do not disappear from historical memory. The contact between Spaniards and North Africa was maintained continuously by Spanish missionaries, especially those who (ironically) continued to be interested in the possible conversion of the exiled Moriscos. One of these was a priest, Father Francisco Ximénez, who settled in Tunis as director of the hospital for (Christian) war captives, and spent fifteen years (1720–35) wandering around Muslim territory, evincing a barely disguised admiration for the culture of the region. In a visit to one village, he met a descendant of exiled Moriscos who informed him that his people still considered themselves Spaniards: 'they threw us out of Spain because we were Muslims, but here they said we were Christians and all the time they kept calling us in contempt "Christian son of a Christian!"[22] In another village the Morisco descendants still held bullfights in the Spanish manner. When Ximénez visited the town of Testour in the summer of 1720 he almost felt himself back at home in Spain:

They have a sheik that those same Muslims call, in Spanish, 'governor', as well as two town councillors and a policeman, in the manner of Spain. There are many of these Andalusian and Aragonese Muslims, but greater still in number are the Arabs who have come in after to live among them, so that at present the Spanish families have been mixed with the Arabs through marriage. And because of this their children are losing the Spanish language. The only ones who speak it well are the old Andalusian Muslims. Every evening that I was in this village, they sent men for me and seated me in the street in the open air, on a special mat with a cushion. And we used to speak together for hours in Spanish. They told me many tales of the old Muslims of the Calahinos, of the Infantes de Lara, of the Moors of Granada, and other tales. They spoke of the very same things that Spaniards speak about when they talk, so much so that I felt I was in some village of Spain.

The exiles left behind them a culture that had struck almost imperishable roots in the Hispanic mind. Al-Andalus was a civilization based principally on towns, for the Muslims, like the Romans before them, were primarily townspeople. The high achievement of large cities such as Córdoba and Granada, with their sophisticated political and civic organization, stands in clear contrast to the modest level of the largely pastoral and rural Christians in the north of the peninsula. Food differentiated their culture from that of Europe. The Valencia of Juan Luis Vives remained down to the seventeenth century a predominantly Islamic territory, and Arab cuisine determined a good part of the Spanish way of life.[23] Though it is difficult to determine with accuracy which plants and fruits entered the peninsula with the Arabs, it can be assumed that they brought the olive, grapefruit, lemon, orange, lime, pomegranate and fig, as well as the date palm. The North Africans were not a wheat-eating people, and relied mainly on legumes for nourishment, so that items such as broad beans, chickpeas, French beans, peas and lentils came to play a fundamental part in Andalusian agriculture. It is possible that rice was (like sugar) a part of the diet by the tenth century, though some scholars hold that it entered Spain much later. The real difference in cuisine was, of course, in the way foods were prepared. The evidence from medieval Spanish Arab cookbooks shows that they flavoured their foods, depending on the dish, with cinnamon, pepper, sesame, mace, aniseed, lemon leaf, cloves, ginger, mint and coriander, a range of spices unknown to the rest of Christian Europe. When they were driven out of the peninsula, the Arabs – and more particularly the Moriscos – took their recipes with them. Emigrants to Tunisia in the seventeenth century enriched the local forms of couscous with tomatoes, potatoes and chilli peppers that had come originally from the New World to Andalusia.[24] At the same time they developed industries in wool, cotton, silk, glass, paper, weapons and leather. Agriculture benefited from efficient irrigation works. The Muslim way of life made a profound impression on the Spanish and European vocabulary, as words denoting items and professions closely identified with the Arabs passed into common usage.

Their buildings survived them. Prominent among the memorials of the Muslim past are the great monuments, of which the mosque at Córdoba is one of the earliest and most striking. Most surviving masterpieces date from the last period of Arab rule. The beautiful Giralda at Seville, originally the minaret of a mosque and subsequently the cathedral tower, dates from the eleventh century, as does the Torre del Oro on the river banks of the same city. The masterwork of Muslim architecture, the Alhambra of Granada, acquired its most beautiful sections in the late fourteenth century. Achievements in written culture equalled those in public building. The language of al-Andalus was Arabic, spoken and written also by many Christians and Jews. All the cultures of the peninsula shared in and carried on the Islamic heritage. Christian rulers hired Arab architects to design and build palaces for them (the impressive palace of the Alcázar in Seville shows every sign of being Muslim and was in fact built by Muslims, but for a Christian king). Christian churches incorporated Arabic music and ritual into their ceremonies (the medieval Arabic-style Mozarabic rite is still used in the cathedral of Toledo). Jewish philosophers wrote their works in Arabic, for that was the cultural language of al-Andalus.

The fall of Granada and the expulsion of the Moriscos did not efface the memory among Spaniards of what it had been like to live in a multicultural society. Most leaders of the Christian state remained, for political rather than ethnic reasons, unswervingly hostile to Islamic civilization. Muslims were the chief military enemy abroad and the chief subversive influence within. On this basis a profoundly hostile image of Islam was constructed in the peninsula. But centuries of living with Muslims and converted Muslims enabled many Spaniards to take a less aggressive view. In 1514 the count of Tendilla, the governor appointed by King Ferdinand in Granada, criticized the king's attempt to make Moriscos abandon their clothing. 'What clothing did we use to wear in Spain,' he protested, 'how did we wear our hair, what sort of food did we eat, if not in the Morisco style?'[25] And in fact the efforts to make the cultures coexist continued for generations. Throughout the century prior to the events of 1609, there were mixed feelings about the role of the Islamic past and even a tendency to romanticize it, for motives that are difficult to explain.[26] Several literary works of the sixteenth century adopted the theme of the difficult coexistence between ex-Muslims and Christians. A notable example is the novel *Abencerraje y Jarifa*, by an anonymous author of 1561, which combines the themes of chivalry, love, honour and social relations between Christians and Muslims.

Perhaps most remarkably of all, the uprising of 1568 and its savage repression were written about with unusual impartiality by Castilian chroniclers. Diego Hurtado de Mendoza, from the great noble family of the Mendozas, wrote an account of considerable literary merit that was also critical of government policy and published only in 1627, fifty years after his death. Luis de Marmol Carvajal, whose history of the war (*History of the Rebellion and Punishment of the Moriscos of the Kingdom of Granada*) was published in 1600, was a soldier of astonishing culture. A prisoner for seven years in North Africa, he picked up enough Arabic to eventually write a history of Africa, then travelled to Egypt, served in Flanders and took part in the Granada wars. Perhaps the most striking work on the wars was by Ginés Pérez de Hita (d.?1619), a native of Murcia. His *Civil Wars of Granada* was published in two volumes in 1595 and 1604.[27] Part romance and part chronicle, it purports to be a narrative based on an Arabic original ascribed to a certain Aben Hamin (Cervantes later used the same trick for his *Quixote*, where the author is alleged to be a Muslim). The first volume is often considered to be an early example of the genre of historical fiction. Written in an engaging style, it offers a remarkably favourable vision of non-Christian Spain, in which the Moriscos are portrayed as sympathetic and cultivated people. A prime example of the romantic vision of Islamic Spain, it depicts the intrigues which led to the fall of Granada in 1492, chivalric combats between Muslims and Christians, and the love affairs of Muslim knights and their ladies. The second volume is an account of various episodes in the war in which he took part personally. Instead of presenting the enemy as an alien force (and he would have been entitled to do so, for there were thousands of Turkish troops who entered Granada in order to fight on the rebel side in 1568), Pérez de Hita describes the conflict as a civil war among brothers, one of 'Christians against Christians, all in the same city and kingdom'. Even in the war, he presents the Spanish troops as brutal and greedy, whereas the Morisco rebels appear as heroic and romantic.[28]

Some Moriscos had over the years made their own contribution towards creating a sympathetic attitude among the majority population. In 1588, when workers were demolishing a part of the former mosque in Granada in order to build a third nave of the cathedral, they found in the rubble a leaden box with a parchment in Arabic. Two prominent Morisco leaders, Alonso del Castillo and his son-in-law Miguel de Luna, were called in to decipher the document. Their conclusion (there was nobody at hand to contradict them) was that it was an early version of the Gospel of St John, but written in Arabic. A few years later, starting in 1595 but continuing through to 1600, the surprising discovery was made in the caves of Valparaiso (later named Sacromonte, or 'sacred hill'), outside Granada, of over twenty leaden sheets engraved in ancient Arabic, which Luna also helped to translate. His conclusion, which he communicated to the expectant (and credulous) Church authorities, was that they added further information to the Christian revelation.[29] The tablets were judged to date from very early Christian times, and depicted a form of religious practice in which features offensive to Muslims did not exist.

A big controversy ensued, with the authorities of the Church in

Granada insisting on the tablets' authenticity, while the very few
Spanish experts who knew Arabic – among them the scholar Benito
Arias Montano – had little doubt that they were forgeries. The tablets
were taken to Rome in 1642, examined and eventually pronounced to
be a fraud (perpetrated almost certainly by Luna and Castillo in an
attempt to fuse together Islamic culture and Christian faith). It was a
notable attempt to claim a place for Arabic Christianity within the
framework of Iberian Catholicism. But the tablets also helped to
reinforce the special sense of identity that the civic leaders of Granada,
whatever their ethnic descent, claimed for themselves. If Christianity
could trace some of its origins to the caves of Sacromonte, they felt,
Granada could claim a special place in Christendom. In 2000 the
papacy returned the tablets to Granada, where they can be seen displayed to the public in a museum.

The attempt of Moriscos like Luna and Castillo to rescue what
remained of the fragile links binding Christian and Islamic culture was
complemented by the remarkable case of Alonso de Luna. Alonso de
Luna was born around 1565 in the town of Linares (near Jaén, in
Andalusia). He seems to have been a son of Miguel de Luna, taking
his first name from his grandfather Alonso del Castillo. He grew up in
Granada, was brought up as a Christian, and spoke and wrote Arabic
as well as he did Castilian. At the age of twenty he converted secretly
to Islam and read the Koran (there must have been many copies accessible) so thoroughly that he claimed later to know it by heart. His
unquestionable gifts as a scholar made it possible for him to form part
of the team that translated the leaden tablets of Sacromonte. He
studied Latin, philosophy and medicine at college, perhaps one of the
colleges set up in Granada by Christian clergy. At an undisclosed age,
he left the city and went travelling through Europe. It was an absence
– we do not know how many years in all – that opened his mind to
new perceptions of the relationship between Islam and the West. He
spent some time in the south of France, then in 1610 (the year, that is,
after the final expulsion of Moriscos had commenced) was in Rome,
where he made contact with some of the pope's physicians. In 1612 he
was in Istanbul, where he met some of the Moriscos who had been
expelled from Spain, and also helped the Dutch ambassador, Cornelis
Haga, to negotiate an alliance between Turkey and the United

Provinces (which were at that date enjoying a truce with Spain, from which they would become independent many years later).[30] During all these journeys he managed to pick up sufficient French and Italian to be able to write in these languages, which suggests that his absence was not a short one, and may have lasted for at least a decade. In those fruitful years, he may have put together the ideas which led to the writing[31] of a mysterious document, known to us only in Italian and Spanish originals, called *The Gospel of Barnabas*, whose authorship has always puzzled scholars and which was probably written in Istanbul.

The *Gospel* seems to have first emerged among exiled Moriscos living in Tunis shortly after the expulsion. It became known on the continent of Europe in the course of the seventeenth century, in an Italian version now preserved in the National Library at Vienna. A version in Spanish certainly existed, for it was consulted by the English scholar George Sale when he was preparing a translation of the Koran (1734), but it later disappeared and only in 1976 turned up in Australia in a partial eighteenth-century copy. The text of this intriguing document[32] claims to be an authentic life of Christ, dating from the same period as the gospels of the Christian Bible. The basic difference is that it disagrees at several points with Christian tradition, states that Jesus (who is quoted as saying firmly, 'I am not the Messiah') was a mortal prophet but not the Son of God, that he was not crucified (Judas Iscariot was), and that he foretold the coming of the true Messiah (described as the 'Messenger'), Muhammad. The gospel was first printed in English in 1907, arousing such interest that an Arabic version was published the year after.

At several points in the *Gospel*, Jesus states explicitly that the Saviour of the world is not himself but Muhammad. 'After me,' he says in one passage, 'shall come the Splendour of all the prophets and holy ones, and shall shed light upon the darkness of all that the prophets have said, because he is the messenger of God.' Another passage states: 'Jesus smote his face with both his hands, and then smote the ground with his head. And having raised his head, he said: "Cursed be every one who shall insert into my sayings that I am the Son of God."' At yet another point:

The disciples asked, 'O Master, who shall that man be of whom you speak, who shall come into the world?' Jesus answered with joy of heart: 'He is Muhammad, Messenger of God, and when he comes into the world, even as the rain makes the earth to bear fruit when for a long time it has not rained, even so shall he be occasion of good works among men, through the abundant mercy which he shall bring. For he is a white cloud full of the mercy of God, which mercy God shall sprinkle upon the faithful like rain.

The *Gospel* was obviously written by a Muslim, and was apparently drawn up in Spanish as its original text, for the Italian version has several significant spelling errors. The fact that it has several explicit references to western Mediterranean society, and even to the writings of Dante, suggest a sixteenth-century authorship,[33] very possibly Alonso de Luna. The intention of the document, to demonstrate that Christianity is a valid religion but that its focus really points to Muhammad as the Messiah, has fascinated Muslims around the world, and it continues to be studied by some today as a serious text. The idea of a compatibility, leading eventually to a convergence, between Christianity and Islam was directly in line not only with the forgeries of Sacromonte but also, remarkably, with Luna's own direct testimony, as given to the Spanish authorities.

For by 1618 Luna was back in Spain. We do not know what motivated him to go back, though it seems likely that his travels had made him develop a sense of a special mission, one that particularly affected Spain and its Muslim exiles and therefore required Luna's presence in the country. He was also in very poor health, and no doubt hoped to end his days in the land that had once been al-Andalus. In 1618, shortly after his return, he was arrested by the Inquisition of Murcia, on the Mediterranean coast some distance from Granada, and questioned over several matters. His answers are vivid proof of the messianic hopes that some Spanish Muslims were developing. The Inquisition caught him with letters written in his own hand, one addressed to the pope and three others to the king. The letters described a vision he had had, according to the statement he made to the Inquisition:

One night in the countryside he was by the power of God carried by angels to the fourth heaven, and from there to the sixth, and he had many visions and saw God our Lord seated on his throne, with his angels who were moving the heavens. And God said to him, 'My son, do not be afraid, I shall give you to know all things, write to the king and to the pope and tell them that it is now the time of the Resurrection, when all heresies will end, and the whole world will convert to the Holy Catholic Faith.' And in the last days he will come to help the Arab nation, and the conversion will be through the Arab language, because it is the most perfect language and God has chosen it as the best, and the angels use it to praise him. And God will punish the Spaniards because they did not wish to use it, even though everybody has a duty to know it.

And every corner of this world will be made perfect, the mountains will be levelled and the waters will be extended and the superfluous waters will be transformed into air, and God will give to his chosen men the earthly Paradise, which is this world but for ever, since they are creatures less perfect than the angels. And he will give the heavens to the angels, as more perfect beings. And the book of the Koran is the book of the things of God.

And God had ordered him to write in the letters that the king should know that during his reign the General Conversion would come about. And God also revealed to him that the books of Sacromonte of this city contain the entire Catholic and Gospel truth. And that there remains one book to be read, which till now no one has managed to read or understand, which God is keeping back for himself, to be read and interpreted and given out at the Conversion and Last Judgment.[34]

It seems likely that in the end the Inquisition released Luna with a simple reprimand. They thought of torturing or imprisoning him, but judged that he was too sick to put up with either. An open condemnation of what he was claiming was out of the question, since that would have brought the Inquisition into direct conflict with the cathedral of Granada, which continued to maintain that the tablets of Sacromonte were part of the divine revelation. So Luna probably got off, and disappears thereafter into the mists of history.

The attempts to create a common ground between the Christian and Islamic traditions were collapsing long before the expulsions of 1609–14. Arabic had never been widely spoken, even among Moriscos, who spoke rather a variant of Castilian (when written, it was in Arabic script). Knowledge of the Arabic language disappeared rapidly. In the 1520s Arabic versions of the Koran were still publicly on sale in the bookshops of Barcelona; by mid-century they had disappeared. The buildings that had been the glory of the medieval past were allowed to crumble, except where they were taken over for use by Christians. Arabic almost entirely ceased to be studied at universities. There were inevitable cultural consequences. Philip II was a great collector of cultural objects and possessed an extensive collection of Arabic manuscripts, but nobody could be found capable of reading the language in order to catalogue them and Alonso del Castillo had to be called in to help. After 1614, for the next two centuries, memory of the Islamic past was preserved only in folklore and in picturesque popular celebrations such as the tournaments between 'Christians' and 'Moors', still commonly re-enacted in towns in the south of the peninsula as a stimulus to the tourist industry, and imitated during the colonial period in Spanish America.

Despite everything, Islam continued to form an extension of the Hispanic experience and could not be wholly uprooted. It was, curiously enough, the absence and exile of the Muslims that made Spaniards accept them back into the mainstream of peninsular culture. Social practices that in former times were seen as unacceptable because they were Islamic passed after the expulsions into general use among Christians and formed part of the style and manners of Spain. In the sixteenth century it was already accepted for Christian women to sit on the floor on cushions in the Muslim manner, particularly in the presence of men. When in 1555 the duke of Alba and his wife visited the queen of England, Mary Tudor, the duchess automatically seated herself on the ground, and the horrified queen made haste to raise her up and direct her to a chair, as befitted her rank. Muslim dress was commonly used among the higher class in the south of the peninsula. Muslim words communicated fundamental aspects of noble life: for example, a knight on horse was a '*jinete*', a word that in ordinary Castilian would be translated as '*caballero*', from the word '*caballo*' for horse. The vocabulary of Christian language was inevitably permeated by words of Arabic origin, many of which worked through into the rest of Europe. Among them were loanwords such as alcohol, sugar, arithmetic, rice, syrup, cotton, saffron and alchemy, which in most cases signified that the Arabs had brought the item with them or had given it an important place in everyday culture.

Throughout Spanish society, Muslim habits and courtesies prevailed until our own time.[35] Ritual washing was a custom common to Muslims and Jews, and was also adopted in medieval times by some of the Christian population. From the 1570s, the dominant Christians took steps to prohibit regular washing and bathing, on the grounds that it denoted heresy, and the habit of cleanliness began to disappear from society. The Islamic custom of having women cover their faces in public survived much longer, and was practised in the peninsula and in South America till the last century. In the seventeenth century, however, Christian moralists decided that the full or partial hiding of the face (the latter, with a fan) was a sexual provocation on the part of women. They denounced it and invited the government to prohibit it, but usually without success, for the use of fans has continued in Castile. Within living memory, travellers to Spain have experienced many courtesies of Muslim origin, such as being told by a host that 'this is your house', or being invited to share food when entering a room where others were eating (to which the obligatory response was always, 'que aproveche', 'may it profit you'). Few remember today that the common Spanish interjections 'ojalá' ('if only it were so!') and 'olé!' come directly from the Arabic ('wa-Allah', 'God will it!'). Exaggerated courtesies were also directly inherited. It was often the custom in old letter writing to sign off with the formula 'I kiss your feet', never actually written in full but expressed in the contraction 'q.s.p.b.' ('que sus pies besa'). Kissing of the feet was paralleled by kissing of the hands; both were acts of respect and vassalage. In the history of western European feudalism, the vassal shook hands with (or rather, put his hands within) the hands of his lord; in Spain the vassal, following Muslim custom, kissed hands. By extension, Spaniards kissed the hands of their parents, or of their ladies, or of their masters.

Even the Catholic way of thinking could not escape from some remnants of seven centuries of Muslim influence. Islamic thought and concepts could be found deep within the mystical ideas of Christians, as Arabist scholars have convincingly suggested. Aspects of the writing of the mystic and poet St John of the Cross, and of the imagery used by Teresa of Avila in her mystical work *The Interior Castle*, were derived from Islamic sources.[36] Some apparently marginal aspects of religious behaviour and thinking in Castile were related to Islamic practice, such as the strange habit in use among the mystical *alumbrados* of Guadalajara in the early sixteenth century, of covering their heads with a cloth when they read the holy scriptures. The only problem of these residual influences is not their existence, but deciding how they were transmitted from one cultural system to the other.

Though Islam had disappeared from Spain, it remained a permanent part of Spain's international confrontations down to our own day. Wherever Spaniards went in the age of their empire, the Moor was there as their traditional opponent, and in the Philippines in the sixteenth century a number of the tribes in the south of the archipelago were dubbed 'Moors' (a name that is still used) because they were Muslims and it seemed the easiest label to pin on them. Within the peninsula, individuals who rebelled against aspects of their own society deliberately adopted pro-Arab attitudes and customs. Because Muslims were perceived as an enemy, those who wished to rebel against Christian values expressed opinions in their favour, or even joined them. Time and again, there were cases of Spaniards who became 'renegades' and either entered Muslim service or embraced Islam.[37] Proximity to North Africa fostered a state of subdued war in defence of the remaining Spanish colonies on the African coastline, but it also promoted kinship based on the ancient memory of a shared history. When an ambassador of the sultan of Morocco visited Spain in 1690 to negotiate an exchange of war prisoners, he encountered persons who criticized the 1609 decision to 'expel this multitude after they were reckoned as Christians'. In Andalusia he met several who claimed to be proud of their Muslim ancestry, and in Madrid an unidentified secretary of the king's council came up to him and declared: 'we are of the race of the Muslims'.[38] Perhaps the last king of Spain to take a personal interest in the forgotten world of al-Andalus was the first Bourbon, Philip V, king from the year 1700, who spent five years of his reign in the province, adopted the Alcázares of Seville as his palace, and even spent a few uncomfortable nights in the Alhambra of Granada. His sleepless nights in the beautiful but semi-abandoned environment of the Alcázares (he suffered from total insomnia) may have played a part in his decision to confirm Spain's presence in Africa by mounting military expeditions across the Straits of Gibraltar.[39] After him, the dust of ruin and neglect settled on to the Muslim heritage of southern Spain.

Historical memories of Islam's fundamental role in the peninsula were consciously blotted out for over three hundred years. A few thinking people, mainly writers and poets, preserved the links, though usually in a minor and subdued way. Ironically, it fell to exiles of a later date, intellectuals who, like the Muslims, were driven out of their country for reasons that others had decided, to restore contact with the culture that had once dominated Spain. In the eighteenth century, a few writers, such as the playwright Moratín, the poet Meléndez Valdes and the essayist José Cadalso (author of the *Moroccan Letters*), made references in their work to Arabs. But apart from literary references little effort was made to explore or save the heritage that the Muslim exiles had left behind them. Neglect of the language of Spanish Arabs was such that when the authorities in 1749 wished to prepare a catalogue of the Arabic manuscripts in the Escorial, they had to call on a Syrian Christian priest to come to Spain to do the work. Foreign visitors to Spain in the eighteenth century reminded their readers back home of what remained in the peninsula from that past civilization, but their references were often resented by native Spaniards, who preferred to think of themselves as a 'European' nation. In his richly informed and illustrated *Travels through Spain in the Years 1775 and 1776* (1779, in two volumes), the English Catholic traveller Henry Swinburne (1743–1803) offered a pioneering perspective of a country that seemed to have lost touch with Europe. The work was subsequently reprinted and also translated into French, but attracted no interest in Spain. Indeed, some who were able to read the work were angered by it. The pro-Enlightenment diplomat Azara claimed that it intended to 'ridicule our government, our customs and our religion'. Swinburne, he protested, 'speaks endlessly of Moors, their history and architecture, especially in Córdoba and Granada; and surpasses himself in praises of that sublime people, in order to humiliate our own.'[40] In fact, when Swinburne was in Granada he was struck, as Washington Irving would be, by the total neglect of Spaniards for their Islamic heritage. 'The glories of Granada have passed away with its old inhabitants; its streets are choked with filth; its aqueducts crumbled to dust; its woods destroyed; its territory depopulated; its trade lost; in a word, everything in a most deplorable situation.'

Active interest in the Arab past was awakened only in the nineteenth century. The first relevant Spanish study was José Antonio Conde's *History of Arab Rule in Spain*, published in Madrid in three volumes in 1820. Conde (1766–1820), like many other intellectuals of the time, had also been an exile, one of the group of enlightened pro-French sympathizers of the early century. A specialist in languages (including some Greek and Arabic), he was educated at the University of Alcalá and in his profession rose to become director of the Escorial and its fabulous library. It was the period when the first students of the Arab language began their work in Spain, and Conde made every attempt to understand and use the manuscripts at his disposal. As an official of the foreign king imposed by the French, Napoleon's brother Joseph, he fled in 1813 to Paris along with other supporters of the regime that was overthrown by the duke of Wellington's military victories. He was able to return shortly, but not permitted back to Madrid until 1816. His substantial *History* was published only posthumously, and had immediate success in terms of interest in other countries. It came out in German in 1821, French in 1825 and English in 1854. A fellow exile living in London, called José Joaquín de Mora, paid him the presumed compliment of publishing in 1826 in London, but in Spanish, a similar history with material cribbed from Conde's work. Among the texts Conde published was a poem by the Muslim ruler Abd-ar-Rahman I, in which the emir addresses a solitary palm tree growing in Córdoba, far away from the land from which its predecessors had come:

> Oh lovely Palm, a stranger thou,
> like me in this foreign land,
> here in the West you languish now,
> far from your native strand.

'You are like myself,' the emir tells the tree, 'in a land where you are distant from your kindred.'[41] Conde in exile in Paris no doubt felt close to the homesick ruler. His approach to the history of the Arabs was pioneering in its use of original sources, and innovative in its attempt to correct traditional pro-Castilian legends, for instance about the greatness of the medieval hero El Cid, who, Conde showed, was really a bit of a thug. However, there were evident shortcomings in the level of his scholarship, and later historians logically tended to dismiss his work. The first authoritative scholar of Muslim Spain, the Dutchman Reinhart Dozy, whose study on the subject came out in 1861, was sharply critical of Conde's work, and his judgement has prevailed.

In the same decade a decisive boost was given to public interest in Granada by, quite improbably, an American. The writer Washington Irving (1783–1859) had already attained considerable success with his books and had visited Europe (1804–6), but a further visit to Spain in 1815 inspired him so greatly that he remained in Europe for seventeen years. From 1826 to 1829 he was attached to the American legations in Madrid, and had a further long stay in Spain from 1842 to 1846 as minister plenipotentiary of the United States. The Spanish years produced a pioneering life of *Columbus* (1828, translated into Spanish in 1834) and a history of the *Conquest of Granada* (1829). 'It is impossible,' he wrote to a friend during his stay in Spain, 'to travel about Andalusia and not imbibe a kind of feeling for those Moors. They deserved this beautiful country. They won it bravely, they enjoyed it generously and kindly.' In 1829 he moved to London and published *Alhambra* (1832), a narrative of the alleged history and legends of Moorish Spain, which he hastened to explain was 'not a historical romance but a romantic history'.[42] When Irving first visited the Alhambra it was a mere shadow of its past, but it fascinated his creative mind. He took up residence in the living quarters there during the summer of 1829, and made an attempt to restore the palace: 'I remained for several months, spellbound in the old enchanted pile.' He pointed out, however, that the Spaniards had grossly neglected the monument. His fictional and fantasy-like evocation of its past caught the imagination of the public everywhere and stirred the Spanish authorities to take an interest in their own heritage.

Irving's work happened to coincide with a vogue in Europe for 'Orientalism', a fashion for Arabic themes that exercised a strong influence on several British, German and French writers and artists during this active phase of European imperial expansion.[43] Men of culture who came into contact with the lands explored by their soldiers, countries such as India, Egypt, Turkey and in North Africa, were fascinated by the novelty of customs and the unexpected sophistication of artistic achievement. It is commonly agreed that the main thrust of the Orientalist movement in Europe came as a result of the interest aroused among writers, artists and archaeologists by Napoleon's 1798 expedition to Egypt. The emperor commissioned several large paintings (invariably, battle scenes) to commemorate the campaign. The French, and in their wake the Anglo-Saxons, rediscovered the Muslim past of the eastern Mediterranean, one however that was romanticized through the themes of exoticism, luxury, fanaticism, death and sensuality. The Spanish dimension of Orientalism came to birth through yet another of Napoleon's military ventures, the invasion and occupation of Spain in the first decade of the nineteenth century (see Chapter 4). Where the French went the English followed, and British appreciation of Spanish culture was extensively enhanced by the Peninsular War (1808–1814).

For perhaps the first time, Spain was discovered and appreciated by the cultured European public. The aspect that caught the imagination was not the Spain of the Romans or that of the Christian epoch, but rather the Spain of Islam, its culture and its music, which seemed to have vanished but was eagerly ferreted out by European visitors. At the end of the eighteenth century the German poet Johann Herder included songs about Granada in a collection of European folk songs he published, and Swinburne included illustrations of Andalusia in his *Travels through Spain*. The translation into English in 1803 of Pérez de Hita's *Wars* is a fair indication of the way in which Spain's Islamic past was arousing interest in other countries. The Alhambra had already, in 1811, been praised by Chateaubriand in his travel memoirs, and featured in Victor Hugo's poem *Les Orientales* (1828). Subsequently, Chateaubriand (d.1848) wrote a historical novel, *Aben-Hamet, Les aventures du dernier Abencerage*, in which he drew directly on his own visit to Andalusia and North Africa. The work gives an unashamedly romantic account of the return of a Muslim noble exile to the land of his fathers twenty-five years after the fall of Granada who meets and falls in love with a beautiful young descendant of the Cid. British contemporaries already had some knowledge of Spain's romantic Muslim past, thanks to Byron's poem *Don Juan* (1819), which was set in Spain. The curiosity for Arab civilization was further fed by Irving's attractive narratives.

The treatment of Granada, however, was not all a matter of literary fantasy. Northern European visitors to the Mediterranean in the late eighteenth and early nineteenth centuries were also inspired by 'classical', that is to say Greek and Roman, themes in art and music, and by the ruins of Roman classical civilization. When they visited Roman ruins in Spain they could not fail to observe what was left of Arabic culture. In London the architect Owen Jones (1809–74), who had previously visited Spain with a French colleague, published the fundamental study *Plans, Elevations, Sections and Details of the Alhambra* (a first version came out in 1836, and the final version was published in two volumes in 1842–5). This was also the period when one of the most discerning and informative of all English tourists, Richard Ford (1796–1858), published his *Hand-Book for Travellers in Spain, and Readers at Home* (1845),[44] based on the years – 1830 to 1833 – he stayed in the peninsula with his wife, when he made over five hundred drawings of Spanish monuments and stayed at one point in the Alhambra. Like Irving, he bore witness to the dilapidated state of the palace, which had been further ruined by the French who occupied it during the Peninsular War. There remained nothing inside the ruins of the Alhambra, he wrote, except

a few gaunt, half-starved, invalids huddled together, their only uniform being ragged misery. These scarecrows form the fit sentinels of a building ruined by Spanish apathy.[45]

On his return from Spain in 1834, he bought Heavitree House in Devon, which he rebuilt in the Andalusian style. Non-Spanish Jews also shared in the passion for the Alhambra. In the mid-nineteenth century, several French synagogues were built in the Moorish style.[46] Spanish Islam began to attract artists like the Briton John Frederick Lewis (d.1876), who spent the years 1832–4 travelling round the country producing sketches and watercolours, which he subsequently published as the superb *Sketches of Spain and Spanish Character* (1836).

Exotic and Andalusian Spain also excited the composers of Europe. Mikhail Glinka came to Spain in 1844 and spent three entirely happy years in the country, picking up musical themes that he later integrated into a *Capriccio* and an *Overture*. He enthused over Aranjuez, Madrid (for him, 'the southern Petersburg'), and inevitably Granada. Nikolai Rimsky-Korsakov, who visited the peninsula very briefly seventeen years later, while he was serving as a naval officer and some time before he turned composer, bought a book of folk-tunes while he was ashore and used the material to explore Arabic fantasies with the symphonic suite *Sheherazade* and a *Capriccio espagnol*. Verdi's *Il Trovatore* came out in Rome in 1853. Georges Bizet in 1875 brought out in Paris his opera *Carmen*, which despite furious criticism at the time for its lack of authentic Spanish melodies (Bizet had never been to Spain, and borrowed his tunes from where he could) soon established itself and was received with delight by Spaniards. The list of great European composers who inspired themselves in exotic Spain was lengthy, but in the country that inspired them there was a remarkable silence. In the first two-thirds of the nineteenth century, not a single musical work of substance was created by Spaniards on the theme of the Islamic culture that had been the driving force of their civilization for around five hundred years.

When Orientalism appeared in Spain in the early nineteenth century, consequently, it was not homegrown but something that Spaniards had caught exclusively from abroad. The main source was France, which in the nineteenth century was the unquestioned centre of Spain's elite culture. Among the few Spanish pioneers of the vogue was the gifted botanical expert Simón de Rojas Clemente (d.1827), a native of Valencia, who became so enthusiastic about the subject that he learnt Arabic, adopted Arabic dress in public, and changed his name to Mohammed Ben-Ali. During an extended visit to Granada, he thrilled to the sensation of walking through the streets dressed as an Arab. The most notorious case was that of his friend, the Catalan Domingo Badía (1767–1822), from Barcelona. His father, secretary to the military governor of the city, was transferred to a job in the province of Granada when his son was aged eleven. Domingo succeeded his father in the post, and was made administrator of the tobacco monopoly in Granada. During these years in Andalusia, he picked up his passion for Arab culture, and got to know Rojas Clemente, with whom he collaborated on a proposal to explore the interior of Africa. He learnt Arabic from Rojas and went with him to London in 1802 to further the interest in botanical studies that they both shared.

In London Badía decided to Arabize himself completely, got circumcised (at great risk to his life, because he caught an infection), and called himself 'Ali Bey', a name that had been used before him by various European adventurers. He returned to Spain and was employed by the government as a spy in the Arab world, and in the summer of 1803 landed in Tangiers. The next two years he spent in Morocco, studying the country and perfecting his Arabic. After Morocco he made his way to Tripoli and Egypt, then travelled throughout the Muslim countries of the eastern Mediterranean; in 1807, disguised as a pilgrim, he entered the sacred city of Mecca, apparently the first westerner to do so. By 1811 he was back in Spain, where his employment identified him as a supporter of the Bonapartist regime, and he was expelled from the country in 1813 along with other pro-French officials. In exile in Paris, he published an account of his travels, *Voyages d'Ali Bey el Abbassi en Afrique et en Asie, pendant les années 1803, 1804, 1805, 1806* (1814). The English published a translation two years later, but in Spain they showed no interest and the book did not appear there until 1836 (in Valencia). He decided to make another visit to the Middle East in 1818 from his home in Paris, and reached Istanbul, but was overtaken by dysentery (some said, by poison) in Aleppo, where he ended his colourful career.

The indifference in Spain to 'the first genuine Orientalist of modern Spain'[47] was compensated only by the interest taken in him by Catalans. In the mid-nineteenth century the Catalans were anxious to back the plans of 'their' general, Prim, in favour of military expansion into Africa. They seized eagerly on Ali Bey as a precursor of the African idea. However, it took some time to find out who he was, a work of research pursued by the great bibliophile of the time, Eduard Toda, who identified Ali Bey's writings. Even so, it was not until around 1934 that the work of Ali Bey managed at last to achieve some recognition in his own homeland.

For better or worse, many Europeans came to look on the Hispanic world as essentially Islamic, forgetting completely that the Spaniards normally preferred to be looked upon as Europeans. For northern European writers, poets and artists, the 'Orient' was right next to them, in hitherto unknown and recognizably exotic Spain. A European writer like Heinrich Heine could write *Almansor: a Tragedy* (1821), in which the tragedy seemingly was the fact that Christianity had triumphed over Islam. For Heine and other Romantics, the authentic Spain was Moorish. Spanish publicists may not have been too happy about it, but they accepted the Islamic image because it seemed fashionable and because at least it allotted a role to some aspect of Hispanic culture, which was very little known outside the peninsula. When the Great Exhibition was held at the Crystal Palace in London in 1851, a section was dedicated to Arabic culture, in which Granada and the Alhambra occupied a central role. Architects were fascinated by the concept of Moorish architecture, and in Brighton the architect John Nash had constructed a mosque-style Pavilion that is still a regular tourist attraction and where a free cup of tea is included in the entry price for visitors. In 1854 the Crystal Palace was re-erected in Sydenham, South London, with a special new building in it called the Alhambra Court, constructed by Owen Jones and including reproduced aspects of buildings from Córdoba and Granada. Though Orientalist styles never became a serious option for architects in England, the Exhibition stimulated other aspects of enquiry. The Catalogue of the 1851 Exhibition included a detailed study of the Alhambra by Jones, and an article giving an idyllic image of the Islamic period of Spain's history. The article was contributed by one of the key figures in modern Spanish culture and the founder of scholarly Spanish Arabism, Pascual de Gayangos.

Gayangos (1809–97) spent a quarter of his life outside Spain, an expatriate who during his absences made a gigantic contribution to the advance of Hispanic learned culture.[48] He was born in Seville (it is memorable that Spain's leading Arabists came from Andalusia) of a military family, and in 1822 at the age of thirteen was sent to study in France, where his family later joined him. He became fluent in French, and also studied Arabic under the expert Silvestre de Sacy. He went to England and at the age of nineteen married an English girl, who returned with him to Spain in 1828. From 1831 the Spanish government employed him to translate Arab documents, and in 1836 made him head of the section of Arab manuscripts in the National Library, Madrid. While working with these manuscripts he made a discovery that revolutionized the study of the Islamic presence in Spain. He found that some of the Arabic documents did not correspond to the normal language, and on transcribing them realized that they were really in Spanish, though written phonetically in Arabic script. This mixed language came to be known by Arabists as '*aljamiado*', or the language of the Moriscos. Gayangos' discovery was reported in the following words in a letter to a friend (Eugenio de Ochoa):

As you used to do, about a year ago I was turning over hundreds of Spanish manuscripts in the library of the British Museum, when I chanced across some *aljamiado* poems by our Aragonese Muslim author. Then in Madrid I was examining some so-called Arabic manuscripts in the National Library, and discovered that most of them even though written in Arabic characters really contained accounts in Castilian and in Catalan, more or less mixed up with Arab words, depending on the education or calling of the writer. I mentioned this discovery to my late master the Baron Silvestre de Sacy, who told me that when Conde passed through Paris he had spoken about the same matter, and he encouraged me to try and decipher some of the documents. I did so, and though it was very hard work at first, because of the corrupt language, the progress I made soon repaid my efforts fully.

The '*aljamiado*' literature raised hopes that an entirely new, secret, culture was about to be unearthed. As it turned out, the manuscripts represented nothing more than the decay of Muslim culture, for they were written in poor Arab grammar and poor Castilian,[49] considerations that did not of course detract from their enormous historical value.

From 1836 Gayangos made extended stays in England, whose language he mastered to such an extent that most of his published work is in it. He wrote important learned articles, and translated al-Maqqari's *History of the Mahommedan Dynasties in Spain* (1840–43) for the Royal Asiatic Society (there were problems finding a publisher in Spain). He also, as we have seen, collaborated with Owen Jones, notably in the book on the Alhambra. Meanwhile, like many scholars after him, he made frequent visits to Morocco to scour the bookshops for old Arab manuscripts, which now form part of the Arabic collection in the National Library at Madrid. In 1844 he returned to Spain as professor of Arabic at the University of Madrid, and in 1881 entered politics as senator for the city of Huelva. Subsequently he retired to London, where he spent the last fourteen years of his life and where his name has become immortal as cataloguer of the thousands of Spanish manuscripts in the British Library, as well as continuer of the catalogue of manuscripts relating to England in the Spanish state archives at Simancas. His death was an accident caused by a passing horse-carriage in a London street. Through his immense bibliophilic activity, erudite studies and learned help to the chief Hispanic scholars of his day (such as W. H. Prescott), Gayangos stands out as one of the greatest Spanish scholars of all time. He was an international scholar who had been formed fundamentally in Paris and London, but fortunately in the field of Arabic studies he did not lack successors in Spain, notably in the form of his pupil, Francisco Codera, who in turn trained the best known of modern Spanish Arabists, Miguel Asín Palacios, a priest specializing in spiritual literature.

Irving's work and the vogue for Orientalism coincided with the beginning among Spanish writers of the Romantic movement (see Chapter 5), which looked for inspiration to the legendary past. The East, including the Arab East, became an integral part of Romantic creativity.[50] Perhaps the first contributor to the vogue was a writer from northern Spain, Telesforo de Trueba (1799–1835), who though born in Santander was educated in England, where he returned in 1823 as one of the Liberal exiles fleeing from the regime of Ferdinand VII and spent most of the remainder of his life there. His entire literary oeuvre is in English, inspired by the novels of Sir Walter Scott. Among several other books and novels dealing with romantic elements in Spain's past, he published *Gomez Arias, or The Moors of the Alpujarras* (1828), the first historical novel by a Spaniard to take up the theme of the Arab presence. His book, however, remained unknown in Spain. The first effective manifesto of the Romantics was a long poem bearing the title *The Foundling Moor* (*El Moro Expósito*), published by the duke of Rivas in Madrid in 1834. Romanticism's taste for medieval history created a school of fiction in which everything associated with the medieval era – the Moorish invasions, the story of the Cid, the history of Granada – was idealized, and accepted into the cultural heritage of the nation. The image of the benevolent Moor, and of a happy medieval past associated with the coexistence of Muslims and Christians, became a recurring theme in verse, novels and drama. In 1830 Trueba published *The Romance of History: Spain*, a collection of romantic narratives of historical episodes, among them accounts of the rebellions of the Moriscos. It was the year that another Spanish exile, Martínez de la Rosa (see Chapter 5), published in Paris in a bilingual edition the play *Aben Humeya*, which dealt with the same theme. The author had read both Hurtado de Mendoza and Luis de Marmol for historical information, but in the text of his *avant propos* emphasized his own origins and his situation as an exile, as the direct inspiration:

The fact that I was born in Granada, and during my youth explored part of the Alpujarras, has been of some use to me, for I have been able to benefit from popular traditions and childhood memories, and I have ended up approaching with a sort of family intimacy, if I may put it that way, a subject that is so closely linked to my birthplace. How wonderful to remember, and to hear repeated, those beloved names, when one is far from one's country!

One of the most striking figures to contribute to the Romantic evocation of the Arab past was the poet and dramatist José Zorrilla (1817–93), who was living as a voluntary exile from Spain when he published in 1852, in Paris, the long dramatic poem *Granada. An Oriental Poem*. In the preface he stated that he was 'ashamed to see that foreign authors have knocked before us at the gates of the Alhambra', and therefore set out to create a poetical narrative of the last days of Muslim Granada (using as his main historical sources the Americans Irving and Prescott). Zorrilla quite effectively conjured up the Moorish king contemplating his territory:

> He smiled as he saw in the distance
> the Moorish ships coming from Africa,
> over a sea that seemed from afar
> a girdle of blue around Andalusia.

Or the dawn breaking over Granada:

> Under its glittering rays
> the fertile earth began to take on hue,
> giving off the gentle aroma
> of the moist night,
> the flowers began to open, the birds to trill,
> and the breeze of unruly dawn
> began to stir the woods and arouse
> the green murmuring leaves.[51]

One of the most prolific and popular poets of his time, Zorrilla spent nearly two decades of his life in exile. When he returned home (see Chapter 5) he was crowned chief poet of Spain in Granada, in the presence of the queen regent. It was a recognition not only of his work but even more of the Romantic obsession with the imagined glories of the Islamic past and their relevance to the creative imagination of Spanish writers. His evocation of Granada remains memorable:

> Leave me in Granada in the middle of paradise
> where my soul swells with poetry:
> Leave me until my time comes
> and I may intone a fitting song.
> Yes, I want my memorial stone in this land.
> Granada! Holy place of the glory of Spain,
> your mountains are the white tents of pavilions,
> your walls are the circle of a vase of flowers,
> your plain a Moorish shawl embroidered with colour,
> your towers are palm trees that imprison you.[52]

In the nineteenth century the European powers turned their eyes to the Muslim north of the continent of Africa. Spain shared in the so-called 'scramble for Africa'. Politicians and intellectuals, driven by the belief that they were a great imperial nation that had once effortlessly conquered America, felt that they were best fitted to bring civilization and religion to the Arabs. They also shared in the vision of a 'Spain' that would hold Spaniards together. In contrast to the conservative traditionalist image of a Spain that had triumphed in the medieval Reconquest, conquered the New World, spread the true faith and extended the civilization of Cervantes, the progressives of the nineteenth century began to create their own myths, which they preferred to present in terms of modernization, republicanism and imperialism. The closest area for imperialism was Africa, a dream that united all shades of opinion, both conservative and liberal, and all varieties of regional sympathy, including Castilians as well as Basques and Catalans. The French occupied Algiers in 1830, prior to extending their control over the coast of North Africa. Spain did not wish to be left behind. In 1859–60 the Liberal generals O'Donnell and Prim led a military campaign into Morocco that was intended to serve as a rallying cry for Spaniards.

The French presence in Algiers gave an important boost to Orientalism, inspiring some of the greatest paintings of Delacroix, who made a visit to North Africa. In Spain, artistic enthusiasm for the Moorish past was still muted, with one outstanding exception. That exception was the Catalan artist Mariano Fortuny y Marsal (1838–74), the century's most brilliant painter after Goya and a restless spirit who was never at home in Spain. Born in Reus (the birthplace also of Spain's leading soldier of the day, General Prim), Fortuny was trained by his family as a painter and at the age of fourteen decided to go to Barcelona to better his talents. His parents did not have the means to finance the journey, so Mariano trekked there (a distance of around 130 kilometres) on his own, and began his training. Impressed by one of his paintings, the Barcelona provincial authority gave him a scholarship to study in Rome, where he spent a highly successful year (1858), visiting museums, admiring Renaissance art, meeting friends at the Café Greco, and even selling some paintings. In 1860 Barcelona chose him to go to Morocco to make an artistic report on the actions of the Catalan troops serving there under Prim. His contact with Africa changed his life as a painter.[53]

He made a number of sketches and notes that served as the basis for subsequent paintings, among them the panoramic scenes of war that the city of Barcelona desired. But it was his contact with the Arab people and the brilliant light of the desert that inspired him with a passion for Orientalism. He even learnt a bit of Arabic. On his way back to Barcelona he passed through Madrid, where he met his future wife, daughter of the painter Madrazo, director of the Prado art gallery. The

African military sketches earned such applause in Barcelona that the city decided to finance a visit through Europe for Fortuny to study how battles were painted. Instead of battles, Fortuny found new things to excite him in Paris, above all the works of Delacroix, who had also discovered Orientalism. He never looked back after this period, was fêted everywhere, duly began painting a series of battles for Barcelona, and returned once more to Morocco, where he regularly dressed as an Arab and completed projected sketches. His paintings, full of brilliant light, impeccable detail and astonishing colour, sold rapidly. He now married, and in 1869 was invited to open a studio in Paris, where he became the centre of artistic attention. His painting *The Vicarage* (1870), an intriguingly rich canvas showing the parties in a gypsy wedding lining up to sign the parish book in the church registry, took Paris by storm. The rage for Arab-gypsy themes was at its height, and the beautifully executed canvas (which Théophile Gautier immediately compared to Goya) showed to perfection the standard images that outsiders expected of Spain: beautiful women in mantillas and folkloric dress, a swarthy bullfighter, Baroque church interiors.

The price that buyers outside Spain were willing to pay for this and other paintings turned Fortuny into a rich man. The next year he took his family to live in Granada, which he had visited before but now for two years became his home, where he could enjoy the Arab environment. After 1872 he moved to Rome, but continued to travel extensively and went to London where he met the artist Millais. In the summer of 1874 he settled in the seaside town of Portici, in the bay of Naples, where the play of sea and light enchanted him. He died unexpectedly of malaria, apparently contracted at Portici, just after moving to Rome that November. He was young, rich and successful, but immersed in depression because he could not devote enough time to what really inspired him, the Arab environment of Morocco and Granada. Leading French and Italian artists vied with each other for the honour of bearing his coffin at the funeral. His achievement echoed as far as the United States, where collectors sought his work and an art critic claimed (in 1887): 'what Chopin is to music, Fortuny is to art, and both of them have more of the gypsy wildness and strangeness of Spain in their works than the sweet classical composure of Italy or the sharp, graceful esprit of France'.[54]

Fortuny's images of Arab culture were often influenced by what he had picked up in France, but in the peninsula they were pioneering. His delightfully erotic *Odalisque* (1861, possibly influenced by the painting of the same name done by Ingres in 1842), was executed during his visit to Morocco, and communicates the rich, sensual Orientalism of a young man of twenty-three years old. His *Court of the Alhambra* (1871) is a sunbathed evocation of the forgotten past of Spain. Across the decade that separates these paintings the consciousness of the Moor as a presence in Hispanic culture was never forgotten in his work. The combination of African presence and artistic brilliance shines through in his virtually perfect *Café of the Swallows* (1868), a watercolour, depicting Arabs sipping tea during a hot Morocco afternoon, which shows Fortuny at his peak. However, he reluctantly had to give priority to the genre painting for which he was most in demand. He stunned European artists with a vision of Spain that they knew of but had never seen depicted on canvas, and pointed the way ahead for other Catalan artists, such as Casas, Rusinyol and eventually Picasso and Miró, to find in Paris a centre of inspiration. At the same time his full-scale battle scenes (notably the unfinished mammoth canvas – fifteen metres long – of *The Battle of Tetuan*, done in 1863), imitated from those painted for Napoleon, evoked for Catalans and Spaniards the dream of a military glory that they had never had in reality and which they could now invent for themselves, firmly caught within the inescapable limits of an artist's canvas. His tragically short creative period – barely fifteen years – served to drag Spanish art out of the generation of sterility it suffered after the death of Goya. Even more than Goya, Fortuny became the first of Spain's painters ever to achieve fame and wealth during his own lifetime, but that was thanks exclusively to his reputation in France and Italy. Spanish fascination for Africa extended into other branches of the arts, and overlapped for example with the renewed cult of the bullfight. From this period dates the convention by which arenas (*plazas de toros*) were built in the neo-Mudéjar medieval style, deemed as being most appropriate to a sport associated with blood, sand and African sun. The striking *plaza de toros* erected in Barcelona at this period is a notable example (made more notable perhaps by the fact that bullfights were until then almost unknown among the Catalans).

The commitment to Africa absorbed Spain's cultural leaders for over half a century. The liberal writer Joaquín Costa viewed North Africa as a mere extension of Spain:

Spain and Morocco are two halves of a single geographical unit, they form a watershed whose exterior limits are the parallel ranges of the Atlas mountains to the south and the Pyrenees to the north. The Straits of Gibraltar are not a wall separating one house from the other. Quite the contrary, they are a gate opened by Nature to allow communication between two rooms in the same house.

The essayist Ortega y Gasset, a strong supporter of the invasion of Africa, pronounced its occupation to be Spain's lot; 'a historical destiny, and in history destiny is a duty'. Others, who had the more unpleasant job of actually fighting there, saw through the hollowness of the imperial dream. An officer serving in the army denounced the perennial Golden-Age mythology that kept them there: 'What has become of the valiant soul who stuck the flag of Castile on the towers of Granada? What brought us to this war? An inspiration from Quixote?'[55] The fears were real, for the subsequent disaster at Annual (1921),[56] when Moroccan forces wiped out a Spanish army, had fatal repercussions on peninsular politics. Ramón J. Sender, who a few years later would become a lifetime exile from Spain, set down in his first novel, *Imán* (1930), a criticism of the society that had sent recruits out to die for their '*patria*'. 'That may be the *patria* there, but this is war, a man fleeing amid mutilated and defiled bodies, feet destroyed by rocks and heads by bullets.' A yet more radical critique came from the writer Arturo Barea, who was already in exile when he reflected on what he had experienced in the African war:

Why do we have to fight against the Muslims? Why do we have to 'civilize' them if they don't wish to be 'civilized'? *We* civilize them? We, from Castile, Andalusia, the mountains of Girona, who don't know how to read or write? Who will civilize *us*?[57]

The commitment to Spain's Arab identity was seen clearly by those who took part in it as a miserable fraud.

*

The presence and subsequent absence of Muslims in the peninsula has had a profound, almost incalculable, impact on the thinking of Spaniards. The absence of the Moor made it possible for writers of the Romantic school, such as José Zorrilla, to idealize him. It allowed Liberal intellectuals of the mid-nineteenth century to create their own highly imaginative vision of what Islam had represented, in order to employ it ideologically against the prevailing conservative view of Spain. The enemies of the Moriscos, namely the monarchy and the Inquisition, also happened to be those who had persecuted and driven out the Liberals. The Liberals therefore identified themselves with the suffering Arabs, wrote plays and poems about them, painted them, and tried to integrate them into the story of Spain's past. This tendency, which reached its peak in the 1840s but continued in attenuated form down to our own day, was not accompanied by any serious attempt to understand Islamic culture, research its roots or learn its language. Arabs were presented as an exotic background against which the tide of Hispanic civilization developed smoothly. Writers like Ganivet affirmed, by poetic instinct rather than through study, that 'the most important influence experienced by Spain, after the preaching of Christianity, was Arabic, which gave life to our Quixotic spirit'.[58] Liberal, Fascist and even Socialist politicians claimed that Spain had developed a 'special relation' with the Arab world,[59] but conveniently omitted to say that the relation had been marked historically by almost unprecedented brutality against the Muslim population. However, using the Arabs as a cultural fiction was somewhat different to accepting the Arabs as 'Spaniards'. That was more difficult to swallow. Arabs were therefore, with very many nineteenth-century historians, pushed into the shadows and consigned to the category of invaders, essentially outsiders to the true Spain. The whole notion of Muslim culture in Spain became, and has remained, profoundly ideological.

The problem was part of the big controversy over whether Spain was part of Europe, or part of Africa. Writers who wished to emphasize the European roots of Spain[60] were particularly insistent, as Ortega y Gasset was, that the Arabs were not an 'essential component' of the true Spain. It was a point of view put forward by influential intellectuals of the later nineteenth century, who knew very little of Arab history but were not afraid to pass judgement on it. Prominent among them was the scholar Marcelino Menéndez Pelayo (1856–1912), a brilliant young Catholic apologist who in a massive display of erudition (a multi-volume *History of Spanish Heretics*, 1880) maintained the view that since earliest times there had been a genuine nation called Spain that drew its strength from the eternal values of Catholicism alone. All other cultures, whether Jewish or Arabic, were passing phases that only contributed distortions (or 'heresies') of the true essence. His views were echoed by scholars after him. The essayist Unamuno allowed himself to write on one occasion: 'About the Arabs, I have a profound dislike for them. I hardly believe in what is called Arab civilization and I consider their passage through Spain to have been one of the greatest misfortunes we ever suffered.'[61] Ramón Menéndez Pidal, one of Spain's most respected philologists and a conservative in outlook, had a similar perspective. His view was a rather more sophisticated one of an 'eternal' Spain (a concept basic to conservative Castilian discourse) that maintained itself through the ages as a 'Catholic' and 'Spanish' entity that neither invaders nor outsiders were able to subvert. The Muslims, in his view, were merely a 'passing' influence, and did not leave their stamp on Spain. Quite the reverse, Spain left its stamp on them. 'The Spanish Muslims distinguished themselves by learning how to Hispanize Islam.' In any case, since the Muslims were foreigners the persecution of their culture was logical. 'Under the Catholic Monarchs, intolerance was necessary in order to unify the nation in its European spirit by the suppression of foreign religions.'[62]

This school of thought formed the background to several full-blooded attacks on the Liberal Arabizers. A scathing campaign was launched by the late-nineteenth-century professor of Arabic in the University of Granada, Francisco Javier Simonet, a dedicated scholar but an opponent of Orientalism and of the Romantic presentation of Muslim Spain. In a lecture in 1876 he attacked 'English and German Protestants' for idealization of the Moorish past, and denounced both Conde and Gayangos as members of a Liberal conspiracy against Spain. In another lecture in 1891 he described Orientalism, with deadly accuracy, as 'in large measure a fiction of poets and novelists'.[63] A similar reaction against the Romantics occurred in the writings of the scholar Sánchez-Albornoz. Claudio Sánchez-Albornoz (1893–1985) was a university professor of medieval history and one of the leading intellectual supporters of the Republic that came into existence in Madrid in 1931. He left the capital in May 1936 to take up the post of ambassador to Lisbon, but barely two months later his embassy was taken over by members of his diplomatic staff who sympathized with the military uprising that initiated the Civil War. He went into exile, first in France for four years, and then – when there was a danger that the pro-Nazi French government might hand him over to the regime in Spain – to Argentina.[64] In 1962 he was named honorary president of the Republic-in-exile, and did not visit Spain again until 1976, just after the death of Franco. He returned to the country permanently in 1983. His best-known work, *Spain, a Historical Enigma*, written during his years of exile and published in Argentina in 1956 in two volumes, is today largely forgotten, not so much because of its inordinately long and turgid 1,500 pages, as because it is imbued throughout with the antiquated conservative ideology and cultural myths of the generation to which he belonged. Gripped by a concern to refute the views of Américo Castro (see Chapter 1), whose name appears on page after page of the work, Sánchez-Albornoz set out to affirm and establish his view of Spain's past by bringing to bear an unrestrained torrent of words, directed not only against Castro but against all other critics, whom he accused of 'total ignorance of Spain's history'.

Part of his argument consisted of a sustained criticism (as we have seen) of the activity of the Jews in medieval Spain, but his principal scorn was directed against the Arabs. His first outspoken attack on the role of Muslims in Spain's past was published as an article, 'Spain and Islam', in 1929 in the *Revista de Occidente*, a journal directed by Ortega y Gasset. In it he argued that 'a bumbling and barbaric Africa warped the destinies of Iberia'. 'Arab culture and way of life,' he maintained, 'was insignificant in a Spain that was western in race, life and culture.' Some years later, in 1943, he expressed the view that the Muslims had diverted 'eternal' Spain from its true destiny. Had it not been for the Muslims, Spain would be a modern country like England and France. At the beginning of his *Enigma* he confessed that it was 'the great genius of Spain', Ortega y Gasset, whose interpretation of

Spain 'inspired me' to seek a similar perspective in Spain's medieval past. As a result, he had delved into history to find the true roots of the character of 'the Hispanic peoples'.

His basic conclusion was uncompromising. Long before the formation of the Arab-Jewish culture with which Castro was erroneously identifying the Hispanic condition, there existed a 'Spain' and 'Spaniards' who owed their vitality to Roman and pre-Roman origins. Those origins survived for centuries, became the basis for peninsular Christian society and modified all aspects of Islam's career in Spain. Chapter Four of *Spain, a Historical Enigma* carries the defiant heading: 'The basic fabric of Hispanic history did not become Arabized'.[65] The Arabs, he insisted, learnt from Spain, not vice versa. Arab influence on culture, customs and language was ephemeral and was never superimposed on Christians. Arab culture soon disappeared: 'two centuries after the year 711, few people in the peninsula knew Arabic well, and very few indeed understood Arabic poetry'. Arab blood also vanished: 'after over two centuries of sexual relationships with peninsular women, there scarcely remained drops of non-Spanish blood'. Spain retained its core essence despite the Arabs and despite the Jews. The greater part of the massive work was dedicated to what he recognized was not his main territory, the world of literature, on which nevertheless he expended hundreds of rambling pages, with the argument that medieval Christian literature owed little to the Islamic world. Even the Moriscos, he argued, were not Arab by origin; most of them 'descended from the Hispano-Romans'.[66] However, they were a threat, and their necessary expulsion saved the country from 'grave dangers and acute political, fiscal, economic and even national crises'.

European Arabists were quick to point out the defects in Sánchez-Albornoz's work. The eminent French specialist Lévi-Provençal, whose researches helped to lay the foundation for the study of the Arab presence in Spain, asked how the author could pontificate about Arab culture when he knew no Arabic. Sánchez-Albornoz hit back and said that Lévi-Provençal's work was basically unreliable and riddled through with errors. The astonishing truth was that for over a generation Spanish essayists, writers and historians engaged in passionate polemics over the Jewish and Arab aspects of their nation's history when they knew no Hebrew or Arabic and had never done any research into what they were arguing over. Of course, they did not need any facts, because the issue at dispute was clear enough. On one side were the traditionalists, who clung to the image of Spain as an integral part of western civilization. In order to substantiate that image, which was essential if Spain was to be identified with European material progress, they traced a direct line of cultural origins from the nineteenth century back to Roman times and even earlier. On the other were the handful of scholars in the early twentieth century, literature experts like Castro and philologists like the priest Miguel Asín Palacios (1871–1944), who took care to learn Arabic and attempted to integrate the seven Muslim centuries into the fabric of Hispanic civilization. They were denounced as propounding an 'oriental' rather than a 'European' view of Spain. Spain, it seemed, desperately wished to be seen as a 'western' or 'European' country.

In the end, and not only because of successful attempts to sell it as a tourist attraction, Granada has left an imperishable mark on the cultural memory of Europe. For many Arabs, the magnetism of Granada is that it represents an Islamic culture that flourished within European territory without losing its essential character, and maintained itself for over seven centuries. As such, it was a phenomenon without equal in the Islamic world, a promise that might again return. In the early years of the twentieth century Granada became the inspiration of the Egyptian poet Ahmad Shawqi (1868–1932), who went into exile when the British installed themselves in his homeland, and chose instead to live in Spain, where he spent six years. He travelled round Andalusia and wrote a series of poems about medieval Spain, the *Andalusiyyat*.[67] Granada survived and survives, as a symbol of resistance but also of cultural affirmation.

3

The Wars of Religion

*We had no religious wars in the sixteenth century, but we have
had them in the twentieth.*

Claudio Sánchez-Albornoz,
Spain, a Historical Enigma (1956)[1]

Spain seemed always to have been a country of believers. From the
sixteenth century onwards, visitors agreed that the culture of the
people was irremediably Catholic. As evidence they could cite the endless religious processions, the ubiquity of clergy, exaggerated number
of saints' days and holidays, universal attendance at mass, the piety of
public personages, and the *autos de fe* of the notorious Inquisition.
There seemed to be almost no deviation from the path of traditional
Christianity, a circumstance that impressed foreigners and of which
generations of Spaniards were logically proud. In medieval times,
heresy made no headway. One of the claims commonly made by
clergy was that Spain was a truly Catholic country. By the end of the
sixteenth century, Spaniards found to their relief that despite possible
threats from the Muslim and Jewish presence and the rise of the
Reformation in Europe, they had been saved from the ravages of
heresy, unlike England which had suffered upheavals and France a
destructive civil war. Church writers congratulated themselves on
living in perhaps the only Christian country in Europe. The image of
a people that retained its Catholic culture unimpaired soon became a
part of the legend. In the nineteenth century the conservative scholar
Menéndez Pelayo affirmed confidently that the essence of Spanish
culture was the Catholic faith.

This was the Spain that, apparently out of zeal for religion, expelled its cultural minorities around the year 1500 and would continue to expel thousands more of its citizens during the next four hundred years. The rite of eviction was almost, it seems, a part of the liturgy of purifying the faith. Christian Spain evolved a process for persistently excluding those aspects of its culture that were judged to be deviant or alien. That at least was the image presented by zealots of the Inquisition, by Protestant and liberal opponents of the tribunal, and by modern scholars, one of whom maintains, 'among the subjects of the Hispanic monarchy there evolved a uniform popular identity based on the Catholicism of the Counter-Reformation'.[2] But did that uniformly ultra-Catholic Spain really exist? Recent scholarship offers good reasons for doubting it. Nearly half the peninsula had been under Muslim domination for up to eight centuries, and aspects of Muslim culture inevitably rubbed off on Christians. In the same way, some Judaic influences continued to play a part in social behaviour. The result was that among both people and clergy it was common to find evidence of a shared community life and of a conviction that all religions could be equally valid. 'Every one will be saved in his own faith', a priest affirmed around 1490, and the affirmation continued to survive for centuries in many parts of Christian Spain. 'Who knows which is the better religion,' a Christian villager asked in 1501, 'ours or those of the Muslims and the Jews?'[3]

There existed an imposing array of magnificent cathedrals and monasteries, impressive public ceremonies and a numerous clergy, all of which left no doubt it was a Christian society. But out in the countryside, where 90 per cent of the people lived, the system of practice and belief was radically different.[4] The absence of dogmatic certainty was accompanied by a widespread ignorance about religion, a common-enough phenomenon in a society and era when illiteracy was high. In 1529 an influential book lamented that 'superstitions and witchcraft in these times are widespread in our Spain', and a bishop reported that people in his diocese 'know nothing about Christianity'. Throughout Spain, among people of all racial and religious antecedents, it was possible to find expressions of disbelief in an afterlife, like the statements made time and again by clergy and laity to the effect that 'nothing exists beyond being born and dying'.[5] In 1554 a prominent friar, Felipe de Meneses, claimed that everywhere in Spain there was ignorance of religion, 'not only among barbarous and uncivilized mountain people but also in those presumed to be civilized, not only in small villages but even in cities. If you ask what it is to be a Christian, they can no more give an answer than savages can.' Trying to find a parallel to the situation, Meneses could only compare Spaniards to the savages of America: 'experience has shown that there are Indies in Castile and that in the very heart of Castile there are mountains, that is, mountains of ignorance'. The description 'Indies' quickly caught on. In 1568 a dignitary of the city of Oviedo in northern Spain appealed to the new Jesuit order to come and preach to his people: 'these are veritable Indies that we have within Spain', he wrote.

The apparently 'Christian' culture of the people of Spain between the sixteenth and nineteenth centuries left much to be desired, since both clergy and people were equally ignorant of basic essentials. Religion ended up (as in many other countries) as an extension of social discourse rather than a system of faith; it was, in other words, what you did rather than what you believed. Religion was the centre of village activity, of community feeling, and of armed conflict. Rather than being only the list of practices laid down by the Church, it was the sum of inherited attitudes and rituals relating both to the invisible and to the visible world.[6] All sections of society, both in town and country, participated in the rituals, which on the one hand determined leisure and work activity, and on the other assigned to people their roles and status within the community. There was no essential contradiction between Spaniards being 'Christian', yet at the same time having no real knowledge of Christianity. There was no formal separation between the sacred and the secular in early modern Europe; the sacred was always part of the profane world, on which it drew for its symbols and functioning.

It was a largely unlettered world, often isolated from the culture of the great cities.[7] The dominant realities were the precariousness of harvests and the insecurity of life. Food and survival, as in primitive rural communities today, dictated social, moral and religious attitudes. Poor diet, frequent crop failures, a high mortality rate, were not mere hazards but part of the very fabric of existence. They were accepted as inevitable, but then as now men took out insurance against what they could not foresee or control. Religion was a major protective force, and where official religion seemed inadequate other rites – such as witchcraft – were used. Life was not, for all that, a pessimistic attempt to ward off disaster. Given that some things were inevitable, there was every reason to abandon oneself to joy and celebration. In rural Spain the full-time labour of modern society was unknown, and towns spent at least one-third of the days in the year on holiday. Ritual festivities – plays, carnivals, processions – were a major, integral and regular aspect of life. They were essential to the life of the community, which normally dictated their form and content; and they were pleasing to the Church, with whose great festivals (Christmas, pre-Lenten Carnival) they coincided. The mixture of communal and religious elements in popular festivities had always caused problems and friction, but long use tended to hallow the ceremonies. In a pre-industrial economy, virtually all rituals were related to the agrarian life of the community. The annual calendar began at Christmas, succeeded very quickly by an outburst of celebration for Carnival, which was the prelude to Lent, the season of waiting and reflection. After the spring equinox, the month of May arrived with its symbols of life and fertility. Work resumed in the fields, and the productive season was crowned by the midsummer fire rituals of St John's Eve. From July the harvest was gathered in, with further celebrations in the community.

Formal Catholic doctrine during the Golden Age of peninsular culture played little part in the essentially folk belief of Spaniards. Religious practice was traditional and sociable rather than theological. People went outside the Church for folk remedies and practices, or for exotic knowledge, or for spiritual and mystical solutions to their anxieties. Within the heart of Spain, the highest nobility of the court of Philip II became supporters of prophetic cranks.[8] Church dogmas barely penetrated daily religion: for example, the doctrine of purgatory was being formally affirmed in Spain only in the 1600s[9] and throughout that century there were bitter quarrels among the clergy over whether the Virgin Mary was born free from Original Sin. Matrimony and even baptism tended to be community rather than religious rituals. The profundity of Spain's Catholicism one hundred years after the period of the Counter-Reformation is still open to debate.[10] In Mallorca, attempts to control a virtually pagan Carnival can be dated back to the fifteenth century. The authorities there banned indecent dances, the donning of clerical dress by carousers, running naked through the streets, and the wearing of masks.[11] In Catalonia the clergy tried to eliminate popular religious practices, enforced the new rituals of worship (Catalonia formerly had a distinct rite of mass), ordered Sunday to be a day of rest from work, set up Sunday schools, changed the imagery in the churches, and stopped the custom of 'playing the guitar and singing profane songs before the Sacrament' (1610).

Discipline of some sort was certainly imposed. Eventually, after a century or more, most people went to church, got married there and took their children to be baptized. They also took part in the great feasts and processions dictated by the clergy. They remained, however, overwhelmingly ignorant of the faith and seldom allowed it to govern their personal lives, their social behaviour or their sexual practice. In the early 1900s the poet Antonio Machado commented on his area of Andalusia: 'the religion of the people consists of superstition and belief in miracles. It is evident that the Gospel does not abide in the Spanish soul.'[12] From as early as the sixteenth century, clergy experienced extraordinary difficulty trying to persuade their parishioners to give up pre-marital intercourse in favour of post-marital. A century later, in Catalonia and in Aragon it was still common for village marriages to be consummated long before the church ceremony.[13] Clergy were particularly concerned about sexual licence: the widespread practice of living 'in sin', the refusal to regard prostitution as wrong, the 'lascivious music and dances' in village celebrations, the semi-nudity of women in stage presentations, and the popularity of 'filthy and devilish' dances such as the saraband.[14] Popular sexual standards survived all attempts at control. In the late seventeenth century an English traveller concluded that 'for fornication and impurity they are the worst of all Nations, at least in Europe; almost all the Inns in Andaluzia, Castile, Granada, Murcia &c having whores who dress the meat and do all the business.'[15] In the nineteenth century, Lord Byron was enchanted by the sensuality, as he saw it, of Andalusia.

From the 1520s the clergy in parts of the country undertook 'missions', intended to bring true religion to the people. The reforming impulse, which had profound evangelical and humanist roots, developed both in the peninsula and in the lands newly discovered in America. At the same time, conservative elements in the Church put themselves on their guard against new religious ideas, which they denounced as 'heresy'. The notion of 'heresy' served to identify people as enemies of the faith. Just as Spanish society had denied a role to Muslims and Jews, it began to deny a role to Christians with whom it disagreed, and consequently brought into existence a further class of potential exiles. Precisely in the 1520s, western Europe was bubbling with ideas of dissent, and Spain did not remain immune. Church leaders learnt of the rise in Germany of a movement of reform inspired by a monk called Martin Luther. The 'Reformation' excited educated Spaniards to take a closer interest in the northern world. Few of them had travelled in those parts of Europe, but the succession of a northerner – Charles V – to the crown of Spain now gave them the opportunity to accompany the royal court and explore the continent. Hundreds of Spanish nobles and clergy were in the entourage of Charles and of his son and successor Philip II when they visited Italy, Germany, France, England and the Netherlands in the first half of the sixteenth century. Among them were many restless spirits who were not satisfied with what their own country offered and wanted to expand their horizons abroad. The contact between Spain and Europe was profoundly positive, but also threw into relief the differences between Mediterranean and northern concepts of Catholicism.

In the early sixteenth century, before religious differences among Christians began to provoke a state of permanent confrontation between Catholics and Protestants, it was normal for scholars, artists, pilgrims and followers of other itinerant professions to spend years and even decades away from their places of origin. There were no firm national boundaries in Europe, and in consequence no fixed languages or loyalties. All classes of people moved far from home, just as in medieval times wandering scholars, adventurers and clergy had travelled from country to country, carrying their culture with them. Soldiers, as in the French case of Martin Guerre,[16] might disappear for decades and turn up suddenly one day. Spaniards, as we know from the extensive wanderings of the author of the *Quixote*, shared in this freedom of movement. The court of Charles V included prominent Spaniards who spent virtually their whole life as expatriates, outside their native country. One of them was the emperor's father confessor, the Dominican friar Pedro de Soto, who spent all his active life in Germany and published all his books there, in Augsburg, Ingolstadt and Dillingen. Another was the poet Cristóbal de Castillejo (c.1496–1550). Castillejo came from a noble family of Ciudad Rodrigo and at the age of fifteen began serving in the royal household, first as page to King Ferdinand and then as secretary to the king's grandson, Prince Ferdinand, four years younger than Castillejo. The prince subsequently left Spain to become king of Bohemia and Hungary, and in 1525 summoned Castillejo (now a Cistercian monk) to join him in Vienna. The poet spent the rest of his life in Ferdinand's service, and never returned to Spain. He travelled throughout the continent, making one visit to England and several to Italy, which remained his source of inspiration for the delicate and elegant poems he continued to write. He published only one work during his lifetime, the fascinating *Dialogue of Women*, which came out anonymously at Venice in 1544.[17] Written in Spanish, it is an Italianate work, courtly in content and construction, a product less of Spanish culture than of the Italian Renaissance.

Since the time of the Renaissance, a few notable centres, among them Paris and Rome, had offered a welcome to university students of all nations. Spaniards went in droves to Italy, nearly half of which was, since the 1500s, a part of the empire governed by the rulers of Spain. In addition, Rome was the one universal attraction in Europe, the seat of the supreme ruler of the Catholic Church. But young scholars also had a strong preference for Paris if they wanted to study, and the city became a meeting-place for Spaniards who, like Luis Vives, were seeking ideas and education. One of the Spaniards who went to Paris, and ended up spending most of his life outside Spain, was a young medical student from the city of Segovia, called Andrés Laguna. Laguna (c.1509–59) was, like Vives, one of the great intellectual prodigies produced by the Hispanic world, and also like Vives he spent the greater part of his life outside his native country.[18] It has been suggested that the operative reason for this virtual self-exile was his converso origin, which seems to have stood in the way of him furthering his studies in Spain. His doctor father educated him in Segovia and then briefly at Salamanca, but he broadened his intellectual formation only on proceeding to the Collège de France in Paris, where he studied medicine and learnt Greek. In Paris he also published his first works, a translation (into Latin) from Aristotle, and a study of anatomy. Laguna then returned for three years (1536–9) to Spain, where he was consulted on one occasion by the royal court, after which he left the country for London and then Flanders. His career thereafter, like that of Vives, belonged no longer to the Hispanic world but to Europe.

For five years (1540–45) Laguna served as municipal doctor to the German city of Metz, years during which he also managed a short stay at Cologne, where he published translations into Latin of works on medicine and botany. These were years of tension in the Germanic lands, when the ideas of the Reformation threatened both religious and political solidarity. The University of Cologne asked him to give a lecture, which he delivered in Latin on an evening of January 1543 before an official audience of professors, in a hall of the university that was lit by the flame of torches. His theme, which has never ceased to be relevant since then, was on 'Europe' and the dangers facing it from internal dissension. Among the problems he had in mind was the threat from the military power of Turkey, a country whose significance he would dwell on a few years later in the best known of his writings. When he left Metz in 1545, by now famous as a scholar, he made a first trip to Italy, where the University of Bologna bestowed on him the title of doctor, and the pope honoured him for services to the Catholic faith. Apart from a short return visit to Germany, he went on to spend the next ten years in Italy, where in 1550 the pope appointed him as one of his doctors and he enjoyed the patronage of a leading Castilian humanist prelate, Cardinal Mendoza of Burgos. It was a period of great productivity for Laguna. He published in Venice six volumes dedicated to the methods and learning of the standard medical authority of the Renaissance, Galen, and also a volume on the gout, based on data 'that I picked up during my travels through Spain, France, England, Germany and Italy'. During that time, one of his pet projects was a translation from Greek into Castilian – almost the only item he ever published in this language – of a botanical work, the

Dioscorides. He travelled northwards with the translation in his baggage, in order to oversee its publication at Antwerp in 1555. He dedicated the book to the emperor's son, who within a few months was to become king of Spain as Philip II. It was a resumption of links with his origins. Early in 1558 he returned to his native city, as an act of piety, in order to place a commemorative brass plaque on the tomb of his dead father. He made one further journey abroad, in an official capacity, but managed to return to die in the nearby city of Guadalajara, and was buried in the family tomb in Segovia.

Though its authorship was long in doubt, there is general agreement that the dialogue known as the *Journey to Turkey* (dated to around 1557) was composed by Laguna. It remained unpublished until as late as 1905, when the editor presented it as a narrative of an actual journey made. Dialogues were a favourite literary form of the Renaissance period. It has been estimated that the number of dialogues written in Spain at that time, both in Spanish and Latin, add up to between one and two hundred.[19] The *Journey to Turkey* was, despite appearances, a fictional narrative in the form of a dialogue between three old university friends who meet many years afterwards and relate their experiences. The central theme concerns the travel experiences of Pedro de Urdemalas ('Peter the Fiction Teller'), who served as a soldier, was captured in Italy by Turkish pirates and taken to Constantinople as a slave. In his eight years of captivity he learns to be a doctor, with such success that he rises to become doctor to the Turkish royal family. He later escapes and makes his way back to Spain through Greece and Italy. His companions in the dialogue ask him questions about his journeys, to which he makes unconventional answers. He loves Spain, it turns out, but finds it backward compared to other nations, especially Italy. As a well-travelled man, he judges that Spaniards are hopeless in languages, especially Latin; their soldiers are poor; their theologians deplorable; their trading methods backward. Of all the professional men the most competent are the doctors. And there is one item of unstinting praise: of all the foods in his experience those of Castile are the most satisfying.[20]

Throughout the 1530s, long before there was any hint of a radical change on the religious front, the Collège de France in Paris 'was a centre that attracted humanists from all countries'.[21] The students were part of the *peregrinatio academica*, as it was called in Latin, a medieval habit of wandering abroad to 'study in foreign parts'. The Spanish colony in Paris included several young men who were in search of new ideas. By the mid-sixteenth century, however, Europe was ceasing to be an area where everyone shared a common fund of ideas, and absence from home took on a special significance, because of serious political and religious differences that might lead to exclusion and even exile. The University at Paris, precisely because it was cosmopolitan, shared in this process of change. In the 1530s it harboured, among very many other students, a small group of international friends who were studying theology and accepted the leadership of a young Basque nobleman, Ignatius of Loyola, founder of the Society of Jesus. Spaniards are proud of the fact that they helped to found the Jesuits. Yet curiously enough this most Catholic of religious orders was constantly the centre of controversy in Spain, where its history from beginning to end was overshadowed by the experience of exile.

Ignatius of Loyola (1491–1556), founder of the Jesuits, was born at the Loyola family castle near Azpeitia in Guipuzcoa, northern Spain. He took up warfare as a career, serving the Spanish authorities who at that time had occupied Navarre and annexed it to the crown of Castile. In an engagement against Navarrese rebels allied to the French, he received a leg wound and had to withdraw. While convalescing, he read a life of Christ and experienced a complete change in his ideas. When he recovered, he decided to set out on a pilgrimage to Jerusalem, but on his way there he stopped at the Benedictine abbey of Montserrat in Catalonia, where he dedicated himself to God. He went on to spend nearly a year in spiritual retreat at nearby Manresa. Here he had the mystical experience that later inspired his handbook of spirituality, the *Spiritual Exercises*. The cell where he mused is still preserved in its original state within the incongruously immense Jesuit building constructed over it more than a century later. He continued his journey to Rome, Venice and Jerusalem. On his return to Spain in 1524, he studied at various universities, including that of Alcalá. In this town he had an experience that was to affect his career decisively.

As a student in Alcalá he developed links with others who were interested in improving their spiritual lives through the formation of small prayer groups consisting not of clergy but only of lay people.[22] Loyola joined a group consisting of three or four other young men, who dressed in a singular way – in long habits with hoods – and met in each other's rooms for prayers. The circle was later widened with the addition of some women. Unfortunately, these happened to be the very months that similar prayer groups in Castile, known as the *alumbrados* or 'illuminists', were attracting the attention of Church authorities because of their apparently unorthodox ideas. At the end of 1526, Loyola and his friends were warned by an officer of the Inquisition to change their spiritual methods and to dress more conventionally. The following April, he was arrested by the bishop's tribunal on related charges, and a couple of months later was forbidden to teach his ideas publicly. In the summer he moved from Alcalá in order to get away from the harassment and settled in Salamanca, but was detained there for the same reasons and warned that he should study more before trying out spiritual methods. In addition to the doubts about his prayer activities, there was a lurking suspicion in the minds of the authorities that he and his friends were Jews or conversos, since the *alumbrados* in Castile were usually of converso origin. Loyola indignantly rejected these assertions, and ever thereafter treated with contempt the anti-Semitic attitude of officials in Castile. In the autumn, he left the hassle behind him, travelled north through Barcelona and took the road for Paris. He never again returned to Spain.

At the end of the nineteenth century, the novelist Pio Baroja felt that there must have been something defective in the culture of Spain for Loyola to become an exile. 'Would he have left Spain permanently if he could have found an active centre of culture in his country?' he asked.[23] For a long time in Spain there continued to be a strong current of suspicion directed against Loyola and his followers. Prominent clergy and prelates, usually from the rival Dominican order, never ceased to insinuate that the Jesuits were heretics. In 1553 a Dominican theologian was still insisting that Loyola had fled from Spain because he was an *alumbrado*.[24] Despite the lifelong absence, in later years Loyola always kept in close touch with his homeland. In Paris he was the guiding influence on the six young men (three of them

Spaniards) who together took vows of poverty and chastity in a little church on the hill of Montmartre in 1534. After considering and rejecting their first intention of working for Christ in the Holy Land, the group decided to offer their services to the pope. The latter, in 1540, gave his approval to the rules for a new religious order, to be known as the Society (Loyola rejected the idea of being yet another 'order', and preferred the term 'company' or 'society') of Jesus, with Loyola as its first general.

The Jesuits increased their membership rapidly and had enormous success in a Europe where they were specially trained to combat heresy. But they also excited opposition, not least in Spain. Many of the clergy, including powerful prelates, were suspicious of the Society because it was foreign in origin (there were few Castilians at first, most were Italians, Basques, Frenchmen and Portuguese), tended to advance itself through influence at court, and counted clergy of Jewish origin among its few Castilian members. Loyola was, as we have noted, particularly conscious of the anti-Semitic attitudes in Castile. From the 1540s he encouraged his clergy in Spain to stand firm against racial prejudice. All through the controversy in Spain about the statutes of *limpieza* (see Chapter 1), and up to his death in 1556, he would not allow his order to discriminate against candidates who were conversos. When conversos did apply to join, however, he advised them to enter the Society in Italy rather than in Spain. When talking of the *limpieza* cult he would refer to it as '*el humor español*' – 'the Spanish whim'; or, more bitingly on one occasion, '*el humor de la corte y del Rey de España*' – 'the whim of the Spanish king and his court'. His immediate successor as general was a Castilian, Diego Laínez. Laínez (1512–65) had been with Loyola since the early days at the University of Alcalá, but was a converso and consequently aroused strong opposition among anti-Semitic sectors of the Spanish Church. Though a Spaniard, like Loyola he also became an exile and never returned to Spain, spending his active career entirely in France and Italy.

However, racialism was not the only problem. Clergy were suspicious of anybody who had contact with the world outside. A Jesuit from Valladolid reported the opinion among some people 'that the Theatines[25] (which is what they call us here in this Babel) have been the source of Luther's errors'. Inquisitors tended to come from the rival Dominican order, and had repeatedly found cause to criticize the Jesuits. The first Index of Prohibited Books issued by the Inquisition in 1559 listed among its prohibitions a volume whose author happened to be the best-known Jesuit in the country. This was Francisco Borja, duke of Gandía and former viceroy of Catalonia, the most distinguished recruit ever to join the Society in Spain. The condemnation fell like a bombshell, because it threatened to bring disrepute not only on Borja but on all the Jesuits. For several weeks the Jesuit leaders carried on an anguished correspondence, some of it in cipher (which proved to be a headache for me when I puzzled over the documents in the Jesuit archives in Rome), over what to do. Some felt that Borja should stay and confront the problem squarely. Borja himself, fearing that he was about to be arrested by the Inquisition, hurriedly left Spain for Portugal and then Rome in the spring of 1560 and never again returned to his homeland.[26]

Borja's exile was a consequence of quarrels within Spain's dominant ideology and within its ruling class. In subsequent years, there would be other reasons for Spaniards to separate themselves from their homeland. Not all did so, however, because of rejection. Many were obliged by professional duty to spend the greater part of their lives outside the country. Some travelled incredible distances and never saw Spain again. Others bore with the voluntary absence but eventually managed to return home, bringing back with them the civilization of Europe, which they grafted on to their own Spanish culture. In matters of the Catholic religion, Europeans inevitably gravitated towards Rome, where there had since Renaissance times been a considerable colony of Spaniards. Some who found the university environment in their country unappealing fled gladly to the more cosmopolitan air of Italy. From Salamanca the Castilian humanist Juan Ginés de Sepúlveda wrote in 1549 to his friend, the physician Luis de Lucena, congratulating him on his decision to pursue his studies not in Spain but in Rome:

To live among excellent and learned persons, to reflect without envy and disrepute, neither deceiving nor listening to deceptions, without putting on a false show of virtue, without fear of calumny and flattery, that to me is not just liberty, it is the commencement of a happy life.[27]

Rome set the standards in questions of music, and Spaniards went there to study. The two foremost masters of sacred music in the peninsula both spent long years in the papal city. Cristóbal de Morales (1500–53), born in Seville, trained as a chorister and sang in the ceremonies at the marriage in the cathedral of the emperor Charles V and Isabella of Portugal. By 1526 he had moved on to Avila, where he directed the chapel choir. In 1535 he began his sojourn in Rome, as a member of the papal choir and also as composer in his spare time. He wrote a cantata in six parts for the ceremonies at Nice (at that time a part of Savoy, but later absorbed by France), when the pope supervised diplomatic negotiations between the emperor and the king of France. Morales' main compositions were published not in Spain but at Venice, in 1542 (his motets) and 1544 (his masses, in two volumes). Thanks to them, he was the first Spanish composer to gain a European reputation. Even though he returned home in 1545 and became chapel master of Toledo cathedral, a Spanish writer of 1555 complimented him as a 'foreign composer', because his melodies had a technical skill and profundity not to be found in the sacred music of the peninsula.[28]

A more prolonged stay abroad was the fate of Tomás Luis de Victoria (1548–1611), universally recognized as Spain's outstanding composer of the late Renaissance. Though the country had boasted good composers such as Francisco Guerrero and Cristóbal de Morales, whose work achieved some recognition in the peninsula, it was not until the end of the sixteenth century that it produced a figure of truly international stature. Victoria came from a prominent noble family in the north Castilian city of Avila, seventh among the eleven children of his parents. His early education included the study of music, and serving as a chorister in the cathedral. At the age of eighteen his widowed mother sent him to further his musical career with the Jesuits in Rome, at the German College, which trained young clergy for the mission field in Germany. Around half the students were Germans, the rest Spaniards, English and Italians. For the next twenty years Victoria lived outside his native land. In Rome he obtained the sponsorship of the cardinal archbishop of Augsburg, and continued his studies, possibly at one time under the supervision of the great master of Church music, Palestrina. While at the College, Victoria was also for a while organist to the church of Montserrat, a church for Spanish residents. In 1573 the students at the College were separated for administrative convenience into two sections, and at the ceremony when the change was put into effect they sang an item specially composed for them by Victoria, a motet on the classical theme of leave-taking, *Super flumina Babylonis*.[29] In 1575 Victoria finally received consecration as a priest, at the hands of an exiled English bishop in Rome, in the English church on the Via di Monserrato.

Shortly after, he entered the newly formed religious order of the Oratory and was made chaplain of a church. Though his whole life was centred in Rome and its music, however, he never lost the desire to return to Spain. In dedicating one of his mass-books (1583) to Philip II he expressed a wish to be able to return to his country. Some time later, the king responded by appointing him chaplain to his sister, the empress Maria, who came back to Spain from Vienna when her husband the emperor Ferdinand died. Victoria returned to Spain in 1587 and served as chapel master to the empress at her residence in the royal convent of the Discalced Carmelites, which continues to be one of the lesser-known treasures of Madrid palace architecture. Apart from a further three-year absence in Rome, when he assisted at the funeral of his master Palestrina, Victoria spent the rest of his life in Madrid, serving the convent as musician and chaplain. With him came the voluminous texts of his precious compositions, which he published over the next few years, both in Madrid and in Rome. Though he wrote a number of lesser pieces of sacred music, which soon became popular because of their profound and plaintive poignancy, his posthumous reputation rests solidly on his masses, of which he composed at least twenty, in the style made familiar by the work of Palestrina. His music gradually became known and sung throughout Spain and Italy, penetrating into central Europe and even into South America. In a sense he was the greatest of the pre-nineteenth-century Spanish musicians, the only one whose music became universal, extending well beyond the Hispanic world.

Beginning around 1525, there were fears that the ideas of Martin Luther in Germany might gain currency in the peninsula. In the event, little of consequence happened for thirty years. Some of Spain's restless spirits, however, were beginning to decide that their future was safer in another country. One of them, Miguel Servet from Aragon, did not choose wisely. Servet (1511–53), from the village of Villanueva de Sijena (ninety-six kilometres north of Saragossa), was at the age of seventeen sent by his father to study at Toulouse in France, and spent the rest of his life outside his native country. A perpetual exile, he was driven by his brilliant mind and restless search for knowledge. He dedicated himself to learning the tongues that opened the way to knowledge, and ended up with a command of Greek, Arabic and Hebrew. He visited the German lands as a member of the court of Emperor Charles V, and met the principal leaders of the Reformation, among them Melanchthon and Bucer. In 1531 he was studying medicine at the University of Paris, but never obtained any qualifications nor practised as a doctor, though he continued to be fascinated by exotic aspects of the science. That same year, at the precocious age of twenty, he published in Haguenau his work *Errors about the Trinity*, in which he argued that the Christian teaching about three persons in one God had no basis in the Bible. The book shocked by its premises and was forbidden even in some cities controlled by the Reformers. Word of his theories got about, and in the course of 1532 the Inquisition in Spain and the French Inquisition in Toulouse made independent moves to bring him to trial. Servet did not ignore the threat, and decided to go into hiding or even emigrate to America. In his own words, 'terrified on this account and fleeing into exile, for many years I lurked among strangers in sore grief of mind. Because of the persecution, I longed to flee to the sea or to one of the new isles [of the Caribbean].'[30] He changed his name to Michel de Villeneuve (from the name of his home village), and began a peregrinating life, moving quietly round France for the next twenty years, always with caution but also burning with the excitement of new ideas.

He was at Paris (where he again studied medicine at the university as an ordinary student), Lyon, Avignon and Vienne, and practised various professions, notably as a printer. In 1535 he published an edition of Ptolemy's *Geography*, in which he made observations on the different peoples of Europe and caustic comments comparing Spaniards to Frenchmen.

The Spaniard is restless in mind, ambitious in his projects, and reluctant to be taught. Even when only half-educated, he thinks he is an intellectual. You will find that all the Spaniards outside their country are intellectuals. They prefer to talk in Spanish rather than in Latin. They tend to cultivate barbaric behaviour in their customs and manners.[31]

After many years away from home, living and thinking like a Frenchman, he belonged less to the peninsula than to the agitated intellectual world of Europe. Finally, in 1553, he published anonymously in Latin at Vienne his principal work, *The Restoration of Christianity*, a fat volume of over seven hundred pages in octavo.

Scholars today remember the *Restoration* because it contains, on pages 169–71, the first statement published in Europe modifying older views on the pulmonary circulation of blood. Doctors had previously followed the belief of the second-century physician Galen that aeration of the blood took place in the heart. Galen held that the blood reaching the right side of the heart went through invisible pores in the cardiac septum to the left side of the heart, where it mixed with air to create spirit and was then distributed to the body. A thirteenth-century Arab physician in Egypt, Ibn Nafis, was the first to suggest that this view was wrong, but his writings were unknown in the West. In his book, Servet concluded that transformation of the blood, accomplished by the release of waste gases and the infusion of air, occurred in the lungs. Blood, he theorized, flows from one side of the heart to the other via the lungs instead of through the wall between the ventricles.

The vital spirit – arterial blood – is first to be found in the left ventricle of the heart, owing to the lungs by which it is produced. This vital spirit originates in a mixture achieved in the lungs, of the air that these inhale and of the blood that the right ventricle of the heart sends to the left one. This communication does not take place through the intermediate wall that divides the heart, as is commonly believed, but rather through a long circuit across the lungs. There is no doubt that the mixture takes place in the lungs. The blood is given its bright colour not by the heart, but by the lungs.[32]

Though his text passed unnoticed at the time, Servet has the credit of being the first European to publish the theory. Effective glory for the medical discovery, however, belongs more properly to his contemporary, the Cremona physician Realdo Colombo, a professor at Padua University whose anatomical researches paved the way directly for the practical demonstration made later by the seventeenth-century English physician William Harvey.[33] Servet was fascinated by medicine but his real purpose was religious – to put into print the dream of a new, radical Reformation to which the work of Luther and Calvin would be only a prelude. His attention to blood arose from the idea, common enough at the time, that the human soul resides in the blood, which alone gives life. The future of the soul concerned him, rather than the movement of blood. His basic idea in the *Restoration* was that the historic Christ was only a man, not God. God was not three persons, as the orthodox doctrine of the Trinity maintained, but simply one. He quoted from both Islamic and Jewish sources on this point, thereby provoking accusations (certainly unfounded) that he was pro-Jewish or of Jewish origin. Salvation of the soul, he maintained, was to be achieved through Christ, the man. The proposition was not simply heretical, it struck at the root of classical Christianity and was seen by all religious leaders as blasphemous. In reality, Servet rejected every single tenet of classical Christianity, whether taught by Catholics or by Protestants.[34] The whole Church, in his view, had been taken over by Satan after the Council of Nicaea in AD 325. 'Two very serious plagues,' he wrote, 'deprived us of Christ: a leaven of Aristotle, and ignorance of the Hebrew language. And then we lost Christ.'[35] The Spanish inquisitors, when informed of the book's contents, took the matter as clear evidence that contact of Spaniards with foreigners could be dangerous.

The book also outraged the leader of the Reformation in Geneva, John Calvin. Michel de Villeneuve was suspected of being the author, and thanks to information from one of Calvin's friends was arrested by the French Inquisition at Vienne. Calvin's friend made the effort of supplying the inquisitors with some letters from Servet which showed that Michel de Villeneuve and Servet were one and the same person. Servet managed to escape from his confinement within a few days, but made the mistake four months later of leaving France and passing through Geneva, where in August 1553 he was recognized when he attended a church service at which Calvin was preaching. He was immediately arrested. What foolishness caused him to tempt fate? In a brief essay a century ago, the Spanish physician Marañón (see Chapter 7) suggested, on the basis of intuitive deductions rather than any clear clinical evidence, that Servet had a profound psychological problem which was sexual in origin. Marañón argued that he had an inferiority complex that was caused by sexual impotence and took the form of an aggressive timidity. In order to overcome his frustrations, Servet deliberately exposed himself to provocative risks. It is one possible way of explaining Servet's mysterious conduct. He was put on trial, and as a result of pressure from Calvin was condemned to be executed as a heretic (for denying the doctrine of the Trinity and the divinity of Christ) by burning. The act took place outside the gates of Geneva, in the area called Champel, on 27 October. It was a slow, painful death, for the logs on the stake were damp and took time to fire up. Servet, who had his book on the *Restoration* strapped to his body, cried out in agony: 'Jesus, Son of the Eternal God, have mercy on me!'

The execution unleashed a fierce controversy among European intellectuals over whether religious dissent (that is, 'heresy') was an offence that should be punished through the death penalty. The debate, oddly enough, never managed to penetrate the frontiers of Spain, where there was little active dissent and therefore no controversy.[36] Servet's death gave him a posthumous fame for reasons that had little to do with him. The minor detail of the circulation of the blood was singled out for importance, whereas the points he considered truly important, about the foundations of Christianity, were ignored. He was treated as a martyr for freedom of conscience, against the clear fact that he never supported such freedom. In a letter to Calvin, he maintained firmly that obdurate heresy 'deserves death'. Only minor offences, he suggested, should be dealt with by 'other punishments than death'.[37] Among these punishments he picked out the most suitable as 'banishment', the condition in which he had spent virtually all his adult life, a perpetual exile from his country, from his Church, and even from himself. The decisive relevance of Servet for European culture came through the writings of a Frenchman, Sebastian Castellio, who used the execution of Servet as an argument to further a defence (in 1554) of the right of individual dissent. In a subsequent work that was not published until half a century after the burning at Champel, Castellio concluded that 'killing a man is not defending a doctrine, it is merely killing a man. When the people of Geneva killed Servetus, they did not defend a doctrine, they killed a man.'[38]

Servet's doctrines and reputation survived unimpaired. His questioning of the Christian doctrine of the Trinity coincided with similar views that began to be aired in Europe, and helped to lay the foundations of the religious movement known as Unitarianism. Voltaire, the great eighteenth-century champion of toleration, was writing a letter in 1759 from his estate at Ferney, on a hillside overlooking Lake Geneva, when he paused and looked out over the lake. 'I see from my windows,' he wrote, 'the city where John Calvin reigned, and the place where he had Servet burned for the good of his soul.'[39]

No other Spaniard suffered death for religious reasons at the hands of the Protestant Reformation. Many, however, were forced to flee from their native land because they sympathized with the new ideas in Europe. One of the most prominent early refugees was the humanist scholar Juan de Valdés. Juan and his twin brother Alfonso came from a prominent family of the city of Cuenca, and were educated at the University of Alcalá. They may have been of converso origin, but the evidence is ambiguous. Both were noted scholars, adding Hebrew to their mastery of Greek and Latin. Alfonso (1500–32) was a prominent court figure and Latin secretary to Emperor Charles V. When the city of Rome, seat of the papacy, was sacked in 1527 by the troops of the emperor Alfonso made haste to justify his master in a tract that circulated only in manuscript, a *Dialogue of the Things that Happened in Rome*. Immediately after, he published a *Dialogue of Mercury and Charon* (1528), sanctioned by the emperor but printed anonymously because it put moral blame on the papacy for the events that led to the sack of Rome. He left Spain the following year, in the company of the emperor's court, and died inopportunely of the plague in Vienna. Meanwhile, Juan (1500–42), who had no official position, published in 1529 his theological study *Dialogue of Christian Doctrine*, which was closely based on some of Luther's early writings. It was the only work he managed to publish during his lifetime, though he left many writings in manuscript. The Inquisition, despite favourable testimony from university experts, immediately attacked the *Dialogue*. The controversy took so dangerous a turn that in 1530 Valdés moved to Italy, just in time to avoid being brought to trial. It was the beginning of a lifelong exile. His treatise was distinguished by its appearance in every Index of Prohibited Books issued by the Inquisition.[40] He lived first in Rome, then more permanently in the city of Naples (a Spanish-controlled territory), where he became the centre of a literary and religious circle that was interested in the spiritual reformation of the Church. The circle included prominent nobles, leading religious figures (some of whom subsequently became Protestants), and top society ladies, particularly Princess Giulia Gonzaga and her sister-in-law, Vittoria Colonna. Among his non-religious works, Valdés composed a *Dialogue* (1533) on the Spanish language, which was published in his native country only two centuries later (in 1737). Valdés was never a Protestant in his beliefs, but he had a strong influence on many Italians who later gave support to the Reformation. He tended to be ambiguous on points of theology, and seems to have stood most for a broad tolerance in matters affecting religion. 'Every man,' he wrote, 'must be careful never to become passionate about things which pertain to religion. Passion should not blind him in such a way that he should come to err against God out of ignorance.' He shared these views with many prominent Italians, some of them cardinals of the Catholic Church. Though there were signs of impending conflict in Europe, when Valdés died it was still a period when harshness and confrontation were not the order of the day in matters of religion. The execution of Servet lay nearly a decade in the future. The flames of the Inquisition seemed to belong only to the past.

The critical moment for Spanish supporters of the Reformation came in mid-century, when for the first time since 1492 a significant number of Spaniards left their country permanently for a life of exile.[41] The development had its origins in the 1530s, when there was a clash of opinions among clergy and theologians over matters that had little to do with ideology and a lot with personal rivalry. The leading scholar on the period, Marcel Bataillon, has shown that the conflicts were a reaction against two intellectual trends active in Castile at that period. The first of these concerned ideas associated with the Dutch humanist and friend of Luis Vives, Erasmus, and the second concerned the homegrown spiritual groups known as *alum-brados*. In the background there also lurked issues of anti-Semitism, since some of the personalities involved were of converso origin. Conflicts and confrontation began to generate exiles. One such was Pedro de Lerma. A former chancellor of Alcalá University, former dean of the theological faculty at the Sorbonne in Paris, and canon of Burgos cathedral, he fell under the influence of Erasmus and publicized it in his sermons. He was denounced to the Inquisition, imprisoned, and finally in 1537 was made to express public regret, in the towns where he had preached, for eleven propositions he was accused of having taught. In shame and resentment, the old man shook the dust of Spain off his feet and fled to Paris, where he resumed his position as a dean of the faculty, dying there in August 1541. According to his nephew Francisco Enzinas (known in the history of European Protestantism as Dryander), people in Lerma's home city of Burgos were so afraid of the possible consequences of this event that those who had sent their sons to study abroad recalled them at once.[42]

In Germany the new beliefs of the Reformation developed inexorably. But in Spain there was little or no reaction to those ideas for a quarter of a century, and the country remained almost impervious to what was happening outside. This was not, evidently, because Spaniards were firm Catholics. Nor was it because of Church reforms, which were not introduced until the end of the sixteenth century. Quite simply, Spaniards and most of their religious leaders managed to show no interest in European currents of thought. During those years, the Inquisition arrested several people on suspicion of heresy, but was unable to establish a clear link between the accused and the new ideas coming out of Germany. Around 1550, this situation changed.[43] The secret import of forbidden Protestant books supplied the necessary proof. Books were smuggled in at the seaports, most notably at Spain's chief port, Seville, where international trade links brought together a broad range of people and opinions that could not fail to have an influence. The authorities and the Inquisition eventually stumbled on a group of suspected Protestants. The circle, which totalled around 120 people, included the prior and friars of the monastery of San Isidro, and several nuns from a nearby convent. They managed to exist in security until the 1550s, when some of the friars, alive to approaching danger, opportunely fled. In the same period, the inquisitors also identified another group of Protestants in the area of the king's court in Valladolid. In 1558 they swooped on both groups, in Seville and in Valladolid. The Protestant movement was broken up, many of its members dying in the flames of the Inquisition. Among those who managed to escape from San Isidro were the friars Cipriano de Valera, Casiodoro de Reina, Juan Pérez de Pineda and Antonio del Corro.[44]

The total number of Protestants arrested and executed at that time was not large. In all Spain probably just over a hundred people were condemned to death for heresy by the Inquisition between 1559 and 1566.[45] Protestants in Spain were always a tiny movement, located mainly in the two cities of Seville and Valladolid, and their importance is small, because they failed to achieve any success. The Spanish Reformation, if we can even speak of such a thing, turned into a movement based exclusively on exiles. Put in perspective, the Protestant crisis in Spain, often presented as a singularly bloody period of repression, seems almost humane when compared with the ferocity of religious persecution in other countries. The English authorities under Queen Mary executed nearly three times as many heretics as died in Spain in the years just after 1559; the French under Henry II at least twice as many. In the Netherlands ten times as many died. In all three countries, very many more died for religious reasons in the years that followed. 'The healthiest country of all is Spain', Philip II observed with some justice to the Inquisitor General.[46] In general terms, Protestants continued to be pursued by the authorities within Spain's borders, but they were never the object of severe persecution, and those who got into trouble were usually foreigners, such as traders, printers, sailors and temporary residents. It has been calculated that between 1517 and 1648 over 2,550 foreigners were arrested by the Spanish Inquisition,[47] proof enough of a degree of repression, but one that produced very few martyrs. The Protestant movement virtually disappeared from sight and memory. The first homegrown study of their fate did not appear until three hundred years later, when Adolfo de Castro brought out a *History of Protestantism in Spain* (1847). Since in reality the Protestants had had very little history in Spain, Castro changed his title in the second edition

(1851) to *History of the Spanish Protestants and their Persecution by Philip II.*

Indeed, Philip II's unfavourable reputation in Europe derived largely from his attitude to Protestants. The government was not complacent about the problem, and asked its spies abroad to keep an eye on the movements and plans of exiles. In 1561 the ambassador in London reported that many Spanish Protestants were escaping to that city. 'They arrive every day with their wives and children and it is said that many more are expected.'[48] Philip's father had in the 1540s condoned the occasional seizure outside Spain of Castilians who became active Protestants. They were packed off home and made to face the music there. The intention was not, as a later ambassador of Philip's in England explained, to eliminate them but to keep an eye on them and hope that others would take the hint and mend their ways.[49] With the help of special funds, a little network was set up to spy on Spanish émigrés living in England, the Netherlands and Germany. Under Philip II, the selective kidnapping was carried out by agents based in the Netherlands, one of them the army paymaster Alonso del Canto. Their most notable success was in persuading the humanist Furió Ceriol (see below) to return to Spain in 1563. In the process, they collected valuable information on Spanish Protestants abroad.[50] Canto in the spring of 1564 was able to inform Madrid of the preparation by Juan Pérez de Pineda of a new version of the New Testament in Spanish.[51]

When we think of Spain, Protestant culture does not immediately spring to mind. Nor at first sight does the history of the Bible seem to be related to the fate of exiles from the peninsula. Yet it was Jewish and Protestant exiles who produced the first full version of the Bible in Spanish. The first full Catholic translation in Spanish came out only in 1793 in Valencia, in an unwieldy edition, obviously not meant for the general public, of ten volumes.

The classic version of the Bible had been in Latin (the so-called Vulgate), of which already by the thirteenth century a king of Castile, Alfonso the Wise, had ordered a Castilian translation to be prepared. Other versions of sections of the Bible followed, sometimes basing themselves on versions made by Spanish Jews (who of course used the

Old Testament). After the expulsion of the Jews, these versions fell under suspicion and were prohibited. The sacred book of Christians was by no means unknown to the Spanish public, but the Church was always reluctant to sponsor translations into the language of the common man. In the early days of the Reformation, there was considerable controversy over whether the Bible should be translated at all.[52] Translation of small sections from the Bible, such as the psalms, met with few problems.[53] But the appearance of various unauthorized versions of the New Testament, which by-passed the Vulgate in order to go back to original Greek texts that were often given an unorthodox interpretation, put the Inquisition on its guard. In the early sixteenth century it began rounding up copies of the translated Bible that had been imported into Spain. In the Index of Prohibited Books it issued in 1559, all translations of the Bible in Spanish were disallowed.

As a consequence, translations into Spanish could only be produced outside Spain. The best known of these was published in 1553, in Ferrara (Italy), by Jewish refugees from the peninsula who felt the need for a text of the Old Testament for their co-religionists, most of whom did not know Hebrew. The publisher was Abraham Usque, who had been born in Lisbon but emigrated in the 1540s to Ferrara and set up a successful printing press. His *Bible in the Spanish Tongue Translated Word for Word from the Original Hebrew* became for Hispanic Jews the standard version of the scriptures, and was re-issued in Salonika in 1568 and Amsterdam in 1611. It was a text based on medieval Jewish translations and therefore written in an archaic style, suitable for use in the synagogue but not calculated to reach the man in the street. Christian Spaniards who based their thinking on direct reading of the scriptures, needed a more accessible text. This was supplied by the exile Casiodoro de Reina.[54]

Reina (1520–94), born near Badajoz (Extremadura) and of Arabic (Morisco) origin, was one of the friars who fled from the monastery of San Isidro in Seville. Like some of the others, he ended up in Geneva, the capital of Calvinism. Dissatisfied with what he found there, he went to Frankfurt and then to England, where he became pastor of a Spanish church, married, began a family, and devoted himself to a frenzy of literary activity on behalf of his fellow Protestants in Spain. After five years in England, he again had problems, and returned to the continent. While he was in London, his stay coincided with that of another of the Seville exiles, Cipriano de Valera (c.1530–c.1602), a firm Calvinist who made England his home and taught at both Cambridge and Oxford. 'Pray for our Spain and principally for the King and all those who govern the state, that God may enlighten them to read and meditate on the Holy Scriptures', Valera wrote in one of his texts. A long list of works came from his pen, among them a *Treatise to Comfort the Poor Suffering in Barbary*, directed to Protestants in Spain, and a translation of Calvin's *Institutes of the Christian Religion*.

During all these years Reina was painstakingly working to realize his great dream, a translation of the whole Bible, on whose preparation he had been consulting with other exile friends. It still staggers the imagination to think of this humble monk from Seville as one of the great humanist scholars of the age of the Reformation, yet that he undoubtedly was. In later years he moved easily through the major languages of Europe, such as French and German. But as translator of the Bible he revealed his expertise as scholar of Latin, Greek and Hebrew. The Spanish Protestant Bible was a long time in the making, and had its origins from well before Reina. A part of the New Testament had been published long before, in 1543 at Antwerp, by the Spanish exile Francisco Enzinas. Enzinas (1520–52) left his native Burgos with his brother Diego at an unknown date, and went to northern Europe, first to the Netherlands and then to Germany, because of his sympathy with the new ideas of the Reformation. Diego chose to go to Italy, where he was later arrested on a charge of heresy and burnt at the stake in 1547. Francisco had better fortune. At the instigation of the German reformer Melanchthon, he studied at Luther's university of Wittenberg and translated the New Testament into Spanish from the Greek edition of Erasmus, managing to get it published at Antwerp in 1543.[55] On the title page Enzinas stated clearly that the edition was dedicated to Charles V, and in an interview with the emperor he did manage to obtain his consent for the publication. Shortly after the interview, however, he was arrested on suspicion of heresy at the instance of Charles's confessor Pedro de Soto, and kept under house arrest in Brussels. He escaped after a year, persuaded by now that he must identify himself with the Reformation. His brush with the authorities convinced him that he could never return to Spain, though he remained loyal to the emperor and indeed dedicated his next book, a translation of the *Lives* of Plutarch, to him. He spent two years in England, where, with the support of Archbishop Cranmer, he obtained a teaching post at Cambridge during the years of freethinking that marked the reign of the boy-king Edward VI. Enzinas returned to the continent two years later in order to supervise the printing of his works, but suffered an untimely death as the result of catching the plague during a visit to Strasbourg.

Enzinas's version of the New Testament was in turn used by Juan Pérez de Pineda, another of the Seville monks, as the basis for an edition which he published in Geneva in 1556, an impressive volume of over seven hundred pages, printed in a small format (13 by 8 centimetres) that could be easily hidden away. The edition formed the bulk of the cargo that a certain Julián Hernández attempted to smuggle into Seville in two huge wine casks the year after. The casks were discovered and confiscated, the smuggler was arrested and later perished in an *auto de fe* in Seville. Pérez de Pineda later completed his own translation of the New Testament, which he intended to publish in Paris. Unfortunately, agents of Philip II managed to seize and destroy almost all copies of the edition. When Reina came to prepare his own effort, he was obliged to do much of the New Testament himself. He followed the guidelines of the text by Pérez de Pineda (who died in 1566), modified some of the translation, and added some explanatory notes. His version of the Bible was eventually published in the Swiss city of Basel in September 1569, the first complete translation into contemporary Castilian. It was known as the Bear Bible because of an engraving on the title page of a bear retrieving honey from a tree, followed by a text in Hebrew to underline that it was based on old biblical sources and not merely derived from the Latin Bible. Years later it was re-touched slightly by Cipriano de Valera, who brought out an edition which he published in Amsterdam in 1602. Known generally today as the Reina-Valera Bible, it has been read and used for centuries by Hispanic Protestants, and remains the standard text of their Bible. It was, for example, the text that the Englishman George Borrow took with him to Spain in 1836, when he set out on a trip to sell the Bible to a population that had never seen it. Reina's later views became thoroughly Lutheran, and he died as a pastor in the German city of Frankfurt, comforted by his wife and his large family.

Reina's long and eventful life was closely tied to what went on in Spain, and he always had Spain uppermost in his mind. Above all, he seems to have been partly responsible for the first, and most deadly, work of polemic directed against the Spanish Inquisition, the *Sanctae Inquisitionis Hispanicae Artes* ('Secrets of the Holy Spanish Inquisition'), published in Heidelberg in 1567. The pseudonym used by the author was Reginaldus Gonzalvus Montanus, but the work appears to have been written by the Seville ex-monks Reina and Antonio del Corro.[56] The authors supplied, for perhaps the first time, a full description of the functioning of the Inquisition and its persecution of dissidents in Spain. Their direct knowledge (there were descriptions of how the monks in San Isidro secretly read forbidden literature during their hours of prayer) gave authority to the account and turned it into an international success. Between 1568 and 1570 it was issued in two editions in English, one in French, three in Dutch, four in German and one in Hungarian. It served for a long time as a basic element in the development of propaganda directed by Protestant writers against the Spanish government. The mid-sixteenth century, we have seen, was the peak period for persecution of Protestants in Spain, though fortunately very few suffered there for their beliefs, thanks to their diligence in escaping overseas to freedom. Despite their valiant work abroad, however, the exiled Protestants made no impact on the culture of their own country and a barely perceptible impact on the movement of events in Reformation Europe.

The controversy over translating the Bible affected the career of at least one prominent Spaniard who was by no means a Protestant but identified himself with the European world and preferred to live outside Spain for most of his life. This was Fadrique Furió Ceriol (1527–92). Furió was one of Spain's most eminent voluntary exiles. Born in Valencia, he followed a respectable tradition in opting to become a soldier-scholar, fighting and travelling along with other gentleman soldiers who served the king of Spain. He appears to have left Spain around 1546, and did further studies in Paris and the

Netherlands. Years later, he stated that he had spent nearly twenty years away from home, 'wandering through France, Flanders, England, Germany, Denmark, Austria and Italy, simply to observe and understand (apart from my studies) the manners, culture, laws and customs of men'.[57] He served with Charles V at the siege of Metz, and in the campaigns in Flanders that preceded peace with France in 1559. He effectively made the Netherlands into a second home, as Luis Vives had done before him. Unlike Vives, he was able to draw on his adult experience of Spain for the material that formed the basis of his books. In 1554 he published in the Netherlands perhaps the most important book written by any Spaniard on the art of communication, his *Rhetoric*. Two years later he developed his arguments further in *Bononia*, which analysed recent controversies about the need to translate the (Latin) Bible into everyday languages. He came out firmly in favour, but there were powerful conservative forces, led by the Inquisition, that disagreed with him, and threatened to act against him. When Philip II became ruler of Spain, Furió, who knew him well and enjoyed his confidence, dedicated to him a volume of advice about how to conduct administration, called *The Council and Counsellors of the Prince* (1559), which was published in Antwerp. The book is remarkable for its declaration of faith in the universality of culture that Furió had encountered outside his native country:

It is foolish behaviour to berate and curse those who have a different belief or are of a different race, whether Jews or Muslims or Gentiles or Christians. The wise man knows that every country has seven leagues of bad roads, everywhere there is both good and bad, he praises and embraces the good and criticizes and rejects the bad, but without blaming the nation where he finds himself.

There are only two countries in the whole world, the country of the good and the country of the bad. All the good, be they Jews, Muslims, Christians or any other faith, belong to the same country, and are of the same household and blood. And the same is true of all the bad.

Furió's intimate knowledge of the Netherlands made him an obvious choice as adviser to the king when events there threatened to turn into a rebellion. Philip valued his advice, but in 1563 ordered him back to Spain, for fear that heterodox influences were at work on him.

In 1573, encouraged by the king's change to a more liberal policy on the Netherlands' revolt, Furió wrote his important *Remedies*, a full-scale programme for change in the north. Its main points seem to have been acceptable to Philip, who in 1574 sent him back to the Netherlands to advise him over the available options. However, thanks in part to the harsh policies of the recent military commander there, the duke of Alba, events had advanced way beyond any possibility of implementing the proposals that Furió recommended. From this date, around 1577, the king lost confidence in him. He continued to protect him and always kept him on hand as a member of his court, which in the case of a person as scrupulous as Philip II meant a great deal, but he no longer consulted him on affairs of state. Furió died of ill health while preparing to accompany the king on a state visit to the eastern provinces of Spain.

As we have had occasion to see, good and prudent Catholics became outcasts from Spain no less than freethinkers. The most remarkable example, so astonishing that it echoed throughout Europe in its day and has been described by its modern historian as a 'real spiritual scandal' of the reign of Philip II, was the imprisonment and exile of the head of the Castilian Church, no less a person than the archbishop of Toledo, Bartolomé Carranza (1503–76).[58] Carranza was born in the Pyrenean kingdom of Navarre, entered the Dominican order, and went on to study in Valladolid and do his doctorate at Rome. He seemed set for great things, but turned down several offers of preferment. In 1545 and 1551 he served as one of the Spanish theologians at sessions of the Council of Trent. He returned to Spain in 1553 and in the following year accompanied Philip on his journey to England to marry Mary Tudor. There he distinguished himself by the zeal with which he crushed heretics and purified the universities of Oxford and Cambridge, winning for himself the title of the Black Friar. In May 1557 the archbishop of Toledo died, and Philip immediately decided to give the post to Carranza, who thus became the holder of the most important see in the Catholic world after Rome. The appointment stirred jealousies and enmities among rival clergy. Only the weapon of attack was lacking. This was supplied by Carranza himself in his *Commentaries on the Christian Catechism*, which he published in 1558 at Antwerp.

The *Commentaries* were considered thoroughly orthodox in doctrine and received the approval both of the Council of Trent and of distinguished theologians in Spain. However, phrases in it were seized upon by hostile critics and denounced as heresy. The bitter personal hostility of a leading theologian of his own Dominican order, Melchor Cano, and of the Inquisitor General, Fernando Valdés, became crucial factors in the development of events. Cano asserted that the *Commentaries* 'contain many propositions which are scandalous, rash and ill-sounding, others which savour of heresy, others which are erroneous, and even some which are heretical'. Led by Valdés, the Inquisition accepted Cano's opinion. What ruined Carranza was the Protestant crisis in Spain, which occurred at precisely the time of his elevation to the see of Toledo. Interrogation of suspected Protestants resulted in detailed denunciations of the archbishop for statements he was said to have made to them. In May 1559 the prosecutor of the Inquisition drew up an indictment calling for the arrest of Carranza 'for having preached, written and asserted many heresies of Luther'. At the end of August the archbishop was arrested by officials of the Inquisition. He was escorted to Valladolid and allotted as prison a couple of rooms in a private house in the city.[59] Here he was kept under house arrest for over seven years. Since he was a bishop, however, exercising powers granted by the papacy, only the pope in Rome could judge the case. Philip II saw the papal claim as interference in Spanish affairs and refused to allow the Inquisition to surrender its prisoner. The case therefore dragged on, with no agreement on legal procedure.

With the accession of a new pope, Pius V, in 1566, a solution came into sight. From his residence Carranza managed to smuggle a message out to Rome in the form of a paper bearing in his handwriting the words, 'Lord, if it be thou, bid me come to thee upon the waters' (Matthew 14:28). This was exactly what Pius intended to do. In July 1566 he managed to reach an agreement with the Spanish authorities to send Carranza and all relevant documentation to Rome. The ageing archbishop reached his exile in Rome and was placed in honourable confinement in the castle of Sant' Angelo. This second detention lasted nine years. The pope died without having decided the case, and it was left to his successor, Gregory XIII, to issue sentence in April 1576. The verdict was a compromise, made no doubt in order to placate Spain. The *Commentaries* were condemned and prohibited and Carranza was obliged to disavow a list of 'errors', after which he was told to retire to a monastery in Orvieto. The sentence was only in part satisfactory to Philip and to the Inquisition, whose authority would have suffered by an acquittal. It satisfied Rome, which had vindicated its sole authority over bishops. In a sense, it may have satisfied Carranza, who was not accused of any heresy despite the prohibition of his *Commentaries*, which was to remain in all the editions of the Spanish Index of Prohibited Books except the last one in 1790. Justice had been replaced by political compromise. Everything had been taken into consideration except the frail old man who, eighteen days after the papal verdict had been read over him, contracted an illness from which he died in the early hours of a May morning in 1576.

The papal city of Rome was also the scene of the other great ecclesiastical drama that concerns us. The only significant spark of excitement contributed by Spain's expatriates in the later seventeenth century was through the now almost forgotten writings of a theologian who spent all his working life outside Spain.[60] This was the 'Quietist' priest Miguel de Molinos (1628–96). Though few people know much about him, it is interesting to recall that the poet Antonio Machado once placed him among 'the four Miguels [Miguel Servet, Miguel de Cervantes, Miguel de Molinos and Miguel de Unamuno] who represent and sum up the essence of Spain'. The term 'Quietism' is applied to a recurring trend in the mystical thinking of all religions, in which a believer attains perfection through repressing his own inclinations and allowing his will to be absorbed into that of God. In this state of quietude, he subjects himself to God and thereby fulfils his existence. The truth is that it is uncertain to what extent Molinos could be described as a Quietist. He was born at Muniesa (Aragon), studied for the priesthood in Valencia, and in 1662 was sent by the Valencian authorities to Rome to promote a petition for the beatification of a Valencian priest. He resided the rest of his life in the Holy City, where with the passing of years he made a reputation as a good spiritual director, and exercised great personal influence over ex-Queen Christina of Sweden during her prolonged and spectacular stay in Rome, holding weekly advisory sessions with her. That would have been the end of the story, but for the fact that in the year 1675 he published two books that sent shock waves through Catholic Europe. The first of these was a little study, so brief that it is better to term it a leaflet, called *Short Treatise on Frequent Communion*. The second book, published the same year in Rome (first in Spanish then in Italian), was a more solid item, with the title *Spiritual Guide*.

The *Guide* printed in its opening pages an impressive selection of approvals by various theologians and by the ecclesiastical authorities, and was so successful that twenty editions appeared in six years. It is hard to explain the success, for the book is a densely written text that is by no means easy to absorb. Moreover, the basic argument – that the believer must be a passive instrument in the hands of God – was neither original nor revolutionary, as Molinos himself kept insisting, and had always formed part of a mystical tradition in the Church. In reality, the success appears to have been personal rather than literary. Molinos was sought out by the whole of Roman society, notably the ladies. His achievement inevitably stirred up envy among other clergy (notably the Jesuits), who took their complaints to the Roman Inquisition and asked that he be investigated. An inquiry was made in 1682 and all the accusations were rejected. Further pressure occurred in May 1685, when the Holy Office drew up charges of heresy against him, and two months later ordered his arrest. During his long custody, he was repeatedly cross-examined about his 'doctrines'. The conclusions of the investigation were read out in September 1687, in the presence of a packed and expectant public in the Dominican church of Santa Maria sopra Minerva. Molinos, who immediately and obediently accepted the findings, was ordered to retire to a monastery for life. Two months afterwards the pope issued a bull condemning sixty-eight propositions he was accused of having taught, and banning all his works. Molinos died forgotten in the Dominican religious house nine years later, but the controversy over his teachings went on in other parts of Europe, notably in France where they got mixed up in high politics.

The fame of Molinos spread even while he was in gaol. In the whole of Spanish history few individuals have made such a mark on European religious thought. The *Guide* was published in Italian, in Latin (in Germany), in French, English, Dutch and German, not to mention a very late version in Russian in 1784. A transatlantic version came out in Philadelphia in 1885. Interest in Germany was due to the fact that this was the great age of German Pietism, a spiritual movement whose founders felt they had a lot to learn from the *Guide*. Molinos' doctrine, which was in essence a harmless application of mystical principles, continued to survive in religious confessions far removed from his own. The Church to which he belonged always refused to admit that it had been harsh to him, and maintained the prohibition on his works. The most ungracious treatment of all was meted out by his own country, Spain, which expunged him from its collective memory and banned all his works. Down to today, there are no substantive studies in Spanish of his life or ideas. He joined the ranks of those who have been permanently exiled from the history of their own homeland.

The firmness with which Spain resisted all the dissenting movements that could have threatened it, from Protestantism to Quietism, confirmed its reputation as the most inflexibly Catholic country of Europe. That reputation was not affected when the government in the later eighteenth century expelled the entire body of Jesuits residing in its territory. The expulsions, as we shall see (Chapter 4), were carried out by a firmly Catholic government and received the support of a good proportion of the bishops and clergy. It would be valid, therefore, to say that all the expulsions carried out from the fifteenth century to that date were in some sense rejections of individuals, groups and minorities whose outlook did not coincide with that professed by the government and by the people over whom it ruled. Exile seemed to be the fate of nonconformists and dissenters. The disinherited were drawn from the ranks of restless spirits alone.

By the nineteenth century, however, a different and more dangerous scenario emerged. For the first time, the Spanish people began to express their detestation of the official Church and the religion it professed. This opened the doors wide to an unprecedented spectacle, a huge upsurge of opinion against the established religion that, for the first time in its history, created a massive emigration of clergy from the peninsula. In certain parts of Spain, the Church was effectively driven out and the practice of religion was suspended. The traditional faith of all Spaniards was driven into exile.

The phenomenon was so astounding that it defied, and still defies, all explanation. Nor will these few lines attempt an analysis of what took place.[61] The growth of violent anticlericalism in the nineteenth and twentieth centuries comes as a surprise only if we accept the traditional view of a solidly Catholic Spain. According to this view, the people remained faithful to their beliefs until the Liberal and Republican parties created a conflict by attacking the Church. This makes sense in political terms, but sidesteps the question of the religious allegiance of the masses. Spaniards seem always, as we have attempted to suggest in the opening section of this chapter, to have accepted little more than the outward forms of the Catholic religion. The religious impulse of the Counter-Reformation in Spain had faded away by the early seventeenth century, and no significant changes in the religion of the people occurred over the next two centuries. People took part in the social activity of the Church – in festivities such as Carnival, Holy Week, Corpus Christi and midsummer celebrations such as the feast of St John – in the way they do today, that is, without necessarily believing in any of it. And all the while, century after century, they might be harbouring resentment against the small and privileged group of people who dominated religious and social life, ran the schools, intruded into details of personal and family behaviour, and dictated all sexual norms. The sexual theme was so recurrent that a recent study has suggested that rejection of the Church's 'authoritarian sexuality' was basic to much anticlericalism in modern times.[62] Hostility to the clergy, both priests and nuns, took so many different forms that it is still impossible to reduce the matter to dimensions that are easy to understand. And it was by no means a development only of our own day. Throughout peninsular history there was evidence of opposition to the clergy. 'The poor,' stated a man in Granada in the 1620s, 'pay tithes to the clergy so they can get fat and rich.' Another stated that 'there should be no more than four priests in the world, and even these should be hanged'.[63]

Hostility to the clergy, it has been fairly argued, did not necessarily mean that people had ceased to be Catholic. If they disliked some priests, it was because these were bad priests. Catholic belief was not affected. Recent studies show, however, that Catholic belief and practice had indeed declined disastrously. Was the situation very different a century before, when such statistics were not available? It seems likely that the image of a fundamentally Catholic Spain was always a fiction. Clergy who in the sixteenth century doubted whether their parishioners were Christians at all, may not have been so far off in their assessment. It is a conclusion that Spanish Catholics have rejected with indignation, but the statistics of the Church in the past century cannot be doubted. A Church survey for the Madrid area carried out in 1909 showed that only 4 per cent of the population fulfilled the Easter precept, that is, the annual confession and communion that is the accepted mark of Church membership. In the 1930s, figures for the city of Alicante show that only 1 per cent fulfilled the precept. A global survey of the Spanish population at the same date found that two-thirds of Spaniards no longer practised their religion.

The first major shock to the image of a solidly Catholic Spain came in 1834, when the Liberal Martínez de la Rosa was head of the government. In the middle of July, during a hot summer made more intolerable by economic and political chaos in the countryside, street riots broke out in Madrid, which ended up with attacks on several religious establishments. The outcome was the murder of a total of seventy-eight clergy (among them eleven Jesuits), whose residences were torched. The events had no immediate explanation or precedent. It has therefore been suggested that it was not a spontaneous (that is, genuinely popular) riot, but a carefully planned action by certain interests. Whatever the truth, 'the events marked a turning point in the history of the Spanish Church'.[64] The clerical murders ('la matanza de los frailes') were of course denounced, but they did not change the opinion of those who felt that the Church had reaped its just deserts. 'The clergy, gentlemen, as a class, is fighting the principles of liberty in every nation, and is combating them in Spain!' These words were spoken in the Cortes by the Liberal Antonio Alcalá Galiano, who had just spent a decade of his life as an exile in England. His view was typical of the opinion of many in government. Though public officials in Madrid were sacked for not taking effective action over the murders, further anticlerical riots took place the year after, in the east of the peninsula and, particularly, in Catalonia. After violent attacks on the leading monasteries of Catalonia in July 1835, an archbishop fled by sea (in a British frigate), and hundreds of monks and priests fled for protection to the army in Barcelona. By September 1835, the majority of Spain's monasteries were closed and empty. A new and potent factor, mob anticlericalism, had entered into Spanish politics. That autumn the new prime minister, Mendizábal (see Chapter 1), introduced unprecedented legislation. By a series of measures that came to be known as the '*desamortización*' ('disentail', which changed the legal status of property), the religious orders in Spain were suppressed and their property confiscated. It was the most radical measure ever taken against the Church, and had profound effects at all levels of society. Some 36,000 clergy were thrown out of work into the streets and were forced to fend for themselves. They were joined by 17,000 nuns.

It was only the beginning of a century of reverses for the Church, which continued to remain structurally intact because the bishops and parish clergy were left in place, with all their property. Educated opinion now joined and stimulated the move against the Church. Galdós's play *Electra* (1901), in which a character takes anticlericalism to the extreme of asserting the need to 'kill the enemy', formed part of a stream of writing that explicitly demanded removing the Church from its privileged position. The full, explosive eruption of irreligion into public view occurred in the events known as the 'Tragic Week' ('*Semana Trágica*') in Barcelona in July 1909. The Madrid government that summer was fully committed to a military intervention in Morocco, and ordered the calling up of reservists. Years had passed since the last census for military service was drawn up in 1903, and many of those eligible in that year were by now fathers of families, and obviously reluctant to risk their lives. Meanwhile the rich and privileged were able to escape recruitment because the old practice of buying exemption from military service still operated. Popular discontent took the form of street demonstrations in Barcelona, where the recruits were waiting to sail. On 26 July a strike was called in the city to protest against the war. It rapidly extended into the suburbs, while gangs of young people and workers went through the streets forcing shops to close and smashing windows. Tramways were halted. The government called out the police, then declared a state of martial law. In retaliation, armed workers attacked the police stations. The violence rapidly escalated, and then inexplicably changed its objective and turned against the Church. During the next two nights and days, the mob sacked and looted churches and religious buildings throughout the city. It was the worst outbreak of anticlerical fury to have occurred in Spain's history. On the morning of Thursday 29 July, Barcelona was a city enveloped in the smoke of burnt-out buildings: 104 people died in the rioting, hundreds were wounded or under arrest. The Tragic Week brought together many aspects of popular protest, radical ideology and traditional grievances.[65] It shocked politicians and intellectuals into rethinking their ideas, and inevitably had a profound effect on the culture of Catalonia. The forces of order arbitrarily picked out as responsible five radicals, who were condemned to death. One of them was a half-crazy coalman, accused of dancing with the exhumed body of a nun. The other notable victim was an educator, Francesc Ferrer, founder of a group of non-religious schools known as the 'Modern School'. Ferrer had himself been an exile for fifteen years in Paris, because of his support for Republican – and, later, anarchist – ideals, and on his return to Barcelona in 1901 set up a school based on his advanced ideas about education as a liberating force. His association with anarchists was enough to bring about his arrest and execution.

The violence continued under the Second Republic, which came to power in April 1931. Articles 26 and 27 of the Constitution of the Republic declared war against the Church: its tax privileges were removed, its schools put under state control, its clergy forbidden to engage in business or trade, its cemeteries confiscated, and the Jesuits were once again, as they were in 1767 (see Chapter 4), disbanded and expelled. Exactly four weeks afterwards, in May, there were riots against the clergy and over one hundred churches and convents in Madrid, Valencia, Seville and other cities went up in flames.' The significance of these outrages can be seen in the light of an often-quoted anecdote told by a minister, Miguel Maura.

When the Republic was proclaimed I received, only a few hours after I assumed my ministry, a telegram from the mayor of a village whose name is not relevant. 'Worshipful Minister of the Interior, Madrid. The Republic has been proclaimed. Please inform what we are to do with the *cura* [parish priest].'

That same month Maura expelled two bishops from Spain for lack of sympathy to the Republic.[66] Meanwhile, throughout Spain anti-clerical elements turned their attention to the hapless *cura*. Both in the cities and the countryside, broad sections of the population, from all social classes, watched with indifference and often with satisfaction as the clergy began to be systematically picked on and persecuted. The years during which the Second Republic was in control witnessed an outbreak of anti-religious violence that shook Spaniards, above all in the period 1934–6.[67]

The worst events took place after February 1936, when left-wing parties won the elections and lost control over their extremist supporters. Between February 1936 and the month of July when the military uprising against the Republic occurred, 411 churches were burnt and 17 clergy murdered. The unrestrained street violence of those months was primarily carried out by Republicans and anarchists, though Fascist groups retaliating also contributed to the climate of fear. Republicans alone, however, pinpointed the Church as the enemy. They were continuing a tradition that had been fostered for over a century by upper-class Liberals. The oft-quoted declaration by President Azaña that 'Spain is no longer Catholic' was far from being shocking. It was a mere commonplace, repeated by all progressives. 'The persecution of the Catholic Church', a historian concludes, 'was the worst ever seen in western Europe.'[68]

The situation became dramatically worse after the military uprising of 18 July 1936 that initiated the Civil War. Generations, perhaps centuries, of anticlerical hatred spilled over into an orgy of church burning and murders of clergy. On the very day of the uprising, as workers in Seville clamoured at the army barracks to be handed arms for defence, churches in all parts of the city were going up in flames. Within the first two months after the rising, around 3,400 clergy in Spain were murdered, and hundreds of churches and convents were burnt and sacked.[69] The peak month was August, when clerical murders in Spain averaged seventy a day. In Barcelona a trade union official told Josep Sanabre, a priest and well-known historian, that 'the plan was to murder you all'.[70] Clergy and nuns from the poorer classes were the chief victims of revolutionary fervour. The worst excesses were in Catalonia, where anarchists eliminated, in the diocese of Lleida, two-thirds of the clergy. The Socialists made their own contribution: in the diocese of Toledo, which they controlled, nearly half of all clergy were murdered. The estimated total for clergy assassinated during the three years of war, often in circumstances of revolting brutality, is around seven thousand. The figures do not include the thousands of lay men and women who were killed because of their beliefs.

In Barcelona the Minister of Justice of the Generalitat government, the Trotskyist Andreu Nin, a man of exceptional culture (his translation of Tolstoy's *Anna Karenina* into Catalan is still the classic version), stated proudly that he had solved the religious 'problem': there were now no more churches and no more clergy.[71] Long-venerated images of the Virgin and of Christ were desecrated, often to the accompaniment of obscene rites, and then destroyed. Throughout Spain, the time-honoured ritual of fire was used to burn not simply sacred objects but also all the documents of Church and municipal archives, which were piled up in the streets and torched. In the village where I now live in Catalonia, activists came from Barcelona in July 1936, seized the parish priest and murdered him, then torched the two local churches. Someone hurriedly bundled up the parish records and took them for safekeeping to the cathedral in Barcelona, where they remain today. Without them I would have been unable to prepare my study, published in 1997, of popular religion in pre-industrial Catalonia. Events justified the comment of the historian Sánchez-Albornoz that 'we had no wars of religion in the sixteenth century but we have had them in the twentieth'.

For all practical purposes, Catholicism ceased to exist in over half the country. From mid-July 1936, in response to the military rising, all churches throughout Republican Spain were closed, and the saying of mass was prohibited. Catholics felt that they were returning to the Church of the catacombs. Most believers, logically, tended to give their support to the Nationalist military uprising. But the brutality was not limited to the Republican side. The Nationalists had their own brand of anticlericalism, and did not hesitate to kill clergy who opposed them, notably in the Basque country. Various members of the clergy collaborated fully in the repression and murders carried out by the Nationalist forces and their sympathizers. A Jesuit army chaplain who was present at the murder of seventy non-combatants in an Andalusian village in August 1936 noted in his diary: 'it is consoling to see how most of them, or rather all of them, die. They all make their confession, and some deaths have been edifying.'[72] The Nationalists subsequently decided to present their struggle as a Crusade to save Christian civilization from atheist Bolshevism, but there was ample reason to disagree with them. The right-wing French Catholic writer Georges Bernanos, who was living with his family in Mallorca from 1934, had direct experience of the way the Nationalist repression functioned, and after he left the island in 1937 he published a passionate denunciation of what he had seen, in *Les grandes cimetières sous la Lune* (1938). The debate over the problem is still a live issue today.

The anticlerical excesses gave rise to one of the forgotten aspects of the conflict: the massive exodus of clergy from Spain, or at least from those parts of it under Republican control. The bishops fled abroad, to the Balearic Islands, to Italy, to France (two Catalan bishops), to Tangiers (the bishop of Málaga), and to the Pyrenean frontier (the primate of Spain, Cardinal Gomá). Thousands of clergy were scattered to the winds.[73] Some went to zones under Nationalist control, others fled abroad and stayed there until the end of the war, others sought refuge in foreign embassies and consulates; very many tried to lose themselves in the anonymity of the bigger cities, while by contrast others felt it safer to hide themselves in remote rural areas. Catholic families hid clergy in their homes at the risk of their lives. Valiant priests attempted to continue their ministry underground. There are no global statistics of these happenings, because for their own security the victims made sure that no records were kept.

The first public gesture of protest, at the highest levels of the Church, was made by Pope Pius XI in a general audience he granted to Spanish refugee clergy at the Vatican on 14 September 1936.[74] Five hundred exiles, led by the bishops of Urgell, Cartagena, Tortosa and Vic, crowded into the audience chamber. The Vatican's secretary of state, Cardinal Pacelli (who became pope three years later, as Pius XII), introduced them to the pontiff. In a substantial allocution, delivered in Italian, Pius XI commented for the first time on the persecution in Spain. He expressed his sorrow at the unprecedented and incomprehensible attack on the Church. At the end of his address he greeted the persecutors, reminding them that they too were brothers of the persecuted. The reaction in Spain was foreseeable. The Republican government rejected the pope's gesture as interference. The Nationalist authorities printed and circulated the Spanish version of the speech, but for their own purposes carefully omitted the ending, one page long, in which the pope had addressed the persecutors as 'brethren'. In 1937 the majority of the bishops issued a collective pastoral letter that called on the faithful to support the Nationalist side. The cardinal of Tarragona refused to append his name to the letter and the new regime did not allow him back to Spain when the war ended. He died in exile in Freiburg in 1943. It was a strange turning of the tables against the Church that had always triumphantly proclaimed that its people were the true Christians and that all others, from Jews and Muslims to Protestant heretics, deserved to be expelled from national territory.

4

The Discovery of 'Europe'

Our aim has been to persuade all Spaniards that we must
borrow from abroad what is in our power to borrow.

Mariano José de Larra[1]

The promise of success for Spain through the benefits of a worldwide empire began to pall very quickly, and no one expressed the consequent disillusion better than Cervantes, at the very height of his nation's imperial power. His novel's hero, the crazy knight Don Quixote, repeatedly castigated his own age for being a disaster, and set off to find for himself and his faithful squire Sancho Panza the possibility of success in another land. His self-exile was intended to be simply a preamble to much better things, the realization of unfulfilled dreams. Cervantes was well aware of the tensions that had led to the exile of other Spaniards. A century had gone by since the expulsion of the Jews, who consequently make no direct appearance in his novel, but the Muslims are everywhere present in its pages, not only as mortal enemies of the nation and antagonists at the battle of Lepanto, but also as victims of the great expulsions of 1609–14. Spain possessed the doubtful honour at the time of being the only European nation to have systematically dispossessed of house and home hundreds of thousands of its own citizens. It seemed, in the judgement of many, both then and later, to be cutting itself off from cultural patterns in the rest of Europe. One of those who devoted half his life to stressing the apparent divide between Spain and Europe was Philip II's private secretary, Antonio Pérez, perhaps the most remarkable of all the exiles of the sixteenth century.

Antonio Pérez (1540–1611) was the illegitimate son of the king's first private secretary, Gonzalo Pérez, a priest of converso origin. Antonio was a man of culture, an aesthete, art collector, writer and political theorist, who, after his father's death, became in 1571 one of the secretaries of state of Philip II. Two years later his patron, Philip's chief minister Ruy Gómez, prince of Eboli, died, leaving Pérez with the effective leadership of the court faction he had led. A contemporary observed that Pérez

climbed so high that His Majesty would not do anything save what the said Antonio Pérez marked out for him. Whenever His Majesty even went out in his coach, Antonio Pérez went with him. When the pope, my lord Don Juan of Austria, or other lords required anything of the king, they had recourse to Antonio Pérez and by his means obtained what they solicited of His Majesty.

Another said, 'Great men worshipped him, ministers admitted his superiority, the king loved him.'[2] Philip confided matters of state to this brilliant young man whose success enabled him to live as a great lord and whose charm led him into a close and still mysterious liaison with the princess of Eboli, the beautiful one-eyed widow of Ruy Gómez.

Ambition eventually led to Pérez's ruin. At the centre of the monarchy he held the king's secrets and controlled the money offered by courtiers seeking favours. His long hand stretched as far as Flanders, where at that moment the king's half-brother, Don Juan of Austria, was acting both as governor and as pacifier of rebellion. Pérez distrusted the implications of Don Juan's policies and disagreed with the attitude of Don Juan's secretary, Juan de Escobedo. He began to influence Philip surreptitiously against them. Suspicious of the way his plans for Flanders were being blocked by Madrid, Don Juan sent Escobedo to Spain in 1577 to make enquiries. On arriving at the court it became clear to Escobedo that Pérez had been playing a double game with his master and with the king. He began to look around for evidence to condemn the royal secretary. But Pérez had already managed to convince Philip that Escobedo was the malign influence in the affairs of Flanders. This would, in his mind, make it easier to get rid of Escobedo. He tried using poison, but this failed. Then on the night of Easter Monday, 31 March 1578, hired assassins came up to

Escobedo as he rode with a few friends through the narrow, dark streets of Madrid, and ran him through.

Popular rumour quickly pointed to Pérez as the assassin. Philip refused to believe in Pérez's guilt, but at the same time he initiated an investigation. It was over a year before any measures were taken. Then, in July 1579, the king ordered the arrest of the princess of Eboli and Pérez. An English diplomat in Madrid at the time evaluated the flood of rumours and reported that 'some think that both she and Perez are imprisoned about the death of Escobedo'. The two accused had to wait a long time in confinement, because the government was about to launch the campaign that would lead to the annexation of Portugal in 1580. Not until June 1584 were charges drawn up by the prosecutor. The investigation that followed led to Pérez being sentenced to two years' imprisonment and an enormous fine. He was still subjected to mild treatment, principally because he had in his possession state papers that (he said) incriminated the king. His refusal to surrender them led to firmer treatment by the government, and in 1588 an accusation of murder was presented against him. After two years of rigorous imprisonment, in February 1590 he was put to torture, which produced a confession of responsibility for Escobedo's death, but did not directly implicate the king. Then in April 1590, with the help of several highly placed friends, Pérez escaped from prison in Madrid and rode across the country to the borders of Aragon. Once he had set foot in that province, which enjoyed independent laws, the crown of Castile was powerless to touch him. In the capital, Saragossa, Pérez was lodged for his own security in the prison of the chief magistrate of the realm, the Justiciar. From this vantage-point he began a successful campaign to win over Aragon to his cause, and provoked in 1591 two major riots, in one of which the viceroy received wounds of which he died a fortnight later. The king decided to send in an army, which occupied Saragossa in November 1591. The first notable victim was the Justiciar, who on the advice of the king's ministers was executed in December. Others who were implicated in the events were executed twelve months later.

Pérez fled across the mountains to the neighbouring Protestant state of Béarn, attempted an unsuccessful invasion of Aragon in 1592 and then went into exile in France and England, still maintaining his campaign against Philip II. In his absence, in the spring of 1592 the Inquisition drew up a list of charges, accusing him of rebellion, heresy, blasphemy and homosexuality.[3] It was the beginning of a complex sparring match between the ex-secretary and his king that gave rise to accusations, counter-accusations and long-enduring historical legends. Pérez almost immediately began to spread the story that he had fallen into disgrace because of rivalry with the king for the love of the princess of Eboli.[4] Like other information that he made available to political circles in England, the story pushed into the background any mention of the murder which had occasioned his arrest. In England he became a member of the coterie around the earl of Essex, and a friend of the philosopher Francis Bacon. To avoid possible conflicts with Spain's government, Queen Elizabeth refused to receive him in an official way at court, but between 1593 and 1595 had several meetings with him in private (she had a good command of Spanish), and received written reports from him. She used to refer to him ironically, even in his presence, as 'the Spanish traitor'. One day, in front of Pérez and some English nobles, she explained: 'Don't be surprised that I do such honour to this Spanish traitor, for I am much in debt to señor Gonzalo Pérez his father, when I was imprisoned during the reign of Philip II and Queen Mary.'[5]

The exile proposed to Elizabeth nothing less than a Europe-wide alliance, to include England and France as well as the Muslim powers, to overthrow the monarchy of Philip II. The queen was far from sharing such futile dreams, which Pérez also took up with the court of France, much to her annoyance. Matters of a private nature, such as Pérez's reputation at court for sexual relations with young men, may have further displeased the monarch.[6] His patron Essex undertook a military expedition to occupy the port of Cadiz in 1596, but Pérez took no part in its planning. His position became extremely shaky when the over-confident Essex attempted a rebellion against the queen, and was arrested and executed in 1601. Events conspired to make it impossible for Pérez to achieve his expressed wish to 'live and die in England',[7] a country he claimed to admire even though he did not speak its language. In 1604 he went to France, where he unsuccessfully tried to gain the support of the court. He never returned to the Spain of his birth and died in comparative obscurity in Paris in the house of an Italian banker friend, where he complained of the cold ('this snow in France') and of his 'depression, because I am alone'. His friend arranged for him to be buried in the nearby monastery church of the Célestins.

Pérez's influence lingered on, for in his writings during exile he presented a vision of Philip II's government and of the Inquisition that had a lasting effect on the way people would think about Spain. The French, Dutch and English happened to be the firmest opponents of Spanish policy, and the testimony of a man who had occupied high office in Spain gave convincing support to their position. Pérez, with his education and culture, turned out to be a superb propagandist. He produced writings and letters incessantly and obsessively, day after day, in Spanish, Italian and Latin, directed to different people of importance whom he hoped to enlist in his campaign against the king. 'The pen was a last resort in his fight for survival and an outlet for his mortification.'[8] During the years of his exile he carried round with him the papers of state with which he had fled and which he claimed would justify him against Philip II. In 1591, just after fleeing from Aragon, he published in the Pyrenean town of Pau a short defence of his cause called *A Bit of History*, which was amplified and republished in London in 1594 under the title *Bits of History, or, Relations*. Further editions came out a few years later in Paris, and there were translations into other languages. Frequently reprinted, it was read eagerly by those who wished to find out about secret affairs of state. Copies were smuggled into Spain, where it also had an eager readership. The little volume came to play an important role in creating among Europeans an image of Spanish tyranny and of the king as a tyrant incarnate. Among his other achievements, Pérez succeeded in presenting to the English and French a completely distorted view of events in Aragon as a struggle for human rights against tyranny, when in reality there had been no repression of privileges in Aragon and no popular revolt. He also used the occasion to further bring into disrepute the Inquisition. The *Relations* helped powerfully to create an image of a Spain that had no part to play in a civilized Europe.

When later historians came to examine Philip II's reign, they did not fail to use the Escobedo murder as a reference point. The first such study, the French historian François Mignet's *Antonio Pérez et*

Philippe II (1845), accepted almost without qualification the version of events given by Pérez. However, the secretary had never managed to produce the documents to support the claim that he had acted on the king's orders, and the affair remained a mystery. Ironically, the best examination of the affair was written nearly four centuries later by another Spanish exile, also resident in Paris and with time on his hands. This was Gregorio Marañón, whose masterly two-volume study (1948) did not resolve all doubts about the Escobedo murder but remains today the classic narrative, setting the figure of the cultured and worldly Pérez within the context of high affairs of state. Concern with the mysterious aspects of the murder, however, has deflected attention from Pérez's true cultural importance, as an exile who contributed forcefully to a vision of Spanish politics that still influences the way many see the sixteenth century and Philip II's part in it.

Pérez, moreover, was a cultural phenomenon in his own right, 'a creative artist who deserves to be ranged among the minor writers of the Spanish Golden Age'.[9] Although his prose works (among them the *Relations*) are undistinguished, his vast corpus of letters is of a much higher quality, leading one of the principal literary experts of that time, Baltasar Gracián, to judge that he was 'the leading example of a serious, conceptual and natural style'.[10] Pérez's ornate, musical and carefully wrought epistolary prose, whether in Latin or in Spanish, was indeed a clear example of the artistic form of expression that we call 'Mannerism'. The ex-secretary, one of the few men of rank in Spain to possess a consciously European culture, always felt ill at ease in his native environment and more at home in the humanist tradition associated with foreign scholars, such as the Belgian humanist Justus Lipsius. When events drove him out of Spain, Pérez drifted effortlessly into the role of a wandering exile, a 'pilgrim', to use his own description for himself. The *Relations* were published under the pseudonym of 'Its authors the Pilgrims', or, in the case of the version published in England, 'Raphael the Pilgrim'.

Pérez's ideas about politics were expressed through the writings of one of his closest admirers and friends, the lawyer Baltasar Alamos de Barrientos (1555–1640). Because of his links with Pérez, Alamos was sentenced by a court in 1587 and then imprisoned by the government in 1590. Released after Philip II's death, he presented to the new king a tract that bitterly attacked the previous regime and may have been inspired by Pérez himself. It painted for Philip III a dramatic (and exaggerated) picture of a Castile in ruins. 'The cities and big towns are empty of people, the smaller villages completely depopulated, the fields with scarcely anyone to till them . . . There is no spot untouched by this misery, which comes principally from the burden of taxes and from spending all the proceeds on foreign wars.'[11] Alamos, who developed into a significant political theorist, was a proponent of the vogue, then spreading through educated circles in Europe and promoted principally by Justus Lipsius, for the ideas of the Roman historian Tacitus. Tacitism implied for its proponents the need to inject reason into politics.[12] By extension, it implied a rejection of the aspects of politics – war, fanaticism, tyranny – which seemed to have gained the upper hand in the late sixteenth century, not only in Spain but throughout the continent. Such theories never gained much of a following in Spain, where, on the other hand, Pérez's *Relations* enjoyed some success as an under-the-counter book, imported from abroad even though prohibited by the Inquisition.

By the seventeenth century many elite Spaniards, weary of the economic disaster, political collapse and intellectual isolation of their country, were pinning their hopes on a new and promising horizon, namely Europe. By 'Europe' they understood a different way of government and a new way of looking at life and culture that would contrast with their failures. Many generations later, the writer José Ortega y Gasset, who liked succinct phrases, coined one that stated: 'Spain is the problem and Europe is the solution'. It was a fantasy vision that political leaders would persist in nurturing from the seventeenth century to today. It remained 'fantasy' because even while they urged the adoption of European norms, writers and politicians resented the need to have to avail themselves of 'Europe', and tended in the last resort to react sharply against it, as the writer Unamuno did in the early twentieth century. The essentially love-hate relationship with the rest of the continent had its origins many generations before but began in earnest only in December 1700, when the last Habsburg king of Spain died without issue, and the crown passed to the grandson of the powerful king of France, Louis XIV. Spaniards greeted with satisfaction the possibility of changes in a nation where, one of their most prominent dignitaries reported, 'justice is abandoned, policy neglected, resources sold, religion distorted, the nobility demoralized, the people oppressed, and love and respect for the crown lost'.[13] It was the beginning, they hoped, of a new lease of life.

Events turned out rather differently. From the year 1700, Spain entered in fact upon a political system that split the country down the middle, intensified internal conflicts among Spaniards, made exile into a permanent reality of cultural life and converted half the political elite into opponents of the monarchy. It was an all-embracing crisis that endured for two and a half centuries, and there was no clear reason why it should have happened, for at first all the signs were completely favourable. However, no sooner had the new king, the seventeen-year-old Philip V, installed himself in Madrid than sharp differences of opinion took place in the governing class. The reasons for tension are easy to understand. Half the population supported the new Bourbon dynasty, the other half remained loyal to their predecessors, the House of Habsburg. For the next dozen years the so-called War of the Spanish Succession cost thousands of lives, both in the peninsula and in the rest of Europe. English and German armies invaded Spain on behalf of their alternative candidate to the throne, the archduke Charles of Austria.

Beneath the surface of political and military events in the War of the Spanish Succession profound issues were stirring. The Bourbon monarchy delivered a mortal blow to Spanish elite culture of the preceding two centuries. Philip V was uncompromisingly French in outlook and brought with him a household and officials who spoke only French. He imposed French taste, furniture and decoration on the court, and changed palace etiquette to that practised in Versailles.[14] French music was introduced, and the French taste for Italian opera. At court, French artists alone enjoyed favour. French menus were adopted, though the queen, Marie Louise, could not always overcome the resistance of the cooks, and often had to make her own meals. In 1707, she was still making 'onion soup' in her own chambers because the kitchens refused to make it.[15] French nobles were given high posts in government and the highest posts in the army.

The entire administration of the Castilian state was entrusted to French advisers.[16] All this provoked protests and a mass of defections among the elite. Though the conflict of those years took the form of a war, it was never a civil war but more exactly a dynastic one, in which the task of each army was to persuade the local population to support their candidate. The opposing armies drifted across the peninsula, capturing and losing and then recapturing towns. Meanwhile a good part of the ruling class had got fed up with one side or the other, and changed allegiances according to events. The consequences can still be consulted in the state archives, where entire volumes of documents are dedicated to listing the supporters of the opposite side who would have to be punished. The lists represent the exiles of the new century. One after another, leading members of the elite, not only in Castile but throughout Spain, voiced their complaints, joined the opposition, and went into exile in protest, while some ended up in prison and died there.[17]

Thwarted ambitions and personal resentment were among the major causes of the crisis. But there was also a stirring of old attachments of honour to the previous Habsburg dynasty. The most startling defection suffered by the government at the very beginning, long before war broke out in the peninsula, was that of a leading noble, the admiral of Castile, who accepted the post of ambassador to France, and left Madrid in September 1702 with an unprecedented retinue of 300 people and 150 carriages filled with his property. Instead of heading for Paris, however, he suddenly changed direction and fled to Portugal, where he denounced the Madrid government and entered the service of the archduke Charles. It was an ominous defection, for friends and family soon followed his example. Resentment of the French, Spain's traditional enemies and now the backbone of the new dynasty, was also important. The government uncovered a plot whose central figure was an Aragonese noble, the count of Cifuentes. According to one accomplice, the count had declared that 'the king was no king but only a puppet through whom his grandfather [Louis XIV] dominates us', and that 'he was bound in duty to hate the French, for they killed his father and his brothers'.[18] Cifuentes was detained in Madrid but escaped to his estates in Aragon, where 'the people rioted in his favour' and he used his influence to stir up popular opinion against the French.[19] Key members of the elite in the eastern realms of the peninsula defected and eventually fled abroad, while in Castile a quarter of the upper 'grandee' nobility and one third of the titled nobility joined the enemy.[20]

A decade after the war, which formally ended in 1714, there were dozens of Spanish nobles living in exile in Vienna, capital of the Habsburg dynasty. The total of nobles, officials and soldiers who fled from Spain to Italy and Austria in the hope of maintaining their links with the dynasty that had employed them has been put at around thirty thousand people.[21] Even if this figure is too high, their numbers were certainly considerable and in the 1730s there existed a plan – never realized – to build in Austria a new city for the exiles, to be called New Barcelona. In the same period one of them, Count Juan Amor de Soria, testified that

from the year 1701 till now the number of those who were victims of the fury of war, of forced exile, of imprisonment and persecution is more than 25,000 people of these realms. Nor has peace opened the doors for the return of the many Spaniards who lived exiled in distant parts.[22]

Clergy at all levels, including bishops, also fled from the French regime. It was reported from Rome in 1713 that over three thousand exiled Spanish clergy had taken refuge there.[23] In addition to voluntary exiles there were others who were expelled from the country, and plans were even made for some to be deported to America.

The scale of defections, and the consequent division of opinion within Spanish society, has seldom received much attention. It was, beyond all doubt, a crucial moment in the country's history, for the eastern realms, which had lost some of their political privileges at the end of the war and were now integrated into a united 'Spain' on conditions they did not choose, continued to demand their rights. Inevitably most of the exiles were political refugees. Among them were two of the more significant figures of the period: Melchor de Macanaz, a government administrator who spent over thirty years in exile in France but managed to return home to die, and the Aragonese noble Juan Amor de Soria.

Melchor de Macanaz (1670–1760) was the first original thinker of Spain's eighteenth century and one of the most ill-fated.[24] Trained in civil law at the University of Salamanca (a province where his personal papers are still guarded jealously by his family in a country villa, and have as a consequence never been consulted),[25] he emerged to prominence during the War of the Succession, when he gained the confidence of the pro-French government and supervised the administrative changes that came into effect in the provinces of the Crown of Aragon, which were deprived of their independent laws. A firm believer in bringing about reforms through the uncontested power of the central government, he favoured the idea of a wholly united Spain, in which neither the provinces nor the Church should have special privileges. In consequence, he earned the enmity of administrators, the Church and the Inquisition. In 1715 he was removed from his post and expelled. An official saw him emerging from his office 'shaken, pale and upset',[26] unable to believe what had happened. He spent the next thirty-three years living just on the other side of the Pyrenees, in the little town of Pau, waiting for the call home. He managed to retain some link with officials in Spain, and was even employed by them as a negotiator in several peace talks with foreign powers in the towns of Soissons (near Paris) and Breda, in 1728 and 1746 respectively. But his views in diplomacy were essentially pro-British, and not to the liking of the government. He was finally permitted to return in 1748, but no sooner did he touch Spanish soil than he was arrested and taken off to the fort of San Antón, in La Coruña (Galicia), where the navigator Malaspina (see below) sixty years later was also to be imprisoned. Macanaz described the fort as 'the most unhealthy and uncomfortable place you could choose in Spain, since it was right on the sea. They held me there three months and seven days, from which they transferred me to a prison in the town.'[27] His family were not allowed to visit him. He remained confined in La Coruña for twelve years. Only in 1760, when he was ninety years old and his health failing, was he released and allowed to retire to his home town of Hellín (Murcia), where he died within a few weeks.

Throughout the decades of exile and prison Macanaz kept himself sane by writing incessantly. As the novelist Carmen Martín Gaite, who shared with the present writer a deep interest in his career, has written:

The more the years passed and all hopes of his cause triumphing seemed to disappear, the more he must have been convinced that nobody was heeding or listening to him, and the more intense became his solitary dedication to filling reams of paper in which he recorded the injustice he had suffered, and presented in a wholly imprudent way the ideals of his cause, protesting in a void, searching for the shape of a non-existent listener, as if his only reason for living was to transform his very breath into ink.[28]

When Carmen Martín and I met in the writers' rendezvous in Madrid, the Café de Gijón, to talk about our common interest in Macanaz, it became clear to us that we had rediscovered one of the crucial but forgotten figures of Spain's history. Her studies concentrated on the fascinating details that emerged in the information collected by the Inquisition as preparation for a possible trial of Macanaz, while my own work looked into his ideas and political role.

Dedication to the written word gave Macanaz some distraction during the long years of exile. His perfectly formed script covers thousands of pages of his almost entirely unpublished oeuvre. By about 1744 – a period that took in almost thirty years of exile – his works amounted to over two hundred folio volumes, and more were to come. The fact of being unpublished sums up his tragedy. As one of the chief ministers of the crown in a period of revolutionary change, he had within his grasp the means of reforming the whole political and economic structure of Spain. He wrote voluminously on the political rights of the crown, the role of the Church, the reform of education and of civil society. Then while in exile in France in 1734, in a strange response to the institution that had excommunicated him, persecuted his family and kept him out of Spain, he began writing a *Critical Defence of the Inquisition*, a puzzling work that was not published in Spain until half a century later. With this notable exception, nearly all his works remained unprinted and unknown, and, what is worse, he became a victim of political interests. Condemned to oblivion in his own country through the fact of exile, he remained almost unknown to posterity, and would have remained so but for the studies that Carmen Martín and I carried out over two hundred years after his death.

Apart from Macanaz, the war years produced few exiles of cultural distinction. An exception was Count Amor de Soria, who eked out his last days in Vienna, and wrote from exile in the 1730s a stinging condemnation of the Bourbon regime and the problems it had brought on his country. A quarter of a century after the achievement of peace, he protested, thousands of Spaniards were still being forced to live in exile, 'searching for tranquillity in far-off regions', and all because of a 'cruel and unjust' regime that imposed its will through 'terror and fear'. The result of this bad government policy, he argued, could be clearly seen. Spain was reduced to a state of 'decline', in which one of the most important causes was the continual expulsion of her subjects, principally the 'two million Jews and three and a half million Moriscos' who had been driven out in previous centuries. The exaggerated figures served Amor de Soria's purpose, which was to question fundamentally any policy of deportation of subjects. 'No reason can possibly justify', he wrote, a government driving out domiciled citizens who were no danger to security and who contributed to the economy of the country.[29]

The upheavals in the peninsula, and subdued resistance to the foreign culture brought in by the Bourbons, gave rise to one of the most dangerous developments of the reign: the birth of a 'Spanish party', as it was called, consisting of conservative members of the elite who opposed the entry of foreign, European ways. Their resistance to the monarchy became critical when in 1724 the king abdicated in favour of his son Luis. Among nationalist-minded Castilians there were high hopes of Luis, who was born in Spain and therefore not a foreign but a native king. However, he died quite unexpectedly, and Philip returned to the throne three months later. In consequence, the legitimacy of his rule began to be questioned. If he had, as some maintained, no right to resume the throne after having solemnly abdicated, then he had no right to rule.[30] The traditionalists, drawn from the aristocracy and clergy, were anti-foreign and pro-Castilian in outlook, and rejected the validity of Philip's second reign. In this way the question of the succession, fated to play a very long role in Spanish politics, emerged to centre stage. The regime's opponents did not cease to campaign, through both rumours and pamphlets, against Philip's second tenure of power. In August 1726 the king had to issue orders asking for an investigation of 'rumours circulating in Madrid and other parts of the realm, to the effect that His Majesty is going to retire from the government of the monarchy'.[31]

It was the first serious split in sympathy between the Spanish crown and the ruling political class, and it had long-term implications that affected the Bourbon dynasty up to the beginning of the twentieth century.[32] In over two hundred years not a single occupant of the Spanish throne, with the sole exception of the Italian Charles III (son of the Frenchman Philip V and the Italian princess Elizabeth Farnese) in the later eighteenth century, could count on the undivided support of the cultured elite. The monarchy began to produce its own exiles. In the five centuries covered by this book, the only occupant of the throne to earn the unadulterated admiration of elite Spaniards (though, it should be emphasized, only Castilian Spaniards) was Isabella the Catholic. She achieved this success, apparently, because she never left the peninsula and could therefore be identified absolutely with her subjects, particularly those of Castile. Every ruler of Spain after her was of foreign origin. It was a phenomenon that the English had to put up with for centuries, since all their rulers after the year 1066 were of non-English origin, and the Spaniards were faced with the same situation. All of Spain's rulers came in for a measure of hostility, and from the nineteenth century six of them were driven into exile. Charles IV was forced by Napoleon to abdicate in favour of his son Ferdinand VII, and spent his last years as an exile in Italy. Ferdinand in turn was removed from his throne by Napoleon in 1808. He was restored to it in 1814, initiating an absolutist regime that lasted for over six years and was reinforced in 1823, when French troops invaded the country and backed him against Liberal reformers. He ruled for another ten years until his death in 1833, but Spanish opinion became permanently polarized, with appalling consequences for public order. Joseph I, Napoleon's brother, had replaced Ferdinand in 1808, but survived only until 1814, when he had to leave, taking his troops with him. Ferdinand's widow, María Cristina, acted as Regent for her young daughter Isabella, but was forced to quit in 1840. Isabella II, after a stormy reign, was forced to abdicate in 1868 and left the country. During her absence Duke Amadeo of Savoy was in 1870 chosen as king by the government, but abdicated and left three years later. The first king of the twentieth century was Alfonso XIII, whose reign lasted until the spring of 1931, when a Republic was proclaimed and he hurriedly left on a British warship. Few European countries can boast such a continuous run of dynastic instability, or a more unequivocal acceptance of exile as a norm of political life. The sustained hostility of the political class to their ruling monarchs bordered on the incredible. Even in the aftermath of a bloody civil war in the twentieth century, a liberal and cultured member of the elite such as Salvador de Madariaga could affirm without any hesitation that one of the greatest misfortunes in Spain's history had been the advent to the throne of the foreign Habsburg and Bourbon dynasties in the years 1516 and 1700 respectively.[33]

The phenomenon of exile was of course resorted to by other European nations at specific moments of crisis in their history. The decades of religious conflict that began in the mid-sixteenth century created permanent refugees, who formed part of what has been termed a 'confessional migration'.[34] Protestants and Catholics refused to tolerate each other within the same country, and had recourse to driving tens of thousands out to live in foreign parts. When divisions reached the level of a civil war, as in seventeenth-century England, temporary exile was inevitable. But there were also periods of military repression that brought about mass emigration in various countries right across the continent, from Ireland to the Czech lands. It is a long and fascinating saga of deprivation but also of resurrection. The motives of those who went into exile were often complex, for many wished not simply to escape repression but also to continue their lives in a better environment.[35] Very many managed to preserve their own culture in a foreign milieu but at the same time make a significant impact on the societies that received them. Refugees helped to transfer technical skills from one country to another,[36] and contributed handsomely to their new economic environment.[37] When all other avenues failed, the homeless and deprived made their way to a new continent, America.

The experience of departure from Spain in the century after 1700 was both new and different from what Spaniards had experienced before. It was new, because for the first time it affected on a substantial scale the upper levels of society, including nobility, clergy and intellectuals, who had never before been obliged to abandon their homeland. It was different, because previous expulsions had always been explicitly racial or religious, affecting Jews and Muslims, whereas the victims now were orthodox Christians (as we have had occasion to see in Chapter 3). There was a third aspect that in time came to play a profound role in the way Spaniards thought about themselves. Expulsion brought many of them face to face with the outside world, and forced them to sort out their role in it. The central reality was that Spain was different, a society in large measure out of step with the values prevailing elsewhere. Foreign travellers certainly noted that entering Spain was a different experience. Though elements of elite culture entered across the frontiers, the peninsula continued to be very much cut off from Europe, mentally even more than physically. Unlike in other countries during the seventeenth century, Spaniards did not produce any travel literature about journeys to foreign lands, whereas Englishmen, Frenchmen, Italians and Germans produced an ample travel literature dealing with Spain.[38]

If the peninsula was isolated from Europe, however, it was never because of repression within the country. Since the time of Ferdinand and Isabella all Spaniards, on a scale unequalled by any other Europeans, had been free to move around the continent. Their military and political duties took them everywhere, and throughout the sixteenth century they continued to study abroad freely if they wished to do so. The isolation of the educated classes in Spain was a cultural phenomenon, not an ideological one. Between the sixteenth and nineteenth centuries every foreign visitor commented on Spain's intellectual seclusion, but few blamed repression for it. 'In all kinds of good learning,' the English traveller Francis Willughby observed in the 1660s, 'the Spaniards are behind the rest of Europe.'[39] The elite was cut off from cultural contact by an inadequate educational system, and by lack of familiarity with any of the languages in which the new thinking was being published. It is significant that we know of no major literary correspondence between Spanish and European intellectuals before the later eighteenth century, when the contacts of the Valencian scholar Gregorio Mayans (who looked to Italy rather than northern Europe for his inspiration) began to take shape. Before that period, only a tiny handful of writers had managed to keep in touch with their colleagues in other countries,[40] mainly through the medium of Latin, a language very little known among Spain's elite and clergy.[41] There was a notable intellectual divide between the peninsula and the rest of the continent. 'If a nobleman wishes to educate his sons,' a prominent government minister reported in 1713, 'he has to send them to colleges in Bologna, Rome, France and other places.'[42] Spain seldom featured as a desirable component of the 'Grand Tour', the trip through Europe made by young nobles in order to complete their education. Its universities were (explained an English traveller in 1664) 'just where our universities were one hundred years ago'.[43] There was no apparent reason for going to Spain, which remained on the outer confines of the western experience. 'No country is less known to the rest of Europe', Dr Samuel Johnson concluded in 1761.[44]

Thinking Spaniards, however, perceived in the broader horizons of Europe a release from the traditional customs that appeared to mark Spain's backwardness. In the course of the late eighteenth century, several gentlemen imitated the Grand Tour practised by other elites and travelled abroad in order to improve their education or pick up technical skills that their country lacked.[45] But it was difficult to escape from the feeling of inferiority. The writer José Clavijo y Fajardo in the mid-eighteenth century commented: 'everywhere we are both little known and little appreciated. A Spaniard who travels must take care to get rid of the low opinion that foreigners have of us.' Contact with the outside world did exist, at least. It demonstrated that Spain was not as cut off from others as some imagined. More important, it at last gave the Spanish elite a real sense of cultural contact. The young José Cadalso, author of the *Moroccan Letters* (an imitation of some essays by the French thinker Montesquieu), in 1757 paid a visit to Paris, as very many other Spaniards were to do, and also a lightning visit to England, Germany and Italy. This was the period when some Spaniards really began to discover Europe for themselves, without worries about the Inquisition back home. The contact opened up a dimension that was worlds away from the traditional Spain they had left behind.

'Europe', or at least what they understood as Europe, became the abiding fixation of forward-looking Spaniards for the next two hundred years. Curiously, the encounter with Europe stirred up wholly confused reactions, of admiration combined with an even more vigorous rejection. Spanish thinkers were happy to learn from other nations, but were always sceptical of what could be gained by imitating them, and had little patience with the idea that any society could be an ideal one, of the type that others tended to call 'utopias'.[46] Some Europeans, led by the distinguished English humanist Sir Thomas More in the sixteenth century, wrote about ideal imaginary societies. Subsequently Italians, Frenchmen, Germans and others dreamed up schemes for utopias, which were meant to offer solutions to current social problems. Only the Spaniards saw no need for it. With good reason Unamuno at a time of national crisis very many years later would cry out: 'Utopias! Utopias! It is what we most need!' The advent of Bourbon rule in Spain did not alter this indifference to the theory of ideal societies. Instead, by a process that is not entirely easy to understand, educated Spaniards began to look for their ideal society not in some imaginary place but in a very real 'Europe'. And when they said 'Europe' they usually meant France, the nation that since 1700 had imposed much of its ideas, culture and customs on the upper classes of the peninsula.[47]

Even while they admired and tried to imitate the world outside, many Spaniards – both progressives and traditionalists – became convinced that other Europeans did not understand them and were interested only in destroying them. Exiles from Spain invariably sought refuge in their immediate neighbour, France, but not because they loved France. Macanaz was typical of the many who disliked the French, accusing them of wishing to destroy Spain. Objections to the Bourbon monarchy were only one aspect of a general objection to the entry of foreign culture. At the end of the War of the Succession, in 1714, a pamphleteer complained that 'the principal reason for our lament is the innate hostility with which all foreigners have always looked on Spain'.[48] Despite all the contact with Europe, even progressive Spaniards refused to admit any superiority of others over Spain. The eighteenth-century traveller and memoir-writer Casanova concluded, after a visit to the peninsula, 'Every Spaniard hates a foreigner simply because he is not a Spaniard.'[49] The passion for Europe was, like the impact of the Enlightenment, a love-hate relationship carried on at a discreet distance, and never deep enough to leave its mark at any point. Spain insisted on remaining impenetrable, dedicated to its own style of life, which was not as changeless as one might suppose. In reaction to foreign influences, Spaniards developed their own preferences.

The almost bipolar split between a preference for Europe and a preference for peninsular tradition turned into a fundamental theme that would permanently affect the fate of cultural exiles. A basic reality in the peninsula was the persistence of popular culture: traditional customs that kept changing their character but never lost force, and indeed began to dominate social manners and the way people thought about Spain. Some foreign influences entered the country, but were quickly absorbed, transformed and integrated into what people already knew. Leaders of culture during the Golden Age made every effort to preserve the country against corrupting foreign influences, seen to come principally from Italy. In the second half of the sixteenth century Italian strolling players brought live theatre to the villages of the peninsula, provoking clerical rage against their 'immodesty' and 'immorality'. The debate over whether theatre was immoral lasted for well over a century, with theologians taking sides on the issue. In any case, popular theatre continued without interruption, despite the moralists, for the people had their own standards on the matter. If the farces and spectacles were really taken away, complained the archbishop of Toledo in 1720, people would no longer come forward to help in the affairs of the parishes.[50] Spain remained different because of the impressively solid dominance of traditional forms in leisure, theatre, music and art. This, evidently, was not to the liking of members of the cultured elite who favoured foreign ways and European influences. They tended to despise indigenous customs and welcomed novelties that came from outside. Since some of them later swelled the ranks of exiles, it would help to identify who they were. On all three counts, opinion in educated circles became highly polarized, and the exiles above all were profoundly influenced by the issues.

The pro-Europe reformers proposed to reform culture by expelling aspects of it which they saw as too popular and too vulgar. This was the spirit in which they attacked bullfights, which the government minister Jovellanos denounced as excessively violent and ferocious.

Ferocity, he proclaimed, should no longer be counted a civic virtue in Spain. The bullfight, throughout history, was rejected by those who associated it with primitive culture. Isabella the Catholic disliked it because of the bloodshed, Philip II disliked it because of the vulgarity, and preferred gentlemanly medieval-style pursuits such as jousts and tournaments. Almost without exception, the Enlightenment elite and the Europeanized intellectuals who looked outside the peninsula for their culture despised it. There is a real sense to affirming, contrary to what we often think, that it was never Spain's national sport. Throughout the northern half of Spain and outside the Basque country, bullfights were unknown. As late as the year 1800 bullfights could not be found in the regions of Catalonia, Galicia or Asturias. Catalans viewed the *corrida* as a symbol of Spain's backwardness relative to European standards. In Barcelona the mayor, Dr Robert, organized in 1901 a public meeting at which he called for the banning of the sport. The Valencian novelist Blasco Ibáñez satirized bullfights in his novel *Blood and Sand*. When in 1767 Jovellanos asked for a report on the sport he was told that *corridas* were customarily held in only 185 of the towns of Spain, and he concluded logically that it could by no means be identified as a national pastime. The government adopted a plan to ban bullfighting within four years from the date of the report. In practice, Spanish inertia took over and nothing was done until a law of 1786 banned the sport. Once again, nothing happened, and four years later a new prohibition was issued. The public was jolted out of this cheerful indifference to the law by a painful event that happened when a bullfighter was gored to death before the eyes of the queen, Maria Louisa. As a consequence, in 1805 her minister, Godoy, prohibited *corridas* for the future. In practice, they continued and actually entered into their heyday, while the figure of the bull became converted into a sort of symbol of Spain's identity.

In the same way, reformers from the seventeenth century onwards set their sights on other popular pastimes. On occasion the Madrid government had issued bans prohibiting public theatre, but they were short-lived (the bans 'have never been successful', a government report of 1672 stated)[51] and did not interrupt the theatrical labours of dramatists such as Lope de Vega and Calderón. Prohibitions were issued against a vast number of aspects of public entertainment, but all without exception came to nothing. One of the most interesting was the ban on carnivals, which was ignored almost as soon as it was issued. Later on, in nineteenth-century Castile, there was a vogue for the folk opera known as 'zarzuela', and for Andalusian song and flamenco. The popularity of these 'authentic' (a translation of the term 'castizo') forms of culture horrified intellectuals, who sought Spain's redemption in the higher elements of European civilization. Unamuno commented that flamenco, bulls and zarzuela were 'a plague' which instead of educating the people to think kept them happy with 'foolishness and stupidities'.

The world of popular entertainment, in other words, was a battle-ground between two ideological tendencies that coincided neatly with the division separating intellectuals in Spain. It was no accident that exiles should have felt themselves alienated from certain ways of thinking and living. Those ways were the traditional ones, firmly supported by a way of thinking that was anti-French, conservative and absolutist. However, by the end of the nineteenth century this polarization became difficult to sustain, for a revolutionary new factor came into play: the beginnings of mass culture. Mass culture – which we shall touch on in the next chapter – changed the face of Spanish leisure, and directly affected the way writers approached traditional problems.

Many reformers felt that the educational system needed to be trans-formed in order to achieve progress in culture. It was one of the issues that played a part in the expulsion of the Jesuits from Spain in 1767. Other nations, such as France and parts of Germany in the seventeenth century, had periodically expelled them but usually because of pressure from local Protestant leaders. Spain, by contrast, had no Protestants and an impeccable record of fidelity to the Church. The Jesuits were well placed in society: they were confessors to the king, ran the best schools and colleges, and virtually controlled the Inquisition. They were indubitably central to what was going on in the cultural world, whether for better or for worse, and their fate was therefore of primary cultural significance.[52] Virtually all the nobles and the intel-lectuals of the mid-century had passed through their schools. Their very prominence, however, stirred up hostility from other sections of the elite, not least from the upper clergy and bishops. Those who wished to reform the educational system also found that the ubiquity of Jesuit control of the school system represented a barrier to change. Even though many Jesuits were clearly progressive in their thinking, a sharp division emerged between their order as a whole and the government officials and others who directed public policy. It reflected the ideological split in Bourbon society between supporters and opponents of Enlightenment thought. The expulsion of the Jesuits, often considered to be a simple act of anticlericalism, and presented as such in their own subsequent writings, was, ironically, supported not only by freethinking reformers but also by most of the bishops of Spain, and was applauded by the most traditionalist sectors of the Church.

How could it have happened? Historians recognize that it was a long time in the making, and a consequence of the opposition of many Jesuit clergy to the reform programme of the ministers of Charles III. Government ministers such as Campomanes were notably critical of the Jesuits, though perhaps the chief pressure against the Society came not from inside Spain but from the governments of France and Portugal, which had already initiated a campaign of propaganda against it and expelled its members in 1759 (from Portugal) and 1764 (from France). What transpired in Spain, therefore, was by no means a complete surprise. At Easter 1766 serious food riots broke out in Madrid and other cities, when rioters called for (and obtained) the resignation of minister Squillace. The government's legal officer, Campomanes, drew up a transparently prejudiced report which claimed that the Jesuits had instigated the riots. A decision to expel the Society was backed up by arguments that reflected ideas then current among progressive thinkers. A government minister, the count of Aranda, was put in charge of the operation to enforce the decree, which was dated 27 February 1767 but kept secret until the last moment. The measure ordered the exile of all members of the Society, and seizure by the state of all its goods, churches, buildings and lands, as well as its documents, books and treasures. At the same time the decree ordered the suppression of the Jesuits throughout the American colonies, where the consequences turned out to be far more dramatic than in Spain.

The first stage of the expulsion was put into effect a month after the date that appeared on the decree. In the night hours on the eve of 1 April, units of the army presented themselves at the doors of the 120 Jesuit institutions in Spain and invited the startled clergy to pack their effects and leave. 'Never has there been a move so well planned, rapid and secret,' a witness reported. 'The colleges which were occupied on the night of 31 March were empty the next morning and all the residents were on their way.'[53] The stunned clergy were allowed to take 'all the clothing and spare attire they wished, without limit, their cases, tobacco, chocolate and utensils, breviaries and prayer books', but not their books and papers, which it was felt would contain information about their plots. The priests were transported immediately to the nearest port.[54] Those from Castile were taken to the north coast, from which they were to join a general embarkation from the Atlantic port of El Ferrol, while those from the east of the peninsula were to sail from the port of Salou. There were also to be sailings from Cartagena and Malaga. In fact there were not enough vessels on hand, so several foreign merchant ships had to be chartered. Nor was there bedding available, which meant that the ships from El Ferrol did not sail until the end of May. Around 5,700 people, all male and mostly elderly clergy, from the most educated levels of the country's cultural elite, were peremptorily put on board the vessels and sent off.

It turned out, however, that they had no destination. The government's decision was that they all be transported to the Papal States, since the Jesuits were unique among the religious orders in having a special vow of obedience to the pope. In the month of May, therefore, four Spanish flotillas converged on central Italy. Just then the pope received notice of the expulsion, and immediately refused – for political and financial reasons – to accept the refugees. The unfortunate priests sailed off again, and in July were all dumped on the island of Corsica, where obviously no preparations had been made to care for them. It was a miserable, botched operation. Comfort and sanitation on the transports had been almost non-existent. One of the priests, Father Isla, sent back to the government a first-hand account of how the ageing priests put up with the sudden journey.[55] In the shipment from El Ferrol, hundreds of Jesuits were crushed into the small space available on two frigates, and had to put up with 'scorching, stuffy air they breathed at the height of the hot season in June and July, insufferable and foul-smelling odours given off by so many bodies stacked into so tight a space', as well as the 'unhygienic food', which was invariably insufficient, and the dirty table linen, which 'they changed only twice in the two long months that we were on board'. The dumping on Corsica was done 'without any care for our well-being or our shelter, since the captains left us on land as abandoned as though we were a herd of filthy animals'. A Catalan priest wrote to his cousin that 'we can say that we lack everything here, except food', and that 'the wretched houses in which we have been left' had nowhere for sleeping.[56] Subsequently several of the Jesuits managed to escape from Corsica and make their way to Italy, Spain or France.

Many of the clergy were of advanced years and unable to deal with the crisis. Around one-tenth of them died, of illness or old age, within a short time of being thrown out of Spain. Some, of course, could not believe what had happened. The measure speaks volumes about the divided state of Spanish society, and the fierce (and traditional) hostility between the main body of the Church (including its bishops) and the castigated order. Campomanes, the minister most responsible for the decree, claimed that the state was acting against a group that had 'promoted ignorance and superstition', and that it was a step towards liberty. On the opposing side, many claimed that – like the Jewish expulsions three centuries before – the measure was a setback for education and science. Distribution of the rich art treasures was entrusted to Antonio Ponz, a minor painter and author of a well-known travelogue of Spain. He sent the paintings and artefacts to several institutions run by the state. In Seville, for example, they formed the first public art gallery in the city. It was logical that the absence of a powerful teaching order should pave the way to changes in the system of public education. But it was also true that many of the refugees were intelligent and cultured men who took their gifts with them into exile. Beyond exile, there was a further test awaiting the expelled clergy, for in July 1773 the pope, Clement XIV, dissolved their order in western Europe. The Jesuits were allowed to continue functioning only in eastern Europe, where they faced no comparable hostility from governments. The order was restored only in 1814.

*

Those who had backed the expulsion of the Jesuits felt that the move would bring Spain into line with an enlightened, progressive Europe. For some, the Europe of the future meant one not simply without Jesuits but without priests. Nicolás de Azara, ambassador to the Holy See in the 1760s and a leading sympathizer of the Enlightenment, is a case in point. In a letter he wrote, 'Though a sceptic I believe in God, but only in his law',[57] meaning that he did not accept the laws of the Church, an attitude he made perfectly clear in his correspondence. He expressed impatience that Spain should be always in the rearguard of movements for progress: 'The whole world is concerned to reform abuses and reduce the usurpations of the priests. Only Spain sleeps.'[58] Other members of the governing elite shared these views. A former ambassador to London and Paris, the count of Fuentes, said during a lecture he gave in 1777 in Madrid that

England and France demonstrate the contribution made by the arts and industry to the public good. The impression that this makes on the heart of a good Spaniard is almost impossible to explain. Immediately it sets up a sad contrast with his own country, deprived of its former splendour by the decay of the arts and practical sciences.

There was a substantial gap between the very small educated elite with European contacts, and the great mass of the largely illiterate public. In matters of religion many in the elite had become freethinking liberals. The Church appeared to be the principal obstacle to all progress, both economic and moral. The Enlightenment in Spain was, however, little more than 'a government-sponsored movement confined to the better spirits of the public administration'.[59] It had a well-meaning programme but not the capacity to effect any change. The fragility of progress could be seen by the outstanding case of Pablo de Olavide, a leading government minister.

Olavide (1725–1803) was born into a rich family in Lima, Peru, and moved in 1750 to Spain, where after some initial problems he married a wealthy widow and entered high society. From 1757 to 1765 he travelled extensively through western Europe, particularly in France, where he imbibed the culture of the great period of the French Enlightenment. During his travels he began buying books, with the intention of building up the finest and most modern collection in

Spain. Nearly all the volumes he accumulated and sent to Madrid were in French, and many were on the Inquisition's list of forbidden books. He had the works of Bacon, Locke, Bayle, Voltaire, Rousseau, and all the latest English novels in French translation.[60] When he settled down in Spain his contacts, his education and his wealth turned his house into one of the cultural centres of Madrid, and he was offered a post in the reformed administration that assumed power after the Squillace riots. The riots became for Olavide a stepping-stone to success. The year after them, 1767, he was appointed to the powerful position of intendant in Seville and Andalusia, but he also continued to play a crucial part in the central government, which in 1769–70 put into effect pioneering educational measures that he had proposed. In Andalusia, he carried out another pioneering project: the colonization of the Sierra Morena zone with immigrants brought in from Germany. These measures, above all where education was concerned, provoked the profound opposition of sectors in the Church, and in 1775 a priest denounced him as 'the most dangerous intellectual in Spain'.[61] It is true that Olavide's conduct as a public official had often been provocative. As a partisan of the Enlightenment, he had criticized what he felt was superstition, decried the worship of images and the public recital of the rosary. On one occasion he had stated jokingly: 'What we need is a bit of Mohammedanism in Spain!' His joviality and openness offended many. He had even – *horribile dictu* – during his travels stayed a week at Voltaire's house in France! When he returned to Madrid from Seville in 1776 he was arrested by the Inquisition on charges of heresy and atheism.

It says much for the power of the supposedly moribund Inquisition that it was able to keep the once-powerful minister locked up for two years. Eventually, in November 1778, he was brought out, put on trial before a select assembly of clergy and officials, and condemned to banishment from the capital, loss of all his goods, and six years' confinement in a monastery. It was a startling affair, in which the Inquisition and conservative sectors of the Church were evidently giving a warning to the government. Olavide was sent to a monastery in the south of Spain, in Murcia. The specific instructions of the Inquisitor General, in June 1779, were that he should have 'a clean and comfortable room, and be allowed at the same time to go out, walking or riding or in a carriage, and be allowed to take the waters when the doctors so direct'.[62] His confinement, it turned out, was more like a paid holiday. He carried out his religious devotions, went to mass daily and ate a frugal diet (for his health), but was accompanied by his family, travelled around taking the waters, and in August 1780 was given permission (for his health) to take the waters at Caldes de Montbuy in Catalonia. Once in Catalonia, he decided it was better to take the waters in Arles, a town just over the French border which he knew personally. In the first week of November, he was free, in France.

He spent the next twenty years in exile, residing mainly in Switzerland and Paris. In the aftermath of the French Revolution and the war waged against France in 1793 by Spain and other European powers, he was rounded up in Paris in 1794 as a suspicious foreigner, and kept in prison for two years. He emerged a disappointed and changed man, angry at all the 'progressive' ideas that had led to the 'horrible Revolution in this country'. In 1797 he published at Valencia a book titled *Triumph of the Gospel*, in which he renounced all his former progressive ideas and praised the Inquisition. At least, that is what the book appeared to be saying. Some scholars suggest that the author had not really changed his attitude, and was framing his message in such a way as to make possible his return.[63] Thanks to the publication, in 1798 he was allowed back to Spain, where he died quietly, far from public life, in a small Andalusian town.

After the French Revolution, the government in Spain began a firm policy of restricting the periodical press and keeping out revolutionary propaganda. When peace with France came in 1795, by contrast, it was difficult to control French ideas and the development of radical thought. A new window had been opened into Hispanic reality. Many intellectuals held up the French model as an ideal and questioned the fundamentals of life in the peninsula. A split opened up between admirers of France – the so-called '*afrancesados*' or 'pro-French' – and defenders of Spanish tradition.

Against all expectation, the century after the year 1700 shook Spaniards out of their old ways and encouraged them to look for new solutions. But they very quickly became disillusioned with what

Europe had to offer. They were happy to pick and choose from what seemed acceptable, but refused absolutely to change their own cultural preferences. Their imperviousness is illustrated by the case of the last outstanding prisoner of the eighteenth century and first illustrious exile of the incoming nineteenth, the explorer Malaspina.

The end of the eighteenth century was the great period of European exploration in the Pacific. The pioneers were the British, in the shape of Captain James Cook's astonishing expeditions in the 1770s. They were followed a decade later by French vessels under Bougainville and La Pérouse. The most important British expedition in this period was led by a young captain who had sailed twice with Cook, George Vancouver. From 1791 to 1795 he led a memorable expedition that mapped the Pacific coast of North America. On his voyage he was surprised to encounter a Spanish naval mission. For nearly three centuries there had been no significant Spanish presence in the seas that Spain theoretically claimed to be within its empire. Not until the 1790s was any serious move made to enforce Spanish claims, through an expedition planned by an Italian naval officer named Malaspina. Alessandro Malaspina (1754–1810) was born in Tuscany of noble parents who, in 1762, moved to Sicily, where an uncle of the family was viceroy.[64] He was educated in Rome and in 1774 went to Spain to enter upon a naval career (the king of Spain since 1759 was an Italian, Charles III). He built up considerable experience of the sea, including two voyages, in 1777 and 1783, to the very distant Philippines. In this period he was also denounced to the Inquisition for certain statements he made in public, but after tedious procedures that dragged out over ten years nothing came of the matter. An original thinker grounded in Enlightenment philosophy, and deeply interested in practical aspects of naval enterprise, his experience as a sailor convinced him of the need for a serious scientific expedition to the Pacific. The idea took shape in his 1786 voyage, when he sailed via Cape Horn to the Philippines, a round trip that lasted twenty-two months. Based on his experience he put forward to the government plans for changing the commercial and navigational aspects of the link with the Pacific. With help from Spanish entrepreneurs, he obtained government support for a special expedition to visit the Spanish possessions in America and Asia. Two vessels, the *Discovery* (*Descubierta*) and the *Audacious* (*Atrevida*), were specially built for the purpose, and sailed from Cadiz in July 1789.

After three centuries of the Spanish presence in the New World, it was the first time that they had carried out an official scientific expedition, with the command entrusted to an Italian. Spaniards took a long time to absorb the world experience. In the sixteenth century Philip II paid for an expedition to Mexico led by Dr Hernández, but the reports he brought back were shelved and never published. In the mid-eighteenth century the French mounted an expedition to South America in which two young naval officers from Spain – Jorge Juan and Antonio de Ulloa – took part, but a crucial part of the report the officers made was suppressed by the Madrid government. For one and a half centuries after the Hernández expedition, almost nothing was done to enquire into the riches offered by the empire. Malaspina's mission was, consequently, historic. The ships under his command carried scientific instruments (purchased abroad), and a team of experts in cartography, astronomy and botany, as well as artists (one Czech, one Spaniard) whose magnificent ink and wash drawings constituted the first 'photographic' record ever made of the native civilizations they encountered.[65] They explored the northern Pacific coast of America up to Alaska, crossed the Pacific to the Philippines, then descended past New Guinea to New Zealand.[66] The four years originally planned soon extended into five. Malaspina eventually returned to Cadiz at the end of 1794. From his observations of administration in the colonies he believed (as Jorge Juan and Antonio de Ulloa had already, and in vain, urged half a century before) that changes and improvements were necessary. Without changes, he felt, the colonies would break free. On returning to Spain, he made his views known and openly criticized the government, especially Manuel de Godoy. It was the wrong time to suggest reform, for the general reaction against the excesses of the revolution in France and the execution of the king had brought about a firm conservative stance in Spain and a war in Europe. Most of Malaspina's contacts in the administration had been removed, but he still believed that his work could contribute something. 'If the experiences of four long years do not deceive me,' he wrote to a friend in Milan, 'I may dare to say that I have put together those few ideas which can restore prosperity, or, even better, can regenerate the Monarchy.'[67]

The nature of that regeneration was highly sensitive, even dangerous. He proposed a 'moderate freedom for the colonies', in the sense of allowing each part of the world empire more political autonomy. He also suggested a 'legal union of the whole empire', meaning a written constitution to recognize the rights and duties of each territory.[68] He lamented the war against revolutionary France, and looked forward to a time when true philosophy would prevail, and the states of Europe would combine to attain peace and progress. His mind went back to the 'benefactress Nature' that he had found among the people of the Pacific, a true hope for Europe. He referred again to the theme in a statement he published in the official state gazette when he arrived in Madrid:

In the immense reaches of our domains Nature has presented us with unimagined products and treasures which will foster new combinations capable of strengthening the Monarchy. And to top off such happiness, none of these surveys has cost humankind a single tear. As a result of this expedition, unlike other such ancient and modern journeys, all the tribes and people visited will bless the memory of those who refrained from staining their shores with blood, but instead set foot on them only to leave useful ideas, tools and seeds behind them.[69]

Malaspina found at the court a complete lack of interest in his ideas. It only impelled him to try to make his views known. He proposed publishing three large volumes on the results of the expedition: the first would include the ships' journals, the second a geographical account, and the third a political analysis. In turn, each volume would have sections on astronomy, meteorology, tides and medicine. The series would eventually include complete cartographical accounts, together with geological, botanical and zoological information gathered by the expedition. It would have been the greatest scientific survey ever carried out by Spain. Malaspina was not too optimistic about what could be done, and expressed his disappointment at the low cultural level of the officials around him. Typical of the reactions he encountered were those of a Spanish colleague who observed that 'Malaspina has sailed the seas and lost sight of the land', citing as an example of his defects 'his veneration for the British, who are detested by all thinking men'. When he tried to present a memo that explicitly criticized Godoy as an obstacle to reform, the favourite persuaded Charles IV to have Malaspina arrested in November 1795 on charges of sedition and sentenced to ten years' imprisonment. In April 1796, Malaspina was transported to the distant fortress of San Antón at La Coruña, where he was fated to spend seven years. His journals, logs and papers had been taken away from him so he was unable to write up the narrative of his expedition.

Three years later a ship left the harbour of La Coruña on its way across the Atlantic. On board was the naturalist Alexander von Humboldt, who commented in his journal:

Our eyes remained fixed on San Antón's Castle, where the unfortunate Malaspina languished in a state prison. On my way from Europe to visit the lands that this illustrious traveller had explored so fruitfully, I would have liked to occupy my mind on a less sorrowful subject.

In 1802, thanks in part to pressure by Napoleon on the Spanish government, Malaspina had his sentence commuted to perpetual exile from Spain, his adopted country. He sailed to Genoa, his last sight of the sea, and settled in Pontremoli (Tuscany), free at last in a country that recognized his merits. In the eight years of life that remained to him (he died prematurely of an intestinal tumour), he must have suffered deep disillusionment knowing that the great schemes developed to aid the country where he had spent twenty-two years of his career would come to nothing. Ten days after his death, far across in the Pacific that he had reconnoitred, the city council of Caracas revolted against its military governor and set in train the revolution that would topple Spanish power in South America.[70] Oblivious to the importance of Malaspina's work, the Spanish authorities made no effort to publish the results of the expedition. Its records, including 300 journals, 450 notebooks, 183 charts and over 800 drawings of places, animals and plants, were impounded or scattered, unpublished and unstudied, as forgotten as the expedition's commander. 'Officially, he became a non-person.'[71] Part of his ship's journal was published in Madrid in 1885, but then forgotten about. Today there are three institutions dedicated to collecting the papers and researching the work of

Malaspina. None of them is in Spain, the country he served. Not until two hundred years after his amazing voyage, in the year 1990, did the Naval Museum in Madrid begin publishing, in response to a British initiative, the rich and forgotten collections of the greatest mariner in Spain's employ after Columbus.

The French Revolution had direct consequences for Spain, provoking on the one hand a policy of repression by the Spanish government against agitators, and on the other giving comfort to sympathizers of the new regime in Paris. Charles IV, king since 1788, backed his chief minister, the count of Floridablanca, in moves to control the press and prevent revolutionary influences entering the country. Inevitably, the government used the standard measures of arrest and expulsion against dissidents, and in 1793 entered on a war against France. The military effort was a failure and Spain was forced into accepting France as an ally. It was an alliance that quickly became a disaster when in 1805 the British defeated the joint Franco-Spanish fleets at Trafalgar. In 1807 a huge French army marched through Spain in order to occupy Portugal, and the following year General Murat effectively occupied Spain by imposing French garrisons on the chief cities. This was accompanied by a dynastic coup whereby Napoleon Bonaparte deprived King Ferdinand VII of the crown and handed it to his own brother Joseph (May 1808).

The French moves, however, had provoked an immediate response from Spaniards of all conditions and opinions. A popular rising in Madrid on 2 May 1808 was suppressed bloodily the day after (not only by the French troops but also by the Spanish authorities), and set in train a series of chaotic struggles. Goya's paintings of the events of those two days continue to shock, as the French repression certainly did. When news of the Madrid events spread, there were uprisings throughout the provinces. In the major cities mobs roamed the streets, looting and occasionally killing. Many motives were brought into play, above all the desire of regional authorities to distance themselves from events in the capital. During these months of confusion the American states of the empire took the opportunity to declare their independence. In the peninsula the Spaniards were too concerned with achieving their own freedom to be seriously disturbed. A Spanish delegation went to London to plead for military help, with the consequence that British troops under Wellesley (better known under his subsequent title of duke of Wellington) sailed to Portugal and Spain to take part in what became known to non-Spaniards as the Peninsular War.

The war began with an unexpected Spanish success at the battle of Bailén (July 1808) against a poorly supplied French conscript force. There were no further Spanish victories, only a continuous series of defeats.[72] The same thing had happened in the War of the Spanish Succession in the early 1700s. Both Napoleon and Wellington were of the opinion that Spaniards were disastrous as regular soldiers. The judgement had a great deal of merit, but was not entirely fair. Though the brunt of the war against the French was borne by British troops, the Spaniards made their own crucial contribution in the form of sporadic but persistent local attacks by peasant 'guerrillas', whose activities tied the French units down. Idealized afterwards as symbols of patriotic resistance against the foreigner, the guerrillas also terrorized the local Spanish population into giving them support. The Spaniards were capable of uniquely heroic acts of resistance, such as the defence of the city of Saragossa against a superior French force. The 'War of Independence', as they later called it, eventually drove the French out, but it also had at least four lethal consequences.[73] The first was to repeat once again the old ritual of exile for those who did not agree. The second, in a country where the 'war' on the Spanish side had effectively been conducted by partisans rather than by a central body, was to sanction regional initiatives and minimize the role of the nation. The third was the glorification of violence. Guerrilla warfare, a Spanish scholar concludes, 'accustomed the Spaniard to live outside the law, to reject the norms of social life and take as his great achievement the maintenance of his own personality'.[74] Finally, the war gave the regional armed forces an initiative in political matters that they never lost, and acted as a prelude to more than a century of army insurrections or 'pronunciamientos'. The widespread and unrestrained violence created an atmosphere of virtual civil war and in consequence a flood of refugees.

In the mythology that later came to be created, first by the Liberal opponents of the French and then by Castilian writers, the anti-French risings of May 1808 signalled the emergence of a Spanish national identity. Certainly the Liberals tried to rally support along those lines. The French forces withdrew to areas of Spain they could more easily control, while the Spanish 'patriots' summoned to Cadiz in 1810 a Cortes aimed at unifying the national effort. Among its memorable acts were the agreement of a new national charter, the Constitution of 1812, and a decree of 1813 abolishing the Inquisition. When the deputy Agustín Argüelles presented the text of the Constitution, he exclaimed: 'Spaniards, you now have a *patria*!' In reality, there was no *patria* nor any feeling of national solidarity, and the measures of 1812 and 1813 were not the measures of healing they appeared to be. Quite the reverse, they had a devastating effect on Spanish public life for the next hundred years. The Constitution was a document that came to be identified with the ideas of the Liberals, and served as an inspiration to many other progressive movements in Europe. But it collided with many traditional attitudes, just as the abolition of the Inquisition (which Joseph I had also, by a decree that was not regarded as legal, abolished in 1809) outraged most traditionalist Catholics.

When, after years of virtual civil war, the French eventually withdrew from Spain and Ferdinand VII was restored to his throne in the spring of 1814, the new king annulled the Constitution, proscribed the Cortes deputies who had voted for it, and restored the Inquisition. His measures established a clear division between two types of opinion current at that time. He became identified with an older vision of Spain, a traditional way of exercising political power (known as 'absolutism'), and a preference for time-honoured customs, culture and belief. It was a tendency that coincided with dislike for the French, and earned Ferdinand massive popular support. Joseph Bonaparte as king, on the other hand, was identified with the other, more reformist, opinion. He received the considered support of many of the enlightened ministers of the previous administration, who felt that the progressive policies identified with revolutionary France would open up for Spain a new era of cultural advances. In June 1813 British troops under Wellington defeated the French army at the battle of Vitoria (a victory commemorated by Beethoven in his exhilarating Opus 91, which he personally directed in Vienna that December), and Joseph with his troops were forced to withdraw to France. He took with him some 20,000 Spaniards who had been driven out by their fellow citizens and who fled across the frontier through any available exit. The first century of the Bourbon dynasty ended as it had begun, exactly one hundred years previously, with a massive wave of elite exiles.

5

Romantic Spain

The heart does not change, the only change
Is in the unhappy man who desires
To evade his destiny by fleeing his native land.
José María Blanco White (1808)

The large number of Spaniards who were obliged to follow King Joseph I in the summer of 1813 after the battle of Vitoria, crossing into France through the area of Bayonne, has never been precisely calculated. Contemporary sources, including the French ambassador in Madrid at the time, offer a round figure of twelve thousand families. 'Almost all have lost their possessions,' an official with them reported to a French minister, 'the rich have lost much and the poor everything they owned.'[1] In perspective, the uncertainty in figures has seemed less important to Spaniards than the suspicion that those who supported the French were betraying their country. Were the defectors traitors, as their traditionalist enemies maintained? Historians appear on balance to have settled the matter satisfactorily.[2] Material circumstances, rather than ideological attitude, dictated decisions. The vast majority of the exiles were military officers, state officials and clergy who, for reasons beyond their control, had taken an oath of loyalty to Joseph and had to live with the consequences. Among them, for instance, was the Granada magistrate Juan Sempere y Guarinos, who stated later that his oath to Joseph had been taken 'not because of treason or of hatred for their lawful king [Ferdinand VII], but because of the conviction that it was the only way to save their fatherland and heal the profound wounds it had suffered from the imprudence and evil of previous governments'. Three-quarters of the refugees were military personnel and their families, and in the remaining quarter there were two hundred clergy (usually state officials) and just over a thousand from the upper sectors of society (including cultural figures).[3] In a decided minority were those who were truly pro-French by political conviction and who continued to support the French king as the main hope for modernization and reform. All chose exile because (as one of them, Canon Juan Antonio Llorente, testified) there was no alternative. The new regime was harassing them, and mob violence was threatening their security and their lives on the ground that they were traitors.

The pro-French émigrés were, of course, hostile to the staunchly conservative (or 'absolutist') position of the returning king, Ferdinand VII. But they were also for the most part opposed to the policy and methods of Ferdinand's opponents, those who supported the Cortes of Cadiz (referred to in the preceding chapter). Heirs to the ideas of the late eighteenth century and the Enlightenment outlook as it had been perceived in Spain, the émigrés firmly supported the idea of a strong reforming monarchy, opposed populist republicanism, and stood up for the maintenance of the Spanish empire, against the independence movement in the colonies. On all three counts their ideas differed sharply from those of a newly emerging tendency that would soon become important, the Liberals. There was, ironically, a further difference. Those who were pro-French among the Spaniards were not necessarily admirers of France. Their views, it has been pointed out, were also based in large measure on what they had learnt from the culture of England and Germany, rather than of France.[4] In terms of practical politics, however, the pro-French and the Liberals were united against the regime of Ferdinand VII.

It was the first great exile of the nineteenth century, and set the tone for the many exiles that would soon follow. The last big movement of expulsion, fifty years earlier, had been limited in nature and impact, since the Jesuits were a small group of ageing single men, drawn primarily from the teaching profession. The pro-French, by contrast, were a broad sweep across the whole elite of Spain, and included officials, military men, clergy, politicians and cultural figures, together with their wives and children. The reasons why they left were also radically different. The Jesuits in 1767 had been removed by a government order. There was no popular pressure against them, no riots directed against their persons or property (though the formal accusation against them was that they had *provoked* riots). The pro-French in 1813, on the other hand, were the first serious victims in Spanish history of mob violence. Those who rioted against the French in Madrid were rising against foreign invaders, as Goya's painting *The Second of May* shows clearly, with its images of anger and passion. But it is invariably forgotten that their violence was also directed against Spaniards. Known sympathizers of the French in Madrid and elsewhere were murdered, their belongings looted. An exile of a later decade, Alcalá Galiano, commented in his memoirs on the outrages committed by street mobs:

There were tragedies of reputable and esteemed generals, civil servants of the highest regard and respect, persons noted through their blood or their wealth, who had till then enjoyed the love and reverence of their fellow citizens in their towns of residence, not to mention other persons of lesser degree in small villages, who because they directly or indirectly opposed the heroic but reckless rising, or because they did not co-operate with it through caution, or because of suspicions that they regarded it with fear and distaste, fell victims of the mob fury and suffered unbelievable atrocities on their bloody remains.[5]

The persecution of Spanish officials in 1813 was brutal but goes unmentioned in the history books, no doubt because it would alter the received image of a patriotic rising directed against foreign invaders. The property of pro-French sympathizers was confiscated, the families they left behind were attacked and maltreated, and minor officials who stayed behind were thrown into prison. The new Spanish government issued a harsh decree expelling from its territory all those (together with wives) who had served the past regime. Fortunately for them, the French government set aside a million francs to pay for the urgent needs of exiles whom Bonaparte's regime had employed in Spain. After Napoleon was thrown out of France in 1815, the situation changed, and the governments in Paris and Madrid tried to work out a scheme to allow the pro-French to go back. It was over five years before some sort of return was allowed. Many of the exiles logically preferred to stay in France, where they often received pensions from the regime.

The sufferings brought about by deprivation and expulsion from their homeland overwhelmed the pro-French in misery, but in some respects exile turned out to have extraordinarily fruitful consequences for Spanish culture. Many of the exiles dedicated their leisure and energy to thinking and writing about the situation that had brought about their departure. In doing so, they notably enhanced the learned culture of their native land. A case in point was Sempere y Guarinos (1754–1830), whom we have mentioned.[6] An official of the government of Charles III, he had in the 1780s begun producing notable writings on the subject of Spain's cultural achievements in that epoch. He was the first Spaniard to attempt the task of compiling a biographical dictionary of contemporary writers, to serve as proof that the peninsula was not quite the intellectual backwater foreigners felt it to be. His point of departure was the question of 'good taste', which he felt had been notably achieved in the reign of Charles III, through whose efforts 'all the sciences and arts in Spain have assumed a new aspect and a certain level of taste that they did not have till now'. He took his inspiration from *Riflessioni sul buon gusto*, a study published in 1715 in Cologne by the Italian writer Ludovico Muratori, which he translated into Spanish in a very free version in 1782.

Sempere's idea, which he expressed in his translation and also in later writings, was that good literary taste in Spain had reached its peak in the sixteenth century, and that the country had subsequently suffered a 'decline', which was now being remedied in his own day. The six volumes of his *Spanish Library of the Best Writers of the Reign of Charles III* (1785–9) was a remarkable compilation, still of considerable use today, offering short summaries of the published work of the authors included: 'My purpose is to include here all those who in their writings have displayed some taste in their style of thought.'[7] In the same years he also brought out the small and highly original volume of his *History of Luxury and of the Sumptuary Laws in Spain* (1788), a study that remains unsurpassed in its scope. The French invasion of Spain and the imposition of Joseph I as king created problems for him, as for all other public servants. He took the oath of loyalty but was then forced to leave the country when the government of Ferdinand VII refused to accept Joseph's officials. He stayed in Bordeaux until 1817, then moved to Paris.

In exile in France he did not cease to publish important studies on the government and laws of Spain. When the Liberals carried out a coup against Ferdinand in 1820 he profited from an amnesty and returned to Spain in October that year, hoping that a period of practical reforms was about to begin. But the king turned the tables on the opposition after three years, and Sempere once again, at the age of sixty-nine, found himself in exile. In Paris he published in French (translated by a friend from Sempere's original text in Spanish) one of the most influential works ever to be written on Spain's history, the two volumes of his *Considerations on the Causes of the Greatness and Decline of the Spanish Monarchy* (1826). That same year he returned to the peninsula, to his native town of Elda (Alicante), where he spent the last years of his life. The *Considerations* turned out to be a seminal book in its influence on French savants, who were just beginning to develop an interest in a country they had until then almost totally neglected. Its thesis of a 'decline' that had somehow been imposed on the otherwise successful evolution of Spanish civilization worked its way into the thought of French and Spanish scholars and determined the postulates of English-speaking scholars down to our own day.

The presence of literary men among the exiles of the early century was notable. It has been commented that 'the return of absolutism in 1814 produced an almost total annihilation of literary Spain. From that year up to 1820, Spanish writers lived either in prison or in exile.'[8] The comment is exaggerated, but serves to emphasize that many elite men of letters left the country. A few went to England, among them the politician and political theorist Flórez Estrada and the writer Antonio Puigblanch. Alvaro Flórez Estrada (1765–1853), from a prominent landowning family in the province of Asturias, had been a colleague of the reforming ministers of the previous generation, and did more than anyone to introduce into Spain the study of the principles of political economy current in England, in the shape of the ideas of Smith, Ricardo and Mill.[9] In the first decade of the century he produced the brief but pioneering writings *On the Liberty of the Press* (1809) and on *The Spanish Constitution* (1810). The latter work was published during a one-year stay in England (1810–11), and received due attention in Blanco White's London journal *El Español*. When absolutism took over in Spain in 1814, Flórez returned to England, accompanied by his son. Apart from a short visit to the continent, he remained in England until 1820, never ceasing to draft ideas, always based on the ideas of the seventeenth-century philosopher John Locke, for a future constitutional regime in his home country. When the Liberal coup took place in 1820, he returned immediately to Spain and resumed his political career as a deputy for Asturias, but was back again in England as a consequence of the French restoration of absolute monarchy in 1823. On the outbreak of the French July Revolution in 1830 he and his son moved, like virtually all the Spanish exiles, to Paris, from which he finally returned to Spain in 1834. Flórez's contribution to Spanish political science demonstrates one of the most beneficial aspects of short-term exile: the way in which cultured émigrés were able to bring back to their country some of the knowledge that they had acquired abroad, provided (as in the case of Flórez) they had mastered the English and French languages. Flórez's best-known work was his classic *Course of Political Economy*, which remained the standard work consulted in Spain for over a century. It was first published in London in 1828, in Spanish, but was also translated soon after into French and went through several editions in Spain.

Antonio Puigblanch (1775–1840) was the pioneer of the movement to abolish the Inquisition. A Catalan from the seaport of Mataró, he was educated in Church schools, then, at the mature age of twenty-four, went to Madrid to complete his studies in law and classical languages. In 1807 he obtained a chair in Hebrew at the University of Alcalá. His remarkable scholarship was matched only by his profound concern for reform in Church and state. In the midst of the passions provoked by the French occupation and the opening of the Cortes at Cadiz, he published in 1811 at Cadiz, using the pseudonym Natanael Jomtob, his *The Inquisition Unmasked* (*La Inquisición sin Máscara*). The pseudonym, he explained, came from the Hebrew and meant 'God has set the day'. The preface stated his purpose clearly: 'My intention is to destroy the Inquisition from its very roots.' Puigblanch made use of a vast range of published sources to demonstrate that both the existence and the methods of the Inquisition (that is, its trial procedure, its rigour, its secrecy, its use of torture and its control of censorship) were against the rules of the Church and of civil society. His substantial volume of some five hundred pages, amply backed up by hundreds of footnotes and quotations in Latin, Greek, Hebrew and French, had an undeniable impact on readers in Spain. 'Can the century of Philosophy calmly allow the Inquisition to survive?' he asked.[10] He was identified as an enemy of the state and fled in 1815 to London, where he stayed for five years; in 1816 he published an English translation of his book. The year after, a German version came out at Weimar. Puigblanch had hopes of furthering his academic studies at Oxford, but he returned to Spain to become a member of the Cortes when the Liberals took over in 1820. However, in 1823, the Liberals were overthrown by French troops and he became an exile once again, settling permanently in England, where he dedicated himself to teaching languages.

Leading cultural figures of the regime of Charles III figured among the pro-French refugees of the year 1813. Among them was Juan Meléndez Valdés (1754–1817), the best-known Spanish poet of his time. Born near Badajoz, he studied law at Salamanca University, where he met intellectuals such as Cadalso and Jovellanos (the latter was soon to be the most distinguished political figure of Enlightenment Spain), and began his literary interests. In 1781 he went to Madrid to further his career and was able to count on the patronage of Jovellanos, who was now a government minister. Thanks to the connection, he was appointed to a chair in Salamanca. Four years later, in 1785, he published the first volume of his poems, which sold well and firmly established his literary reputation. However, he was unable to resist the temptation of a political career. Thanks again to Jovellanos, he was rapidly promoted to high legal posts and ended up as prosecutor of the supreme court in Madrid in 1797, the year that Goya painted a gracious portrait of him,[11] signed 'your friend Goya'. When Jovellanos fell from royal favour, Meléndez was ordered to give up his posts, and retired to live in Salamanca. These ups and downs were merely the beginning of his troubles. In 1808 he accepted office from the government of Joseph Bonaparte, but in doing so he fell foul of the popular reaction against the French. Pro-French long before his Bonapartist days, Meléndez had a personal library in which over half the books were in French, and several were works prohibited by the Inquisition.[12] Identified as a French sympathizer, in Oviedo he fell victim to the mob fury of May 1808, and was only saved from lynching when priests came out to intervene and exposed the sacred Host to the angry crowd.[13] After the anti-French party returned to power in 1813, he was compelled to flee with his wife to France. He lost everything: his house, his library and his poetry manuscripts. In France he passed four years of misery, and died at Montpellier poor and neglected in his sixty-fourth year. Half-forgotten today in Spain, and completely unknown to the European cultural world of his time, Meléndez was a typical figure of the Spanish version of the Enlightenment. His verse, light and lyrical, belongs to a different age, but was appreciated by the very people who drove him out of his country.

Another literary figure, Leandro Fernández de Moratín (1760–1828), was a prime example of a writer who not only made attempts to learn from the culture outside his country, but also ended his days in exile. Born in Madrid into a literary family, he became apprenticed to a jeweller but devoted his energy to poetry (his first poem to win a prize was on the conquest of Granada). Through family influence he obtained a post as secretary to the embassy in Paris, and spent two fruitful years in the French capital. On his return in 1788 he took the first stage of holy orders in order to be able to enjoy the income from a benefice in Burgos, but dedicated his time to writing plays. A shy, retiring person who never had enough confidence in himself to propose marriage, he felt more at ease outside his native environment, and in 1792 secured enough money to be able to travel through Europe. He spent a year in London, where he made extensive and entertaining notes on the English and their civilization, learnt enough of the language to attempt a prose translation of *Hamlet* (published in 1798), and studied in the British Museum. He next went to Holland, Germany, Switzerland and Italy, enjoying the sightseeing and expressing his creativity in a sensitive correspondence. His visit to Rome only confirmed his anticlerical opinions: 'I would forgive Rome its decadence, if within the ruins of its former dominion one could find more justice, more order, more good policy, more good faith, more honour, better manners, less impostures and less hypocrisy.' They were five enriching years. The portrait by his friend Goya in 1799 shows a gentle, earnest young man with a fair complexion, pursed lips and light brown hair.

Back in Spain in 1796, Moratín was appointed translator in the administration, and wrote several plays, of which the last and most successful was the romantic comedy *The Maidens' Consent* (*El Sí de las Niñas*) (1805), which played to crowded houses and was later translated into several foreign languages. The work, classical in form and wholly traditional in outlook, dealt with the reaction of society to a proposed marriage between partners of unequal age. It was a theme he had already broached in his first play, *The Old Man and the Young Girl* (*El Viejo y la Niña*), twenty years before. *The Maidens' Consent* presented an uncle and a nephew as rivals for the hand of a young girl, and argued for the right of the girl to make a free choice (in favour of the nephew) in defiance of family pressures. The dramatist used the plot in order to portray with delicate irony the problems presented by the gap between young and old. Unfortunately, Moratín was unable to write any plays after this, because he became caught up in the politics of the French occupation of Spain. When in 1811 he accepted the post of director of the Royal Library it identified him with the rule of Joseph Bonaparte, and like other state officials he had to face the threat of mob violence against pro-French sympathizers. He fled from Madrid in 1812, in the company of the French army. For the next five years he was with the French in Valencia and Catalonia, and eventually fled from Spain in 1817, going first to Montpellier then to Bordeaux, where (apart from a fleeting return to Spain in 1820) he spent the greater part of his remaining years, dying in Paris. Unlike other exiles, once he was uprooted he ceased to be creative, a circumstance to be explained by his refusal to accept the new tide of events.

Perhaps the most historic change of this turbulent period was the abolition of the Inquisition. It had been the most powerful instrument of exile in traditional Catholic Spain, and enjoyed considerable influence during the many centuries before its eventual abolition in 1813 (it was restored briefly after, abolished again in 1820, then restored but abolished definitively in 1834).[14] The opposition to Joseph Bonaparte was centred on the Spanish Cortes that had been meeting in the port of Cadiz since 1810. Around three hundred deputies took part at one

time or another in the Cortes' sessions, all of them from the propertied classes, mainly clergy, lawyers, public functionaries, army officers
and nobles. The high point of the sessions was the proclamation in
1812 of a national Constitution, in which the Catholic religion was
declared to be the official and sole permitted religion. After that, however, there were profound disagreements, mainly over abolishing the
Holy Inquisition, which about half the deputies, and indeed most of
the public, still wished to retain. Despite the disagreements, a decree
abolishing the Inquisition was eventually passed in February 1813, by
a margin of ninety votes to sixty. The deputies who abolished it felt
sure they understood what the tribunal signified in Spain's history –
intolerance, obscurantism and clericalism; in brief, all the factors
against which they were fighting. This made the Inquisition an ideal
explanation for all the ills that seemed to have plagued the country
since the fifteenth century. It was blamed for destroying freedom of
thought and freedom of the press, condemning Spain to intellectual
backwardness, destroying the economy, and excluding progress. One
deputy, named Calatrava, proclaimed passionately: 'I shall leave the
country if the Inquisition is restored! I am and remain a Catholic,
apostolic and Roman, but I wish to be free!'

The two Spaniards who did most to engrave in our minds the image
that we still have today of the Inquisition were at the centre of the
debates and struggles of those years, and passed a good part of their
last years in exile as a consequence of the events associated with the
fortunes of the monarchy. They were the priest Juan Antonio Llorente
and the painter Francisco Goya. Llorente (1756–1823), from the
village of Rincón de Soto in Aragon, lost both his parents when still a
child, and was brought up by his uncle. He studied at the University
of Saragossa, and after taking holy orders became vicar-general to the
bishop of Calahorra in 1782. Three years later he became an official
of the Spanish Inquisition in the town of Logroño and in 1789 was
promoted to being one of its secretaries in Madrid. In those decades
the Inquisition had little or no role in religious matters, and was far
from being what it was in past times. Resident in Madrid from 1805,
Llorente was among the many who took an oath of loyalty to Joseph
when he became king in 1808. After this, he was engaged for a few
years in carrying out the decree for the suppression of the monastic

orders, and in examining the archives of the Inquisition. In 1809, when Joseph abolished the Inquisition, he recommended to Llorente the preparation of a history of the tribunal. With all the archives of the Holy Office at his disposal, writes Llorente, 'I collected an immense amount of material at the cost of both labour and money, since I employed many persons during two years to copy, summarize and note what I indicated to them'.[15] The unimaginable wealth of sources enabled him to produce the first documented histories of the tribunal, which he managed to publish in Madrid: *Annals of the Inquisition of Spain*, in two volumes, which came out in 1812, and *Historical Memoir on What Was the National Opinion in Spain about the Tribunal of the Inquisition*, in the same year. The *Annals* were written when he had direct access to archive documents, and were the first unprejudiced and reliable works ever to open up the secrets of the notorious institution. The *Historical Memoir* served as the main source of historical information for the deputies in the Cortes of Cadiz when they carried out their own abolition of the tribunal.[16]

At the time of the eventual withdrawal of French forces from the peninsula, Llorente crossed the Aragonese frontier into France in 1813, 'fleeing from the peril of anarchy', and the evidence of 'the murders of many illustrious gentlemen' who had chosen to stay.[17] He was fortunate to escape poverty in France, since he figured among the few exiles who managed to receive financial help from the French state for their services to the Bonapartist monarchy. During his absence the mob, egged on by the new anti-French government, sacked his lodgings and destroyed his library, one of the finest in Madrid with over eight thousand rare books and manuscripts, many of them unique originals whose loss was irreparable. He managed all the same to take a considerable quantity of manuscripts with him into exile, and they formed the most solid part of his great work, *A Critical History of the Spanish Inquisition* (Paris, 1817–18), the four volumes of which were published in French, after being translated under his supervision. There were problems. The hasty translation contained many errors, and when news got out that he was about to reveal the secrets of the tribunal he began to receive poison-pen letters from French clergy. The work was not brought out in Spanish until 1822, in Madrid. Meanwhile it had also come out in German and Dutch, and would soon be published in English and Italian. Its success was – for that period – phenomenal (four thousand copies sold in one year), one of the first real best-sellers of modern times, which meant that Llorente would no longer have to worry where his next meal would be coming from.[18] The negative side was that it attracted much attention for the wrong reasons in Europe, particularly among Protestants and anticlericals who felt it backed up their views. The enthusiasm with which the book was greeted by enemies of the Church involved its author in considerable persecution by Catholic authorities.

When Llorente went on to publish (in French) a rather too frank *Political Portraits of the Popes* in 1822, he received a peremptory order to quit France. The real reason for his expulsion seems not to have been this matter of the popes, however, but rather the close contact he still maintained with Spanish Liberals.[19] He left at the end of the year and made his way back to Spain, travelling in the dead of winter through a freezing, snow-covered landscape. He was sixty-eight and still suffering from the effects of the cold when he arrived in Madrid, where he died exactly four weeks later, on 6 February 1823. French newspapers indignantly denounced the expulsion, which was seen as the direct cause of his death. One newspaper stated: 'men of position have hastened to pay a last tribute of esteem and regret to this energetic defender of humanity and of true religion, this lamentable victim of intolerance'.

The nine years of Llorente's exile in Paris (he also made a brief visit to London, where 'although the temperature and climate were not congenial to me, I liked the city very much') were extraordinarily fruitful ones, but he also had the disappointment of being suspended from his functions as a priest for daring to write about the Inquisition. His unprecedented incursion into the secret archives of the Inquisition made him the first historian of Spain ever to have access to the dark secrets of the notorious tribunal. Those secrets were many, and he revealed them all. 'Having been myself the secretary of the Inquisition at Madrid, during the years 1789, 1790, and 1791, I have the firmest confidence in my being able to give the world a true account of the secret laws by which the interior of the Inquisition was governed, laws which were veiled by mystery from all mankind.' 'In 1809, 1810, and 1811,' he went on to say in the preface to his *Critical History*, when the Inquisition in Spain was suppressed, all the archives were placed at my disposal; and from 1809 to 1812 I collected everything that appeared to me to be of consequence in the registers of the council of the Inquisition, and in the provincial tribunals, for the purpose of compiling this history.

He was also the first scholar to publish (in Paris in 1822) a critical edition of the works of the famed sixteenth-century friar Bartolomé de Las Casas.[20] But he reserved for some future day the preparation of a special book. In his own words, 'I have almost completed another work, titled *History of the Life and Happenings of Antonio Pérez*. If I have time, I will finish the work, which should interest those who care for historical truth.'[21] That study was, alas, never completed, though most of the papers he consulted in its preparation were handed over to the National Library in Paris, where they were consulted over a century later by another exile, Gregorio Marañón, author eventually of the most reliable life of Philip II's secretary. It is significant of the permanent ideological division in Spain that even today, those who wish to downgrade the exiled Llorente insist above all on his 'treason' to his native country in removing from it valuable archival documents which he then 'sold' to a foreign power, namely the French library authorities.

It is difficult to exaggerate the scale of Llorente's achievement, even though both his personal character and historical accuracy have been assailed, primarily by his own countrymen. The Catholic scholar Menéndez Pelayo, whose fame rests principally on the enormous multi-volume attack against Spain's great heretics that he published (1880–83) when he was just twenty-four years old, was not sparing of invective when it came to Llorente. He brushed him aside as 'lacking in erudition, puerile in criticism, insipid in style, without vigour or charm', and the *History* as 'a pile of calumnies, dry and sterile, malicious, indigestible, vague and incoherent'.[22] Menéndez Pelayo had all the passion of a young zealot when he used these phrases, and Llorente is among the very few people so passionately denounced in his great study. There were inevitably weaknesses in a work so vast that it would normally have taken several years and several scholars to produce, but Llorente's *Annals* and *History* were the first fully documented accounts of the Inquisition to have seen the light of day in the over three hundred years of the tribunal's existence. They opened up and exposed to public view hitherto darkened corners of Spain's history, and for those who doubted his account the author published not only details of his sources but also *pièces justificatives* to confound criticism. Both as a pioneer, and also as one not specifically trained for the task he undertook, Llorente made many important slips, with the consequence that a powerful conservative and Catholic tradition in his home country dismissed his work as inconsequential, in the same way that it would later dismiss the impressive work on the same theme of the American Henry Charles Lea, in 1907, as inconsequential. Llorente's *History* disappeared into the obscurity of libraries, and was not republished in Spain until 1980, nearly two centuries later. In the same way the work of Lea, whose writings on the Inquisitions of Europe revolutionized historical science, remained unknown to and unread by Spanish historians until the year 1983.[23] It was a remarkable example of the way in which a single vision of the past could be imposed on a nation's reading public, and on its historians, for nearly two hundred years.

It is – as we shall see – an exaggeration to think of Goya as an exile, but because, as Spain's greatest painter, he played a crucial part in depicting the culture of his time, we cannot fail to bring him into our story at this point, above all for his attitude to the Inquisition. Goya's portrait of Llorente (1810) is a beautiful achievement, a gentle portrayal of the man who first brought the history of the Inquisition into the light of day. By contrast, his depictions of the Inquisition itself are angry, caustic and dripping with indignation. His large canvas of the Inquisition, painted at a time (1819) when there were feverish debates in Spain over whether it should be abolished, repays long study because of its almost unbelievable dexterity in depicting the character of the institution. Francisco de Goya y Lucientes (1746–1828) was one of the supreme creative artists of all time, and therefore never quite at peace with the society in which he lived. He was born in the village of Fuendetodos (Aragon) but his family later moved to the Aragonese capital, Saragossa. He studied art locally, then spent a short time in Italy with the same intention. On his return he took up various commissions for frescoes, and created designs for tapestries that were produced in Madrid. By 1780 he was an established artist, and shortly after, in 1789, he was appointed as one of the court painters to Charles IV. A few years later, in 1792, he was struck by an illness that left him almost completely deaf. In 1799 he was elevated to principal court painter. Deafness inevitably affected the way Goya perceived the world round him, though it would be wrong to think of him as locked into a silent universe. From the 1790s he began to produce the penetrating and disturbing caricatures known as *Los Caprichos* (*The Caprices*), but they were not the whole Goya. When the French took over in Spain he was confirmed as chief court painter. The subsequent period of civil war gave him the opportunity to present another series of comments, this time on the *Disasters of War*, a series that depicted the ghastly tragedy and atrocity of a society tearing itself apart, which remained unknown until brought to light in 1863.

As a solid, believing Catholic and an official court painter, Goya had no reason to fall foul of the Church. However, his friends tended to be ministers (Jovellanos, Moratín) who had little sympathy with the Inquisition and its political role. This is an indication of the personal opinions of the painter, who in the 1790s from time to time included satirical references to the Inquisition and the clergy in his work. Among his *Caprices*, for example, two (nos. 23 and 24) are explicitly critical of the Inquisition. Goya's appointment as chief painter to the king (he painted his *Family of Charles IV* in 1800) presumably gave him protection against malicious critics, but some of the *Caprices* were denounced to the Inquisition and in self-protection he donated the whole series to the king as a gift. It was a highly unstable period in politics, when court power was in the hands of the favourite Godoy, for whom Goya painted the two portraits of the *Majas*, one dressed and the other naked, depicting not (as popularly believed) the duchess of Alba but in fact Godoy's young mistress Pepita Tudó. From this time Goya bore witness through his paintings to some of the most decisive events in Spanish history, notably through his emotionally overwhelming canvases on the impact of the 1808 popular rising against the French in Madrid in *The Second of May*, and the repression of the subsequent day (*The Third of May*). Despite their intensity and impact, the canvases were painted, surprisingly, not in the shadow of those events but five years later, after the French had been expelled from Spain. Nor were they publicly exhibited during his lifetime. Among the arresting portraits the artist executed in this period was that of the hero of the war against the French in the peninsula, the duke of Wellington.

Goya's pro-French friends took office in 1808 under the new king, Joseph I, in the hope of securing political reform. Goya, by contrast, refused to identify with any of the political groupings. His clearest ideological statement at this time, however, left little room for doubt about his opinions. The Liberals, as we have seen, were influential in the sessions of the Cortes that met from 1810 at Cadiz, where they led the parliamentary debate on the subject of abolishing the Inquisition. Goya's contribution to the proceedings was to paint two powerful satirical canvases depicting the Inquisition. Though the notorious tribunal was abolished by the Cortes, it refused to die and was restored to life by Ferdinand VII after the French had left Spain, and with them Goya's pro-French colleagues. Because Goya did not meddle directly in politics, and carried on his functions as painter despite the change in regime, neither the Liberals nor the absolutists harassed him. In 1816 he published in Madrid one of his classic works, a series of thirty-three etchings on the theme of bullfighting (*Tauromaquía*). From 1819, when he moved to reside just outside Madrid, his work developed in a more bizarre direction, and he began to cover the walls of his home with the strange Black Paintings, touching on the world of witches and monsters. Among the paintings, which were later moved to the Prado, is the *Duel with Clubs* (*Duelo a garrotazos*), depicting two peasants fighting, a strange and gripping parable of the conflicts in a society where the struggle between Cain and Abel was unceasing. The paintings also included the bizarre and grotesque *Saturn Devouring His Son*, in which one of the legendary Titans, his mouth dripping with blood, bites off the head of one of his children.

In terms of what we now perceive about his work, these were crucial years in the artist's development. However, he made a wholly unexpected decision. Soon after his wife died, he took into his home Leocadia Zorrilla, who had a five-year-old daughter Rosalie. At the time, Goya was seventy-eight years old. In 1824 he packed up all he had and took Leocadia and her daughter to live with him in France. The departure was meant to be definitive, because before leaving the

painter drew up a will leaving the house where he lived to his grandson Mariano. There is no logical reason why he should have chosen
to exile himself, least of all to Bordeaux, from where Moratín wrote
in June that year: 'Goya has arrived, deaf, old, clumsy and weak, and
not knowing a single word of French'.[24] The artist had complaints
about the government of Spain but he had not in fact been exiled and
was not in bad standing with the king, from whom he continued to
receive his official pension. Some have surmised that he decided to go
away because Leocadia had reasons for leaving the country. He chose
Bordeaux principally because his friends Moratín and Manuel Silvela
were there. The absence was therefore a voluntary exile, but one he
had chosen for peace of mind and not because he was fleeing from any
problems. Despite his age, he worked as never before, walking round
the city with his sketchbooks, looking for material, drawing, and even
making an adventurous trip to Paris to do some sketches there.[25] The
stay in Paris, from June to August, elicited a report from the government's police spies that 'because of his difficulties in speaking and
understanding French, he stays at home, going out only to see the
sights and take a walk in public places'.

  'Goya is fine,' Moratín reported from Bordeaux, 'he busies himself
with his sketches, goes walking, eats, takes a siesta, I think that there
is now peace in his household.'[26] The artist continued to draw more
Caprices, about which he had declared in 1799 that 'criticism of
human errors and vices can be an objective of painting, as it is of oratory and poetry'. He also did several sketches based on the local
madhouse, and published (in 1825) a collection of Bulls of Bordeaux.
The collection consisted of four large lithographs in one hundred sets,
and was a significant technical achievement for him. Instead of leaving
the original sketches to professionals who would use traditional
engraver's tools to produce the lithographs, he learnt to produce his
own pictures directly with etching and aquatint. The years in
Bordeaux were a strange form of exile that was no exile, for in 1825
he also made a quick trip back to Madrid to make sure that his pension would be paid despite his absence from the country. He seems to
have been happy in France, where one of his last etchings shows a
little wizened old man, cackling to himself in merriment, riding high
on a swing. It was Goya himself, high in the air.[27] He died in 1828 and

was buried in Bordeaux. Sixty years later the Spanish government initiated moves to bring his remains home, but when his grave was opened to make a preliminary examination it was found that his body lacked a head. His tomb may have been the victim of gravediggers looking for items that they could sell to medical dissectionists, for there is no other explanation of the strange disappearance. Regardless of the deficiency, his remains were moved to Spain in 1899.

The generation of Moratín, Goya and Llorente was formed in and belonged to the eighteenth century, the age of reformism and Enlightenment ideas. Those who hailed from the upper class were without exception of a classic, conservative, frame of mind. The expulsion of pro-French refugees severed brusquely the link between that age and the new, more radical movements that arose after the French Revolution. The change of times and mentality did not, however, modify the tradition of political emigration, which continued with full force. The departure of King Joseph was followed by the return of Ferdinand VII, called 'el Deseado' ('the Desired one') because his return was desired by those opposed to the French. His rule turned out to be disappointing to his supporters, however; he sided with the traditionalists and restored the Inquisition. The Liberals put together a plot against his government and gained power in 1820 through a military uprising led by a young officer, Colonel (later General) Riego. It was the absolutist politicians who now had to leave the country. When Ferdinand VII was restored with French help in 1823, thanks to troops – traditionally called 'the ten thousand sons of St Louis' – sent in under the duke of Angoulême, it was once again the turn of the Liberals to leave. At the king's death in 1833 the country was effectively thrown into a period of dynastic civil war, between on the one hand the partisans of the young queen Isabella and her mother the regent María Cristina, and on the other supporters of the late king's brother, Don Carlos. The followers of Don Carlos, known as 'Carlists', backed his right to succeed to the throne, and set in train a powerful armed movement that played a significant part in the politics of northern Spain for nearly a century (see below). There were further exiles when the regent was driven out in the years 1840–44. Throughout the early part of the century there was a continuous stream of

Spanish political exiles towards France, where the high point for progressives was the July Revolution (1830) that overthrew the Bourbon
monarchy there and installed the pro-Liberal Louis-Philippe, duke of
Orleans. Spanish exiles took an active part in the events.

The emigration that took place when Angoulême and his army
entered the country across the Pyrenees in April 1823 was substantial.[28] There was a dash for the ports, as generals, politicians and
bureaucrats took advantage of their superior financial resources to
seize all available means of transport. It is generally accepted that
around 20,000 émigrés left Spain. Among the elite the largest group
was made up of people such as army officers and administrative
officials, who tended to return as soon as possible since their entire
income came from employment by the state. The generals and politicians, on the other hand, stayed abroad much longer because they
could be clearly identified with a certain type of political affiliation.
The exile turned out to be lengthy enough to receive the name of 'the
ominous decade'.

Among the thousands who poured across the border into France in
these decades of war and revolution was a man who had nothing to
do with war or politics, but who made his mark nevertheless on the
world in which he became a permanent exile. This was the opera
singer Manuel García (1775–1832). Born Manuel de Populo Vicente
Rodríguez, a complex surname that he later changed to simply
García, he came from a humble family in Seville.[29] Trained as a
chorister in the cathedral, over the years he added music composition
to his singing abilities. He married a girl from nearby Cadiz who was
also an accomplished singer. Their first great legacy to the world
was to bring into it several children who all became singers of international repute. When the occupation of Spain by the French began a
decade of turbulence, they decided in 1808 to flee from the upheaval,
and ended up in the centre of world music, Paris, where García began
his European reputation by appearing in Italian opera. Three years
later, the family moved to Naples, where García struck up a close and
lasting friendship with the young composer Rossini, who wrote *The
Barber of Seville* especially for his voice. In the same months, García
also premiered one of his own comic operas, possibly inspired by the
Orientalism that was then in fashion in Paris, called *The Caliph of*

Baghdad. In 1815 the plague appeared in Naples and the family returned to Paris and then went on to London, where he left his daughter Maria Felicia at boarding school. Within a few years Maria Felicia established her family's fame. She sang successfully in both London and Paris, and then in 1825 accompanied her brother, sister and parents (García now had a second wife, having separated from his first) to New York, where they stayed for two years and made history by establishing the earliest Italian opera company in the United States. To all these places García and his family introduced for the first time the operas of Rossini (notably *The Barber*) and of Mozart.

On the voyage from Liverpool to New York in 1825 the Garcías had as a fellow passenger the Scottish socialist Robert Owen, who was on his way to the New World with family and friends to set up his pioneering Utopian community at New Harmony (Indiana). The Owen group composed a hymn, later adopted as an anthem for New Harmony, that García and his family sang for them:

> Land of the West, we fly to thee,
> sick of the old world's sophistry,
> haste then upon the dark blue sea.
>
> Land of the West, we rush to thee,
> home of the brave, soil of the free.
> Hurrah! She rises o'er the sea.[30]

A couple of days after arriving in New York in November 1825, the Garcías staged Rossini's *Barber of Seville*. The illustrious audience included Joseph Bonaparte, lately king of Spain (who had abandoned Europe and moved to New Jersey after quitting the Spanish throne), and a host of other dignitaries. The programme sheet announced the opera as 'the first representation of an Italian musical drama in America'.[31] It created a sensation. Though many were enthusiastic, American critics who had never encountered the art-form were baffled as to why a stage drama had to be sung, and poked fun at it. Not to be outdone, the Garcías took their music on a tour of the States and then of Mexico, experiencing adventures and dangers at every stage. Their achievement, bringing opera to the New World, was pioneering and a resounding success. Maria Felicia became known by the professional name Madame Malibran (from her wealthy husband, whom she married in America and later left) and achieved immense fame as a mezzo-soprano on both sides of the Atlantic (except in Spain), as well as success with a number of famous men. She died inopportunely of a riding accident in England when she was only twenty-eight years old. Her brother Manuel went on to become a well-known music teacher in Paris and London, counting Chaliapin and Jenny Lind among his students. The senior Manuel, meanwhile, dedicated himself to teaching and composing music in the years up to his death in Paris. Despite his world fame, he remained almost completely unknown in his original homeland. In 1859 the Spanish musicologist Mariano Soriano complained that 'Spain has relegated him to oblivion and forgotten his works'. Apart from a few songs, all of García's oeuvre – over fifty operas, and several songs, symphonies, masses and chamber works – remains unpublished.[32]

Among the long-term exiles in this decade were cultured individuals, such as the duke of Rivas and Francisco Martínez de la Rosa, who played a crucial role in changing literary tastes and introducing the Romantic movement into Spain. Angel Saavedra, better known by the title he later inherited as duke of Rivas (1791–1865), came from the aristocracy of Córdoba and went into exile with other Liberals in 1823. An army officer, he was wounded in a previous campaign and, during his recovery, composed the drama *Lanuza* (1822). He was also a poet, producing his first book of poems in 1814. On the ship to England in 1823, he penned the sort of verse to be expected from someone driven from his native country, with classic titles such as *Super flumina Babylonis*, and *The Exile*. He stayed for less than a year in London, where he became a firm Anglophile and familiarized himself with the works of Sir Walter Scott and Lord Byron. Scott through his historical novels, and Byron through his narrative poems, revealed to the Spanish exiles possibilities for serving up their ideas and their vision of the past in a way that could be communicated effectively to the Spanish public.

After London, Saavedra's main residence in exile was Malta, where he spent five years as a personal guest of the British ambassador. He then moved on to France where he stayed four more years. While in

Malta he wrote a long ode to *The Malta Lighthouse* (1828), in which the beacon that illuminated the way ahead was a symbol of Liberalism and Romanticism. He also began composing (as we have had occasion to note, Chapter 2) a piece of narrative verse, *The Foundling Moor*, which took as its scenario his own home city of Córdoba in the tenth century. The work was in part modelled on the romances of Scott, but possibly owed more to the romantic pro-Moorish literature circulating in London at that time, notably Byron's *Don Juan* (1819). He finished it in France in 1833, publishing it the next year in Madrid, with a preface by Alcalá Galiano. This long and tedious poem, which has little intrinsic merit for the reader today, is commonly taken to be the manifesto of the Romantic movement in Spain. Shortly after his return from exile, he published perhaps the most successful theatrical work of Romanticism, *Don Álvaro, or, the Power of Destiny* (1835), which acquired a more solid and lasting fame a generation later when Verdi used its argument as the basis of his opera *La Forza del Destino* (1862). In retirement at his residence in Seville, the duke of Rivas became more conservative in outlook and dedicated his time to writing trivial historical romances, choosing his themes not from those which had inspired the Romantic movement, but from largely mythical military victories that fed the patriotic imagination, such as *The Victory of Pavia*, or *Bailén*.

Francisco Martínez de la Rosa (1787–1862), statesman and dramatist, was one of the most important refugees of these years. A native of Granada, he went to the university there and then turned to writing. During the struggle against Napoleon he took the patriotic side, entered the Cortes as deputy for Granada, and continued writing plays. His drama *The Widow Padilla*, in 1812, depicted the widow of the sixteenth-century *Comunero* leader Juan de Padilla sacrificing her life in the struggle against the tyranny of a foreign monarch, Charles V. Meanwhile he became drawn more deeply into politics, and in 1814 when Ferdinand VII came back Martínez was banished to the fortress of La Gomera on the North African coast, where he remained until 1820. It was an excellent opportunity for him to develop his ideas on how Muslim civilization had suffered under the tyranny of the monarchy ever since the time of Charles V. When the African exile ended he returned to Spain and his political activities.

In February 1822, when he was only thirty-four, the king chose him to head the government. Politics in Madrid was a delicate balance between the interests of multiple schemers, among them the king himself. Outside Madrid, disorder reigned as conflicting groups literally went to war against each other. Martínez was pushed out of government, and in April 1823 the French troops under Angoulême put an end to Liberal rule. Martínez found himself once more in exile, this time in Paris. It was the beginning of a long and fruitful absence of eight years, during which he continued writing and publishing. The most prominent of the Paris émigrés, thanks to his wealth and position he lived comfortably and presided over soirées at which French and Spanish intellectuals mixed. A French diplomat observed him to be handsome and elegant, 'with the straight and proud bearing of an hidalgo from Granada'.[33] He returned to Spain in 1831 and when the regent María Cristina took over after the death of Ferdinand VII, became prime minister in January 1834. He proved incapable of coping with the insurrectionary movement that was tearing the country apart, and resigned eighteen months later. In subsequent years he served as ambassador in Paris and Rome, and held many important political offices. He was not a great success in politics, but in literature he was one of the chief promoters of the Romantic movement in Spain. Fluent in French, he moved easily in the literary and political world of Paris. He was the first to take themes from Spanish history and serve them up to audiences as Romantic drama. The pioneer work was (as we shall see) his play *Aben Humeya* (1830), staged with great success in Paris and with a Spanish composer, Gomis, for its music. On his return to Spain he continued in the same vein, notably with *The Venetian Conspiracy* (*La Conjuración de Venecia*) (1834), about a medieval political scandal, and with a romantic novel imitating the style of Scott, *Doña Isabel de Solís* (1846).

During his years in government the great thorn in Martínez's side was a young Spanish journalist who made a name for himself by his attacks on political incompetence. This was Mariano José de Larra (1809–37), a native of Madrid, who had been only four years old when he accompanied his father, a doctor, out of Spain in 1813 as one of the pro-French exiles. The family returned in 1818 and Mariano was educated in various colleges in Spain, chosen according to where his father's job took him. He began writing, and in 1828, aged only eighteen, brought out his own satirical journal, modelled on the English satirical tracts of the eighteenth century. He married the year after, an unhappy match that ended in separation a few years later. By the 1830s young Larra was an established essayist, publishing scathing attacks on all the regimes of his day. It was also the year that he met a married lady called Dolores, with whom he soon had a passionate affair. In early 1833 he began writing for the Liberal *La Revista Española*, under the pseudonym 'Figaro', a name he borrowed from the French dramatist Beaumarchais. This was the period in which he wrote his most memorable articles attacking the authorities. With his radical politics and his youthful vigour, Larra became one of the symbols of renovation. 'Our aim,' he wrote, 'has been to persuade all Spaniards that we must borrow from abroad what is in our power to borrow.'[34] In 1835 he went abroad to refresh his intellectual roots, visiting Lisbon, London and, in particular, Paris, where he stayed several months and met Victor Hugo and Alexandre Dumas. On returning to Spain, he began to write for the journal *El Español*. He also extended his commitment to politics by getting elected as a deputy in 1836.

His world, however, was crumbling. He found no satisfaction in any of the politicians of the day, was deprived by events from taking his seat in the Cortes, and was profoundly depressed by the collapse of his relationship with Dolores. In February 1837 Dolores came to see him and confirmed that the love-affair was at an end. No sooner had she left his house than he shot himself. His Byronic career gave added life to the Romantic movement whose adepts gathered at his funeral, where an ode for him was read by its young author, José Zorrilla. A product of exile (when he returned to Spain in 1818 at the age of eight his principal language was French), Larra never really came to accept his circumstances and remained a sort of exile all his short life. A sharp, caustic writer, specializing in irony and wielding a pen that all the politicians feared, he has with reason been looked upon as the father of Spanish journalism. He mocked bitterly everything that in his eyes made the country and its government a laughing stock before the world. Perhaps no writer till then had been so merciless in pointing out the defects of Spain. 'Larra killed himself,' the poet Antonio Machado commented a century later, 'because he did not find the Spain that he sought, and when he had lost all hope of finding it.'

The reality of exile had a profound impact on the young men who had emigrated mainly for political reasons only. It brought them into direct contact with European culture, forced them to imbibe foreign languages, art and music, and educated them in political ideas that were unknown in Spain. Above all, it cultivated a sense of patriotism that was (and is) unknown to the Spanish frame of mind. 'Patriotism' may have seemed a noble sentiment, especially when directed against invaders and enemies of the recent present and also of the faraway medieval past, but it was out of place in a peninsula where loyalties were exclusively regional and never national. Spain had never managed to put together a programme for national consciousness that would combine the passionate causes of the present with the lost causes of the historic past, nor had it ever accepted a recognizable role for the peoples – the Jews and Arabs – who had been among those lost causes. Romanticism supplied the exiles and their friends with the tools for creating a new vision, and at the same time a new ideological aspiration.

Perhaps most typical of the new breed of Romantic poets was José de Espronceda (1808–42), a born rebel who was held in high esteem during the nineteenth century but whose writings were never of high enough quality to stand the test of time or to make any impact outside the peninsula. He was born in Almendralejo (Badajoz) and while still young adopted the cause of the struggle against absolutism. At the age of fifteen he and his friends were condemned by the authorities for belonging to a secret society, but fortunately the sentence of five years was commuted to a stay of a few weeks in a local monastery. When he was eighteen Espronceda left Spain for the Portuguese capital, Lisbon, where he met a young lady, Teresa, a Spanish colonel's daughter, whom he followed to London. In the English capital, he was the youngest of the political refugees, and managed to publish his first poems there, poor imitations of English originals.[35] Teresa got married in London, to a Spanish businessman, and eventually had two sons by him. Espronceda, in part to escape from his love for Teresa, left in 1829 for Holland and the next year went to Paris, just in time to take part in the July Revolution which brought a liberal regime to power under King Louis-Philippe, popularly known as Philippe 'Égalité'. In 1832 Espronceda returned to London to see Teresa, whom he persuaded to abandon all and join him. When the Spanish government proclaimed an amnesty for Liberals, he returned home in 1833, taking the colonel's daughter with him.

In Spain he continued to be involved in plots and political agitation, but carried on writing and won recognition in particular for his poem *Song of the Pirate* (1836), imitated unashamedly from Lord Byron[36] and typical of the romantic adventurism of his themes. He was active in journalism, and in 1835 helped to found the Ateneo club of Madrid. The poet José Zorrilla described him as having a

pale, sickly face, topped by curly black silky hair that was divided down the middle of his head and hung on both sides over his small, fine ears, whose lobules peeked out through the curls. His thin, straight, dark eyebrows crowned clear, restless eyes protected by thick eyelashes.

The frequent wanderings and absences proved to be too much for Teresa, who decided to separate from him, taking with her the daughter he had sired. Still appreciated today by some for his lyrical verse, Espronceda personified several of the virtues and defects of the Liberal writers of his time: active, idealistic, romantic, but also mediocre and derivative. His poems are ideal for declamation, but the sentiments appear theatrical. Typical of his style is the long ode to Teresa he wrote after her death in 1839:

> Exiled on a foreign shore
> I with ecstatic gaze
> followed the silver furrow of the brave vessel
> as it flew to the port of my native land.
>
> When the sun sinks in the west,
> alone and lost in my shady grove
> I feel that I hear in the breathing of the wind
> the melodious voice of a woman.

Spaniards went abroad, picked up new ideas, and returned home with them. It was only one part of the process of cultural transfer. The

French who had so decisively invaded the life of the peninsula, and the English who had intervened to restrain them, were also part of the mechanism that exported to other Europeans some knowledge of what Hispanic culture offered. The French, who professed to despise the Spaniards, were astonished by the richness of the art that could be looted from the peninsula. Napoleon looted half the Spanish state archives (they were returned a century later, after being carefully catalogued in a way that the original archives were not), while his generals stole works of art from the royal palaces. In Seville the French commander Marshal Soult ordered all the city's art treasures to be collected in a central location so that he could pick and choose paintings at his leisure. For the first time in their history, the French, Germans and English began to appreciate the rich and exotic aspects of Hispanic creativity. The epoch of expulsions in the opening decades of the nineteenth century initiated a trend that opened up the peninsula to foreign gaze. The British were fascinated by Spain's Arab past, their troops were deeply committed to intervention against the occupying French, and their politicians in Parliament were sensitive to the commercial possibilities of the American colonies. From the peninsula the English artist G. A. Wallis wrote home in 1808: 'If you had time and could bear the horrors of travelling in Spain, it would be worth while to visit this country', where he had discovered 'Velasquez, Alonzo Canno, del Greco, really first-rate men whose works are quite unknown out of Spain'.[37] 'I am at home in Spain', the essayist Charles Lamb confessed in 1815 to the poet laureate Southey. Robert Southey, author of the poem *Roderick*, which had a medieval Hispanic theme, was fluent in Spanish, had travelled in the peninsula, and translated the chivalric narrative *Amadis*. It was a decade when Scott, Byron and Wordsworth all showed concrete interest in Spanish matters. Byron visited Andalusia briefly in 1809 and gave Spain a prominent spot in his narrative poem *Childe Harold's Pilgrimage* (1811). Military intervention, together with sympathy for Spanish exiles because they were allies against Bonapartist France, stimulated appreciation for peninsular civilization and gave a push to English creativity. In the same decade, as we have had occasion to note, the German poet Heine, through his dramatic poem *Almansor* (1821), expressed his deep fascination for the culture of the south.

Passion for the exotic also gripped Paris. For the rest of the nineteenth century, Paris became a centre of Hispanic creativity. Exiles who fled to the French capital brought their tastes with them. It was a period, for example, when the exotic music of the Spanish guitar became the rage in social circles, and even inspired several paintings. The impact on French appreciation of Spain was unstoppable. The year 1830 was particularly fruitful for stimulating interest on the part of northern nations: Victor Hugo put on his *Hernani, ou l'Honneur castillan* in Paris, Mérimeé visited Spain for the first time, Richard Ford began his three-year visit to the peninsula, and in Paris the July Revolution brought King Louis-Philippe to power. In 1838 Louis-Philippe, friend of the Spanish Liberal émigrés, bought some four hundred Spanish paintings for the Louvre, where they constituted the Galerie Espagnole. Prior to that period, Spanish artists were largely unknown in France and in northern Europe generally. Two generations previously, when Diderot published his *Encyclopédie* (1758–68) he identified eight schools of art in the history of European painting, but Spain did not appear on his list.[38] The Galerie Espagnole was one of the influences that changed all that, giving to Spanish painting a recognition and a status that it had never previously enjoyed.[39]

Artists and writers who yearned to free themselves from domination by Italy embraced with enthusiasm the influences they discovered in Spain. One of the most influential painters of the century, Manet, went to Madrid in 1865 and pronounced Velázquez to be the greatest painter of all time. After him, the painter Gustave Courbet based his social realism on what he found in Velázquez. The peninsula and its seeming exoticism became the great hunting ground that greeted artists looking for inspiration, writers looking for themes, and musicians looking for new ideas. Among the immediate results were Victor Hugo's *Hernani*, Prosper Mérimée's *Carmen*, Théophile Gautier's *Voyage en Espagne* and Giuseppe Verdi's *Don Carlo* (which premiered in Paris in 1867). The American painter John Singer Sargent, who was strongly influenced by Manet and shared his enthusiasm for Velázquez, paid a visit to Spain and did a canvas of the Alhambra (1879). Ironically, therefore, the members of the elite who were exiled and had to live in Paris found themselves the centre of attention and helped to initiate a fashion for things Hispanic. Expelling its luminaries was, it turned out, one of the great favours that Spain did itself.

When they viewed their country in perspective, one of the first things that the political exiles of the nineteenth century realized was that it had no adequate narrative of its past. They agreed in rejecting the old clericalist and heroic histories, but found that there was nothing to put in their stead to allow Spain to have a recognizable place in the story of western civilization. Contemplating their country from outside it, the refugees realized that a new portrait of Spain's past must be presented. One consequence was the import of pro-Romantic history writing into Spain. Curiously enough, the early samples of this new history were written and published outside Spain, not in it. A key figure was the Liberal politician Antonio Alcalá Galiano (1798–1865), an aristocrat who had helped to bring about the Revolution of 1820, and had entered the Cortes, but in 1823 was obliged to seek exile in England at the onset of the 'ominous decade', when the French army invaded the country and restored the absolutist monarchy of Ferdinand VII. He spent the next eleven years as a refugee, seven of them in London, and recalled later that:

Nearly all of us who went to England arrived in a state of total penury, only public charity could give us the necessary food and shelter. Those who had property in Spain were unable to receive aid from that source, or received what little the circumstances permitted, thanks to decrees that confiscated or sequestrated their private income, or mob violence that did not respect their property. Most of the refugees consisted of persons who worked for their living, military men, clergy, lawyers, civil servants, doctors, writers, in short the nucleus of the so-called Liberal party in every village, or let us say the most active and prominent part of it.

Among the other Liberals who made London their home in that period were the former finance minister Canga Argüelles, and the secularized Dominican Jaime Villanueva, author of the splendid multi-volume *Literary Journey round the Churches of Spain*, who died in London the year after he arrived. Alcalá Galiano was fascinated by history, and devoted his leisure hours in exile to translating works of history into Castilian from English and French, languages in which, thanks to his elite education, he was completely at home. George Borrow, who subsequently met him in Madrid, testified that 'he spoke and wrote English nearly as well as his own tongue'. In 1828 Alcalá Galiano was appointed to the first (and short-lived, since it functioned for only two years) chair in Spanish language ever established in England, at University College, London. Among those backing him for the post was the writer Jeremy Bentham. Alcalá Galiano devoted his inaugural lecture to attacking the Inquisition, which he accused of having repressed liberty of thought and crushed all intellectual initiative. He claimed (with considerable justice) that no history had been written in Spain since the middle of the seventeenth century, when the country entered into 'absolute mental darkness'.[40] The professorship encountered administrative difficulties and attracted few students, so Alcalá Galiano resigned after two years, leaving for Paris in 1830 in order to take part in the events of the July Revolution.

The exiles collaborated among themselves to help publish a short-lived Barcelona journal, *El Europeo* (1823–4), the first important bridge for the transfer of foreign ideas to Spain. Above all, they were impressed by the relevance of literary fiction to the understanding of the past, as achieved through the works of Sir Walter Scott and Lord Byron among the British, and those of Victor Hugo and Alexandre Dumas among the French. When Alcalá Galiano and other exiles returned to Spain in 1833, they brought their new vision with them. The movement of ideas was not, for all that, only in one direction. The Peninsular War brought Britons and Frenchmen into contact with many aspects of Spain's traditions and landscape, such as in the case of the Arab past of Andalusia. In the same way, there was sympathy abroad for the struggle of liberal Spaniards against absolutism. Foreign visitors therefore absorbed Hispanic influences, and in their turn influenced Spanish exiles. A case in point was that of a young French scholar of liberal sympathies called Louis Viardot, who at the age of twenty-three accompanied the French army that invaded Spain in 1823. He used his time to study and observe Spanish customs and culture, and on his return to Paris became a close friend of the Spanish nobles who had been exiled by that very invasion (notably Martínez de la Rosa and the count of Toreno), accompanying them back to Spain in 1834 when the regime changed.[41] The Spanish exiles were a great success in the Paris of Louis-Philippe; they were fêted at social gatherings and took part in the literary and musical life of the capital.[42]

Alcalá Galiano's preface to *The Foundling Moor* of the duke of Rivas (1834) was the first manifesto of the Spanish Romantic movement. The exiles who returned in 1834 brought back with them a sense of the past that had been heightened by their reading. They set about creating a historical narrative for Spain, through the medium of textbooks. The membership of the creaking Academy of History was renovated, through electing historians to be members of the august body. Until then the Academy had been used (as it still is) as a club for retired generals and bureaucrats. Along with the new history of the past that they were creating for Spain, the Liberals brought a new mythology, most of it manufactured in London, Paris and Brussels. In the official speech he made on being received into the Academy of History in 1834, Rivas pointed specifically to Scott, Byron and Victor Hugo as the inspiration behind the historical revolution the Romantics were proposing.[43] They pinpointed the ideological enemies of the present, and re-wrote the past accordingly.[44] The present enemy was the absolutist monarchy that had sent them into exile, so the traditional monarchy of Spain, that is to say the sixteenth-century monarchy of Charles V and Philip II, was presented as absolutist.

A central feature of this new history, created exclusively by Spaniards but written up on the basis of insights gained during the years of exile, was the systematic denigration of the person of Philip II, through whom they targeted the monarchy of their own day. In an early play, *Lanuza* (1823), Rivas had drawn the main outlines of the thesis. Juan de Lanuza was the hero of the liberties of the kingdom of Aragon, who was cruelly and illegally executed by the tyrant Philip II in 1591. Similarly, in his preface to *The Foundling Moor*, Alcalá Galiano condemned 'the barbaric state into which the Spanish nation fell under the house of Austria'.[45] Philip II came to be viewed as the historic enemy of 'progressives' not only in Spain but also in England, France and Belgium. The independence of the new state of Belgium was being prepared in those years, and among the tasks the Belgians set themselves was the creation of their own history. This took an important step forward when they selected as chief archivist of Belgium a French scholar, Gachard, who among his early achievements gathered archive material on the reign of Philip II. The Spanish king now appeared in Liberal writing as the historic oppressor of all peoples, including his own. Among the works written in exile in Paris by Martínez de la Rosa was the drama *Aben Humeya, or the Revolt of the Moors under Philip II*, which immediately achieved success when performed on stage. The hero of the play was the romantic-tragic-noble figure of the rebel leader, Aben Humeya. As in several other works produced in these years, Philip was presented as an arch-enemy of liberty, destroyer of the rights of the Aragonese, the Portuguese and the Dutch, patron of the tyrannical Inquisition and assassin of his own son Don Carlos. One after another, the plays, poems, novels and operas attacking Philip II and the 'decline' he inflicted on Spain rolled off the presses. It was one of the most successful achievements of the exiled Liberals, and left a permanent mark on European perceptions of the king. The denigration of Philip II fitted perfectly into the political programme of Liberals struggling against the 'absolutism' of Napoleon, Ferdinand VII and Metternich, and was also adopted by Anglo-Saxon scholars who followed the Romantic school.

The blatantly romanticized version of Spain's history had been offered already to the English public in 1830, when the Liberal exile Telesforo de Trueba (see Chapter 2) published in London *The Romance of History: Spain*, a collection of fictional narratives in the style of Washington Irving. Fortunately, not all the historical production was literary fantasy. Alcalá Galiano was serious about giving Spaniards their own history books, but since they had none of their own he translated and published (in 1844) a textbook in English,[46] adding annotations by himself, Martínez de la Rosa and the diplomat Donoso Cortés. Until that period the only authoritative history of their country known to Spaniards was by the sixteenth-century Jesuit Juan de Mariana, which had the advantage of being a work open to liberal interpretation but the disadvantage of covering only the period down to the year 1516. This did not deter nineteenth-century writers, who republished the text of Mariana and then 'completed' it down to their own time.[47] A typical work of this type was published in ten volumes in Valencia in 1839. However, no serious surveys by

Spaniards appeared. A French scholar who published his own *History of Spain* in 1839 commented that while there were modern authorities one could cite for the histories of other nations, 'there is unfortunately no Spanish name that can be cited'.[48]

There was obviously a real need for a genuine researched history. This was supplied at last by a Liberal writer and member of the Cortes, whose work began to emerge in the 1850s. Modesto Lafuente (1806–66), son of a pro-French doctor from the province of Palencia, never lived outside the peninsula but knew something of foreign scholarship and had done work in the state archives. He entered the priesthood at an early age, but left it definitively at the age of thirty in order to plunge into the world of writing and politics in Madrid. He got married in 1843, became a prosperous writer of articles for the Madrid press, and in 1854 successfully obtained a seat in the Cortes. His contribution to the new Spanish historiography took the form of a thirty-volume *History of Spain* (1850–67) that ranks, beyond all doubt, as the most impressive one-man history ever written in Spain, a work that after a century and a half is still valuable to consult and a pleasure to read. It immediately became a classic, which subsequent Liberal writers 'completed' to bring up to date. Lafuente was ideologically conservative and strongly pro-Castilian, an adherent of theses that not everybody supported about the unity of Spain as a political and cultural entity, or about the tyrannical absolutism of the kings of the Habsburg and Bourbon dynasties. His approach was scholarly enough to win the applause of most opinions in the political landscape. But it also hallowed views that were later seen to be partisan and divisive.

Most of the elite exiles eventually came back and played important roles in politics and society. One at least stayed abroad. This was José María Blanco White (1775–1841), an exceptional case whose career touched on several key aspects of Hispanic culture. Born José María Blanco y Crespo in Seville, his father was an Irish merchant, William White (rendered into Spanish as 'Guillermo Blanco'), who had settled in Spain and married a local woman. The boy studied at the University of Seville, where he proved to be a gifted student, and became a follower of one of the professors, the literary figure Juan Pablo Forner.

Already in this period Blanco began using his rudimentary English to translate verse into Spanish and was composing poetry. In 1799 he became a priest, even though he had misgivings about the faith, and was appointed as chaplain to a religious community. His doubts increased. 'Believing religion a fable,' he explained later, 'I still found myself compelled daily to act as a minister and promoter of imposture.' His testimony on the question of religion offers important evidence of the real roots of faith among Spaniards at this time. From 1806 he worked in Madrid, where he had a secret love affair (which later produced a son, whom he supported and subsequently brought to England). The events of the Napoleonic invasion now impinged on his life. In 1808 the people of Madrid rioted against the French occupation, and Blanco joined the rebels in Seville, where he helped to publish a weekly newspaper which was soon closed by the authorities. During this period he became aware that he no longed believed in his role as a priest, and also became disillusioned with the deteriorating political situation. 'For several years,' he wrote (in 1832) in his autobiography, 'I had been forming in my interior the intention of leaving my country, and I identified myself with it to such an extent that there was hardly a thought or wish of mine that did not have some connection with my plan.' Tormented and adrift, in 1810 he took the decision to leave Spain.

It was not an entirely voluntary decision. He was one of thousands of Spaniards who that spring fled for their lives from Andalusia in 'a general panic' (Blanco's own words) as the French forces advanced without resistance on the city of Seville. In Seville, 'we raised anchor at dusk in the midst of violent explosions that you could hear from a distance, and as soon as night fell we could see clearly the flashes that accompanied them. The spectacle lasted all night.' Downriver, in Cadiz, he boarded an English frigate and sailed to England, never to return. He was immensely sad at the decision he had taken. As the port disappeared from sight, 'a shade of sadness passed over my spirit, to think that I would never again see those tall white buildings, and I tried to console myself by gazing at the sublime expanse of ocean that spread out in the immense loneliness before my eyes'. Lines he wrote in 1808 reveal his frame of mind at this time:

The heart does not change, the only change
is in the unhappy man who desires
to evade his destiny by fleeing the native land
that made him lament his troubles.[49]

In exile he blossomed into an international figure.[50] He had already
made contact in Spain with the English radical Henry Fox, Lord
Holland, who took a special interest in Spanish affairs, and under
Holland's tutelage in England dedicated himself to a variety of causes.
The British were keen to secure the services of a cultured person who
could serve their interests by making contact with anti-French sympathizers in the Hispanic world. Blanco started a magazine, *El
Español*, which was distributed in Spain by the British authorities. Its
contents were not to the liking of Spaniards. Urged on by the British,
Blanco turned his attention to the independence movement in Spain's
South American colonies, and wrote several important articles that
the Americans hailed as support for their cause. In turn, he was
fiercely criticized by 'patriotic' Spaniards for extending sympathy to
the rebels. 'The French because of their ideas and tastes, Castilians
because of the old pattern of their policies, were openly hostile to
England and considered the American colonies to be their own.'[51]
Blanco began to realize that his perspective differed from that of his
countrymen, and he became more critical of them. Why, he asked, had
Spaniards never been able to rid themselves of an oppressive Church?
Why had they not been able to defeat Napoleon as the Russians had
done? Why did Spain continue to use the slave trade, instead of abolishing it as the British had done? Over the years, he began to despair
of Spain's capacity to reform itself, and placed his hopes more and
more on a regenerated Latin America.

The distancing from Spain encouraged him to make a special effort
to accept his new environment and integrate into the British way of
life. 'Setting aside the painful separation from my own family,' he
wrote to his parents from London in 1812, 'I have never been so
happy as I am in England.'[52] Though the greyness of the capital was a
disappointment, the green countryside landscape enchanted him, and
he felt he could put up with the cold and foggy climate. He improved
his command of the language rapidly ('for very many years I studied

untiringly the language of the country') and was soon writing as easily in English as in Spanish. By the end of his life he had composed a significant corpus of poems, novels and essays in both languages. He also converted to the Anglican faith, became a clergyman in that Church shortly afterwards, and succeeded in obtaining a teaching post at Oriel College, Oxford, where his colleagues in the Senior Common Room included several Anglican clergy, among them John Keble and John Henry Newman, who were reconsidering their position within the Established Church. Both Blanco White and Newman played the violin. The latter's diary at this period includes entries like: 'played music with B. White in evening', and 'music quartet with B. White in evening'. A friend who saw them playing described 'Blanco's excited and agitated countenance' and 'Newman's sphinx-like immobility'.[53] From 1821, based in the quiet Berkshire rectory of Ufton Nervet, White wrote for the *New Monthly* a series of portraits of life and society in the Spain he had known as a boy and a young man. They were published the following year in book form as *Letters from Spain*, which can still be read with profit as an informed and perceptive description of distinctive Spanish customs in the opening years of the nineteenth century. From 1823-5 he edited *Variedades*, a magazine for Spanish America that made his reputation among readers there.

Blanco gave his firm support to the Liberal exiles who came to London in 1823, just as in the same period he helped the Venezuelan exile Andrés Bello, for whom he obtained employment as a tutor in Oxford. The poverty that some of the Spanish Liberals faced made him write to the press to plead in their support. They were by no means a small group, totalling according to one account around a thousand families,[54] most of them with no financial resources. In reality, there could have been few more pathetic images than that of the exiles. The scholar Thomas Carlyle penned this portrait of them:

In those years a visible section of the London population, and conspicuous out of all proportion to its size or value, was a small knot of Spaniards, who had sought shelter here as Political Refugees. 'Political Refugees:' a tragic succession of that class is one of the possessions of England in our time. Six-and-twenty years ago, when I first saw London, I remember those unfortunate Spaniards among the new phenomena. Daily in the cold spring air, under skies so unlike their own, you could see a group of fifty or a hundred stately tragic figures, in proud threadbare cloaks; perambulating, mostly with closed lips, the broad pavements of Euston Square and the regions about St. Pancras new Church. Their lodging was chiefly in Somers Town, as I understood: and those open pavements about St. Pancras Church were the general place of rendezvous. They spoke little or no English; knew nobody, could employ themselves on nothing, in this new scene. Old steel-gray heads, many of them; the shaggy, thick, blue-black hair of others struck you; their brown complexion, dusky look of suppressed fire, in general their tragic condition as of caged Numidian lions.[55]

There were apparently so many Basques among them that the tree round which they habitually gathered in Somers Town became known as 'the tree of Guernica'. Some of the Numidian lions died in exile; others made it back home to fight again. In reality they were not condemned just to pacing the streets. Most of the men came from the elite class, and were therefore wholly useless for any sort of practical activity involving work or earning a living. True to Spanish practice, they devoted themselves to more important matters such as holding regular meetings in each other's houses in order to discuss politics, and once a month held a general meeting (a *tertulia*) in the local coffee house, where they could spread their wings. The women, by contrast, learnt to work at several handicrafts and helped to bring in money. The more influential of the exiles were able to go to meetings in Holland House, where the English aristocracy who favoured their cause could be contacted. When the 1830 revolution took place in Paris, most went to France immediately. The social and political climate there was more amenable, and the language easier to cope with.

Blanco was one of the few to stay put. But, like most involuntary exiles, he never quite fitted into his new home. Behind the thin, relaxed face with its firm lips and bright, penetrating eyes, perceptively depicted in the portrait at the Unitarian church at Ullet Road in Liverpool, lurked a permanently restless soul eager to pursue the logic of his ideas. A recent biographer has commented that 'though an idealised England might be his rational home, the real England was a place in which spiritually and emotionally he would always be an alien'.[56] He was, inevitably, uncomfortable in the Anglican Church. In 1832 he moved to Ireland as a guest of his friend Richard Whately, the archbishop of Dublin. The change gave him an opportunity to reconsider his religious ideas, and his *Second Travels of an Irish Gentleman in Search of a Religion* (1833) was written in Dublin. In 1835 he returned to England, not however to Oxford but to Liverpool, where he joined the Unitarian community and published his *Observations on Heresy and Orthodoxy*. The Unitarians, we should recall, deny the divinity of Jesus. Poor health and hypochondria dogged his last years in Liverpool. His autobiography was published posthumously in 1845. When he received a copy of it, John Henry Newman, who was then at his parish in Littlemore, Oxford, agonizing over whether to make the change that would take him in a direction quite the reverse of that taken by his friend, commented:

When a person feels that he cannot stand where he is, and has dreadful feelings lest he should be suffered to go back, if he will not go forward, such a case as Blanco White's increases those fears. For years I have an increasing intellectual conviction that there is no medium between Pantheism and the Church of Rome. If intellect were to settle the matter, I should not be now where I am. But other considerations come in, and distress me. Here is Blanco White sincere and honest. He gives up his country, and then his second home, —Spain, Oxford, Whately's family,—all for an idea of truth, or rather for liberty of thought. True, I think a great deal of morbid restlessness was mixed with his sincerity, an inability to keep still in one place, a readiness to take offence and to be disgusted, an unusual irritability, and a fear of not being independent, and other bad feelings. But then the thought forcibly comes upon one, Why may not the case be the same with me?[57]

Like all Spanish exiles who flew too far from the nest, Blanco suffered disdain and neglect at the hands of his fellow countrymen. His offences were many: he had turned his back on his roots, embraced heretical beliefs, and written in a language that his fellow countrymen could not read. For over one hundred years he was consigned to oblivion. It was left to fellow exiles and dissidents to call attention to his achievements in the 1970s.[58] Even today, nevertheless, he is for Spaniards a lonely, forgotten figure, and is remembered mostly by South Americans, who know that he was one of the first Spanish defenders of their independence. Belatedly, in 1984 the city of Seville set up a commemorative plaque on the house where he was born. His personal papers and letters, however, repose in exile and far from Spain, in Liverpool and Princeton.

The Romantic period also took exiles very far afield, less for political reasons than (as was the case of Blanco White) because of an irrepressible restlessness. The sentiment was personified in the poet José Zorrilla (1817–93). He was born in Valladolid, of a stern traditionalist father who supported the cause of the Carlists, and from an early age shared the enthusiasm, fashionable in educated circles, for the swashbuckling aspects of Spain's medieval past. He began higher studies in Toledo but abandoned them in favour of a bohemian life in Madrid, where he became a successful but always penniless poet. The change of direction was typical of his constant restlessness and refusal to conform. Aged just twenty, he made himself famous in Madrid by reciting an elegy at the funeral of Larra in February 1837. A few months later he managed to publish his first volume of verse, and when it was well received continued to publish more poems, mostly imitated from French poets. His work may not have been of quality, but it was certainly prolific. Though now recognized as a literary figure, he could not settle down in the capital and decided to live abroad, inspired by the wish to escape from the wife he had married in 1839, sixteen years his senior.

In 1845 he went to Paris, where he finally met the French writers who had helped contribute to the growth of historical Romanticism, such as Dumas and Gautier. The mother on whom he doted died that year, and after a short return home the rootless and restless Zorrilla decided to abandon his country permanently, moving first to Bordeaux and then to Paris and Brussels. He took with him the mental baggage of his home country and in 1852 published, in Paris, his long narrative poem *Granada*. He appears to have been in a state of deep depression, and when Paris dissatisfied him he moved to London, then in 1854 to Mexico City, where he spent twelve relatively barren years (including a year in Cuba), writing little of merit and unsure of his own ideas. When the Austrian Archduke Maximilian became (for a brief and tragic period, from 1864 to 1867) emperor of Mexico, Zorrilla was given employment at court and appointed director of the national theatre. He returned to Spain in 1866 and managed with some success to resume his literary career, though he always lived on the edge of poverty. An opera he wrote on the basis of his play *Don Juan Tenorio* failed after only one week at the theatre. However, the Romantic writers greeted him with acclaim, and in 1889 in a curious medieval-type ceremony he was crowned chief poet of Spain in Granada by the duke of Rivas (son of Angel de Saavedra), in the presence of the queen regent. It was a recognition not only of Zorrilla's work but even more of the Romantic obsession with the imagined glories of the Islamic past and their relevance to the creative imagination of writers at that time. Zorrilla replied with a long poem, reminiscent of that which he had read over the grave of Larra, thanking the assembly for their recognition of his work. He died shortly afterwards during an operation to treat a brain tumour.

Of the more than forty dramatic works he produced, the one that stood the test of time was the drama *Don Juan Tenorio* (1844), still a firm favourite of Spanish popular theatre and film thanks to the unsophisticated simplicity of its plot and diction. Though by no means great literature, the work is performed each year in many Spanish towns on 1 November, the eve of All Souls' Day, the day that the Don Juan of the play meets his maker. The story of Don Juan seems to have first been given literary form in the 1630 drama *El Burlador de Sevilla* (*The Prankster of Seville*) by Tirso de Molina, but in the epoch before which Zorrilla wrote had been used by artists as diverse as Molière, Mozart (in *Don Giovanni*), Byron and Alexandre Dumas *père*. In 1830 Pushkin also produced a poetical drama, *The Stone Guest*, on the Don Juan theme. The broad lines of the story were therefore well established. Don Juan is an unrepentant libertine who seduces Inés, the daughter of a military official, Luis Mejía, the Comendador of Seville. Inés subsequently dies of a broken heart. The Comendador challenges Don Juan to a duel, but is killed. Don Juan celebrates with a feast at the stone tomb of the Comendador, whom he mocks, but the Comendador's statue comes to life and tries to drag him down to hell (the doom he receives in previous versions, including that by Mozart). Don Juan evidently deserves his fate, but Zorrilla changes the ending and allows the libertine to be saved after a last desperate confession.

As the statue pulls at his hand, the desperate Don Juan pleads:

> Let go! If it be true
> that a moment of contrition
> can give a soul salvation
> for all eternity,
> Holy God, I believe in You!

At this moment, the ghost of Inés appears and confirms that her love for him has saved him.

> I gave my soul for you
> and through me God grants
> your despaired-of salvation.
> . . . Love saved Don Juan
> At the brink of the tomb.

Instead of being condemned for ever for his debauchery, Don Juan is saved through the love of Inés and through his own repentance. Indubitably the reason for the enduring success of Zorrilla's play in Spain was the new happy ending, allowing the audience to share in the conviction that love redeems.

The nineteenth century in Spain was an epoch of continuous exile, provoked by interminable political and military upheavals that, bit by bit, came to engulf all social classes. The strangest group in the comings and goings of exiles during the Romantic period were the Carlists, a movement that still enjoys support in Spain. Their central doctrine was male dynastic legitimacy: the Spanish throne should go to the male line heirs of Ferdinand VII, namely his brother the Infante Carlos, rather than to his female-line heirs (who included Queen Isabella II). Beyond the dynastic question, Carlism was in essence a traditionalist movement that developed both reactionary and revolutionary tendencies. It supported the Catholic Church against Liberalism, called for the restoration of the Inquisition, and defended regional rights (the '*fueros*', mainly of the Basques and Catalans) against central government. The broad base gave it immense support throughout northern Spain, and triggered several small civil wars. In consequence, it produced floods of exiles. The first Carlists to become refugees fled in the years before 1839, at the end of the first war they fought against the state. The government tried to root out its popular support by deporting activists to the New World. In 1836 there were around 2,200 Carlists languishing in Cuba, most of them young peasants from the mountains of Navarre. Prisoners were also sent to Puerto Rico. In theory they were meant to serve a six-year exile to allow them to cool off, after which they could make their way back. Upper-class Carlists, on the other hand, shifted for themselves when they lost their battles, and simply crossed the frontier into France, where they rubbed shoulders with Liberal exiles. One Liberal in Paris in 1839 described how 'the two emigrations, republican and Carlist, were on good terms. Sometimes they had bitter arguments, but they shared a friendship based on common sufferings, above all at lunch time', when they met in the same café.[59] At the end of the First Carlist War in the summer of 1839 possibly over 30,000 left the country and crossed the Pyrenees into France,[60] but most were ordinary soldiers with neither the resources nor the inclination to stay in another country, and they returned in 1840 after the queen issued an amnesty. The root cause of all the problems, Don Carlos himself, left Spain in 1839 and spent the rest of his life in exile, first in France then in Italy. The second round of exiles left the country in 1848, after an attempted rising (known as the Second War) failed. A final round of refugees left in 1876 after the last war involving the Carlists. With the passing of time, Carlism gave up its dynastic ideas and ultra-Catholic outlook, developing after around 1880 into a conservative party that also included many radical tendencies. The Carlist exiles contributed nothing significant to Hispanic culture, for they never gained the support of the intellectual urban classes and their ideas were too contradictory to make any sense. Their movement was 'a romantic epic in which selfless devotion to an ideal was soiled by treason, desertion and incapacity'.[61]

6

Searching for a National Identity

I am a Spaniard, a survivor of the sterile struggle to which we
are subjected by the ignorance and indifference of our country.
Enrique Granados, New York, 1916[1]

Absence from home meant for an exile an environment where everything, from language, food and clothes to customs and entertainment,
was different. Spaniards travelling through the continent felt the
contrast keenly, for their culture was perceptibly different from that
of northern Europe. The Mediterranean was a society of warm nights,
street activity, conversation into the early hours, and morning
sunshine that shocked by its brilliance. In the north there were things
to admire, such as the perpetually green fields that enchanted Blanco
White when he first discovered England; but Spaniards were per-
plexed by the language barrier, the damp, dark evenings, the stodgy
food, the closing down of social contact at dusk. Despite the differences, visitors to the north felt strongly that Spain needed to learn
from other Europeans if it wished to be more in accord with the modern world. Comparing themselves with Europe, many writers were
sharply critical of peninsular culture. It was not difficult to arrive at
this point, since traditional culture in Spain was fundamentally rural,
based on popular customs rather than on elite inclinations.

In the nineteenth century, there was no single Spanish culture, but
rather a range of regional modes of life that varied radically across the
peninsula. To foreign travellers, the strangest aspect of the peninsular
way of life was the small role played in society by the ruling classes,
who seemed unsophisticated and whose daily entertainments differed

little from those of the society around them. Spanish life appeared to be based on low culture rather than on elite preferences. Already in the 1650s the Belgian traveller Antoine de Brunel felt that the Spanish nobility were effete: 'they rarely go out of Madrid, they never go to war or visit foreign countries unless they are sent there'. In consequence, public life was based on the people, 'and there is no country with more equality'.[2] When the Englishman Joseph Townsend visited Spain in the 1780s he commented likewise on the absence of an effective aristocracy in the countryside. 'Throughout the whole of Spain I cannot recollect to have seen a single country residence like those which everywhere abound in England.'[3] From the time of the eighteenth-century Enlightenment the educated Spanish elite began to feel that they had a duty to bring their civilization into line with what they had experienced in other European countries. The creation of a recognizably national culture began, however, very late, in the final decades of the nineteenth century. It owed everything to the development and subsequent dominance of the big cities, whose limits were not significantly extended until the 1860s, when in Madrid, for example, the new suburbs of Salamanca and Retiro were created. Even then Madrid remained a small town, with less than a quarter of a million residents (in contrast to the two and a half million of London at the same epoch), and with no dignified avenues, elegant residences or even street lighting. In mid-century a writer, Mesonero Romanos, observed in the course of a trip through France and England that the Spanish capital was a 'disgrace' compared to other European towns.[4] At the end of the century Ortega y Gasset lamented that it had no creative culture, and was still provincial. The rebuilding of Madrid and Barcelona at the turn of the century, along lines imitated from other European capitals, created for the first time cosmopolitan centres in which culture could be nurtured. With a respectable and modernized centre from which to work, the permanent features of what we know as 'Spain' fell into place.

To some, the advances were not enough. Young men with an urge to better themselves and contribute to culture were soon dissatisfied with what the capital had to offer. There was a lot of political activity, indeed Madrid in the nineteenth century became one of the most active and chaotic political centres of the continent, with a constant succession of coups, revolutions, government (and dynastic) changes and troop movements. Poets and writers took part in the excitement, but invariably became disillusioned or had to leave for their own safety. Their dissatisfaction became the fuel for a tendency to look outside Madrid, and outside Spain, for new hope. They became intellectual rather than political exiles. Indeed, most of the figures that appear in this chapter were not formally émigrés but, rightly or wrongly, thought of themselves as alienated from the values prevailing in their society. Much that was truly modern appeared to be available only outside the peninsula, and Spain seemed, despite all its progress, to be a backwater. After a stint in Germany and Paris, in 1866 the diplomat and writer Juan Valera returned to a Madrid that seemed by comparison a desert: 'Madrid has theatres, fiestas, women, courting, intrigues and people in the streets, which are always full of life. But in intellectual matters it seems a tomb.'[5] The future seemed to lie in 'Europe', or more precisely, in the city of Paris, which for over a century had been the model for Spanish political and cultural aspirations. The peninsula began to modernize, but the intellectual elite had its eyes fixed on exterior horizons. Elite culture began to develop, but nurtured itself essentially on the work of expatriates and exiles.

Paris was, for all westerners and even for Americans, the centre of the civilized world. By the 1890s, new architecture transformed it into a modern capital of two million people. It was a city of wealth and poverty, but for the young culture-hungry artists and writers it combined history, decadence and inspiration. Spanish exiles had gravitated automatically to Paris since the Napoleonic occupation of the peninsula, and they continued to do so for the next four generations. This was the city of Baudelaire and Victor Hugo, of modernism, surrealism and cubism, of poster-art and music, of political agitation and the *affaire* Dreyfus. Even more than a centre of inspiration for creative Spaniards, it was the crossroads where they made contact with every other nationality.[6] The main foreign émigrés living in the capital were Germans and Poles, but the dominant artistic inspiration – apart from the French – came from the Russians, Americans and English. These three nations together represented half of the foreign artists putting on exhibitions in Paris in the year 1909. The Spaniards represented less than 5 per cent.[7]

A basic condition for having a modern and 'national' life in Spain was the possibility of sharing experiences across the peninsula, without being limited only to regional modes of conduct. By the end of the nineteenth century, the fundamental push towards cultural change was given by the growth of mass communications, in the form of roads, railways, the telegraph, the radio and – eventually – the cinema. Most of these new developments were associated with foreign influence. The modernization of the peninsula would have been delayed much longer had it not been for foreign help, since Spanish financiers did not have the capital or courage to invest in their own country. The exploitation of the rich mineral deposits of Asturias was financed by a Belgian, and the copper mines of Andalusia by the British. In those decades the textile industry of Catalonia began to develop with British help, followed soon after by the Basque industries. In order to transport industrial goods, the investors needed reliable communications. Over half the capital that financed development of the railway system after 1855 came from France.[8] The first line to be built in the peninsula was a short link from Barcelona to Mataró in 1848, and government legislation in the 1850s facilitated further foreign investment in railways, with the main network being completed by the 1870s. Unfortunately the decision was made to construct national lines with an unusually broad track gauge about twenty-three centimetres wider than that used in most of Europe. This made it impossible for France to invade Spain by rail, but was more expensive to construct and also cut the country off from direct access to Europe. To make up for the decision, some narrow gauge railways were constructed in some of the provinces but broad gauge continued to be the national standard until 1988. It was symptomatic of the way in which modernization, whether in technology or culture, was carried out.

Improvements in technology were followed by the beginnings of mass entertainment, which began to change the nature of Spanish cultural life. As with technology, the changes came from abroad. All the successful entertainments were visual, and none made a serious impact on illiteracy, of which Spain had (excepting Portugal) the highest levels in western Europe. In 1887 some 65 per cent of the Spanish population did not read or write (by comparison, around the same date illiteracy in England was 15 per cent and in New England

10 per cent). Within this general figure the variations ran from Madrid with 38 per cent illiteracy to Granada with 80 per cent. In the long run the most powerful cultural change to be brought in was popular sport, which created a focus of entertainment that transcended regional and social barriers across the peninsula. The major innovation was football, introduced by the British into the peninsula in the late nineteenth century and first played in the Basque country in the 1870s. The first operative football club was founded in the southern town of Huelva in 1889, the year that the first leather football seems to have been used in Spain. From then on the sport snowballed. A football association was formed in 1913 and achieved recognition by the International Olympic Committee in 1924. The first league matches were initiated in 1928. Radio, roads, the motor car, the train and football brought town and country together, gave Spaniards a means of communication, and made the 'nation' into a collective experience. However, was it the type of nation that everybody wanted? And could everybody share in it? The coming of mass culture dismayed at least one writer, Ortega y Gasset, who thought that 'Spain is falling apart, falling apart. Today it is less a people than the dust cloud that remains when a great people has passed by on horseback along a great highway of history.'[9]

The import of mass entertainment, communications and sport was also creating a firm basis allowing Spanish civilization to build bridges to the non-Hispanic world. The process was of course one-way only, for though Spain became a rich source of ideas for other Europeans in art, literature and music, in everyday material matters it exported very little directly and continued to preserve its longstanding cultural isolation. Traditional Spanish culture was rooted in the villages, among people who were almost wholly illiterate and whose way of life had little to offer the upper classes. The educated elite appreciated aspects of folk culture, but had little doubt that a more sophisticated option could only be sought outside the country, in Europe. This conviction accelerated the tendency for many to search for cultural inspiration elsewhere than in their own country, principally in terms of creative leisure, art and music. Those who did so became – like the musicians discussed below – in some measure cultural (rather than political) exiles, accepting the need to spend long years abroad in search of a new way to understand and revitalize their own country. In effect, they looked abroad for the possibility of creating culture at home. Logically, this led to profound doubts about the nature of what Spanish civilization had on offer. It tended to perpetuate the classic division between the world of virtual exiles (those, that is, who looked to Europe) and the world of traditional Spain.

The search for ideas from abroad determined the attitudes of an influential section of the elite. Spanish thinkers had always been strong on political attitudes and theological concepts, but had never since the seventeenth century produced a systematic school of ideas. A country with few philosophers, it tended to borrow its fundamental ideas from others, and the nineteenth century was the great period when elite Spaniards, whether as travellers or as exiles, drew on the intellectual concepts of other nations. It was a trend that Angel Ganivet later (as we shall see) denounced, when he swept those concepts aside as 'purely external means'. But the trend was a powerful one. The Romantic exiles in the early century learnt from the political and literary ideas of the British and the poetical styles of the French. And in the mid-century, for perhaps the first time, contacts with Germany gave life to a pro-Germanic influence that endured for two generations.

The first significant intellectual bridge to Germanic Europe took the form of a quaint, pseudo-religious movement called Krausism that few today would be able to identify or define. It was an aesthetic, almost religious, outlook created by Julián Sanz del Río (1814–69), who in 1843 gained a scholarship to study abroad in northern Europe. Already an admirer of the German writer Karl Krause (an obscure philosopher friend of Hegel who died in Munich in 1832), he made contact in Brussels with one of his followers and went on to study Krause's ideas during a lengthy stay at the University of Heidelberg. He returned to Spain a devotee of the ethical idealism proposed by Krause. Under him and a few devoted followers, the fund of ideas known as 'Krausism' became adopted not so much as a philosophical doctrine but as an ethical guide for transforming individuals and society and thereby bringing about a regeneration of Spain's long-stagnant cultural levels.[10] Because of its non-Catholic precepts it was attacked by the

Church and the state authorities, and in 1867 the leading Krausists (including the writer Francisco Giner de los Ríos) were expelled from their university posts. Converted into exiles in their own country, they turned the tables on their persecutors. As an alternative, the year after they founded the Free Institute of Education (the *Institución Libre de Enseñanza* or ILE). It was intended to be an alternative university, dedicated to a liberal education free from the control of state or Church. When the vocation as university met with no success, the ILE turned to secondary education and to reforming the attitudes and tastes of the public. Non-ideological by nature, it was enormously important because it offered for the first time in Spain a middle-class, reformist approach free of partisan dogmatism. Inspired in good measure by English liberalism, it embodied a programme that aimed to change the face of Spanish culture:

to establish personal contacts between teacher and taught, to embody advances in European educational method, to widen the syllabus by courses on art, folklore and technical subjects, to play games and take excursions in the countryside.[11]

The supporters of the ILE can be classified in general as individuals who looked to Europe and were proponents of reformist ideas that later developed into the movement for 'regeneration'. Their educational programme took many different and unexpected forms. For example, an emphasis on contact with the countryside (which in England continues to play some small part in the system of instruction) excited Spanish reformers. One of the astonishing aspects of traditional Spanish culture had been its indifference to gardens and landscaping. Even a cursory glance over the range of painting in the Golden Age reveals an absence of countryside scenes, which tend to creep in only as part of a depiction of mythological stories. Philip II in the sixteenth century made prolonged but futile efforts to introduce landscaping, and not until a century later did the new Bourbon dynasty manage to develop the idea of country-house gardens. The aridity of most of the peninsula was a powerful obstacle. In the nineteenth century, the influence of English ideas turned the leaders of the ILE towards the artistic and moral benefits of contact with the countryside. The classes of the ILE took their pupils on 'excursions', and hikes into the countryside soon became established as a cultural activity of the elite all over Spain. The visible landscape, 'the land of Castile', became viewed as in some way an expression of the soul of Spain, and therefore as an object of devotion. For the essayist Azorín, a solution to the 'problem of Spain' lay in cultivating 'generations who get to know the land of Spain'. Ortega y Gasset felt that landscapes 'teach us morality and history, two exalted disciplines that are sorely lacking among Spaniards'.[12]

The renewed vision of the present served also to observe the past through different eyes. 'The spirit of the ILE,' Azorín wrote, 'has stimulated love for nature and in consequence love that has renewed our painting.' The man who succeded Giner de los Ríos as director of the ILE was Cossío, an art historian who rediscovered the forgotten figure of El Greco. In the same period, artists rediscovered the Velázquez and Goya who had already received the attention of the French. But the real change took place in the depiction of the present day. Azorín pinpointed the artists who most reflected the philosophy of the ILE: Beruete, Sorolla and Zuloaga. To their number we may also add Rusiñol. The regional artists, inspired usually by the techniques of French Impressionism, dedicated themselves to local themes and landscapes. Particularly notable were the contributions of Basque painters such as Ignacio Zuloaga, and Valencian painters such as Joaquín Sorolla. It seemed as though Spain was discovering itself for the first time. What remained to be explored was the projection of this culture on to an international stage, a move that took place thanks to the help of American patronage. Perhaps the first Spanish artist to achieve success in America was Sorolla. When he was asked in 1911 to do the series of panels *Regions of Spain* for the Hispanic Society in New York (see Chapter 8), he travelled through the peninsula in an attempt to catch the right sentiment and idea for each province. Through education, art and literature, the handful of bourgeois intellectuals tried to give form and substance to a different Spain.

The ILE had a fundamental importance for the evolution of ideas among Spain's cultural elite, and however indirectly played a part in the way that intellectuals distanced themselves from the official culture, traditional and Catholic, defended by both Church and state. Among the institutions that arose out of it were research bodies such as the *Junta para Ampliación de Estudios* (Committee for Further

Education), which in turn in 1910 founded the *Residencia de Estudiantes*, where students pursuing higher studies could apply to reside. Situated on a quiet and shady hillside in the northern part of Madrid, the Residencia subsequently became well known because in the 1930s it housed students who included Juan Ramón Jiménez, Unamuno and, later on, Federico García Lorca, Luis Buñuel and Salvador Dalí. These students did not, of course, share any of the original aspirations of the ILE, but they all ended up excluded from the official Spain that the ILE had originally attempted to combat and change.

In some way, the ILE and its supporters – many of whom fought hard for their principles – can be seen as part of the background that explains why some individuals ended up in real or voluntary exile. They were cut off from traditional Spain, or, as a subsequent scholar of conservative views put it, 'they did not manage to become Spanish'.[13] Their ambitious programme stood little chance of acceptance and it has been argued that the ILE failed in all its main objectives, because 'a heroic minority cannot hope to change an intolerant society by quiet persuasion'.[14] Though the ILE did more than any other body to give form and meaning to a more 'Spanish' culture, and helped to rear a whole generation of significant intellectuals, it never succeeded in rooting that culture firmly within Spain.

Above all, the intellectual class felt that it lacked a reliable outline of the past to which it could appeal for support and inspiration. What was the historical process that had led to the emergence of Spain as a nation? The only way to find out was, obviously, through a fresh historiography and an innovative portrait of past events. The problem was uncertainty over the political identity of 'Spain', for the various pieces of the country were still uneasy with each other, and the 'Spanish state' kept changing according to political, ideological and dynastic preferences. One way round the political obstacles was to concentrate on the emergence of a shared culture. The way forward, then, was to identify three aspects of Spanish life: past traditions; current achievements; and aspirations for the future in terms of ideas and values. This was the scheme proposed in Germany by the philosopher Herder, and borrowed from him by the Krausists and their followers.[15]

The exploration of 'Spanish' culture had the significant consequence that many Spaniards came to discover not what they shared
with other peoples in the peninsula, but rather what was special about
their own regional way of life. In Catalonia the attempt to restore an
authentic 'national' voice took shape in what came to be called a
Renaissance, the *Renaixença*. Unfortunately, after generations of
Castilian domination the would-be regenerators could find suitable
cultural material only in the distant (and imagined) medieval past or
in the confused mass of peasant folklore. Teams of researchers were
sent through the villages in order to collect oral testimony to surviving
folklore, information that would reinforce a sense of Catalan identity.
The result was that Catalonia possesses the best folklore records of
any province of Spain. But little of this served to regenerate identity.
Even the much-publicized revival of the Catalan language, through
public poetry readings, was little more than symbolic lip-service.[16]
Those who recited medieval-type Catalan verses in public continued
to use Castilian as their main spoken language among themselves. The
most emblematic expression of linguistic renewal was a poem that a
Catalan writer 'exiled' in Madrid, Aribau, addressed to a mountain
peak that symbolized for him the Catalonia he longed for. In fact,
Aribau had never before published anything in Catalan, and never
again did so. This was hardly the basis on which to construct a modern,
industrial identity. Catalonia was a thriving, forward-looking society,
with solid roots in imperial enterprises in Cuba and the Philippines,
and an active interest in European trends. The key to a new orientation came in 1884, when a group of young intellectuals founded
the review *L'Avenç*, financed by profits from Cuba. Calling themselves
'Modernists', they sought their inspiration *outside* Spain.

These well-heeled, upper-class young men had lots of leisure time,
and spent much of it in the cosmopolitan world of Paris, the store-house
of progressive thought and art for Spaniards. The bookstore they
founded in Barcelona, called also *L'Avenç* (1891), was stuffed with
French books. Catalan Modernism was in effect simply an extension of
the intellectual concepts of Paris.[17] Through Paris, however, many
Modernists managed to tap into the sources of all European culture.
The young poet Juan Maragall observed that their inspiration was not
merely the French novelist Zola, but also non-French writers such as

Ibsen, Tolstoy, Maeterlinck and Nietzsche. The young men of that generation were fortunately not forced into political exile, as the Romanticists had been two generations earlier. They chose all the same to drink of the wisdom available abroad, and a stream of cultural celebrities went to Paris and London. Perhaps the most exciting of them was the Catalan Ramón Casas (1866–1932), indubitably one of western Europe's greatest *fin de siècle* painters. In 1881, at the age of fifteen, with his father's aid he left his native Barcelona to study art in Paris, which influenced him decisively as a painter. Paris became his semi-permanent home, from which he made periodic visits to the peninsula, drawing inspiration from Andalusia above all. In 1890 he went again to Paris, where for two years he shared an apartment and studio in Montmartre with his close friend the artist and writer Santiago Rusiñol. From 1894 he settled down to work in Barcelona, but visited Paris every year. In 1897, along with his friends, he helped open the café *Els Quatre Gats* ('The Four Cats'), the central meeting place of his artistic circle, and still today an active centre for creative artists. His work in stunning portrait painting, and flamboyant poster art, made a decisive contribution to the cultural consciousness of Barcelona's upper classes.

This vast quantity of foreign influence inevitably gave rise to doubts. There were doubts even among the intellectual exiles, whose view of things Spanish was strongly influenced by their extended stay outside the Hispanic environment. A prime example of the problem of rooting a modern cultural identity securely in the contemporary world was a painter of this generation, who made his name in Europe but remained for decades virtually unknown in his home country. This was Juan Gris (1887–1927), a key figure in the Cubist movement of the early 1900s. He gravitated northwards in part because all European artists were focusing their interest on Paris, but also because of the simple fact that in cultural terms Spain was a satellite of France. His baptismal name was José González, the thirteenth of fourteen children born into a comfortable middle-class family from Madrid. As a child he became interested in design and did a course in it, but in 1904 – the same year that Picasso decided to settle permanently in Paris – he decided that his future lay in avante-garde painting. In order to earn a living he became an illustrator. Two years later he determined to escape from his unmistakably plebeian name and changed it to 'Juan Gris', then sold all he had, including his bed and mattress, and with the proceeds paid for a journey in September to Paris. He arrived in the capital with sixteen francs in his pocket. Gris never returned to Spain, preferring to convert himself into a Frenchman, even to the extent of changing his first name to 'Jean'. 'It is by this name,' wrote his friend and agent Daniel-Henry Kahnweiler, 'that he lives on in the memory of his intimate friends. Only Gertrude Stein used to call him Juan.'[18] 'He was infatuated by France, French civilization and culture, and the French language', Kahnweiler reported. Ironically, though his correspondence was in French, Gris habitually signed his name as 'Juan'. The only remaining evidence of his Spanish origins lay in his dark, swarthy complexion and his square-cut face, unmistakably a man of the Mediterranean, who detested bullfights but never managed to lose his fondness for flamenco music.

He plunged into painting, becoming a convinced supporter of the Cubism of Picasso and Braque. Typical of his work at this stage was his Cubist oil *Hommage à Picasso* (1912), in which, he boasted humorously, he 'cut Picasso into small pieces'. He quickly built up a reputation of his own, counted the writer Gertrude Stein as one of his supporters, and did commissions for Diaghilev. He married a French girl, Josette, from whom he became inseparable. He never travelled outside France, because he had failed to regularize his civil status as an immigrant and therefore did not possess a passport (his application for French nationality was interrupted by his untimely death), but his work featured in exhibitions throughout Europe. From around 1922 he based himself in the seaport of Boulogne, where he died after over a year of serious illness (caused by uraemia) and a brief seventeen years of life as an artist. The procession at his funeral was a roll-call of the great musicians, artists and poets in France, among them Picasso, Chagall and Miró.[19] The poet Paul Éluard commented: 'For us today, Gris represents unforgettable images.'

Few artistic geniuses have been so effectively excluded from the memory of their own country. Though it took some time to develop, Gris's reputation grew and by the 1960s his paintings were fetching the same level of prices as those by Picasso. From the 1930s, exhibitions of his work were put on in Paris and other European cities, and shows in the United States were capped by that at the MoMA in New York in 1958.[20] His works featured in galleries and collections in Europe and the New World. But not in Spain. In Spain he remained unknown. When a study on the artist was published in Barcelona in 1975 the author wrote, 'this is the first Spanish book devoted to him'.[21] The first significant exhibition in Spain of his work was put on only in the 1980s.

Though artists, writers and men of culture drank from the sources of inspiration in Europe, many of them in subsequent decades ended up turning their backs on it. A notable example was the essayist and novelist Angel Ganivet (1865–98), the son of a small businessman in Granada who had committed suicide at the age of thirty-two, leaving his wife to bring up five children and care for the family mill. Fortunately the business prospered, and Ganivet was able to complete his education in Granada and at the University of Madrid, where he gained a doctorate. He developed a capacity for languages and entered the consular service, serving from 1892 in Antwerp and then in Helsinki and Riga. His active career was spent well away from Spain, in the very different environment of northern Europe, where he pursued the deeply introspective and profoundly religious reflections that had already begun to develop in his doctoral dissertation. Contemplating his country from his northern eyrie, he felt convinced that it needed spiritual regeneration, which it could find only within itself rather than from outside. The problems that he surveyed on the outside were, as is often the case, embedded in his own inner being. In Antwerp, where he wrote a social novel, La Conquista del reino de Maya (The Conquest of the Kingdom of Maya, set actually in East Africa and not published until 1897), he experienced an intellectual and spiritual crisis, aggravated no doubt by his stormy relationship with a Cuban girl, Amelia, and by his contraction of syphilis.

He travelled by train from Antwerp to take up his post in Helsinki in the bitter cold of January 1896. There were problems of communication, since Swedish was still the society language in Finland, while the people spoke Finnish and his landlords were English. He tried to get by on French. With little to do, he dedicated himself to writing, in a congenial room that looked out on woods and an open sea. It was a perfect setting, and he managed during the year to write his best-known work, the *Idearium español* (1897), as well as a partly autobiographical novel, *The Travails of Pío Cid* (*Los trabajos del Pío Cid*) (1898). He was soon joined by the persistent Amelia and their son, Angelito. However, at the same time he had a secret affair with his neighbour, a Russian girl known as Masha, who coached him in languages. Two and a half years later, in August 1898, he was transferred to Riga, where there were further communication problems, since the elite spoke German but the common languages were Latvian and Russian. It seems that the climate, his own introspection, and the emotional tensions with the jealous Amelia worked together to produce a crisis (he was also suffering from progressive syphilitic paralysis). On a freezing November day in Riga, two months after his arrival there, he threw himself into the River Dvina. They fished him out alive, but he repeated his suicide attempt, this time successfully.

Ganivet is traditionally associated with the generation that was affected by the loss of Cuba (which will concern us presently), yet he had little in common with them other than his dreams and prejudices. He was not too concerned about the loss of Cuba and felt it might even be a blessing. From Riga he wrote to a friend: 'the loss of useless colonies is a blessing and may be the beginning of a decent life'.[22] His *Idearium* was an extended essay offering a perspective of Spain, viewed from his exile in the Baltic. Its few strong points were those reflecting his own direct experience, but his general opinions and analysis were both unoriginal and immature, reflecting the fund of ideas current in the previous half century. Little more, perhaps, can be expected of the first political musings of a thirty-year-old who had seen little of the world. In essence the essay was yet another text, like the very many written by Castilians from the seventeenth century onwards, offering solutions to everything that made Spain a backwater of Europe. 'The central motif of my ideas,' he wrote, 'is restoration of the spiritual life of Spain.' 'Wherever we care to pass over the roads of Spain we will encounter the eternal sphinx with the eternal question: is it better to live as we have done till now, or should we break definitively with bad traditions and transform ourselves into a modern nation?' His answer was that neither alternative was desirable. Other countries might be richer and more advanced than Spain, but Spain had the inestimable wealth of her spirit. That must be purified and conserved. Technology and science were not part of the Spanish spirit ('there is no way of establishing them in Spain'), and that aspect of Spain could not be changed. It was an unfortunate aspect of non-Hispanic civilization that 'by bad luck they give more importance to kilometres of railway than to works of art'. Nor was there any point in embarking on a period of militaristic empire-seeking in Africa. Spain had to realize her true mission and develop into a great nation and culture. The solution to its weaknesses, which were many, was not to go outside looking for a panacea. Spain contained its own riches within itself and hence its own salvation. 'We need to shut with bolts, keys and locks all the doorways through which the spirit of Spain escapes and spills over into the four points of the horizon.' Spain alone had virtue, and it should not be allowed to escape. The frontiers must be sealed.[23] Unfortunately, Ganivet offered no convincing presentation of the native virtues that Spanish culture could develop once it sealed its frontiers. The only way forward he could suggest was for Spain to develop (peacefully) its links with Muslim Africa: 'seek a support in the continent of Africa in order to maintain our personality and our independence in front of Europe'. 'If you look to the future, there are a thousand signs that indicate that Africa will be the field for our future expansion.'[24]

The search for a true Hispanic identity was inevitably concentrated across the Atlantic, where the two inescapable realities were the colonial heritage of Spain's empire in South America, and the rise of the United States in the north. When upper-class Spaniards at the end of the nineteenth century visited the United States they were in no doubt that they went as representatives of a superior culture. Juan Valera (1824–1905) was no exception. Born in Córdoba of a leading noble Liberal family (and related to Alcalá Galiano), he started his literary vocation as a poet, studied law at university, and began his diplomatic career in Lisbon, Rio de Janeiro and Dresden. In 1858 he became a deputy in the Cortes, and seven years later a diplomat in Frankfurt. In 1872 he was named minister of education in Madrid, and also became a senator. It was the high tide of his literary and political activity, and in 1874 he began publishing sections of his novel *Pepita Jiménez* in the press. At the end of 1883 he was appointed to a diplomatic post in Washington. During all these years he was effectively separated from his wife, and had many affairs with women abroad. In Washington he had a passionate affair with a lady who committed suicide when Valera left to take up his next appointment, in 1886, in Brussels. His last years, spent in Madrid, were overshadowed by the onset of blindness.

Though Andalusian by origin, Valera felt uneasy in Andalusia and in the rest of Spain, and was typical of those many Spaniards who felt strongly that they were exiles within their own country,[25] but once outside it could not wait to go back. He never ceased to condemn the backwardness of his own nation in every conceivable aspect. 'This pitiful land of chickpeas', was his phrase for it in 1860, and he compared Spaniards to 'the chickpeas that make up our main nutriment'.[26] No sooner was he abroad, however, than he saw matters differently. 'I am a patriot,' he explained, 'through a spirit of contradiction and of pride, whenever I am abroad; and when I am in Spain – without ceasing to esteem her – I usually have a very bad opinion of her.' In his mature years he displayed these contradictions during a stay of several months in 1884 as a diplomat in Washington. He used his time to visit the northeast, and supervise a translation into English of *Pepita Jiménez*, the first modern Spanish novel to enter the American market.

He was familiar with the names of America's Romantic historians (Irving, Ticknor, Motley, Prescott) who had studied Spain, and with those of a few poets (Longfellow, Emerson), but had read none of them. 'The only one of whom I have read a little is someone called Henry James, all right but not in any way noteworthy.'[27] On the whole he was surprised by the friendliness of Americans: 'they care for us more than you might think'. According to him they were culturally inferior, because in Spain cultured people 'do not give way to such extravagances and madnesses and depravities'. He was happy, however, that Americans knew about the greatness of Spain, 'the immortal memory of our glories, greatness and exploits in America', and felt that this called for Spain to recover its leadership of the New World. 'Spain has to become once again a nation worthy of its past, to the point of exercising a certain domination in the New World, above all in the Spanish-speaking world, and the departure point for our activity has to be New York.'[28] It was ironic that he should be writing in this way on the eve of the biggest military defeat to be suffered by Spain since the humiliations piled on it by the Turks in 1560 and the English in 1588 and 1805, all of them – significantly – naval actions but with much less impact on Spanish popular opinion than the Spanish-American War.

The Disaster,[29] as the war came to be known in Spain, was a consequence of a rebellion against Spanish rule in Cuba, led by the poet José Martí, who counted on the support of the United States government. The rebellion inspired a response from anti-Spanish groups in Puerto Rico. Cuba, quite logically, had most of its trade contacts with the United States, which stood on the sidelines while the conflict in the island continued. In February 1898, however, the visiting American battleship *Maine* was suddenly blown up off Havana, with the loss of over two hundred men. In Washington the Spaniards were held responsible (historians now consider the explosion to have been an accident) and war was declared in mid April. The press and public in Spain were enthusiastic about defeating the American 'pigs' (the standard image in Madrid), who were jeered at as cowards whom the Spanish lion would quickly devour. 'The children of Cortés and Pizarro', a Madrid writer enthused, 'cannot retire as humble lackeys from the region they discovered, populated and civilized.'[30] The government was more pessimistic. Spain was totally unequipped to fight a campaign thousands of miles away, and American forces mopped up with ease what was left of the empire. An American fleet besieged Manila and on 1 May sank the entire Spanish fleet. A further American expedition left San Francisco on 25 May, occupied Hawaii (not a Spanish possession) and Guam along the way, and began to take over the Philippines. In June the Americans landed in Guantánamo Bay in Cuba and began military operations. In July a further force occupied Puerto Rico. When the Spaniards sent a fleet out to Cuba there was a quick encounter in which the Americans lost one man dead and nine wounded, while the Spaniards lost all their ships, with five hundred dead, two hundred wounded and thousands of prisoners. In mid-August Spain agreed to the American peace terms. In December, by the Treaty of Paris, Spain gave up sovereignty over Cuba, Puerto Rico, Guam, the Philippines and the Mariana Islands.

Though it has become customary to present the Disaster as a decisive influence on a group of writers who have been dubbed 'the Generation of 98', in reality it did little more than bring to the surface a number of ideas that had been maturing for some time. The writers who came to accept the label were by no means the most sophisticated level of Spanish intellectualism. They were all very young (Unamuno was only thirty-four that year), and their thinking was inevitably immature and subject to sharp changes and contradictions in the years that followed. The phrase 'Generation of 98' was in any case not used at the time, and emerged only fifteen years later, in 1913, from the pens of Ortega y Gasset and (later) of Azorín.[31] Azorín summed up the significance of the writers concerned in these words:

the Generation of 98 has merely continued the ideological movement of the previous generation, together with a cry of passion, a corrosive spirit and love of reality. It has had all this, and mental curiosity for things foreign and the spectacle of the Disaster – the failure of all Spain's political life – have enlivened its sensibility and given it a character that did not exist before in Spain.[32]

The Disaster brought home to many Spaniards the ineptness not simply of their government, their army and their navy, but of their country. The demand for reform took shape in the fund of ideas known as 'regeneration'.[33] Writers and publicists raised their fists to the skies in anger, but ended up beating themselves on the breast. Once again, as in the seventeenth century, they began to lament that the country was in decline. The only way out of the impasse, writer after writer proclaimed, was to modernize Spain and bring it into line with Europe. One of the most agitated debates to arise was over Spain's scientific incapacity. The well-known Aragonese physician Santiago Ramón y Cajal (1852–1934), subsequently the first Spaniard to win the Nobel Prize for medicine,[34] was taking a peaceful walk out in the country with a friend, when he heard the news of the sinking of the Spanish fleet off Cuba and the surrender of the city of Santiago to American troops. The news fell on him like a thunderbolt. He had done his military service in Cuba, after graduating in medicine at the University of Saragossa, and had firm ideas on the matter. There had been belligerent speeches in the Cortes in Madrid, and articles in the newspapers suggesting that Spain was about to teach the United States a lesson. Nobody imagined that the real outcome would be 'the Disaster'.

Spaniards had always been taught that theirs was the most powerful empire in the world. What had brought them to this debacle? Cajal felt that the crisis offered food for thought, and put down his ideas in a text that was originally a discourse to a scientific group (1897) but re-edited several times and published in 1913 under the title *Advice on Scientific Research* (*Reglas y consejos sobre investigación científica*). It was translated into several languages. Cajal appears at this point of our narrative because he was, figuratively speaking, an intellectual exile, standing well outside the mainstream of elite opinion as to what Spain represented and where it was heading. His argument in the tract was that the United States had won because it was a modern society that had embraced science, whereas Spain was still living in its past. 'We have been defeated by the United States,' he wrote, 'because we were ignorant and weak. We need to regenerate ourselves through work and study.' He called in particular for the teaching of science to be given a central role in the university syllabus. In response to the stock affirmation that Spain had once been great, and was now merely weakened, in a state of decline, he affirmed roundly that the excuse of 'decline' was false. 'Is it acceptable,' he asked, 'to claim that we have degenerated in comparison with our predecessors of the sixteenth and seventeenth centuries?' The real problem, in his view, was that Spain had never been a modern country: 'Spain is not in decline, it is intellectually backward', and had never emerged out of its medieval backwardness.[35]

They were daring words that no one wanted to hear, but by then people had to listen because he had become world famous. Ramón y Cajal was born in a village in Navarre, though he always identified himself with his home town of Ayerbe in Aragon. He served in the army in Cuba (1874–6), gained his doctorate in medicine at Madrid in 1877, and then held top university posts consecutively in Valencia, Barcelona and Madrid. The real breakthrough in his career occurred in 1887, when he became acquainted with new histological techniques pioneered in Italy and Paris. He went abroad, contacted foreign scholars, and pioneered his own theories and methods about the mapping of the human nervous system, which resulted in his sharing the Nobel Prize in 1906 with the leading Italian scholar in the field, Camillo Golgi, 'in recognition of their work on the structure of the nervous system'. A universal scholar, he was also a keen writer, photographer and artist. He lived an introspective, solitary life, preferred his laboratory to social contact, and enjoyed nothing better than slow, quiet walks and a solitary coffee outside. Yet his fertile mind was always active and continued to be so into ripe old age. His wide vision enabled him to take a perspective that purely literary men were unable to do. Cajal's views on the Disaster were bitterly attacked by Castilian writers, notably Ortega y Gasset and Pio Baroja, who felt that he was completely out of line with their own nationalist approach. The writers of the 98 generation were united in the conviction that their country was potentially the most advanced and civilized in the world, and that the Americans were the real barbarians. Their disdain for science was logical, for despite the efforts of a few individuals from the eighteenth century onwards, the peninsula had never kept pace with western technology or industry. If there was any backwardness in the country, Spain's elite maintained, it was the fault not of Spain but of the Inquisition. This was an argument that Cajal attacked vigorously. The Inquisition, he said, disappeared over a hundred years ago, yet had Spaniards done anything since then? Not a single voyage of world exploration had been organized by Spaniards, not a single Spanish writer was being read in the rest of Europe, not a single scientific success could be chalked up for Spaniards. Spain, compared with the rest of Europe, was 'deplorably backward and shabby . . . it has been in a semi-barbaric state, almost entirely alien to any concern to broaden the horizons of the spirit'. 'While our people were sleeping the centuries-long sleep of ignorance, the nations of central and northern Europe overtook us decisively.'[36]

Castilian contempt for science was, of course, merely a defensive posture. But it was a posture adopted by the majority of writers from Valera and Ganivet onwards, and typical of the pedestrian metaphysical level on which many such questions were debated. Despite the shock of the Disaster and the clamour everywhere for 'regeneration', in practice nothing happened. The novelist Pio Baroja published in

1903 a novel, *The Search (La Busca)*, in which he mentioned seeing over a cobbler's shop the sign 'footwear regenerated'. He commented:

The historian of the future will certainly find in this sign a proof that at certain times the idea of national regeneration was widespread, and it will not amaze him that this idea which began with wishing to reform and regenerate the Constitution and the Spanish race, should end in our time in a corner of the slums, where the only thing carried out was reforming and regenerating footwear.[37]

The agitated controversies of the 98 generation appeared, even to those who took part in them, notably sterile. Américo Castro commented in 1962 that 'the Generation of 98, and those of us who continued it, brought forward nothing decisive'. Seen in perspective, the published debates of those years reveal one of the basic and perennial defects of elite culture: the tendency to manufacture a smokescreen of words rather than face reality head on. Instead of analysing the logistical shortcomings that had led to the loss of Cuba, the political class preferred to treat the affair as a moral disaster, just as in the seventeenth century Philip IV had viewed Spain's military reversals as a punishment for sins. One consequence was to give special importance to the men of letters, who were treated as though they were prophets or social analysts able to explain what had gone wrong. If there had been a disaster, the first priority was to talk about it; action could be postponed. So-called 'intellectuals' were idolized, and their pronouncements were accepted as the real issue; the other issue, the loss of the empire and of thousands of Spanish lives, was quietly swept under the carpet. The elevation of the so-called 'intellectuals' to a position of eminence, as though they were a sort of 'aristocracy of the spirit', encouraged people to believe that beyond their cultural qualities they offered answers to the pressing problems of society.

The emergence of 'the intellectual' as not simply a writer but also a prophet was one of the strangest but also most typical aspects of *fin de siècle* Spain, where members of the tiny educated elite could claim the right to impose their preferences in a pre-industrial country on a mass public that was over two-thirds illiterate. The origins of this phenomenon are normally associated with what was happening across the frontier in France, where in the same year, 1898, the novelist Émile

Zola burst into politics over the Dreyfus case with his historic article, 'I accuse', in the newspaper *L'Aurore*. From that moment the middle class in western Europe began to pay special heed to what writers and journalists chose to communicate.[38] If the writers adopted the flamboyant posture of martyrs, condemned for example to an unjust exile, they were adored even more as redeemers. The term 'intellectual' became accepted across much of Europe. Chekhov appears to have been the first to create, in that same year 1898, a Russian word for it, 'intelligentsia'.[39] In Spain, it came to be used more specifically of writers who became journalists, using their newspaper columns as podiums from which to inform and instruct the masses who were presumably waiting for a mere gesture from them. Around 1900 the 'intellectuals' came to be seen (not least, of course, by themselves) as one of the hopes remaining to Spain after the fruitlessness of 'regeneration'. 'Peoples progress', Ramiro de Maeztu wrote in 1915, 'when they produce intelligent men and support them with the power of the government. And if not, not.'[40] They were aware, certainly, that in a nation that was heavily illiterate, where very few read any newspapers and even fewer read books, their writings would circulate only among their own social class. They were, however, quite used to speaking only to each other, whether in literary '*tertulias*' or 'gatherings', or within the shelter of exclusive upper-class clubs (such as the Royal Academy of Language). To identify themselves as unique, they adopted specific manners of dress. Azorín put on a monocle and went everywhere carrying a red umbrella; Valle Inclán let his beard grow down to his waist; Pio Baroja wore a cap and a dark overcoat; Maeztu dressed like an English gentleman. Their limited readership did not dent their conviction of their vital role. There was more than mere courtesy in the sentiments expressed by the poet Antonio Machado to the 'intellectual' Unamuno when the latter was living in exile in Hendaye, on the Basque coast of France, in 1927. 'Here', Machado wrote from Madrid to Unamuno, 'we suffer the absence of Unamuno, his articles, his poems, his spirit watching over the spirituality of Spain.'[41] Few individuals in human history have been thus elevated to the supreme position of guardian of the spirit of their country.

The subject of the encomium, one of the best-known writers of that generation and a declared enemy of modern science, was Miguel de

Unamuno (1864–1936). Unamuno, the third of six children of a Basque baker, was born and educated in Bilbao, studying later at the University of Madrid for a doctorate on the Basque language. In 1889 he made a quick tour of western Europe, paid for by his uncle, and saw the new Eiffel Tower in Paris, constructed that year for the Exposition Universelle. In 1891 he obtained the chair of Greek at Salamanca, a city in which he spent the rest of his professional life, save those of his exile. It was a good indication of the academic standards at the university that Unamuno knew no Greek, but the chairman of the committee that selected him, Juan Valera, was quite clear on the matter. 'None of them knows Greek,' he stated, 'but we gave the chair to the one most likely to know it!' In the same year Unamuno married a Basque girl, by whom he had ten children. He kept up his links with Bilbao, where he began writing (in 1894) for a socialist paper, *The Class Struggle*. His socialist affiliation continued for three more years. He combined his social writing with an active interest in philosophy, and Salamanca became his permanent home. In this early period he published the short essays known as *On Authenticity* (*En torno al Casticismo*) (1895, issued as a book in 1902), in which he broached many of his ideas, including his conviction – which he later modified substantially – that Spaniards must save themselves by modernizing towards Europe.

And what does all this have to do with the other idea, *casticismo*? A great deal, because *casticismo* is the response of the old national spirit that reacts against Europe-ization. It is the work of the immanent Inquisition. The characteristics that in another age were able to give us leadership, now leave us prostrate. The Castilian soul was great when it opened itself to the four winds and spread round the world, but later it shut the valves and we have not yet awoken.

Is everything moribund? No, the future for Spain's society waits within our past society, in its intra-history, in the yet unknown people, and will not gain strength until the winds and tempests of the European environment awaken it. Spain remains to be discovered, and only Europeanized Spaniards will discover it.

Between 1896 and 1897, and more specifically in March 1897, he went through a religious crisis which shattered his previous belief in reason as a way of approaching God and the meaning of life. He turned his back on universal concepts of philosophy and reality and focused attention on the individual consciousness. Convinced that reason (and science) did not supply answers but led to despair, he concluded that one should take refuge only in faith. This, obviously, was a type of existentialism that was beginning to get known in Europe through the writings of Kierkegaard, whom Unamuno tried to read. A product of this evolution was his best-known group of essays, *The Tragic Sense of Life* (1911, published as a book in 1913), the only one of his works to make an impression on a European public. His 'conversion' at a young age – he was just over thirty – set the stage for the new Unamuno, more volatile in his ideas, less at ease with the political and religious establishment.

In 1900 he was appointed rector of the university, but he was relieved of the post in 1914 because of political disagreement with the government. Then in 1924 an essay he published attacking King Alfonso XIII earned the displeasure of the military dictator Primo de Rivera and in March he was sent to Fuerteventura in the Canary Islands, far away off the African coast, and lodged at government expense in a hotel. It turned out to be a six-year absence, longer than he could have imagined. But it was also a make-believe exile. 'Persecution of the intellectuals has begun', the essayist Azorín protested when Unamuno's exile was made known. 'Where will it end?' 'This unique man has been transformed into a great national figure. Everybody in Spain is talking about Miguel de Unamuno.'[42] In fact, Unamuno had deliberately put himself in the limelight, and the regime retaliated more as a gesture than as a real punishment. 'They did not throw me out,' he claimed later, 'I made them throw me out, so I wouldn't have to bow to censorship.' He was by no means a prisoner in the Canaries; he sailed off in the yacht of a Paris newspaper director in July, and took ship at Las Palmas for Cherbourg. That very month Primo de Rivera issued an amnesty to Unamuno, whose 'escape' from Fuerteventura was planned specifically so as to avoid benefiting from the amnesty.

On 28 July the writer was in Paris, this time as a voluntary exile. He confessed to feeling old and isolated, and on the brink of depression. There was work on hand, because he collaborated with the

Valencian novelist Blasco Ibáñez, who also happened to be in exile in Paris, and for much the same reasons. The two launched a weekly paper called *España con Honra* (*Spain with Honour*), which lasted about a year. Blasco had little faith in Unamuno's temperament: 'the only thing I'm afraid of is that since this don Miguelito is a mystic, one day if his arm hurts he will call a priest, enter a monastery, and make us all look like fools.'[43] Members of his family joined Unamuno a few months later. In August 1925 he moved to Hendaye, a French Basque town near the Spanish frontier, where he lived five comfortable years, managed to write in leisure, and received visits from Spanish admirers. His writings in exile amount to 275 articles in Spanish and in French, written both for home and for foreign consumption. As a noted figure, he adored being the centre of attention. 'We, the so-called intellectuals,' he was to proclaim two years later, 'are saving the historic honour of Spain.'[44] He and his friends were conscious of the precedent set in France by Victor Hugo, who had ostentatiously exiled himself for ten years to the (conveniently close) island of Guernsey because of a difference with the government of the day. Two weeks after Primo stepped down from power in 1930, Unamuno made the dramatic gesture of walking over the bridge at Hendaye that crossed into Spain. He went back to Salamanca, was reappointed rector, and exchanged his chair of Greek for that of Castilian Language.

He returned, he hoped, like a Moses about to lead his people into the Promised Land. His exile had converted him into the centre of attention and he profited from it, addressing public meetings and plunging into politics, first in the city council and then, when the Republic was proclaimed in 1931, as a deputy in the Cortes. He very quickly lost faith in the politicians, and did not present himself for the Cortes elections in 1933. In 1935, as the violence mounted on all sides, he denounced 'the disgusting state of politics at present'. In December that year, he foresaw that 'Marxists and Fascists between them are going to destroy the soul of Spain', and lamented 'Spain's national leprosy, the resentment, the envy, the hatred for intelligence'.[45] His writings had by now made him a European figure, and in February 1936 he went to Oxford to receive a doctorate *honoris causa* from the university. While in Oxford he learnt of the victory of the left-wing Popular Front in the Spanish elections and on his return made no secret of his antagonism to government policy, which he perceived as a negation of what the Republic had originally stood for in 1931.

Unamuno's basic attitudes date from his conversion, and his exile had little effect on them. This was not surprising, since he did not like accepting the views of others. He had an exceptional intellect and great imaginative sensitivity, but never put his ideas together in a systematic way and never elaborated any coherent philosophy. The early influences on him had been foreign, mainly drawn from German Romanticism and positivism, but the spiritual experience of 1897 turned him into a purveyor of mystical language and an opponent of the modern world. He disliked dogmas such as Marxism, but at the same time felt that Catholic dogma was at the heart of Spain. His essays, especially during the period of the Republic of 1931–6, were all firmly liberal in tone, but his method of expressing himself was frequently extremist and illiberal. Since he changed his views often, it is not easy to figure out where he stood on any issue. His problems in 1936 with both the Republic and the rebel military (referred to in Chapter 7) were a typical product of his confusions.

While the intellectuals anguished over the culture of their country, the politicians were convinced that there could be no country without the lineaments of a political state. Culture and politics were in reality two faces of the same problem: the fragility of Spain as a shared experience. 'Modern Spain,' a government official complained in 1775, 'can be considered a body without energy, a monstrous republic formed of little republics which confront each other because the particular interest of each is in contradiction with the general interest.'[46] When Henry Swinburne travelled through the peninsula in the 1770s he was similarly struck by the complete lack of solidarity between provinces. Though the elements of a national culture were beginning to converge, observers recognized that it was little more than a gloss. In 1897 the Santander novelist José María Pereda spoke up for what he called the regional novel, for he felt that regional life – 'love for the land of one's birth, its laws, habits and good customs, its air, its light, its views, its traditional fiestas and celebrations' – was the authentic reality of Spain. 'In reality,' his fellow novelist Pérez Galdós agreed with him, 'we are all regionalists, for we all work in some sizeable corner of the Spanish landscape.' At the turn of the century the intellectuals felt, as Ortega y Gasset did in 1917, that 'Spain lacks any national feeling'. In his *The Redemption of the Provinces* (1931) Ortega concluded that 'local life' was the only driving force and that the 'province' was 'the only vital reality that exists in Spain'. The creative culture of that period certainly derived its inspiration from local life. Juan Valera in *Pepita Jiménez* (1874) depicted the society of Andalusia, Clarín in *La Regenta* (1895) exposed the conservative society of Oviedo, Blasco Ibáñez in the series of novels that he published from 1894 onwards offered a panorama of Valencia, and Narcís Oller in *Gold Fever* (1892) opened up the life of Barcelona. The researches of Joaquín Costa confirmed what was evident – that Spaniards lived local rather than national lives. The sociologist Julio Caro Baroja saw what he called the 'sociocentrism' of Spanish towns as perhaps their most fundamental, traditional and therefore most dangerous attribute.[47]

Regionalism became the catchword at the turn of the century and logically took on political overtones, with the Catalans in the vanguard. In 1885 a group of Catalan personalities handed to Alfonso XIII a 'Memorandum of Complaints' with the request 'that a system of regions, attuned to present conditions, be introduced into Spain'. One of the sponsors was Francesc Romaní, a conservative and nationalist lawyer who the next year helped to found in Barcelona the journal *La España regional*, which came out monthly for seven years and mobilized a campaign in favour of regional autonomy as the best defence of Spain's unity. The campaign had no political pretensions, and regionalism continued to be what it essentially was, a sentiment based on environment and roots. The emotion overlapped, however, with another dynamic tendency, 'nationalism', which had the same origins but drew its vigour from two more persuasive cultural sources: language and history. It was, all the same, a curious kind of nationalism, with shallow roots that literally had to be invented, because the nationalists were unsure about their antecedents, their ideas and their aspirations. The generation after the Disaster, then, found itself in a dizzy spiral of perplexity: trying on the one hand to piece together

Spain's newly discovered national culture and on the other to promote the regional and provincial identities that had held the stage before the evolution of the twentieth-century state. The disappearance of a world profile in 1898 threw further fuel on the fire, as Spaniards of all persuasions attempted to save their lost honour by re-inventing the greatest of all their identities – the 'empire' – and tailoring it to the needs of the new age.[48]

It was not exactly chaos, for that would come later. Rather, it was a generation of dissension and instability that seemed to call for rigid measures of control against a tide of workers' strikes and political uncertainty. The control was supplied, at least for a time, by the military dictatorship of General Miguel Primo de Rivera who, with the complicity of King Alfonso XIII, took control of government for a seven-year stint (1923–30), promising to solve the national crisis and bring to an end a disastrous war that had been dragging on in Morocco since the first decade of the century. Political control soon created victims, and a number of prominent figures were arrested. The physician and writer Gregorio Marañón was imprisoned for a month. He later recalled: 'Primo de Rivera put me in gaol and imposed a savage fine on me, then afterwards one fine day we turned into the best of friends'.[49] It was a notably mild 'dictatorship', but had the consequence of attracting the hostility of the now self-conscious 'intellectuals', who were convinced that they knew better than anyone what the country needed. The confrontation led in true Hispanic style to a further round of exiles, who included opposition politicians such as the Catalan Francesc Macià and the Liberal minister Santiago Alba, as well as writers such as Unamuno. During the latter's stay in Paris he collaborated in the literary efforts of other exiles from the dictatorship, such as Blasco Ibáñez (whom we shall encounter later, in Chapter 8) and Ortega y Gasset.

José Ortega y Gasset (1883–1955), the most respected essayist of that generation and one of the few to achieve any international recognition, did not escape the burden of exile. Born in Madrid, he was educated in Málaga and Bilbao and obtained his doctorate (1904) at the University of Madrid. Following in the footsteps of the Krausist intellectuals who had looked to Germany for inspiration, he spent three years abroad in the universities of Berlin, Leipzig and Marburg

(1905–7), where he imbibed neo-Kantian influences. To Marburg, he wrote later, 'I owe at least half my aspirations and almost all my education'. After returning to Spain he obtained the chair of metaphysics at Madrid (1910). His stay in Germany convinced him that his own country was living only on the fringes of modern civilization. 'The history of Spain is little more,' he suggested, 'than the history of its resistance to modern culture.' The medium he chose for addressing the public was the short essay. His published work consisted entirely of fragmentary pieces that emitted brisk, pontifical judgements on a vast variety of themes, from history, politics and art criticism, to philosophy and ethics. Unlike contemporaries such as Unamuno who expressed themselves in rambling and sonorous prose, Ortega preferred short, striking phrases that caught the reader's attention. He never produced a solid volume or any systematic expression of his thought, an aspect that his critics later stressed when they questioned his achievement. Logically, like many other writers he was dedicated to journalism (what Spaniards called 'ensayismo'), and helped to found several magazines, of which the most influential was the *Revista de Occidente* (1923). He was the archetype of what Spaniards came to understand by the word 'philosopher', that is, an essayist or journalist who applied his opinions to an issue without necessarily being an expert on it.

Coinciding to some extent with work being produced in that period by 'mass society' analysts in Germany (such as Karl Mannheim and Erich Fromm), he began to look at the old theme, given new life by the Disaster, of 'the grave illness Spain is suffering'. His most fecund comments took shape in a short 1,500-word essay titled 'The empire of the masses', which criticized the individualism that ignored the interests of others. 'When in a nation the masses refuse to be masses, the nation falls apart, society splits up and social chaos ensues, a historic *invertebración* ['loss of backbone']. We are living through an extreme case of this *invertebración* in Spain today.' The essay came out in a small volume published as *Invertebrate Spain* (1921). It was the prelude to his best-known work, an essay on *The Revolt of the Masses* (1929), in which he argued that in twentieth-century society the initiative had been taken out of the hands of intelligent minorities and passed to the vulgar, unqualified masses. It became perhaps the most widely commented-upon work produced by any Spanish writer of the age, but people took widely differing views of it. Some considered that Ortega was criticizing mass movements like Russian Communism or Italian Fascism; others felt he was predicting a civil war in Spain; others again considered his views elitist and proto-fascist.

Though a Liberal he gave some support to Primo de Rivera's dictatorship,[30] but had little faith in the monarchy behind Primo. Like others of his generation in Europe, Ortega found it difficult to come to terms with the pace of civilization, and many of his essays (such as *The Revolt of the Masses*) show a clear rejection of the direction being taken by politics, art and literature. He belonged, almost, to another time. In 1925 he denounced *The Dehumanization of Art*, meaning by 'dehumanization' the emergence of modern painting, with its apparent elimination of the human figure and human feelings. In the same way he was unhappy about aspects of democracy that set the individual aside and gave priority to mass values, which for him were always bad values. From the late 1920s his thought showed the influence of the German philosopher Martin Heidegger, and his ideas drifted into an imprecise form of metaphysics which inspired him to make affirmations such as: 'I am not my life. This, which is reality, is made up of me and of things. Things are not me and I am not things', and: 'I am myself and my circumstance'. It was a form of existentialism that he never developed sufficiently and in any case found few adepts in Spain, so that his most memorable essays remain simply those where he offers his thoughts on the human condition, as seen of course from Spain.

As an opponent of the monarchy, he became in 1931 a firm supporter of the Republic, entered the Cortes as a deputy (1931–2) and was appointed Civil Governor of Madrid. A year in professional politics was enough to disillusion him. In a public lecture in December 1931, called 'Reconsidering the Republic', he outlined some of his disagreements with current policy. The following June he published a newspaper article on the same theme. He continued to support the Republic but was horrified by the violence of the Popular Front. Just after the military uprising of July 1936 he was forced to sign a statement of support for the Republic, but considered it 'intolerable pressure', since the Republic he had supported in 1931 was very clearly not the pro-Communist one that emerged in 1936. Thereafter he kept his lips sealed on political issues, left for Alicante in August and took ship for France. It was the beginning of a nine-year exile.

One of the most interesting consequences of intellectual questioning after the Disaster of 1898 was the rise in Spain of the cult of Cervantes, and particularly of his novel *Quixote*. Cervantes was by no means an exile from his country, though he spent many years outside it. Nonetheless he took on, in time, a special significance, because he came to represent for all Castilian exiles the values of their traditional culture. When trying to explain what their country had offered the world, they unanimously settled on the literary output of one man. That man represented in their eyes an eternal, unchanging, centre of certitude in a world that had been thrown into confusion by the destruction of Spain's imperial role and by the inability of reformers to come forward with new solutions to the problem of what Spain was and where it was going.

Little is known of the early life of the novel's author, Miguel de Cervantes (1547–1616). He was born in Alcalá de Henares, son of a doctor, but emerges into the light of history only when he left the country to go to Rome, where he resided several months, prior to volunteering as a soldier for the naval battle at Lepanto (1571), where he was wounded in his left hand. After a further year serving in the Mediterranean he returned towards Spain but was captured by Algerian corsairs and spent five years as a slave in Algiers. He was ransomed and eventually returned to Castile, where he managed to devote himself to writing while trying to work for his living. Towards the end of the century he was working in Andalusia as a tax collector, and ended up briefly in gaol in Seville in 1597. In 1605 he succeeded in publishing the first part of his novel *Don Quixote*, and settled in Madrid. His subsequent published works included the *Exemplary Novels* (1613), and the second part of *Don Quixote* (1615). Because Cervantes' life is largely unknown, there has been ample room for speculation and fiction. It is certain that he did not loom large on the cultural horizon of Spain's great imperial age. Not until 1738, a generation after the end of the Habsburg dynasty, did a critical study of the author appear, in the form of a biography by the Valencian scholar Gregorio Mayans. Not until the second half of the nineteenth century were Spaniards alerted to the qualities of the *Quixote*, which began to be presented as the epitome of the nation's cultural achievement. Since then Cervantes has become a worldwide phenomenon. Hundreds of studies and biographies of him have been published in virtually all the languages of the globe. Few of them have advanced textual knowledge, because the unique quality of *Quixote* is that it can be interpreted subjectively in an unending number of ways, and always according to the individual's viewpoint. That, in some measure, was also the appeal of the book for Spaniards.

At various points in the later nineteenth century the novel *Quixote* had been commented upon by literary figures, who used its central character in order to point a moral.[51] After the drama of 1898, however, the literary aspects became almost completely irrelevant – the only pertinent factor being the ability to read into the novel an interpretation of Spain's moral status in a world threatened by the materialism and technology of the United States. In a letter that year to Angel Ganivet, Unamuno claimed that the novel was 'the eternal symbol of humanity in general and of our Spanish nation in particular'.[52] Probably the first literary commentary came from the exiled Nicaraguan poet Ruben Darío, who was in Spain when the crisis occurred and expressed his rage through an essay, *D. Q.* (the initials of Cervantes' hero), which he published the following year in Buenos Aires. Darío saw in Quixote a personification of those high ideals that had made Spain great and would eventually rescue Hispanic culture from the monster (the United States) now threatening it. The Uruguayan writer Rodó, whose essay *Ariel* (1900) was a feverish response to the invasion of Cuba, subsequently went on record with the opinion that 'the philosophy of *Quixote* is the philosophy of the conquest of America', in the sense that Quixote represented spiritual values that had dignified the Spanish conquest, whereas the American aggression represented vulgar materialism. The Quixote cult received its most powerful boost with the celebration in 1905 of the third centenary of the novel.[53] Less than a decade had passed since the Disaster, and commentators used the novel in its historic past as a means of analysing what had gone wrong with Spain's present. In a subsequent essay Unamuno wrote: 'It may be that we have to seek the hero of our way of thought not in some philosopher of flesh and bone, but in a being of fiction and action, more real than all the philosophers, namely don Quixote.'

The tone was set by Unamuno's *The Life of Don Quixote and Sancho* (1905), in which the author used the novel as a tool for his own presentation and disowned any connection with Cervantes. The book fused together material from Cervantes and from a life of the founder of the Jesuit order, Ignatius Loyola, in order to describe a spiritual quest, in which Quixote searches for new spiritual values in the world of materialism. The apparent subject is the errant knight, but the real subject is Unamuno, trying to present himself as an intellectual with a message. The message is little heeded, just as the insensible flocks of sheep do not really hear the speech made to them by Quixote. 'It is a terrible thing if wherever one goes in our Spain, scattering heartfelt truths, people come to you and say they don't understand, or understand the reverse of what you are saying.' But the knight carries on, challenging (like Unamuno) windmills that 'today do not have the appearance of windmills but of locomotives, dynamos, turbines, steamships, automobiles, telegraph wires', in sum, the paraphernalia of detestable material civilization. The task of Spaniards does not consist in finding solutions for the future. 'There is no tomorrow! What will happen to us today, now? That is the only question!' This wholly fantastic rendering of the novel paved the way to yet more extensive liberties with Cervantes' text by other writers. From being a work of literature, *Quixote* was converted into the essential tool of every commentator on the spiritual and social situation of Spain. A whole new world of philosophical discourse was opened up. Every significant exile from Spain made his contribution, so that the *Quixote* became the surgical tool par excellence which writers used to prise open and analyse the inert corpse of their native country.

The new concern with Cervantes had little to do with culture and much to do with national pride and mysticism. The president of the Second Republic summed it up nicely in the 1930s: 'We claim to see in the defeat and disappointment of Don Quixote the failure of Spain itself.' Writers like Unamuno and Ortega paid attention to the morally uplifting principles of the novel, while would-be reformers (the 'regenerationists') found modernizing values. The leading Aragonese intellectual, Joaquín Costa (d.1911), whose researches on the rural economy of Spain were meant to prepare the way for an era of economic reform that would 'regenerate' the country, had no doubt that on a moral level Spain had to seek its salvation across the Atlantic

as a counterweight to the Saxon race. To confront the Saxon Sancho [that is, the United States, typically seen as an inferior lackey] there must always be the pure luminous Spanish Quixote, a Quixote who through passion and faith and sacrifice makes the earth become something more than a factory and a market.[54]

The last phrase was a swipe at what was seen as the mercenary materialism of United States' culture.

Unamuno's study was accompanied in the same year by Azorín's *The Route of Don Quixote*. In 1914 Ortega published his *Meditations on Quixote*. Two years later, in 1916, a competition was held for a statue to be placed in the centre of the Plaza de España in Madrid to commemorate the author of *Quixote*. The diplomat Salvador de Madariaga in his inimitable way produced a *Guide to the Reader of Quixote* (1925), the same year that Maeztu brought out his penetrating *Don Quixote, Don Juan and the Celestina*. For Maeztu, 'the whole of Spain has been a Quixote. We were sleepwalkers who roamed through the world thinking we were awake, but we were asleep.' The sole academic study of the novel's text came from Américo Castro in his *The Thought of Cervantes* (1925). Of all the studies produced in these years, only that by Maeztu was conceived in exile, after fifteen years of absence had modified and matured the way in which he arrived at a perspective of Spain's role within western civilization. All the writers we have mentioned, however, ended up at loggerheads with the regimes under which they lived, so that in a sense the experience of exile was built into the construction of the Quixote myth. The idea continued to haunt writers, who seemed to have no other substantial basis for their discourse.

The studies of the exiles inevitably offer some clue to the reasons why differences of opinion over a novel should give rise to heated ideological debate. Perhaps the most ironic comment on the theme of Quixote came from the pen of Ramón y Cajal, whose comments were as usual out of step with his literary colleagues. In a short lecture that bore the title 'Quixotism and the psychology of Don Quixote' (1905), delivered in response to the book published that year by Unamuno, he tried to bring the literary theme back to the solid world of reality. 'Let us admire the book by Cervantes, but let us not sidetrack the message towards realms the author did not have in mind.' 'Authentic *quijotismo*,' he went on, 'has ample scope for action in Spain', by which he meant that there were contexts in which the story of Quixote gave food for thought. He then turned the theme towards the question of modernization. Spain had been a disaster in questions of science, and why? Because 'its intellectual leaders had little of the truly Quixotic passion'. The true spirit of Quixote was the spirit of enquiry, because enquiry is adventure. Where, he demanded, 'are the Quixotes of industry and commerce?'[55] Another critic of the literary fantasies surrounding Cervantes was an Aragonese engineer from Huesca named Lucas Mallada (d.1921), one of the early promoters of Darwinism in Spain and a sharp critic of writers who (like Unamuno) preferred dreams to the possibility of scientific progress. In a penetrating study dated 1890, Mallada wrote: 'Among us there exists in all social classes a defect that I shall express in one sole word: fantasy. The land of Don Quixote is a land of dreamers.'[56]

The accumulation of names writing about the Don Quixote theme, over a span of two decades, shows that the obsession – unparalleled in any other European country – with a two-centuries-old work of fiction was a serious cultural phenomenon. The obsession has developed over the generations into an almost religious veneration, repeated in the centenary celebrations of the year 2005, in which the novel served as a Holy Bible (read aloud solemnly by public figures, paragraph by paragraph, by day and night and from beginning to end) and its commentators as apostles. It is worth recalling that those 'apostles' of Quixote in 1898 were, without exception, not venerable prophets but snobbish young upper-class men who were simply searching for a place to hang their still-undeveloped thoughts. In 1898 Ganivet was thirty-three, Unamuno thirty-four, Ortega fifteen (he was thirty when he came round to meditating on the novel). They would soon modify and develop their ideas about the novel, just as they would soon modify their ideas about Spain. In the long journey towards eventual maturity, for each of them a fundamental role would be played by the reality of their eventual exile. But within that exile the theme of Quixote would continue as a permanent flame of optimism, and virtually the only hope of salvation. Unamuno defended 'my worship of *quijotismo* as the national religion'. An exile of those years, the Valencian novelist Blasco Ibáñez, expressed perhaps better than anybody the celestial significance of the mad knight of La Mancha. He affirmed the role of the novel as 'the Bible of our people', and as 'the representative of the spirit of Spain and of all humanity'.[57]

The problem of establishing a recognizable national identity shone through clearly in the case of music. The nineteenth century was the period when Spanish non-sacred music managed for the first time to claim a place in the international arena, almost entirely through the achievement of musical exiles. In family and social gatherings, Spaniards of every rank obviously enjoyed, played and developed folk rhythms, ballads and musical compositions, which combined both sacred and secular themes. Music was a central feature of everyday culture. The songs known as *villancicos* had served, with or without musical instruments to accompany them, as entertainment at public occasions and feasts for generations. This popular tradition was continued uninterrupted into modern times, but growing contact with music from outside the peninsula modified the tastes of the elite. At least from the time of Ferdinand and Isabella, the royal court gave preference to what was imported from other countries. Like the Tudor royal court in England, the Spaniards imitated Burgundian clothes, ceremony, art and music.[58] Rites of chivalry came to Spain from Burgundy. Spain's great age of empire, the sixteenth century, was also the great age of imported music, which entered in part from the north, in part from Rome. A good part of the music was sacred, based on voices. Philip II developed the music of his chapel in the direction of Flemish choral styles, while the most relevant Castilian composers of the period were men such as Morales and Victoria, both of whom spent years abroad in Rome learning the choral styles that their contemporary Palestrina had been composing in Italy.

By the eighteenth century little had changed at popular level. Folk rhythms, ballads and dances were the staple fare of the people in their celebrations. But at the king's court in Madrid there were important developments: the new French dynasty of the Bourbons rigorously excluded native Spanish music. The elite consequently lived with and came to appreciate the quality of European music, particularly when Charles III, late in the century, brought an Italianate court with him. Those who appreciated traditional Spanish music were irritated by these trends. A librettist (Luciano Comella) complained in 1791 that 'some people in our country applaud only what is foreign'. When intellectuals in the middle of the nineteenth century tried to identify what was authentic about their music, they were sorely troubled. Everything, it seemed, had come from Italy, little from Spain. Typical of this concern was the controversy raised about the relative merits of domestic and foreign opera. Some sort of 'opera' had been known in Madrid in the later seventeenth century, when Italian music began to enter the peninsula. Distinctively Italian opera, with more musical instruments and a more developed plot, became established under Philip V in the early 1700s and spread rapidly when the Italian Charles III became king in the later part of the century. By the opening of the nineteenth century Italian music, represented by Rossini, reigned supreme in Spain. It was the type of music written by the Valencian composer José Melchor Gomis (1791–1836), who trained as a choir-master, but during the struggle against Ferdinand VII joined the forces under the rebel General Riego and composed music for patriotic songs, including, it seems, the music for Spain's only historical national anthem, *The Hymn of Riego* (*Himno de Riego*).[59] As a pro-French official, he fled to France in 1823, living the rest of his life in exile. From 1826 he spent four years in London, where he tried to make a living by giving music classes and selling sheet music of popular Spanish songs, but he failed to find any outlet for his compositions. Like most of the exiles in England he went to Paris when the 1830 pro-Liberal revolution took place. He was more successful in the French capital, where he composed the music for Martínez de la Rosa's opera *Aben Humeya*.

Italian success did not displace the native operetta known as the zarzuela, which, however, had to fight for survival. From the 1840s, 'there was a reaction to the invasion by Italian opera, and the first attempts to create national opera took place'.[60] In part this took the form of reviving the zarzuela. When Tomás Bretón wrote his *The*

Lovers of Teruel, he defended the idea that opera could be Spanish and not simply derived from Italian music. In opposition to this idea, others argued that only the zarzuela was genuinely Spanish, because both words and music were based on popular tradition and melodies. In order to further the idea that Spain had its own music and did not simply borrow from others, the music critic Antonio Peña, a Basque who published in 1881 the first history of zarzuela, developed a myth that the zarzuela was the authentic expression of the Spanish people. The claim was not untrue, for over the preceding generation a group of musicians, mainly from Madrid, had set about rescuing folk melodies and composing comic operettas (the '*género chico*') with easy tunes. The composer Barbieri in the 1860s enjoyed great success with his works, to be followed by Chueca in the 1890s. The zarzuela, presented in the Apollo Theatre in Madrid, reigned almost supreme well into the 1930s, and Chueca (wrote one critic) was to Madrid what Offenbach was to Paris under the Second Empire.

The success of zarzuela, however, condemned Spain to isolation in its forms of music.[61] Multi-instrumental orchestral music remained unknown in the peninsula. This was ironic, for the obvious richness of popular peninsular melodies never failed to appeal to and stimulate musicians, both in and out of Spain.[62] Spanish folk tunes were used in their work by early European composers such as Scarlatti and Boccherini, and also later by Glinka, Strauss, Rimsky-Korsakov (*Capriccio espagnol*), Debussy (*Iberia*) and Ravel (*Bolero*). A curious tradition in opera also resulted in leading European operas choosing Spain, and particularly Seville, as a venue (Bizet's *Carmen*, Rossini's *The Barber of Seville*, Mozart's *Don Giovanni*, Verdi's *Il Trovatore*, Beethoven's *Fidelio*). Stravinsky was typical in his sentiments: 'In 1916, touring Spain made a tremendous impression on me. I'm in love with her popular music, those gypsy dances!'[63] A typical case of the penchant for Spain was the French composer Édouard Lalo (d.1892), who began his musical career at Lille but ended up working in Paris, where he composed his rich and elegant *Symphonie espagnole* for violin and orchestra (premiered 1874), which took the form of a concerto in five movements. The work was written especially for the Spanish violinist Pablo de Sarasate, who was then initiating his career in Europe. The successful combination of

Sarasate and Lalo demonstrated that Spain had a distinctive musical message for the world.

Sarasate (1844–1908) was born in Pamplona (Navarre), in the mountains that form the frontier between Spain and France. His father was a bandmaster in the army, and he learnt to play the violin at an early age, giving his first public concert in the north of Spain when he was only eight. He later studied in Madrid, and performed at court. The queen was impressed and helped to finance him going to Paris in 1856 to study, when he was aged twelve. He was meant to be accompanied by his mother, but she died on the way, and the boy musician was brought up by adoptive parents in Paris. Five years later, he won a prize at the Conservatoire for his playing, and never looked back from that moment. It was the beginning of a highly successful career that involved almost permanent absence from Spain. He was patronized by Saint-Saëns, who wrote a special piece for him (Violin Concerto No. 1 in A, Op. 20, to which he gave the name *Concert-stück*). Impresarios from London to Russia clamoured to have him play: in 1861 he performed at the Crystal Palace in London and then went on a tour of eastern Europe. At the peak of his career Sarasate was a phenomenon without equal, incessantly touring the world of culture, from America to Russia, with commitments in every country of note. In 1870 he toured the United States in a group that included the famed opera singers Adelina and Carlotta Patti. He helped bring fame in the New World to Max Bruch, whose Violin Concerto No. 1 in G Minor had recently premiered in 1867 at Coblenz. Sarasate performed the piece to perfection at the Steinway Hall, New York, and repeatedly thereafter during his visit. A year after his return to Europe, Lalo composed the *Symphonie*, which Sarasate performed in Paris and London (spring 1874). The violinist subsequently travelled by horse-coach down the Rhineland with Bruch, who was inspired to compose a second violin concerto (in D Minor, 1878), in which the motif was the Carlist wars in Navarre, a theme the two had talked about as they admired the magnificent scenery.

As with other exiled artists, Sarasate was virtually ignored by his country, which did not possess the musical infrastructure – orchestras, theatres, public taste – to appreciate him adequately. He played occasionally in the peninsula, in the context of the zarzuela, but even when he played he did so to empty houses,[64] and public indifference to his music, even in Navarre, was almost complete. Not until 1880, two decades after he achieved fame in Europe, was he invited to Spain, where he performed in the big cities with such success that he repeated the tour the following year. This second tour was disappointing, and he did not return until ten years later. The cultural world of northern Europe was more to his taste. In the spring of 1884, he wrote from London: 'I have played in Germany, Belgium, Paris, and here I am pinned down as though I had never left home.'[65] During this visit Whistler painted his portrait, *Arrangement in Black: Portrait of Señor Pablo de Sarasate* (now in the Carnegie Museum, Pittsburgh) in his studio at Cheyne Walk, London. The artist went on to decorate a music room in Paris for Sarasate, who professed to Whistler he was his 'devoted friend and ardent admirer'.

At the beginning of his career, Sarasate performed opera fantasias (most notably the *Carmen* fantasia) and other pieces that he himself had composed. His pieces inevitably had a Spanish flavour, and helped to bring folk melodies to the attention of European composers and public. His best-known composition, the *Zigeunerweisen*, showed that apart from his masterly performances he owed his success to exploitation of the gypsy theme, which Europeans and Americans took to be the real soul of Spain. Sarasate extended his interest to the folkloric music of other nations as well. He had a great affinity for Scottish folk melody, wrote a piece called *Scottish Airs*, and had Max Bruch write specially for him in 1880 the *Scottish Fantasia*. His contact with Lalo, Bizet, Saint-Saëns and others was fruitful to everybody concerned, since composers were always on the lookout for good performers, and Sarasate was universally esteemed as the best. George Bernard Shaw heard him in England and proclaimed that he 'left criticism gasping miles behind him'. Sarasate was always impeccably dressed. The young cellist Pablo Casals met him in Madrid:

he was an elegant gentleman, very debonair, with flowing black hair, a long slender moustache and gleaming black eyes, and he smoked cigars incessantly. At one point he offered me some brandy. When I declined he exclaimed: 'What! You intend to be an artist and you don't drink? *C'est impossible!*'[66]

His female fans adored him, but he remained all his life a bachelor.

Though Sarasate became very wealthy, he was also quite generous. He settled down in a villa in Biarritz, but every year he would return to Pamplona to perform during the Fiesta Mayor, the traditional annual week of celebrations. While he watched from a balcony as the bulls charged through the streets beneath him, the citizens would cheer their native son. And when Sarasate died of chronic bronchitis at his Biarritz home in 1908, he left his earthly goods to his two sisters and the city of Pamplona, which brought his body back, gave him a civic funeral, and later opened a museum in his honour.

Sarasate's career was stunning proof that Spanish artists could flourish brilliantly in an international environment. The downside of this situation was that they could not enjoy similar success in their own country. A virtuoso like Sarasate had to live in absolute exile from his own country, where his music did not have a public unless it was watered down into popular tunes. The problem of Spain's musical estrangement, despite this widespread admiration of its folk culture, and the irritating identification of the peninsula only as a land of gypsies (the theme of *Carmen*), was of deep concern to those musicians who, like the Catalan musicologist Felip Pedrell, wished to profit from folk music and make it the basis of composition (*Por nuestra música*, 1891), but also desired a more European perspective. The gypsy theme was, however, impossible to shake off, and from Sarasate to Falla it remained firmly at the centre of musical composition. It was, above all, a theme that appealed strongly to foreign writers and composers, who prized highly the exotic element it supplied.[67] From Borrow's romantic image of Spanish gypsies in *The Zincali* and *The Bible in Spain*, to Victor Hugo's gypsy girl Esmeralda in *The Hunchback of Notre Dame*, Spanish culture was projected on to outsiders as essentially a gypsy one. Spain seemed to be a source of creativity among others, but not a creator in its own right nor within its own musical environment. This situation changed radically with the appearance of the Catalan pianist Isaac Albéniz, a colleague of Pedrell.

Born in the foothills of the Pyrenees at Camprodó, of a Basque father and a Catalan mother, Albéniz (1860–1909) was an autodidact child prodigy who gave his first public concert at the age of four, at the Teatre Romea in Barcelona. His father was a state official whose duties took him round Spain. This made it possible for Isaac to study music in Madrid; he composed his first piano piece at the age of nine, and was soon giving concerts throughout the peninsula. Piano music played in elite salons was a typical product of the Romantic movement in Europe, but had gained in popularity in Spain after visits to the peninsula by Liszt (1844) and Gottschalk (1851). Isaac's constant movement seems to have been also an expression of his restless personality, for in later years he made up stories of places to which he had allegedly been. When his father had to go to Havana in 1875 he accompanied him and stayed there for a year. On his return he made short visits to Europe to study in Leipzig, Vienna and Brussels, settled for a while in Madrid (where he achieved great success and was honoured by Queen María Cristina), then from 1889 in Barcelona. The piano concert he gave at the Salón Romero in Madrid in January 1886 was a brilliant tour de force. He played chosen pieces by all the major European composers, then rounded off the presentation with his own *Suite espagnole*. Albéniz was particularly inspired by a visit he made to Granada in 1886, when he became especially attracted to flamenco music and the strange wail of the *cante jondo* ('deep song', a vocal form associated with flamenco). He wrote of the visit: 'I am looking for tradition, which is a goldmine . . . the *guzla* [an Arabic stringed instrument], lazily dragging the fingers across the strings. And above all the heartrending, off-key wail. I love Arab Granada, which is all art, all – it seems to me – beauty and emotion.'[68]

In 1889 he established his European reputation by being received with wild acclaim at a concert in Prince's Hall, London, a success that led to four more piano recitals. But he was also badly in debt, and while in London (his main place of residence from 1900) he signed a contract giving exclusive rights over his music to an English agent, who then sold them to the society banker Francis Money-Coutts. Coutts wanted Albéniz to compose a musical trilogy on the theme of the Arthurian epics. Since the composer needed the money he began work on the scheme immediately, but also managed to finish his lyric comedy *Pepita Jiménez,* based on Valera's novel. In Brighton he suffered his first severe attack of Bright's disease or nephritis, a urinary infection. He appears to have been careless of both his diet and his health, but never lost his good humour. An aspiring young Polish pianist named Arthur Rubinstein, eighteen years old when he met Albéniz in Paris in 1904, described him as 'a fat little man with a round face, black beard and upcurled abundant mustachios, a jovial fellow, whose eyes had a charming, smiling twinkle'.[69]

Albéniz's success in England in 1889–90 brought Spain to the attention of Europe. Europeans in 1800 had been still unaware of Spanish art, and in 1900 were equally unaware of Spanish music. A London newspaper in 1900 observed that 'there is no distinctive school of musical art belonging to Spain, and its music is but a pale reflection of French or German thought'. Albéniz's music also drew on the French and Germans, but his recitals began to open a few eyes. After hearing them, a London critic commented: 'for several generations Spain is supposed to have been in the background in the matter of high-class music', but 'we begin to be doubtful' of this idea.[70] Albéniz spent the greater part of the next ten years in England and northern Europe, travelling and giving concerts, a deliberate exile on which he entered because it gave him access to the sources of his music, to a public that truly appreciated him, and above all to the necessary financing, which he would not have found in Spain because of the absence of any musical infrastructure. 'Mine has been,' he wrote, 'a Homeric struggle against poverty.' During those years, however, he lived too well; his health gave way and he longed for the sunshine of Spain. 'I haven't stopped for a minute: trips to Paris, trips to London, trips to Belgium, concerts, competitions, in short, a life that is no life!' In August 1907 he wrote to a friend: 'my physical self turns every day more nationalist, complaining bitterly that it is not toasting in Spain; I am getting old, my bones, flesh and mind are slowing down.'[71] His musical imagination was centred on his native Catalonia, and like his mentor Felip Pedrell he was a musical nationalist, wedded to the idea of using folk music as the basis for composition. Casals said of him that 'the music he composed was greatly affected by his homeland of Catalonia, by its wonderful scenery and its folk melodies, and by the Arabic derivations of some of them. "I am a Moor", he used to say.'

Though his constant musical inspiration was Spain, he had no time for political Spain. News of the 1898 Disaster only confirmed him in his feeling of alienation from his country. 'I have decided to ignore what happens or might happen in Spain', he insisted.[72] Precisely because of this feeling, he made an effort to conjure up the authentic Spain he carried in his mind, and the years of absence from home gave birth to the most memorable of all his works. In 1897 in England he began a suite based on poems by his friend Money-Coutts. They were originally given the title *Alhambra*, but ended up with the title *La Vega*, meant to be a reflection on the plain ('*la vega*') before Granada. Between 1905 and 1908 he composed the twelve pieces, divided into four books, of his immortal suite *Iberia*, certainly the most significant piece of music composed by a Spaniard in the twentieth century. The first book was completed in Paris (which was now his main residence) in December 1905, and had its premiere in the same city the following May. At the end of 1906 the work was also premiered by a Catalan pianist in Barcelona and Madrid. The last book of the work was finished in Paris in the summer of 1907. The twelve pieces – beginning with 'Evocation', which conjures up a lyrical and nostalgic image of Spain – are picturesque and sometimes complex presentations of landscapes, places, festivities, dances and folk music. Poor health prevented Albéniz from undertaking their orchestration, which was carried out after his death.

Though Albéniz was a convinced enthusiast of European music, his absence abroad made him vividly aware of the need to create a musical tradition in Spain that was not a mere imitation of continental fashions. Years later, the Seville composer Joaquín Turina recounted an incident when he, Manuel de Falla and Albéniz were taking coffee in a Paris café in 1907. Albéniz, according to Turina, 'played the role of missionary, urging us to abandon all foreign influence and follow him in the task of creating a genuinely Spanish music'.[73] The insistence on orientating all his imagination towards Spain, from which he also drew most of his inspiration, is the reason why he chose voluntarily to exile himself from his country, as though he could attain creativity only outside its frontiers. The duty of Spain's artists, Albéniz affirmed, was to 'make Spanish music with a universal accent'.[74]

In April 1908 his deteriorating health obliged Albéniz to follow his doctor's advice. He left Paris and went with his wife and children for a rest cure in the Pyrenees, at Cambo-les-Bains, where in May he was visited by his friend the pianist Enrique Granados. Seated at Albéniz's bedside, Granados explained that he was just off to the United States for a round of concerts. Albéniz asked him to play something. Granados began to play a piece, then without warning changed to the barcarole *Mallorca*, written during a trip that the two had made there together. It was one of Albéniz's last lucid days, for the heavy doses of morphine he was taking rendered him unconscious. He died in May 1909, a few weeks before his forty-ninth birthday. The next day, by coincidence, the Grand Cross of the Légion d'honneur arrived from Paris for him. His body was taken back to Barcelona, where he was given a great civic reception, and then buried on the hillside of Montjuic.

Albéniz's friend and fellow Catalan Granados also died young. Like Albéniz, he was beginning to convert himself into a creative exile, for he also combined in the same measure a fervent love for Spain together with a profound rejection of established Spanish attitudes. In many respects his story parallels that of Albéniz. Enrique Granados (1868–1916), was born in Lleida (Catalonia) but his father had been born in Cuba and his mother came from Santander. The family moved to Barcelona, where from the age of thirteen he studied music under the pianist J. B. Pujol and won a prize in front of a jury that included Albéniz and Felip Pedrell. When his father died, Enrique had to help out his family by playing the piano in a cafeteria for five hours a day. His earnings helped in part to pay for a visit (1887–9) to Paris, where he took music classes at which his fellow students included Maurice Ravel and the Catalan Ricard Vinyes. He was also in contact with the most important French composers, especially Camille Saint-Saëns. In 1889 he returned to Barcelona to begin his career as a virtuoso and composer, arranging for the publication of his *Twelve Spanish Dances*, the first work to gain him international recognition, and the basis of his lasting popularity both in Spain and with the European public. In 1891 he helped to found the musical society Orfeó Català, but disliked the politicization of culture among both Catalans and Castilians. 'They wish,' he wrote, 'to give the Orfeó a politically Catalanist colour, and I do not agree with this. It seems to me that art has nothing to do with politics. This has earned me some unpleasant moments, even to receiving disdainful accusations that I write Andalusian dances! As though that were a crime! I consider myself as

Catalan as anyone else, but in my music I wish to express what I feel, what I admire and what pleases me, be it Andalusian or Chinese!'[75]

Granados's successes in the 1890s occurred mainly in Madrid and Barcelona, the two cities he made his home. In Barcelona he founded the Granados Academy, whose aim was to teach music to students in a way that broke with antiquated and (in his experience) fruitless methods. In Madrid he achieved success with a zarzuela called *María del Carmen*, effectively a Spanish version of Bizet's opera *Carmen*. He also had the opportunity to see in the capital some of the paintings of Francisco Goya, which inspired him to compose the piano suite *Goyescas* (1909–10), which he first performed in Barcelona in 1911. This remarkable work opened up new international horizons. He met the American pianist Ernest Schelling, and in 1913 Schelling performed the London premiere of the music. His next venture was to make the piano suite the basis of a one-act opera of the same name, written specially for the Metropolitan Opera in New York. Timed to last one hour, *Goyescas* described the tragic love-story of two couples, the bullfighter Paquiro and his friend Pepa, and the lady Rosario and her lover Fernando. A New York premiere was planned for 1916, so Granados and his wife sailed there at the end of 1915, even though the First World War had broken out in Europe. A few days before the night of the premiere, Granados and the Catalan cellist Casals put on a small concert together at the Ritz Carlton Hotel. The opera performance was a great success, so much so that he was invited in March to give a concert at the White House for President Wilson.

That same month he returned with his wife to England and then boarded the vessel *Sussex* for Spain. It was torpedoed by a German U-boat in the Channel and most of the passengers, including the pianist and his wife, were drowned. There was a stunned international reaction. A memorial concert was held two months later in New York, organized by Schelling and with performances by Paderewski, Kreisler and Casals. At the end of the concert a solitary candle was left flickering on the piano in the darkened hall, while Paderewski played Chopin's *Funeral March*. Granados had already in those months come into contact with a world with wider horizons than those of his own country. One of his last letters from America, written in Catalan, betrayed the potential exile: 'I am a Spaniard, a survivor of the sterile struggle to which we are subjected by the ignorance and indifference of our country. I dream of Paris and have a world of projects!'[76] The words were testimony to the strange situation of Spain's leading composers, who attempted to give musical identity to their country but failed to receive recognition. The work of Albéniz and Granados was little known to their contemporaries in Spain, and the two musicians achieved success and found an appreciative public only in cosmopolitan circles outside their own country.[77] Modern music in the European idiom was neither played nor practised in the peninsula, and symphony orchestras did not come into existence in Madrid or Barcelona until around 1910.

7

The Elite Diaspora of 1936–9

*Are those who throw us out of our country any less exiles than
we are?*   Gregorio Marañón (1947)[1]

The Second Republic came into existence, like the First (formed after
the expulsion of Isabella II, and short-lived), on the heels of dynastic
revolution and royal exile. In January 1930 Alfonso XIII forced the
highly unpopular Primo de Rivera to resign as prime minister, and the
latter retired to Paris, where his health gave way and he died within a
few months. The king found it hard to recover for the monarchy the
confidence that it had lost among the political classes during the seven
years of dictatorship from 1923. There were anti-monarchic plots in
the provinces, in the unions and in the army. An attempt at a rising
against the regime in 1930 failed, and it looked as though the king had
triumphed. But when municipal elections were called in the spring of
1931 they produced sweeping gains for the republicans, and the
politicians persuaded Alfonso that he must abdicate. The king collected his effects hastily and left by car for the port of Cartagena,
where he took ship for France. Every attempt since 1700 to establish
a stable monarchy had ended in kings and queens periodically pack-
ing their bags and leaving, some (Charles III of Habsburg, Isabella II,
Amadeo of Savoy, Alfonso XIII) for ever.

The Second Republic was proclaimed amid great hope and expectation, on 14 April 1931. The poet Antonio Machado described how
he and a group of other republicans raised the flag over the city hall
in Segovia:

With the first leaves of the poplars and the last almond blossoms, spring led in our Republic by the hand. Nature and history seemed to melt together into a fairy tale or a children's story. A day of peace, that astonished the whole world.

The intellectual class dreamed that the moment had come to right all the errors of the past and return to the Golden Age. One of the posters released for the occasion in Madrid showed a beautiful young girl, the 'Spanish Republic', wearing the red cap that the French normally used to depict their republic. For its supporters the early Republic continued to be '*la Niña Bonita*', the pretty girl. To underline the parallel, it was decided to hold the first session of the national assembly on 14 July, the date commemorating the French Revolution. In elections for a new Cortes, the Socialists emerged as the biggest party, though a controlling majority was held by the various groups who reflected different 'republican' persuasions. It was certainly the most 'intellectual' parliament in Spain's history. Men from the professional and bureaucratic middle classes, led by lawyers, teachers and university professors, made up over 80 per cent of the membership. Never before in European history had 'intellectuals', who since 1898 considered themselves potential saviours of the country, been given the opportunity to put their words into action. They took the chief posts in government. A Madrid newspaper, *El Sol*, remarked on 'the systematic promotion of intellectuals to all the executive positions in the state'.[2] But there were grave deficiencies in this potentially optimistic picture.[3] The collapse of and confusion among various right-wing groups that had supported the monarchy meant that the substantial conservative and Catholic sector in society was inadequately represented. By contrast, the overwhelming Socialist and republican victory misled deputies of those persuasions into believing that they alone represented Spain. That misapprehension was carried through in the framing of the new Constitution, which in Article 26 advanced towards open confrontation with the Church. 'We are going to carry out a surgical operation', the prime minister, Manuel Azaña, declared in a speech in October, adding the comment that the operation was going to be fatal for the patient. As it turned out, the operation would be fatal for the Republic.

In the streets and countryside the anarchist parties and trade unions, which distrusted parliamentary democracy, began to take measures, such as collectivization of landholdings and seizure of private property, that provoked armed reprisals. The first significant attempt at political violence occurred in the summer of 1932, when an attempted coup in Seville by General Sanjurjo and a group of right-wing officers failed. Over the next four years the situation deteriorated. Between 1934, when the army (on behalf of the Republic) brutally put down a revolutionary insurrection in the region of Asturias, and 1936, an increasingly embittered confrontation developed within Spanish society. The government attempted to placate all sides by accepting a coalition with conservatives, who finally demonstrated that they had strong electoral support, but this proved to be no solution.

In February 1936 general elections were held, in which a Popular Front coalition won 43 per cent of the vote, while the Right won 30 per cent and the Centre 21 per cent.[4] The biggest single party (the CEDA, of Catholic ideology) was on the Right. Under the prevailing electoral system, the votes translated into quite a different situation in the Cortes. The Popular Front swept up 60 per cent of the seats, giving it a controlling position that was confirmed when the electoral committee of the Cortes, run by a pro-Front group, manipulated a number of doubtful results in order to give the Front 67 per cent. An election that was evenly cast therefore ended in a solid Front majority. The new government proved unable to establish public order, which immediately deteriorated alarmingly as armed groups of anarchists, revolutionaries and (in retaliation) Fascists intensified the spiral of violence. For all practical purposes, the Republic collapsed.[5] Its failure, as a scholar has recently explained,[6] was provoked by the anti-democratic stance of all the principal protagonists: the left-wing anarchists, Socialists and Communists, who believed that the revolution was on its way and must (as in Soviet Russia) be accelerated by violent means; the Azaña government, which depended on them for survival and was afraid to choose more moderate allies; and the Right, which knew that if public order collapsed they could rely on conservative figures in the armed forces.

After the victory of the Popular Front, in both Barcelona and Madrid the streets passed into the control of radicals who set out to gain the initiative in a situation that had given them the electoral advantage. A rapid descent into street bloodshed and anticlerical attacks ensued. The principal target was the Church. Violence and coercion created an atmosphere of fear, which had its most terrifying impact on Madrid. In the sessions of the Cortes the conservative leader, José María Gil Robles, read out every week lists of statistics published in the press. In June 1936 he summarized the figures to date. From February to now, he said, the effects of the street violence were: 'churches totally destroyed 160, attacks on places of worship 251, deaths 269, wounded 1,287, acts of violence against persons 215, robberies 138, attempted robberies 23, political centres destroyed 69, centres attacked 312, general strikes 113, partial strikes 228, newspaper offices destroyed 10, attacks on newspapers 33, bombs 146'. Unamuno was among those who expressed publicly his shock and disgust at the way in which the Republic had handed the streets over to thugs. For the right-wing political opposition, the last straw was the murder of their parliamentary leader, Calvo Sotelo, in reprisal for that of an officer in the security forces. The killing could have been stomached had it been just another in the long line of murders taking place at that time. But this time it was different, for the victim had been seized in his house by members of the Republican state security.

Right-wing politicians were in little doubt that order would have to be imposed through an army rebellion, but some Communists and Socialists were optimistic that they could deal with the threat. Any coup, they felt, would be crushed as Sanjurjo's had been in 1932. However, when the expected military rising took place on 18 July 1936 it opened a Pandora's box that intensified polarization in the country, because it pushed most leftist groups immediately into an uncompromising policy of revolution. The Republic had, over a period of five years, failed to be the democratic regime for which people had hoped. Armed conflict was already in some measure the order of the day when the miners of Asturias revolted in 1934 and leftist parties began to turn to revolution as a solution. The entry of the army into the struggle completed the process. A full-blown civil war might still have been avoided if either side had won the initiative at the outset, but the coup failed to win Madrid, Barcelona and the greater part of Spanish territory, making a prolonged conflict inevitable.

Unamuno gave his support to the uprising, which seemed to offer a hope of law and order. He was removed from the rectorship of Salamanca University by the Republican ministry in Madrid, but the Nationalists had control of Salamanca and confirmed him in office. A week after the rising the rebels constituted a new city council, which Unamuno attended as an elected member, expressing his solidarity with the army because 'we have to save western civilization, which is in danger'. Already in those few days the rebels had rounded up and summarily executed hundreds of people, but Unamuno felt it was simply a 'cleaning-up operation'. Soon the executions came to include university colleagues he knew, friends, officials, even his students. At the beginning of October Franco was in Salamanca, as new Head of State, and on the twelfth Unamuno as rector, and in Franco's name, presided over a celebration of the 'Day of the Race' (see Chapter 9), which coincided with the opening of the university year. University professors spoke of the evils of the moment, of communism, of the treason of Catalans and Basques, all punctuated by approving cries from the public of 'Spain! Spain!' Finally Unamuno said a word. 'I said I did not intend to speak,' he said, 'but I cannot be silent.' He spoke concisely and openly. He had until now believed in the 'war to defend Christian civilization', but what was happening now was an 'uncivil war' charged with hate, and 'hate that leaves no room for compassion cannot win'. 'You have neither right nor reason on your side', he went on. His last words were lost in the ensuing protests, cries and confusion; soldiers came forward, waving their guns and insulting the speaker. General José Millán Astray, Franco's bizarre right-hand man and founder of the Foreign Legion, screamed out, 'Death to intellectuals!' and 'Long live death!' The expletives were revelatory of the limits of the general's originality: the first was by now a standard one directed against the 'intellectuals' who had supported the Republic, the second was the slogan of the Foreign Legion. Unamuno had to be helped out of the angry crowd. He had, shortly before, denounced the murders committed in the name of the Republic in Madrid. Now, in one of his last letters, he denounced the new rebel state as 'a stupid regime of terror', which threatened to bring 'death to freedom of conscience, freedom of investigation, the dignity of man'.[8] Shortly after, on New Year's Eve, he died of stroke in the course of a heated argument over Fascist Italy. Ortega y Gasset, who was in Buenos Aires when he received the news the following day, wrote:

I do not know the medical details of his end, but whatever they are I am sure he died of 'the Spanish sickness'. His individual death has joined the innumerable deaths that today make up the life of Spain. He did well. His task is completed. In these months so many of our fellow citizens have died, that we survivors feel strangely ashamed at not having died as well.

Another writer who expressed his detestation of both sides was the novelist Pio Baroja (1872–1956), who by the year 1936 had developed a firmly held view about the barbarism of both factions in the political confrontation, detested the political class, and despised both the Left and the Right, not to mention the allegedly democratic Republic and Spain itself, which he saw as inadequate and pathetic. Born at San Sebastian in the heart of the Basque country, the son of a mining engineer, he studied medicine in Madrid, qualified as a doctor and found a post in his home province. However, after a year he gave up his practice and moved to Madrid where he helped his brother to manage a bakery. He combined the work with a dedication to writing, which soon occupied all his time. In 1899 he visited the literary capital, Paris, where he met fellow Spaniards as well as Oscar Wilde. On his return, he became immersed in the world of journalism, and made several journeys abroad, mainly to Paris. A solitary, sullen, figure, he never married and his outlook towards others tended always to be resentful. This attitude is easier to understand when we realize that his favourite thinkers were the great German pessimists Schopenhauer and Nietzsche. From 1912 he came into possession of the country house 'Itzea', in the beautiful mountain area of Vera de Bidasoa in northern Navarre, where he lived alone with his mother until her death in 1935. As a misanthrope, he was hostile to most norms and ideals, professing himself at various times to be anticlerical, anti-Catholic, anti-Semitic, anti-democratic, anti-capitalist and anti-socialist. 'I have always been a radical liberal, an individualist and an anarchist', he declared on one occasion. His first publication, called *Lives in Shadow* (*Vidas sombrías*) (1900), was written on the basis of material jotted down during his year as a doctor. Later he was producing books at the rate of two a year, novels that appeared to be randomly written, almost fragments of narrative.

He used to spend the summer months away from Madrid, in 'Itzea'. When the military uprising of July 1936 took place, Baroja was staying there with a doctor friend. A military column of Carlists, a political group that supported the uprising, had orders to detain the two men, but they were released the next day. Baroja explains: 'in the village nobody could guarantee that the incident would not recur, so I decided to go to France, which is only five kilometres away from Vera'.[9] He collected what he needed, set out walking, and a passing motorist gave him a lift to the frontier. During a stop at Hendaye, he wrote:

in this revolutionary and absurd adventure on which Spain was fully embarked, I felt incapable of putting my confidence in politics. It was difficult for a Spaniard, unless he were a fanatic or a dreamer, to be optimistic about the possibility of supporting one or other of the sectors into which our country appeared divided. As for ideology, I found it difficult, since both sides seemed to me equally poor, wretched and mediocre.

He eventually ended up in Paris, where he lived in the Colegio de España in the university city, writing articles for the Buenos Aires press and keeping in touch with events in Spain. Alone in Paris, he quickly got depressed. He visited Spain briefly in 1938, but never felt safe and left again for Paris. When the imminent German invasion threatened Paris, he left in 1940 for Bayonne, on the Basque frontier. That autumn, he returned to Vera de Bidasoa and Madrid.

He wrote his memoirs many years later, and only in 2005 has the final volume emerged into print. The deeply misanthropic vision at which he arrived had been a long time maturing. In these final memoirs he says: 'I have never professed to have any special political attitude. I had none. I am a spectator, a curious onlooker, nothing more.' About the men of quality who directed public life, he held that 'there have been very few, because the majority were mediocrities, at least in Spain'. After condemning both Left and Right, he yearns for (this part of his memoirs referred to the 1950s) 'the great men who tried to explain the world: Democritus and Epicurus, Lucretius and Marcus Aurelius, Copernicus and Kant'. He goes on to say: 'our age is not one of explanation, but of darkness and a stupid fury'. On the Civil War, he wrote: 'No one can maintain that the governments of the Republic were effective, or fair or sensible. It was an orgy of unchecked appetites.' His final judgement in that period was: 'There is no way of knowing how we are going to emerge from this terrible convulsion, which is the most serious disease that Spain has had in centuries.'[10]

The so-called 'intellectual' class, meaning the educated middle class of the educational, political, medical and other professions, with its long-standing adherence to republicanism, liberalism and socialism, faced some difficult decisions but failed to come up with any adequate answer. Intelligence alone was no guarantee of solutions. Indeed by 1933 the role of so-called 'intelligence' in politics was being openly, and justifiably, questioned. Writers of all political persuasions directed their attacks against those who, they felt, had betrayed the Republic into the hands of chaos and demagogy. They took as their point of departure one of the most influential essays of that generation, the French scholar Julien Benda's La trahison des clercs (The Treason of the Intellectuals) (1927). Benda accused the intellectuals of his time of abandoning the programme of the Enlightenment, the search for truth and scholarly ideals, in favour of political ideologies of race and class. They were, he claimed, fostering 'the intellectual organization of political hatreds', and therefore committing treason against society and humanity. The failure of those who had promised a better future through the Republic was evident. On the Right, Ramiro de Maeztu criticized the literary men who now ran politics. From the Left, the poet José Bergamín blamed intellectuals directly for the collapse of the Republic: 'the Republic slipped out of their hands',[11] a statement that betrayed his conviction that the educated elite had it in their power to save the country. Among the most perceptive judgements was the report sent home to his newspaper in Buenos Aires by a journalist who wrote in 1937: 'this superstition of the all-knowing "intellectual" is at the root of the tragedy we are witnessing'.[12]

In the spring of 1936 there was still cohesion among writers who supported the Republic, although some, like Rafael Alberti, were working actively to by-pass non-Communist supporters and concentrate instead on a core of 'anti-Fascist' names, who included particularly Buñuel, Machado and García Lorca. As late as the end of May 1936, when a group of French writers under André Malraux visited Madrid in the name of France's Popular Front government, there was still enough broad support to unite at a dinner of honour names as diverse in tendency as Alberti, Sánchez-Albornoz and Américo Castro. This common front quickly collapsed. The theme is relevant at this point because it explains why some Spaniards saw immediate exile as the only viable option, and others committed themselves to the struggle until they ended up on the losing side and were also forced into exile. It was a time to take sides, but the degree of commitment was tempered always by the knowledge that terrible atrocities were being perpetrated. There was fear in the street and fear in the home. We can observe events more closely through two specific murders of those days.

The poet Federico García Lorca was in Madrid when the rising occurred. Lorca (1898–1936), the best known of Spain's modern poets, was also an active dramatist. He was born in Andalusia, near Granada, and educated in Granada and later in Madrid, where he lived (in 1919) in the Residencia de Estudiantes. He learnt music from Falla, becoming proficient on both the guitar and the piano. As a poet he collaborated with Juan Ramón Jiménez, and built up a special friendship with the thoroughly nonconformist young men Dalí and Buñuel. Dalí, who met Lorca in 1923, was excited by him: 'the poetic phenomenon in its entirety presented itself before me suddenly in flesh and bone, viscous and sublime, quivering with a thousand fires of darkness and of subterranean biology' (he wrote later in his *Secret Life*). Lorca's homosexuality determined his friendships but in the case of Dalí the element of intellectual excitement was undoubtedly stronger. Lorca quickly became established as a poet, in particular for his literary rendering of the gypsy music of Andalusia. He was also profoundly committed to the theatre, and in 1927 gained fame with his romantic historical play *Marina Pineda*, where the scenery was constructed by Dalí. He was soon the best-known poet of his day, thanks to the publication in 1928 of his *Primer Romancero Gitano*. He visited New York briefly (1929–30) but hated it, and escaped to Havana (the American experiences were the basis for his *A Poet in New York*, published after his death). He was back in Spain by 1931, an active supporter of the Republic and director of a theatrical company which put on plays for the people in the provinces. The death of a bullfighter friend, Ignacio Sánchez Mejías, inspired his best-known and possibly most-quoted poem, *Lament for the Death of a Bullfighter* (1935). This was also the period of his theatrical trilogy of peasant life, *Blood Wedding*.

The themes of his work, pride, passion and death, also marked his own life. Exactly four weeks before the military rising of 1936, he had just finished writing his play *The House of Bernarda Alba*, and decided to return to his home town of Granada, before undertaking a visit he had planned to New York.[13] Madrid was in the throes of violence and tension. Lorca was in full career as a successful poet and director of popular theatre, working actively in Madrid to support the crumbling Popular Front. He returned to a Granada that was in full control of the rebels, busy purging the city of 'reds', and hid in a friend's house. He was flushed out on a Sunday afternoon, 16 August, and taken to the military headquarters. Since the prisoner was well known, the commander consulted with his superior, General Queipo de Llano, about what to do with him. 'Give him coffee, lots of coffee (*café*)' was the reply (at that time the initials CAFE signified, to those who knew, '*Camaradas, ¡Arriba Falange Española!*', that is, 'Comrades, long live the Spanish Falange party!'). Two days later the prisoner was taken outside the city and murdered together with three other victims. One of the executioners, who claimed to be 'sick of queers', for added measure fired two shots up Lorca's backside.

Lorca was never in outlook or intention an exile (though some commentators claim to have discerned suicidal elements in his writing), and was passionately committed to his art, his friends and his convictions. He appears in this narrative because he was the most notorious victim of a period of violence that wreaked extensive damage on Spain's cultural scene. He also became in time a symbol of the violence exercised by the vulgar and ignorant element of the Nationalists against all cultural figures who did not share their views. It is easy to understand, on the basis of what happened to Lorca, why thousands among the educated elite of Spain opted for exile rather than run the risk of living in a country where uncontrolled mortal confrontation was the order of the day. It is of course true that the violence and cruelty of those supporting Franco was visibly greater only because the Nationalists turned out to be the victors of the civil conflict, and continued the violence from a position of military superiority. The violence and cruelty on the losing Republic side was no less intense, and was in the same way carried out by vulgar, ignorant and fanatical elements, as any conversation with those who have memories of that war will confirm.

In Madrid the military uprising added fire and fury to the already lawless state of the capital. Control of the streets passed into the hands of '*comisiones de investigación*' ('commissions of enquiry') set up by leftist political groups and trade unions associated with the Popular Front government, who rounded up suspects and herded them into empty prisons and churches. The committees received the grisly name of '*checas*', from the Russian name for the secret police[14] set up in that country after the Soviet Revolution. In reality, it has been pointed out, the whole city became a *checa* in the second half of 1936,[15] with about 250 *checas* active, according to a priest who had direct contact.[16] Thousands (the numbers have never been established) of guiltless citizens and clergy were dragged from their homes, locked up for days and weeks without any access to the outside world, then, without any formal accusation, taken from their cells and shot. There was no legal process, no written record of either arrests or executions, and the committees of judges were secret. Victims were seized because they were politically inconvenient, because their money could be taken, or simply because they had personal enemies. One of these victims was the writer and parliamentary deputy Ramiro de Maeztu, perhaps the most noted intellectual of the Right, whose fortunes we shall follow later (Chapter 8). At the time of his arrest and murder there were around five thousand people detained by the *checas* of Madrid. On 7 and 8 November, with the forces of General Franco threatening Madrid, and at a time when the Communist Santiago Carrillo was one of the officials in charge of Public Order, a fleet of buses transported two thousand of the detainees to the outlying villages of Paracuellos del Jarama and Torrejón de Ardoz, where they were summarily massacred and their bodies thrown into mass graves. Further mass murders took place in the following weeks. A few months later the Comintern agent in Madrid, Georgi Dimitrov, reported to Voroshilov in the Kremlin: 'When the Fascists were nearing Madrid, Carrillo, who was in control at the time, gave the order to shoot the arrested Fascist functionaries.'[17]

The brutality of the year 1936 in Republican Madrid had its equal in the city of Barcelona, where *checas* also operated. The Church was the principal victim, as we have had occasion to observe, with over five hundred clergy murdered that year in the diocese of Madrid alone. For our purposes, there is no point in giving details of the thousands of Spaniards of all ranks, conditions and ideologies who were pitilessly done to death on both sides, whether supporters of the Republic or supporters of the uprising.[18] The end result was the creation of an inhuman situation from which families tried to save their loved ones. The onset of war only made the situation worse. In towns and villages that the military rebels came to occupy, they made it their first duty to exterminate all opposition, with inevitable and horrifying consequences. At the same time, in areas of the Republican zone the authorities sanctioned executions by putting the apparatus of repression into the hands of '*jurados populares*' ('people's juries').[19] In so-called democratic Spain, terror became commonplace. The Nationalist repression, for its part, had two significant features with a permanent impact on the memory of Spaniards. First, unlike the Republican massacres, which often took place because of a loss of control, the Nationalist massacres were officially approved and carried out by the forces of the military authorities. Second, the repression continued relentlessly into the post-war years.

The uncontrolled violence of those weeks in the summer of 1936 explains why thousands fled when there appeared to be no other option. A radical deputy of the Cortes, a woman, testified to the fear that gripped the upper classes in the Republican zone: 'the appearance of Madrid was incredible: the bourgeoisie giving the clenched-fist salute, men in overalls [instead of suits], women bareheaded . . . people who humbly begged permission to remain alive'.[20] They addressed each other as '*camarada*' instead of '*señor*', and farewells dropped the form '*adios*', because it mentioned God, in favour of '*salud*' ('greetings!'). In Barcelona the middle classes immediately hid their suits and ties, because it was dangerous to be seen on the streets in elegant dress. The intellectuals had to make their own decisions. The cellist Casals escaped to France. The diplomat Salvador de Madariaga was urged by the government in Madrid to leave because the anarchist vigilantes had him on their extermination list. He passed through a Barcelona in total chaos, and by good fortune the Communist guards allowed him to cross over the French frontier on 1 August, two weeks after the military uprising. President Azaña admitted openly, in 1937, that the situation was out of control: 'we were the prisoners of anarchists and Communists. We really were.'[21]

The majority of intellectuals who chose exile did so not out of support for one side or the other, but because their lives were not safe under the Republic. On 16 June 1936, over a month before the beginning of the rebellion, a deputy of the Lliga Catalana party, Joan Ventosa, asked his colleagues in the Cortes:

Are we perpetually condemned in Spain to live in a regime of successive conflicts, in which the rise to power or triumph in elections initiates the hunting down, persecution or liquidation of adversaries? If that were so, we would have to renounce being Spaniards, because civilized life would be incompatible with our country.[22]

From the first, the poet Rafael Alberti supported the killings as an acceptable way of defeating the military uprising and bringing about the Communist revolution. He attacked the middle-class Republican supporters and commented sourly later that 'Ortega, Marañón, Ayala, deserted when they found out that the policy of white gloves had to become stained with the blood of the enemy'.[23] Alberti also took the lead in pointing out who should be purged from public life. Under pressure from a committee he headed, and on the very day that Maeztu was arrested, a group of thirteen intellectuals, including Ramón Menéndez Pidal, Antonio Machado, Gregorio Marañón, Ramón Pérez de Ayala, Juan Ramón Jiménez and José Ortega y Gasset, were pressured into allowing their names to appear on a document declaring their support for the Republic. Ortega later explained laconically how his signature had been obtained (Marañón's was obtained the same way): 'With a pistol at my head, I had to sign what four young men demanded.'[24] The Republic later used the document in its propaganda, but most of those whose names were on the list were already preparing to flee.

1. The expulsion of the Jews from Spain in 1492, stipulated in the decree illustrated here, generated many myths and prefigured the expulsion of disapproved minorities in subsequent centuries.

2. Juan Luis Vives, an exile from the age of sixteen, became a luminary of Renaissance humanism in northern Europe and an example of Spaniards who triumphed outside their homeland but were forgotten inside it.

3. Excluded almost completely from the cultural memory of Christians, Moorish Spain had to wait till the nineteenth century before Europeans recognized its importance. Mariano Fortuny's romantic evocation of the Muslim past, as in his *Judgement in the Alhambra of Granada* (1871), contributed to the rebirth of interest.

alias Reves.   Sichem fecit.

MICHAEL SERVETVS HISPANVS DE ARAGONIA

4. A brilliant and restless spirit, resident outside Spain from the age of seventeen, Miguel Servet drew on radical religious ideas circulating in France and Germany, but fell foul of the Calvinists and was burned alive at Geneva, as shown in this eighteenth-century print.

5. The refugee ex-monk Casiodoro de Reina published the first complete text of the Protestant Bible in Spanish in 1569 in Basle. It became known as the 'Bear Bible' because of the print on the first page.

PRAGMATICA
SANCION
DE SU MAGESTAD
EN FUERZA DE LEY
PARA EL ESTRAÑAMIENTO DE ESTOS
Reynos á los Regulares de la Compañia, ocupacion
de sus Temporalidades, y prohibicion de su restableci-
miento en tiempo alguno, con las demás pre-
cauciones que expresa.

Año   1767.

EN MADRID.
En la Imprenta Real de la Gazeta.

6. Following the example of France and Portugal, in 1767 Spain took the surprising step of expelling members of the Society of Jesus from all its territories. For the first, but not the last, time Catholic clergy suffered a punishment previously imposed only on non-Catholic Spaniards.

7. Goya's *The Second of May*, referring to the Madrid anti-French riots of the year 1808 but painted six years later, depicted the violence that made the early decades of the nineteenth century the peak period for exile but also for cultural regeneration, especially among refugees.

8. Rediscovery of the Muslim heritage, triggered in part by foreign writers and artists, encouraged Spaniards to produce their own revaluation of the past. *Odalisque*, by Fortuny, painted in Rome in 1861 shortly after a visit to Morocco, emphasizes the exotic and erotic aspects.

J. A. *Llorente,*

Auteur de L'histoire de l'Inquisition

mort à Madrid le 5 Février 1823

9. Juan Antonio Llorente's four-volume *History of the Inquisition*, published in exile in Paris in 1817, revolutionized understanding of the tribunal and remained the standard history for a century.

J. Slater. 17 Newman Street. 1812.

10. A refugee from the wars in Spain, José María Blanco White settled in England in 1810 and made significant contributions to literature and ideas, in both Spanish and English, but was scrupulously forgotten for two centuries by his former countrymen.

11. The Navarrese violinist Pablo Sarasate made a brilliant career in Europe and achieved fame on both sides of the Atlantic, but was largely forgotten in Spain.

12. Isaac Albéniz's suite *Iberia* gave Spain for the first time a piece of music that earned a European reputation. His autographed sheet notes, in English and in French, identify Paris as the place of creation.

13. The highly successful novelist Vicente Blasco Ibáñcz photographed in exile, surrounded by friends at the Café de La Rotonde in Paris in 1928, the year of his death. Blasco is third from the left; on his left sits the exiled writer Miguel de Unamuno.

14. An early work, *Bottle and Fruit Dish* (1917), by Juan Gris, whose entire oeuvre was produced in France and who remained unrecognized in Spain for most of the twentieth century.

15. Castile's principal essayist of modern times, José Ortega y Gasset, who argued for regeneration in Spain's culture and was among the many who sought safety in exile in 1936.

16. Dalí's *Soft Construction with Boiled Beans (Premonition of Civil War)*, created in Paris in 1936.

17. The most famous artistic commentary on the Spanish Civil War, Picasso's *Guernica*, painted in 1937 in Paris, achieved worldwide fame before eventually finding a permanent home in a Madrid art gallery.

18. An exception to Joan Miró's normally apolitical stance, this angry appeal for help was painted in the shape of a large postage stamp.

19. Composer Manuel Falla, seen here in the early days of his international fame, spent the last years of his life in exile.

20. The poet Rafael Alberti dedicated his creative energy to the Communist cause in the Civil War, when this photo was taken, but wrote the bulk of his verse in exile in Argentina and Italy.

21. A rebel against society, the film director Luis Buñuel had little opportunity to develop his talents because of the outbreak of the Civil War, and his best-known films were produced in Mexico and France. He is seen here during the shooting of *Belle de Jour* (1967) with Catherine Deneuve.

22. A child prodigy who quickly achieved world fame, the cellist Pablo Casals pursued his musical career in exile in the south of France and in the United States, particularly in Puerto Rico. The photo shows him and his young wife Marta being received by the Kennedys at the White House.

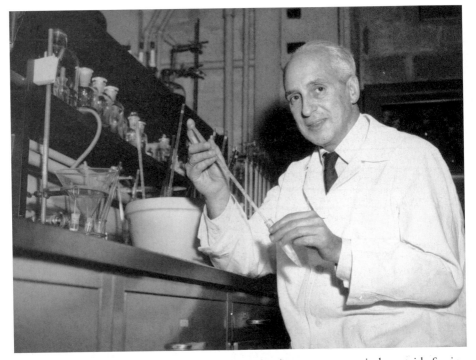

23. Severo Ochoa's distinguished career as a scientist was spent entirely outside Spain, particularly in the USA, where his research earned him a Nobel Prize in 1959.

24. Seen here shortly before his death, the poet and Nobel winner Juan Ramón Jiménez was a depressive who owed much of his inspiration to his wife, Zenobia. 'It is she', he informed the Nobel Prize committee, 'who really deserves the prize.'

25. Doyen of Spain's liberal intellectuals in the early twentieth century, Gregorio Marañón combined his achievements in medical science with those in the humanities.

26. An active scholar and politician, best known for his work in international peace-keeping bodies, Salvador de Madariaga (*in the foreground*) is seen here in 1948 at a session of the Political Commission of the Congress of Europe at The Hague.

27. Through his historical studies at Princeton from the 1940s Américo Castro influenced a whole generation of non-Spanish scholars, but his views were frowned upon in Spain.

When he got wind of the military uprising, Ortega feared that he would become a victim of the Republican vigilantes in Madrid and moved house to live with his father-in-law. The French embassy arranged for him to obtain a passport, and he and his family left by train on 31 August for the port of Alicante, where they took ship for France. By November he was in Paris. He was chronically ill for the next few months, and remained bedridden. His two sons, meanwhile, enrolled in the Nationalist army, as did those of Marañón and other exiles. Opinion among French intellectuals tended to support the Republic, leaving Ortega somewhat isolated. 'These past months,' he commented in 1937, 'dragging myself alone through the streets of Paris, I realized that I didn't really know this great city, only the statues. And since I had no one to talk to, I chatted to them about the great themes of humanity.'[25] Bound more to German culture than French, he felt isolated in Paris, but ruled out the Anglo-Saxon countries as a refuge since his sympathies were with Germany rather than with its enemies. In 1942 and 1943 he was still publishing works in Germany.[26] In 1939 he moved to Portugal. Soon afterwards, he accepted an invitation to lecture in Argentina, where he spent the next three years. When he returned to Portugal in 1942 he spoke of Argentina as a 'country where things did not go well for me', an opinion shared by Sánchez-Albornoz, who wrote to Ortega that 'my life in this extremity of the world is a sequence of unhappy days, loneliness and misery, life has forced me to endure with Iberian pride my relations with this riff raff'.[27]

In December 1936 Gregorio Marañón, who received various threats to his life in Madrid, also fled with his family to Alicante and managed to get away in an English destroyer. Years later he testified:

Eighty-eight per cent of the university teachers of Madrid, Valencia and Barcelona have had to flee abroad, abandon Spain, escape in any possible way. And do you know why? Quite simply because they were afraid of being murdered by the Reds, even though many of the threatened intellectuals were known to be men of the left. Do you understand, dear friends? Among those who are outside their country, refugees from Red Spain, are [here follows a long list, which I have abbreviated]: D. Ramón Menéndez Pidal; D. José Ortega y Gasset; D. Gregorio Marañón; Pérez de Ayala; Pi y Suñer, a Catalan doctor with a world reputation; Puig y Cadafalch, former president of the autonomous government of Catalonia and a leading architect; Baroja; Azorín; Agustín Calvet, director of *La Vanguardia* of Barcelona; Carlos Soldevila, Catalonia's intellectual; Eugenio d'Ors; José María de Sagarra, the poet of Barcelona; Pedro Salinas, professor and poet; Salvador de Madariaga; Juan Ramón Jiménez; Américo Castro, who shares together with Ramón Gómez de la Serna and other intellectuals the nostalgia of exile in Buenos Aires; D. Rafael Altamira, professor of history; the professor and Arabist D. Miguel Asín Palacios . . . I won't go on. I could continue filling sheets of paper. Among those who are deemed incompatible with Red Spain are a president of the Republic, D. Niceto Alcalá Zamora; a president of the Cortes of the Republic, D. Santiago Alba; three presidents of the Council of Ministers of the Republic; . . . and the cream of the ex-ministers and personalities of the Lliga Regionalista (Cambó, Ventosa, Rodés, Bertrán y Musitú) are now outside their native land . . . I could cite you twice the number of refugees . . .[28]

The breakdown of order was, very clearly, the direct cause of the first great wave of emigration of cultural figures from Spain. It has become habitual to affirm that progressive intellectuals left the country 'in 1939', thereby associating their exile with rejection of the Franco regime.[29] The truth is that the most prominent cultural figures went into exile not at the end of the war but at its beginning, around 1936. And they chose exile because they were disillusioned with the failure of the Republic rather than because they opposed a hypothetical future Fascist tyranny. The cream of those who left, virtually all of them liberals and supporters of the democratic regime that had come to birth in 1931, did so long before 1939 and mainly because they were fleeing from the Republican terror. Some, of course, were fleeing from the violence of the assassins on both sides, both Nationalists and Republicans. Yet their disappointment was principally with the Republic, which they had supported, and not with the army, to which they had never given support. The testimony of the poet Juan Ramón Jiménez is unequivocal:

My wife and I realized very quickly that like the majority of writers and artists we were doing nothing in Madrid, and were in constant and stupid danger, since Madrid was full of people of all parties and all persuasions and all intentions, and we decided to ask my friend premier Azaña for permission to leave for the United States. It was arranged in one day. I was offered some diplomatic posts which I did not accept, save for one as 'honorary cultural attaché' in Washington. We left with two cases, a change of underclothes, a suit, some medicine (I was very ill) and our wedding rings.[30]

His wife Zenobia added her own testimony in her diaries: 'The worst thing about Madrid was the murder that threatened behind the front lines, and the terrible suspicion of one's neighbour. You cannot die happy in the company of assassins.'[31] Jiménez was offered a Communist guard as protection by Alberti but he turned the offer down. He was later criticized, as were other refugees, for abandoning ship at a moment of crisis, but explained that he had long-standing commitments that year in New York and in Puerto Rico.[32] He and his wife left via Valencia and Catalonia, then crossed France and took the steamer from Cherbourg. He remained a Republican all his life, despite his experience. In an interview in 1937 he stated: 'I regret very profoundly many things that happened in Republican Spain, but my position is unchanged, and because such things have happened on one side I am not going to defect to the other.'[33]

Azaña recognized that the blame lay on his side, and noted sourly in his diary in June 1937: 'Leading and even eminent Republicans have deserted (unfortunately, very many). Why? I don't know. They have all left without my agreement and against my advice, and some (I can name them) deceiving me. All of them had the duty to serve the Republic until the last moment, and to stay at my side as long as I remained standing.' Yet the Republic was unable to guarantee the safety of those who supported it.

Among the refugees of those days was the writer José Martínez Ruiz (1873–1967), who used the pen-name Azorín (taken from the name of a character he invented in a novel in 1902). Born in Monóvar (Valencia), he was a close friend and admirer of Blasco Ibáñez, though the two later had serious differences of opinion. He first went to Madrid in 1896, afire with wild anarchist ideas that he slowly modified, though he never lost the urge to shock and provoke. One of his significant public acts was the visit of homage organized in 1901 to the grave of Mariano José de Larra, when Azorín read out a speech honouring the dead master. Like some other writers he adopted poses, combining his revolutionary ideas with a disconcerting appearance of well-greased hair, a monocle and a trimmed moustache, carrying everywhere what became his hallmark, a brilliant red silk umbrella. Known to be a shy, introverted person, he progressed through a surprising range of political tendencies. In his youth an advocate of revolution, then in the 1930s a supporter of federalism and socialism, in his last phase he matured towards liberal conservatism and coexistence with the Franco regime.

His essential medium of expression was the essay, which he filled out with vague, flowery phrases that seemed to soar above reality without quite getting to grips with it. In this way he carefully avoided committing himself to specific causes, or at best was able to give support to some matters while avoiding others. One of his best-known works was the collection of newspaper articles published as *Castile* (1912), which communicated poetic impressions of elements of the landscape – railways, cathedrals, inns – and what they signified to the viewer.[34] When the Republic was born in 1931 he greeted it enthusiastically: 'Spain will recover its historic meaning, its true tradition, interrupted by the succession to the throne of the Habsburgs and the Bourbons'.[35] By 1933 his sympathies had cooled, and he came to see communism, on the one hand, and militarism on the other as the two great enemies. He was shunned by both camps, a situation in which several other writers found themselves and which made their exile virtually inevitable. In 1934 he commented that 'there have always been Spaniards who have called other Spaniards "anti-Spain"'.[36] When the February elections gave power to the extreme Left he no longer had doubts. In his articles he lapsed into a total silence on political matters.

Early in August 1936, when the Republican terror in Madrid appeared to be sparing nobody, Azorín and his wife made their way to Catalonia and thence to Paris, where he could breathe more freely and write without fear. From Paris he wrote articles for *La Prensa* of Buenos Aires, and published his books there. Though he wrote about Spain, he avoided mentioning the conflict or its implications. When the war was ending, in January 1939, he tried to press the new regime to allow the non-combatant exiles back. He wrote to Marañón, whom he saw as the leader of the small group of exiles in Paris:

You must try to bring about the return to Spain of its exiled intellectuals, without distinction of ideology, you must act so that they do with the intellectuals, the opposite of what the duke of Lerma, to the shame of Spain, did with the Moriscos.

A week later he sent the same message to the Franco government:

Spain will be deprived of one thousand of its intellectual workers. Of this number, three hundred are indisputably eminent. You will conquer the territory but the area of the nation will be deprived of its spirit. What sort of Spain is it – the world will ask – from which its most illustrious sons flee voluntarily, even if not proscribed?[37]

He received no response, but returned to Madrid at the end of the summer. Though he made several gestures towards the Franco regime, Azorín was in reality, as his writings show, a committed liberal, a dedicated colleague of writers of all opinions, and a profound admirer of French creativity. He returned briefly to his esteemed Paris (even though, as he confessed, 'I don't speak French, I have an absolute incapacity for learning languages'), but his home thereafter was in Madrid.

One of the noted sympathizers of the military uprising to remain in exile was the Catalan Eugenio d'Ors. Ors (1881–1954) was one of the most outstanding intellectuals of Spain, today undeservedly relegated to the shadows because of the way his political views developed. Born into a rich Barcelona family, he was raised and educated in the Catalan capital, where during his formative years the cultural movement known as Modernism exercised almost total control over all aspects of artistic and literary creativity. Imported wholesale from Paris, where it had originated, Modernism rose to new heights of expression in the hands of the imaginative and vigorous Catalan upper class, which peppered the capital with decorative art and luxurious residences in the new style. Ors became a brilliant star in the Barcelona firmament, as newspaper columnist and art critic, frequenting groups in the café *Quatre Gats*. But he also began to question whether Modernism really held anything of promise for Catalonia. In rejecting the romanticism of Modernist art and the naivety of appeals to the folkloric past, he attempted to formulate new approaches, in both artistic and philosophical terms. He coined a term for this new approach, *Noucentisme* ('twentieth-century-ism'), which he defined as being essentially a programme for 'civilizing' the city and province. For a young man of only twenty-five, it was an ambitious start.

From 1906 he began a stay of four years in Paris as correspondent of the Barcelona paper *The Voice of Catalonia*, sending home regular contributions to a daily column titled 'The Glossary' (*El Glosari*), over the pseudonym 'Xenius'. It became the vehicle for his ideas, and brought the cosmopolitanism of Paris to the backwoods of Catalonia. The writer Josep Pla commented: 'young people today cannot imagine the sensation produced in our intellectual world by the *Glosari* of *La Veu de Catalunya*'. Ors communicated to his readers the excitement of new ideas from Europe and even from America (after discovering the work of William James he declared himself to be a 'pragmatist' as well). However, it was another matter to get people back home to accept the possibility of a new way of thinking.

After he returned to Spain he attempted to get a university chair in Madrid but was turned down. That same year, 1914, his friends in Catalonia secured for him the post of director of education in the province. His entry into politics excited envy and hostility, and a carefully planned campaign among sections of the Catalan elite removed him unexpectedly from the post in 1920. In profound disgust, he exiled himself from his native soil (and its language) and moved his activity to Madrid, where he was received with open arms, found employment, and received the honours that his own region had always denied him. In 1927 he took up a post in Paris, where he continued to write and publish (in Spanish and French, but not in the Catalan of his early career). In 1931 he took another radical step and divorced his wife (they had married in 1906 and she retained custody of their sons). It was a long and fruitful absence from Spain, but when the Civil War broke out he decided for reasons of security to remain abroad, while his three sons fought in the Nationalist army. From 1937 he was based in Pamplona, capital of a province (Navarre) that was in Nationalist hands; he joined the right-wing Falange party and wrote regularly for its newspaper. From this point on, he dedicated himself to the rescue of Spanish culture, and managed to recover for the Prado Museum the works of art that had been exported for security to Switzerland by the

Republic in the early months of the war. He returned to Madrid as soon as the war ended, and played a leading role on the cultural front for a regime that badly needed support from figures who, like Ors, were respected abroad. In the 1950s he returned to Catalonia to pass his summers on the coast at Vilanova i Geltrú, and died in nearby Vilafranca del Penedès.

During the Civil War there were five main waves of refugees,[38] most of whom logically went to the most accessible land frontier, that of France. In addition to them there was a continuous emigration, particularly in the summer of 1936 when people fled from the military uprising and from the counter-terror unleashed by supporters of the Republic. The truly sizeable movements resulted from successive phases in the war and included two main categories: soldiers retreating from the front, and ordinary people fleeing from the occupying forces. The first wave occurred in September 1936, when the Nationalists took over much of the northern coast of the peninsula. The second took place in the late summer of 1937, when the rebels completed the occupation of the Basque provinces. The third wave, from the region of Aragon in the summer of 1938, was made up of 45,000 civilians, of whom a quarter were children. The biggest and most decisive wave left in January and February of 1939, when the Catalan front collapsed and the entire resistance, both military and civilians and including President Azaña, the Basque leader Aguirre and the Catalan leader Companys, had to withdraw to France; the numbers who left in those weeks were close to half a million. The collapse of Catalonia convinced the Republican leaders, who still controlled about a third of Spain, from Madrid to the Mediterranean coast, that further resistance was hopeless. At the end of March, Madrid surrendered. A communiqué issued from Burgos by the new government on 1 April stated: 'Nationalist troops today took their last objectives. The war is over.' A final, desperate exodus from the Mediterranean seaports then took place. Studies tend to neglect the relevance of the other land frontier, that with Portugal. The country was in the hands of the right-wing dictator Salazar, and therefore less attractive as a political refuge than France. However, an estimate by an English Communist writer suggests that in the course of 1936 as many as 40,000 Spaniards fled to Portugal from the violence in both Republican and Nationalist Spain.[39] Statistics of the total emigration are of small importance since the movement of population was always temporary, and most refugees managed to return within a few months. Of the half million who left Catalonia in 1939, for example, possibly only a fifth were permanent refugees. It was, all the same, a colossal tragedy that had no precedent in Spain's entire history. The tragedy became worse for many who eventually became trapped in France when the Nazis took over that country. From 1940 onwards, around 24,000 Spanish refugees in southern France were transported by train to the Nazi labour camp at Mauthausen in Austria. Around 16,000 of them died, with some 8,000 surviving the ordeal.[40]

The Soviet Union, which at that period was systematically eliminating whole sections of its population through deportation and persecution (and had incidentally lost a total of some three million refugees in the post-revolutionary period between 1917 and 1929), generously offered to accept the children of Republican (usually Communist) supporters. In September 1936 about 1,200 children from Asturias (centre of the miners' strike) aged between two and twelve were shipped off from Gijón to St-Nazaire and from there to Leningrad. In the same way, a proportion of the 14,000 children evacuated from the Basque country in the early days of the war ended up in the Soviet Union.[41] It has been calculated that between 1936 and 1937 around five thousand children were sent to the Soviet Union, where they were initially treated as heroes but gradually subjected to political pressure and personal mistreatment, with the consequence that by 1943 only two thousand of them remained.[42] In 1956/7 contacts between Spain and the Soviet Union allowed around half the remaining emigrant children to return home, but many of them were unable to adapt to conditions in Spain and soon returned to Russia, where in 2005 around six hundred could still be identified. The evacuation of children continued until almost the last days of the war in 1939. Thousands ended up in Mexico, and were put up in far from satisfactory conditions. The first ship to take them there was the Méxique, which arrived from France in June 1937 with 450 children. Most never saw their parents again, and long after it was possible to return home many preferred to stay in the country – whether Russia or Mexico – that fate had prepared for them. Only in the last decades has their story begun to be told. Most children, logically, remained in France, where there were around 11,000 in the summer of 1938. Other countries accepting them were England, Belgium (around 5,000), Switzerland and Denmark.

A substantial part of the privileged classes joined the refugees. As we have seen, their exile had already begun around 1936. Apart from the war refugees of 1939, who inevitably included a large number of Catalans as well as some stragglers like the poet Antonio Machado, the well-known names left the peninsula at different stages of the struggle that began in 1936, and some went even before. Each left for a different motive, though the driving force was always the need for self-preservation rather than simply opposition to a specific regime. It would be correct to say that every single emigrant was fleeing from the lawlessness that reigned in Spain from around 1934 and particularly in the days of the Popular Front government of 1936, a lawlessness that became more tragic and acute as the war ended and the victors sought vengeance. In a chaotic civil war where both sides had shown their disregard for human life and civilized culture, there was of course no pressing reason to abandon family, property and country merely because of ideological disagreement, no matter how strong. In most of the documented cases, those who left did so simply because they were under threat from one side or the other. Many preferred to stay in Nationalist Spain, but took care to behave prudently.

As had happened in the case of the pro-French exiles of 1813, in the late 1930s there were many refugees who came from the administrative and educational elite. If we apply to them the imprecise category of 'intellectual', it may be possible to estimate that they numbered around five thousand, among them the many who crossed over the Catalan frontier into France in the last weeks of the war. Estimates suggest that the refugees with professional qualifications included around two thousand doctors, one thousand lawyers, five hundred engineers, and one hundred and fifty university professors.[43] Among them were names that went on to attain eminence in their respective fields, such as the palaeographer Agustín Millares Carlo (1893–1978), who spent his exile in Mexico and Venezuela but eventually returned to Spain; the Americanist José María Ots Capdequi

(1893–1975), from Valencia, who died in Colombia; and the ancient historian Pere Bosch-Gimpera (1891–1974),[44] who spent all his exile in Mexico. These educated émigrés were only a tiny fraction of the Spaniards who left their homes, and their absence probably had few material consequences on the country they had left.[45] Moreover, similar exoduses had recently occurred from Bolshevik Russia and Nazi Germany, so that the mass exit of exiles from Spain attracted little attention or interest outside France and Hispanic America.

Very many, of course, never made it into exile and left their bodies and their memory interred in the native soil for which they had fought and which received them when their struggle was over. Their lives are no formal part of our story, but it is impossible to think of Spanish culture without briefly mentioning one man, Miguel Hernández, who was perhaps the finest Spanish poet of the twentieth century. Hernández (1910–42), a native of Orihuela, was a unique product of the rural working class of Murcia in southwestern Spain. Completely self-taught as reader, writer and poet, though cut off by poverty from access to higher culture, when very young he began producing verse of remarkable intensity relating to his immediate material environment. His first book of poems was published in the provinces, in the city of Murcia. Later he gravitated to Madrid, where he managed to make contact with established poets, and impressed Juan Ramón Jiménez with an 'Elegy' (1935) on the death of a friend. On the outbreak of the Civil War, he embraced with passion the causes of liberty and Communism. Early in 1937 he married an Andalusian girl from Orihuela, and had two sons by her (the elder died within a few months). He fought on the war front, and visited the Soviet Union in the fall of 1937. During all these months he continued to produce poetry. When Republican resistance collapsed in 1939, he returned home to Orihuela and then decided to escape across the frontier into Portugal. The Portuguese police sent him back to Spain, where after a few weeks in prison he was released. He made the mistake of returning to Orihuela, where he was again arrested, sent to Madrid and condemned to death. The sentence was later commuted to thirty years in prison, but he was already seriously ill with typhus and tuberculosis, and died in a prison at Alicante. His themes were the war, love, death, his children, and his young wife.

> Nobody will save me from this shipwreck
> If not your love – the plank I cling to,
> If not your voice – the star to guide me.
> Evading in this way the dark fear
> That not even in you would I find haven,
> I smile between one grief and another.[46]

Possibly the best known and most emblematic of the refugees was the poet Antonio Machado (1875–1939), who died in France at the very end of the war and was therefore in a sense the proto-martyr of the exile. Born in Seville, he moved with his family to Madrid and then later to Soria, where he taught French. In Madrid he worked together with his brother Manuel, also a poet (he died peacefully in Madrid in 1947). Antonio's early poetry, including *Solitudes (Soledades)* (1903) and *Solitudes, Galleries and Other Poems (Soledades, Galerías y otros poemas)* (1907) was strongly influenced by the French Modernist movement. In generational terms, he belonged to those affected by the 1898 Disaster, and has often been studied in that context. But unlike those thinkers, he carved out a new, creative, world for himself, in the countryside of Soria. His marriage in 1909 to a sixteen-year-old girl, Leonor, resulted in his happiest and most fertile poetic period, including what is arguably his best work, *Fields of Castile (Campos de Castilla)* (1912). It was a book that marked him out immediately as the most distinctive poet of the Castilian landscape, its fields, sky, clouds, towns and people. During this time, the dominant themes in his poetry were nature, Castile and the *Romancero* medieval ballads (one of his poems is the haunting ballad *La Tierra de Alvargonzález*, about two sons who murder their father in order to have his land). Passages in his work leave in the memory unforgettable images of the eternal, unchanging reality of the traditional landscape. He conjured up the tangible present and the lost past in verses that fix both in the mind's eye:

> Castile the wretched, once the mighty,
> Draped in her rags despises what she does not know.
> Is she in waiting, sleeping, dreaming? Does she remember
> The blood shed when she possessed the fever of the sword?[47]

Tragically, his wife died after only five years of marriage and Machado left Soria for the Andalusian town of Baeza, where he taught in the school and the pupils, joking at his stolid, rather shabby appearance, called him 'Don Antonio *Manchado*' ('the stained'). In Baeza, where he tended to shun external life and became more timid and alone, he returned to a more simplistic approach in his writing. He dabbled in philosophy and wrote, under the pseudonym of 'Juan de Mairena', newspaper articles with a notably religious undercurrent. During the troubles of 1936 he stuck firmly to his Socialist ideas and was among those evacuated by the authorities when they moved the capital of the Republic from besieged Madrid to the safety of the port of Valencia. His great years of poetry were long behind him, but he remained as a distinguished symbol of support for the crumbling Republican cause. When the war ended in February 1939 he was already gravely ill, but was taken across the Pyrenees with his sick mother and his brother. He did not survive long, and died soon after in the frontier port of Collioure. Because Machado's ideas were wholly traditional it is not surprising that there was no problem about publishing his works in the period after the Civil War when more overtly radical writers were banned. At the same time, he had accepted some of the premises of socialism, always entertained a certain naivety about Soviet Communism ('the greatest thing in the world today, is what Russia is achieving'[48]) and in Collioure even mentioned the possibility that he might seek refuge in Russia. Juan Ramón Jiménez's wife Zenobia was in Florida when she made an entry in her diary in February 1939. 'Juan Ramón had just dictated to me the text for opening a subscription in *La Prensa* [of Buenos Aires] to help Spanish intellectuals suffering in the concentration camps in France, when he opened the paper and his head fell in grief to read about the death of Antonio Machado.'[49] The poet's death was a prefiguring of the terrible future that faced those who were forced to flee from the ruins left by the Civil War.

The crisis of the war claimed one of its most prominent victims in García Lorca, but Lorca himself was part of a literary and artistic group that was uneasy in either of the political camps, and had already prepared itself for a future of internal exile because of the homosexual orientation of some of its members. One of the names associated with the group was Luis Cernuda (1902–63), a native of Seville and an outspoken homosexual who faced his character squarely in his principal collection, *Reality and Desire* (*La Realidad y el Deseo*). He began the work in the 1930s but continued to expand it almost until his death in 1963. His major themes, about desire, love and sexuality, arose from what he drew from the work of others around him, in terms of both romanticism and surrealism. Even more outspoken was his *Forbidden Pleasures* (*Los Placeres Prohibidos*), in which he used avant-garde expression to approach the question of his sexuality. When the Civil War broke out he had just arrived in Paris as secretary to the Spanish ambassador. He returned to Madrid, then in 1938 went to England to give lectures on behalf of the Republic. He stayed on, taking up posts teaching Spanish at various universities. In 1947 he accepted a post as language teacher at Mount Holyoke College, Massachusetts. A timid and solitary person, he was depressed by the long New England winters and moved to California and Mexico. From 1960 to 1962 he held a visiting post at UCLA. The Hispanic south, despite its poverty and backwardness, seemed to him alive and vibrant, in contrast to the deadness of the Anglo Saxon world. Restless in all the places he chose to live, excluded from Spain by both his politics and his sexual orientation, he felt deeply conscious of his marginalization:

> I am a very strange writer,
> without a country, without a people: subject more than most
> to the wind of oblivion which when it blows kills.[50]

The overwhelming majority of refugees had left Spain by the only available route, the land frontier of the Pyrenees. 'More than half a million fugitives made their way across the Pyrenees in the dead of winter,' the cellist Casals recalled. 'And in that exodus were the best and noblest of Spain – the soldiers and poets, the workers and university professors, jurists and peasants who had championed freedom and would not bow to tyranny.'[51] Casals' passionate vision embroidered the reality to some extent, for there were few poets or jurists, and the tyranny had not been only on one side. Since 1936, refugees had been fleeing Spain. A leading scholar admits that 'reliable records do not exist', but suggests that in the Republican areas during the war the number of murders may have totalled 60,000, and in the Nationalist areas possibly 70,000.[52] The number of war casualties is not included in these estimates, nor the extensive number of executions carried out by the Franco regime (possibly 30,000 people) after its victory. The exiles were seeking to save their lives not just from one side but from both. As the Catalan writer Carles Riba affirmed six months after reaching the safety of France: 'I fought well, against the two real enemies, Fascism and Marxism'. Over half of the emigrants returned home within a few months, but those who were politically compromised could not afford to do so, and the permanent exiles across the Catalan frontier have been estimated at around 162,000. Conditions in the host country rapidly deteriorated; the year of their arrival coincided with the outbreak of the Second World War, and Germany invaded France in 1940. Supporters of the Spanish Republic had, of course, already fought against Germans within Spain. The pressure was made worse by the policy of the collaborationist Vichy regime of helping the Germans to identify and arrest Jews. France became an unsafe country, and many had to attempt to flee overseas to America.

The handful of Catalan leaders and intellectuals who escaped were thrown into further despair in 1940 by the news that the Catalan president, Lluís Companys, had been handed over by the Vichy government to the Nationalist troops, and shot in Barcelona as a traitor. The French refused to give any guarantees to the remaining Catalans. 'We are in a cataclysm,' Carles Riba complained, 'in respect of everything we love and which is worth living for.' We owe to Riba a description of the flight from Barcelona to Girona and thence to the frontier:[53]

We left Girona very late, when the city was black, frozen with the imminence of its occupation. Two military ambulances took us, a group of writers and Catalan and Castilian university professors, the most notable Antonio Machado. A whole night and day to arrive at Cerbère. At the frontier, a confused mob, panic-stricken.

The Catalans did not wish to move far from Catalonia, nor indeed from France, which for all of them had been the centre of their ideas and aspirations. They could not imagine leaving Europe and transplanting themselves to America (by which they usually meant Mexico, whose language was not theirs). Catalans represented nearly two-fifths of the emigration created in the last days of the war, because their province was the final area of resistance, but only one-fifth of the eventual emigrants to America were Catalan.[54] 'America does not exactly repel me, but it does not attract me,' Riba wrote. 'Can you imagine Rilke living in America?' In the summer of 1940 he felt that 'in the long run our dilemma is America or Spain. I am horrified by both extremes.' By 1942 he had decided not to emigrate to the New World. It was a decision shared by other Catalan writers, who felt that their roots were in France and in Europe, and they could not imagine an exile that involved Mexico.[55] The situation in France, however, was so difficult, between pressure from the police and the Germans, and the lack of income and food, that several decided in 1943 to return, 'like the most humble refugee who goes back', commented Riba, who was one of them. In clinging to France the Catalans were clinging to their permanent source of inspiration.

Other Catalans saw little alternative to the New World, and like the Castilians they went to Mexico. Perhaps the most emblematic of those who chose France was the creator of the modern Catalan language, Pompeu Fabra (1868–1948). Though he is now thought of as a lexicographer, Fabra in fact trained as an engineer, and his main professional experience were the ten years (1902–11) he spent in Bilbao as a professor of chemistry in the school of engineering. He combined this technical expertise with an obsessive interest in the problems of the Catalan language, which like several other minority tongues in Europe included various regional dialects and few grammatical rules. Concerned that it should have a more logical structure and vocabulary, he began publishing studies such as his *Essay on Modern Catalan Grammar* (1891) and collaborated with others in trying to systematize the language. The fruit of his years in Bilbao turned out to be not some engineering textbook but a *Grammar of the Catalan Language* (1912). The Catalan authorities chose him as the ideal person to put into effect a cultural counterpart of their political aspirations, and backed him so absolutely that he became in some sense a sort of dictator who almost single-handedly laid down, often very arbitrarily, new rules and norms concerning the way Catalan should be spoken and written. The end product of twenty years' labour was the great *Diccionari general de la llengua catalana* (1932), still today the one essential book in every educated Catalan's library. Even in exile it was the standby of Carles Riba, who in 1940 wrote from France to Joan Gili, a Catalan bookseller long resident in Oxford: 'Since yesterday we have the two Fabra dictionaries. One is specifically for me, I lost mine in the odyssey of the evacuation.' Fabra, a quiet, unassuming and self-taught devotee of words, became transformed into a unique national symbol. Like other prominent Catalans on the losing side in the Civil War, he went into exile in France in 1939, living first in Paris, then finally in the little Pyrenean village of Prades, where he participated in the cultural activity of the still partly Catalan-speaking area (part of French territory since the year 1659).

Repeating the experience of the Liberals in the early nineteenth century, many exiles headed for England. One of them, the author and diplomat Salvador de Madariaga (1886–1978), was already Anglicized. He was born in La Coruña, one of the eleven sons of an army officer. In his own words:

In 1898 a stroke of intuition persuaded my father that we had lost the War through lack of technology, and a stroke of decision made him send me to Paris to study engineering. Thus began an exile that would make me spend the greater part of my life outside Spain and extend my training towards a sector that I, who was born a poet, would never have discovered or imagined.

It turned out that my literary vocation did not, as is often the case, represent any obstacle to my scientific studies. Besides, passing one day from the Batignolles to the Latin Quarter, I made contact with a group of English and Americans of both sexes, and met a Scottish girl, whom I married in 1912. All of this furthered my Europeanization. In 1916 I threw over my technical career and went to London to write. In 1920 I published my first book, *Shelley and Calderon*.[56]

From 1916 he worked for *The Times* and published his writings in both Spanish and English. He then worked a few years with the disarmament section of the League of Nations in Geneva, and returned to take up the chair of Spanish literature at Oxford (1928–31). A typical product of this period was his *Englishmen, Frenchmen and*

Spaniards. When the Second Republic was declared he served as ambassador in Washington and Paris, since his complete command of the languages and broad international experience made him ideal for the jobs. From 1934 he was in the government at Madrid, first as minister of education in the Lerroux government, then (for ten days) as minister of justice. As an active politician he earned the hostility of both Right and Left. When the Popular Front government took over, he disagreed with the attitude taken to the League of Nations and withdrew from active politics to his house at Toledo. He wrote in his memoirs:

In 1936 I was a liberal and European member of parliament, at a time when people were not interested in Europe or in the parliamentary system or in liberalism. This was the real reason why I emigrated.

Witness to the fear reigning in the streets of Republican Madrid, he declared that there was no effective difference between Marxism and fascism. On the outbreak of the Civil War he distanced himself from both sides and went off to exile in Oxford, which became his permanent home and where he produced an impressive range of publications, written directly in Spanish, French and English, on a broad sweep of themes, above all history, international relations, literary criticism and social psychology. My memory of him at Oxford is of a venerable, gentle but firm and soft-spoken gentleman, with an instinctive sense of humour. He travelled in the New World but refused to respond to questions put to him there about Spain:

My reasons were obvious. I could not speak for the rebels, for they stood against all that I hold true. I could not speak for the revolutionaries, not only because I did not believe in their methods (nor, in the case of most of them, their aims) but because they did not stand for what they said they stood for. They filled their mouths with democracy and liberty but allowed neither to live.[57]

After the Second World War he returned to the defence of the humanist values in which he most believed, notably peace, co-operation and education. In supporting the movement for a united Europe, he also helped to found the College of Europe in 1949. His tireless work for European understanding earned him the Goethe

Prize in 1972 and the Charlemagne Prize in 1973. Three years earlier, a widower at a ripe old age, he married for the second time. The new life may have emboldened him to abandon his comfortable home in Old Headington, Oxford. 'I can face no more northern winters,' he commented, 'and I cannot go to my country because of its political winter', so he and his wife moved to Locarno in Switzerland. He returned to Spain only in April 1976, after the death of Franco, and paid his respects to the king. Two years later he died at Locarno. With Blanco White and Alcalá Galiano, he was one of the few convinced Anglophiles among the exiles of modern times. He was also the only authentic intellectual among them, a committed and cultured European, conservative in character but liberal in outlook, the only Spaniard of his day to acquire an international reputation as a participant in the effort to re-create the world after its wars. As an exile, Madariaga had his own curious, but also provocative and good-humoured, way of looking at Hispanic history. His gently belligerent literary style made his books path-breaking. His *Spain* (1935, 1958) offered a bird's-eye view of the country's history, and his *Christopher Columbus* developed the argument, first put forward by the German writer Kayserling, that the explorer was of Jewish origin.

Of a different social complexion among the emigrants to England was Arturo Barea (1897–1957), who was born in Badajoz of humble origins, and later moved with his family to Madrid where his mother earned a living as a housemaid. After military service in Morocco (his experiences are described in his novel *The Track*) he found a steady job, married and became a Socialist. As an enthusiastic young Socialist he had ambitions to better himself, but soon found that there were class barriers within socialism when it was made clear to him that he did not have the correct social status to be able to enter the Residencia de Estudiantes in Madrid. During the Civil War he worked as the director of the press and censorship bureau of the Republican government. He had as an assistant a 'short, plump' (his own description) Austrian girl who, out of sympathy for the Socialist cause, went to Madrid when the Civil War started, met him and never again left his side. The task of the censorship bureau was to prevent journalists, especially the foreign press, publishing anything but optimistic news about the Republican forces. One of the first active radio broadcasters in Spain, he acquired some fame as the 'unknown voice of Madrid'. He left Spain with Ilsa in 1938 and after a few months in France eventually married her and settled in the village of Eaton Hastings near Faringdon in Berkshire. 'More than expected and more than seemed likely in a Spaniard, I took to English life at once, and fell in love with the English countryside.'[58]

He worked for the BBC during the Second World War, mainly in the Latin American section where he did a weekly fifteen-minute talk under the pseudonym 'Juan de Castilla'. In total he did about 850 scripts for the BBC. His direct knowledge of events in Spain formed the basis of several articles he wrote for the press, but his real energies were spent on creative literature, novels and short stories as well as books of criticism, including *Lorca, the Poet and His People* (1944) and *Unamuno* (1952). He was never at home in English, which he found difficult to master. In an incident in 1941, when his knowledge of the language was still rudimentary, he retorted to a salesman who came to the door asking for his wife, with the statement 'My wife she is not!'[59] His best-known work, *The Making of a Rebel* (1941-4), was an autobiographical fiction trilogy (*The Forge, The Track* and *The Clash*) written in Spanish and then translated into English by Ilsa. It did not achieve any notable success until published in New York in 1946. Later it came out in Spanish in Buenos Aires (1951) and finally in Spain (1978, after the end of the Franco regime). The Buenos Aires publication enabled him to make a promotional trip to Argentina in 1956, when he delivered lectures directed not only against the Franco regime but also against the murders of Maeztu and of clergy under the Republic. In 1951 he published *The Broken Root*, in which he approached the theme of a rootless Republican exile who goes back to Franco's Spain but has problems accepting his new situation, with the result that he leaves again. It was a problem he never faced in his personal experience, not only because the political environment made it impossible but mainly because he felt deeply rooted in England: 'I do not intend ever to return permanently to Spain,' he said.

The path to England was also taken by an eminent man of medicine, Josep Trueta (1897-1976). Born into a good family of Barcelona, he was given a superb education and wished to become an artist, but was influenced to take up medicine, in which he graduated from university in 1921. He devoted the rest of his life passionately to medical surgery, and was one of the foremost military surgeons of the century. After graduation he was contracted to a hospital in Barcelona, worked for his doctorate, and made an illuminating visit to Vienna, where he extended his experience of traumatology. In Barcelona he happened to be one of the doctors on duty the day (in June 1930) that they brought in the body of the architect of the Sagrada Familia church, Gaudí, who had been struck by a bus. By 1935 he was head of surgery at the hospital of Sant Pau. When the Civil War began he devoted himself to the treatment of its victims, putting into practice his own new methods for preventing gangrene among patients, with a corresponding saving of lives. He is said to have personally operated on 1,073 victims during the war, losing only six of them. When Barcelona surrendered he left the city with his family for France and then England, where he was invited to visit the Nuffield Hospital at Oxford, a visit that turned into a stay of twenty-two years. During his leisure moments as an assistant surgeon he would visit the Bodleian Library and read up material for a little book that, he felt, would serve to introduce his homeland to the English. Published in 1946, *The Spirit of Catalonia* is a modest but moving essay on the early history of Catalonia and its struggle for freedom. My copy of it – given to me by the author – sits proudly amid the other books on my shelves in Barcelona. Trueta was an imposing, courteous and good-humoured gentleman with a serious vocation and an intense love of his homeland. He was never entirely separated from Catalonia, because in Oxford he enjoyed the company of the only other Catalan family in the city, that of the publisher Joan Gili, an Anglophile who had settled there in 1934. In 1943 he published his authoritative *Principles and Practice of War Surgery*. In 1949 he was appointed Nuffield Professor of Orthopaedic Surgery. On retiring from the chair in 1965 he returned to Barcelona.

The preference of the émigrés for Spanish-speaking countries may have restricted the public to whom they could address themselves, and their voice was little heard in the outside world. Unlike the emigration of elite figures from Russia and Germany in the same generation, the Spanish emigration to Latin America included no literary or intellectual talents that would later become household names.[60] Virtually all the relevant names among the émigrés of 1939 maintained their reputation only within the ambit of the Hispanic world, and were almost unknown to westerners. Even a name like Machado failed to leave its mark. A culture in exile is one that is normally most vociferous when raising its voice in protest, as the examples of other nations have amply demonstrated. This did not happen in the case of Spain. Many voices protested against the Franco regime and the way the West accepted it, but those that attracted attention were limited to Spaniards who became citizens of the United States or of western Europe. The émigrés in Latin America had to be content with a low profile. They were, moreover, denied any recognition of their cultural significance. The Nobel Prize was awarded to three Spaniards in the middle of the century, but two were citizens of the United States (see Chapter 8), and only one resided in Spain.

The Nobel Prize for literature was awarded to the poet Vicente Aleixandre, who had remained in Spain but was almost unknown outside the peninsula. Aleixandre (1898–1984) was born in Seville and grew up in Málaga, but the family later moved to Madrid, where he went to school and university. He graduated in 1920 and took up a job in the railway administration, devoting his leisure moments to composing poetry. Within a couple of years he had serious health problems and became a semi-invalid. He gave up work and lived in his family's house, writing poetry. His first poems were published in 1926 in the magazine *Revista de Occidente*. Aleixandre remained in the country despite the Civil War and dictatorship. His health did not allow him to move but his personal inclination also kept him aloof from political life. *Destruction or Love* (1935), which some critics see as his principal work, was his last significant publication before the epoch of cultural repression. The military regime in power after 1939 frowned on him and for some time prohibited him from publishing. He became in effect an 'internal exile', unwelcome to those who were in power but also cut off from those who had gone abroad. During this period of uncertainty and poor health, he wrote to a correspondent:

Between pain and joy, there is something in me that saves me from my own destruction or abandonment, from crumbling before the blind pointlessness of living, and it is the sudden blinding consciousness that I am also an expression of the dark forces of life. My faith in poetry is my faith in identifying myself with something that transcends my visible limits.[61]

His first work after nearly ten years of silence came out in 1944, *Shadow of Paradise*. In it the poet speaks to himself and recognizes that 'love and grief are your realm'. His persistently poor health and reclusive life (he never married) were inevitably powerful influences on the type of poetry he wrote. 'I have always envied good health,' he wrote in 1954, 'it is the only thing I envy.'[62] Over and above the appeal to Freudian images of love, dreams and death, Aleixandre's verse moves in a mystical and romantic haze that is distinctly removed from reality. The award of the Nobel Prize to him in 1977, two years after the death of Franco, was for 'creative poetic writing which illuminates man's condition in the cosmos and in present-day society', and was clearly a gesture to newly democratic Spain.

In Europe the protest names that made the greatest impact were of two exiles from the world of creative art, Casals and Picasso. The world-famous cellist and conductor Pablo Casals (1876–1973),[63] born in El Vendrell (Catalonia), was encouraged by his parents to develop his musical talent, with such success that he gave a solo recital in Barcelona at the age of fourteen. Albéniz heard him play and gave him a letter of introduction to the private secretary of the queen regent, María Cristina, in Madrid, where Casals was asked to play at informal concerts in the palace. He studied in Madrid and after a year in Paris returned to take up professional posts in Spain as a cellist. In 1899 he began a round of international concerts, and played before Queen Victoria. 'After dinner', the queen noted in her diary, 'a young Spaniard, Señor Casals, played on the violoncello most beautifully.' Next he made a grand tour of the United States (1901–2) and South America. The United States took him by surprise. 'For me,' he said later, 'America was an emancipation.'[64] Recalling the vastness of its countryside, he said: 'Never before had I been so overwhelmed by Nature's grandeur and diversity.' In 1914 he married an American socialite, the singer Susan Metcalfe (from whom he separated fourteen years later). He was now at the peak of his career. 'I lost track of the number of concerts I gave. I do know, it was often around two hundred and fifty a year.' He played throughout Europe and with the world's leading musicians.

The violence of the Republic that emerged in 1936 affected him profoundly. Wherever the anarchists took over in Catalonia, they drew up death lists of members of the bourgeoisie. Inevitably Casals, in his opulent villa on the coast at Sant Salvador, became a prime target. Both he and his brother figured on the execution lists in the village. They remained untouched only because those responsible for selecting the victims kept saying in his case, 'Not yet, not yet'. Some people in the village disappeared for ever.[65] On the day of the military uprising, 18 July, he was in the Orfeó theatre in Barcelona rehearsing Beethoven's Ninth Symphony, when a message came giving the news and telling them to disband because of the danger of a military coup in the city. 'Dear friends,' Casals addressed the orchestra and chorus, 'I do not know when we shall meet again. As a farewell, shall we play the Finale?' The answer was a loud 'Yes!' At the end they put away their instruments and went out into the street, where people were already erecting barricades.[66] In September he had to go to Paris for a performance, and in view of the dangerous situation at El Vendrell he decided to stay in France, where he settled in Prades, a village in the French Pyrenees near the frontier with Catalonia. He continued to make visits to Barcelona. In July 1937 he performed there at the Orfeó, then five days later took ship at Boulogne for a concert trip to South America.

He finally left Barcelona with the other Catalan exiles in 1939, refusing thereafter to play in any country that recognized the Franco regime. When the Allies normalized their relations with Franco after the end of the Second World War, Casals protested in a letter to the press in London that 'the exiles hounded out of Spain by Franco's rebellion, represent the best elements in our country'. He subsequently turned down honorary degrees offered him by the universities of Oxford and Cambridge. From Prades, where he stayed seventeen years, he went to visit the emergency camps set up for refugees from Spain, and began organizing a campaign to help. 'The scenes I witnessed might have been from Dante's "Inferno". Tens of thousands of men, women and children were herded together like animals, penned in by barbed wire. There were no sanitation facilities or medical provisions.' Prades became the centre of his extremely active professional life. Visitors came to see him, among them the American violinist Alexander Schneider, who soon became Casals' most important point of contact with the professional music world. With Schneider's help, from 1950 he began organizing at Prades an annual musical festival that has become famous. He also continued giving international concerts, and began his custom of concluding performances with his rendering of the traditional Catalan carol the *Song of the Birds* (*Cant dels Ocells*).

Catalonia was among the last fronts of resistance held by the Republicans in the Civil War, and Catalans therefore featured prominently in the final flood of refugees that poured over the Pyrenees into France. One of the exiles was a relatively unknown composer who has been identified by experts as 'the most significant figure of the generation after Falla', and even (by a Catalan musician) as 'Catalonia's most important composer in four centuries'.[67] In a real sense he can be regarded as a symbol of the culture that was expelled from the peninsula in 1939, for the type of music he represented did not return to Spain for two decades. Robert Gerhard (1896–1970) was born in Valls to parents of non-Catalan origin. His father, a Swiss-German, was a wine merchant, who sent his son to Switzerland to study. When abroad, Robert changed the direction of his studies and decided to become a musician. He studied music in Munich then returned to Catalonia, where he took piano lessons from Granados and helped the leading folklorist Joan Amades to collect popular songs. After 1920 Robert furthered his musical studies in Paris, Berlin and London, and was accepted as a pupil by the great pioneer of modern music, Schoenberg. In Vienna he made contact with the modernist composers Berg and Webern, and also met the young lady he later married. He finally left Catalonia only when Barcelona was about to fall in 1939, and eventually settled in Cambridge, England, where he did work for the BBC's Spanish service and became a British citizen. His compositions were modest and brought him little recognition, but typically one of his first works written on British soil was a ballet, *Don Quixote*, for chamber orchestra, which was aired on the BBC and also used in a Sadler's Wells ballet production.

*

Perhaps the most universally known protest name was that of Picasso. The best known and most successful artist of his age, and the only Spaniard to feature in *Time* magazine's list of the hundred most influential persons of the twentieth century, Pablo Picasso (1881–1973) was born in Málaga, but at the turn of the century lived and worked as an artist in Barcelona. From 1904 he was permanently resident in Paris, the centre of a brilliant group of international artists and poets. His painting style developed through several phases, during which he moved towards Cubism around 1909. From the 1920s he was involved with Surrealism, and took up sculpture. By 1932, thanks to outstanding exhibitions in Paris and Zurich, he was famous. At that time he had also renewed his links with the peninsula. The Second Republic, anxious to gain the support of international figures, named him honorary director of the Prado art gallery. Picasso was flattered, and in 1933 and 1934 made brief visits to Madrid and Barcelona to renew his personal contacts (and also to see a bullfight or two). He was fundamentally apolitical at this time, even though some of his closest associates were leftists.

The outbreak of the Civil War helped to change his attitude, thanks to one incident. On 26 April 1937, a busy market day in the Basque town of Guernica, German and Italian warplanes in the service of the Franco forces appeared in the sky and dropped incendiary bombs that killed around three hundred people, wounded several hundred more and levelled three-quarters of the buildings. It was an unexpected assault on defenceless civilians in an age when air attacks were relatively unknown, and shocked opinion everywhere. Nationalist forces blamed the Republicans for the outrage, and the Germans denied any knowledge of the affair. Exaggeration of the number of casualties further helped to inflame opinion. Picasso saw the news in Paris when he opened his daily paper on 28 April (photos of the results of the bombing did not appear until two days later). In January the Madrid government, seeking to win support from an international public, had asked the architect Josep Lluís Sert to approach Picasso about participating in the Spanish Pavilion of the World Exhibition being prepared for that spring in the French capital. Sert asked him to contribute a large mural, but though Picasso accepted he was unenthusiastic about the idea. He had never done a huge canvas, and was doubtful about participating in political propaganda, although precisely that month he had begun a series of etchings on *Dreams and Lies of Franco*, a sort of comic strip with grotesque postcard-size images depicting violence and screams. In the same weeks he had also come up with an image, a raised arm defiantly grasping a hammer and sickle, that he released to the press as an indication of his opposition to the policy, practised by the western powers, of non-intervention in the Spanish Civil War. In some sense, then, he was prepared for the plunge into propaganda. The news of the bombing evidently gave him the impulse he needed to begin the proposed mural.

He began his sketches on 1 May 1937, while outside in the streets of Paris there were mass demonstrations against the bombing. Ten days later he began the full-size execution. In principle, the details of the painting were not triggered by the bombing but rather were variations of ideas and themes that had long featured in his work. He eventually produced an enormous oil painting, 3.5 metres high and 7.8 metres long, the largest he had ever done, painted in greys, whites and blacks with small touches of colour and incorporating images from photographs. *Guernica*, the most famous work of art inspired by the Civil War, took two months to complete and was put on show when the Spanish Pavilion opened on 12 July. Both the public and later art critics had mixed feelings about what the overpowering work was meant to express and whether it succeeded in its purpose. The initial reception to the canvas was muted. Spanish government officials were disappointed that the painting was not more explicit, others did not like its obscure symbolism. The Soviet writer Ilya Ehrenburg, an intimate connoisseur of the cultures of both Spain and France, defended Picasso stoutly against his colleagues. It was clear, however, that this was not a painting of war.[68] The canvas showed in the foreground a man on the ground, his body pierced by a pike, lying beneath a horse that rears up, its head turning leftwards. On the left of the scene a woman cradles a child in her arms. To the right of the picture there are three figures, one kneeling, one at a window, one apparently floating. Two more animals, a bull and a bird, fill out the space, which is littered by various objects. There are no signs of war, no sky, no aeroplanes, no apparent violence. The only thing in common between the several heads, of humans and animals, is that all are screaming in terror. Picasso had arranged for each stage of the painting to be photographed, and kept all his sketches, which later accompanied *Guernica* when it went on tour. Despite this unusual opportunity to observe the creative process, the complexity of the work baffled many, and it took years for its symbolism to mature in the minds of critics.[69] Throughout the year 1937 the only work by Picasso to really excite international attention was his 1907 work *Les demoiselles d'Avinyó* (with the placename in Catalan rather than French), which was put on show (and sold) in New York. The impact of *Guernica* on Picasso himself was, however, indubitable. The images he had used for the painting continued to obsess him, and in June he completed his etchings on *Franco,* while also dedicating his time to a new canvas on *The Weeping Woman*, a theme directly related to his *Guernica*.

The painting had been commissioned and paid for by the Second Republic, which decided to use it as a work of propaganda. It was taken to London in September 1938, and had a brief tour round the country before being returned to France. In April 1939, two months after the defeat of the Republic by Franco's forces, it was shipped from Le Havre to the United States, accompanied by the Republic's last prime minister, Negrín. America was the biggest single market for Picasso's works, and American sympathizers of the extinct Republic hoped the painting would influence public opinion. In New York it was put on show at the MoMA, chosen by Picasso as official custodians of the work. It was the only work, whether in literature, art or music, produced by any exiled Spaniard in the course of five centuries to make an immediate impact on the consciousness of the outside world. For those permanently affected by the consequences of armed conflict, it continues to convey a resounding message.

The painting drew on imagery – the horse in the bullfight, the minotaur, weeping women – that had characterized his work for several years.[70] In that sense, it said nothing new. However, the context to which it referred, its sombre colours and its overwhelming dimensions soon overcame any initial doubts about its effectiveness. The desire to find an appropriate symbol of protest against brutality overcame the rest. *Guernica* became initially a fund-raiser for the victims of the Civil War, then an emblem of opposition to fascism. New York was gripped with Picasso-mania as visitors flooded into the MoMA. Other world artists were impressed by the possibility of using art to protest against dictatorship. There were dissenting opinions, notably from Soviet artists who were committed to 'Socialist realism' and found the images 'monstrous and pathological', but the painting had established itself. So too had Picasso. In wartime France, he managed to command enough respect to remain safe from the occupying Germans, and at this period developed an active association with the Communist Party. It was an affiliation that made it impossible for him ever to return to his native land, since Franco lived longer than he did. After the war, he continued to triumph with his symbols for peace, specifically the dove that featured on a poster designed for the Communist-organized Paris Peace Congress in April 1949. In 1961, he married Jacqueline Roque, and continued his prolific work in painting, drawing, prints, ceramics and sculpture until his death in April 1973.

Meanwhile, *Guernica* continued its triumph. It travelled to Brazil and toured Europe throughout 1955 and early 1956, was exhibited in Munich, Cologne, Hamburg, Brussels, Amsterdam and Stockholm, and returned for Picasso's seventy-fifth birthday to New York, where it was installed in the third-floor gallery at the MoMA. It inspired imitators, and featured in progressive films. Publicity posters against other war tragedies used it as a basic image for peace. Even those who hated it came round to accepting it. The work managed, nevertheless, to stand up to the obvious ideological over-exposure that it was suffering. Perhaps its most significant triumph was in getting accepted by those who had actually carried out the massacre at Guernica. In its early years the painting had received jibes from officials of the Franco government, and it was forbidden to reproduce it in Spain. By the 1960s, the regime had come round to recognizing that although it might be a loathsome piece of art it formed part of Spain's history. Ministers opened negotiations about getting it for the Spanish people. Picasso's ninetieth birthday in 1971 was celebrated, even though in a subdued way, in Spain. The issue of the painting was complicated, however, when the artist released a statement which said that 'since 1939 I have entrusted *Guernica* and the studies that accompany it to the MoMA in New York for safekeeping, and they are intended for the government of the Spanish Republic'.[71] Further long negotiations followed. Eventually, in 1981 by agreement with Picasso's heirs it was transferred to Spain and is now housed permanently in the Queen Sofía Museum, Madrid. A journalist on the Madrid paper *El País* wrote in September 1981 that 'its exile has always been an offence to our dignity and highlighted our inability to live in peace'.[72] When it was put on show after its arrival, five thousand visitors lined up to see the painting in the first two days. True to form, Spaniards immediately started to quarrel about the painting, notably over where it should be located. But, at last, another exile had come home.

The first exiles were profoundly concerned to continue the fight against Franco through their writings, in order to establish the validity of their Spain as opposed to the one that had triumphed. Others felt they were carrying the real Spain into exile, that they alone were now the real spirit of Spain and that they had left a corpse behind. A minor poet, León Felipe, addressed his peninsular colleagues from the safety of Mexico:

> Brother, yours is the estate,
> The house, the horse and the gun,
> Mine is the old voice of the earth.
>
> You have everything.
> Yet I leave you voiceless, voiceless,
> I go off with the song.

However, though the exiles felt that theirs was an unprecedented experience, in substance they were re-enacting the migrations of the mid-nineteenth century. Many of them had been educated in the style of thinking common to the writers of 1898, and that was the style they continued to preserve, antiquated and full of vague philosophic idealism. Like the idealists of the 1890s they believed that they, as 'intellectuals', were the torchbearers of their people's culture. They also felt their view of Spain to be distinct from the one held by those who supported the new regime. In substance, however, it was remarkably similar, just as the visions of Liberals and conservatives in the 1850s had had much in common. In Paris forty-four writers set up a Union of Spanish Intellectuals, which organized meetings, lectures and soirées at the Hispanic Institute in the rue Gay-Lussac. In March 1939 some of them founded a Committee for Spanish Culture, proclaiming that their aim was to rescue 'authentic' Spanish culture from the enemy. In February the following year the Committee published in Mexico the first issue of a journal, *Spain in Exile* (*España Peregrina*), edited by the poets José Bergamín and Juan Larrea, which managed to survive for eight more issues, contained fifty pages in each issue, and attained a circulation of about one thousand.

What was the culture they wished to preserve? Their eyes were set not on the earth but on the heavens. Rejecting the Nationalist regime, while at the same time distancing itself from the Communists, *España Peregrina* spoke up for 'that universal awareness that is characteristic of the Spanish people'.[73] Their own awareness was, however, curiously non-universal and ultra-nationalist in content. Taking up the thread of arguments that had been put forward half a century before by the Generation of 98, writers such as Juan Larrea affirmed that Spain alone had the secret of universal salvation. Spain was, he wrote in *España Peregrina*, 'predestined to be the leaven that will raise us to the heights to which the human race aspires'. The first number of the journal modestly presented the editors as

the kernel of a more profound type of humanity, a synthesis of the experience of the West, launched by Spain in these fertile soils of America where they speak our language and from which it will radiate over the Peninsula and over the whole world. We are the projection of the Spanish soul, of its identity with the highest human values.[74]

The frustrations of the past, the decline of the empire, the loss of Cuba, the defeat of democracy in Spain, were of minor importance, for Spain had a special value, its spiritual leadership, which no other country had. Indeed, Spanish culture was the highest form of western culture, and the Spanish language, the language of Cervantes, was its highest expression. The *Boletín* of the intellectuals in Paris issued in 1947 a special number to celebrate the fourth centenary of the birth of Cervantes, and proclaimed that their aim was to 'recover the genius of Spain'.[75] The rest of the western world, particularly England and the United States, seemed to most of them to be sunk in decadent materialism, and the course of the Second World War was proof of the diseased state of the West.

It was a line of thought shared by many of the same generation. Sánchez-Albornoz, who was nominal prime minister of the Republic's government-in-exile from 1962 to 1971, likewise argued in 1943 that because of humanity's 'gigantic' debt to it, Spain was the 'inextinguishable torch' illuminating mankind's way towards the future.[76] No hope could be entertained of the materialist culture of the United States and England; only Spain's spirituality was the way forward. It is ironic to observe that precisely the same views were serving as the basis of the thought of the Franco regime.[77] Both sides claimed that Hispanic culture was the only authentically human form of civilization.[78] Typical of this tendency was the view of the exiled essayist Francisco Ayala, who in *The Reason for the World* (*Razón del Mundo*) (1944) argued from Argentina that the Protestant and Anglo-Saxon part of the world had sunk into the mire of barbarism, and that Spain (the exiles' Spain, of course, not the Spain of Franco) remained the sole reserve of western culture. In an essay written in 1949, when the war was over and with the Franco regime still firmly in place, Ayala tried to reassure his colleagues who felt they had been forgotten and their voice virtually silenced. In answer to the question that formed the title of his essay, 'For whom are we writing?', Ayala admitted that they could not go on forever writing about the destiny of Spain, and that 'our words are lost in the wind'. But, he said, 'we trust that some of them will not be lost', because there was still a task for them. They must remain conscious of 'the function that the intellectual has in society today and the responsibility he may have for its disasters and disorders'. As Spanish writers had done half a century before, he reverted to the image of the intellectual as the saviour and prophet of society. He and his friends clung on to the vision that despite their circumstances they were the true hope. They should not be depressed by the fact of exile, Ayala added in one of his more extraordinary utterances: 'considered properly, all writers today, wherever they may be, live in exile'.[79]

The consequence of this survival of nationalist idealism, in a nation that had little experience of democratic thinking, was that the mainstream of exiles failed to offer an alternative vision of Spain, or to create a new identity as an alternative to the Fascist regime. Indeed, the identity they projected was so similar to the ideas of the new regime that a writer in a Falange paper in 1940 commented with approval on the sentiments set out in the first issue of *España Peregrina*. In their turn, the editors of the expatriate publication reprinted his comments, in which he had compared their wanderings with that of the Chosen People, the Jews, after they had left the Promised Land:

Through these worlds of God, shattered and bitter, goes pilgrim Spain, with all the maledictions of exile on its head. And like those fugitive Jews, whose fate was like theirs, for both were members of a chosen race, they put their despair and distance into words.[80]

In a letter to the novelist Max Aub in 1968, Américo Castro, then in Princeton, commented on the Spaniards in exile as 'these poor, deluded and amiable creatures, who have no notion of who they themselves are and are therefore incapable of making their own future. If they really get round to knowing who they are and why they are, maybe one day they will be able to assume the reins of their own collective destiny.'[81] Since the handful of writers associated with *España Peregrina* had clearly lost themselves in a desert of their dreams, the only viable substitute vision available to the anti-Franco émigrés was offered by Marxism, which therefore became the sole vehicle of protest and creative activity, even though the upper-class exiles avoided it like the plague.

Since they disagreed radically with the ideology of both the winners and the losers in the Civil War, for strategic reasons the outstanding figures among the intellectuals abroad kept clear of politics, and were notably silent about the regime in power in their country. This made it easier for some of them, like Marañón, to return early. Gregorio Marañón (1887–1960) was, like Miguel Servet, Ramón y Cajal and Salvador de Madariaga, one of those universal intellects that Spain produced from time to time, and like them he found his inspiration as much outside the country as within it. From a cultured upper-class family, he chose medicine as his career and in 1910 completed his doctorate and studied for part of the year in Frankfurt am Main. When only twenty-four, he became head of the Department of Infectious Diseases at Madrid's principal hospital. His chosen subject was endocrinology, and the practical research he did (mostly in Germany) was on the secretion of the glands, the actions of hormones and the relationship between glandular functioning and sexual determination. He came to the conclusion that glandular secretions were an important determinant of human behaviour, a view that he applied to his reading in history and literature.[82] He became fascinated by the possibility of applying the results of medical research to an analysis of the physiological and psychological make-up of historical personalities. As a result he produced a number of historical biographies that were in every sense pioneering works of research, based on exacting historical evidence but also relying on diagnosis over time in order to understand and explain the conduct of the subject. 'History', he wrote in a book published in 1936, 'is a true auxiliary science of medicine. Studying it improves the doctor's ability to penetrate into the souls of men.'[83]

Spain's history, like that of other countries, is full of leaders who had personality problems, and Marañón enjoyed attempting to analyse them. His first study (1930) was about the fifteenth-century king of Castile, Henry IV, whose root problem was an alleged sexual impotence, so that when his wife eventually produced a daughter as heir the paternity was attributed not to him but to his chief minister. His next fully researched essay, which has inevitably been superseded by the work of professional scholars[84] but is still eminently readable, was on the seventeenth-century politician the count duke of *Olivares* (1936), seen as a case study in the psychological effects of the search for power. Marañón's next study, written in Paris (1939) when he was far away from the Civil War, was an analysis of the Roman emperor *Tiberius*, whom he diagnosed as a case of 'resentment'. His most memorable historical biography was also researched in exile, but published after he returned to Spain. This was his classic masterpiece in two volumes on Philip II's secretary *Antonio Pérez* (1947), which was also in effect an in-depth analysis of the character of the king. Marañón considered the king to have been a weak, timid personality, easily influenced by the smooth-tongued and more worldly-wise secretary.

Beyond these historical cases, in whose study he employed the tools of documentary research rather than the new Freudian techniques of psychoanalysis, Marañón made a contribution to the psychiatric analysis of a fictional personality who was also a perennial human phenomenon: Don Juan. 'Don Juan' was a traditional figure, that of a profligate pursuer of women, to be found in many cultures. In the classic account, as we have seen (Chapter 5), the notorious Don Juan is a seducer who ends up in hell. Several literary studies on the theme had been produced since the 1880s, mainly in France and Spain. With a European tradition on which to base his analysis, in 1924 Marañón set out to examine the psychological roots of Don Juan's personality.

In common with other moderates such as Ortega, he gave public support to the new-born Republic in 1931 and entered the Cortes, but never opened his mouth in a debate. The excuse he gave was that 'in default of other virtues, I am learning more every day the courtesy of talking only about what I know'. He was soon disillusioned by the political chaos and street violence that became endemic after the first stage of the Republic. However, his status as a moderate was high, and he was even invited to form a government at the end of 1933. But it proved impossible to get the groups to agree on his basic points: a coalition government of all forces, to create stability and tolerance, and the dissolution of the existing assembly. As the situation deteriorated, he expressed his loss of faith in the men who had set themselves up as saviours. In 1933 he felt that 'with some exceptions, the intellectual should not take part in government'. The following year, he concluded: 'the intellectual has failed in his task, and is now paying the price'.[85] When asked to play an active role in the chamber, he wrote back to his correspondent, the leader of one of the political groups: 'I don't need to shift from my leftism, which is if you like very mild, but no less firm. I am sad to think that there may be great and tragic sorrows in Spain. I prefer not to add to them and to continue being a liberal spectator and worker for science.'[86] Fundamentally non-political, Marañón did not share the extremism of others, avoided being dragged into politics and concentrated instead on his writing and his patients. He greeted the February 1936 election results with characteristic moderation. 'A policy of the left should now be put into effect in Spain,' he wrote in the press, 'but without destroying the opinion of the right. Both need to work together.' No such co-operation ensued. His views on the subsequent anarchist and Communist terror can, curiously enough, be found in the preface he wrote to a historical work about exiles by another scholar many years later: 'The resentful sectors of humanity, envious or cruel, which make up three-quarters of our species, take advantage of the outbreak of freedom to remove their masks and surge into the streets.'[87]

When the military rising occurred in July 1936 he received threats to his life from Republican vigilante committees. 'In July 1936,' he wrote later, 'I heard on the radio in San Sebastián the news of my own execution. A friend was pleasantly surprised a few days later to hear my voice.'[88] He stated later that 'I had to present myself twice before the *checas*; one was presided over by a woman, in the walls of the Casa de Campo; the other time they summoned me to make a declaration before the so-called People's Court.'[89] The French government offered to protect him and arranged for him and his family to leave from the port of Alicante on an English destroyer, the *Active*. In Christmas week two cars left Madrid for the coast, one with Marañón and his family, the other with the medievalist Ramón Menéndez Pidal. The escort was headed by an anarchist official, a nephew of Angel Ganivet. In a talk to the PEN club in Paris a week later, Marañón said: 'I venture to declare my mistake in having at times served under the banners of a humanism that was not a real humanism'. His restrained but biting testimony came out in a booklet he wrote a few months later, defining how impossible it had become to maintain liberal ideals in Spain:

Last November a newspaper columnist told me in Madrid, 'You have always been a liberal, you will support us'. On the same day, however, a workers' committee banned the reprinting of one of my books because the following phrase appeared on one page: 'I have always been a liberal, thank God'. When I left Spain and commented that their decision did not seem to me very liberal, they declared me an 'enemy of the people'. A South American writer, communist and Catholic, referred to me in an article as 'the new Spanish Torquemada'.[90]

Almost immediately he made a trip through Argentina, Chile and Brazil in 1937, following it in 1939 with another that added Peru and

Bolivia to the itinerary. The visits opened up his imagination, for the first time, to the vastness of the Hispanic experience. 'The Spaniard who has been in America,' he wrote after his return, 'adds to his heart for ever an imperishable element, nostalgia for America that will never leave us.' He continued to be closely occupied with the Hispanic world, writing regular articles for the press in Cuba, Argentina and Mexico. At the same time, his residence was the centre of numerous visitors, including exiles in Paris such as his close friends Pérez de Ayala and Ortega y Gasset. Ramón Pérez de Ayala had been ambassador of the Republic in London, but resigned soon after the Popular Front victory in February 1936 and left Spain with his family at the end of the year. In those years of intense personal pressure, Marañón came to terms with exile and the choices it offered. His isolation also helped him to come to terms with himself: 'I had time to get to know myself'.

He was able to continue as a doctor in Paris, and when he had leisure moments he resumed his writing. His apartment in number 7, rue Georges Ville, near Avenue Victor Hugo, filled up with books and papers but he had no time to decorate his walls. His friend Josep María Sert visited him one day, said 'You have no pictures!', and made him a gift of the sketches for the murals he had been commissioned to do on the ceiling of the League of Nations building in Geneva. Marañón worked with patients and hospitals, finding time to write and also to travel and give lectures, all within the context of a country that the Germans were occupying. He was present in Paris in June 1940 when the German army marched in to occupy a silent and sullen city. A photo taken by a friend shows him standing in the Place de la Concorde with columns of German infantry in the background. Life became difficult as food supplies ran short and fear mounted. But there was time for research. He and his wife, Lola Moya, could be seen periodically, wrapped in blankets, working on sixteenth-century documents in the cold of the National Archives. The problem of exile, his own and that of other Spaniards over time, occupied his thoughts constantly. They were most vividly expressed in the lecture he gave in Paris, eventually published in 1947 in Buenos Aires, in which he reflected on the history of his country and the way in which the fact of exile had determined its destiny. When members of his family fell seriously ill in Spain, he could not resist the pressure to return.

One personality of this time moved so frequently between his different activities that he falls into none of the categories we have touched on, yet his absences were also so prolonged that he belonged to no fixed world, least of all Spain. Salvador Dalí (1904–89) was a curious figure on the fringes of international culture, and a natural outsider. The consciousness of territorial or political exile was not present in his work and never formed part of his creative makeup, but he was an exile – it would be more correct to say 'fugitive' – from all types of reality, never identified himself explicitly with any religious, political, sexual or even artistic inclination, and was all his life in flight from himself. His international projection was remarkable, and he remains after Picasso the best-known Spanish artist of the twentieth century. Born in Figueres (Catalonia), son of a prosperous notary, his early years were spent in the countryside of Ampurdán and in the quiet fishing village of Cadaqués, where with the support of his parents he set up his first studio (later in life he set up both home and studio in the neighbouring seaside village of Port Lligat). At the age of eighteen he went on to study art in Madrid, and first achieved international recognition when three of his paintings were shown in an exhibition in Pittsburgh in 1928. From this period he was active in Paris, where he joined the Surrealist group led by the writer André Breton (and was later 'expelled' by them). Surrealism began as a literary movement in France, but became most popularly connected with the art world and exercised a special attraction over Spaniards: in art Miró and in cinema Buñuel were conscious followers of the Surrealist imagination. In 1929 Dalí was visited in Cadaqués by the French poet Paul Éluard and his wife Gala. Gala (a Russian, her real name was Helena Diakonova) became Dalí's lover and changed his life completely. She made her life with him, managed his business affairs and was the inspiration of countless paintings. His best Surrealist work dates from this period (*The Persistence of Memory*, 1931).

Dalí was based mainly in France, and consequently escaped the pressures of the Civil War. The conflict back home presumably had a role to play in the inspiration of his compelling oil on canvas *Soft*

Construction with Boiled Beans (Premonition of Civil War), which was painted in 1936 and for some commentators reflects far more vividly than Picasso's *Guernica* the shock of bloody conflict. In its agony of movement, the painting is an obvious reflection of Goya's horrifying depiction of Saturn devouring his children, and stuns the viewer into admiration. The unanswered question is whether it is an authentic expression of suffering or simply a grotesque piece of surrealism, since it was done in Paris before the outbreak of the Civil War, and the worst was yet to come. Dalí explains the painting as follows in his notorious *Secret Life*:

When I arrived in Paris I painted a large picture which I entitled *Premonition of Civil War*. In this picture I showed a vast human body breaking out into monstrous excrescences of arms and legs tearing at one another in a delirium of auto-strangulation. As a background to this architecture of frenzied flesh devoured by a narcissistic and biological cataclysm, I painted a geological landscape, that had been uselessly revolutionized for thousands of years, congealed in its 'normal course'. The soft structure of that great mass of flesh in civil war I embellished with a few boiled beans, for one could not imagine swallowing all that unconscious meat without the presence (however uninspiring) of some mealy and melancholy vegetable.

Dalí's lengthy absence from Spain was due largely to work rather than to politics. Disagreements with the regime in power never turned him into an exile. However, when the Germans invaded France in 1940 he and Gala moved to the United States (they had already been there in 1934). 'They spent the next eight years at the seaside resort of Carmel, California, with money-making forays to New York and Hollywood.'[91] As a result of his endless extravagant postures and statements, *Life* magazine proclaimed him 'America's Number One public madman'. He put on his first big retrospective exhibition at the MoMA in 1941. Always eager to shock, the next year he published his scandalous autobiography, *The Secret Life of Salvador Dalí* (Dalí knew no English, and he – or Gala – wrote the book in French). His years in America propelled him to fame and fortune, since the public found no difficulty in understanding the combination of romantic and exotic to be found in his large, compelling canvases. Significantly, the National Gallery in Washington DC acquired emblematic works such as his *The Discovery of America by Christopher Columbus*. He was now a world figure, and after nearly thirty years outside his country he had no difficulty in returning to Spain when he wished, and giving his approval to the Franco regime. His gripping depiction of *The Crucifixion* (1954) was another example of the way in which he was able to appeal at one and the same time to his commercial instincts, to the official religious ideology of the regime, and to his subdued erotic preferences. His sexual explorations, aided and abetted by the equally adventurous Gala, had specific preferences, about which he made no secret. His quasi-homosexual relationships had bound him in the early days to Buñuel, Lorca and others, but as he aged he chose younger bisexuals. In 1974 his home town of Figueres opened the Dalí Museum, which has now been converted into the main centre of the Dalí cult. After Gala's death in 1982, Dalí tended to live more in Catalonia, where he died in very poor health.

Dalí's private life influenced and infused all his art. He liked to expose the most intimate and scatological aspects, claiming that they explained his art, as in some sense they do. He is the artist of his century who most often painted the human backside, a reflection of his obsession with Freudian concepts, the fundamental inspiration of much Surrealism. In fact he met Freud briefly (in London) a year before the latter's death. Freud thought, with good reason, that Dalí was strange. 'That boy looks like a fanatic,' he murmured. 'Small wonder that they have a Civil War in Spain if they look like that.'

Perhaps the only innovative vision broached in these turbulent years had arisen on the Left, in the ranks of the anarchists and the Communists. Both these movements rejected elite culture, but they also attracted the adherence of significant writers, who all ended up in exile since there was no room for them in Franco's Spain.

Rafael Alberti (1902-99) was born in Puerto Santa María (Cadiz), from which his family moved to Madrid in 1917. Instead of finishing his school education he took to painting, which became a lifetime hobby ('what I wanted was to paint, and paint a lot!'). He also attempted writing plays, and only later switched to composing poetry. Despite his initial aversion to the capital, he soon took to the life of Madrid and the variety of experiences it offered. He made contact with other young writers, most of them associated with the Residencia de Estudiantes, such as García Lorca and Juan Ramón Jiménez. 'We were going to be the new and authentic vanguard', he recalled in his memoirs.[92] His first poems in the 1920s contained the recurring theme of the sea and were finally published as *Landlocked Sailor* (*Marinero en Tierra*). He took part in student protests against the rule of Primo de Rivera, the beginning of a lifetime devoted to radical causes. In 1929 he brought out one of his principal collections, *About Angels* (*Sobre los ángeles*), which were influenced by Surrealism. In the 1930s he managed to obtain from the new Republic a scholarship to study abroad, and began an unprecedented – at least for Spanish writers – spate of travels. By 1931 he was in France, where he came into contact with Picasso and Latin American writers living in Paris such as Miguel Angel Asturias. He happened to be in Germany when the Nazis were preparing their coup against the Weimar Republic and saw enough of the Soviet Union (in 1932) to remain a convinced admirer, a position he shared with friends such as the Chilean poet Pablo Neruda. In 1934 he formally became a member of the Communist Party. That year he also visited New York briefly (long enough to write an anti-American poem, *The Stars and Stripes*), and spent a year in Mexico. After returning to the peninsula in 1935 he visited Ibiza, where he heard of the military rising.

He immediately went to Madrid and joined the struggle to defend the Republic. Alberti was an unusually vigorous figure, tall, strikingly good-looking, with penetrating eyes and a full head of fair hair, a dynamic figure in the manner of the Russian poet Mayakovsky. With his wife María Teresa León at his side, he worked tirelessly for the cause, placing his poetry at the service of propaganda and political activity, in the manner of Soviet writers.[93] He also took his art to the people, holding poetry readings in workers' clubs and public squares. It was part of the educative programme entered into by intellectuals who supported the Republic. He went to Moscow in 1937 (his third visit there) to seek Soviet help, and was received personally by Stalin for a two-hour visit in the Kremlin. The enthusiasm he thought he found among Russians for revolutionary Spain overwhelmed him: 'a feeling for Spain as felt through Moscow, a joint but single enthusiasm'. He returned to Spain determined to serve the revolution, enrolled briefly as a pilot (though he never flew a plane), and helped in the evacuation of works of art from the Prado Museum in Madrid. The paintings were transported by truck to Valencia to save them from the air bombardments, Alberti travelling with a pile of Goyas heaped up on his lap. For the duration of the war he remained in Madrid, but in March 1939 he left for Alicante, where various Republican leaders were hoping to arrange evacuation. He and his wife left in a light plane for North Africa and from there went by boat to Marseilles. In Paris Picasso helped them and arranged for him to get a job. Neruda was busy arranging for left-wing sympathizers to leave for the New World, and got the Albertis passports for Chile, but after crossing the Atlantic the couple decided to remain in Buenos Aires. 'When we arrived in Argentina we had absolutely nothing, nothing, nothing.'[94]

The Albertis spent the next twenty-four years in Argentina, and he produced most of his work there. In exile, he expressed at times his feeling of estrangement and solitude:

> A poet, his roots
> Broken, scattered to the wind,
> His voice dried up, waterless,
> A man alone, exiled,
> Ineluctably exiled,
> Who watches the dusk fall
> And fears the night.[95]

His verse was simple, lyrical and always conscious of Spain, presented as a bull in agony on the other side of the sea (*The Bull in the Sea: Elegy on a Lost Map*):

> My windows
> No longer open on to the poplars and rivers
> of Spain.

But the reality of exile was mitigated by the presence of love:

> I am beset at times by catastrophe:
> My homeland lost,
> My seas and woods far off,

Without me and in despair.
Yet you, in the distance, rise up
A true Venus of foam and leaves,
Body of green sap and saltpetre
That cling to you as you rise.
Happy are those who after the storm,
Or even amid its red rays
Sigh for you, touch you and die
For you, for you, who are also the dawn.[96]

He was not cut off from the world, as other Spanish exiles came to be. Thanks to his active links with the Communist Party, whose programme he supported unquestioningly, he had at his grasp the resources of left-wing contacts and publishers, and was always on the move, particularly after the Second World War. The first time he returned to Europe was in 1950, as an honoured guest at the Soviet-inspired World Peace Festival held in Warsaw. It was the occasion when Picasso, who the previous year had invented his symbol of a dove for peace, was awarded the Stalin Peace Prize. In subsequent years Alberti did not cease to travel, always as a paid guest of the Russians. He visited the Soviet Union again, and after a trip to China wrote poems about the successes of Chinese socialism. Thanks to the active promotion of his hosts, he achieved an international profile that no other Spanish intellectual of the twentieth century ever had the fortune to enjoy. He was in Buenos Aires when Stalin died in 1953, and penned a long elegy:

There are no races, no peoples, no corners,
Not even the smallest fragment of the world
Where the voice does not reach, the voice that
    announces with sadness:
Joseph Stalin is dead.

Quite apart from its pedestrian quality, the elegy revealed the impoverished ideology of the only well-known Spanish exile who was still following the party line. When he eventually decided to leave Argentina, he had no problem settling in Italy in 1963, in the Trastevere district of Rome, where he continued to enjoy the attentions of progressives and received visits from intellectuals. Apart from that, his exile in Rome bored him:

> Always walking down or up,
> Entering, leaving and entering . . . going to the market.
> How much are eggs today? And the fish?
> Life spent eating and emptying the bowels.
> Going to churches, when I have no faith,
> One's soul feeling like a cat in a cage.
> Returning outside . . . drinking wine with water.
> Going to the river . . . and, once again, eating.[97]

The summit of his success was the Lenin Peace Prize, awarded in 1965. Eventually, in 1977, two years after the death of Franco, he returned triumphantly to Spain, where the Communist Party secured him a seat in the parliament. He was fêted and showered with honours, but many of his ambitions had changed. He gave up his seat within a year, and returned actively to his distant artistic past, producing publicity posters in the Surrealist style that he now followed. His wife died in 1988, and he re-married a couple of years later. He died in his native town, Puerto Santa María, to which he bequeathed much of his creative work.

Mass communication, as we have noted, was slow to penetrate Spain, but the impact of radio and film was immediate, at least in the cities. The first (foreign) film in Spain was shown in Madrid in 1896, but Spaniards were late in entering the field. The first fiction film made, by film pioneer Fructuoso Gelabert, was in 1897. Barcelona was the main centre of production for the next twenty years, before Madrid took over. The first sound film came out in 1932, but there was slow progress because of the absence of supportive technology. All the same Spaniards brought out 109 films between 1932 and 1936, a respectable figure even when compared with the 700 produced by England and the 2,000 produced by the United States in the same period.[98] It was a time when producers everywhere were conscious of the social possibilities of the medium, and in the Second Republic officials were keen to imitate the striking experiments made by Soviet propaganda. The highly combustible state of opinion in Spain, however, called for some caution. The massacre (for which the government was held responsible) at the village of Casas Viejas in January 1933 was typical of the problems that might excite opinion. In consequence, it was the Republic that tried to proceed carefully. When the Soviet director Eisenstein's pioneering film *The Battleship Potemkin* was shown in Madrid, a member of the audience, Luis Buñuel, remembered that people got so excited that 'we wanted to put up barricades and the police had to intervene'.[99] Understandably, the government banned the film. Buñuel subsequently faced the same type of obstacle.

Luis Buñuel (1900–83) was the son of a prosperous merchant in the small town of Calanda (near Teruel, in the province of Aragon) and saw his first film when he was eight years old, in a cinema in the Aragonese capital, Saragossa. He studied at a Jesuit school in the capital but was expelled for his behaviour. In 1917 he was studying to be an engineer in Madrid, where thanks to his father's money he was accepted into the Residencia de Estudiantes. He soon developed a close personal relationship with two of the other residents, García Lorca and Salvador Dalí, and started writing instead of studying. He was also a dedicated sportsman, and started boxing. We have an image of what he was like in the year 1924, when he graduated from the University of Madrid, in the form of a striking portrait painted by Dalí. Buñuel moved on to Paris, where he spent a total of four years, developing his new interest in filmmaking. During his extended stay, in 1929 he collaborated with some friends, including Dalí, on the script for *Un Chien andalou* (*Andalusian Dog*), a Surrealist film that shocked the public (the opening shot showed a razor slicing through an open eye) and made cinema history through its enduring impact on later filmmakers. He went on to film *L'Age d'Or* (1930), which also provoked a scandal, mainly because of its anticlerical tone. The police banned the showing and seized copies of the film, but Buñuel was in Los Angeles when it all happened, on the first of his many visits to Hollywood, where MGM had shown interest in his work. He returned to Spain in 1931, just as the Republic was being proclaimed, and offered his services to the authorities. It was potentially one of his most fruitful periods, when he planned many ambitious projects, and brought out *Las Hurdes* (*Land without Bread*), about a region in the water-starved province of Extremadura, in which he contrasted the poverty of the peasants with the wealth of the Church. Controversial in Spain, he also continued to carry out projects for the American film industry, both in Paris and (with Warner Brothers) in Spain.

Las Hurdes was first shown in Madrid in 1933, and touched a sensitive spot at a very sensitive time. Among those present at the showing was Gregorio Marañón, who criticized the film for high-lighting only the misery of the region and ignoring completely its architecture and churches. The Republic needed to sell its achieve-ments rather than underscore problems it could not solve. The film was banned and continued to be banned. The outbreak of the Civil War, however, ended censorship, and Soviet films began to be shown freely in areas under Republican management. Buñuel was encour-aged to do propaganda projects, of which the best known was a film, *España 1936*, that he made in collaboration with a French director. He was also put in charge of the film section of the Spanish Pavilion in the 1937 World Exhibition in Paris. This was, however, almost the end of his career as a Spanish director. In 1938 he left France to go to America in pursuit of work. His exile (for it turned out to be such, since he was unable to return to the Spain he had known), like that of many creative artists and scholars such as Picasso and Severo Ochoa, was brought about directly by his need to have access to the sources that made his work possible. Political motives never entered into it. He settled in Hollywood, where he was given good contracts for work for the MoMA, New York. His aggressive character, however, soon brought him into conflict with his paymasters. The Hollywood moguls disliked his work for its offensiveness and realism, and even-tually he lost his job in 1943.[100] He hung around for three more years, looking for work, but never made a single film during the seven years he spent in Hollywood. Smarting under the failure, in 1946 he moved to Mexico, where he became a citizen in 1949.

In Mexico he was able, after over a decade of frustration, to create the films he wished, and in so doing he earned the international recog-nition that had eluded him. Of all the exiled artists who had supported the Republic, he was the only one whose name entered popular culture and became known to millions. He continued to apply Surrealist touches to a presentation that was basically savage social criticism, relieved by heavy irony and pessimism. Inevitably, his *Los Olvidados (The Forgotten)* (1950), perhaps his best-known film, earned him harsh criticism from the Mexican government for its negative rendering of social reality. The plot follows a young boy, Pedro, through misadventures associated with the low life, crime, immorality and poverty of the shanty towns. In effect Buñuel broke all conventions by questioning the stereotypes that had until then reigned supreme in Mexican cinema. Only after its triumph at the Cannes Film Festival, where Buñuel won the best director award, did the authorities and critics tolerate the film. He went on to produce successes, based on Mexican life, such as *Nazarín* (1958). Nazarín is a priest who attempts to lead a truly Christian life by surrounding himself with the dregs of the earth in a Mexican village, but finds that his charitable efforts are all counterproductive. He is expelled from the Church by his superiors for befriending a prostitute, and sets off with her to find his role in the world. The film won an award at the Cannes festival of 1959.

A director of international reputation after his triumph with *Los Olvidados*, he went to France in 1955 to make a series of highly successful films. In an unusual departure from its normal boycott of Communist exiles, the Spanish government, desperate to achieve some sort of success at the Cannes Film Festival, offered to finance a film by him if they could agree on a script. The result was his *Viridiana* (1961), which Buñuel ensured Spanish officials did not see before its premiere. A novice nun, Viridiana, visits her only living relative, an uncle who lives alone on his large country estate. He is struck by her resemblance to his late wife, and attempts to seduce her. When she refuses, he commits suicide. Struck with guilt, Viridiana returns to the country house and engages in charitable work by inviting in a group of beggars whom she lodges and feeds. One day while she is away, the beggars repay her kindness by holding a bawdy dinner party in the house. She returns and is shocked, whereupon they rape her. The plot was bold enough, but the Spanish government censors were not prepared for the unscripted shots, of which the most notorious was the obscene re-enactment of Leonardo's *Last Supper*. The film won the Golden Palm at the Festival, but was immediately disowned by Spain and banned in the country.

Buñuel went on the following year, 1962, to direct in Mexico his *The Exterminating Angel*, a macabre comedy which soon became a cult movie. The film describes the situation of a group of upper-class guests who come to dinner, find they cannot leave, and end up in a grotesque and surrealist orgy of degeneration. The wish to shock also informed most of his productions in France. His films insisted obsessively on sexual perversions (*Belle de Jour*, 1967; *Tristana*, 1970, both starring Catherine Deneuve) and the constant theme of anticlericalism. Curiously, he benefited from the new political environment in the United States, where protests against the Vietnam War were increasing, and he finally won an Oscar from the Americans for his *Discreet Charm of the Bourgeoisie* (1972). He died in Mexico City.

Buñuel, clearly, was one of the many exiles who like Picasso ceased to be formally Spanish (though his basic perceptions continued always to be Spanish) and became universal. He threw himself wholeheartedly into both the creative and meretricious aspects of the film industry, and was never afraid to reveal his own combination of genius and vulgarity. His public, however, could never be sure whether his message was to be taken seriously, since behind his realism (or Surrealism, or nihilism, or any other 'ism') it was difficult to find any sustained set of attitudes or beliefs. Some of his statements, like the following, are credible:

I feel it necessary to say here (since it explains in part the trend of the modest work which I later accomplished) that the two basic sentiments of my childhood which stayed with me well into adolescence, are those of a profound eroticism, at first sublimated in a great religious faith, and a permanent consciousness of death. It would take too long here to analyze the reasons. It suffices that I was not an exception among my compatriots, since this is a very Spanish characteristic, and our art, exponent of the Spanish spirit, was impregnated with these two sentiments. The last civil war, peculiar and ferocious as no other, exposed them clearly.[101]

He took his surrealism seriously, but principally because it might serve 'to explode the social order, to transform life itself'. He accordingly bulldozed his way through most of the values that he had imbibed and that his society nurtured, and for the same reason he was attracted to the revolutionary possibilities of the Republic.

The preference of creative artists for communism was a common enough phenomenon in the Europe of that time, and Spain was no exception. There was, however, no such thing as a single set of attitudes among the pro-Communists, and the war quickly brought out the latent differences among the exiles. Shortly after the war the English writer George Orwell exposed in his *Homage to Catalonia* the machinations of those members of the party who accepted their orders from the Soviet Union of Stalin. Among the exiles the dissension could be seen through one of the most expressive writers of his generation, Jorge Semprun (1923–), who escaped from Spain with his family in 1937, and grew up as a permanent resident of France. Of upper-class origin, he was a grandson of Alfonso XIII's prime minister, Antonio Maura, and his father was a lawyer and poet. He joined the Spanish Communist Party in its French exile in 1942. As a member of the French Resistance he was arrested by German forces in 1943 and sent to the concentration camp of Buchenwald, from where he and other survivors were eventually rescued by the Allies. Driven from Spain, driven from France, confined in the camp among a vast community of deportees (around 50,000, with twice that number also working in the adjoining areas), his experience as a refugee changed his life. He returned again and again in his writings to the themes of exile and deprivation. They were the subject of his successful novel *Le Grand Voyage* (*The Long Voyage*, 1963), which narrated in semi-autobiographical form his experience of the journey to and internment in Buchenwald. He told a Spanish journalist in 1994 that 'All I really am is a deportee'.[102] Interviewed for *Le Monde des débats* in May 2000, he said:

For me, there is nothing about the camps that cannot be put into words. Language makes everything possible for us. But the writing is interminable; it is never done, because an isolated work by itself cannot do more than allude to fragments of reality, because an infinite work of memory or anamnesis goes hand in hand with the infinite work of writing. You have never finished telling the story. An example is the smell of the camps and of the crematorium – something that all the survivors know and remember, which sometimes comes back in their dreams. That is how we identify ourselves as former deportees; it is these memories that set us apart from everyone else alive.

In the same year he told a German reporter about his choice of theme:

'Today I am convinced that only one thing is important: Buchenwald.'

He wrote almost exclusively in French. In the 1960s he added screenwriting to his other occupations as interpreter (for UNESCO) and novelist: his first script was for Resnais' film *La Guerre est Finie* (1966). During the 1950s he returned to Spain illegally as part of his work for the Communist Party. In 1964 his disagreement with the Stalinist line of his party earned him expulsion from it, and he returned to Spain only briefly in 1988–91 (he has seemingly always retained his Spanish citizenship) as minister of culture of the second Socialist government. Though much of his work has been translated into Spanish, Semprun has been somewhat neglected in Spain, not because of his politics, but because as an expatriate with a career abroad his writings deal with themes that do not fall within the historic experience of Spaniards.

The emigration of the greater part of the cultural elite between 1936 and 1939 was wholly unprecedented. For over four centuries, there had been periodic expulsions and departures, but never before had such a systematic flight of the educated classes occurred. Taken together with the massive exodus of refugees from the Civil War, it represented a truly momentous event in the country's history. Commentators suggested that a major cultural tragedy had taken place, comparable for instance to the expulsion of the Jews. It may be that we are too close in time to see events in proper perspective, but on balance the negative significance of the elite diaspora was probably much less than it first appears. Nearly all the major literary figures had come safely back, as we shall see in the final chapter of this book, shortly after the war ended. Some of those in exile stuck to their ideological guns, and gradually drifted apart from events, until old age called them home. Meanwhile, the whole process of departure gave rise, as we have already seen in the diasporas of previous centuries, to an enormously fruitful opening of horizons. Both first and second generation exiles integrated themselves into the mainstream of western culture, opened doors and windows and brought new life to their own creativity and, in the long run, to Hispanic civilization.

8

The Search for Atlantis

We Spaniards find ourselves divided into two hemispheres,
and also divided within each of the hemispheres.

Juan Ramón Jiménez[1]

From the earliest stage of Spain's contact with the New World, commentators speculated about the strange situation that had created advanced civilizations like those of the Aztecs and Incas, living within a world of far less developed peoples. What were the origins of the high American cultures? It was not an empty question, for in answering it the Spaniards hoped to define their own place in the New World, and their relation to the indigenous peoples there. Some sixteenth-century historians of the Inca world had the theory that the Incas were remnants of the advanced civilization of Atlantis, referred to in the classical writings of the Greek philosopher Plato. In two of his dialogues, written four centuries before Christ, Plato referred to a great island civilization that existed at the beginning of the world but was eventually destroyed and disappeared beneath the waves. Was Plato talking about a real event, or simply using Atlantis as a myth to put forward his ideas? Since they were continually discovering strange and incredible things, some early Spanish explorers did not discount the possibility that survivors of Atlantis – a city that gave its name to the great ocean between Europe and America – might have made it to the New World. Exacting scholars discounted the possibility, but others insisted that the myth was true and that it was one of the original links between the two Atlantic worlds. The explorer of the Amazon, Orellana, claimed for example to have found proof of contacts with Atlantis. When he wrote his essay on political philosophy, the English Renaissance lawyer and politician Francis Bacon gave it the title of an ideal territory, *The New Atlantis*. Since that time, scores of books have been written about Atlantis and scores of theories put forward, usually at the level of popular fantasy.

The real vogue in theories about Atlantis began in the nineteenth century, in France, Germany and the United States. One of the most vivid depictions of the lost continent of Atlantis came in the French novelist Jules Verne's tale *Twenty Thousand Leagues Under the Sea* (1869). In the same years that Verne was writing, the possibility of new horizons across the Atlantic was being explored directly and personally by one of the most restless spirits of the nineteenth century in Catalonia, the priest and poet Jacint Verdaguer (1845–1902). As a young student in the seminary he was already a poet, winning prizes for his verse in 1865. He was fired by the vision of Columbus's voyage to America (when Columbus announced his discovery in 1492 he did so in Barcelona, capital of Catalonia). Stray bits of a poem were forming in his mind. Shortly after his ordination as priest in 1870 he fell ill, and the doctors recommended that he take a rest and seek some sea air. He took the advice literally. Catalans at the time were heavily involved in the tobacco industry in Cuba. Verdaguer secured a passage as chaplain on a Catalan vessel that set out from Cadiz bound for Havana. On his return he had the virtually complete text of his Odyssey-style poem, *Atlantis* (in Spanish and Catalan the word is *Atlántida*) (1876), written in antiquated Catalan and in the best tradition of the Romantic style of Byron. He entered it for a public competition, where it was acclaimed and awarded a prize. With time, he was greeted as the national poet of Catalonia. His later years were less triumphant. He suffered depressions and mental crises bordering on madness, was pursued by the police, and shut away in a monastery.

Verdaguer's story of *Atlantis* told of a great civilization of the West, located in the island of Atlantis, which is destroyed by divine wrath, and the Titans who inhabit it are buried in the depths of the ocean. On the ruin of this old civilization, its protecting angel takes leave and ascends to heaven. But on the way he passes his authority to another angel, who descends to the surface of the earth. This is the angel of Spain. 'The angel of Atlantis,' says Verdaguer's summary at this point, 'turning to heaven, gives to the descending angel of Spain the crown of the queen of the worlds.'

> Since I see rising in the East the star that is setting here,
> Here is the crown of fine gold that Atlantis wore
> When she was queen. Place it on her brow.[2]

Dominion over the western world has collapsed, but will be replaced by the new star in the East, the rising star of Spain. The poem closes with Queen Isabella sending Columbus out towards the New World across the Atlantic.

Columbus's contact with the New World in 1492 set in train a process of population movement that changed the appearance of the globe. But the changes happened extremely slowly, because Spaniards were in no hurry to go to the unknown expanses of America. It was literally a lifetime, over thirty years, before they founded the first township in the Caribbean, the settlement of Santo Domingo on the island of Hispaniola. Many of the Europeans who entered the capital of the Aztec empire had not even been born when the new continent was 'discovered'. For the greater part of the sixteenth century, the American experience was not a significant component of Hispanic culture. At the most mature period of their imperial adventure, Spaniards continued to be ambiguous about what the New World represented for them. Cervantes, in *The Jealous Old Man from Extremadura* (1605), knew enough about America to describe it as 'refuge and shelter of the desperate of Spain, a disappointment to many and a remedy for few'. However, he knew little about it. In his *Quixote*, published at the same date, America is a distant land of promise, but little more. The word 'America' is mentioned only once in the novel, the New World only once, and 'the Indies' six times.[3] In the time of Cervantes, emigration across the Atlantic was slowing to a trickle, and people seem to have been losing interest in what was happening there.

Spaniards did not always see inhospitable America as the land of opportunity. Historians have suggested that in the period 1500–1650 perhaps 437,000 Spaniards went to the New World.[4] However, there is no reliable evidence that so many crossed the Atlantic, and it seems more probable, as has recently been argued,[5] that the numbers were much smaller. At the end of the colonial era, a census for Mexico in 1790 revealed that only 0.2 per cent of the population was of Hispanic origin, of whom the majority had been born in America and not in the peninsula. When the Wars of Independence broke out in the New World territories, many Spaniards were driven out and deprived of their properties: in Mexico by 1830 the number of Spaniards had fallen by half.[6] The peninsula did not have enough people to send to the New World, and of those who went a very high proportion returned to Europe disillusioned. As we can see from the correspondence of those who were successful in the New World and wished to attract their families over, it was not easy to convince Spaniards of the benefits of emigration.

Those who emigrated had no wish to be exiles and did not necessarily decide to settle. From the beginning there was always an impressive return flow. But the enormous divide of the Atlantic inevitably made it difficult for many to come back, so that thousands of Spaniards who had committed themselves to participating in the life of the worldwide empire, whether in Italy or Mexico or the Philippines, inevitably looked on themselves as true expatriates. They missed the sights, smells and above all the food of home, but in their new places of residence came to terms with the problem, got together with other expatriates, and reminisced about what they had left behind. Thousands, no doubt, found themselves in the position of the settler in Potosí, Bolivia, who wrote to his family: 'I don't know what to do. To tell the truth I have no wish to die in this country, but back where I was born.'[7] Another in Cajamarca, Peru, wrote in 1698: 'though my body is in America, my soul is in Navarre'.[8] For generations of Spaniards, there was a perennial pull between their adopted homeland and the one they had left behind. The persistent longing for home, however, had to compete with (and seldom overcame) the practical satisfaction that emigrants found in their corner of the empire.

Two widely different Hispanic cultures grew up, sharing in common little more than language, which in its turn was influenced and altered by the difference of environment. Those who lived outside the peninsula felt that they now belonged to a different world. Bit by bit, the expatriates began to identify themselves more with their new home than with the place where they had been born, the *patria* of their hometown, their village, their kinfolk, their familiar countryside. When a citizen of Cartagena wrote in 1590 urging his wife to come over and join him, he told her to forget about the pain of leaving her homeland: 'don't keep thinking about your *patria*, because the real *patria* is the country that looks after you'.[9] 'I always used to have the deep wish to return to my *patria*,' explained a merchant of Mexico City in 1592 to his parents in the Canary Islands, 'and if I had done so I would have been greatly mistaken.'[10] Instead, members of the family were urged to come over to join him. Colonists observed the clear contrast between their lifestyle in the New World and what they had known in the Old. 'I am not saying to you that I don't wish to go to Spain,' a husband wrote from Lima in 1704 to his wife in the peninsula, 'for I really do wish to go.' The problem was, he explained, 'the ruin that is Spain, with so many debts and dues and taxes, none of which we have over here'.[11]

Long-term emigration – the mass equivalent of the 'exile' that a specific few suffered – became a permanent feature of the Hispanic condition. At the end of the nineteenth century every European state was unloading its unemployed on to the New World. Spaniards made up a fair part of this emigration. Though only a few managed to make their fortunes across the ocean, the dream of America as a place of refuge and hope never faded. In the middle years of the nineteenth century there was a new wave of emigration, mainly to Cuba. The biggest movement of population came after 1880, when economic changes and financial instability drove millions of Europeans out of their continent, mainly across the Atlantic. The exodus from Spain was explosive. Over three and a half million Spaniards crossed the ocean between 1880 and 1936 in search of a better life, though very many returned home and fewer than half stayed on permanently. The areas most favoured by the newcomers were Cuba and Argentina, with the United States beginning to feature as an important destination. In the peak period of 1880 to 1930, 34 per cent of Spaniards went to Cuba, 48 per cent to Argentina, and 2 per cent to the United States.[12] The last-named country was already being inundated by other Europeans, and began to impose restrictions from 1924. By then, in any case, the number of emigrants from the peninsula had begun to fall drastically, as the countries of Latin America started to close their doors to workers who competed with their own population. Emigration was consequently not permanent, and many came back. It has been estimated for Spain that 'between 1882 and 1914 nearly four returned for every five who left'.[13] A Spanish politician admitted in 1907 that 'departures are very many, but so are the returns'.[14] In the year 1931, 27,000 people left for the New World but 62,000 came back, a reverse trend that continued throughout the early 1930s.[15]

Emigrants went also to other lands in Europe, but always as temporary labour rather than long-term displacement. After the First World War, in which it had not been a participant, Spain was able to send men to other countries to find jobs. The official figures for Spaniards resident in France in 1921 was 255,000, about 16 per cent of the number of foreigners in the country, employed mainly in the area along the Atlantic (Bordeaux) and Mediterranean (Nice) coasts.[16] After the Second World War, in which Spain again did not take part, the same type of labour emigration took place. When the Franco regime began its economic reforms, it was forced to export labour in order to solve its own employment problems and also to earn foreign exchange. Between 1960 and 1973, the number of 'guest workers' (as the Germans called them) who emigrated from Spain exceeded one million people, representing according to one estimate as many as a quarter of the country's active labour force.[17] By 1972, there were still some 590,000 Spanish workers resident in France. Spaniards, therefore, were always on the move. But America was the great obsession.

The last great emigration from the peninsula took place, we have seen, in the 1930s, the very decade when all countries were reluctant to accept newcomers. It affected not only the propertied classes, whose reactions have been touched on, but all sections of the population. Unlike emigrations of the preceding century, this was exclusively political and entirely involuntary. In the last eighteen months of the Civil War, some 400,000 refugees crossed over into the most accessible refuge, France. Most, as we have noted in the previous chapter, returned to Spain in 1939. The Nazi occupation of France in 1940 changed conditions dramatically for those who remained. Most were forced to go back or were forcibly repatriated. Those who could manage it undertook a second journey of exile, this time to Latin America, where some governments suspended their restrictions and welcomed the refugees. It was not a decision to be regretted, for the immigrants usually had something to offer their host countries.

One positive effect of the repeated transatlantic contacts in the nineteenth century was a greater consciousness in the New World of the roots of Hispanic identity. 'Progressive' writers, poets and political agitators in Latin America had always rejected the imperial and colonial heritage in favour of authentic native roots. In narratives of the conquest of Mexico the good guy had been Cuauhtemoc, last legitimate ruler of Nahua Mexico, the bad guy had been Cortés. Subsequent political movements, especially in Mexico, favoured the culture of the Indians and rejected the culture of the Spaniards. In the half century after the independence of the Latin American nations, Spaniards were reluctant to accept freedom for America. As a consequence, when Blanco White began to express his support for a free Spanish America he earned fierce criticism in Spain. By the end of his life White had lost faith in Spain's capacity to regenerate itself, and looked instead to America as the hope for Hispanic culture.

By contrast, Spaniards continued to be indifferent to the Hispanic heritage. In the 1740s, the government officials Jorge Juan and Antonio de Ulloa, who had spent a dozen years in America, commented indignantly on the total lack of interest shown by Spaniards in their empire. Blanco White, nearly a century later, had the same impression:

The animosity raised against me in Cadiz was because of my defence of the right of the Spanish colonies to a liberty equal to that of the mother country. Even in these moments [1845], when all hope of reconquering the Spanish American dominions has been lost, the spirit of the conquests of Mexico and Peru is not extinguished, and during the years when the colonies began to shake off their yoke, the pride of conquest was as great in Spain as in the sixteenth century. Since that century the Spaniards have lived in the most profound ignorance of the course of human affairs in the rest of the world, and for this reason the prejudices inherited by successive generations remain as strong as in the time of Cortés and Pizarro.[18]

Half a century after Blanco, the situation was unchanged. Ganivet commented in 1898 that 'our colonization has been almost a fiction. The majority of the nation has always been ignorant of the geographical location of its territories.'[19] Apart from a few writers, mostly of conservative persuasion, Spaniards had no interest in their colonial past and continue still to be remarkably indifferent to the culture and peoples that formed part of it. Down to the present day, 'the idea of empire is almost totally absent from the collective imagination of Spaniards'.[20] Study or analysis of the phenomenon of empire does not feature in university courses, and for the general public the imperial age is associated not with real events but exclusively with stereotyped heroic images of the great feats of superhuman versions of Cortés and Pizarro. In the years before the Disaster a few daring spirits, among them Juan de Valera, had travelled to America to explore its culture. Though Valera professed disdain for the Spain that he hoped to regenerate, he could not bring himself to believe that the New World might offer a solution. Quite the contrary: what most satisfied him about the United States was that its people appeared to be dazzled by the greatness of Spain. 'The immortal reflection of our glories,' he wrote to the historian Menéndez Pelayo, 'discoveries, adventures, greatness and exploits in America, produce and sustain a sympathy, admiration and love for Spain and the Spanish!'[21] As we have seen, his solution was that Spain should re-create its 'hegemony' in the New World. After the Disaster, that was no longer possible, and intellectuals began to give a different meaning to the magic word 'empire'. At the beginning of the twentieth century the idea of bringing new life to a moribund Spain through a re-vamped concept of 'empire' played a key role in the writings of some right-wing writers, especially in Catalonia,[22] but the idea was never more than a bizarre fancy. Meanwhile, a fictional image of the empire as an expression of Spain's capacity and might continued to influence the minds of the public, which devoured with enthusiasm (and never more than today)[23] novels about Spanish achievements in Flanders and in the Andes but remained indifferent to the real empire of the past.

Spain's political presence in America north of the Gulf of Mexico had always been negligible, and shrank to nothing during the first half of the nineteenth century. When the United States gave up Texas to

Mexico by treaty in 1821, it seemed that the main area of Spanish influence would remain south of the border. Then came the US-Mexican war of 1846–8, when Mexico lost half of its territory, including all of Texas, to the Americans. The border changes had profound consequences for Hispanic culture. The United States, the world's biggest reserve of Anglo-Saxon civilization, would within a century begin to develop into the world's most important Hispanic nation. That may not have been the vision facing the refugees from the Civil War in 1939. Almost without exception,[24] they avoided the United States and preferred at first to go elsewhere.

Confronted with the undeniable power of the United States, which after the Spanish-American War of 1898 went on to intervene in the territory of Panama in 1903, Spain and its former colonies found that they had no resources in common other than the language they spoke. In the view of some, however, the heritage was not merely one of language but rather of a whole 'culture', one that united the Spanish-speaking peoples against the expanding power of the United States. The concept of 'culture' was never explained or identified, but readily took shape in two specific myths that became the stock-in-trade of the new conservative reaction. One, which we have commented on already, was the myth of the figure of Don Quixote, taken to represent spiritual values as against the materialism of the Anglo-Saxon nations. The second, which we shall touch on in Chapter 9, was the myth of 'the language of Cervantes', representing claims to universal cultural hegemony.

From the time that the colonies in America freed themselves of Spanish rule, they rejected the old imperial heritage. A tradition inherited from the early nineteenth century insisted that Spain was an imperial power that had bled America dry, destroyed its people, and left only the husks. By contrast, the United States had helped to liberate the colonies. The Argentine politician Domingo Sarmiento was among those who rejected the Spanish heritage and embraced the future offered by America. 'Yankee civilization,' he wrote, 'was the work of the plough and primer, while the cross and the sword of Spain destroyed Spanish American civilization. There [in the United States] they learned to work and to read, here we learned to loaf and to pray.'[25] There was an active debate about the relative contributions of

English-language (or 'Anglo') and Spanish culture to the well-being of Latin America. Meanwhile, the anti-Spanish tendency was aggravated, notably in Mexico, by a pro-indigenous movement, which turned its back on what the Europeans had brought and preferred to insist on the values of the pre-conquest peoples. The debate between the respective merits of Anglo and Hispanic values was soon overtaken by the development of intensely anti-Yankee attitudes.

Eventually the pendulum swung back to favouring the idea of Hispanic origins. In part this was a gut reaction against the United States, provoked by the total Spanish military and naval collapse in 1898. The Nicaraguan poet Rubén Darío, who was at the time in Spain, where he spent many fruitful years, took up a theme based on Shakespeare's play *The Tempest* and contributed energetically to the tide of anti-Yankee sentiment with an angry essay denouncing *The Triumph of Caliban* (1898), in which he poured intemperate scorn on 'pink, fat, vulgar' Americans and 'the greed of the Anglosaxon'. In *The Tempest* Caliban represented the malign spirit, whereas the good spirit (that is, the Hispanic spirit) was the fairy Ariel. The literary reference was extended in a highly influential tract titled *Ariel*, published in 1900 by the Montevidean writer José Enrique Rodó. The way forward, many argued, was for a pan-Hispanic alliance against the United States, based on the evident superiority of Spain's spiritual values over the crude materialism of the West. The assertion of moral superiority was part and parcel of the feeling of material inferiority that had depressed many Spaniards at the time. Coincidentally, the pan-Hispanic idea was also a deliberate propaganda move by the Spanish government. As early as the 1850s the Spaniards had initiated a cultural offensive, which became more intense after the defeat in 1898, and in the 1930s gave birth (among writers such as Maeztu) to the notion of 'Hispanidad' ('Spanishness'), later taken up with gusto by the internationally isolated government of Franco. 'Hispanidad', substituted later by other similar words, became a rallying cry that gained widespread support among Hispanic American writers. Even in Argentina, which with its substantial Italian and British elements was not normally categorized as an Hispanic country, the writer Manuel Gálvez could claim that 'we belong to the Spanish caste'. The Chilean Communist poet (and Nobel winner) Gabriela Mistral drew a radical antithesis between 'the language God gave us', namely Spanish, and 'the misery which the United States gives us'.[26]

The active links between Spain and the New World were reinforced, inevitably, by exiles from Spain who not only looked towards America but drew from the New World inspiration for their own ideas and projects. One of the most remarkable of them was the Valencian novelist Vicente Blasco Ibáñez, who achieved only limited fame in his home country but became one of the truly international figures of Hispanic culture. He achieved what no other Spanish writer had until then: global recognition. This was in good measure because his own horizons were never limited to Spain but embraced both Europe and the Atlantic. Blasco Ibáñez (1867–1928), born in Valencia city of a good family, studied law at university but soon left the legal profession and turned to writing. Bilingual in Catalan and Castilian, he produced all his significant works in the latter language, which he used to portray realistically the lives of everyday people in Valencia. He also became active politically, as a federalist, anticlerical republican. In 1890 the police tried to arrest him for his work as an agitator and he fled in a fishing-boat to Algeria, then to Marseilles and Paris, where he lodged in the Latin Quarter. Paris represented for him, as it had for previous exiles, the fount of inspiration. He revelled in the intellectual environment, and above all came to admire the writings of Victor Hugo and Émile Zola, whose social realism definitively influenced his own work. A year later an amnesty was declared by the Spanish government and he returned, founding in 1894 the anti-monarchist newspaper *El Pueblo*, in which he began to serialize the first of his regionalist novels, *Rice and Cart*, heavily influenced by Zola. It narrated life among the lower-middle classes and shopkeepers of the city of Valencia.

In 1895 he took part in protests against the Spanish repression in Cuba and had to flee to Italy, where the atmosphere stimulated him to continue writing; on his return in 1896 he was arrested, imprisoned and exiled from Valencia. His experiences gave rise to *La Barraca* (*The Shanty*, sometimes translated as *The Cabin*, 1898), the most typical of his regionalist novels and the one to achieve most success in Spain. It described with great realism the life of the poor peasants in the plain of Valencia, living in their crude mud-huts or shanties, and the hatred and violence faced by a new family trying to make their way in the region. A French reader persuaded him to have it translated; it immediately became an international success and was translated into the major European languages. The regionalist novels, among them his *Reeds and Mud* (*Cañas y Barro*, 1902), were set in the environment of the labourers and fishermen of the villages of the Mediterranean coast, with a realistic and sensitive portrayal of their conflicts, loves and struggles, and remain that part of his work which is most appreciated by his Valencian countrymen. The debt to Zola was deeply personal. When the Dreyfus affair was brought into the open through Zola's press article 'I accuse' in January 1898, Ibáñez backed him energetically, collected mass signatures of support in the streets of Valencia, and went personally to Paris to visit the author and kiss 'the hand that created so many immortal works'.

Ibáñez was now an active politician and member of the Cortes. In 1906 he and the Valencian painter Sorolla received the Légion d'Honneur. He was a celebrity, but a permanently restless one. Personal conflicts and political tensions induced him to withdraw, disillusioned, from active political life in 1907. By that date he had taken part in fifteen duels (one of them was nearly fatal), and had been imprisoned over thirty times. The good income from his books encouraged him to change the direction of his life, and he set out to discover the world, travelling through Europe and into Turkey. His absence served only to direct his attention to what he had left at home, and when he came back he wrote probably the most memorable of all novels about bullfighting, *Blood and Sand* (*Sangre y Arena*, 1908), which was filmed in 1922 and again in 1941 in Hollywood, and in an execrable Spanish version in 1989. Often supposed to be a Hemingway-style eulogy of the sport, it is rather the opposite, since like many progressives Blasco Ibáñez did not like bullfighting. The story concerns Juan Gallardo, a bullfighter who finds that his humble origins are the barrier to success both in love and in the ring. He is merely a plaything for his public, who throw him over when he gets gored. He then realizes that his real enemy is not the bull, but the crowd.

Still young (he was only forty-two) and active, Ibáñez changed direction again and set out to discover the New World. In 1909 he spent a year in Argentina, where he was acclaimed rapturously by the public in Buenos Aires and explored the possibility of founding utopian colonies in the savagely beautiful lands of Patagonia. His reception excited him. 'I come here,' he told his cheering public, 'representing an intellectual Spain, a new Spain!' At heart still a revolutionary and republican, he was inspired by the vision of compensating for Spain's failures (especially that of 1898) by creating a new and better society on the other side of the Atlantic, where the only fundamental requirement would be Spanish language and culture. The year 1909 was that of the Tragic Week (see Chapter 3) in Barcelona. Ibáñez expected the usual flood of refugees from Spain, and hoped to offer the exiles a new world in Patagonia. In later years he directed the operation from Valencia. 'I shall found there,' he wrote, with reference to Patagonia, to which he returned time and again, 'a colony with the name Cervantes. Before raising a single house, I intend the first construction to be a statue of the author of *Quixote*.' A second planned colony was given the name 'New Valencia'. Landless labourers from Valencia in Spain were encouraged to go out to populate the new settlements. The Atlantis-style vision also had its literary side. He wrote *The Argonauts* (1914), which was translated into French and became a success in Paris. The hero of the novel is a young Spaniard who goes out to America to achieve his fortune, on a crossing that lasts two weeks and involves conflicts in the lives of passengers both rich and poor. The author felt his work to be in some degree autobiographical:

Out of everything I have written the first chapter of *The Argonauts* is the only thing I can read without effort, and many times reading it has brought tears to my eyes, I know why and I do not wish to say anything more.

Blasco Ibáñez, however, did not have corresponding good fortune with his social experiments. For reasons beyond his control, the colonies collapsed. Many settlers, ancestors of those who are still there today, continued to live in the region.

When the First World War broke out, he went to Paris to give support to the French, and later, while staying at a friend's château in

Provence, began the text that emerged as *The Four Horsemen of the Apocalypse* (*Los cuatro jinetes del Apocalipsis*, 1916), the novel that brought him world fame and inspired two Hollywood films (1921 and 1962). The novel was unique in Spanish literature as the first work of fiction to bring its author world renown in their lifetime. It was exceptional also for the complete indifference with which it was received in Spain, where neither the cosmopolitan theme nor its European environment was understood by the public that read the first serialization in a Madrid newspaper in 1916. Set in both Buenos Aires and Paris, the novel follows the fortunes of the Desnoyers family in the generation leading up to the outbreak of the Great War. Marcel Desnoyers, from Marseilles, emigrates to Argentina and works successfully for a wealthy landowner, whose elder daughter he marries. The younger daughter marries a German. When the land-owner dies, his sons-in-law return to Paris and Berlin respectively, and with his fortune Desnoyers buys a château on the Marne. The outbreak of war disrupts everything. When the Germans invade France, the officer responsible for occupying and destroying the château, where Desnoyers is now living, turns out to be the son of his German brother-in-law. Marcel finds hope in his son Julio, a ne'er-do-well who has returned from Argentina and opportunely changes his life, distinguishing himself fighting for the French. Unfortunately, he dies at the front. Desnoyers is left to ponder on the vision of the four terrible Horsemen of the Apocalypse – war, conquest, famine and death – who remain as the scourge of humanity. 'It appeared to him that from afar was echoing the gallop of the four Apocalyptic horsemen, riding roughshod over all his fellow creatures.'

Blasco Ibáñez expected little of a version in English, and sold the translation rights for a nominal $300. But the American edition sold over 30,000 copies a month in its first three months, and went through twenty printings; in all it probably sold half a million copies. The novel's enormous success in the United States was of course because it coincided with the early stages of the war, and because of its strong pro-French stance. By contrast in Spain it excited the hostility of the literate elite, who had drawn many of their ideas from Germany. The author was invited to the States in 1920 and awarded an honorary doctorate by the University of Washington. In his speech at the award ceremony, Ibáñez was so moved that he proclaimed that Don Quixote now belonged to the New World: 'Don Quixote grew tired of living in Europe and now lives in America!'[27] He gave lectures, and was fêted right across the nation. The Hearst newspaper chain signed him up to write articles at the then princely figure of a thousand dollars each. In Los Angeles, MGM bought the rights and released a film (1921, with Rudolph Valentino), which was deservedly successful. It was followed by one of *Blood and Sand* (1922, again with Valentino). Blasco Ibáñez had already been interested in the possibilities of film as a way of communicating literature to the public. In 1916 he wrote the screenplay for an early Spanish (silent) film version of *Sangre y Arena*, which was on show to the public in Madrid for an uninterrupted run of seven months. His great dream had been not to put his own work on the screen but rather the *Quixote*. This dream was swamped in the success of his novels as Hollywood films.

He admired the political system in the United States. 'I have always been a republican', he once told a meeting in Valencia, 'but don't think that my inspiration was France. I have sympathy for its culture and literature, but it is not my ideal. I have always loved the United States, because it is a federal republic. If federalism did not exist there, believe me the country would not be as great as it is.' An enormous civic reception, literally a triumph, was held for him on his return to Valencia in 1921. He drove into the city at the wheel of a Cadillac which he brought back with him. The international success meant little in Spain, however, where he found himself in trouble because as a stubborn republican he continued to criticize the monarchy and, from 1923, the dictatorship of Primo de Rivera. Police harassment made it impossible for him to live in the country. He remained in exile for the rest of his life at his luxury villa, Fontana Rosa, which he constructed at Menton on the Côte d'Azur, importing rose bushes, orange trees and ceramic tiles from Valencia to decorate a garden in which he set up ten columns with busts of the world's ten greatest writers (the biggest bust, naturally, was of Cervantes). Apart from further novels, he continued publishing subversive tracts against the monarchist and dictatorial regime and earning fabulous dollars from his articles for Hearst. At this period he summed up his life:

I have been a political agitator, I have passed part of my youth in prison, I have been a convict, I have been mortally wounded in fierce duels, I know all the physical privations that a man can suffer including that of absolute poverty, and at the same time I have been in parliament until I grew weary [seven times], I have been an intimate friend of heads of state, I knew personally the former sultan of Turkey, I have lived in palaces, for some years of my life I have been a businessman and handled millions, I have founded towns in America.

But it was not the end of his travels. Drawing on his fund of dollars, in 1923 he began a six-month round-the-world trip in a luxury ocean liner. It was a way to refresh his mind, but it did not stop him using his social sensibility to observe that the Horsemen of the Apocalypse were also stirring in Asia:

We whites have been in the driving seat until now, but what if one day the hundreds of millions of Asiatics find a leader and a common ideal? This voyage has helped me to see that the demon of war is far from dead.[28]

What remained of his free time was spent writing, or dictating. He died four years later at Menton with an evocation of Victor Hugo on his lips, the richest novelist in the entire cultural history of Spain. As an exile with an international culture, he did not fit into any of the categories recognized by Spaniards, regardless of their political affiliation. They did not understand how he could be both a rebel and successful. He was therefore consistently marginalized down to recent times in the cultural memory of official Spain, which refused to act on a request that his villa be preserved as a museum. After the monarchy was overthrown in 1931, his body was brought back home by the administration of Valencia in October 1933, and the immense procession of honour through the streets was headed by ministers and the president of the Republic. Fontana Rosa became a ruin after the death of Blasco Ibáñez's widow in 1939, but after half a century of neglect the authorities at Menton have recently begun to restore the gardens and the ceramic tiles to something of their former glory.

The New World, or a fantasy version of it, never ceased to be viewed by Spaniards as a source of possible solutions to their problems. From the mid-nineteenth century politicians attempted to restore links with the American colonies, alleging that they belonged to a single 'Hispanic race' (see Chapter 9). The word race (*raza*) was never used in an ethnic sense. Rather, it was meant to include all those – principally Spaniards and *mestizos* – who had lived in the New World and were therefore heirs to the two cultural benefits supposedly brought by the empire, namely the Catholic religion and the Castilian language. Men in public life in Spain in the 1870s believed firmly in the virtues and eventual destiny of this *raza*. By contrast, they despised the United States, which they felt was based on two false values, that of materialism (i.e. capitalism) and that of democracy. Spain alone retained the true values, based on the spirit. All political groups in Spain, whether conservative or Liberal, shared these views.[29] The rebirth of the imperial vision was, above all, a consequence of the 1898 Disaster, which deprived the ruling elite of its last historical and cultural dreams.

The vision of America as the great new hope for Hispanic culture was expressed most precisely by Ramiro de Maeztu, who contended quite simply that Spain had civilized both America and the world. That was its legacy, and Spaniards had to return to it. Maeztu referred to 'the great achievements of the Reconquest, the Counter-Reformation and the civilization of America'. Those three peaks remain, even today, firmly fixed in the historical perception of many Spaniards, who would not give a second thought to the possibility that they might be ideological fictions. Maeztu (1874–1936) had a Basque father who married the daughter of the British consul in Paris, was born in Vitoria in the Basque country, and grew up speaking both English and Spanish.[30] The family income came principally from a sugar plantation in Cuba, to which Ramiro travelled in 1891 in an effort to help his father stave off bankruptcy. He took the opportunity to travel through Central and parts of North America, returning to Bilbao in 1894 when his father died. The long stay in Cuba was crucial to his formation. He then worked as a columnist in Madrid until, in 1905, he made the great decision of his life: to work in England, where he remained for fifteen years as a correspondent of Spanish newspapers and *La Prensa* of Buenos Aires, alternating his stay with travels through Europe. In 1910 and 1913 the visits were to Marburg

University, the Mecca of Ortega y Gasset, who had recommended that he imbibe some German civilization there.

Like other Spaniards before him, he found London especially difficult to accept because English literary men did not have the continental custom of discoursing long and earnestly in public bars until the early hours of the morning. Cooped up in a boarding-house in Bayswater, he wrote to Rubén Darío in 1913: 'I have lived for eight years in London, the most solitary and boring existence invented by civilization.'[31] He was in England when the Great War broke out, personally visited the Belgian front for his reports, and also acted as a war correspondent in Italy. In 1916 he married an English girl, Alice Hill. It may have been the best thing he ever did, because she kept his feet on the ground. Salvador de Madariaga was with him at this time in London, and described him as having a 'well-shaped, expressive face, aquiline nose, large mouth, firm chin, deep eyes and a broad forehead crowned with black hair'. Of Alice he commented: 'Maeztu, who always gave the impression of living on the limits of extravagance, never revealed his deep wisdom more than in marrying her'.[32] Young and elegant, Maeztu dressed in the manner of an English gentleman, and expended his energy on an astonishing amount of writing. He expressed his ideas in short, aggressive articles which he produced at the rate of at least one a day, representing an estimated total during his life of fifteen thousand items. Like Ortega, he never had the patience to write long texts and never produced a considered book.

Those fifteen years of absence worked a fundamental change in his thought.[33] At the outset he had been, like other Spanish writers, drawn to the propensity for Germanic thought inherited from the ILE (see Chapter 6). Because of this he admired Nietzsche (whose *Zarathustra* first appeared in Spanish in 1899), and Germanic discipline. During his years in England he did not lose this thread in his thought, for he was in close contact with the literary circle run by A. R. Orage, a mysterious radical journalist who was also an admirer of Nietzsche. He was also influenced by the liberal thinker T. E. Hulme and by the group of Catholic radicals associated with Chesterton and Belloc. The literary environment was not enough to make him overcome his inability to write more than a few words at a time. The most he could do was put together in English a number of articles under the title *Authority,*

Liberty and Function in the Light of the War (1916), a surprisingly sustained and intelligent exposition of his social ideas, consisting of regular contributions to the radical socialist journal directed by Orage, *The New Age*, and writings for other journals. However, his direct experience of the war forced him to reassess his previous admiration for the northern countries and the radical ideas he had shared with his friends in London. The Europe in which he believed was destroying itself through war. What was the way forward? When he returned to Spain with his wife in 1919 ('weary', he complained, 'of the climate of London, I hate rain and fog') his ideas had changed substantially. Spain, which did not take part in the war, now seemed to offer a solution. In 1899, after the Cuba disaster, his essay *Towards another Spain* (*Hacia otra España*) had called for the country to sever links with its fatal history and enter the European mainstream. That option now appeared closed, and Maeztu searched for the answers within Spain's own past. He still carried with him, however, a fund of influences from England and the theorists of *The New Age*: the belief in a form of socialism, in the primacy of spiritual values, in the value of authority. He also made a three-month visit to the United States in 1926, in an attempt to understand how that country had succeeded where Spain had failed.

When Primo de Rivera seized power in 1923, Maeztu, like other writers, did not hesitate to support him, and served as ambassador to Argentina until Primo's fall in 1930. His stay in Argentina, which began in February 1928, was of capital importance, for it enabled him to understand directly the historical background of the New World's links with Spain, and it brought him into contact with the brothers Irazusta, who ran the newspaper *La Nueva República*. The brothers had travelled widely in Europe and drunk deeply of the new radical Catholic thinking represented by Chesterton in England and Maurras in France; they were also familiar with the Catholic thought of Donoso Cortés and Balmes in Spain. Maeztu and his new friends, all writers of the newspaper, held informal meetings at the embassy where they exchanged and developed ideas. He was present at the public ceremony at which the president of Argentina proclaimed the Twelfth of October to be the '*Día de la Raza*', a label that had originated in Mexico about a decade previously and later spread through the Hispanic world. Maeztu reports how a modest weekly publication in Buenos Aires protested that the day should more properly be called 'Día de la Hispanidad'. He took up the idea enthusiastically. His stay helped him to mature an outlook favouring a historic collaboration of the Hispanic nations against Anglo-Saxon America, and this was finally expressed in his last book, *Defence of Spanishness (Defensa de la Hispanidad)* (1934).

It was the ultimate attempt, coinciding with the 'new imperialism' dreamt up in the same period by Catalan nationalists,[34] to find Spain's salvation overseas. Beginning with the observation that 'Spain is an oak tree half suffocated by ivy', Maeztu conceded that within the previous century his country had not contributed a single original idea to the world. This 'sterility' arose simply out of 'our adulation of the foreigner'. It was time now for a resurgence of 'Spanishness', which had not ended with the end of empire. 'The community of Hispanic peoples cannot be one of voyagers on a ship who, after living together for a few days, take their leave and never see each other again.' Spanishness, for him, was unique.

When it discovered the sea routes of East and West it created the physical unity of the world, when it affirmed at Trent the dogmas that assure to all men the possibility of salvation and therefore of progress, it formed the unity that makes it possible to talk with reason of the moral unity of the human race. In consequence, Spanishness created Universal History, and nothing in the world, apart from Christianity, is comparable to it.

'Not only have we carried civilization to other races, but also something else that is worth more than civilization, the consciousness of the moral unity that they share with us.' 'There is no achievement in Universal History comparable to that of Spain.' 'The classic example of Spain must be the guide and the model from which all the peoples of the earth have to learn.' The nations of Spanish America have to be true to themselves, 'and they will not achieve it if they are not at the same time more Hispanic', because 'Hispanidad is their common spirit and at the same time the condition for achieving success in the world'. The little work is replete with similar observations, made with an impressive ignorance of the history of Spain's role in America, but with an irrepressible hope for the future. And that future, expressed clearly by the author, lay in the direction of a spiritual regeneration based on a rejection of the democracy that had failed Europe.

On his return to Spain he helped to found the conservative paper *Acción Española*, and published several collections of essays, of which the most significant was *Don Quixote, Don Juan and the Celestina*. Maeztu's ideas had become reactionary, in the sense that he looked backwards to a wholly imaginary past, whose characteristics he created straight out of his head without pausing to consider whether they were historically true. He urged Spain to recover its historic religious mission, which in his view had involved not only Spain but also the peoples of the former empire. In a letter to an Argentine friend he wrote:

Threatened spiritually on all sides, the Hispanic peoples need to affirm themselves and that will force them to dig into their roots, which are not as some think based on slavery but on independence, because the spirit of independence is at the root of all things Spanish.

His ideas fitted into a line of thinking that had been developing steadily in the Atlantic world ever since the Disaster. Among the intellectuals he was conspicuous in not supporting the Republic of 1931, but agreed to be elected to the Cortes of 1933 as a deputy for Guipúzcoa. When the army uprising began in July 1936 he was singled out by Republican leftists as an enemy. He hid in the apartment of a friend, but on 30 July was flushed out and detained by the police. He asked to be kept in detention for his own safety but was released, and immediately picked up by the Popular Front militia. The distinguished philologist Menéndez Pidal phoned the prime minister, Indalecio Prieto, to ask if he could intervene. It was as good as done, Prieto replied; but from the way he said it Pidal understood 'that they were not going to do anything. And nothing was done.'[35] Locked up in the prison at Ventas, after three months of detention Maeztu was taken out with thirty others at midnight on 29 October and murdered.

Thousands of refugees from the Civil War managed to make their way across the Atlantic. That was seldom a first option, for it was clearly preferable to live closer to home, in Europe, in the hope that circumstances might change. The factor that forced them to choose

America was the outbreak of the Second World War and the occupation of France by the Germans. Even then, the choice was limited. Half of Latin America was in the control of right-wing regimes that were favourable to Franco or else unwilling to provoke the Germans. The exiles of 1936–9 did not go out into the unknown. Awaiting them in Latin America was a cultural world that their own country had helped to create, and to which they could make a possibly unprecedented contribution. One of the refugees of 1939, Manuel Andújar, who eventually returned to Spain in 1967, observed that many of the intellectuals who went to Mexico in 1939 felt they were participating in a new voyage of Columbus, a new attempt to discover America.[36] The New World was, it seemed, opening its arms in welcome. That, at least, is how the poet Jorge Guillén greeted it:

> Thanks to you, saving shores
> That receive me, dry me, dress me and feed me,
> You raise me on your shoulders, innocent new world
> To leave me on high.

Mexico, for reasons of culture and politics, was the nation that most transatlantic exiles chose.[37] The country had a left-wing government headed by General Lázaro Cárdenas, who needed international political support. After the Civil War began in Spain, the Mexican representative in Portugal, Daniel Cosío Villegas, suggested to his president in 1937 that it might be a good idea to offer asylum to a handful of exiled intellectuals. He suggested a few names, among them Marañón, Fernando de los Ríos and Sánchez Albornoz (none of whom in fact settled in Mexico). The idea of accepting refugees, once agreed, soon grew out of all proportion, but Cárdenas was firm about the plan to attract brains to his needy country. In 1938 he founded a 'Casa de España' in Mexico, 'to serve as a centre for meetings and work to those invited up to now and others who will be invited later'. In 1940 the Casa changed its name to the 'Colegio de Mexico', which evolved into a centre for the Spanish writers and their culture. Cárdenas also offered the exiles a chance to become Mexican citizens and some four-fifths eventually accepted. It has been calculated that Mexico accepted possibly 20,000 refugees from the Civil War.[38] The professional qualifications the émigrés took with them were not to be scorned. For example, of the five thousand or so who arrived in Mexico from France on thirteen vessels in 1939, among them the ship *Sinaia* which carried the first big batch of immigrants (13 June), a third were unqualified workers, but another third were professionals with good educations, and the rest family members.[39] Mexico was still seeking its cultural bearings in the twentieth century, and the presence of the educated Spaniards (dubbed '*transterrados*' by one of them, that is to say, 'transferred') would, it was hoped, give it a boost in terms of status and show the world that Mexico was identifying itself with the advanced civilization of Europe and of Imperial Spain.

The educated groups (the 'intellectuals') who left for the New World in 1939 were heirs to an elite culture that had venerated them as though they personified the spirit of their country. They were conscious of it, and their attitudes reflected it. As we have seen, some felt that they were repeating the journey of Columbus and rediscovering America. 'Here is Spain', one of them – Larrea – wrote, 'seeking material and spiritual truth for men'. Three years before, in 1936, the exiled Menéndez Pidal in Cuba had already presented a similar image. His theme was Arabic poetry, but he slipped the following comment into his lecture:

The Spaniards here are like the fugitives from burning Troy, scattered over lands and seas, dreaming of being able to collaborate in the sacred task of Aeneas, to rebuild the fallen city, guarding with us the household gods of Spain.[40]

The émigrés of 1939, perhaps less versed in classical lore, used other images. The *Sinaia*, a vessel that had served in the past in the Mediterranean for the mass transport of Muslim pilgrims to Mecca, became a symbol for the penniless, homeless and virtually unknown handful of Castilian writers who found themselves in a country that seemed at first to be their own, because it shared a common language, but turned out in practice to be different, alien and sometimes even hostile. The expatriate journal *España Peregrina* decided to compare the vessel with the coming of the Pilgrims to New England: 'one cannot but remember the *Mayflower*', it concluded. 'The captain does not know that his *Sinaia*, which used to take pilgrims to Mecca, has been transformed for ever into the holy, the unconquered city of liberty.'[41] The passengers, according to the journal, included a select group of writers who brought with them the spirit of Spain ('we are the essence of the soul of Spain'), a Spain 'discoverer of new worlds', a Spain that brought new hope ('Spain personifies, absolutely, human aspiration towards a universal reality'), a spirit that was 'a missile advancing towards a better world'.[42]

We can see from these declarations that the so-called international views of many exiles were curiously traditionalist and nationalist. Most were going to a continent 'about which they knew next to nothing before arriving'.[43] In contact once again with the New World, they assumed unashamedly the mantle of Spain's imperial past and adopted notions of grandeur that were precisely those of the regime in the peninsula. Their views were 'based on the idea that the former Spanish empire constituted a unique cultural whole, believed to embody a series of spiritual values whose preservation was of crucial importance to the future of human civilization'.[44] In practice, the specific spiritual values contributed to humanity by Spain were never identified or specified. The exiles (and, in common with them, the Franco regime) felt themselves outpaced by the ideologies and technologies of the twentieth century. The only hope in sight seemed to be that offered by the New World, 'these lands of America where they speak our language', as Larrea put it. The Spanish language, consequently, became the liferaft of Spain's culture, and the base of the political myth called 'hispanismo' by some Republicans and 'Hispanidad' by the Francoists.

Though it is politically correct in Spain to lay stress on the brotherly help received from Mexico, in reality the Mexican government's attitude was not firmly supported by Mexican opinion, which was as divided over the Civil War as Spanish opinion had been. Political groups – both liberal and conservative – as well as peasant organizations, protested over the unlimited entry allowed to tens of thousands of foreigners who might threaten their jobs. Sections of the press presented the 'invasion' as a 'prolongation of the Conquest'. One newspaper claimed that 'eighty per cent of Mexicans are against this invasion by Spaniards'.[45] The majority of the Spanish colony in the country was pro-Franco, opposed the immigrants, and held public celebrations for the Nationalist victory in the spring of 1939. By contrast, the Communists (notably the painter Siqueiros) and the governing PRI party gave firm support to the immigration. There was a lively debate in the press over the defects and virtues of the newcomers.

In most other countries of Latin America the reception of refugees was affected by internal political instability, and relatively few Spaniards were able to settle. Some three thousand were received into the Dominican Republic, where the dictator Trujillo ruled, but most of them left as soon as they could and went to Mexico. The poet Pablo Neruda, who was at that time consul for Chile in Paris, arranged for a ship, the *Winnipeg*, to transport two thousand Spanish workers (with preference given to left-wing activists) from Bordeaux to Valparaiso. Argentina, which had a large population of peninsular origin and had always been looked upon by Spaniards with admiration, was unfortunately ruled by a government that inclined to support the rebels in the Civil War and showed little wish to help the Republican refugees. However, private bodies managed to help some exiles, who came inevitably from the professional classes.

Unlike the immigrants of the sixteenth century, the new Spaniards did not come to conquer or to get rich, but simply to survive. Most had no intention of staying, for they had usually left families and children behind. Some, like the 460 children that Mexico arranged to bring over from Barcelona and Valencia in 1937, had left their parents behind. The only hope sustaining them all was that the regime in Spain would soon collapse and they could return home. It was a vain hope, as Franco demonstrated that he had a solid grip on the country, and was astute enough to survive by not allying with either side in the Second World War. As far as the exiles could see into the future, the continent of America was their new home, and within that continent not just Spanish America but the United States as well. Once in the New World, the literate refugees devoted themselves when possible to expressing themselves in print, for they had little else to contribute. The printed word, in any case, carried on the message that the Civil War had interrupted. The Catalans in Mexico, for example, were not discouraged by the fact that they were writing for a virtually non-existent public, and produced publications that attempted to establish continuity with journals back home. Apart from small cultural items,[46] they managed to bring out a number of novels and essays.[47] Some of them, like the novelist Pere Calders (1912–94), gave fluent expression to the sentiment of exile. Though he returned home in 1962 he failed to gain recognition and it was not until 1978 that his work became known to the Catalan public. His brother-in-law, who later in life adopted the pseudonym 'Tisner', returned to Catalonia in 1965 (after twenty-five years of exile), in the last and milder phase of the dictatorship, and became known as a caricaturist in the Catalan press. Tisner's memoirs, *Living and Seeing* (*Viure i Veure*) (1989, 1995), treat the years of exile with humour.

From the middle years of the nineteenth century Spaniards were suspicious of the culture of the United States, seen as a threat to nationalist dreams of the unique moral role of Hispanic civilization. By contrast, many Americans (for example Irving, Merriman and Huntington) showed great enthusiasm for the traditions of the peninsula, visited Spain and studied its history and art. They managed to deliberately overlook the poverty of Spain in favour of its romantic and exotic aspects, as Irving had done and as Ticknor did in the field of literature and Prescott in the field of history. Artists visited the peninsula, copied pictures in the Prado and painted the Alhambra. The sum total was an impressive state of receptiveness on the part of America. Without that receptiveness an important dimension of Spain's modern exile culture, from Severo Ochoa and Juan Ramón Jiménez to Picasso and Dalí, would have fallen on stony ground, since there would have been no other nation with the resources to patronize it.

The importance of American receptiveness was crucial in the area of art, where the key figure was the New York collector Archer M. Huntington (1870–1955). Huntington's multi-millionaire stepfather made his money through the railroads, and hoped his son would follow him in the business. Archer, however, had already from the age of twelve decided he wanted to become a collector, although he remained for long uncertain about what he wished to collect. On a visit with his mother to England in 1882, he noted in his diary:

On July 2 we went to Sefton Park and saw some birds in cages. Then to a bookstore and bought a book by G. Borrow. It is called *The Zincali* and is about the gypsies of Spain. The most interesting book I have found here. Spain must be much more interesting than Liverpool.[48]

Borrow fascinated him. '*The Bible in Spain* followed, and I was launched on a sea of wonder.' Subsequently, a visit to Mexico in 1889, when he and his parents dined with the dictator Porfirio Díaz, opened up the wonders of the colonial world and he decided to become a collector of Hispanic things. 'Mexico was a revelation. This was my first encounter with something that would fill my whole life.'[49] In 1892 he made his first trip to Spain, but busied himself during the previous year learning Arabic, which he considered essential to any concern for Spanish culture. In the peninsula he began buying thousands of old editions, a task he continued in two further visits in 1896 and 1898. His stepfather introduced him to Hispanic art by purchasing for him in 1896 Antonis Mor's impressive 1549 portrait of the duke of Alba. In 1900 Huntington inherited a third, worth some $150 million, of his stepfather's estate, making him one of the richest men in America. He employed a good part of the money in collecting books and other items from abroad, becoming in the process perhaps the greatest philanthropist Hispanic culture has ever had the fortune to possess, either within or outside Spain. In 1904 he founded in New York the Hispanic Society of America. The Society, destined to become not only a centre for Hispanic culture of all the Latin countries but also a major museum in its own right, first opened its doors in 1908 at the Beaux-Arts building on Audubon Terrace in Upper Manhattan, which is still its home. Among its endless services to culture, the Society put on major exhibitions that brought Spanish artists to the attention of the American public for the first time. The outstanding example was the Valencian artist Joaquín Sorolla, whose exhibition in 1909 beat all records for attendance (160,000 visitors in the first four weeks), converted the artist into a world figure and made him rich. When he left New York to go back to Spain, he thanked his patron effusively: 'I know what the splendid work of the Hispanic Society has meant in my life as a painter'.[50] As a follow-up, Huntington two years later commissioned him to create a series of paintings representing the

Regions of Spain. The impressive work, which occupies the main hall of the Society, consisted of twenty-nine panels up to three metres high and totalling seventy metres in length. It took seven years to complete (from 1912 to 1919) and was installed only in 1926.

Huntington's enormous contribution to Hispanic culture was paralleled by that of Charles Deering (1852–1927), from Maine, whose family's fortune was made in the production of farm equipment and harvesters. Both Charles and his younger brother James became passionate collectors of Old Masters and devotees of Spanish art. Charles was one of the most important benefactors of the Art Institute of Chicago, for which he purchased works by El Greco and Zurbarán. In 1901 he happened to see Ramón Casas's painting *The Execution (El Garrote vil)* in a gallery in Munich, and was fascinated. He brought Casas to the States in 1908, took him around the entire country from coast to coast, and also brought him over in 1923 and 1924. In 1909 he bought a former hospital at Sitges, in Catalonia, which he converted into an art museum, named 'Maricel' ('sea and sky'). Casas scored an immediate success in America, where he made a small fortune in painting portraits ('this is a vineyard!', he wrote home delightedly in 1924). He also made contact with Huntington: 'Yesterday I went to dine with that gentleman whose name I forget, who brought Sorolla and Zuloaga over, and I think we arranged to put on an exhibition next year.'[51]

Spaniards found the United States daunting, and difficult to fit into their perspective. Despite the experience of the Disaster, many unexpectedly accepted contact with it. Among them was the writer Federico de Onís (b.1885), a pupil of Unamuno who was invited in 1916 to set up the department of Hispanic Studies at Columbia, took up a permanent position there, and taught at the University of Puerto Rico from 1952 to his retirement in 1954. From his outpost in United States territory, Onis managed to nurture a fierce passion for the incomparable values of Spanish literature, and in particular for the virtues of the *Quixote* as a unique statement of universal culture, 'the highest moment of Spanish spirituality'.[52] Many exiles from the Civil War chose to go to the United States when it appeared that they could obtain satisfactory employment in colleges specializing in Hispanic literature. It gave them a privileged platform from which to project themes of Hispanic achievement. Among them were the poets Pedro Salinas and Jorge Guillén, touched on in Chapter 9. For a couple of decades the United States became the chief repository of aspects of elite peninsular culture.

The two Hispanic exiles who obtained a Nobel Prize in those years were not part of the world of political émigrés. They were, indeed, citizens of the United States rather than of Spain. In 1959 the Nobel Prize for medicine was awarded to Severo Ochoa, not for achievements in Spain but on account of the research that he and his co-winner Arthur Kornberg (his first doctoral student, from Stanford) had done in biochemistry in the United States. Ochoa (1905–93) was born in the village of Luarca, in the province of Asturias in northern Spain. After graduating from Madrid in 1929, he did research for two years at the University of Heidelberg, in the laboratory of Otto Meyerhof. 'Meyerhof,' Ochoa testified later, 'was the teacher who most contributed towards my formation, and the most influential in directing my life's work.'[53] Apart from two brief stays in Madrid, the rest of his professional career was spent outside Spain. He was in Madrid in 1936 when the Civil War began, and with help from his friend Juan Negrín managed to get papers allowing him and his wife to leave. He resumed work in Heidelberg, then spent three years (1937–40) in England. The war situation in England encouraged him to accept a post in 1940 in the United States. In 1942 he moved to join the faculty at the New York University School of Medicine. His first postdoctoral student, who worked with him for a year in 1945–6, was Arthur Kornberg.[54]

Ochoa's research was mainly on enzymatic processes in biological oxidation and synthesis, and his pioneering achievement was in helping to define the genetic code that helped scientists to further understand the structure and function of DNA. In 1953 the scientists Watson and Crick had already argued that DNA (deoxyribonucleic acid) was the material of inheritance, but a couple of years later Kornberg and his colleagues identified the DNA-copying enzyme, ribonucleotide polymerase, which was later recruited for many kinds of DNA technologies. The article announcing the research was published by Ochoa and his assistant, Marianne Grunberg-Manago, in the 1955 edition of the *Journal of the American Chemical Society*. The Nobel Prize in 1959 went to Kornberg for the enzymatic synthesis of DNA, and to Ochoa for the enzymatic synthesis of RNA (ribonucleic acid). In 1956 Ochoa became an American citizen, and returned with his wife to Spain only at the end of his life, in 1985, dying there in 1993. Like the artists and musicians of his generation, he always formed part of a universal community rather than being a refugee from one country.[55] His contacts with scientists from Spain were few, notably visits he made to conferences in 1969 and 1975, and because he was marginalized by Spanish officials he apparently had little practical impact on the state of Spanish research. By contrast, in the United States he was always eager to help young colleagues from the peninsula.

Three years earlier, Juan Ramón Jiménez had also won the Nobel, for his lyrical poetry. Jiménez (1881–1958), son of a landowning banker, was born in Moguer, on the southern coast of Spain. He was meant to study law but turned his interest first to art then to poetry, and moved in 1900 to Madrid, where he began his links with leading poets such as Rubén Darío. 'In around 1896 (I was fifteen years old),' he wrote later, 'the state of Spanish poetry was truly lamentable. We young poets were looking for a figure to satisfy us and set an example. It was then that Rubén Darío arrived in Spain.' The death of his father that year forced him to return to Moguer, and triggered off the series of depressive illnesses that hounded him for the rest of his life. He lived in Moguer from 1905 to 1911, moving subsequently back to Madrid, where he lived in the Residencia de Estudiantes. In these months he wrote *Platero y Yo* (*Platero and I*) and collaborated with the Catalan-American poet Zenobia Camprubí (whom he met in 1913 in Madrid) in translating the work of the Indian poet Tagore (winner of the Nobel Prize in 1913) from English to Spanish. In 1916 he took ship from Cadiz to New York in order to marry Zenobia, who became the mainstay of his life. Jiménez's great loves were Zenobia, the sea – his permanent memories, as with Alberti, were of the sea coast of Andalusia – and the United States. All three infused his most typical work, *Diary of a Newlywed Poet*, which he wrote in America and published in the same year, 1917, and his widely read and loved *Platero and I*. *Platero* became, after *Don Quixote*, the most popular work of all time in Hispanic literature. A prose poem in short, simple sentences, it evoked the countryside and people of Andalusia as seen through the eyes of a young boy and his friend the donkey.

> Platero is a little donkey, so hairy, smooth, and soft on the
> outside that you might say he is made of cotton, without
> any bones. Only the jet-black mirrors that are his eyes
> seem to be hard, like two beetles of black glass.

> I turn him loose and he goes off to the meadow, caressing the
> blossoms gently with his nose, barely brushing the sky-
> blue and golden flowers . . . I call to him softly, 'Platero?'
> and he comes to me with a happy trot, almost as though
> he is laughing, in an imagined tinkle of his bell.

Progressive left-wing figures like Buñuel and Neruda greeted it and what it was attempting to do with derision. In opposition to Ramón Jiménez's defence of 'pure poetry', the latter published a 'Manifesto of impure poetry'. Antagonism between Jiménez and the Communist writers continued throughout the years of exile after 1936.

In all his early work he had been a lyrical poet, producing short poems that – like some French poets, such as Verlaine, who influenced him – communicated gentle sounds, landscapes and images. All that changed in 1916, when his new life with Zenobia encouraged him to choose a *depuración*, a 'purification', a move towards 'naked poetry'. He abandoned rhyme and assonance and opted for free verse. The *Diary* was an extended prose poem, combined with verse, that served also as a record of his stay in New York. He permitted himself flights of fancy, imagining that 'New York is the same as Moguer'. Apart from his own reflections, the pages show that he had come to know and appreciate the poetry of Poe, Dickinson and Whitman, as well as Frost and Amy Lowell. 'The *Diary* is my best book', he later affirmed: 'Love, the high seas, the sky above, free verse, the different Americas and all my travels up to now brought it to me as an entity.'[56] Despite the change of style, what he maintained throughout the writing of his later years, including those of exile, was an absolute clarity of imagery that made his poems wholly subjective and almost completely cut off from the crude reality of the outside world.

He had rendered signal service to his fellow poets in Spain in the 1920s when he published their works in his review *Indice*. Alberti recalls him as then having 'a deep black beard, the perfect profile of an Andalusian Arab, and a soft voice'.[57] His trim profile is caught perfectly in the portrait Sorolla did of him in 1916. Much of Jiménez's most significant work was done before he finally left Spain, and he never let politics intrude into the purity of his work. All his life he suffered from manic depression, the dark side of his sparkling, limpid verse. When the military uprising took place in July 1936, he was pressurized to sign a common manifesto in favour of the Republic, but like other signatories left the country immediately after, with the excuse that he had to take up an appointment as honorary cultural attaché to the embassy in Washington. He remained strongly attached to the Republic, but found he had little in common with the violence and hatred that dominated Spanish politics in the last months that he was in Republican Spain.

A special place among the exiles is occupied by the novelist Ramón J. Sender (1901–82), whose work attracted international attention very quickly. He grew up in the countryside of Aragon and began his university career in Madrid but never finished it, dedicating his time instead to journalism and politics. He returned to Aragon where he edited a local newspaper, was then called up for military service in the Morocco War, of which a product was his novel *Imán* (1930, translated into English as *Earmarked for Hell* in 1934). His subsequent novels all narrated some aspects of his own experience in politics and trade-union activity. An active anarchist in the 1930s, like other anarchists he revelled in the hypothetical blood that had to be shed for the future revolution to succeed. The main character in his *Siete domingos rojos* (1932, translated as *Seven Red Sundays* in 1936) declares: 'A bourgeois is not a person. Nor an animal. He is less than anything else. He is nothing. How can I feel sorry that a bourgeois has died, since I myself am going out to kill them?'[58] He joined the Communist Party and went to Moscow in 1935; in the same year he married his wife, Amparo. The outbreak of the Civil War affected his life deeply. He fought at the front, where a friend described him as 'handsome, with a belt, pistol, leading a group of militia'.[59] His writings glorified the 'strong people's army, serene, invincible'. The militancy had dire personal consequences. His brother Manuel was murdered by the pro-army forces, and four months later his wife was interrogated and then murdered (along with her two brothers). Sender's position with the Communist Party also became shaky, and he was expelled from it in 1938.

He left the country to carry out propaganda work for the Republic, stayed in Paris for a while and then, in the spring of 1939, went to New York with his two children. 'I am leaving my country,' he explained, 'because I have in France two children who cannot yet speak Spanish or French. Their mother was killed because they could not kill me.'[60] He spoke no English, and decided to settle in Mexico, where he founded a publishing house and wrote several novels, all based on his experiences in the war. In 1942 he returned to the United States on a scholarship, accepted various teaching jobs, and eventually in 1946 became a US citizen. For a while, thanks to the good offices of Buñuel, he worked as a translator for MGM, but for the seventeen years from 1946 he taught at the University of New Mexico, Albuquerque, from where, after divorcing his second wife, he went to teach in Los Angeles and later moved to San Diego. He finally made return visits to Spain at the very end of the dictatorship, in 1974 and 1976, and succeeded in moves to recover his Spanish citizenship in 1980. But he never returned to Spain. After his death at San Diego his ashes were taken out to sea by family members and his ex-wife, Florence Hall, and scattered over the Pacific.

For most of his working life he remained excluded from Spain, where his books were not published until the 1960s. Meanwhile, he turned out to be the most prolific of the writers in exile, notching up around a hundred titles in his lifetime. Perhaps his most emblematic novel was *Requiem for a Spanish Peasant* (*Requiem por un campesino español*, 1953), which he published in Mexico originally with the title of *Mosén Millán*. The action, which takes place in an Aragonese village during the Civil War, centres on the *mosén* (the word means 'priest'), who is officiating at the funeral of a peasant whom he unwittingly denounced and who was later executed. The only people to turn up for the requiem are those who were responsible for the peasant's death. The narrative is related through flashback memories that the priest has of the executed man. In Mexico between 1942 and 1966

Sender also brought out the nine autobiographical novels titled *Chronicle of Dawn* (*Crónica del Alba*). The chief character is an officer of the Republic's army, an alter ego of Sender himself bearing the name Pepe Garcés, who ends up in a refugee camp in the French border town of Argelès, where he narrates his history, divided up into the nine sections of the work. *Chronicle of Dawn* was allowed to come out in Spain in 1965, and from then on Sender did not look back, as his books began to sell. A Spanish friend wrote in the press that 'After nearly sixty years of ostracism Sender has returned literarily to Spain.'[61] He won a literary prize in 1969. In 1975 he was at last able to publish *Requiem por un campesino español* in Spain. *Alba* was made into a series for Spanish television in 1978, and *Requiem* was made into a film in 1980. However, like all the exiles Sender was never received back on the terms that he merited. Few creative writers in all Spain's history were as marked by exile as he was. The experience infused everything he wrote, and he wrote obsessively and at times excessively.

In a rather different category were those creative artists whose professional work was not restricted to the use of the Spanish language and who consequently moved about with greater freedom of choice. Among them were two members of the same Catalan aristocratic family, Josep María Sert and his nephew Josep Lluís Sert. The former (1874–1945), was perhaps the leading mural painter of his time, whose world reputation can be seen through the works he carried out on both sides of the Atlantic. The son of a notable artist, he was in part educated at home by tutors and developed as a painter of large-scale murals. From 1900 he was resident in Paris, a base from which he travelled regularly to Italy to improve his method and style. His reputation very soon brought him commissions, starting with the decoration of the interior walls of the cathedral of Vic (Catalonia), contracted in 1900 but completed only in 1927. He was chosen to paint the murals in the meeting hall of the League of Nations at Geneva, and was called over the Atlantic to paint the frescos in the huge main hall of the Rockefeller Center in New York, because the directors of the Center were unhappy with those that the Mexican Marxist Diego Rivera had started painting. Rockefeller wanted a series of murals depicting the triumphs of American civilization (or 'Man's Conquests', to give the official title), done in black, white and grey. Begun in 1932, the work was completed in 1941.[62] Sert's style was possibly even more unusual than Rivera's. His figures are immense, dark Goya-type fantasies that glower over the humans looking up at them, and bring a feeling of unease to the casual visitor who may be walking through the Center simply to pick up a lunchtime sandwich and is quite unprepared to be faced by the Titans of the universe. Sert was also capable of more traditional work, as with his murals for government buildings in Barcelona, where he reverted to using heroic medieval images. His other outstanding works included the banqueting hall of the Waldorf Astoria hotel and the hall of the Hispanic Society, both in New York. His commissions kept him constantly on the move. He was in Geneva in October 1936 to inaugurate his work in the hall of the League of Nations, and returned to Spain only to find that his magnificent work in the cathedral at Vic had been destroyed by anarchist anticlericalists. The act made him a convinced supporter of the Nationalist military uprising, and after the Civil War he painstakingly restored the entire series of murals.

Josep Lluís Sert (1902–83), also from Barcelona, took a degree there in architecture and later went to Paris for a while to study with Le Corbusier. He quickly gained a reputation as an upcoming designer and planner. Sert was dignified and aristocratic: in the 1930s he had 'large, almost fierce eyes, a mouth fringed by a short curly red beard that made him look like a pirate, arms like a gladiator, everything in him embodied vigour and strength'.[63] He made his name with his design for the Spanish Pavilion in the 1937 World Exhibition in Paris, which the struggling Republican government, beset by a military rebellion, hoped would be a showcase for their cause before an international public. Sert approached Picasso, then permanently in residence in Paris, asking him to contribute a large mural to the exhibition. The result was his memorable work on *Guernica*. When the Civil War ended Sert opted in 1939 to move to the United States, where he eventually became an American citizen. His important book *Can our Cities Survive?* (1943), which drew in part on Le Corbusier, initiated his career as a town planner. Subsequently he toured and lectured on planning and design projects both in the States and in Latin America. In 1955 he was an established and prominent professional, and founded in Cambridge, Massachusetts, in collaboration with Hudson Jackson, the firm of Sert, Jackson and Associates, which went on to design several prominent buildings at Harvard University, notably the striking Holyoke Center (1963) and the substantial Science Center.[64] He also had a teaching post at the university and from 1953, on the recommendation of the Harvard designer and professor Walter Gropius, was appointed dean of the Harvard Graduate School of Design, a post that he held until his retirement in 1969. Sert's style was a faithful reflection of his origins: though a true modernist, he expressed the spirit of the Mediterranean. After his retirement he returned to Barcelona.

The worldwide projection of Sert's approach to architecture had its parallel in the work of his lifelong friend and colleague the artist Joan Miró (1893–1983), who coincidentally died in the same year. Sert designed Miró's studio on the island of Mallorca. In order to repay him, the artist flew over the Atlantic to Sert's house in Cambridge, measured the wall over the sofa and created a painting to fit the space exactly. Apart from the impressive buildings at Harvard, Sert's most accessible work is the emblematic Miró Museum (1975), a brilliant group of white structures that sits atop the hill of Montjuic in the city of Barcelona. Unlike Sert, Miró did not need to exile himself, since he already formed part of the permanent Spanish emigration of artists centred on Paris. He was born in Barcelona, studied business and art, and eventually opted for the latter as a career. In 1920 he made the first of several visits to Paris (already the home of Picasso) and settled permanently in the city the following year. For approximately the next twenty years it was the centre of his activity, precisely because it was also the world centre of modern art. He returned to his home at Mont-roig (near Tarragona) periodically, and began several of his key paintings there, so that he was never continuously absent.

His choice of Paris as a permanent base obeyed the old imperative by which Catalans of all persuasions (and especially their artists) had looked to the city as their inspiration. His returns, however, were normally restricted to the periphery of Spain, and when he later moved back it was to the Mediterranean islands rather than to the mainland. He married his wife in Palma de Mallorca in 1929 and took her to live with him in Paris, but moved his base to Barcelona in 1932. In 1936 he travelled to Paris with a collection of his work, scheduled to go to an exhibition in New York (he had already exhibited there twice before), and when the Civil War broke out he decided to stay where he was, together with his family. The following year he contributed a large mural on *El Segador* (*The Peasant Reaper*) to the Spanish Pavilion at the Paris Exposition, to indicate his support for the Republican cause. Perhaps his best-known poster, called simply *Help Spain!* (*Aidez Espagne!*) and in the shape of a large four-colour stamp, showing a Catalan worker shaking his fist at the sky, was produced in this period (1937) to call for support for the Republic. The poster included Miró's optimistic words in his own hand: '*Dans la lutte actuelle, je vois du côté fasciste les forces périmées, de l'autre côté le peuple dont les immenses ressources créatrices donneront à l'Espagne un élan qui étonnera le monde*' ('In the present struggle, I see on the Fascist side forces that are spent, and on the other side a people whose immense creative forces will give to Spain an energy that will astonish the world'). In 1941, when the war situation in France was becoming critical, he returned with his family to Palma de Mallorca. The next year he returned to Barcelona, where he found conditions acceptable. Though his paintings diminished after this period (he did not return to painting until 1944), he continued to be richly productive in an extensive range of other illustrative work, and his international reputation grew to become immense.

Early in his career Miró had flirted with styles such as Fauvism and Cubism, and from the 1920s moved to the Surrealism associated with such names as André Breton and Max Ernst. By 1930 he had discovered his own approach, which disconcerted many but was original and distinctive enough to propel him to fame and international recognition. He applied his style not only to painting but also to sculpture, ceramics and murals, a range of decorative applications that opened up endless commercial possibilities and helped him achieve world fame. Commissions for the decoration of public buildings poured in, and in 1941 he put on a general exhibition at the MoMA in New York. He did not visit the States in person until 1947, when he did a mural at a hotel in Cincinnati. The most direct recognition of his work, however, always came from Paris, where he put on major exhibitions at the Museum of Modern Art in 1962 and 1978. His new-found success also enabled him to construct in Mallorca the lush studio-residence designed by Sert, into which he moved in 1956 and which from 1992 became the island's Miró Museum.

Miró was a quiet, unassuming man who said little about politics or art, but his style offered the postwar world a new and original approach to modern imaginative design. Commentators have seen in his work a reflection of the colours and forms of the Mediterranean world that inspired both him and Sert. The achievement of both artists consisted in carrying to the world outside Spain a sense of modernity and creativity that ironically could not be found within the country from which they came. On a more extensive and profound level than was achieved by artists who worked with words alone, they took into exile a perception of Spain that Spaniards themselves could not see at the time.

Among the writers who successfully bridged the gap between Europe and the New World was the novelist Max Aub (1903–72). An exile all his life, his career illustrates a crucial phase in Hispanic literary activity. He was born in Paris, of a German-Jewish father and French mother who moved to Valencia in 1914. Though his subsequent formation was Spanish he was always intimately associated with France. As cultural attaché to the Republic's embassy in Paris he collaborated with André Malraux in making the film *Hope* (*L'Espoir*) (1937) on the Civil War. He crossed the frontier into France with other exiles in 1939, but was denounced as a Communist and interned by the Germans in 1940 in a camp at Le Vernet, where one of his fellow detainees was the writer Arthur Koestler. Later he was deported to a Vichy prison camp in Algeria. In all he spent over two years in camps, an experience that marked him deeply. He escaped from Algeria in 1942 and took ship at Casablanca for Mexico, which then became his home (he acquired Mexican nationality in 1956). He had published verse, plays and prose before the war, but his principal work appeared in Mexico, where he published the novel cycle *The Magic Labyrinth* (*El laberinto mágico*) (1943–68), among other works. His modernist style, consisting of semi-fictional elements and often playing games with the reader, never caught on: few read his books and his theatrical works did not reach the stage.

Aub was happy in Mexico but felt professionally isolated, mainly because he was not read by those who should have read him. His work was eventually translated into French, English, German and Italian, but Spanish readers never came to appreciate him. He also fell out with other exiles, whose quarrels he could not stand. 'The emigration,' he noted in his diaries, 'is finished.' He felt that the émigrés 'are imbeciles, blinded by sectarianism'. Aub remained largely forgotten, and was buried in Mexico City in 1972.

For writers, exile was a long wait for an outcome that many did not live to see. In a sense they were prisoners of their own circumstances. Little known in the non-Hispanic world when they began their creative careers, they immersed themselves in a further Hispanic environment that continued to be unknown to outsiders for decades to come. Those who insisted on the theme of the Civil War were doubly unfortunate, for that soon became a subject overtaken by other political realities. Remembered by a few in the peninsula, they were forgotten to the outside world. One case, typical of many, was the writer María Zambrano (1904–91), still completely unknown in the non-Hispanic world. Zambrano, a native of Málaga, was trained in philosophy at university but later devoted herself more to writing. She was among the refugees who left at the end of the Civil War and went to Mexico, but the greater part of her stay in Latin America was (from 1940 to 1953) in Cuba, where she gave classes, and also taught in a brief visiting capacity in Puerto Rico. From 1953 she lived successively in Italy, France and Switzerland, finally returning to Spain in 1984, after forty-five years of absence. Her observations in 1961 show that she shared with others of her generation the conviction that the mission of the refugees, both in the New World and Europe, revolved exclusively round Spain. 'It seems that we have been thrown out of Spain in order to serve as its conscience, and scattered as we are through the world we have to speak up for her. We are memory.'[65]

Obsession with the Civil War created a cultural blockage that affected novelists, but had less impact on other creative artists. Manuel de Falla (1876–1946), the only Spanish composer of the twentieth century to become known to an international public, belonged to the generation that preceded Aub and Buñuel. His exile completes the long intellectual odyssey of those who incorporated the Atlantic world into their cultural vision. Born in Cadiz of a Valencian father and a Catalan mother, he began his career as a pianist. When he was twenty his family moved to Madrid, where in 1899 he won a prize for piano playing. There was little interest among Spaniards in European-style music, and Falla limited his efforts to composing zarzuelas and writing pieces for the piano. In these years in Madrid he studied musical composition with the Catalan scholar Felip Pedrell (1841–1922), the key figure in Spain's musical rediscovery during the late nineteenth century, who had just moved to the capital. Pedrell brought home to him the importance of the country's folklore heritage. Falla's first serious composition, the opera *Life is Short* (*La Vida Breve*), was based on a poem and won a prize in 1905, but was not staged, a clear sign of the difficulties facing creative music in Spain. Falla went to Paris in 1907 and spent seven fruitful years there, learning, talking and composing, in touch with prominent composers. Paris was the Mecca of European musicians, and it was a good moment for Spanish music. Falla met Albéniz, who was finishing his *Iberia*, he listened to Granados playing the *Goyescas*, he met Debussy, who was completing his *Iberia*, and Ravel, who was writing his *L'Heure espagnole*. Thanks to the creative environment in Paris, Falla managed to write his *Three Melodies*, based on texts by Théophile Gautier, and began work on *Nights in the Gardens of Spain* (*Noches en los jardines de España*), a nocturne for piano and orchestra. Debussy helped him finally to stage *La Vida Breve*, first put on in Nice in 1913 and then in Paris the year after. Though the work was thoroughly Andalusian in inspiration and set in Granada, its overall impact was cosmopolitan, infused with French elegance and occasional Wagnerian touches.

Falla's international contacts helped to spread his music, and he himself performed some of his own piano works in London in 1911. The outbreak of war in 1914 forced him to return home. When they realized in Madrid that the French had considered Falla's *La Vida Breve* worthy of attention, they finally agreed to put it on, at the Zarzuela theatre in November 1914. Falla was then asked to write an opera with a gypsy theme, typical of his native Andalusia. The result was *Love the Magician* (*El Amor Brujo*), which when first put on in

Madrid in 1915 failed to evoke much enthusiasm in critics and a public looking for a more 'Spanish' type of music. Some said the work was too French, others that it had too much flamenco. Falla later commented that 'the audience is unfair and never managed to understand . . . Let time pass, and when we are able to appreciate, justice will be done.' A revised version, first staged in Paris in 1925, was certainly a success. A flamenco ballet, *Amor Brujo* had a gypsy theme, in which the gypsy girl, Candelas, is haunted by the spirit of a dead lover, so that a new suitor, Carmelo, has to fight the spirit in order to win her through a kiss. The work's lasting popularity owes much to the memorable 'Ritual Fire Dance', which was first popularized by Arthur Rubinstein in a solo piano version and then repeatedly adapted and elaborated by a score of musical performers in the United States.

In 1916, while relaxing at the seaside resort of Sitges, Falla completed work on *Nights*, which turned out to be his most ambitious and successful concert work. In form a symphony in three movements for piano and orchestra, it was first performed in Madrid in April 1916, a haunting, somewhat melancholy combination of musical impressions in the style of Debussy, specifically evoking the countryside of Andalusia. The impresario Diaghilev was visiting Spain that year and asked Falla to write a work for the Russian Ballet. He adapted *El Amor Brujo* and the result, after several revisions, was *The Three-Cornered Hat* (*El sombrero de tres picos*), which became an international success. The rehearsals and production took place not in Spain, which did not have the resources or the audience, but in London in 1919, with choreography by Massine and designs by Picasso. Staged as a ballet in two scenes, the plot revolved around a rough miller and his pretty young wife, on whom the local law official (a *corregidor*, whose symbol of rank was a three-cornered hat) has dishonest intentions. After several comic confusions, the miller and his wife are reconciled to each other, and the *corregidor* is spurned. Full of folk tunes, the music caught on immediately with the public. During his visit for the production, Falla reiterated that his inspiration came from Spain and France, but not from German music, 'which knows nothing of the special music implicit in our Spanish scene, in the manners and speech of our people, in the outline of our hills'.[66]

The year 1919 marked a turn of the tide in his personal life. Just before Falla went to London his father died. While he was in England he received news that his mother was gravely ill, and left at once for Spain (thereby missing the premiere) but arrived too late. Falla was a frail, diminutive figure, with a high forehead and sunken eyes, wholly immersed in himself and dependent for outside help entirely on his parents. He never showed any interest in the opposite sex, and his obsessive religious dedication converted his life into that of an ascetic. Solitary now after the death of his parents and even more withdrawn, he decided to leave Madrid and settled in Granada, with his sister Carmen as housekeeper and secretary. Juan Ramón Jiménez recalled that Falla 'went to Granada seeking silence and time, and Granada gave him harmony and eternity'. Before leaving the capital he finished his *Fantasia Baetica*, commissioned by the pianist Rubinstein. It was greeted with hostility by the Spanish critics. His *Concerto for Harpsichord* (1923–6), commissioned by Wanda Landowska, did not receive their approval either. Anything that ranged beyond peninsular experience seemed to be unacceptable in Spain. One consequence was that he earned only a modest living from his work, and went abroad periodically for concerts, to London, Paris, Italy and Switzerland. He was in Paris in January 1920 at the French premiere of *The Three-Cornered Hat*. When a performance was later put on in Madrid it was attacked for political rather than musical motives, because it allegedly mocked the Spanish character and represented, as one alleged expert stated, 'a chapter out of the Black Legend'.[67]

Like other Spanish artists, Falla was influenced by the *Quixote*. He used an incident from it as the basis of *El Retablo de Maese Pedro* (*Master Peter's Puppet Show*), which was commissioned by the Princess de Polignac.[68] The work had its premiere in Paris in August 1924, after a preliminary presentation two months before in Seville. It went on to play in New York in December 1925. The Civil War tied him down in Granada, where he experienced directly the anticlericalism of the Republic (with which as a Catholic he had no sympathy) and the murder by the Nationalists of his close friend Lorca, with whom he had collaborated on some projects. He denounced at the time the 'satanic outrages in Granada' represented by the deaths of Lorca and other friends. On balance, however, he welcomed the advance of the Nationalists as contributing to 'the salvation of Spain'.[69] Though invited by the Nationalists to compose martial music for them, he took no public stand in their favour. Alien to the politics of both sides, he withdrew into his own deeply religious world.

He continued to nurture one dream, to compose a work that would encompass the Hispanic experience in America. His idea was a cantata that would centre on the emergence of Spain, but would take in the evolution of Spain's role in America, concentrating all the while on the theme of religious destiny. The idea took shape in 1926, when he was planning a dramatic work in collaboration with the artist Josep María Sert. They asked the French Catholic writer Claudel for a possible libretto, but did not like what he came up with. Salvador de Madariaga happened to visit Granada at this time, and Falla asked: 'Why don't you write me a poem on the discovery of America?' Madariaga demurred. Falla subsequently came across Verdaguer's epic poem, and after deciphering its Catalan with the help of a dictionary began using it as the basis for an enormous 'scenic cantata' to which he gave the name *Atlantis* (*Atlántida*), composed for a chorus and large orchestra. In his mind's eye, the poem celebrated Spain's birth out of the ashes of the lost continent, and the extension of its religious mission into the New World of America. It was a difficult period in Falla's life, when he began to reach out beyond nationalist music to a more universal conception of creativity. It was a time, however, when he was also overwhelmed by depression, poor health and bizarre behaviour which did not go away but occupied the later years of his life. When the British Hispanist Walter Starkie visited him in 1935, he encountered a Falla who was 'emaciated and ethereal, his face that of an ascetic monk, whose life was divided between meditation in his cell and his tiny garden'.[70]

In 1939, shortly after the victory of Franco, Falla left the country to take up an invitation to direct a series of concerts in Argentina. His departure had no political motives. It is possible that his principal reason for leaving was the endemic poverty of his life in Spain,[71] though it also appears that he had begun his bizarre phase and was convinced that people were conspiring against his health. He spent the rest of his days enclosed in a house in Alta Gracia, near Córdoba in

Argentina, with 'two or three regiments of medicine bottles and packets' by his bedside.[72] Certainly, Falla was well advanced into the unreal world in which he spent these last seven years, during which he composed almost nothing. The *Atlantis* was left unfinished. It was continued by a disciple and fellow exile, the composer Ernesto Halffter, who presided over the first public performance of extracts at the new Opera House in Berlin during a music festival in 1961. The first Spanish performance, in November that year in Barcelona, with the singer Victoria de los Angeles, also consisted of excerpts. The first full staging took place only in 1962, at La Scala in Milan. Falla's *Atlantis* centres round the figures of Columbus and Hercules.[73] It begins with a prologue in which a boy (Columbus) is rescued from a sinking ship, and the promise is given that Spain will be saved, while a 'hymnus hispanicus' is sung. The main work consists of three parts. The first part details the labours of Hercules in the Catalan Pyrenees, which are burning but from whose ashes will rise a new Barcelona. The second part describes how, after vanquishing a monster, Hercules sees the vision of a new land: old Atlantis sinks beneath the waves, but a new Spain rises from the sea. In the third part, Columbus hears a prophecy that the limits of the new Spain will extend beyond the Pillars of Hercules, and the work ends with his three ships sailing to the unknown promised land.

After his death the authorities in his country, which had seldom recognized his merit and which rejected his most original work to the extent that nearly all his premieres had to be put on outside Spain, decided to bring him home. He was interred in Cadiz cathedral. An exile to the end, Falla was, ironically, fêted after his death as his country's greatest composer. He was, for all that, also one of the great puzzles among composers. One might well ask how the deep and intense passion of his music, the lyrical beauty alternating with sensual rhythm, could have proceeded from the imagination of a timid, dry, ascetic man who shut out from his life all the pleasures of the bodily senses. By coincidence, in the same period that Falla was nurturing his final work, the theme of Atlantis was also adopted by Juan Ramón Jiménez as an invisible thread to bind his writings together. Jiménez was thoroughly happy in America, which for him became a paradise reborn. Writing to Gregorio Marañón in 1948 he referred to 'this

Atlantis' as his place of residence.[74] He hoped to publish the poems of the first six years of his exile as a single volume with the title *Lyrics of Atlantis* (*Lírica de una Atlántida*), but the dates were then extended and he failed to put together the whole work in his lifetime. The poems were published with this covering name in 1999.[75]

9

Hispanic Identity and the
Permanence of Exile

Departure! In order to . . . set an example and prepare the way
for a fatherland that I do not at present have?

Eugenio María de Hostos,
The Pilgrimage of Bayoán (1863)[1]

One of the most enduring legacies of Spain to the Hispanic world was
the permanent experience of disintegration and exile, with a consequent loss of focus and insecurity of identity. Unable to agree on what
they were or where they were going, Spaniards over a timespan of five
hundred years resorted to the option of expelling dissidents in the
belief that it would help to solve the problem. (Ironically, the exiles
who left usually turned out to have a more balanced perspective of
matters than those who had expelled them.) This by no means helped
the process of national awareness. Since the Bourbon epoch,
Spaniards have been irreversibly split down the middle, often for no
apparent or logical reason. The division has also been characteristic
of the New World territories that formed part of the Spanish empire.

From the time of their independence in the early 1800s, the
Hispanic nations of Latin America shared the ambiguities and doubts
over who they were. In simple terms, this was a matter of 'nationalism',[2] a question of defining who they were, what territory was theirs,
what races made up their people, and what language they were meant
to speak. Through consideration of past experience and present
concerns, they could settle on an 'identity' and on future aspirations.
The nature of culture – a term embracing political practice, traditional
customs and elite achievement – lay at the heart of this search for

identity. Unfortunately, even after several generations it seemed impossible to resolve the issue satisfactorily, and recent commentators have been virtually unanimous that none of the Hispanic countries of America, with the possible exceptions of Mexico and Cuba, has achieved a cohesive national identity. It did not help that many writers and thinkers who might have contributed to the debate were periodically forced to abandon their homelands. Like historic Spain, Latin America has persistently produced exiles and a corresponding exile culture. Since the nineteenth century, its writers of all ideologies have habitually preferred to live abroad. One of the best-known, Andrés Bello, spent thirty years of his life in London. Since that time, many of the region's most prominent cultural figures have lived, and still live, in exile.

When the Hispanic Americans were struggling for freedom from Spain, several leaders relied heavily for help on their great neighbour to the north, the sleeping giant of the United States. From that time onwards, the USA played an increasingly important role in the developing fortunes of the former Spanish colonies. The treaty of Guadalupe Hidalgo in 1848 at the end of the Mexican-American War gave an enormous fillip to the United States, which bought from Mexico for $15 million the vast span of territory that was to become the states of California, New Mexico, Arizona and Texas. The Spanish-American War of 1898 completed the process. When Spain was pushed to the outer fringes of the Hispanic world in 1898, the nation responsible was the USA. As a consequence many Spaniards, of all political complexions, have harboured a permanent resentment, at times obsessive, against Americans.[3] The occupation of Cuba and Puerto Rico was the last stage in the southward movement of the United States frontier, which had already made a decisive advance to the Rio Grande. That new frontier created for the first time an urgent problem of identification among the peoples of Hispanic America who were affected by the displacement of homes and loyalties. Very many woke up, figuratively speaking, to find themselves in a world that was not their own. In Arizona (around Tucson) and New Mexico, citizens of New Spain had to accept becoming citizens of the United States. They were often propertied people, and eventually adjusted without problems. But a different development also occurred. Over the greater part of the south-west frontier, thousands of Mexicans began to enter the United States because of the demand there for a workforce. Immigration from the Hispanic into the Anglo world became a major social and cultural phenomenon.

By the end of the nineteenth century the relationship between Anglo and Hispanic America was patently one between rich and poor. California may serve as a classic example. When the state was absorbed into the Union in 1846, it had a resident Mexican population that felt at home. The Gold Rush a few years later brought in a flood of poor whites who transformed the ethnic balance, heavily disfavouring Mexicans. The coming of the railroad completed the process. By 1900 the Hispanic population, at every point of contact with the Anglo world, was in an inferior position. The regular immigration of poor Mexicans in search of a living confirmed the picture. By the twentieth century the normal situation of Hispanics in the northern half of the New World was that of immigrants. In one special case, Puerto Rico, the immigrants took on the character of exiles.

Most of the citizens of Puerto Rico welcomed American intervention in 1898, hoping that it would serve as the prelude to a new future. The island's role as a Hispanic addition to an essentially Anglo-Saxon territory, however, created a unique situation and provoked differing responses. Spaniards always thought of the island as theirs, created by them. They did little, however, to advance its cause. The first significant patriot of the struggle against Spain was Ramón Betances (1827–98), son of a wealthy landowner of Mayagüez.[4] He was educated in Paris, where he qualified as a doctor of medicine, and returned to the island to lead the struggle against slavery. Repeatedly exiled several times by the Spaniards for his revolutionary activity (he led an abortive rising in 1868), he remained permanently exiled in France, his home for forty-five of the seventy years of his life. For a quarter of a century his apartment in Paris was the centre of the comings and goings of activists dedicated to the independence of Cuba and Puerto Rico. He died in France, where his literary work in exile earned him the award of the Légion d'honneur.

Another outstanding defender of Puerto Rico's culture was Eugenio María de Hostos (1839–1903), whose life and work were profoundly marked by the reality of exile. Born in Río Cañas, a settlement in the jurisdiction of Mayagüez, on the west of the island, he went to school in San Juan and then travelled to Spain (1852) to complete his higher education in Bilbao and Madrid. In Madrid one of his professors was the father of Krausism, Sanz del Río. Hostos became a firm Krausist and republican Liberal, as well as a supporter of freedom for the slaves of Puerto Rico and Cuba. In his leisure time, at the age of thirty-three he wrote his principal literary work, the Romantic political novel *The Pilgrimage of Bayoán* (1863), a reflection in some measure of his own life. Written in the form of a rambling and wordy poetical diary, in which the hero Bayoán travels ceaselessly as an exile because his only dream is to liberate his homeland Borinquén (an old native name for Puerto Rico, used today mostly in the forms Boriquén, Borikén and Boricua), the author is faced at every point by the necessity of departure:

Departure! In order to find the way to make my unhappy Borinquén happy, to set an example and prepare the way for a fatherland that I do not at present have? To travel through the continent of America, think on its future and advance it? To Europe, to convince it that America is the predestined site for a future civilization?[5]

I complained, they persecuted me; I proclaimed the truth openly, it cost me exile. I have travelled through all America, I have the firm conviction that the peoples best prepared for a great civilization are the peoples of America, and I am distressed by the condition in which I see them.[6]

However, he soon fell out with his fellow Liberals when they showed no interest in his idea of a free Puerto Rico, which continued to be a colony of Spain until the end of the century. His private diaries, which he began writing at the age of eighteen as a form of therapy, and which were published only in 1939, thirty-six years after his death, show that he suffered from constant depression and a profound feeling of solitude.[7] He left Spain and in 1870 settled in New York, which over the next twenty-eight years became his base for the extensive travels he made through Latin America, proposing the abolition of slavery and (his pet idea, which he launched in New York in 1876) a federation of free Antillean nations made up of Cuba, the Dominican Republic and Puerto Rico. He also devoted his energies to educational schemes.

When the United States took over Puerto Rico in 1898 he welcomed the liberation but protested against the act of conquest, 'the shame of an annexation' as he termed it. He was one of the members of a so-called Commission which the administration in Washington consulted, but his voice counted for nothing. He lamented the situation: 'an America diverted from its path, the statue of Liberty with flames instead of torches, shadows instead of light'.[8] Finally, after thirty-five years of restless exile, he returned to Puerto Rico in the hope of joining with others to demand independence, but received little support from the population, which instead welcomed the liberation that the Americans offered. Disappointed, he left Puerto Rico on a now definitive exile and spent the last years of his life in the Dominican Republic. He even wrote his own epitaph: 'My wish is that they will say: In that island [Puerto Rico] a man was born who loved truth, desired justice, and worked for the good of men.'

Writers like Hostos welcomed the possibility of participating in the achievements of the United States. That possibility dimmed when it became clear that Puerto Rico would have to live for a long time not on equal terms but merely as an associated entity. Gradually a division grew up between those who felt the island should cut free of the United States, and others who felt it had much to gain from even a secondary association. The crucial and dominating factor that imposed itself was the movement of population, an aspect that determined everything in the century after annexation and brings Puerto Rico inevitably into a central position in our narrative. The general phenomenon of Hispanic exile affected the island in at least four main ways. First, it was a community created largely by Spanish immigration, since there was no indigenous population after the beginning of the imperial period. Second, it became the only Hispanic territory to be politically absorbed into an Anglo culture, since other territories where United States influence prevailed were either large entities with their own civilization, such as Cuba and the Philippines, or were sparsely populated with scattered settlements, such as in Texas and California. Third, it was the only society in which exiles from peninsular Spain felt themselves at home, since it combined aspects of Spanish and European culture with an undeniably New World Hispanic environment. Fourth, it was the only Hispanic territory in which emigration ('exile') became a fundamental aspect of social evolution.

Puerto Rico was a small society in 1898, and to defend (or create) an identity it had to try being a big one. But over the subsequent hundred years several tendencies blocked its progress along this path. In trying to decide who they were, Puerto Ricans were pulled in three directions, none of them necessarily advantageous. The first was the pull of the United States; the second was towards their own undefined and usually mythical origins; and the third was towards the Spanish element of their past. It was a three-way pull that actually affected all sectors of the Hispanic population in the New World. It was almost impossible to escape from a profound ambiguity when it came to defining attitudes in each of these spheres. The first and certainly the most destructive reality was the drainage of population to the United States.

The exodus began a couple of years after annexation and took off as problems of transport eased with the coming of the aeroplane. In 1917 the Jones Act was passed by Congress, granting United States citizenship to everyone born in Puerto Rico and its islands. Benefiting from the country's status after 1952 as a 'commonwealth' (or, in Spanish, ELA or 'free associated state') of the Union, thousands of islanders took part in a massive airborne migration to the mainland United States, and principally to New York. In 1920 Puerto Ricans resident in the States numbered 12,000. Between 1945 and 1965 around half a million moved to the mainland, and between 1991 and 1998 a further quarter of a million. The figure for 'migrants' was in reality less important than the figure for those finally identifiable as 'residents'. In the nationwide census of the year 2000, the number of people of Puerto Rican origin resident on the mainland of the United States was 3.4 million, and those on the island 3.8 million. Very many were no longer an active part of the island, since at least half had been born on the mainland, which was their real place of origin. The peculiar constitutional status meant that concepts such as 'emigration' and 'exile' no longer applied, because people were really moving within their own country rather than between two different countries. It was never simply a question of poor islanders moving to the mainland, since the ineradicable poverty among Puerto Ricans in urban areas of the mainland also created a regular pattern of emigration back to the island. The situation produced two consequences of profound importance for the identity of Puerto Rico. The permanent cycle of emigration/immigration created an unbreakable chain of movement that determined, perhaps for ever, the evolution of Puerto Rican society. And by 1980 the number of Puerto Ricans resident in New York surpassed that of San Juan, converting New York into the biggest Puerto Rican city in the hemisphere.[9]

The special situation of Puerto Rico gave a new dimension to the notions of exile and migration. Exile no longer exists if there is always the possibility of unimpeded return. This state of 'immanent exile', or of permanent movement back and forth, in what has been called a 'circular migration' (a *vaivén*),[10] is obviously of crucial importance in determining a sense of identity and the evolution of cultural values. Puerto Ricans usually viewed their time in the United States as a temporary situation, since they wished to work there for a while and then return with enough money to settle down. Some succeeded; many did not. For the latter, the temporary exile became permanent, since they could not afford to go back. The constant flux in population undermined, for all practical purposes, the attempt to determine an identity, since Puerto Rico ended up with two identities, derived from the two halves of its population.

The duality presented a problem for writers and novelists who were trying to approach the basic question 'Who are we?' Were the Puerto Ricans a product of their unique identifiable past, associated for example with the traditional figure of the original farmer inhabitant, the *jíbaro*, with his symbol of the *pava* or straw hat?[11] Or should they somehow find their roots in the vanished indigenous people of the islands, the *taínos*? Or were they, as some Spanish writers liked to think, simply an extension of Hispanic culture? Many felt that the loss of population was a threat to the stability and identity of the island. In his play *The Ox-Cart (La Carreta)*, staged in New York in 1953 and in San Juan a year later, the nationalist writer René Marqués presented a pessimistic vision of the extent to which emigration was undermining island identity, and suggested that the only hope for Puerto Rico was for its people to return to it. The play centred round a *jíbaro* family that migrates from the poverty of the countryside to the slums of San Juan, and then to the ghetto in New York, falling into further degradation with each move.

The most agonizing question was over the status, social condition and future of the exiled half of Puerto Rico. On the island the Boricuas had clear status levels and class differentiations that were the result of their own history and the immigration of Spaniards and Caribbean peoples. By contrast, on the mainland the expatriates tended to represent a depressed social sector, logically so since they had emigrated in search of a better life. In New York, they formed in those days the lowest economic level of the entire Hispanic population, with one-third of families below the poverty line. It was a situation that Puerto Rico's leaders found difficult to accept. It did not help that in addition to the poorer immigrants, many of them uneducated *jíbaros*, there was also a good number of the intellectual elite, writers and scientific workers who were attracted by the higher wages in the USA and so created a brain drain that the island administration tried in vain to control.

The concentration of Boricuas in specific zones of the city of New York contributed also to the import of aspects of island culture to the mainland. 'When I came in 1916,' wrote Bernardo Vega (1885–1965), a Boricua activist who wrote his memoirs in the 1940s, 'there was little interest in Hispanic culture. For the average citizen, Spain was a country of bullfighters and flamenco dancers. As for Latin America, no one could care less. Cuba and Puerto Rico were just two islands inhabited by savages.'[12] Vega was a left-wing activist who spent most of his life in New York, where he worked on behalf of the pro-independence groups on the island, but returned to Puerto Rico at the end of his life. His work was not published until 1977, rendering him totally unknown outside the island. Another relevant activist for the identity of Puerto Rico was Jesús Colón (d.1974), who lived in New York for half a century, working at menial jobs but devoting his leisure to writing articles for the Communist Party.[13] These two men were typical of the protest movement that saw its fight for social justice as a necessary part of the fight to clarify the problem of Puerto Rico's identity.

The metropolis of New York served as a shop window for the presentation and slow acceptance of Hispanic culture. By force of numbers, the Boricuas were able to project an image that had a bigger impact than those of other Hispanic minorities. Almost every aspect of that image was at first unfavourable. With time, however, their religious practice, their carnivals, their street markets and stores, their restaurants, especially on the Upper West Side of Manhattan, transformed them into an integral part of the New York scene. Most of all, their sporting activity determined their social importance. By 1950 the city had about twelve Boricua baseball leagues, which by 1960 totalled one hundred and ninety teams.[14]

A crucial aspect of exile culture was the development of popular music. In the Latin world, song and music were always used as a direct expression of exile. Since the sixteenth century, lamentation had been the daily comfort of indigenous and black slaves in the Caribbean, whose songs drifted through the twilight of haciendas and plantations. A Basque musician from Spain called Sebastián de Iradier (d.1865), who found himself in Havana, was fascinated by the mournful music of the Cubans and wrote a tune for guitar called *El Arreglito* (1840), reputed to be the first habanera (though the slow Tango dance and song of that rhythm may have had earlier origins). Imported to Spain, the habanera in time became a standard feature of Spanish folk music. Bizet stole the tune *Arreglito* as the popular 'habanera' of his opera *Carmen*. Iradier's compositions – the best known of which was the habanera song *La Paloma*, first performed in Havana in 1855 – became popular on both sides of the Atlantic. His achievement as an itinerant composer carved out a special place for Hispanic music. Another emigrant to Cuba was the Catalan Xavier Cugat (1900–90), whose parents left their native Girona in Spain when he was only five years old and settled in Cuba. A highly gifted child, he took up the violin and in his teens emigrated to the United States, apparently at the insistence of Enrico Caruso. He displayed his virtuosity by becoming an illustrator for the *Los Angeles Times*, and then from 1920 became a band leader, composing and popularizing Latin rhythms derived from the Caribbean tradition. His dance band played regularly at the Coconut Grove in Los Angeles, then went on to non-stop success in New York, where for sixteen years they were the resident orchestra of the Waldorf Astoria Hotel. Cugat's success was phenomenal. Criticized for devoting his talents to commercial music, he retorted, 'I would rather play "Chiquita Banana" and have my swimming pool than play Bach and starve'. He returned to his native Catalonia only at the very end of his life, continued to live boisterously and died happy at a ripe old age.

Music became an essential element in the integration of Boricuas with the New York scene. At the same period that Cugat and other musicians were introducing the American public to Caribbean rhythm, recently arrived Boricuas in the 1930s began to develop music with which they could identify. The most distinctive composer of the 1930s was Rafael Hernández (1892–1965), whose sister Victoria ran a music shop in Spanish Harlem. He did not limit himself to island rhythms, but incorporated Spanish and international styles in order to create messages with a patriotic content. His brilliant and tuneful *Lamento Borincano* was first recorded in 1930, a purely New York song of exile that was taken to Puerto Rico in 1931 and caused a sensation. It became in the process a sort of national anthem that was adopted in the 1940s as the theme song of Governor Luis Muñoz Marín's party, the PPD (Popular Democratic Party).[15] It narrated the story of a *jíbaro* who goes to town to sell his produce, fails to sell anything, and returns home crushed:

> You can hear this song anywhere,
> Of my unhappy Borinquén, yes,
> Sadly the *jibarito* goes
> Thinking this, saying this,
> Weeping along the road,
> What will happen to Borinquén, dear God,
> What will happen to my sons and my home?

Another bolero composed by Rafael, first recorded in 1935, expressed the nostalgia of a New Yorker for his native Puerto Rico, which is addressed as the 'beautiful' (*Preciosa*):

> The poets call you Beautiful
> They sing your story
> No matter if the tyrant treats you
> With black evil
> You will be Beautiful

> With no flag, no laurels, no glory
> Beautiful, Beautiful they call you,
> The children of liberty.[16]

The romantic and confident song became a key item in the repertoire of Puerto Ricans everywhere, but the touchstone of one's
political stance vis-à-vis the status of the island was the word 'tyrant'
('*tirano*'), which clearly pointed at the USA. From the late 1940s
Muñoz Marín added the song to his party's theme music, but changed
the word '*tirano*' to 'destiny' ('*destino*'). Hernández returned to live in
Puerto Rico from 1947, but appears not to have commented on the
change. In popular use, the word 'tyrant' continued to prevail.

It would not be an exaggeration to say that the decisive cultural
event for Puerto Ricans in New York, in terms of social acceptance,
was the opening in 1957 at the Winter Garden Theater, Broadway, of
the musical *West Side Story*, with lyrics by Stephen Sondheim and
music by Leonard Bernstein, which went on to achieve even greater
success when it was filmed in 1961. It was the background against
which the community in New York – the Nuyoricans – mounted in
Central Park in 1965 the first Puerto Rico Folk Festival. However, the
integration of Boricuas into mainland society represented a clear
divergence from what was happening on the island, where the government, especially under Muñoz Marín (governor from 1949 to 1964),
adopted a conscious policy of 'cultural nationalism', which involved
an active stimulation of island folklore (nearly all Spanish in origin),
Catholic religion and Spanish language. Where citizens on the mainland were using English as their main language, on the island the
schools and administration favoured Spanish. This helped to intensify
the cultural divide within the same people, turning many into effective
exiles. But was the 'exile' genuine? Is the United States the homeland,
or is it alien territory? For nearly a century, thinking people in Puerto
Rico have been divided over the two basic issues of who they are and
where they are heading. The divisions were highlighted in successive
plebiscites that were held in an attempt to clarify the state of opinion.
In the last two plebiscites, in 1993 and 1998, a consistent number of
Puerto Rico citizens (46 per cent) supported greater integration with
the United States ('statehood'), but on each occasion a (narrow)

majority favoured a simple continuation of the status quo as 'commonwealth'.

The splits that seem to be inherent in Puerto Rican society across the United States – between loyalty to island and mainland, or to Spanish and English as languages – have given rise to an emphasis on the theme of exile that is often difficult to understand, and is equally often meaningless. It is common for Puerto Ricans who have made their careers on the mainland to proclaim that they are suffering in exile. A poet who currently earns his living in New York affirms: 'I define myself as a foreigner – *un extranjero*; and an exile – *un exiliado*. Being an *exiliado* means I long night and day for a return to the land I have rejected.'[17] At the other end of the spectrum are writers – and scientists and university professors – who were born in Puerto Rico but recognize the obvious fact that the mainland United States gives a scope for creativity that cannot be found in Puerto Rico. Among them are the writers who in 1975 founded the Nuyorican Poets Café in New York.[18] While insisting on their roots in the island, and their loyalty to its language and traditions, the Nuyorican Poets accept the need for English as a means of communication, and the importance of multiculturalism (that is, of all ethnicities and not only Hispanic) as a springboard to future experiments.[19] One of the Café's founders, Miguel Algarín, made the attempt to go back to his roots, but on his visit to Puerto Rico became conscious of the rejection faced on the island by those who lived in the big mainland city:

> We thought
> That getting off the plane
> Would drop us into the lap
> Of '*la familia*', we thought
> We'd find a noble feeling
> That we'd be sure and secure
> That there would be a *madre*
> *Alma* to kiss our New York
> Soot-filled bodies and soul.[20]

Instead, there was rejection. Was there a way forward?

*

Spanish immigration had made an important contribution to Puerto Rico in the nineteenth century, and continued to be significant in the twentieth. One of the first cultural contacts between the peninsula and the island was through the writer Federico de Onís (1885–1966). Onís, a disciple of Unamuno, pioneered the participation of Spaniards in universities of the United States, where he taught at Columbia in the 1920s. He never accepted integration into American culture and always maintained the outlook of his own generation, namely that Hispanics had little to learn from America. His services to Hispanic literature were many, including the publication for the American public in 1922 of a work by the Chilean poet Gabriela Mistral. He was also the first to coin the literary term 'postmodern' to mean an aesthetic and literary tendency that reacted against aspects of modern creativity. He was at the quayside in New York in 1929 to receive García Lorca when the poet made his ill-fated visit there. Lorca disliked the city, was completely at sea with the English language, did not fit in at Columbia, and had mixed feelings about the black neighbourhoods he insisted on visiting in search of inspiration. In Puerto Rico, Onís helped to found the Department of Hispanic Studies at the University of Puerto Rico, Río Piedras.

The first of the Civil War exiles to choose Puerto Rico as a haven was the poet Pedro Salinas (1891–1951). Born and brought up in Madrid, Salinas began his career by giving classes in Spanish for three years at the University of Paris (1914–17). In 1918 he obtained a chair at the University of Seville, from which he later transferred to Murcia. In this period he also developed links with England, where he taught at Cambridge on a brief one-year contract (1922). In 1933 he helped to convert a summer school for foreign language students at Santander into a 'Universidad Internacional', based on the magnificent royal summer palace of the Magdalena, and became its first general secretary until the advent of the Civil War. In 1935 he accepted an offer of a one-year visiting post at Wellesley College in upstate New York, and left Spain to take it up in 1936 just as the war began. Though he was a supporter of the Republic, his testimony in the spring of 1936, when he was preparing to leave for America, confirms the way in which liberals of sensitivity reacted to the terrible breakdown of order in a Madrid controlled by the anarchists and leftists in the Popular Front:

Apart from the attraction of America, I am delighted to be able to save myself from this Hispanic environment, every day more envenomed, more full of hatred and bad blood, more hostile to good relations and cheerful work. I have the impression that everything is going to get worse, and this trip is a salvation, I can feel it.[21]

By the end of the year he was teaching in Wellesley. Adapting to America was not easy, particularly because he found it difficult to learn English, and never got over his rough Spanish accent. In the collection of his correspondence titled *Travel Letters (1912–1951)* he expressed clearly to his wife, whom he had left behind in Algeria with his children, his sentiments as an exile:

Reading the newspapers these days, seeing the photos of houses levelled in Madrid by the bombing, something in me breaks. You tell me to give up the idea of returning to Spain, something which is so natural, so logical, that it surprises me. In my classes I speak of Spain, of the land of Castile, of Andalusia, and I cannot figure out if any of it still exists, or not. I'll tell you in confidence, almost in secret, that now that I have the chance to spend another year here, I feel an inner urge to go to Europe, or rather to Spain. I know that it is absurd, of course, but when I think about certain things over there, certain places, the gardens of the Alcázar in our October of 35, the Escorial, I get the urge to give up. Starting a new professional life here is so demanding! We do not yet realize how much we have lost. When peace comes I shall find out that I have no career, no post, no money, everything that I built up in forty years of life will have gone up in smoke. But what I have lost most, and that is the worst, is something intangible, the air, the light, the way of speech, the countryside and the skies, that make up Spain.

He confessed to 'spending a huge amount of energy trying to adapt', and how much he longed to hear the Spanish language spoken.[22] However, in 1938 he made an important step forward when his poems were first translated into English, gaining him the hope of a wider public. Two years later he accepted a post at Johns Hopkins, which he held until his death. Meanwhile, in 1943 he took up a visiting one-year post at the University of Puerto Rico, Río Piedras. What he experienced when he arrived on the island – sunshine, palm trees, Hispanic language and food – was like a sudden discovery of Eden.

The one year became three years. They were possibly the most creative period of his life. He would sit and write his poems on the terrace of the Afda Club in San Juan,[23] facing the Atlantic. Logically, his verse included the feel of sea and sun, but within fundamentally introspective themes of love, absences and departures.[24] Salinas's poetry turned out to be somewhat restricted in its themes and too private in vision ever to appeal to a wide public. When he left the island in 1945 he observed that 'one of the biggest reasons for personal satisfaction that I take from Puerto Rico is that in the free time outside classes I have worked with pleasure and constancy in my literary work. I have worked here as seldom in my life.'[25]

Though an enthusiastic supporter of the United States, which had given him shelter, a fine job and citizenship, Salinas never lost touch with his Spanish roots and in consequence became more critical of his host country, particularly after 1945 when it became clear that the Allies had no intention of liberating Spain from Franco. He began to feel that he was an 'American by residence only', not in his soul, and preferred to retire to the Hispanic environment of Puerto Rico, where he felt more in touch with his own language and culture. In Puerto Rico he was the centre of contact for other exiled academics, among them Vicente Llorens and Jorge Guillén. Llorens was invited by Salinas to give courses at Río Piedras and was then sponsored by him for a post at Johns Hopkins. Personal links between the exiles made it possible for Llorens, backed this time by Américo Castro, to move to Princeton, which became his final post. Salinas died during a visit to Boston, but his body was brought back to Puerto Rico for burial.

Jorge Guillén (1893–1984) came from a privileged family in Valladolid, studied in Switzerland and Madrid and spent six years (1917–23) as a language assistant at the University of Paris, where he married a French girl. His earliest verse was published from 1920 onwards. In 1925 he obtained the chair of literature at the University of Murcia, and subsequently spent a couple of years teaching Spanish at Oxford (where he learnt no English), before moving to take up a chair at Seville. When the Civil War broke out he and his wife went to Navarre to leave their children in France with her family for safety. They were detained by pro-rebel elements in Pamplona in August 1936, but released after five days. When they returned to Seville, the city was in rebel hands, and Guillén contacted friends in England and the United States to try to obtain a post abroad. The couple eventually managed to leave Spain in July 1938 and sailed to America. Guillén took up short-term university jobs, one of them at McGill University in Montreal. He was delighted to be free, and wrote to Salinas:

We are out of Spain. That is a privileged situation, a highly privileged one. Besides, we are in America, and in non-Hispanic America, and in ideal university posts, ideal despite everything![26]

From September 1940 he succeeded Salinas at Wellesley. He taught at the college from 1940 until his retirement in 1957, and made frequent trips to visit family and colleagues in Spain. After retiring he took up visiting posts at several campuses, including Harvard and Puerto Rico. From the 1960s he began to spend his summers in the city of Málaga, in which he settled permanently in 1976. The lyricism of Guillén – expressing faith in life and in nature, so that some critics found his poems too intellectual and dehumanized – was mirrored in his first main publication, the *Cántico* (1928). He subsequently reissued the *Cántico*, adding new poems each time. The edition of 1928 contained 75 poems, one in 1936 125, and those of 1945 and 1950 270 and 334 respectively. In his second major work, *Clamor* (1963), he did not avoid the brutality of the world. This may have made his verse more amenable to his various translators, who helped to bring his work to a larger public than most Hispanic poets were fortunate enough to reach. His 'Blood in the River' ('*La Sangre en el Río*') seems to be a reflection on the Civil War:

> So profound a horror is never absurd.
> Between the ups and downs of events
> – selfless, sublime, gloomy, ferocious –
> The crisis clamours out
> Truth or lies,
> And as it goes it creates its own history,
> Heading towards an unknown future,
> Where it is awaited by hope and the awareness
> Of so many, so many lives.

The most prestigious of Spain's Civil War exports to Puerto Rico was, of course, Juan Ramón Jiménez, the island's first Nobel Prize winner, whom we have touched upon in the previous chapter. He arrived in New York from Spain with his wife Zenobia in 1936 and soon moved on to Puerto Rico (Zenobia's mother was from the island). He subsequently visited Cuba, where he tried to get away from the constant demand for him to give lectures. He was relieved finally to settle down in Miami, where the setting reminded him of Europe and Spain and allowed him to resume his creative work. His enthusiasm for the United States was such that when the Japanese attacked Pearl Harbor he wrote to the State Department offering his services, leaving it to them to decide 'in which way a poet of fifty-nine years and young in spirit can serve this nation'. The quaint gesture betrayed the belief of his generation that an 'intellectual' signified something, but also demonstrated his commitment to the country that had given him a home. 'For me,' he wrote to Pablo Neruda from Miami, 'Spain was my upper side and the United States my reverse, now they are two reverses or two upper sides totally distinct from each other.'[27]

'I started to write poetry again in Florida', he wrote in 1943. He also felt that the ocean brought him within striking distance of the Spain he knew: 'it is fortunate,' Zenobia wrote, 'that he can still see Moguer [his birthplace] from a distance'. From 1939 to 1942 he did some language teaching at the University of Miami at Coral Gables, then from 1943 to 1951 he and his wife were employed by the University of Maryland, College Park, where he enjoyed tranquillity and wrote a substantial amount of verse incorporating elements of his new environment (such as American street names) into his Spanish. The lush vegetation and trees of the south enchanted him. 'Juan Ramón has been happy,' Zenobia noted in her diary in 1949, 'leaning like a madman out of all the windows and saying, "This is splendid!"'[28] From Maryland the couple moved in 1951 to Puerto Rico, where 'JR' (as Zenobia referred to him in her diaries, which she wrote in English) did occasional teaching at the university at Río Piedras. The moves from one base to another were distressing. 'With every trip, the whole house on our backs, moving everything, losing so many things . . . And in every place, starting again, and all the time, from start to finish, illnesses, illnesses, illnesses.'[29] Throughout those years Jiménez never escaped from his permanent affliction: he had extensive periods of depression, and his only support, personally and professionally and in dealings with others when English had to be spoken, was Zenobia. She could not help confiding to her diary that life with a depressive was terrible. 'JR,' she wrote, was 'always unable to adapt to his surroundings, he finds relaxation only when he is alone'. In 1951 she was diagnosed with cancer and operated on at Boston while her husband remained in Puerto Rico. From 1954 the poet entered a final critical phase of depression, from which he did not emerge. It is easy to imagine the impact on him of Zenobia's death in October 1956. Three days before she died, he received news that he had been awarded the Nobel Prize. His own death transpired in May 1958. A week afterwards, though he seems to have expressed the wish to be buried on the island, his body and that of Zenobia were taken to Spain and buried together in the cemetery at Moguer.

No doubt because of the completely apolitical quality of his verse, he was scorned by other exiled writers, who felt that he should adopt a political stance. The Franco regime scorned him for its own good reasons, did not publish his work, and paid little attention to the Nobel honour. Juan Ramón Jiménez, however, never budged. He attacked the political activists, fell out with several of them, and branded the poet León Felipe a 'fake'. When José Bergamín brought out an opportune edition of Machado, he commented: 'Unamuno, Machado, García Lorca are now enjoying a fame based on the [civil] war, thanks to the manipulators of cadavers and reputations. Whoever knew those three well, will know their repugnance for all the noise over their publicized deaths.'[30]

Juan Ramón Jiménez's reputation became more solid as a result of the Nobel Prize, but because of the barrier of the Spanish language and the nature of his lyrical verse he never reached a wide public. Pau Casals, by contrast, always enjoyed a universal fame. Towards the end of his stay in Prades in the French Pyrenees the cellist, then aged seventy-eight, developed a personal relationship with one of his music students, Marta Montañez, aged eighteen at the time. The appeal of the very attractive young cellist may have been enhanced in part by her resemblance to Casals' mother, a native (of Catalan origin) of Puerto Rico. He became highly receptive to the idea of Puerto Rico. When he was invited to celebrate his seventy-ninth birthday in the island in 1955, a grand concert was put on in his honour and Governor Muñoz Marín held a reception for four hundred guests at which Casals and Marta played. Four days after the reception Casals flew to Mexico, where nine hundred Civil War exiles attended a banquet arranged by the Spanish Republican Centre. The re-creation of a Spanish environment in the New World must have been deeply moving for Casals. At the beginning of his visit to Puerto Rico he was taken to visit the house where his mother had been born. By early 1956 he found the setting he was in and the attention he was receiving to be irresistible, and decided to settle on the island. 'Wherever possible, I have lived by the sea', he confessed. Puerto Rico and his new life with Marta (whom he married in 1957 after securing a divorce from Susan Metcalfe, whom he had not seen in thirty years) gave him the tranquillity he desired. His lifestyle was unchanged. 'For the past eighty years,' he explained, 'I have started each day in the same manner. I go to the piano, and I play two preludes and fugues of Bach. It is a sort of benediction on the house.' The morning music was usually from the *Well-Tempered Clavier*. Bach had been his permanent inspiration since the day when, at the age of thirteen, he had come upon some old sheets of Bach cello suites in a Barcelona shop and gone home to practise them, in a state of excitement.

He was enchanted by the new phase in his life. 'I am in love with this country,' he wrote to a friend, 'I feel so much at home here that I have had a wonderful idea. What would you say of a Prades Festival in Puerto Rico in April 1957?'[31] The idea appealed greatly to the governor, because it coincided with his attempts to enhance the cultural identity of Puerto Rico. The presence of Casals would at one and the same time underscore the Hispanic character of the island, and add an international star to its firmament. When the first Casals Festival was held as scheduled in 1957 (Casals could not take part because he had suffered a major heart attack during rehearsals), over half the seats were reserved for foreign and mainland United States sale, in order to make sure it would be an international event. For the next sixteen years of his life, Casals moved between his two festivals, in Puerto

Rico in June and at Prades in early summer. The benefit to Puerto Rico was that musical performers accepted invitations to the festival, for a long time the only venue on the island where classical music was performed. Artists who played in it during its early phase included Rubinstein and Rostropovich. Soon, however, there were pressures over the monopoly exercised by the event. Critics felt that more Puerto Rican music should appear in the repertoire, and more Puerto Rican musicians be allowed to take part. While this continues to be an issue, the festival has survived various ups and downs and is still the island's main cultural attraction.

Casals, meanwhile, was adjusting to life in America. He had sworn never to play in any state that recognized the Franco regime, and the United States was clearly one of them, just as Puerto Rico was clearly part of the USA (he got round that by citing the island's status as an 'associated' rather than a full state of the Union). In the event, he stretched his own definition of what an official concert might be, and continued to play in the United States without problems of con-science. In 1958 he took part with other leading musicians in a concert at the United Nations in New York, the first of many success-ful performances on the mainland. The most contentious decision was an invitation to play for President Kennedy at the White House in November 1961 (it was not Casals' first appearance in that location, for he had played there in 1904). He accepted when the concert was given the status of a private performance preceded by a private dinner in honour of Governor Muñoz. He also insisted on playing, as he normally did at the end of every concert he had given since leaving Spain, his rendering of the traditional Catalan folk melody *The Song of the Birds* (*El Cant dels Ocells*), which was his permanent gesture in favour of freedom and which the Catalans themselves came to accept as a piece of patriotic music. The following year he took part in a public concert in San Francisco at which his main contribution was the two-hour oratorio *The Crib* (*El Pessebre*), which he had first begun writing in 1943. Based on a poem by a fellow Catalan exile, the work was premiered in Mexico in 1960, and developed the Christmas theme as part of his campaign for peace in the world. It received a mixed reception in San Francisco because of its conservative content and style, but it was Casals' favourite creation and he continued to receive invitations to stage it. For him, it combined Catalan tradition with the longing for peace. He performed it in the general hall of the United Nations in October 1963, and before the highest authorities of the nation in Washington in October 1967.

Over and above these specific events, he became drawn into American musical life, notably through his participation in the annual Marlboro Music Festivals in Vermont. Throughout his last thirteen years he led the orchestra in the weekend festivals, inspiring both public and performers. The cellist Yo-Yo Ma felt his four summers there were 'magical' ones that 'led me to a commitment to music I could not have received from one school or one teacher'. Casals composed several musical pieces, one of them the 'Hymn of the United Nations', first performed at a session of that body in 1971. In 1972 he conducted a celebrated concert of eighty cellists at New York's Lincoln Center. The following year he died in Puerto Rico, where his casket was draped with the flags of that island and Catalonia. The dictatorship in Spain came to an end in 1975, when Franco died. Casals' remains were returned to Catalonia in November 1979 and interred at El Vendrell.[32] He always retained an intense feeling for his homeland. 'I have travelled in many lands and have found beauty everywhere. But the beauty of Catalonia nourished me since infancy. When I close my eyes I see the ocean at Sant Salvador and the seaside village of Sitges with the little fishing boats.'

The Hispanic environment of the New World, and of Puerto Rico in particular, offered expatriates from the peninsula the hospitality of language. It was the most fundamental aspect of identity, without which the homeless became truly exiles, cut off in an environment of unfamiliar and unreceptive sounds. The age of empire had contributed to the spread of Castilian, which in the twenty-first century is the principal language of up to a fifth of the human race. The fact seemed to give substance to the old Castilian dream, ironically stimulated by the 1898 Disaster, that if they had failed in the material pursuit of power they had succeeded in establishing a cultural hegemony based on their language. The cults of Quixote and of Hispanidad were at the heart of this deeply held conviction, which saw the national culture as comprising fundamentally the language of Castile.

Hispanic culture across the centuries was, of course, not simply a matter of language. It took various forms at different periods and was a rich mixture drawn from the experience of many peoples, climates, creeds and races, and among those who contributed to it were the exiles, living beyond the normal scope of an Hispanic environment. The Castilian language had a smaller role than might at first appear. The situation in the Iberian peninsula during the Golden Age was typical. Spanish books might have been the best-sellers in Barcelona shops, but in the streets there nearly everyone spoke Catalan. 'In Catalonia', claimed a priest from that principality in 1636, over one hundred years after the beginning of the Habsburg dynasty, 'the common people do not understand Castilian.'[33] The situation could be found elsewhere in the coastal provinces of Spain. As late as 1686 regulations for shipping in Guipúzcoa had to stipulate that vessels carry a Basque-speaking priest, since among the seamen 'the majority do not understand Spanish'.[34] The absence of a common national tongue was a fairly normal phenomenon in most European states at that time, but in Spain it was particularly striking. About a quarter of all Spaniards around the year 1600 did not use Castilian as their daily language, and Castilian was not understood at all by a good part of the natives of Andalusia, Valencia, Catalonia, the Basque country, Navarre and Galicia.[35]

The problem existed throughout the length and breadth of the empire. At the end of the colonial regime, around 1800, a very small proportion of the population in Spanish America could speak some form of Spanish, but they could neither read nor write it. Because of the high level of illiteracy, the newly independent states were barely able to find personnel fit to carry out the necessary administrative duties. Spanish as a spoken and written language of the population became a reality only after the Spaniards were no longer there, thanks to the educational programmes devised by the emerging states of Latin America. The fate of Spanish in Asia was even more unfortunate. During the age of early European commerce in Asia, the accepted lingua franca was Portuguese,[36] spoken even by Asian traders to each other and adopted perforce by Spaniards who wished to communicate with them. The Navarrese Jesuit Francisco Xavier used the language as his main medium of communication in Asia. As late as the eighteenth century, officials of the British East India Company in India had to learn to communicate with their employees in it. In the Philippines, ignorance of the Spanish language was almost total, after three centuries of Spanish colonization.[37]

In Europe, curiously enough, despite the seeming weight of Spain's power, Spanish never became the language of diplomacy. A Castilian writer boasted forcefully in 1580 that 'we have seen the majesty of the Spanish language extended to the furthest provinces wherever the victorious flags of our armies have gone'.[38] In fact, there were no victorious armies in Europe, and the only language with any pretension to cultural universality was Italian, soon to be succeeded from the seventeenth century by French. Italian was, after Latin, the most common language used by diplomats in Renaissance Europe.[39] In the early eighteenth century over half Spain's ambassadors were foreign: among them were four Englishmen, two Dutchmen, one Belgian and fifteen Italians.[40] When not written in Spanish, their dispatches were regularly in French or Italian.

In a world of strange tongues, expatriates could face a severe problem of communication with others. The logical solution was to take their language with them. The Jews expelled in 1492 took their spoken Spanish, as well as their residual Hebrew. The Muslims and Moriscos expelled between 1492 and 1614 took their Spanish, which seems to have disappeared rapidly. Exiled Protestants were too few in number to make a significant contribution to the diffusion of Spanish. In the eighteenth century the language problems of elite Spanish émigrés virtually disappeared. The early Bourbon court established French as the main medium of polite conversation, so that most elite exiles thereafter were probably able to manage a few words of that language. By the nineteenth century the establishment of Paris as the fount of elite culture meant that young men completed their education in France and ended up speaking its language. In a trend that stretched from the Enlightenment to the Second Republic, many elite Spaniards became fluent in French,[41] which added to the attraction of France as a logical place of refuge. The Valencian scholar Gregorio Mayans, a fervent admirer of Italian culture, admitted in 1734 to Spain's chief minister, the Italian José Patiño, that Spain had failed to extend the influence of its language. 'One of the things that a nation should take particular care to achieve,' he wrote, 'is that its language become universal.' But Spanish had now been superseded by English and French, whose literature, science and languages were supreme in the world. 'The fault,' he said, 'is ours, through our inadequacy.'[42]

Inadequacy or not, exiles found themselves continuously battling against alien tongues. Blanco White confessed in his *Autobiography*:

Firm as I have remained under the most difficult circumstances, in my resolution never to return to Spain, the only loss that experience would make me fear if I were to relive the past, would be that of my native tongue. Among the many examples in the works of Shakespeare of a surprising knowledge of human nature, few have impressed me so much as that to be found in a passage (which those who are not in my circumstances would probably have passed over) in which he describes the great misfortune of a man exiled from his country who has to support living among those who do not understand his tongue.

Spaniards living out their days in a foreign environment could hardly fail to share the same sentiment if they had arrived as adults and never mastered the host tongue. 'Deprived of my country and my tongue,' wrote Juan Ramón Jiménez in the United States, 'I believe that not a single Spaniard of those I know outside Spain, speaks Spanish, Spanish, the Spanish that I am losing.'[43] His wife Zenobia testified that 'not hearing or speaking Spanish makes him forget it, and he gets depressed'.[44]

The European nations exported their languages to the New World but in revenge the New World often chewed them up into exotic and barely recognizable versions, as those who attempt to speak standard English in the Caribbean or metropolitan French in Louisiana and Haiti know very well. The Spanish language, which had never attained much diffusion in colonial times, was saved from this fate by the local elites of post-independence Latin America, who attempted to convert it into an acceptable and literary form. From the same period, the Hispanic peoples of the New World were faced with several linguistic challenges that profoundly affected their culture. Hispanic exiles, by virtue of being forced out beyond the confines of their own language, found themselves at the frontier where the question of language affected that of their own identity.

The first important issue for nations in the Hispanic New World was whether the language of the conqueror, Spain, would continue to be their language. Around the year 1900 writers such as the Peruvian Manuel González Prada called on South Americans to restore the native Indian to the forefront of their cultural programme. The pro-native or *indigenista* movement became highly influential in the subsequent generation, but was looked upon as unprogressive by those who aspired to modernization and a convergence of cultures. Some Peruvians, like José de la Riva-Agüero, commented that the Indian past 'has much that is exotic and strange for us [from Lima]: we do not feel for it the close affection that we have for the colony', and stated that 'we are proud of our enduring Spanishness. That has been and is our physiognomy, our evident destiny, which we cannot and will not give up.' One of the fundamental problems of the nativist movement was that it lacked a coherent language or literature on which to base itself. None of the surviving Indian languages could be used as a vehicle for modernization. In territories such as Puerto Rico there was not even a native language, for the *taínos* had – through enslavement and imported diseases – become extinct in the sixteenth century. Most writers recognized the problem. The pro-native Cusco writer Luis Valcárcel opined in *Tempest in the Andes* (1928): 'that is our national history, a perennial conflict between invaders and invaded, between Spain and the Indies, a war without a truce, and still without hopes of peace. Five centuries of daily battle!' But within half a century the pro-native tendency was rejected, above all by writers who employed the Spanish language inherited from the colonial period. In Peru, Mario Vargas Llosa stated firmly that 'there may be no other realistic way to integrate our societies than to ask the Indians to pay this high price ['give up their culture – their language, their beliefs, their traditions and habits – and adopt that of their old masters']; it may be that the ideal, that is, the preservation of the primitive cultures of America, is a Utopia incompatible with the other more urgent goal, the establishment of modern societies'.[45] He affirmed:

It is tragic to destroy what is still living, the possibility of a culture even though it is archaic; but I fear that we shall have to choose between one or the other. I know of no case in which it has been possible to choose both, except in those countries where two different cultures have evolved more or less simultaneously. But when the economic and social divide is so great, modernization is possible only through the sacrifice of indigenous cultures.

The debate over coming to terms with Indian culture took different forms in different Latin countries. In Mexico, a special case, it was the conservative ruling class that took charge after independence, and created a new formula which seemed viable. Mexico was seen as a society consisting almost entirely of people of mixed race, known strictly as *mestizos* in Spanish but in formal language always referred to as the 'race' (*raza*). In 1918 the writer Antonio Caso picked out October the Twelfth, the date normally identified as that of Columbus's arrival in America, as a day on which to celebrate the 'Mexican *mestizo* race', the *Raza*, or mixture of Spanish and indigenous cultures. Ten years later, the 'Day of the Race' (*Día de la Raza*) was declared an official national holiday by the government, though there were many who questioned whether there was anything to be celebrated. The Indian more or less disappeared from sight, subsumed in the *mestizo*. The established and essentially reactionary theory of *mestizaje*, promoted notably in the 1940s by José Vasconcelos (d.1959), a writer who had been minister of education but went on to develop a highly mystical and messianic vision of his people's historical experience, was that the Conquest period combined the best of the cultures of Spain and the New World and had produced a 'cosmic race'. This allowed the pro-Spanish programme to be adopted under cover of a multicultural formula that pushed the Indian into the background.

The second challenge to literary culture was posed by Spain itself, which began a campaign of linguistic imperialism that coincided with the ideas of the supporters of '*Hispanismo*' in Latin America and is still an essential part of Spanish policy. '*Hispanismo*', especially after 1898, was directed principally against the United States and the English language. It also, however, fuelled the fires of Castilian nationalism, and was directed against the minority languages of the peninsula, which were in danger of becoming active vehicles for provincial separatism within Spain. Unamuno, a Basque by origin, showed himself an intractable enemy of all threats to the language of

Cervantes. He recommended that the Catalan language be eliminated, and predicted the 'inevitable death' of Basque as a language. 'Every day,' he announced, 'I am more of a fanatic for the language in which I speak, write, think and feel.'[46] At the same time he advocated the suppression of all languages apart from Spanish in the former Hispanic lands of the New World. The sentiments were echoed by Ortega y Gasset, who believed no less firmly in the unique virtues of Castile. 'Only Castilian heads,' he maintained in *Invertebrate Spain*, 'have adequate capacity to perceive the great problem of a united Spain.' Castile alone had created Spain, and Castile's language alone was the true language of Spain.

Shortly after the loss of the colonies, Spanish writers took part with politicians in a movement to affirm the benefits that their culture had brought to the New World. The moves were continued during the dictatorship of Franco through the granting of state funding for the establishment in key cities of institutes for the promotion of the Castilian language. The broad lines of this attempt to recover status in the world may be summarized as follows. The doctrine of '*Hispanismo*' included, among many other postulates, 'the existence of a unique Spanish culture, lifestyle, traditions and values, all of them embodied in its language; the idea that Spanish American culture is nothing but Spanish culture transplanted to the New World; and the notion that Hispanic culture has a hierarchy in which Spain occupies a hegemonic position'.[47] The New World, in this post-imperial view, was perceived as a virtual tabula rasa that had had little coherence of its own before it received the decisive imprint of the Castilian language. That language immediately created the Hispanic *raza*, the highest form of civilization. This attitude was carried to the New World by cultured exiles from the peninsula, and was also promoted by Latin Americans at international gatherings, in which writers such as Carlos Fuentes were invited to back up Castilians in eulogies of the culture that Spain had conferred on America. In a typical pro-*Hispanismo* speech in Rosario, Argentina in 2004, Fuentes put forward the idea that 'in the beginning, America was a vast unpopulated territory', waiting only for cultural input, which it received when 'indigenous America was infected by the immense Hispanic legacy, from the most multicultural land of Europe: Celtic and Iberian, Phoenician, Greek, Roman,

Jewish, Arab and Christian Spain',[48] a highly optimistic vision of the impact that Spanish emigrants had really had on the New World.

The third challenge came from the Anglo world, as the contamination of Hispanic populations by the commerce and culture of the English-speaking world threatened to change and swamp the 'language of Cervantes'. It was a problem that had its origins in the nineteenth century but was not at first seen to pose any danger. When Juan Valera visited America, a few years before the Disaster, he was convinced that the superiority of Castilian literature of the nineteenth century reaffirmed the validity of the sixteenth-century conquest, and that there was no threat from the Americans. 'In the field of letters,' he reassured his friends, 'both in quantity and quality, the Spanish language has conquered English America.' It was a touchingly naive observation. Others were rather more conscious of the real situation. In an effort to affirm Spain's cultural role, from 1861 the Spanish Academy of Language began a campaign to confer 'corresponding memberships' on writers from Spanish America. There was no doubt of the political relevance of language. In 1885 when the Unión Ibero-Americana was founded in Madrid, a speaker saluted the peoples of Latin America, 'who constitute a common *raza*, to arrest the march of Saxon civilization'.[49] The theory, widely diffused from the mid-nineteenth century among writers in Madrid, was that Spain represented the pure spirit of moral values while the United States represented a corrupt materialism that would end in self-destruction, leaving Spain as the supreme leader of civilization. Exiles from Spain arrived in the New World secure in the pride that the most precious thing they carried with them was their language. Brought up in the high tide of Hispanism, they became effectively missionaries of the linguistic gospel. Unamuno was echoing Valera when he claimed that the Castilian language was 'the basis of our spiritual *patria*, and Cervantes gives us firmer claims of possession over America than Columbus gave to our forefathers'.[50] Since all else had failed to hold the empire together, language would be the new way forward. 'The day will come,' the director of the Unión Ibero-Americana announced in Madrid in 1904, 'when from Mexico to Cape Horn there will be an autonomous people, confederated by ties of blood, language and history, united by the vital interests of the *raza*, stretching a hand across the Atlantic.'[51] That dream of linguistic imperialism never, of course, materialized.

A successful confrontation with English was, however, difficult to sustain. In a number of fundamental areas Spanish vocabulary proved unable to stand up to changes that were taking place in the western world. First, the diffusion of international culture, most notably in the field of sports such as football, tennis and golf, imposed the use of foreign languages and excluded Spanish. In Spanish, the essential vocabulary of these sports is still drawn from English. Second, the rise of modern technology, medicine and science introduced a flood of wholly alien terminology that could not be translated into Spanish and produced headaches above all for programmers in the computer age. Finally, the close physical and cultural contact between Hispanic and Anglo populations in North America gave rise to a new convenience vocabulary that has come to be known as Spanglish, a virtually new language that the guardians of the purity of Cervantes' tongue have rejected with horror. The combination of the three factors has helped to create an angry but somewhat impotent reaction on the part of those who feel themselves to be guardians of the Castilian language.

Spanglish, a form of speech used extensively by Hispanics in the Anglo world, is par excellence a consequence of exile. Although in Spain it is habitual to believe that Hispanics in the United States are about to impose their language on the nation and thereby bring about the long-hoped-for cultural conquest, the real threat is directed against traditional Spanish culture, as the case of Puerto Rico shows clearly. The island government's different policies on language are a reflection of the problem. In 1991 the PPD government, which Muñoz Marín had founded and led, decided to recognize Spanish as the only official language. In 1992 the opposition PNP (New Progressive Party) came to power and reverted to the traditional support for English. The different stances reflected what was really happening to the language of Puerto Rico. In Puerto Rico, Boricua literary activity is in Spanish, the main language of the island. However, Nuyoricans tend to write in the language of their environment, English. Nuyorican culture, and with it Hispanic culture in the United States, is firmly bilingual. This was in a sense a gain for the Spanish language. In 1974, in their decision in *Lau* v. *Nichols*, which arose out of a conflict in California, the Supreme Court decided that the exclusive use of English for children beginning their education in state schools without any knowledge of the language, was discriminatory. The decision has helped minorities to absorb the English language at an acceptable pace. In practice, however, the universality of bilingualism among Nuyoricans has made Spanglish an everyday phenomenon that has penetrated both Spanish and English, introducing ingenious neologisms that fuse both languages and also in some measure create a new one, especially among the younger generation. A number of academics and writers defend Spanglish[52] and even publish in it, but traditionalist Castilian speakers look askance at the trend because they see it as a threat to standard Spanish. (English speakers, in a nation where their language has come to terms and learnt to live with over two centuries of immigration, tend to be more tolerant.) Spanglish is a legitimate form of speech used by Hispanic expatriates (in the Bronx, Spanish Harlem, East Los Angeles, San Antonio and South Florida), but the debate over whether it can be identified with a distinct cultural identity is still open.[53]

10. The Return of the Exiles

Exile is always a mistake, because one has to return or at least try to.　　　　　　　　　　　　Max Aub, *The Return: 1964*[1]

For five centuries the attitudes, culture and ideology of the Hispanic world were profoundly and extensively shaped by the reality of exile and the consciousness of not belonging.[2] When Gregorio Marañón in 1947 published the text of his Paris lecture on the exiles, he dedicated it to his friend and co-exile, a supporter like him of the Second Republic of 1931, 'Ramón Pérez de Ayala, who is in Spain even though he is outside it'. It became a permanent feature of the Hispanic condition to live voluntarily or involuntarily outside the homeland, for a few years maybe but often for a lifetime. That separation from home brought with it an inevitable sense of loss. From the end of the fifteenth century, many Spaniards learnt perforce to live outside their country, but the feeling of deprivation was confined to things associated with family, village and region. A sense of national identity did not yet exist and those who lamented the absence of 'Spain' were in reality yearning not for a country called by that name but for the many different experiences that the word represented. Fifty thousand Jews left in 1492, tens of thousands of Muslims left between that date and the year 1502, a trickle of emigrants became expatriates in the Caribbean. All of them had to learn to live without the familiar comforts of life at home, the everyday sounds, and the warmth of a common language. In those early decades, it is possible that a majority of those who left were not formally expelled but were expatriates forced out (like the conversos of Jewish origin) by an inhospitable environment, or fleeing from social conditions they could not endure. As the centuries rolled by, tens of thousands more left the peninsula, but nearly always under the same conditions of duress. The fact that departure was almost a normal situation rendered it somehow invisible to those who were not direct victims. The seventeenth-century diplomat Saavedra y Fajardo commented that northern Europeans 'reconnoitre the world and learn languages, arts and sciences; Spaniards remain in tight seclusion in their country'.[3] Ramón y Cajal in the 1890s had the impression that 'during the epoch of military supremacy we travelled little'; half a century later Marañón as historian affirmed that 'the Spaniard is little inclined to travel';[4] and Ramón Menéndez Pidal likewise affirmed that 'the Spaniard is not interested in obtaining general cultural knowledge of foreign countries, hence he is not a lover of travel'.[5] Despite these opinions, travel – above all, involuntary travel – was in reality a permanent feature of Hispanic culture.

Long absence created a persistent yearning for the sounds, smells and tastes of home. All the expatriates were familiar with the problem. The Valladolid writer Cristóbal Suárez de Figueroa (d.1644), who spent half his life in Italy, recognized that 'even spirits that are most opposed in the *patria* become reconciled when they are outside it, and learn to appreciate each other'. He meant that the feeling of being part of the same nation created a strong mutual bond among exiles, and gave greater meaning to the homeland. Suárez expressed forcefully the yearning of those who had left Spain, and with it the 'skies, rivers, fields, friends, family and other pleasures that we look for in vain when we are away'.[6] Sooner or later emigrants would mention in their correspondence their heartache for the shape of the hills, the slope of the valleys and the curve of the sea that had formed a deeply ingrained part of their lives and left them deprived of a dimension of being.

Second only to the yearning for one's own language, touched on in the previous chapter, came the nostalgia for home cooking. Food in the host country never quite matched up to expectations, least of all in the New World where the basic essentials of an Hispanic diet – wheat, wine, oil, even salt – were for a long time unknown. Contact with something akin to those lost tastes and smells might stir up a deep longing for the past, as in the familiar case of the nineteenth-century French novelist Marcel Proust, for whose protagonist the flavour of a small madeleine cake in Paris evoked an immediate memory of his distant and forgotten childhood. This seems mere literary artifice when compared to the experiences of those whose entire expatriate lives were punctuated by remembered tastes, smells and sounds. A Spanish friar who was travelling in 1512 through Bethlehem came across some of the Jews who had presumably left Spain in the 1480s, and they confessed to him that they 'yearned for Seville and the meats and dishes they used to make there'.[7] Spaniards in the peninsula possessed one of the richest diets of Europe, a product of the culinary heritage of Muslims, Jews and Christians, drawing on the produce of the wheat fields of northern Spain, the fisheries of the Mediterranean and Atlantic, the olive groves of Andalusia, the vineyards of Castile and Catalonia, and the rice-fields and orange groves of Valencia. The Mediterranean food that they knew was the first thing they yearned after when far from their native land. Differences of diet were, and are, basic to defining identity. The Muslims of al-Andalus had a distinctive diet that drew on origins in Persia and the Maghreb but was solidly based in centuries of Andalusian life. It was one of the aspects they most missed when they left the peninsula. During his exile in the Maghreb Ibn al-Azraq of Málaga (1428–91) composed an *urjuza* or form of didactic poem in which he wrote about the favourite dishes of his former homeland and mentioned in comparison those of his new environment in North Africa.[8]

There are few more poignant examples of an exile deprived of his native food than Juan Luis Vives. His experience of England was the worst. He was very well treated there, he confessed, but 'this windy, heavy, damp climate ill suits me, together with the type of food, so different from what I am used to'.[9] In his dialogues a character who has been long absent from Valencia returns there and invites a friend: 'let us go for a walk, I have an irresistible desire to see my native city that I have not seen for so long'. The visitors comment on the beauty of the streets ('pebbled streets', Vives recalls), and the quality of the food in the market. 'What a big square! What order in the layout of vendors and goods! What a perfume of fruit!' 'The wine of Spain is firm, takes water and lasts long', and as for olives, 'their taste is more exquisite than those from Mallorca'.[10] It is doubtful if Vives, who left Valencia when he was aged sixteen, retained much memory of wine. But he was right about the mixing of wine and water. Around the same period the exile Servet remarked that in contrast to French wine, that produced by Spaniards had to be drunk with water: 'the French drink it neat, the Spaniards diluted with much water'. Until a generation ago, this was still the normal way of drinking wine among the people of Spain. The insistence of Vives on food can be paralleled by the attention given to the same subject in Laguna's *Journey to Turkey*, where the principal protagonist gives more importance to aspects of diet than to any other feature of European culture.

The contrast between England and Spain was also the background for the sufferings of the Spanish ambassador in London in 1672. English food so disgusted him that he never bothered to eat outside the embassy. 'There is no way he can accept the customs of that nation,' the Genoese ambassador reported of him. 'He stays indoors and refuses to speak to people.'[11] Generation after generation, thousands of Spaniards left their native shores and went into exile or to seek a better life, and in all cases their thoughts turned back to the food that was no longer accessible. Their case was never as extreme as that of Francisco Pizarro, who went everywhere in the expanses of Peru carrying with him a pocketful of wheat grain, in the hope of planting the seeds and at last achieving the bread of home. In the 1760s a Spanish noble was immensely pleased to be dining in Berlin on Spanish food and wine imported specially to the city by an English general who had lived for years in Spain and regularly got supplies of the food that he greatly missed.[12] 'I am fed up,' the artist Ramón Casas wrote from the luxury of the Waldorf Astoria in New York in April 1909, 'with steak,[13] I yearn for a plate of beans with ham. For nearly six months I have not tasted salad.'[14] A longing for the food of Valencia inspired the writer Azorín, in exile in Paris in 1937, to dedicate his pen to the theme, not however in the inaccessible press of his native province but in the far-distant newspaper *La Prensa* of Buenos Aires. Even so humble an item as a yearning for water could cause an exile in the United States in 1936, the poet Salinas, to complain that Americans did not drink water for pleasure, for theirs was not like 'the water of Spain, drunk sensually, Bacchus-like'.[15] Second only to the Castilian language, food defined the cultural identity of Spaniards in exile. 'In the migrant experience', a recent scholar has pointed out, 'food is not just a question of regular consumption for maintenance purposes. It plays a multiplicity of roles in the social, political, economic and cultural lives of new immigrants and those who become long-term settlers.'[16]

The main Spanish dish to impress foreigners in modern times is the rice stew of Valencian origin known as 'paella', which appears not to have been documented before the nineteenth century. Paella was, however, certainly eaten in London in the early decades of that century. During the years of their exile in England the Liberal politicians met at each other's houses to share meals. Among them were the brothers Jaime Villanueva (priest and author of the *Literary Journey*) and Joaquín Lorenzo, who would meet every Sunday at the house of a fellow Valencian exile, Vicente Salvá, and feast on a weekly paella. Another exile in London at the time was the brother of the general, Riego, who had brought about the *coup d'état* of 1820 in Spain and been brutally executed by the government three years later. He settled down permanently in London as a bookseller and, thanks to his contacts with the peninsula, on one occasion acquired for the delight of his friend Richard Ford, author of a well-known travel book on Spain, Spanish sausage ('real genuine Extremadura *chorizo* sausages') and chickpeas ('sweet and rich').[17]

Exiles, then and now, have always lamented the unavailability of their native food. Curiously, Hispanic cuisine has never been easy to export and has tended to remain confined to Hispanic communities. Western countries have accepted with alacrity all types of additions to their diet, but not Hispanic (the acceptance of Mexican food in the United States is a notable exception). Immigrants have normally had to take their food with them. The most striking example can be found in the Puerto Rican emigration to New York in the early twentieth century. By the late 1920s there were over 125 Puerto Rican-owned restaurants in the city, especially in the Upper West Side of Manhattan and in East Harlem, selling standard Puerto Rican food based on Caribbean produce such as rice, bananas and coconut. A journalist in 1950 noted open-air stands in Park Avenue (between 111th and 116th Streets) as a 'center for vegetables, minor fruits, textiles for retail . . . small carts selling tomatoes, potatoes, beans and avocado . . . carts with ripe bananas, toasted peanuts and sausages under the wide three-coloured umbrella'.[18]

The phenomenon of exile kept repeating itself generation after generation. But why did some citizens feel they had a right to eject others? It is a curious fact that, in the case both of the Jews and of the Moriscos, though the authorities regularly resorted to expulsion there were always grave doubts expressed by other Spaniards as to whether they had any right to do so. The reason usually given – whether 'religion', in the case of the Jews, or 'security', in the case of the Moriscos – was never the whole explanation. Far more significant was the social confrontation that had developed over the years. Was it no longer possible for different cultural groups to coexist? Very many people at the time thought that it was indeed possible. The government, however, declared that the relevant minority groups did not belong there. It was a claim that drew from the Morisco leader Aben Humeya the outraged retort in 1569: 'Do you not realize that we are in Spain, and that we have owned this land for nine hundred years?' The Muslims had been an integral part of al-Andalus long before the Christian incursion into their territory, and arguably had an even greater right than the Christians to claim it as their home. The fragile legal basis for expulsion explains why very many Spaniards, from the nobility and clergy down to the common people, continued to feel that it was unjustified. A lingering feeling of guilt persisted for generations among the Christian majority, and eventually found expression in the Romantic literature and art of the nineteenth century. The authorities claimed, however, that they were cleansing the land of ideas and beliefs that were alien to it and a threat to its integrity. From the expulsion of Jews and Muslims to the ejection of *rojos* ('Reds') by the Franco regime, an assertion of 'exclusiveness' – the Fascists referred to their opponents as 'anti-Spain' – became the normal justification for expelling fellow citizens.

Some commentators have felt that the continuous urge to perform a form of surgical purification on its own body is an innate characteristic of the Hispanic mind. The persistent and long-term resort to expulsion, it has been suggested, springs from some element hidden in the Spanish psyche. The idea appears inherently unlikely but has been taken up by some Castilian writers eager to grasp at a general explanation that avoids the need to look for specific and concrete reasons. Commentators of all persuasions have generally felt that this sinister element can be traced back to the first and most elemental of all crimes, as narrated in the Bible story of Cain, who killed his brother Abel out of envy after their parents, Adam and Eve, had been expelled from the Garden of Eden. The almost eternal crime of 'fratricide' became referred to in Castilian as '*cainismo*'. The idea appeared in Unamuno's 1895 essay *On Authenticity*, and was the central theme of his minor novel *Abel Sánchez* (1917). The novel, which Unamuno insisted was a parable of Spanish reality (and of Spain's 'national leprosy') rather than a fiction, describes the lifelong friendship between two friends, Abel and Joaquín, which turns to hatred and envy when the woman that Joaquín loves, Helena, marries Abel instead. Writing the preface to the second edition of the novel from his exile in Hendaye, France, Unamuno wrote:

In the nearly five years that I have had to live outside my Spain I have felt how the old traditional – and traditionalist – Spanish envy, its innate (*castiza*) envy, which embittered the efforts of Quevedo and Larra, has come to form a kind of political movement.

Since then the parable of Cain has flourished among all who wield a pen. In his writings, Américo Castro used the verb 'cainize' to refer to the periodic brutality throughout history of some Spaniards to others.[19] Other writers have suggested that *cainismo* is Spain's particular and original sin, and the word is used almost daily in the Spanish press as though it were a self-evident aspect of Hispanic political and literary life.

Fratricidal polarization tends to occur mostly in civil wars, but in Spain the polarization was of such long standing that Marañón did not hesitate to affirm that 'the history of Spain has been a continuous civil war, in which we can find the principal cause of our national misfortunes'.[20] In his own day Marañón was labelled by Fascists as 'anti-Spanish', a bizarre title for this most Spanish of middle-class intellectuals. He had no hesitation in retorting that 'the great glory of Spain is made up of the achievements of all the anti-Spanish!' Like other liberals, he felt that he was no party to the polarization and could survey it with some detachment. 'On one occasion,' he noted, 'Unamuno said to me: "If you want to be sure that a liberal person is really one and not merely on the surface, there is an infallible sign, if he has been labelled a traitor by both sides."'[21] The confrontation, however, was not necessarily between two sides only. The enemies were also on one's own side, as events revealed throughout Spain's history. From the 1480s, when Jews in some synagogues were urged to protect themselves by denouncing conversos to the Inquisition, to the 1930s, when in Barcelona George Orwell revealed for the first time the fraternal assassinations that occurred among supporters of the Republic, Spaniards fled from violence at the hands of their own kind. The image comes to mind of Goya's 'black painting' of two men locked in struggle with each other, the *Duel with Clubs* (*Duelo a garrotazos*). Exile was not simply the consequence of an impersonal *diktat* by an oppressive state, as happened to Jews and Moriscos, it was also a conflict of brothers. During the five centuries covered in this book, Spaniards were constantly threatened by the malice and treachery of neighbours, family and colleagues. Anti-Semitism fed on social resentment. Resentment between neighbours fed the social hatred in the early months of 1936. In that summer of 1936, the affable concierges of middle-class apartments in the smart quarters of Madrid were the most useful sources of information for the groups of Republican assassins who carried out their nightly *paseos* or raids. It was a long history of a coexistence that failed to function adequately, a sort of collective *cainismo*. From the fifteenth century onwards, Spaniards were driven into exile no less by the social violence of other Spaniards than by institutional decree.

In retrospect, however, it became uncomfortable to present Spaniards as a people who were always at loggerheads with one another. It consequently became more fashionable to present the conflicts and expulsions as minor blemishes on a society that was essentially one of understanding and tolerance. The key word was at one time '*convivencia*' ('coexistence'), a word that claimed to describe the way in which Christians, Jews and Muslims lived together and worked for a better future. The word continues to be used by political figures and tourist agencies who wish to present Spanish society as the ideal alternative to the conflicts prevailing everywhere else in the world. After the 1930s the key word became '*mestizaje*' ('mixing' or 'fusion'), which implied that despite unpleasant moments (genocides, obliteration of cultures) the peoples of the Hispanic world came together and shared a common set of values which in the long run was more lasting than the unpleasantness. This interpretation, fundamental to the thinking of the Mexican writer Vasconcelos and the Spanish writer Maeztu, has become rooted in the thinking of many university academics and sections of the Spanish press. One Spanish historian[22] feels that it is a question of the

common links, the varied histories of declines and shipwrecks, histories like rivers that flow down into the map of daily life, being rewritten and reborn in new fusions (*mestizajes*) of long and immense routes that join together in a heritage that is for most of the time despised and mistakenly thrown aside but despite everything continues to live.

With the phrases '*España mestiza*' (a motto employed by some ideological groups on the Right) and '*historia mestiza*' the course of Spanish history runs smooth again, after a few bumps along the way.

But there were naturally constant irregularities on the surface, and these were not simply a consequence of political or religious intolerance. Throughout these centuries, the basic anxiety of many creative artists in Spanish culture was the recognition that cultural achievement had to be something more than the simple rituals of traditional folklore. The massive, even stifling, weight of opinion from the fifteenth to the twentieth centuries affirmed that what was good in Spain came from within it, and that Spain did not need anything from outside. Well-known names, including (as we have seen) the most prominent figures of the 1890s, gave support to this attitude, which is still firmly rooted at many levels: in political life, in culture, in the universities, in public life. Part of the problem, as Larra indicated in the early nineteenth century, was that only a small minority was interested in learning from Europe. The vast majority was opposed to what came from outside, because they believed they already knew better and were superior. Many writers and thinkers consequently reacted against this attitude, and felt that it was essential for Spain to search outside itself in order to advance its culture by updating it from outside sources. Ironically, one had to become an exile in order to promote

Spain, a situation that happened over and over again. Perhaps the clearest comment on the situation was made by Albéniz in an interview he granted to a Madrid journalist in August 1894. The journalist asked the composer why he chose to live outside Spain instead of in it. Didn't that mean betraying Spain? Albéniz's answer (as summed up by the reporter) was as follows:

Albéniz is more Spanish than the most Spanish, but for Albéniz being Spanish does not consist in writing sheets of music at five cents a page, nor in resigning himself as a consequence to eating cold stew in a garret. Albéniz lives in Paris and in London, because in Paris and in London he can eat and sleep. He is not a bullfighter, so Spain is not a country where he can live well.[23]

It was a forthright way of commenting that Spain had no musical infrastructure or musical public to compare with England, France or Italy, and that an ambitious composer could find his way and make his living only through expatriation. The story was the same throughout Spain's history. Juan Luis Vives' biggest doubts about Spain were not over the Inquisition, which hurt his family but never threatened him directly. His fears were reserved for the lack of study resources, since there was no environment for research in Spain comparable to that in northern Europe or Italy. From his time onwards, scholars, artists, composers and writers preferred to live in exile because that was where they could tap the roots of international culture and creativity. Down to the time of Ochoa, who did his research in Germany and Oxford before going to the United States, Spanish scientists could advance science most profitably when they did not live in Spain. When the retired Américo Castro returned to Spain in the 1970s, what he most missed was the fund of scholarship available in American libraries. There was, and still is, nothing comparable anywhere in Spain to the university libraries of England and the United States.

A different tendency among some exiles, however, upheld the uniqueness of Spain. Its partisans continued to share the vision that they alone held the Golden Fleece, and refused to see the need for borrowing anything from non-Hispanic cultures. In practical terms, they either were protagonists of intense political beliefs (of both the Right and Left) or else were creative writers (mainly poets) who felt no affinity for such areas as scholarship and science. This division of opinion led to profound disagreements among the émigrés of the 1936–9 generation. Many felt that it was a betrayal of Hispanic values for intellectual exiles to live in the United States and accept employment there. For them, Spain was the sole and indispensable source of wisdom. Those who disagreed with them felt, however, that living outside the Hispanic ambit offered the opportunity of learning from other cultures. Américo Castro commented in a letter of 1957 that

The refugees cannot swallow me for living in the United States, for not being a fellow traveller, for not believing in the Two Spains, for not having fought in the trenches. Since I belong to no party, church or fraternity, I am turning into a sort of Blanco White of the twentieth century, driven into a corner with clergy and pastors.

The recipient of the letter, Menéndez Pidal, who was politically more conservative than Castro but shared his non-partisan outlook, came to the defence of the idea of 'Two Spains', a concept he had done most to popularize. There was no way, he pointed out to Castro, to escape from the constant tendency of Spaniards to split into two bands. 'Unfortunately they are two, and there are always two on all sides. Here [in Spain] we have half of the half fighting against each other, just as with the exiles.'[24]

The theory of the 'Two Spains' became another way of referring to *cainismo*, though constant use of the phrase in the daily press eventually reduced its meaning to the level of banality. As outlined by Menéndez Pidal, the theory served to explain some of the context that provoked the constant stream of exiles in Spain's history. Born in La Coruña in Galicia, Pidal (1869–1968) came from a prominent Asturian family. His parents moved in 1884 to Madrid, where he eventually gained a doctorate on medieval ballads and in 1899 secured the chair of philology at the university. When he married, in 1900, he took his bride on a honeymoon trip that covered the sites associated with the medieval military hero, the Cid. His career thereafter was that of a wholly dedicated academic. In 1909 he gave lectures at Johns Hopkins and Columbia, and the following year was instrumental in founding in Madrid the Centre of Historical Studies. His lasting claim to fame came from encouraging the history of language in Spain as a scientific subject. He published a historical grammar of Spanish in 1904 and in 1914 established the *Revista de Filología Española*. In 1925 he was elected director of the Royal Academy of Language, and within a few months published *Origins of Spanish*, his first serious contribution to what he hoped would be a lengthy work on the formation of the Castilian tongue. In 1929 he brought out the book for which he became best known, *The Spain of the Cid* (which came out in English in 1934).

A quiet, slim, bespectacled figure with an unmistakable two-pointed beard, Pidal was a firmly conservative figure who had, however, no interest in politics and no sympathy for either of the factions in the Civil War. Like other prominent personalities, he was at risk from the Republican murder squads in Popular Front Madrid. In March 1936 he commented to Marañón that in a city of 'murders every night', 'the only hope must be survival'.[25] When the city turned ugly at the end of July, just after the military uprising, he took refuge first in the Residencia de Estudiantes, where he was horrified to hear the maids calmly discussing '*paseos*' that had happened during the night, and then in the Mexican embassy. He accompanied Marañón into exile in 1936. Projects that he had been directing, such as one on constructing a linguistic atlas of the peninsula, also disappeared into exile when the researchers went abroad carrying their valuable papers with them.[26]

Menéndez Pidal wrote in 1947 an essay in which he developed and made explicit an old theme, about the constant divisions among Spaniards. The text, which formed the introduction to the multi-volume *History of Spain* that he directed from the 1930s, was translated by Walter Starkie and published in English in 1950 as a small book with the title *The Spaniards in Their History*, which came out in a Spanish edition nine years later. Where Unamuno had chosen to refer to the fratricidal strife between Cain and Abel, Pidal referred to a struggle between 'Two Spains'. The phrase could be found in many writers, from Larra down to Maeztu, Ortega y Gasset and Machado. Ortega wrote in 1914 that 'two Spains are locked in an unending struggle'. Machado penned an often-repeated verse:

Little Spaniard, born
Into the world, God bless you,
One of the two Spains
Will freeze your heart.[27]

Pidal presented the idea of 'Two Spains' as a way of looking at the various ideological attitudes in Spain's history. 'In Spain, difference of opinion degenerates into a contest of irreconcilable animosity.' The contradictions within Spain which had apparently been reconciled by the imposition of religious uniformity broke out time and again until the period of the Civil War. It was a struggle – often mute, never suppressed – between Two Spains.[28] The interplay between African and European Spain, isolationist and international Spain, liberal and conservative Spain, caused the tensions that explained the strife in Spanish history. The Two Spains followed 'the fated destiny of the two sons of Oedipus, who would not consent to reign together and mortally wounded each other'. Menéndez Pidal looked forward to an age when reconciliation would eventually occur, and reintegration would lead to unity of purpose in a tolerant society.

Did exile have a negative effect on the homeland? One of the inevitable claims of exiles was that their opponents were to blame for everything that had gone wrong in the country. The classic enemy they picked on was the Spanish Inquisition, recipient of the greatest volume of obloquy ever heaped on a single institution in the whole of European history. It was reviled by the Jews and conversos, loathed by the Moriscos, damned by the Protestant refugees, denounced by the Enlightenment and, finally, censured for all time by the Liberals as the primary cause of their nation's backwardness. In his *Critical History*, Llorente held that it had ruined the country, 'arresting the progress of arts, sciences, industry, and commerce, compelling multitudes of families to abandon the kingdom; and instigating the expulsion of the Jews and the Moors'. In his lecture at University College, London, in 1828, Alcalá Galiano picked on it as the *fons et origo* of all his country's ills. Though subsequent Liberals did not cease the attack, Juan Valera in 1878 made a valiant attempt to place the issue in its proper perspective. The Inquisition, he said, had not been uniquely bad, nor was it the direct cause of

Spain's cultural decadence. Spain's backwardness was the fault of Spaniards themselves, who felt they were 'the new chosen people of God', an attitude that provoked 'our separation and isolation from the rest of Europe'.[29]

However, it continued to be much easier to clear Spain's elite of all responsibility and lay the blame squarely on the tribunal. Without attempting to offer evidence for their argument, writers continued to affirm that Spain's backwardness relative to Europe was caused by the Inquisition. Unamuno pontificated (in *On Authenticity*) that 'the mental poverty of Spain began with the isolation into which we were put by the protection of the Inquisition'. Ortega y Gasset, using more poetic licence than historical accuracy, claimed that the Holy Office had 'Tibetized' Spain, meaning that it had been an 'instrument of isolation' that had theocratized the country, depriving it of its rightful place at the forefront of civilized nations. Américo Castro concluded that 'Spaniards had already felt very little inclination to cultivate science, but terror of the Holy Office dissuaded them even more'.[30] 'Inquisition' has, after five centuries of vilification, continued to be a useful expletive in the political vocabulary. Much more to the point is the fact that through their new historiography, which drew heavily on that of the French, the Belgians and above all Juan Antonio Llorente, the Liberals managed to create an interpretation of their nation's past that influenced all other historians. In a scenario of Two Spains, the Inquisition quite clearly belonged to the 'other' Spain, the one that was firmly ensconced in the country and directly responsible for the sufferings of its exiles, whether Jews, Muslims or enlightened Christians.

But the exiles themselves became the focus of an even more pronounced tendency, to claim that Spain's backwardness was a consequence of their absence. Had there been no emigration, the argument ran, Spain would today be the most advanced society in Europe. If the country lacked merits, it was because the people of most merit had been expelled. It became a standard dogma that the expulsion of the Jews robbed Spain of its capitalist and economic potential. According to a recent English scholar, 'it weakened the economic foundations of the monarchy'.[31] The next stage was to blame the backwardness of Spain's agriculture on the absence of the Moriscos, who by 'common agreement' (the words of a leading

American scholar) 'were the most industrious, intelligent, persevering and thrifty inhabitants of Spain, and almost the only subjects who did not disdain manual labour'.[32] These views, based on no historical evidence whatsoever, were shared by all progressive writers, both Spaniards and foreigners. In the nineteenth century the liberal American historian John Motley concluded in his *Rise of the Dutch Republic* (1855):

The highest industrial and scientific civilization that had been exhibited upon Spanish territory was that of Moors and Jews. When in the course of time those races had been subjugated, massacred, or driven into exile, not only was Spain deprived of its highest intellectual culture and its most productive labour, but intelligence, science, and industry were accounted degrading, because the mark of inferior and detested peoples.

Writers who explained Spain's problems with the thesis that evil forces were continually at work exiling its best citizens and denying the country access to enlightenment had little difficulty applying their ideas to subsequent epochs, and above all to the early twentieth century. The elite emigration of the late 1930s gave rise to a claim that the Civil War destroyed all the burgeoning scientific and cultural potential of the nation. A typical recent view is that

the Civil War cut short the beginnings of a scientific system in Spain. The ideological and cultural bases of the dictatorship of General Franco represented an enormous step backwards for the weak and fragile scientific structure in Spain. It was a genuine blood-letting from which Spanish science did not recover, and whose consequences lasted throughout the entire second half of the twentieth century.[33]

The vision of a developing scientific community in Spain that was destroyed through the expulsion of its best members was comforting as a belief in Spain's capacities, but is certainly baseless. A number of personnel with technical and medical qualifications – a high proportion of them state employees whose jobs had been taken away by the new regime – certainly left Spain as a result of the Civil War,[34] but there was no significant emigration of 'scientists', nor any identifiable impact for good or ill on Spanish science, least of all a 'blood-letting'.

The Franco dictatorship has in the same way been blamed for inadequacies in the Spanish system of education,[35] in the cinema industry, and even in historical writing.[36] It has been claimed that Spain's curious achievement in not producing a single school of philosophy to make an impact on Europe, and the complete absence of Spanish names from any roll-call of the leading thinkers of post-medieval western history,[37] are due to the intellectual impact of exile and, in particular, the Franco repression. A commentator blames the phenomenon on 'the continuous persistence into our most recent history of repeated waves of exiles, that mark our intellectual evolution', a claim that, as we have seen, is the exact reverse of what happened, since in reality exile helped to stimulate innovation and it was contact with the outside world that brought new ideas into Spain. The same writer suggests that 'in the three years of war (from 1936 to 39) there occurred an immense blood-letting of emigration, which affected the discipline of philosophy in a fundamental way, so much so that it left a complete desert in the field'.[38] One may suspend belief for a moment and imagine that Spain was a paradise of philosophical creativity in 1936, but the crude reality is that few if any significant philosophers can be identified among the refugees of those years.

The great convenience of attempts to pin the guilt exclusively on the undeniable fact of repression is that they serve a dual purpose: to condemn an obvious wrong, and at the same time to give an irrefutable reason for Spain's inability, after four centuries of empire, to produce philosophers, scientists and historians on a par with those of other European countries. From the political writers of the seventeenth century (known in the literature as *arbitristas*) to Ganivet and Ortega y Gasset in the nineteenth, and publicists and historians in the twentieth, the standard argument was that factors beyond its control robbed Spain of success and condemned it to 'decline'. The apparent solidness of the reasoning made it unnecessary to enquire any further, because the facts were (it seemed) plain enough. Time and again Spain had persistently destroyed its richest part, devouring its own children in the manner of Goya's terrifying 'black' painting of Saturn, thereby condemning itself to a back seat in the concourse of nations when its innate values should have placed it at the very forefront, the true if not the only leader of world civilization.

The problem of science was one of the key issues. Throughout its imperial history Spain had drawn on the technology of its allies without making any decisive contribution of its own. There were many relevant achievements in navigation and medicine, especially during the age of discovery and exploration, but Spaniards themselves, according to the leading authority, had an 'explicit awareness of scientific backwardness in Spain'.[39] The fact was glaring enough for Ganivet to suggest that by their nature Spaniards were not meant to be scientists ('there is no way of making the sciences take root in Spain', and 'until recently we did not know how to construct warships, and until very recently our engineers were foreigners').[40] Unamuno went to the extreme of declaring that other nations were welcome to their science, for Spain did not need it and had something better, its own philosophy. Azorín had the same idea: 'it is absurd to blame Spain for its lack of creativity in science, that was not its path'.[41] Unamuno expressed his outright opposition to the promotion of the works of Darwin and Spencer, whose writings first appeared in Spanish in 1878. Ortega summarized the matter succinctly in 1908: 'There is no science in Spain, but there are a good number of fervent young men who are ready to dedicate their lives to scientific endeavour.'[42] Américo Castro seemed also to be convinced that Spaniards were not cut out to be adepts of science: 'Spain has always maintained her right,' he commented, 'to live on the margin of scientific and industrialized Europe'.[43]

As many diligent scholars have shown, it was not quite true that Spain during its years of international power lacked persons of scientific merit.[44] However, the leading biologist Faustino Cordón (d.1999) followed his colleagues in affirming a few years ago that 'science has had a very slow growth in Spain. Not a single scientific discipline began in Spain.' A recent study by a scientist concludes, 'the fundamental fact is that scientific discoveries were produced in other countries and not in Spain'.[45] Not only (the same scholar concludes) did Spain fail to make a single significant contribution to theoretical and applied sciences, in chemistry, physics, medicine or technology, but every pioneering Spanish researcher (down to today) has had to rely on foreign laboratories. She comments on the Spain of the 1960s that 'the dependence of the Spanish scientific community and the politicians responsible for it, on the more developed countries, has been twofold: technological and scientific. The technical instruments were neither designed nor constructed in Spain, nor were the knowledge and areas of research evolved in the Spanish scientific community.' Progress in science came from what could be brought in from outside, often by Spaniards who had lived outside in virtual exile. In that sense, the Franco regime's political colour may not have been responsible for backwardness, but its state of isolation from the western world had an inevitable impact on scientific culture.

Laments over exile were often artificial, especially when uttered by mediocre writers. It is difficult, for example, to take seriously the following lines of bad verse by the twenty-year-old Espronceda in London, when we know that his social life in that city, alternating between social receptions and young women, was far from being a vale of tears:

> Exiled, dear God, from our homes,
> The pain makes us weep,
> Spain! Who will soothe our grief for you?
> Who will wipe our tears?[46]

However, for many others the return home could be, as it was for José Zorrilla when he came back from Mexico in 1866, a final satisfaction:

> Spain! I see you again!
> God took me so far from you
> That I feared I would never return.
> If my happiness today does not kill me
> I shall never die.
>
> Spain of my soul!
> Not a single day has passed
> That I did not pray to God for you.
> Who knows if you still
> Remember me?[47]

Zorrilla's unequivocal sense of relief, however, was far from being a common experience of upper-class exiles, many of whom reconciled themselves to their situation. There was nothing inherently bad about the permanence of absence. New realities, such as a recent marriage, a family, a job, a profession, or simply old age and ill health, turned exile into a permanent and not unwelcome alternative. Falla kept repeating his desire to return. 'My only wish is to return to Spain,' he claimed, 'when the war ends, when the means of travel are faster and safer, to live the last days of my life quietly in some Spanish village.'[48] But he made no move to do so. He had never liked cities, and in 1942 moved 800 kilometres away from Buenos Aires to a restored chalet in Alta Gracia, in the province of Córdoba, in order to enjoy the clean air and the mountains. Persistent bad health, among other problems, made it difficult to move again. Return was out of the question.

An exile that began in deprivation and suffering could therefore become, in almost every sense, an enriching experience that opened new horizons.[49] Exile was not entirely a loss. After his return in the 1830s (admittedly, to a privileged life that few others enjoyed) Alcalá Galiano mused: 'in days of tranquillity I have often looked back in my mind to those times of exile and poverty, and have considered them almost a lost happiness'.[50] In theory the sole horizon of an exile was return. In the seventeenth century, Cervantes in *The Jealous Old Man from Extremadura* spoke of the 'natural desire that all have to return to their homeland'. Return was the great aspiration throughout all the years of suffering, poverty and alienation. Return dictated ideas, activity, writing and creativity; it inspired music and poetry. After we accept the overwhelming priority of return, it comes as a surprise to find that for possibly the majority of exiles, and above all the cultural exiles, it not only ceased to be a priority but became an option that few desired.

The most notable example was that of the Jews. A century after the 1492 expulsions, several tried going back to Spain, above all to promote the business interests that many maintained there through family links with Portuguese financiers, highly favoured at the court of Madrid.[51] In the seventeenth century Jewish financiers and writers, as well as ordinary citizens (mainly from Portugal), came back to rediscover their roots. This was part of the normal reaction of exiles, many of whom felt that beyond their religious ties there were also ineradicable social urges (the call of their Spanish language, for example) that drew them back.[52] The passing of Gibraltar to British hands in 1713 allowed hundreds of Spanish Jews from North Africa to reinstall themselves on their native soil. A census of 1826 in the Rock showed that it had a population of 15,500 persons, of whom 1,660 were Jews from Morocco. From the mid-nineteenth century, however, even though there were no longer cultural or religious barriers, very few came back to Spain. Prominent exceptions were the Sephardi Jews based in Tangiers. When Morocco became independent of Spanish control in the 1950s, several thousand Jews from Tangiers and Tetuán moved to Spain. Among them were the Toledano family, who became commercially successful and established a leading position in the Sephardi community.[53] Though Jews preserved a distant respect for their Sephardic origins, centuries had passed and they were too integrated into their existing (and usually more flourishing) societies to wish to return to a land of romantic memory with which they had little in common. Today, in 2006, there are fewer than 20,000 Jews resident in Spain, not all of Sephardic origin, and the few non-Hispanic Jews who have applied for Spanish nationality in recent years tend to come from the Balkans or North Africa. By way of comparison, Israel has 4.7 million Jews, the United States 5.6 million and France 600,000. Evidently, historic Sepharad has long since lost its appeal for Jews, attracted rather by the ideological inspiration of Israel or the material promise of the United States.

From a strictly religious point of view, in any case, absence was a normal condition of Jewish existence. Poised between two deprivations – the destruction of the Temple on the one hand and the unrealized hope of the Messiah on the other – Jews conducted their faith and their material existence in a virtual no-man's-land that was also acceptable as home. It was 'simultaneously possible to be ideologically in exile and existentially at home'.[54] It therefore turned out that, though Jews continued to be shuttled from one place to another throughout their history, they never made return to their origins a priority. They made formal laments about the expulsion from Sepharad, but when given the chance to go back found that they were equally at home in the countries of adoption. In a very profound sense, Jews in 1492 did not go into exile, for exile was their permanent condition, and they took it with them from one place to another.

In the twentieth century the American sociologist Thorstein Veblen categorized Jews as 'aliens of the uneasy feet', who, because they are perpetually 'wanderers in no-man's-land, seeking another place to rest, farther along the road, somewhere over the horizon', enjoy a greater capacity than others to reinvigorate themselves. The idea of returning was not therefore a primary goal. How could it be when the ultimate goal was Jerusalem, from which the Jews of Sepharad had always been exiled?

For Hispanic Muslims the story was somewhat different. The tide of Muslims who wish to immigrate (the word 'return' has no historic meaning here) to al-Andalus has risen by leaps and bounds. Until the end of the 1990s there was virtually no Muslim immigration. In 2006, by contrast, the total of legal and illegal Muslim residents in Spain was around one million. The myth of return has been actively fostered by most of the leaders of the Spanish Muslims, who have attempted to assert a historic right to settle once again in a province that has regained, in their writings, the name al-Andalus. Washington Irving was well aware of the sentiment. He quoted a ruler of Tetuán of the nineteenth century who believed that 'a time would come when the Moors would reconquer their rightful domain, when worship would again be offered up in the mosque of Córdoba'." One may ask, of course, whether there was any 'rightful domain' for a people that had its feet firmly planted on both sides of the Mediterranean.

The refusal of exiles to return raises an important issue that is at the heart of the present book. The Hispanic diaspora changed Hispanic culture, but it also changed the nature of those who left their country. Many of those who left entered voluntarily into another scheme of things. When expelled Spaniards could also feel themselves at home in another culture, they immediately overcame the problems of so-called exile, and by their capacity to adapt proved that they were citizens of a broader world than the one they had come from. The exiles of the sixteenth century, from Vives and Servet to Loyola, Borja and Casiodoro de Reina, were European figures who made an imperishable impact on the culture of their time. Without necessarily losing sight of their origins, they ceased to be Spaniards and became Europeans. It makes no sense to consider them as extensions of Spain, for their ideas and writings drew primarily on what they encountered outside Spain. They had, like very many others, from Blanco White to Picasso, left Spain behind them and become part of a universal civilization.

The capacity to integrate into the broader world, however, was a characteristic only of those whose cultural horizons were flexible, for Spain also possessed a far stronger tradition of exiles whose horizons seldom extended beyond its borders. This was the case above all of poets and novelists, whose work was inevitably rooted in the world they knew and whose creative inspiration suddenly made little sense when uprooted. The Liberals of the early 1800s, too, were politicians who waited patiently in exile for the summons home, but their cultural work in exile was exclusively orientated towards Spain. The poems, plays and essays of the Romantic movement may sometimes have used foreign models, but their themes were exclusively Hispanic and contained little to interest a reader from outside the peninsula. As a result, great swathes of Hispanic cultural activity made little or no mark on the outside world. Some of the literary exiles of the 1930s present the clearest cases. Obsessed by their private circumstances, which they arbitrarily identified with those of their country, they formed little groups in Paris, Mexico and Buenos Aires, published ephemeral journals, spoke only in their own language, and gradually discovered, as Francisco Ayala and Bergamín did, that they had ceased to have a public in Latin America and in Europe. Their written work, like that of Sender and Aub, centred exclusively on what they had experienced in the Spanish war, and on little else. In consequence, with their gaze focused only on their immediate tragedy, they never managed to connect their creativity to that of western civilization. Fascinating memoir/novels, like Arturo Barea's *The Forging of a Rebel*, remain almost unknown today both in the country they describe and the one in which they were written. Yet even those who were obsessed with their experience of Spain might be unsure of their final destination. Though Ramón J. Sender seems to have prepared the way for a possible return home, when his time arrived he instructed his former wife to make sure that his ashes were scattered over the Pacific at San Diego.

The Jesuits expelled in 1767 were an extraordinary example of how it became possible to accept exile and turn it into victory. A great and good scholar has described how the beleaguered priests in Corsica took with them a level of learning that was severely lacking in the land they had left. 'We can see how universal and modern was the intellectual fibre of those exiles even before they made contact with Italy, more open than Spain to the literary, critical and scientific currents of eighteenth-century Europe.' In the textbooks they recommended in their classes in Corsica, 'nothing was missing of the best and most choice of what was to be found in France, Italy, Germany, England and Holland'.[56] They went on to accept with resignation the abolition of their order by a politically pressured pope, and immersed themselves in the Italian society that became their new home, contributing magnificently to its intellectual life. When the new king of Spain, Charles IV, decided in 1798 to allow the expelled clergy back, a difficult decision faced those who no longer felt that they belonged to Spain. An aged priest, the abbé Pavesio, wrote from Milan:

I grieve at the pain of leaving Italy, where I have received so much kindness and where I have spent the best years of my life, more than thirty years of absence. I fear that in the end I shall give in out of respect and shall have to return to my fatherland, which for me has become a foreign country. Wherever I end up, I shall carry in my heart the memory, love and gratitude of those illustrious Piedmontese, who are bound to me by so many debts and so much veneration.[57]

In reality, absence presupposed for very many the need to re-create their culture in another land. It was the classic fate of exiles, and those from Spain were in principle committed to following the same path. Hispanic culture could plant its flag on foreign soil, though in practice the exiles were always too few, their material resources too meagre, and their willingness to integrate rather too hesitant for any significant progress to be made. The educated middle-class professionals who left Spain in 1939 were adamant that their purpose was to 'save Spanish culture', but they achieved little more than the publication (in Paris and in Mexico) of short-lived journals that had a minute circulation. Publication with the specific purpose of political propaganda, usually with the help of the Communist Party, had a more hopeful future. The outstanding example was the success of the firm of Éditions Ruedo Iberico, which published authors in Paris with the intention of sending their works into the peninsula.

In practical terms, the survival of culture outside Spain came to depend entirely on the issue of language. The Catalan writer Rovira i Virgili stated in 1946 in Montpellier that 'far from the material fatherland of the country, we live in the spiritual fatherland of our language',[58] and it proved no problem to cultivate the language in question, particularly since the south of France was amenable to the reception of Catalan culture. But it was another matter to maintain and develop language in exile. Expatriates in Mexico soon discovered that though they had imagined their language to be the same as that of their new home, the reality was somewhat different. Integration into a host community would always result in the downgrading of one's own tongue. Although the example is not typical, since he was educated within the host culture, Jorge Semprun's contribution was significant. With one exception, every novel he wrote was in French. His explanation was unhesitating: 'For my part I chose French, the language of exile. I chose new roots. I made exile into a homeland.'[59] At the same time, Semprun was not betraying his own language. 'Despite everything, the Spanish language did not stop being mine, it belonged to me. Consequently I did not cease to belong to it. I would continue at times to express my most intimate self with its words, its sounds, its flamboyance. In short, in terms of language I did not become French but bilingual.'[60]

For creative artists, and especially writers, return home had a driving purpose: to reclaim the public that did not exist in exile. Writers at other times and in other cultures, like the Russian poet Marina Tsvetaeva, isolated in 1938 in a Paris that did not read or understand her, have felt the need to go back. Tsvetaeva's own words were: 'The poet cannot survive in emigration.'[61] When the Jewish writer Antonio Enríquez Gómez (see Chapter 1) went back to Seville in 1650, he was driven by the need to find once again the public that was not available to him in the France where he lived. Return in such cases had little to do with political regimes or yearning for the homeland. It was fundamentally the recovery of one's voice, the contact with a lost audience, the ability to move within the environment marked out by one's habitual language. Max Aub, resident in Mexico but tied to Europe by his culture, complained in his diaries: 'As never before, the lack of a public gnaws at me. In short, my failure.'[62] The failure was particularly poignant for those exiles who felt that by staying in Latin America they had a ready-made public. In reality they found that the language was dissimilar, the themes different, and the impact disastrous. In *The Outcome* (*El Remate*), which like everything he wrote was acutely subjective, Aub puts into the mouth of his protagonist the following observation: 'The Republican exile, above all if he is a writer, lives and works in a void, silenced in his country of origin and only half integrated in his country of adoption. We rot, we disappear. Because, as is natural, even in Mexico we are nothing.'[63] Writing in Spanish in England or in the United States was already a lost battle, since at the time there was almost no reading public for the language or the strongly Spain-orientated themes. But the situation was not much better in Spanish America, where novels and poems by the exiles ended up virtually as soliloquies.[64]

Poets, acquainted with the peculiar nature of poetry as soliloquy, were – despite Tsvetaeva's opinion – perhaps best able to cope with exile and find their home within it. A case in question was Luis Cernuda, who did not see a physical return as the most suitable answer:

> Return? Let him go back who
> After long years, after a long journey,
> Is weary of the road and yearns for
> His land, his house, his friends,
> The love that awaits his faithful return.
>
> But you? Return? You do not think of returning
> But of going on freely,
> Always forthcoming, whether young or old,
> With no son to seek you, as Ulysses was sought,
> No Ithaca awaiting you, no Penelope.[65]

In another of his poems he was even more specific:

I prefer

Not to return to a land whose faith, if it has one, is no longer mine,

Whose ways were seldom my own,

Whose hostile memory comes back to mind,

And from which both absence and time have separated me.[66]

When the Franco regime began to be accepted back into the community of nations, particularly after the United States began cultivating links with it in the 1950s as a useful ally in the Cold War against the Soviet Union, some exiles began drifting back. Their motives were inevitably wide-ranging. There had been too much suffering and antagonism in the Civil War for return to be an easy option, and the regime in any case refused to accept back active enemies of that period. Anyone associated with the Communist Party was permanently barred. One of them, an exile as a child but now an adult agent of the Communist Party in exile, was Semprun. He slipped back into Spain and headed for the residence he remembered at Alfonso XI street in Madrid.

In 1953, when I returned to Madrid for the first time to work there in the underground Communist organization, I ran all the way to Alfonso XI. The city of my childhood had not yet become the sprawling industrial metropolis, so savagely magnificent and dilapidated, that it is today. There one still breathed the dry, pure air of the neighbouring hills, the sky was still a deep blue, the water was still deliciously cool and clear. But above all, the neighbourhood around El Retiro, remembered from my childhood, had not changed at all.

Never, during those years lived abroad, had I ever experienced such a poignant feeling of exile, of strangeness, as in the privileged moment of my return to my native land.[67]

Cultural figures with some standing in the outside world might have been welcomed back because it was thought that their presence would help to soften the country's unfavourable image. The problem for the émigré 'intellectuals' was that, with very few exceptions, they were completely unknown outside Spain and therefore had little to offer the regime. The prominent exception was Ortega y Gasset, who had been living in straitened economic circumstances in Paris, Argentina and Portugal.

He was a classic example of the fall of the mythical figure of the 'intellectual', worshipped by Spaniards since the turn of the century. In 1944 he observed: 'Intellectuals have passed from being everything to being nothing, from being the glories and eminences of nations to being wiped off the social landscape.'[68] Something of the old myth remained, however, for the regime was interested in bringing him back. From 1941 he began to receive his stipend as a university professor (the moribund Republic had deprived all who left in 1936 of their posts and wages). When the time was ripe, he was permitted to enter Spain from Portugal. Driven across the frontier in August 1945, on the same day that news broke of the dropping of the atomic bomb on Hiroshima, his arrival was greeted with fulsome praise in the press. He desisted from any open identification with the regime, asking only for help to resurrect his review, the *Revista de Occidente*. He never regained the status he had enjoyed in the 1930s. The writers still in exile spurned him for having returned to Franco's Spain, where in fact he had a minor role, became increasingly depressed and irritated,[69] and ventured abroad only to congresses (in 1949 to the United States, his first and only visit there) on the theme of Germanic culture.

Among the first figures to come back was Menéndez Pidal. As we have seen, he left Spain when Marañón did. After stopping a while in Bordeaux he went to Cuba, where he stayed six months and gave lectures. He then spent a year at a university in the United States, and moved to Paris in the summer of 1938. All the time, his overriding obsession was with his books and papers, which had remained in their totality in Madrid. 'What is most at risk is my beautiful library', he bewailed to Marañón. 'Without it what will my old age be like?' Cut off from it, he appears, unlike other émigrés, to have done little creative work during the years he was absent from Spain. He was now seventy years old. When he returned to Madrid, in July 1939, the first place to which he headed was his library. He continued to have problems with the functionaries of the new regime, but clung stubbornly to his independence,[70] which he maintained against factions of both the Right and Left. His response to continuous sniping from other exiles, who felt he should not have returned to Franco's Spain, was expressed brilliantly in 1952:

If every time that Spain had a government I disliked I were to exile myself, I would have lived virtually forever in exile. My *patria* belongs more to me than to the various governments that manage it.[71]

Precisely because he was a conservative, however, the sniping continued. Pidal had two great passions, for the Castilian language and for the unity of Spain. His views on both tended to coincide with those of the dictatorship, a fact that anti-Francoists emphasized. The most disagreeable pill for him was the use made of his study on the Cid. The *Song of the Cid* (*Cantar del mío Cid*) is a poem written in the mid-twelfth century about the Castilian hero Rodrigo Díaz de Bivar, relating events of his exile from Castile in 1081 until shortly before his death in 1099. The Cid achieved the remarkable feat of becoming ruler of the Muslim kingdom of Valencia, and was the first of the Christian leaders to defeat the new Muslim invaders of the peninsula, the Almoravides. Menéndez Pidal produced an edition of the *Cantar* in 1908, and then a political study, *The Spain of the Cid* (1929, in English 1934), that gave historical substance to a figure who until then had been merely a literary legend. Spaniards had never shown much interest in the subject. It was left to the Italians and French to write operas on him (Antonio Sacchini in 1773, and Jules Massenet in 1885, based on Corneille's seventeenth-century play), and to the Americans to make the first film (1961). Pidal's study excited the interest of the Franco regime, which adopted the figure of the medieval hero as an emblem of Spain's religious and military glory.

Some exiles from the Civil War period came back in order to spend their last days on their native soil. That, at least, was how many in Spain imagined it to be. What could be a greater gesture of support for the nation and its cause than the return of the absent son? Yet the real motives of those who came back seem to have had little in common with such noble considerations. They returned simply because home was where they belonged, regardless of the regime. Azorín, d'Ors and Menéndez Pidal returned immediately after the conflict. Pio Baroja came back in 1940, Marañón in 1942, Pérez de Ayala only in 1954. Because of his speedy return, in August 1939, Azorín was stigmatized as a Fascist, but it is clear that he had long since divorced himself from the tempo of active politics. His articles indicate an intense sense of relief at coming home, at the sensual and aesthetic satisfaction of contact with things once known. He was sixty-six years old. 'The first and capital impression of Spain: all the food has a more intense flavour. There is a firmer, tastier feel to the meat, the vegetables, the fruit, the bread. Brown bread, wholemeal bread, that I am eating, really delicious.' Even the half-ruined capital could be seen as it once had been. 'In Madrid everything is the same. Spain is as it always was. Under the high and bright blue sky, the paper sellers cry out raucously.'[72] He knew of course that Spain was not the same, for his essays scrupulously avoided any reference to the political situation. Marginalized for a time by the regime's hardliners, he became even more of a recluse than before, and took refuge in writing. Gradually he was accepted back into the fold and began to receive official recognition. In 1952 he announced, in a newspaper interview, that he was retiring from the literary world. He died at a ripe old age, in 1967, but the subsequent generation tended (with typical partiality) to spurn his work for political reasons.

Azorín was no threat to the regime, or indeed to any regime, and was received back tranquilly. In the same way, several other apolitical exiles were able to return without problems. One such was the musician Joaquín Rodrigo (1902–99). Rodrigo was born in Sagunto (Valencia), youngest of the ten children of a landowner. In 1905 an epidemic of diphtheria in the region made him virtually blind, and helped turn his education towards aural culture. In Valencia city he attended music classes, and his family employed a reader to help him with reading and writing. He began to compose music in the 1920s, and wrote orchestral pieces. In 1927 he moved to Paris, the Mecca of Spanish musicians, and studied under Paul Dukas at the École Normale de Musique. Among the contacts he made in Paris was Manuel de Falla, who helped to make the young Rodrigo's work known to his colleagues. He also met his future wife, the Turkish pianist Victoria Kamhi, whom he brought to Spain and married in 1933. Her international culture, knowledge of languages and, of course, her sight stood him in good stead during his career. By 1934 the couple were back in Paris, where Rodrigo resumed music composition. They were in Germany in the summer of 1936 when the Civil

War broke out, and found themselves deprived of all income when the Academy of San Fernando, which had given Rodrigo a scholarship, informed him that because of the war it was no longer possible to send funds.

Instead of returning to Spain, as others did, they decided to earn a living for themselves by giving Spanish and music lessons at the institute for the blind in Freiburg, in the Black Forest, where they had the status of 'Spanish refugees'. 'One came into contact,' his wife recalls, 'with some generous people who knew how to find ways of helping without wounding our pride.'[73] Apart from a brief visit back to northern Spain early in 1938, Rodrigo remained abroad, in Paris. It was there that some Spanish friends suggested he should write a concerto for guitar. The result was the *Aranjuez Concerto*, which he completed in Paris (he named it as a homage to 'the happy days of our honeymoon, when we walked in the park of Aranjuez').[74] He took the manuscript with him when the impending outbreak of war with Germany made them decide to return finally to Spain in September 1939, eight months after the end of the Civil War. 'World War Two broke out two days after we crossed the Spanish border.'[75] The concerto premiered in Barcelona in 1940, and was an immediate success. Rodrigo accepted a post in Madrid that would allow him to compose. After working for some time in a college for the blind, and in national radio, from 1947 he was Professor of Music at the University of Madrid. The concerto became one of the most widely performed concert pieces of the century, though usually not with a guitar as its main instrument. It took the form of three movements, with a key central adagio that offered a lush romantic sweep combining folkloric intensity and soulfulness. For both foreign and Spanish audiences it seemed to incarnate Spain, and brought the composer world popularity. Thanks to it, he was showered with honours both inside and outside Spain, though his later music did not develop beyond the unsophisticated style of the concerto.

Logically, the returnees had no wish to explain why they were back. Marañón made a brief return in December 1941, exactly five years after his departure, for family reasons, but went back to Paris almost immediately. He was escorted to the frontier by a police official who apologized to him for the necessity of keeping him under surveillance.

It was during this second stay in Paris that he wrote his essay on the exile of Luis Vives, in which he observed that:

When you are compulsorily exiled, you feel as never before the living flame of patriotism. But he who exiles himself voluntarily through excess of love does so because he has created an intangible hope for his distant country, he adores it not as it is but as he would like it to be.[76]

In a letter to Menéndez Pidal he stated that 'I am not going to Spain, because I prefer to work here'.[77] But family needs came first. Marañón had to make another family visit in October the following year, when his daughter fell seriously ill. Thereafter he remained in the country, commenting that he chose the lesser of two evils: 'I prefer the Inquisition to the Inquisition plus pedantry plus lies plus hypocrisy.'[78] 'He went back and enjoyed the light of the day in Spain and the incomparable nights', an envious Madariaga commented.[79]

One by one, and always urged on by those who were in Spain, the great names returned. Politics became in time a secondary consideration, particularly for those who realized that they had to accept current reality. Those who had transformed their professional and personal horizons felt little need to revert to the antiquated excuse of wishing to leave their bones in their native land. The claim has been made that Américo Castro returned because of a patriotic wish to die in Spain. The truth seems to be that he came back because it was the wish of his wife, who died shortly before he did. His own preference was to end his days not in Spain, 'as a prisoner in a country scarcely his own', but in the United States he knew and loved, in a house 'not far from Widener Library' at Harvard.[80] In Spain he was virtually unknown. Max Aub wrote, during a visit to Spain: 'the overwhelming majority have no idea that Américo Castro is here living in Madrid'. A figure such as Castro's scholarly antagonist Sánchez-Albornoz, who had been nominal president of the self-styled government-in-exile, was clearly not free to return under the Franco dictatorship. In the 1973 edition of his *Spain, an Enigma* he stated: 'I have lived in exile thirty-seven years and will die in it'. Ten years later, he returned. One of the last to return was Alberti. Even he made his peace. Shortly after his return in 1977, he was asked to pronounce the traditional address (the *pregón*) at the Carnival celebrations in his home city of Cadiz. He was greeted and embraced by an old friend and fellow native of Cadiz, the ageing poet José María Pemán, a monarchist and one of the literary stars of the Franco regime. In that embrace the perpetual struggle between the Two Spains, between the returning exile and the son who remained at home, seemed at last to have been resolved.

However, return was not a simple option. Exiles who refused to change their ideas found themselves increasingly alienated from a changing homeland. With an eye on foreign opinion, in the 1950s the regime began to slacken its hold, and press laws were relaxed. New journals began publication. Pens reverted to classic debates, which now seemed daring because they allowed a bit of controversy into public life. One such debate, in the style of the Generation of 98, was broached by Pedro Laín Entralgo, in his *Spain as a Problem*, which received a response from one of the regime's writers, Rafael Calvo Serer, in his *Spain without Problems*. The universities began to buzz with activity, and a press law of 1966 opened the door to freer publication. Even the hermetic world of Spanish academic life began to change. Younger scholars looked for employment abroad, especially in the USA and England. Among them were many second-generation exiles, such as politics professor Juan Marichal (born in Tenerife 1922), whose active career was spent as head of the department of Hispanic Studies at Harvard. The exiled 'intellectuals' who had proclaimed Hispanic culture to be the great future of human civilization (with themselves as its only guardians) became increasingly irrelevant in a context where the contact of their old homeland with the outside world, and the slow but sure advance of technology imported from Europe and the United States had changed the entire cultural landscape. What Spain had on offer quickly became less relevant than what foreigners offered to Spain. Writers who had left the country thinking they were taking the Ark of the Covenant with them found that they had in reality taken very little and that Spain remained Spain, capable always of producing new fruit. León Felipe, who in 1939 had claimed to represent the cultural elite – 'I go off with the song' – found that twenty years after the end of the war the landscape had changed, though Franco was still there. 'I feel ashamed now,' he explained in

1958. 'I did not go off with the song. We did not go off with the song. You kept everything, both the land and the song. Now we are here, we the Spaniards of the exodus, astonished to hear you sing.'[81]

The passing of decades made it very difficult to cross bridges. Though there was some common ground in political matters, the cultural gap remained immense. Fifteen years after the end of the Civil War, early in 1954, Ramón Sender published an article in Paris pouring scorn on the cultural pretensions of writers living in Spain and asserting the moral superiority of those who worked in exile. In the same year, one of those based in Spain, José Luis Aranguren, a respected Catholic monarchist who later became a notable supporter of democratization,[82] published an essay in the review *Cuadernos Hispanoamericanos* assessing the writings of the exiles and welcoming their work (even though the Spanish regime continued to prohibit most of it). A handful of exiles in Buenos Aires published an answer to the article, expressing their appreciation for its tone but reasserting their own moral superiority over those who lived and worked in Spain. As the years passed, it seemed that the exiles became more entrenched in an exclusivism that at times bordered on the sublime. An example of this was the reply to Aranguren's article by a minister of the government-in-exile, Fernando Varela, in 1957. Rejecting the hand offered by Aranguren, he stated that Aranguren failed to understand the great sufferings endured by 'Pilgrim Spain', sufferings that constituted an 'immense tragedy, only comparable in its dimensions with the millenary dispersion of Israel, and in its intensity with the crucifixion of Christ'.[83] Not surprisingly, it took an entire generation for many who lived abroad to recognize that theirs was not the only Spain, and that there was also one inside Spain itself. The polarization between exiles and returnees was only one part of the constant bickering over who was the real keeper of Spain's culture.

The return to Spain was, as Aub had discovered, by no means an easy process. The democratic government after Franco's death issued an amnesty decree on 4 August 1976, but in practice those Spaniards who lived abroad had long since dipped their feet in the water. When Aub arrived at Barcelona airport in 1969 he declared, 'I have come, but I have not returned'. In the event he was disappointed to find that he was not read and few knew who he was. 'The problem over returning or not to Spain, thirty years later, is not Franco but time: and oneself. The exile perished, what has changed is Spain. Quite different.'[84] Part of the motive for his visit was to gather material for a biography of his long-time friend Buñuel, but he was shocked that people appeared to have swept the Civil War under the carpet. He recorded his negative reactions in *Blind Man's Buff* (*La gallina ciega*, 1971), written in the form of a diary covering the two months of his visit. The rambling, verbose volume trudges page after page through Aub's account of his profound disappointment. 'Spain has changed inside out,' he observed. 'At no moment did I have the feeling of forming part of this new country which has usurped the place of the one that was here before.' The excitement, the suffering, the pain, the ideology, were no longer there. 'Spain is no longer romantic. It is no longer the Spain of "Death or victory!" or, if you like, "They shall not pass!" It is a Spain of mediocrity, of the refrigerator and the washing machine.'

'The streets are full. People walk, run, fill the sidewalks and streets. Nobody remembers.' 'All these people go or meander to their jobs in absolute tranquillity. This is a controlled population that does not protest.' Like other exiles, and indeed long after most of them, he refused to accept that the Spain he preserved in his mind was now outdated. 'Really, nothing is there in this splendid Madrid morning to stop you filling your lungs with fresh air and deciding that you live in the best of all worlds!'[85] He made a second visit in 1972, but his impressions were no more favourable. He sensed resentment, a desire to shut him out. 'There clearly exists in Spain a feeling hostile to "those who left" and are coming back. Especially against those aged from forty to fifty. What are they afraid of? That they will take their jobs from them, tomorrow?' Above all, he was disappointed at the almost total ignorance among so-called intellectuals of anything that went on outside the borders of their country. 'How Cela pronounces French!', he noted. 'He shows off his knowledge of England, yet doesn't speak the language. I was surprised by the absolute lack of foreign books in his library. What depressing ignorance!'[86]

From his point of view, Aub was absolutely correct. But the decades had opened up an irreparable fissure between those exiles who still lived in their past, and the newer generation of a different Spain, one that was emerging from its Third World status into the new era of tourism, cocktail bars and football. The two poles were presented clearly in a brilliant essay by the young writer Francisco Umbral in the newspaper *Ya* in October 1969, written at the time of Aub's first visit:

He and all the others return in glory, but they return late. They are the American cousins with Spanish culture. They didn't speak out at the time and it is now too late for them to speak. The return of the magi does not bewitch us. We esteem them, we await them. But it difficult now for them to bewitch us.[87]

Like the half-forgotten Ortega who returned to a world in which the 'intellectuals' no longer ruled, Aub recognized that the old tribal gods had been removed from their pedestals. Aub wrote: 'those of us who left don't count any more, it would have been better to have stayed . . . We were wiped off the map. A clean sweep. No one knows who we were, and even less what we are.'[88] Those who made the effort to stay felt lost in the new Spain. The poet José Bergamín confessed that he felt 'more and more a wanderer in my country'.[89] His was a classic case of the restless and homeless exile. Bergamín (1895–1983) was from Andalusia and in the 1920s a friend of Juan Ramón Jiménez and the Madrid circle. A firm Republican in 1931, in 1936 he was appointed cultural attaché in Paris by the new government because he knew French. The Nationalist victory in 1939 meant that he could not return home so he went to Mexico, where (as we have seen) he and the poet Juan Larrea founded the short-lived journal *España Peregrina*. Perpetually quarrelsome in character, in Mexico he fell out with his hosts, and moved on to Caracas, then later to Montevideo, and when he had exhausted that he went back to Paris, from where he applied for permission to return to Spain. A strong Catholic, and relatively conservative in outlook, he had little trouble with the decision. In 1958 he at last trod on native soil, but the problem of settling in became acute, and he itched for trouble. It came when the government disapproved of him signing a declaration in support of a miners' strike in the Asturias in 1963. He went off into exile again and returned to Montevideo, but quickly moved back to Paris, where he lived six eventful years. He was witness to the revolutionary enthusiasm that shook the French university world in May 1968, but did not approve of it. At last in 1970 he was allowed to return to Spain, but it was by no means a final destination, for a month after his return he was back in Paris and continued going back to it. In Spain he inevitably fell out with everybody, and withdrew into being an 'inner exile'. One of his last poems stated:

> I was a pilgrim in my homeland
> From the moment I was born
> And all the time I lived there
> I continued to be so,
> Pilgrim from a Spain
> That is no longer within me.[90]

The year after writing this he died, a strange exile who seems to have made exile his required way of life and who, as Juan Ramón Jiménez well knew, was unable to come to terms with the special effort required to maintain one culture while living within another. Unhappy with any of the regimes through which he had lived, as a self-styled republican he also energetically rejected the monarchy that came with the restoration of democracy after Franco. In the end, he confessed that he was fed up with being a Spaniard, and went off to die in the Basque country, where he ended up writing for radical pro-Basque papers. His was not the only case of a disappointed exile. Many who returned expected to be treated as heroes, but the country had changed and the culture had evolved well beyond the postures of the 1930s. Among those who met with Bergamín in the literary cafés of Madrid was the writer Antonio Espina, who came back to Madrid in 1960 but found himself surrounded by a different generation, which took little notice of him. Espina died forgotten in 1972. Over the years, with the separate ways taken by cultural patterns on both sides of the Atlantic, exiles who believed their devotion to their own language had earned them a place in their own country found that belief disappointed. From his direct knowledge of the individuals affected, José Luis Aranguren commented that

> So long as the exiled conserve their state of mind as exiles, they cannot return; accustomed to live among their memories and nostalgias, in a Spain that exists not in reality but in their hearts, they have become blind to the crude light of a present that is alien to them and that has evolved without them.[91]

All too often, the home country did not want its exiles back. In normal circumstances, returning exiles are greeted with open arms, especially if they have managed to become successful and even famous. Through new knowledge that they have gained abroad, they become a force for cultural and technical change in their home communities. 'Our experiences made us see that there are alternative ways for China to develop and for us to lead our personal lives', stated one of the thousands of Chinese students who returned home in the 1990s after years of training in the United States.[92] Statements like this were not made in the environment that greeted returning Spaniards.

Time and again, would-be returnees found to their chagrin that the authorities, both under the dictatorship and under the subsequent democratic regimes, turned their backs on them. Old and retired exiles, unlikely to represent any competition for jobs or honours, were welcomed back without problems. Those who represented the possibility of change were not. The fate of science repeated itself. Since the turn of the century, when the professor of biochemistry in the University of Madrid complained that he 'had to teach biochemistry as though it were metaphysics, since there were no laboratories', budding researchers (like Ochoa) had to go abroad to access the latest research or the most recent laboratory methods. In their turn, these scientific exiles, absent not for their political convictions but simply because their country had no resources, attempted to help their colleagues in Spain. One of the exiles was a Catalan named Joan Oró (1923–2004), who made his career at the University of Houston, in Texas. In 1970 Oró helped to found the new Institute of Biology in Barcelona, with a governing body that included Josep Trueta. One of their aspirations was to create an adequate environment in which Ochoa might be able to work after retiring from New York. When news of their proposal got around, there was an outcry from colleagues and politicians about having to accept back 'émigré brains'.[93] Instead of returning to Spain, therefore, Ochoa went on to work for the pharmaceutical firm of Roche in New Jersey. 'I moved to the Roche Institute on July 1,' Ochoa wrote to a colleague in 1974, 'and I cannot tell you how happy I am here with the splendid facilities for work.'[94] Nothing comparable would have been available to him in Spain, to which he returned only after retiring from Roche. The case is relevant, because the same happened with Oró, who obtained his doctorate in the United States and went on to teach for nearly forty years at Houston. He did pioneering work in the early stages of DNA analysis, and was particularly involved with research on life in outer space. When he retired in 1994 there were promises that he would be accepted to do research in Spain, but the promises were empty ones and he went back to the States. In default of conceding him a laboratory, the government generously in 2003 bestowed on him the noble title of 'marquis'. Titles and prizes were deemed a good substitute for investment in science.

Ochoa's return in the 1980s was by no means the triumph that some Spanish officials thought it was. Like Américo Castro and many another returnee, Ochoa found that he had come from a progressive, modern environment to one that was far from being so. 'When you have lived in New York, you cannot live anywhere else', he commented to a friend. The biggest disappointment was in the financing and facilities available to scientists in Spain. Ochoa stated unambiguously: 'Spaniards have nothing of which to be proud.' When pressed to explain why, despite everything, he had come back, he said: 'Because I was old. In the United States they back the young, it is a country where youth has a great future. They respect the old but no longer pay attention to them, a position I find reasonable. We came back because at eighty it was time to go back to where your roots are.'[95]

Doors in the mother country that had been opened to allow exit were therefore seldom opened again to the exiles, except those who shared the political ideology of the government in power. It was a rule followed almost inflexibly across five centuries. A scholar, himself an exile of the 1930s, observed that 'from the point of view of national continuity, exile comes to be, in a literary as well as political sense, a shipwreck from which few remains – and not always the best ones – can be salvaged'. This created a sort of dilemma for the Spanish establishment, which had contributed nothing to the success of its exiles abroad, but did not wish to dissociate itself wholly from them. The achievement of those who had left could never be seen, or even accepted, as a contribution to their original country. Exile continued to be in some sense an expulsion, a deprivation.

However, the triumphs of exiles, even if resented by the official ideology in the home country, could still be viewed as a contribution to the larger and vaguer concept of Hispanic culture. From that viewpoint, 'Hispanic culture' across five hundred years could lay claim to one of the richest heritages available to any European nation, since all who had left the peninsula could still by a process of association be seen as still within Spain. Blanco White made immense efforts to convert himself into an Englishman, loved England and wrote in English, but he could be claimed as part of the cultural fund of Spain. The achievement of Servet or Ochoa was made possible only by the educational system of other countries, but it could still be claimed for Spain. A tendency therefore developed to reclaim as part of Spain's heritage all those who had for one reason or another been excluded from it. It was an attempt at cultural hegemony that did no harm and offended no one, but had the advantage of mitigating the painful story of continuous exile inflicted on millions of Spaniards. There was only one, though fundamental, drawback to this presentation. Could those who had integrated into other worlds, as Vives had integrated into the city of Bruges and the mainstream of European humanism, be considered in any meaningful sense still linked to their origins?

The refusal of the mother country to accept the exiles had many legitimate reasons. The most important reason was simply that the country was too poor to accept professionals who had lived in better-endowed environments. University men who had lived and worked in the United States, England, France and Germany could not hope for the same level of salary or departmental budget in Spain. On the same principle, without special financing scientists could not hope for adequate facilities. Only special government favour, and logically a government salary, enabled Jorge Semprun to return to Spain. Other non-elite exiles came back to modest professions and low-level expectations. In general, Spaniards were happy to see their émigrés only after they had retired, and on these conditions Américo Castro and Ochoa, both citizens of the United States, ended their days in the homeland. The possibility of a final return seems to provide a happy conclusion to the story, yet it also serves to blur perspectives, by downplaying the role that exile has played in cultural history. In a post-exile situation, all those who lived abroad and continue to live abroad, regardless of the reasons that took them there, become invisibly integrated into the permanent fabric of Hispanic achievement. From Luis Vives to Albéniz and Ochoa, the narrative of Spanish culture thereby becomes (misleadingly) transformed into a long story of continuous success.

Looking back, two astonishing aspects of the centuries of Hispanic peregrination leap out. The first is the inability of many exiles to distance themselves from their roots and place themselves within a universal environment. There were a tiny handful, mainly scientists and artists, who immediately identified themselves with new issues that transcended old perspectives. Their novel surroundings gave life to their creative energy, and drew them into a different culture and language that they learnt to share. From Vives to Picasso, Ochoa and Madariaga, there were Spaniards who ended up belonging to all mankind because their perception was universal, not national. As Pío Baroja once pointed out perceptively, 'Vives, Servet, Loyola and others had nothing Spanish about them except their place of birth'.[96] These, and numberless others, spent all their active lives outside Spain and their contribution to European culture was not primarily Hispanic. In the nineteenth and twentieth centuries, intellectual refugees from Poland, Russia and Germany fell into this same pattern of cultural adaptation. Literary figures such as Joseph Conrad and Vladimir Nabokov, and a seemingly endless stream of artists, musicians, writers, philosophers and scientists of Central and East European origin, transformed the experience of absence into an enrichment of universal values. Edward Said wrote in *Reflections on Exile* that:

most people are principally aware of one culture, one setting, one home; exiles are aware of at least two, and this plurality of vision gives rise to an awareness of simultaneous dimensions, an awareness that – to borrow a phrase from music – is contrapuntal. For an exile, habits of life, expression, or activity in the new environment inevitably occur against the memory of these things in another environment. Thus both the new and the old environment are vivid, actual, occurring together contrapuntally.

The experience was, however, not normally true of Spanish exiles. Perhaps because they felt they were an elite, whom the homeland would soon summon back, many educated Spaniards refused to integrate into their host communities. Jorge Semprun was exceptional in deciding to 'make exile my homeland'. The majority, by contrast, accepted no alternative home. Though thousands of educated Spaniards in the nineteenth century, for example, went to live in England and France, they resolutely refused to learn the language of their new home, which they treated as alien and hostile. One of the nobles who lived for ten years in England in the 1820s as a refugee from Ferdinand VII returned under the subsequent Liberal regime as ambassador to England. The embassy secretary in London asked him why he still spoke no English despite having lived there so long. The ambassador explained: 'It is a mistake to think that I was an émigré here for ten years. The truth is that I was one for only a week, because every week I expected a revolution in Spain and lived with my case packed for returning to Spain.'[97] The problem was the same even when the language seemed to be no obstacle. In Mexico in the 1940s, peninsular exiles for the most part maintained their cultural activity almost completely on the margins of Mexican society, dedicated their political activity to Spanish themes, and sent their children to foreign rather than Mexican schools. Like all émigrés, those of the first generation remained wedded to their origins and refused to accept the culture of the lands that received them. This gave rise to a persistent feeling of alienation.

The vast majority of Spanish cultural exiles tended not to adapt to any culture that was not their own, or to dedicate themselves to issues that were not primarily centred on their place and language of origin. Ganivet, even while he looked out of his window over the pines and grey sea of the Baltic, shut the present out of his mind and concentrated his thoughts only on the problem of regenerating Spain. Absentees from Spain were usually unable and unwilling to absorb the culture and language of the new host society, and limited themselves to dreams of going back to their own society. Poets exiled in the New World, whether in Mexico or Argentina, ignored the environment in which they lived, and wrote instead about Castilian landscapes and Andalusian coastlines. The past they had experienced froze their vision and thus determined the parameters of their creativity. It was not surprising that they could not always get their message across to the people in their new environment. The Civil War, for example, wiped out all other themes in the work of Aub. 'For the people of my generation, and for the two preceding as well as the subsequent,' he explained, 'the war was the Big Thing, with capital letters; it determined our way of life, how we looked at the world, how we died.'[98]

Clinging to one's past was an old phenomenon, but raised the question of whether the exiled were really exiled, an issue that had many antecedents. In an interesting lecture given at a PEN conference in 1939 in the United States on the theme 'Can Culture Survive Exile?',[99] the poet Pedro Salinas argued that when there is a hostile cultural environment at home, any intellectual has the right to become an exile in order to further cultural survival. Flight into exile becomes not a negative but a positive and creative act. However, Salinas was speaking, whether his audience realized it or not, within very specific margins. Rooted exclusively in his own Spanish context, his sights were set only on the culture he had left behind. Very many of the writers who left during the Civil War felt, as we have had occasion to emphasize, that they were the sole bearers of the Ark of the Covenant. They were convinced that they represented their country's culture and had the duty to preserve it and take it back home. The fact that they now lived in Mexico or in Maryland was of little moment. Though he was quite certain about his message, Salinas was unable to cite any historical intellectuals who fitted into his argument about Hispanic culture surviving unchanged outside the peninsula. He named just three exiles of the early sixteenth century, Leone Ebreo, Luis Vives and Juan de Valdés, but failed to demonstrate in what way they preserved their roots. (Had he delved further, he would have found that all three wrote well outside the limits of Hispanic culture and that their public was overwhelmingly non-Spanish.) He therefore had to fall back on the classic standby adopted by writers of his generation: presenting the argument through the fictional prism of Cervantes. 'Many of our national heroes,' he stated, 'have acquired their full stature in exile.' The 'national hero' he actually cited was Don Quixote, who (Salinas said) exiled himself from the restricted life of being a village squire and marched off to discover new worlds. 'Only when he breaks with the past and takes the road of exile does he become himself and achieve immortality.'

The situation of being trapped within personal exile made it in many cases almost impossible to readjust one's bearings. This led to the second astonishing aspect of much Spanish exile: the inability to arrive at a clearer definition of personal and, by extension, national identity. Throughout the centuries of conflict and expulsion, those who had left clung doggedly to the concept and memory of 'Spain', a word that in the earlier centuries referred merely to the baggage of personal experiences, since 'Spain' did not exist politically. In theory, exile and the wish to return should have contributed powerfully to consolidating the idea of nationhood, and reinforcing what 'Spain' meant in cultural and political terms. But this development never occurred. Spain is the only nation in Europe to claim to have had a 'War of Independence' (what other nations call the 'Peninsular War' of 1808–1813), without ever celebrating an 'Independence Day'. The long years of struggle, the thousands of dead and exiled, the aspirations and ideals, all led nowhere. The political groups of the early nineteenth century, including pro-French, Liberals and Carlists, were too busy fighting each other to devote any time to consolidating the independence they had won. The lack of solidarity was felt even more profoundly in the refusal to have a national anthem, and in the reluctance to share a common flag. The Liberals boasted an anthem, the *Hymn of Riego* (1820), which after more than a century of oblivion was intoned solemnly at the instauration in 1931 of the Second Republic. After that occasion it fell back into oblivion. By failing to decide their own identity, exiles failed to decide the identity of their origins. The creative spirits of Spain, whether or not driven out of their homeland, remained prey to their own consciousness of alienation, of not belonging to the environment that had produced them. Many of those who have passed through these pages were intellectual nomads, who did not fit in and had problems identifying themselves not only with their own country but with other countries as well.

The homeland, the *patria*, failed to become a rallying point for exiles, and in turn the exiles did little to promote a feeling for it. For Spaniards both inside and outside their country, the sentiment of 'patriotism' has never existed. In Mexico, for example, the Spanish communities held interminable feasts to celebrate '*mi tierra*' ('my land') and '*mi país*' ('my country'), but they were celebrating only their regions, never their nation.[100] This has had a profound effect on the phenomenon of exile. Whereas Russian exiles in the early 1900s were able to re-create Little Russias all over Europe and North America, not a single expatriate community from the peninsula managed to create a Little Spain. The Russian émigrés 'united around the symbols of Russian culture as the focus of their national identity'.[101] As soon as they were outside their home country, by contrast, Spanish exiles all but lost their interest in a possible national identity. Buñuel's films during his exile speak of proletarian Mexico and bourgeois Europe, but when they speak of Spain it is only to cast doubt on everything that constituted the official Spain of the day. In Buñuel one discovers a Spain that is putrefying, eaten through by the maggots of clericalism, greed and sexual hypocrisy, and there is no promise in sight that a more desirable, more optimistic nation might be waiting to emerge from the rubbish heap.

The experience of exile became for creative spirits almost a need, one that gave them liberty to find a context where they would achieve wholeness. The travail of not-belonging was a way through to discovering where one belonged. They did not entirely lose their grip on the homeland, which supplied a point of orientation, but they seemed to use that homeland merely as a way to define or justify their own absence from it. They wished to flee from Spain, knowing full well that it was their only home. The attitude took very many shapes and forms. In 1523 Juan Luis Vives expressed a sentiment that became common among those who were really much happier away from home. 'I am deeply distressed because I do not know what to decide. I hate to go back home,' he wrote to his friend Cranevelt, 'but to stay here is not possible.'[102] Rejection of Spain was already in the early sixteenth century a problem for him. He had missed opportunities of returning, and turned down invitations because he had no confidence in the opportunities for study available. The worst experience was the injury done to his father and mother by the Inquisition. In the summer of 1527 he wrote to his friend, the humanist Juan de Vergara: 'One has to speak well of one's own homeland, even though the opinion you have of it is quite different.'[103]

Three and a half centuries later, a cultured intellectual such as Juan Valera felt so deep a rejection of Spain's backwardness that he yearned to be away from it and outside it, yet when he travelled to Paris, Frankfurt, Brussels and Washington he felt an equal rejection of what those places had to offer. Even the good food in France was not enough. 'There is no doubt that they cook better here, and do everything better, than in Spain, but I prefer to eat badly and live badly and be in my own land.'[104] Spain, he felt, was uncivilized and primitive: 'there is a great deal that has to be done in Spain, everything is unexplored, virgin, uncultivated: philosophy, history, the sciences, even literature'. The big problem was 'the backwardness of Spain', because the country was 'a country of idiots'. 'In Spain instead of advancing we keep going backwards.'[105] He condemned all the political parties, despised those responsible for the military adventures in Africa, and thought it significant that the Krause whom some Spaniards had regarded as a philosophical revelation was unknown and unimportant in his native Germany.[106] Very many of the elite felt as he did, and considered expatriation a desirable option, because they were not quite sure what sort of Spain they wished to belong to.

Exile intensified a dual problem of identity: that of the exile himself, but also that of the homeland. The exile did not feel totally deprived of his former self if he could at least preserve part of the lost past within himself. Carles Riba explained, a few months after leaving Catalonia in 1939, that 'I do not miss my homeland, and if it depended on me I would not return to it for a long time, for what is essential about it, the idea, I carry within me'.[107] However, in the difficult environment of Vichy France he found it impossible to lead a normal life, and along with several other Catalan exiles he chose to return in 1943, after four years of absence. In the mind of the exile, perspective and distance allowed him some possibility of defining more clearly what the homeland was, and what it meant to him. The issue was not simply one of deprivation, of giving vent to vapid verse like that of Espronceda or the other Liberal exiles as they made their way to London. Beyond the direct sentiments of the exile lay the important question: Did he belong to the homeland any longer? The answer can be looked at on an individual or a global level. On an individual level it is obvious that the exile belongs to his roots as long as he wishes to identify with them, and the eventual return home may confirm this axiom. On the other hand, by adopting during exile (as

Blanco White did) a scale of cultural values that had little in common with one's origins, the involuntary emigrant in fact voluntarily ceases to share in the home that he knew. The problem arises at its most extreme in the case of Puerto Rico, where (it has been pointed out)[108] the main theoretical problem is whether the half of the nation that lives permanently outside the island shares any longer to a convincing degree the identity of the homeland. The exile, in brief, may in some sense yearn for his country, but because he has a different perception of its identity he ends up rejecting what he no longer recognizes.

Scholars have called attention to 'the lack of impact Spain has made in recent times on the European mind'.[109] There were indubitably weaknesses in cultural interchange. The relative backwardness of peninsular society, which lagged one or two centuries behind western taste and technology, was a significant factor. The Spanish tongue could also be a barrier. Despite much-vaunted claims by writers in Spain and South America, the language was little read outside the Hispanic regions, and even less translated. The practical consequence for some creative figures, especially if they used the printed word, was that they remained relatively unknown both within their country of origin and outside it. It was this seemingly unfavourable situation, however, that the exiles helped to resolve. And they were able to do it because of their contacts with the non-Hispanic world. The situation for Hispanic culture had not always been difficult. In the great imperial age of the sixteenth century, Spanish culture had had access to international links. Printing presses in the two most developed European nations, Italy and the Netherlands, made their resources available to Castilian authors.[110] Unlike the English, who could expect to publish a book in English only in their own country, Castilians had the choice of publishing in any of the realms of the peninsula, as well as in the other states of the monarchy and in France and Portugal. By the 1540s, more books by Spaniards, whether in Latin or in Castilian, were being published outside than inside the peninsula. They appeared mainly in Antwerp, Venice, Lyons, Toulouse, Paris, Louvain, Cologne, Lisbon and Coimbra.[111] The standard of presses outside Spain was much higher, and controls less onerous.[112] The diffusion of printed Castilian literature helped to spread to the rest of Europe the great Castilian writers and also a genre that soon bred imitations, the *pícaro* novel. The diffusion of books in the Dutch Netherlands was particularly remarkable. Between the sixteenth and the eighteenth centuries, private and public libraries there stocked over one thousand editions by Castilian authors, and 130 editions in translation from Castilian.[113] The steady disappearance of the Spanish Empire, however, also cut off access to cultural contacts. From that time it was the exiles who became the new bearers of Hispanic civilization. Refugees from Spain, not only Jews and Protestants but also prominent members of the clergy such as the Jesuits, and later on the great waves of nineteenth-century exiles, published their works outside Spain and made an impact that they would not have achieved by printing within the peninsula.

Thanks to the phenomenon of exile, key aspects of the Spanish achievement developed and matured conspicuously outside the peninsula, where they benefited from the help of two great nations, France and the United States.[114] The role of these nations in stimulating Spanish creativity has seldom received the attention it deserves, yet it was extensive, powerful and fundamental. Without it, peninsular culture would have limped into the contemporary world. From Renaissance times, and even more fundamentally from the age of the Enlightenment, Paris became the great magnet that attracted creative spirits from the peninsula. From the eighteenth century, Spain's Bourbon monarchy trained its elite to develop a taste for the works of French and Italian philosophers and writers. In return, the French elite in the nineteenth century introduced their Spanish colleagues to the vogues of Romanticism and Orientalism, and taught them art, music and architecture. Paris became the cultural capital of Spain, as a seemingly unending stream of singers, composers, poets, novelists, artists and creative people of every political hue settled in the city and made it their ultimate home.[115] It also became the cultural focus of Hispanic America, as indeed it had been since the era of independence in the 1800s. The poet César Vallejo, who felt that the Latin countries 'lack a cultural home of their own', saw that Paris offered an 'intellectual centre that fosters and promotes individual culture'.[116] Artistic figures from Spain incorporated themselves, via Paris, into the European cultural circuit (Albéniz's complaint, as we have seen, was of 'trips to Paris, trips to London, trips to Belgium, concerts, competitions, in short, a life that is no life!'), where their contribution was more highly appreciated than in the peninsula. For others, such as Picasso and Semprun, it became home. When a Spanish visitor chided him for living in Paris when he could be living in Spain, Picasso shrugged and replied, 'Our face is our passport!'[117] Granados's cry of 1916, 'I dream of Paris!', expressed the yearnings of every creative Spaniard over five centuries. A few absentees in Europe were eventually received home after their deaths, like Albéniz or Blasco Ibáñez, but others (from Luis Vives to Madariaga) were never repatriated. They remained abroad, in the international environment that had made them great, far from their native Spain.

The American contribution was no less significant. Spaniards remained hostile to the success of the United States, because their hearts could not forgive the humiliation of 1898. But at almost every stage it was the United States that took over from France the task of universalizing Hispanic culture. When Juan Valera visited the States in order to promote the American translation of his *Pepita Jiménez*, he was pleasantly surprised to see that the Americans knew who Cervantes was, but he showed little interest in their 'inferior' culture and dismissed Henry James as worthless. American interest in Valera, on the other hand, was both positive and pragmatic. The attention extended to his novel was symptomatic of the American genius for identifying what was durable and profitable in culture. In those very decades, Sarasate was playing his way across the States, and Archer M. Huntington and Charles Deering were beginning the great enterprises that gave classic Hispanic culture its window on the world. No one who has visited the impressive galleries of the Hispanic Society in Manhattan or the Art Institute in Chicago can doubt the unique importance of America in fostering Spain's heritage. 'I have left half my life as an artist in America!', Sorolla recognized when he left New York in 1909. The United States offered to Spanish artists and scientists a public that could appreciate their work, and patrons who could finance their needs. Among the expatriates, Picasso, Blasco Ibáñez, Dalí and Buñuel were conscious that their livelihood depended on the American market. Without the United States, there would have been little scope for the contribution of exiles such as Casals, Juan Ramón Jiménez, Américo Castro or Severo Ochoa. The last three of these were, of course, citizens of the United States, as were many other stars of the Hispanic firmament. The development of science in post-Franco Spain also owed everything to the patronage of expatriate Spanish researchers by the United States.[118] In its peculiar position as one of the world's largest Hispanic nations, it was appropriate that the United States should also have been the principal luminary of the Spanish achievement in culture. Nobody expressed his appreciation better than Pablo Casals, in the banquet speech he made before state dignitaries in Washington DC in October 1967, after a performance of *El Pessebre*. He thanked 'America, the country I love. The country I love so much and that I have known long before most of you. You are the richest nation, but you are also the most generous of any nation. You have helped advance every noble thing.'[119] Years later, Jorge Guillén was asked in an interview whether the years of his exile had been painful. His answer was probably not what the questioner expected:

In the United States, where I was very well received, my exile has not been unhappy. Besides, exile has not been for me a crucial phenomenon, because I can find in any point of the earth what is essential: air, water, sun, people, human company.[120]

Exile could be either imposed or self-imposed. Perhaps the most widely appreciated book of the Middle Ages was the *Consolation of Philosophy*, written by the Roman aristocrat and scholar Boethius in his prison cell in exile in Pavia in Italy, shortly before he was put to death by government decree in the year 524 of the Christian era. His head filled with laments about the injustice of exile, he is suddenly confronted by Philosophy, who appears in the form of a venerable woman. Philosophy tells him frankly that he has to rise above his individual concerns. As long as he ponders only his own miseries, his exile is merely self-inflicted:

> You have not really been banished far from home,
> you have strayed. If you wish to call it expulsion,
> then you expelled yourself. No one else
> had the power to do it to you.[121]

In the same way, the obsession with their own plight and a corresponding inability to adjust their focus marked very many exiles.[122]

They became trapped within their own vision of what should have been, and effectively exiled themselves, in the sense referred to by Boethius. The true flowering of exile culture came about when it discovered new and universal horizons that were not accessible to those who remained physically or mentally locked away in the homeland. Many expatriates, inevitably, had problems in understanding the way other people thought. They wrote prose, poems and music inspired solely by the private and localized environment from which they came. Salvador de Madariaga, who saw the premiere of Falla's *The Three-Cornered Hat* in London in 1919, was enthusiastic about it but also asked himself a question that was a valid criticism of the cultural achievements of those who came face to face with the outside world. 'Why,' he asked himself, 'is it only Spanish composers who cling to stylized popular forms, while Beethoven and Debussy express themselves in a universal language?'[123] Despite some sophisticated pieces, such as the very brief *Harpsichord Concerto* (1926) written for Wanda Landowska, Falla seems not to have strayed far from the Spanish element.[124] Many exiles limited themselves to the narrow world they had come from. Others, however, achieved universality because they grasped at the new horizons beyond their homeland, and chose an idiom that was not parochial but accessible to all. That, in sum, was the great gift of exile. The disinherited went through deprivation, alienation and loss of identity, but some achieved for Hispanic culture what they would certainly not have been able to accomplish had they eked out their days at home in tranquillity.

Glossary

aljamiado	Castilian dialect of Muslims and Moriscos, when written it used the Arabic script
alumbrados	Illuminists, groups of mystics who minimized the role of the Church and of ceremonies
arbitristas	writers, mainly of the seventeenth century, who drew up proposals for economic and political reform
auto de fe	'act of faith', the ceremony at which accused were sentenced by the Inquisition, either in public or in private. The burning of heretics was never technically part of an *auto*, but took place afterwards
Call	name given to the Jewish quarter in Barcelona
cante jondo	'deep song', a vocal form associated with Andalusian flameno dance
casticismo	cultural concept referring to 'authenticity' or popular roots; the adjective is *castizo*
checa	Soviet-type tribunals set up in major towns by left-wing militants in 1936, responsible for numerous death sentences. The name was taken from the Soviet secret police, the Cheka, set up after the 1917 Revolution
Comendador	a dignitary of the Castilian military orders
Comuneros	participants in the rising of Castilian cities against Charles V in 1520
conversos	term applied to Christianized Jews and their descendants
Cortes	the parliament of each realm of Spain, and also of the whole of Spain
Día de la Raza	'Day of the Race', name given in the nineteenth century in Latin America and Castile to 12 October, day of the discovery of America, celebrated in this case as the day of triumph of the Spanish 'race'
Diputació	the executive organ of the government of Catalonia

flamenco	Andalusian dance and music, of gypsy origin
fueros	local laws and privileges, in particular of the non-Castilian provinces of Spain
intendant	in the eighteenth century, a state-appointed provincial adminstrator
jíbaro	peasant, in some Latin American societies, notably Puerto Rico
Kabbalah	type of medieval Jewish mysticism associated with interpreting the Old Testament
Krausism	nineteenth-century school of thought, derived from the ideas of a minor German philosopher
ladino	Castilian Jewish language, written in Hebrew script
limpieza de sangre	'purity of blood', meaning freedom from any taint of Jewish blood
Marranos	term, of uncertain origin, applied to Jewish conversos
mestizaje	'mixture', most commonly used of the mixture of races in colonial Latin America
Morisco	a Christianized Moor, term used from the sixteenth century
Mozarabic	adjective from 'Mozarabes', Christians who lived under Muslim rule
Mudéjar	a Muslim living under Christian rule; in art, the Muslim style of decoration and architecture
paseos	in everyday Spanish, 'a walk' or stroll; in the context of Spain in 1936, calling for victims at their homes and taking them out to be shot
pícaro	rogue, a profession made famous in Spain through the 'picaresque' novels of the sixteenth century
qasida	verse form developed in pre-Islamic Arabia and used since then by Islamic poets
remença	Catalan peasantry who rebelled in the late fifteenth century
urjuza	medieval Islamic didactic poem
villancico	popular ballads of medieval origin, especially Christmas ballads
zarzuela	Spanish operetta

Select Bibliography

The sources cited in this bibliography and in the endnotes refer specifically to the theme of exiles and the cultural impact of exile. They are not intended to be a guide to all the reading on, for example, the question of the Jews as touched on in Chapter 1, or the question of literary Romanticism as touched on in Chapter 5. With few exceptions, works authored by the exiles – and which I have consulted directly – are dealt with in the relevant chapter and are not therefore cited here. Some items consulted on the Web are cited in the footnotes as being 'on-line'. Coverage of most themes is obviously partial. The items cited should give scope for further exploration of the aspects of culture I have tried to present.

Albala, Ken, *Food in Early Modern Europe*, Westport, Conn. 2003

Alberti, Rafael, *La Arboleda Perdida. Memorias*, Barcelona 1959

Alcalá, A., ed., *Judíos, Sefarditas, Conversos*, Valladolid 1995

Al-Da'mi, Muhammed A., *Arabian Mirrors and Western Soothsayers. Nineteenth-century literary approaches to Arab-Islamic history*, New York 2002

Alegria, Fernando and Jorge Ruffinelli, *Paradise Lost or Gained? The literature of Hispanic exile*, Houston, Tex. 1990

Alted, Alicia and Manuel Aznar, eds., *Literatura y Cultura del Exilio español de 1939 en Francia*, Salamanca 1998

Aronsfeld, Caesar C., *The Ghosts of 1492. Jewish aspects of the struggle for religious freedom in Spain 1848–1976*, New York 1979

Aznar, Manuel, ed., *El Exilio Literario español de 1939. Actas del I Congreso Internacional*, 2 vols., Barcelona 1998

Bainton, Roland, *Hunted Heretic*, Boston 1953

Balcells, J. M. and J. A. Pérez Bowie, *El exilio cultural de la Guerra Civil (1936–1939)*, Salamanca 2001

Baldock, Robert, *Pablo Casals*, Boston 1992

Balfour, Sebastian, *El fin del Imperio español (1898–1923)*, Barcelona 1997

Barnette, Douglas, *El Exilio en la Poesia de Luis Cernuda*, El Ferrol 1984

Bataillon, Marcel, *Erasmo y España*, Madrid 1950

Batllori, Miquel, *La Cultura Hispano-Italiana de los Jesuitas expulsos*, Madrid 1966

Beckwith, Stacy N., *Charting Memory: Recalling medieval Spain*, New York 2000

Benbassa, Esther, ed., *Mémoires juives d'Espagne et du Portugal*, Paris 1996

Bernardini, Paolo and Norman Fiering, eds., *The Jews and the Expansion of Europe to the West, 1450 to 1800*, New York 2001

Camprubí, Zenobia, *Diario*, 2 vols., Madrid 1991, 1995

Cárcel Orti, Vicente, *La persecución religiosa en España durante la Segunda Republica (1931–1939)*, Madrid 1990

Caro Baroja, Julio, *Los pueblos de España*, Barcelona 1946

Caro Baroja, Julio, *Los Judíos en la España moderna y contemporánea*, 3 vols., Madrid 1962

Carr, Raymond, *Spain 1808–1939*, Oxford 1966

Carrasco Urgoiti, M. S., *El Moro de Granada en la literatura (del siglo XV al XX)*, Madrid 1956

Casals, Pablo, *Joys and Sorrows. Reflections as told to Albert E. Kahn*, New York 1970

Casanova, Julián, *De la Calle al Frente. El Anarchosindicalismo en España (1931–1939)*, Barcelona 1997

Castro, Américo, *The Structure of Spanish History*, Princeton 1954

Castro, Américo, *The Spaniards. An introduction to their history*, Berkeley 1971

Caudet, Francisco, *Cultura y Exilio. La revista 'España Peregrina' (1940)*, Valencia 1976

Clark, Walter A., *Isaac Albéniz. Portrait of a Romantic*, Oxford 1999

Coleman, David, *Creating Christian Granada. Society and religious culture in an Old-World frontier city, 1492–1600*, Ithaca, NY 2003

Coll, Isabel, *Ramón Casas 1866–1932*, Murcia 2002

Cotarelo y Mori, Emilio, *Bibliografía de las Controversías sobre la licitud del teatro en España*, Madrid 1904

Crichton, Ronald, *Falla*, London 1982

Cutter, Donald C., *Malaspina and Galiano. Spanish voyages to the North-west coast, 1791 and 1792*, Seattle, DC 1991

Defourneaux, Marcelin, *Pablo de Olavide ou l'Afrancesado (1725–1803)*, Paris 1959

Díaz-Más, Paloma, *Sephardim*, Chicago 1992

Dreyfus-Armand, Geneviève, *L'éxil des républicains espagñols en France, de la guerre civile à la mort de Franco*, Paris 1999

Duany, Jorge, *The Puerto Rican Nation on the Move. Identities on the island and in the United States*, Chapel Hill, NC 2002

Dufour, Gerard, *Juan Antonio Llorente en France (1813–1822)*, Geneva 1982

El Exilio Español en México 1939–1982, Mexico 1982

Faber, Sebastiaan, *Exile and Cultural Hegemony. Spanish intellectuals in Mexico, 1939–1975*, Nashville 2002

Figes, Orlando, *Natasha's Dance. A cultural history of Russia*, London 2002

Fraser, Ronald, *Blood of Spain*, Harmondsworth 1979

Friedman, Jerome, *Michael Servetus. A case study in total heresy*, Geneva 1978

Fusi, Juan Pablo, *España. La evolución de la identidad nacional*, Madrid 2000

Gampel, Benjamin R., ed., *Crisis and Creativity in the Sephardic World 1391–1648*, New York 1997

Ganivet, Angel and Miguel Unamuno, *El Porvenir de España*, Madrid 1912

Glasser, Ruth, *My Music is My Flag: Puerto Rican musicians and their New York communities, 1917–1940*, Berkeley 1995

Godzich, Wlad and Nicholas Spadaccini, eds., *The Crisis of Institutionalized Literature in Spain*, Minneapolis 1988

Gómez-Martínez, José Luis, *Américo Castro y el origen de los españoles: historia de una polémica*, Madrid 1975

Gómez-Santos, Marino, *Vida de Gregorio Marañón*, Madrid 1971

Gómez-Santos, Marino, *Españoles sin fronteras*, Barcelona 1983

González, Isidro, *El retorno de los judíos*, Madrid 1991

Goytisolo, Juan, *Disidencias*, Barcelona 1977

Harrison, Joseph and Alan Hoyle, *Spain's 1898 Crisis. Regenerationism, modernism, post-colonialism*, Manchester 2000

Hensbergen, Gijs van, *Guernica: The biography of a twentieth-century icon*, New York 2004

Hess, Carol A., *Enrique Granados. A bio-bibliography*, Westport, Conn. 1991

Hess, Carol A., *Manuel de Falla and Modernism in Spain, 1898–1936*, Chicago 2001

Hess, Carol A., *Sacred Passions. The life and music of Manuel de Falla*, Oxford 2005

Historia General de la Emigración española a Iberoamérica, 2 vols., Madrid 1992

Holguin, Sandie, *Creating Spaniards. Culture and national identity in Republican Spain*, Madison, Wis. 2002

Iberni, Luis G., *Pablo Sarasate*, Madrid 1994

Ilie, Paul, *Literature and Inner Exile. Authoritarian Spain, 1939–1975*, Baltimore 1980

Jiménez, Juan Ramón, *Selección de Cartas (1899–1958)*, Barcelona 1973

Jiménez, Juan Ramón, *Guerra en España (1936–1953)*, Barcelona 1985

Jiménez, Juan Ramón, *Time and Space. A poetic autobiography*, New York 1988

Jiménez, Juan Ramón, *Lírica de una Atlántida*, Barcelona 1999

Jiménez, Juan Ramón, *Diary of a Newlywed Poet*, Selinsgrove 2004

Juliá, Santos, ed., *Víctimas de la Guerra Civil*, Madrid 1999

Kagan, Richard, ed., *Spain in America. The origins of Hispanism in the United States*, Urbana, Ill. 2002

Kamen, Henry, *The Spanish Inquisition. A historical revision*, New Haven, Conn. and London 1993[a]

Kamen, Henry, *The Phoenix and the Flame. Catalonia and the Counter-Reformation*, New Haven, Conn. and London 1993[b]

Kamen, Henry, *Spain's Road to Empire. The making of a world power 1492–1763*, London 2002

Kedourie, Elie, ed., *Spain and the Jews*, London 1992

Keller, Gary D., *The Significance and Impact of Gregorio Marañón*, New York 1977

Kilduff, Martin and Kevin J. Corley, 'The Diaspora Effect: The Influence of Exiles on Their Cultures of Origin', *M@n@gement*, vol.2, no.1, 1999

Kirk, H. L., *Pablo Casals*, New York 1974

Kornberg, Arthur, et al., eds., *Reflections on Biochemistry. In honour of Severo Ochoa*, Oxford 1976

Küster, Lutz, *Obsession der Erinnerung. Das literarische Werk Jorge Sempruns*, Frankfurt 1989

La Expulsión de los Judios de España (II curso de Cultura hispano-judia y sefardi), Toledo 1993

Laín Entralgo, Pedro, *La Generación del Noventa y Ocho*, Madrid 1959

Lisón Tolosana, Carmelo, *Belmonte de los Caballeros. A sociological study of a Spanish town*, Oxford 1966

Llorens, Vicente, *Liberales y románticos: una emigración española en Inglaterra, 1823–1834*, Madrid 1968

Llorens, Vicente, *Aspectos sociales de la literatura española*, Madrid 1974

Llorens, Vicente, *El Romanticismo español*, Madrid 1989

Llorente, Juan Antonio, *Noticia biográfica*, Madrid 1982

López-Baralt, Luce, *Huellas del Islam en la literatura española*, Madrid 1985

López-Baralt, Luce, 'Un codice adicional del Kama Sutra español', in http://www.alyamiah.com/cema/ (2002)

Machado, Antonio, *Poesías completas*, Madrid 1962

Madariaga, Salvador de, *Españoles de mi tiempo*, Barcelona 1974

Manfredi, Dario, *Alessandro Malaspina*, Nanaimo, BC 2001

Marañón, Gregorio, *Españoles fuera de España*, Buenos Aires 1947

Marañón, Luis, *Cultura española y América hispana*, Madrid 1984

Marco, Tomás, *Spanish Music in the Twentieth Century*, Cambridge, Mass. 1993

Martín, José Luis, *Claudio Sánchez-Albornoz*, Valladolid 1986

Melammed, Renée Levine, *A Question of Identity. Iberian conversos in historical perspective*, Oxford 2004

Menéndez Pelayo, Marcelino, *Historia de los Heterodoxos españoles*, 6 vols., Madrid 1963

Menéndez Pidal, Ramón, *The Spaniards in Their History*, trans. Walter Starkie, London 1950

Mestre, Antonio and E. Giménez, *Disidencias y Exilios en la España moderna*, Alicante 1997

Molas, Joaquim, ed., *1898: Entre la crisi d'identitat i la modernització*, Barcelona 2000

Monroe, James T., *Islam and the Arabs in Spanish Scholarship*, Leiden 1970

Moore, Joan and Harry Pachon, *Hispanics in the United States*, New Jersey 1985

Morán, Gregorio, *El Maestro en el Erial. Ortega y Gasset y la cultura del franquismo*, Barcelona 1998

Moreno Alonso, Manuel, *Historiografía romántica española*, Seville 1979

Murphy, Martin, *Blanco White. Self-banished Spaniard*, New Haven, Conn. and London 1989

Naharro-Calderón, J. M., ed., *El Exilio de las Españas de 1939 en las Américas: adonde fue la canción?* Barcelona 1991

Netanyahu, Benzion, *Don Isaac Abravanel*, Philadelphia 1968

Netanyahu, Benzion, *The Origins of the Inquisition in Fifteenth-Century Spain*, New York 1995

Newman, Jean Cross, *Pedro Salinas and his Circumstance*, San Juan, Puerto Rico 1983

Nino Rodríguez, Antonio, *Cultura y Diplomacia: los hispanistas franceses y España de 1875 a 1931*, Madrid 1988

Otte, Enrique, *Cartas privadas de emigrantes a Indias 1540–1616*, Seville 1988

Ouimette, Victor, *Los intelectuales españoles y el naufragio del liberalismo (1923–1936)*, 2 vols., Valencia 1998

Payne, Stanley G., *Spain's First Democracy: The Second Republic 1931–1936*, Madison, Wis. 1993

Payne, Stanley G., *The Spanish Civil War, the Soviet Union, and Communism*. New Haven, Conn. and London 2004

Peers, Edgar Allison, *A History of the Romantic Movement in Spain*, 2 vols., Cambridge 1940

Pérez Villanueva, Joaquín, *Ramón Menéndez Pidal, su vida y su tiempo*, Madrid 1991

Pike, Fredrick B., *Hispanismo 1898–1936. Spanish conservatives and Liberals and their relations with Spanish America*, Notre Dame, Ind. 1971

Pimentel, Juan, *La Física de la Monarquía. Ciencia y politica en el pensamiento colonial de Alejandro Malaspina (1754–1810)*, Madrid 1998

Pitt-Rivers, Julian, *The People of the Sierra*, 2nd edn, Chicago 1971

Prescott, William H., *History of the Reign of Ferdinand and Isabella the Catholic*, London 1841

Radomski, James, *Manuel García (1775–1832). Chronicle of the life of a bel canto tenor at the dawn of Romanticism*, Oxford 2000

Ramón y Cajal, Santiago, *Obras literarias completas*, Madrid 1947

Raphael, David, ed., *The Expulsion 1492 Chronicles*, Hollywood 1992

Riba, Carles, *Cartes de Carles Riba*, 3 vols., Barcelona 1991

Romero, Justo, *Isaac Albéniz*, Barcelona 2002

Roth, Norman, *Conversos, Inquisition and the Expulsion of the Jews from Spain*, Madison, Wis. 1995

Rubia, José, *Américo Castro and the Meaning of Spanish Civilization*, Berkeley 1976

Rubio, Javier, *La emigración de la guerra civil de 1936–1939*, 3 vols., Madrid 1977

Ruspoli, Enrique, *La Marca del Exilio*, Madrid 1992

Sachar, Howard M., *Adios España*, Barcelona 1995

Said, Edward W., *Reflections on Exile and Other Essays*, Cambridge, Mass. 2000

Sánchez-Albornoz, Claudio, *España. Un enigma histórico*, 2 vols., Buenos Aires 1971

Sánchez Mantero, Rafael, *Liberales en el exilio*, Madrid 1975

Santesmases, María, Jesús, *Entre Cajal y Ochoa*, Madrid 2001

Sarrailh, Jean, *L'Espagne éclairée de la seconde moitié du XVIIIe siècle*, Paris 1954

Serrano, Carlos, ed., *Nations en quête du passé. Le péninsule ibérique (XIXe–XXe siècles)*, Paris 2000

Sorolla y la Hispanic Society, Madrid 1999

Starkie, Walter, *Spain. A musician's journey through time and space*, 2 vols., Geneva 1958

Stavans, Ilan, *The Hispanic Condition. Reflections on culture and identity in America*, New York 1995

Stillman, Y. K. and N. A. Stillman, *From Iberia to Diaspora*, Leiden 1999

Swinburne, Henry, *Travels through Spain in the Years 1775 and 1776*, 2 vols., London 1787

The New Grove Dictionary of Music and Musicians, 2nd edn, London 2001

Tinterow, Gary and Genevieve Lacambre, *Manet/Velazquez. The French taste for Spanish painting*, New Haven, Conn. and London 2003

Torrecilla, Jesús, *El Tiempo y los Márgenes. Europa como utopía y como amenaza en la literatura española*, Chapel Hill, NC 1996

Townsend, Joseph, *A Journey through Spain in the Years 1786 and 1787*, 3 vols., London 1791

Ucelay-Da Cal, Enric, *El imperialismo catalán. Prat de la Riba, Cambó, D'Ors y la conquista moral de España*, Barcelona 2003

Ugarte, Michael, *Shifting Ground. Spanish Civil War exile literature*, Durham, NC 1989

Ungerer, Gustav, *A Spaniard in Elizabethan England: The correspondence of Antonio Perez's exile*, 2 vols., London 1975, 1976

Valera, Juan, *Epistolario de Valera y Menéndez Pelayo 1877–1905*, Madrid 1946

Valera, Juan, *151 Cartas inéditas a Gumersindo Laverde*, Madrid 1984

Valle, José del and Luis Gabriel-Stheeman, *The Battle over Spanish between 1800 and 2000. Language ideologies and Hispanic intellectuals*, London 2002

Valverde, José María, *Azorín*, Barcelona 1971

Valverde, José María, *Antonio Machado*, Madrid 1975

Vived, Jesús, *Ramón J. Sender. Biografía*, Madrid 2002

Vives, Juan Luis, *Epistolario*, ed. J. Jiménez Delgado, Madrid 1978

Wiegers, Gerard A., *Het Inquisitieproces van Alonso de Luna*, Nijmegen 2004 (on-line)

Willughby, Francis, *A Relation of a Voyage through a Great Part of Spain*, London 1673

Yerushalmi, Yosef Hayim, *From Spanish Court to Italian Ghetto. Isaac Cardoso: A study in seventeenth-century Marranism and Jewish apologetics*, New York 1971

Notes

PREFACE

1. The almost limitless varieties of recent diaspora are shown by the Internet web page listing, titled 'Border Crossings', drawn up by scholars at the University of Iowa.

2. Said, p.173.

3. However, the United States has had its own share of exile-expatriates, from the 80,000 Loyalist settlers who fled the coming of the American Revolution, to the thousands of Southerners who left the country when the Civil War ended, and the thousands of black slaves who fled to Canada and Africa in the nineteenth century. Nor should one omit the elite cultural figures (the artists Whistler and Sargent, for example, and, above all, the novelist Henry James, who became a British citizen in 1915) who chose Europe as their inspiration in the same century, to be followed a generation later by prominent literary figures (Hemingway, T. S. Eliot, Ezra Pound, Hart Crane and, much later, James Baldwin).

4. Thomas Sowell, *Migrations and Cultures. A world view*, New York 1996, mentions every nation but Spain, and touches only briefly on Spain's Jews.

5. Dreyfus-Armand, p.20.

6. It is common to refer to the 'union' of Castile and Aragon, as Marañón does here, but in reality there was no political union until over two hundred years later.

7. Marañón 1947, p.22.

8. Cf. the magnificent presentation in Orlando Figes, *Natasha's Dance*.

9. Here, and at very many other points of this book, there is a temptation to draw parallels (in this case with the Slavophiles of Russia), but comparisons would have led to an extraordinarily long work. The informed reader can make his own comparisons.

10. Said, p.175.

PRELUDE

1. Prescott, p.327.
2. Isabella's authority was accepted in Catalonia only because she was the wife of the king; otherwise she was queen only of Castile and had no right to rule in the realms of the Crown of Aragon, of which Catalonia was a part.

1. THE SURVIVAL OF THE JEW

1. Quoted in Yerushalmi, p.437.
2. Cf. David Romano, 'Rasgos de la minoría judía en la Corona de Aragón', in C. Barros, ed., *Xudeus e Conversos na Historia*, 2 vols., Santiago 1994, II, pp.229–30.
3. Yitzhak Baer, *Die Juden im christlichen Spanien (Urkunden und Regesten II)*, Berlin 1936, pp.411–13.
4. Joseph Ha Cohen and Rabbi Capsali, in Raphael, pp.17, 106.
5. C. Carrete Parrondo, 'Nostalgia for the past', *Mediterranean Historical Review*, vol.6, no.2, 1991, p.35.
6. For a discussion of figures, see Henry Kamen, 'The Mediterranean and the Expulsion of Spanish Jews in 1492', *Past and Present*, 119, 1988.
7. Jaume Riera Sans, 'Judíos y conversos en los reinos de la Corona de Aragón durante el siglo XV', in *La Expulsión*.
8. Rabbi Ha Levi, in Raphael, p.87.
9. Recent opinions include those of Maurice Kriegel, in Barros, *Xudeus e Conversos*, I, p.188: 'no document drawn up by the sovereigns makes any reference to the idea that liquidation of religious plurality was desirable'.
10. Alonso de Zurita, *Historia del rey Don Hernando el Catholico*, 6 vols., Saragossa 1610, I, p.9.
11. The point, well known to specialists in the period, is reaffirmed by Roth, p.313.
12. Caro Baroja 1962, I, part 1, chaps. xi–xiv, gives a useful summary of where they went.
13. Raphael, p.120.
14. Caro Baroja 1962, I, part 1, p.220.
15. Raphael, p.42.
16. Beinart, in Kedourie.
17. From a lecture delivered at Brandeis University in 1959, printed in *Orbis*, 1967.
18. Raphael, p.54.
19. Netanyahu 1968, pp.201–4.

20. Netanyahu 1968, p.249.
21. Eric Lawee, *Isaac Abarbanel's Stance toward Tradition*, New York 2001, p.162.
22. Though Jews had been expelled from the peninsula, they were tolerated in all the other territories that were ruled by the monarchy of Spain.
23. Seymour Feldman, *Philosophy in a Time of Crisis*, London 2003, p.167.
24. Angel Sáenz-Badillos, 'Literatura hebrea y pensamiento entre los judíos en el siglo XVI', in *La Expulsión*.
25. Most Jewish immigrants to France came from Portugal: see Gérard Nahon, 'Cristianos nuevos españoles y portugueses en Francia', in Alcalá, pp.282–97.
26. Some Jewish historians continue to use the term crypto-Jews when talking of conversos, apparently because they feel that conversos would never really have been Christians.
27. Excellently summarized in Netanyahu 1995, pp.995–6, from whom I take the examples that follow.
28. Cited in Kamen 1993[a], p.42.
29. Riera Sans, op. cit., p.85.
30. For a general survey, see Kamen 1993[a].
31. Quoted in Raphael, pp.136–7.
32. Cf. José-Carlos Gómez-Menor, 'Linaje judío de escritores religiosos y místicos españoles del siglo XVI', in Alcalá, pp.587–600. However, Gómez-Menor gives no documentary sources, and there is certainly no evidence for the Jewish origins of some names he cites.
33. The 'converso' interpretation was expressed most forcefully by the Harvard professor Stephen Gilman, in his *The Spain of Fernando de Rojas: The intellectual and social landscape of La Celestina*, Princeton 1972.
34. The useful summary by Carlos Mota-Placencia, 'Más sobre el presunto judaísmo de *Celestina*', in Stillman and Stillman, p.294, gives full references to other essays on the theme.
35. For all my quotes from Vives, see his *Epistolario*, and Angel Gómez Hortiguela, *Luis Vives entre líneas*, Valencia 1993.
36. The circumstances of this invitation are explained in my *The Duke of Alba*, New Haven, Conn. and London 2004, chap. 2.
37. Miguel de la Pinta Llorente and J. M. de Palacio, *Procesos inquisitoriales contra la familia judía de Juan Luis Vives*, Madrid 1964.
38. J. L. Vives, *On Assistance to the Poor*, Toronto 1999, p.18.
39. Cited by Marañón 1947, p.145.
40. Castro 1954, p.578. The emphasis is Castro's.
41. Yosef Kaplan, 'The travels of Portuguese Jews from Amsterdam to the

"lands of idolatry" 1644–1724', in Kaplan, ed., *Jews and Conversos. Studies in society and the Inquisition*, Jerusalem 1985.

42. Miriam Bodian, '"Men of the nation": the shaping of converso identity in early modern Europe', *Past and Present*, 143, 1994, p.66.

43. Constance Rose, 'Antonio Enríquez Gómez and the Literature of Exile', *Romanische Forschungen*, 85, 1973; N. Kramer-Hellinx, 'Antonio Enríquez Gómez: desafío de la Inquisición', in Barros, *Xudeus e Conversos*, I, pp.289–307.

44. David L. Graizbord, *Souls in Dispute. Converso identities in Iberia and the Jewish Diaspora, 1580–1700*, Philadelphia 2004, p.1.

45. Cf. Moshe Idel, 'Religion, thought and attitudes: the impact of the expulsion', in Kedourie, p.130.

46. Cf. Sáenz-Badillos, op. cit., pp.182–5.

47. Nikolai Kochev, 'Sephardic Jews and printing in the Balkans', *Annual*, vol.xxiv, Sofia 1989, p.26.

48. Menahem Schmelzer, 'Hebrew manuscripts and printed books among the Sephardim before and after the Expulsion', in Gampel, p.264.

49. Yerushalmi, p.64.

50. Ruspoli, p.99.

51. Yerushalmi, p.153.

52. On Sabbatai, of course, the classic study is that of Gershom Scholem, *Sabbatai Sevi, the mystical Messiah, 1626–1676*, Princeton 1973.

53. The view that the world is made up of atoms.

54. Cf. Yerushalmi, pp.271–301.

55. One example is Benito de Peñalosa, *Libro de las Cinco Excelencias del Español*, Pamplona 1629.

56. Quoted in Yerushalmi, p.383.

57. Graizbord, op. cit., pp.6–7.

58. Details from the superb study by Yosef Kaplan, *From Christianity to Judaism. The story of Isaac Orobio de Castro*, Oxford 1989.

59. Ibid., p.329.

60. None of the authors in Bernardini and Fiering (see Select Bibliography) identifies any Spanish Jews in the New World before around 1800.

61. Some Jewish historians, of course, continue to search for proofs that Jews were the pioneers in the New World. Cf. the comments of Michael P. Carroll, 'The debate over a crypto-Jewish presence in New Mexico: the role of ethnographic allegory and orientalism', *Sociology of Religion*, spring 2002.

62. A useful short survey is Donald McGrady, *Mateo Alemán*, New York 1968.

63. Francisco Márquez Villanueva, 'El canto de cisne de Mateo Alemán', in *Inquisición y conversos. III Curso de Cultura Hispano-Judía*, Toledo 1994.

64. Cf. J. A. Maravall, *La literatura picaresca desde la historia social*, Madrid 1986, p.253.

65. *Guzmán de Alfarache*, p.438.

66. Carr, p.174.

67. On Amador and the nineteenth-century historians who dealt with the Jews, see Roberto López Vela, 'Judíos, fanatismo y decadencia. Amador de los Ríos y la interpretación de la historia nacional en 1848', *Manuscrits* (Barcelona), 17, 1999.

68. Quoted in Isidro González, *El retorno de los judíos*, Madrid 1991, p.160.

69. 'The entire field of Sephardic research was introduced by non-Jewish scholars and is even today dominated by scholars whose only training is in Spanish literature and language and have no knowledge of Hebrew literature.' Norman Roth, 'What constitutes Sephardic culture?', in Stillman and Stillman, p.252.

70. *Attitudes Toward Jews in 12 European Countries*, Anti-Defamation League, New York 2005 (on-line).

71. Isidro González, op. cit., p.68.

72. Sara E. Schyfter, *The Jew in the Novels of Benito Pérez Galdós*, London 1978.

73. Aronsfeld, p.12.

74. Caro Baroja 1962, III, p.208.

75. The chair was a flop, apparently because there were no students, and the professor left a few years later.

76. Cited in Ucelay-Da Cal, p.659.

77. Benbassa, pp.13-14.

78. Yitzchak Kerem, 'The Europeanization of the Sephardic community of Salonika', in Stillman and Stillman, p.73.

79 Ucelay-Da Cal, p.662.

80. Díaz-Más, p.160.

81. Cf. Israel J. Katz, 'El legado musical de la diaspora sefardí', in Alcalá, pp.365-92.

82. There is a good short discussion of *ladino* in chapter 3 of Díaz-Más, notably pp.75-7.

83. Depending on the part of Europe, the language was also known as Espanyol, Sephardi, Judio or Judezmo.

84. The arguments of Isaac Jerusalmi, 'El ladino, lengua del judaísmo y habla diaria', in Alcalá, pp.301-18, are convincing.

85. See in particular Mark Mazower, *Salonica, City of Ghosts: Christians,*

Muslims and Jews, 1430–1950, New York 2005. I am grateful to Simon Winder for this reference.

86. Sánchez-Albornoz, II, pp.206, 258, 164. A penetrating look at Sánchez-Albornoz's views on Jews is given by Benzion Netanyahu, 'Una vision española de la historia judía en España: Sánchez-Albornoz', in Alcalá, pp.89–117.

87. The fullest outline of Castro's views is given by Guillermo Araya, *El pensamiento de Américo Castro*, Madrid 1983.

88. Goytisolo, p.142.

89. The loyalty of his followers was impressive. When during a visit to Harvard I called on one of Castro's former students, who by then was a well-known professor, he sat me down and his first question to me was: 'Tell me, Professor Kamen, what is your position on Don Américo?'

90. For example, Eugenio Asensio, *La España imaginada de Américo Castro*, Barcelona 1976.

91. Haim Avni, *Spain, the Jews and Franco*, Philadelphia 1982, p.186.

2. THE PERSISTENCE OF THE MOOR

1. Quoted in Beckwith, p.284.

2. Irving, *Tales of the Alhambra* (several editions, also on-line), chap. 8. Irving relates that when Charles V, on a visit to Granada, was told of Abdallah's story, he exclaimed that he 'would rather have made this Alhambra my sepulchre than have lived without a kingdom in the Alpujarra' mountains.

3. Diego Saglia, 'The Moor's last sigh: Spanish-Moorish exoticism', *Journal of English Studies*, vol.3, 2002.

4. M. A. Ladero, 'Mudejares and repobladores in the kingdom of Granada', *Mediterranean Historical Review*, vol.6, no.2, 1991.

5. For *aljamiado*, see below, this chapter.

6. Mercedes García Arenal, *Los Moriscos*, Granada 1996, pp.33–41.

7. Louis Cardaillac, *Morisques et chrétiens. Un affrontement polémique (1492–1640)*, Paris 1977.

8. L. García Ballester, *Medicina, ciencia y minorías marginadas: los Moriscos*, Granada 1977.

9. Cardaillac, op. cit., p.100.

10. Diego Hurtado de Mendoza, *Guerra de Granada*, Barcelona 1842, p.80.

11. Don Juan to Ruy Gómez, 5 Nov. 1570, *Colección de Documentos Inéditos para la Historia de España*, XXXVIII, 156.

12. The following details are drawn from the authoritative study by Henri Lapeyre, *Géographie de l'Espagne morisque*, Paris 1959.

13. For some cases, see Rosa Blasco, 'Los Moriscos que permanecieron en el obispado de Orihuela después de 1609', *Sharq al-Andalus*, 6, 1989.

14. Quoted in R. L. Kagan and Abigail Dyer, *Inquisitorial Inquiries: Brief lives of secret Jews and other heretics*, Baltimore 2004, p.126.

15. Martine Ravillard, *Bibliographie commentée des Morisques*, Algiers 1979.

16. Cited in G. Gozalbes Busto, *Los Moriscos en Marruecos*, Granada 1992, p.115.

17. Beebe Bahrami, 'Al-Andalus and Memory: the past and being present among Hispano-Moroccan Andalusians from Rabat', in Beckwith, pp.127, 137.

18. For aspects of the continuing Hispanic memory among exiles, see Míkel de Epalza and Ramon Petit, eds., *Recueil d'Études sur les moriscos andalous en Tunisie*, Madrid and Tunis 1973. I am grateful to Luce López-Baralt for this reference.

19. Susan T. Rivers, 'Exiles from Andalusia', *Aramco World*, vol.42, no.4, 1991.

20. On Cervantes' views, cf. F. Márquez Villanueva, *Personajes y temas del Quijote*, Madrid 1975.

21. Luce López-Baralt, '"Al revés de los cristianos": la España invertida de la literatura aljamiado-morisca', in J. M. Díez Borque, *Culturas de la Edad de Oro*, Madrid 1995, p.215.

22. Cited in López-Baralt 2002, who draws on the research of Mikel de Epalza.

23. For what follows, see Expiración García-Sánchez, 'Agriculture in Muslim Spain', and David Waines, 'The Culinary Culture of al-Andalus', in S. K. Jayyusi, ed., *The Legacy of Muslim Spain*, Leiden 1992.

24. Rivers, op. cit.

25. Quoted in Helen Nader, *The Mendoza Family in the Spanish Renaissance*, New Brunswick, NJ 1979, p.187.

26. López Baralt 1985: 'El Moro en la literature española renacentista'.

27. I follow in part the exposition in Barbara Fuchs, *Mimesis and Empire. The New World, Islam and European identities*, Cambridge 2001.

28. I have consulted the Madrid 1913 reprint of the first edition of 1595.

29. D. Cabanelas, 'Intento de supervivencia en el ocaso de una cultura: los libros plumbeos de Granada', *Nueva Revista de Filología Hispánica*, 30, 1981. There is a good discussion of the matter in Coleman, pp.189–201.

30. Wiegers, p.12.

31. Wiegers, pp.13–14, puts forward the idea of Luna as the possible author. However, he also says in another essay: 'It seems most likely that the author

was a European convert to Islam who wrote in Istanbul and was in close contact with Moriscos in Tunis, Spain and Morocco' (Wiegers, 'European converts to Islam in the Maghrib and the polemical writings of the Moriscos', in Mercedes García-Arenal, *Conversions islamiques. Identités religieuses en Islam méditerranéen*, Paris 2001, p.212).

32. Available in several published editions, and also as an e-document on the Internet.

33. The best summary of research on *The Gospel of Barnabas* is by Jan Slomp, 'The Gospel of Barnabas in recent research', *Islamochristiana*, 23, 1997. Basic contributions to the idea of a Morisco origin came from M. de Epalza, 'Le milieu hispano-moresque de l'Évangile islamisant de Barnabé (XVI–XVIIe s.)', *Islamochristiana*, 8, 1982, and more recently from Luis Bernabé, 'Los mecanismos de una resistencia: los libros plúmbeos del Sacromonte y el *Evangelio de Barnabé*', *al-Qantara*, XXIII, 2, 2002.

34. Our information on Alonso de Luna comes from his statements to the Inquisition in Archivo Histórico Nacional, Madrid, Inquisición leg.1953, reproduced for example in Bernard Vincent, 'Et quelques voix de plus: de Francisco Núñez Muley à Fatima Ratal', *Sharq al-Andalus*, 12, 1995, pp.142–4.

35. Castro 1954, chapter VIII, 'Islamic tradition and Spanish life'.

36. López-Baralt 1985, p.95; and in more detail in her *The Sufi trobar clus and Spanish Mysticism: A shared symbolism*, Lahore 2000.

37. Anita González, 'La Inquisición en las fronteras del Mediterráneo. Historia de los renegados, 1540–1694', *Areas*, 9, 1988, pp.51–74. The phenomenon of renegades could also be found among Christian Italians.

38. *Account of an Embassy from Morocco to Spain in 1690 and 1691*, no date or place given.

39. For Philip V and Africa, see my *Philip V of Spain. The king who reigned twice*, New Haven, Conn. and London 2001.

40. Ronald Hilton, *La Légende Noire au 18e Siècle: Le monde hispanique vu du dehors*, 2002 (on-line).

41. Cited in Monroe, p.55.

42. Al-Da'mi, p.168.

43. A good introduction is A. L. Macfie, *Orientalism*, London 2002. It is usual to cite the work by Edward Said as an explanation of the cultural trend, but a more scholarly look at the topic is offered by John Mackenzie, *Orientalism, History, Theory and the Arts*, London 1995.

44. Richard Ford, *A Hand-Book for Travellers in Spain, and Readers at Home*, 3 vols., reprinted, Carbondale, Ill. 1966.

45. Ford, II, p.554.

46. Dominique Jarrassé, 'Sefarad imaginaire: le style hispano-mauresque dans les synagogues françaises du XIXe siècle', in Benbassa.

47. Josep M. Fradera, 'Domingo Badía Leblich/Ali Bey: una idea sin Estado', in A. Morales, ed., *1802. España entre dos siglos*, Madrid 2003, p.453.

48. Much of what follows is derived from Monroe.

49. Cf. López-Baralt, 1985, pp.123–6.

50. Raymond Schwab, *The Oriental Renaissance*, New York 1984, p.482. Schwab's work first appeared in French in 1950.

51. José Zorrilla, *Obras Completas*, 2 vols., Valladolid 1943, I, pp.1207, 1220.

52. Ibid., II, p.620.

53. The best survey of Fortuny is the exhibition catalogue *Fortuny 1838–1874*, Barcelona 1989.

54. Edward J. Sullivan, 'Fortuny in America: his collectors and disciples', in *Fortuny 1838–1874*, p.105.

55. Ernesto Giménez Caballero, *Notas marruecas de un soldado*, Barcelona 1983, p.28. See also the useful article by Luis J. Sánchez Marco, 'La identidad nacional y la guerra de Marruecos', in *Actas de las III Jornadas de Historia de Llerena*, Llerena 2002.

56. The definitive study is D. Woolman, *Rebels in the Riff*, Oxford 1969.

57. Arturo Barea, *La forja de un rebelde: la ruta*, Madrid 1984, p.79.

58. In Ganivet and Unamuno, letter to Unamuno printed in the press in Granada in 1898.

59. The new Socialist government in 2004 proclaimed that its aim was a new 'Alliance of Civilizations', based on an alliance between Spain and Morocco, to bring peace to the world.

60. The important and scholarly study of Spanish literature by Otis H. Green, *Spain and the Western Tradition*, 4 vols., Madison, Wis. 1968, completely omits any mention of Muslim (or Jewish) influence on Hispanic literature.

61. Quoted in Monroe, p.247.

62. Menéndez Pidal, p.216.

63. J. A. González, 'El auto fallido sacromontano', *al-Qantara*, XXIV, 2, 2003, p.553.

64. Mariano Peset, 'Claudio Sánchez-Albornoz, un medievalista en el exilio', in Balcells and Pérez Bowie.

65. Sánchez-Albornoz, I, p.189.

66. Sánchez-Albornoz, II, p.714.

67. Reuven Suir, 'Al-Andalus arising from Damascus', in Beckwith, p.264.

3. THE WARS OF RELIGION

1. Sánchez-Albornoz, II, p.563.

2. José Alvarez Junco, *Mater Dolorosa. La idea de España en el siglo XIX*, Madrid 2001.

3. C. Carrete Parrondo, 'Nostalgia for the past', *Mediterranean Historical Review*, vol.6, no.2, 1991, p.33.

4. William Christian Jr., *Local Religion in Sixteenth-Century Spain*, Princeton 1981.

5. C. Carrete Parrondo, *Fontes Iudaeorum regni Castellae, vol. II: El Tribunal de la Inquisición en el Obispado de Soria (1486–1502)*, Salamanca 1985, pp.37, 79. The statement, attributed to a priest, went on to state: 'and have a nice woman friend and eat well'.

6. Kamen 1993[a], p.82.

7. For what follows, cf. Kamen 1993[a].

8. Cf. Richard L. Kagan, *Lucrecia's Dreams. Politics and prophecy in sixteenth-century Spain*, Berkeley 1990.

9. J. Le Goff, *The Birth of Purgatory*, London 1984.

10. Lisón Tolosana's opinion is that despite profanity, excess and ignorance, the villagers he studies had become Christian by the nineteenth century: Lisón Tolosana, p.281.

11. P. P. Delgado Alemany and J. Serra i Barceló, 'La reglamentació del Carnaval', in *Espai i Temps d'oci*, Palma 1993, pp.341–6.

12. Valverde 1975, p.104.

13. Lisón Tolosana, p.264.

14. Cotarelo y Mori, pp.57, 129, 217.

15. Willughby, p.496.

16. Natalie Davis, *The Return of Martin Guerre*, Cambridge, Mass. 1983.

17. Cristóbal de Castillejo, *Diálogo de Mujeres*, ed. Rogelio Reyes, Madrid 1986.

18. For what follows, I rely on Bataillon, pp.676–92, still the best summary.

19. Jesús Gómez, *El diálogo en el Renacimiento español*, Madrid 1988.

20. Cf. Bataillon, p.685.

21. Ibid., p.511.

22. Cf. Alastair Hamilton, *Heresy and Mysticism in Sixteenth-Century Spain: The Alumbrados*, Cambridge 1992, pp.91–7.

23. Quoted in Laín Entralgo, p.127.

24. Hamilton, op. cit., p.97.

25. The Theatines were a new religious order founded in Italy at this period, noted for their spiritual discipline; Spaniards used the term to disparage the newly formed Jesuits.

26. Cándido de Dalmases SJ, 'San Francisco de Borja y la Inquisición española, 1559–61', *Archivum Historicum Societatis Iesu*, 41, 1972.

27. Quoted in Luis Gil Fernández, *Panorama social del humanismo español (1500–1800)*, Madrid 1981, p.488.

28. Starkie, I, p.106.

29. Robert Stevenson, 'Tomas Luis de Victoria', in *The New Grove High Renaissance Masters*, London 1984, p.293.

30. Bainton, p.74.

31. Quoted in part in Bainton, p.94. I have retouched parts of the quotation.

32. My text is shortened and adapted from that given in Josep Trueta, *The Spirit of Catalonia*, Oxford 1946, p.71.

33. Matteo Realdo Colombo (1516–59) was pupil and then successor of Vesalius at the University of Padua. His work, *De Re Anatomica*, was published after his death in 1559, then translated into English in 1578 and German in 1609. One of his patients was Michelangelo.

34. Cf. Friedman, pp.17, 133.

35. Ibid., p.99.

36. In the late fifteenth century, by contrast, many writers, such as Queen Isabella's secretary Hernando del Pulgar, had questioned whether the death penalty was an appropriate punishment for heresy.

37. Cf. Joseph Lecler, *Toleration and the Reformation*, 2 vols., London 1960, I, p.329.

38. *Contra libellum Calvini* (1612), cited ibid., I, p.355.

39. Quoted in Lawrence and Nancy Goldstone, *Out of the Flames*, New York 2002, p.257.

40. J. E. Longhurst, *Erasmus and the Spanish Inquisition: The case of Juan de Valdés*, Albuquerque 1950; J. C. Nieto, *Juan de Valdés (1509?–1541)*, Michigan 1968; Bataillon, *Erasmo y el Erasmismo*, Barcelona 1977, pp.245–85; Carlos Gilly, 'Juan de Valdés: Übersetzer und Bearbeiter von Luthers Schriften in seinem *Diálogo de Doctrina*', *Archiv für Reformationsgeschichte*, 74, 1983.

41. A good brief introduction is A. Gordon Kinder, 'Spain's little-known "Noble Army of Martyrs" and the Black Legend', in Lesley Twomey, ed., *Faith and Fanaticism. Religious fervour in Early Modern Spain*, Aldershot 1997.

42. Henry Charles Lea, *A History of the Inquisition of Spain*, 4 vols., New York 1906–08, III, p.419.

43. Edward Boehmer, *Bibliotheca Wiffeniana: Spanish reformers of two centuries, from 1520*, 3 vols., London 1874–1904.

44. A. Gordon Kinder, 'Cipriano de Valera, Spanish reformer', *Bulletin of*

Hispanic Studies, 46, 1969; and his *Casiodoro de Reina*, London 1975. For the Seville community, Ernst Schäfer, *Beiträge zur Geschichte des spanischen Protestantismus und der Inquisition*, 3 vols., Gütersloh 1902, I, pp.345–67; II, pp.271–426.

45. The exact number is uncertain. For the figures in this paragraph I have been guided in part by W. Monter, 'Heresy executions in Reformation Europe, 1520–1565', in O. P. Grell and B. Scribner, *Tolerance and Intolerance in the European Reformation*, Cambridge 1996.

46. Philip to Valdés, 23 Aug. 1560, Collection Favre, Bibliothèque Publique et Universitaire, Geneva, vol.29 f.4.

47. Thomas Werner, *La represión del protestantismo en España, 1517–1648*, Leuven 2001, p.viii.

48. Quadra to Philip II, London, 11 Oct. 1561, Archives du Ministère des Affaires Etrangères, Paris, Correspondance Politique, Mémoires et Documents vol.234 f.105.

49. Guzmán de Silva to Philip II, London, 26 Apr. 1565, *Colección de Documentos Inéditos para la Historia de España*, XXVI, p.540.

50. Canto's detailed memorandum of 1563, in Archivo General de Simancas, section Consejo y Juntas de Hacienda, leg.55 f.174, gives a good sketch of Spanish heretics in Europe.

51. Canto to Eraso, Brussels, 12 May 1564, Archivo General de Simancas, section Estado, leg.526 f.125.

52. Cf. Bataillon, pp.552–5.

53. Laurie Kaplis-Hohwald, *Translation of the Biblical Psalms in Golden Age Spain*, Lampeter 2003, p.3.

54. Jorge A. González, *Casiodoro de Reina*, Mexico 1969.

55. Cf. Bataillon, p.514.

56. Nicolas Castrillo, *El 'Reginaldo Montano': primer libro polémico contra la Inquisición Española*, Madrid 1991, p.31.

57. Fadrique Furió Ceriol, *El Concejo y Consejeros del Príncipe*, Madrid 1978 edn, p.190.

58. This brief account is based on Menéndez Pelayo, V, pp.9–82; G. Marañón, 'El proceso del arzobispo Carranza', *Boletín de la Real Academia de la Historia*, 127, 1950, pp.135–78; Lea, op. cit., II, pp.48–86; and J. I. Tellechea, *El arzobispo Carranza y su Tiempo*, 2 vols., Madrid 1968, I, pp.23–6. The various studies by Tellechea on Carranza are definitive; but there is still no adequate biography.

59. Cf. J. I. Tellechea, in *Historia de la Inquisición en España y América*, 2 vols., Madrid 1984–1993, I, p.566 (the best summary of the case).

60. Cf. J. I. Tellechea, 'Molinos y el quietismo español', in R. García-Villoslada,

ed., *Historia de la Iglesia en España*, vol.IV, Madrid 1979, pp.475–521.

61. Some recent discussions include Ullman, mentioned below, note 65; and Frances Lannon, *Privilege, Persecution, and Prophecy: The Catholic Church in Spain, 1875–1975*, Oxford 1987.

62. Timothy Mitchell, *Betrayal of the Innocents. Desire, power and the Catholic Church in Spain*, Philadelphia 1998, p.56.

63. M. A. Fernández García, *Inquisición, comportamiento y mentalidad en el reino de Granada (1600–1700)*, Granada 1989, p.247.

64. William J. Callahan, *Church, Politics, and Society in Spain, 1750–1874*, Cambridge, Mass. 1984, p.155.

65. The classic study is Joan Connelly Ullman, *The Tragic Week. A study of anticlericalism in Spain, 1875–1912*, Cambridge, Mass. 1968.

66. Cárcel Orti, p.109.

67. For anti-religious terror in the Madrid diocese, see J. L. Alfaya, *Como un río de fuego. Madrid 1936*, Barcelona 1998.

68. Stanley G. Payne, *El catolicismo español*, Barcelona 1984, p.214.

69. Juliá, p.154.

70. Quoted in Cárcel Orti, p.210.

71. Juliá, p.20.

72. Ibid., p.353.

73. Cf. Julio de la Cueva Merino, 'El anticlericalismo en la Segunda República y la Guerra Civil', in E. La Parra López and M. Suárez Cortina, eds., *El anticlericalismo español contemporáneo*, Madrid 1998, p.285.

74. Cárcel Orti, p.275.

4. THE DISCOVERY OF 'EUROPE'

1. Torrecilla, p.56.

2. Here I use quotations from the one-volume English edition by Gregorio Marañón, *Antonio Pérez, 'Spanish Traitor'*, London 1954, pp.11, 13.

3. Isabel Martínez Navas, 'Proceso inquisitorial de Antonio Pérez', *Revista de la Inquisición*, 1, 1991, p.191.

4. Ungerer, I, p.42.

5. Ibid., I, pp.73, 145. Elizabeth was kept under close watch during the reign of her sister Queen Mary, who had married Philip II, but she was protected both by the king and by Gonzalo Pérez.

6. Pérez's homosexual propensities are lucidly discussed in Ungerer, I, pp.191–202.

7. Cited in Ungerer, I, p.304.

8. Ibid., I, p.69.

9. Ibid., II, p.324.

10. Cited in ibid., II, p.325.

11. 'Discurso al Rey nuestro Señor del estado que tienen sus reynos', dated 'en la cárcel y Otubre 7 de 1598': Biblioteca Nacional, Madrid, MS.904 f.284–5. The text has recently been published (Madrid 1990).

12. The variety of ideas shared by Tacitists is difficult to summarize.

13. Marquis of Villena, November 1700, in Manuel Danvila, *El poder civil en España*, 6 vols., Madrid 1885, III, p.369.

14. Miguel Morán, *La imagen del rey. Felipe V y el arte*, Madrid 1990, pp.81–3.

15. Yves Bottineau, *El arte cortesano en la España de Felipe V (1700–1746)*, Madrid 1986, p.197.

16. The technical details of the changes are summarized in the useful essay by José Antonio Escudero, 'La reconstrucción de la administración central en el siglo XVIII', in his *Administración y Estado en la España moderna*, Valladolid 1999.

17. Henry Kamen, *The War of Succession in Spain, 1700–1715*, London and Bloomington, Ind. 1969, pp.96–9.

18. Archivo Histórico Nacional, Madrid, Consejos legs.7240, 7243, 7244.

19. Fray Nicolás de Jesús Belando, *Historia civil de España desde el año de 1700 hasta el de 1733*, 3 vols., Madrid 1740–4, I, p.207.

20. Kamen, *The War of Succession in Spain*, op. cit., p.99.

21. Juan Amor de Soria, *Aragonesismo austracista (1734–1742)*, Saragossa 2000, p.125. For names of some political exiles, Virginia León Sanz, *Entre Austrias y Borbones. El archiduque Carlos y la monarquía (1700–1714)*, Madrid 1993, pp.184–7.

22. Amor de Soria, op. cit., p.94.

23. Cited by Antonio Domínguez Ortiz, *Sociedad y Estado en el siglo XVIII español*, Barcelona 1976, p.95.

24. Henry Kamen, 'Melchor de Macanaz and the Foundations of Bourbon Power in Spain', in Henry Kamen, *Crisis and Change in Early Modern Spain*, London 1993.

25. Carmen Martín Gaite, *Macanaz, otro paciente de la Inquisición*, Madrid 1975, comments that Macanaz's handwritten memoirs 'are in the possession of Don Francisco Maldonado, who has refused to let me consult them': p.344. The same gentleman also refused me permission to look at the papers, on the excuse that the villa where they are housed had no light or water. It will soon be three centuries since the memoirs were written. The question is, will they survive this deliberate neglect?

26. Ibid., p.307.

27. Ibid., p.439.

28. In *Cultural Albacete*, Jan. 1985, no.12.

29. Amor de Soria, op. cit., p.89.

30. Cf. Henry Kamen, *Philip V of Spain. The king who reigned twice*, New Haven, Conn. and London 2001.

31. Archivo Histórico Nacional, Madrid, Estado leg.2530 no.139.

32. Cf. Teófanes Egido, *Opinión pública y oposición al poder en la España del siglo XVIII (1713–1759)*, Valladolid 1971, p.148: 'The loss of respect for king Philip, who had been sacred till then, was the central fact marking the change of direction in criticisms made against the government.'

33. See his *Memorias (1921–1936)*, Madrid 1974. For Madariaga, the other great misfortune (for Spain) was the discovery of America.

34. H. Schilling, 'Confessional migration', in *Le migrazioni in Europa sec. XIII–XVIII*, Istituto F. Datini, Florence 1994, p.175.

35. Andrew Pettegree, 'Protestant migration during the early modern period', in *Le migrazioni*, op. cit., p.447.

36. Fred A. Norwood, *The Reformation Refugees as an Economic Force*, Chicago 1942.

37. H. Schilling, 'Innovation through migration: the settlements of Calvinistic Netherlanders in 16th and 17th century central and western Europe', *Histoire Sociale – Social History*, 16, 1983.

38. Among very many studies, cf. J. N. Hillgarth, *The Mirror of Spain, 1500–1700*, Ann Arbor 2000, which shows how foreigners saw Spain.

39. Willughby, p.497.

40. One example is the correspondence of Justus Lipsius with Spaniards: Alejandro Ramírez, *Epistolario de Justo Lipsio y los españoles (1577–1606)*, St Louis, Mo. 1967.

41. For an overview of the low level of Latin in Spain, see Luis Gil Fernández, *Panorama social del humanismo español (1500–1800)*, Madrid 1981.

42. Macanaz, cited in Henry Kamen, *Spain in the Later Seventeenth Century 1665–1700*, London 1980, p.313.

43. Willughby, p.474.

44. James Boswell, *The Life of Samuel Johnson*, 2 vols., London 1949, I, p.226.

45. Sarrailh, pp.337–72.

46. 'There were practically no writings about utopias in Spain': Torrecilla, p.19.

47. 'By "Europe" one means an abstraction usually embodied in France': Torrecilla, p.53.

48. Cited in Kamen, *The War of Succession*, op. cit., p.392.

49. Quoted in Sarrailh, p.373.

50. Cotarelo y Mori, p.580.

51. Cotarelo y Mori, p.389.

52. José Antonio Valero, 'Razón y nación en la política cultural del primer dieciocho', *Espéculo, Revista de estudios literarios*, no.22, 2002.

53. Quoted by Teófanes Egido, 'La expulsión de los jesuitas de España', in R. García-Villoslada, ed., *Historia de la Iglesia en España*, vol. IV, Madrid 1979, p.750.

54. The following details come from E. Jiménez, ed., *Expulsión y Exilio de los jesuitas españoles*, Alicante 1997.

55. J. F. de Isla, *Memorial en nombre de las cuatro provincias españolas de la Compañía de Jesús desterradas del Reino a S.M. el Rey D. Carlos III*, Alicante 1999.

56. Batllori, p.62.

57. Sarrailh, p.627.

58. Ibid., p.365.

59. Carr, p.71.

60. Defourneaux, pp.476-91.

61. Ibid., p.327.

62. I take the details that follow from Manuela Moreno, 'Breve biografía de Olavide', in *Inquisición española. Nuevas aproximaciones*, Madrid 1987.

63. Sarrailh, p.622, who cites also the opinion of the French scholar Morel-Fatio.

64. The biographical details that follow come principally from Manfredi.

65. Many of the drawings are reproduced in Cutter.

66. Malaspina's journal is edited by Andrew David et al., *The Malaspina Expedition 1789-1794: The journal of the voyage by Alejandro Malaspina*, 3 vols., London 2002-5.

67. Manfredi, p.77.

68. Pimentel, p.376.

69. Manfredi, p.78.

70. Cf. Pimentel, p.385.

71. Cutter, p.139.

72. Carr, p.106.

73. See ibid., p.109.

74. Quoted ibid.

5. ROMANTIC SPAIN

1. Luis Barbastro Gil, *Los afrancesados. Primera emigración política del siglo XIX español (1813–1820)*, Madrid 1993, p.11.
2. Miguel Artola, *Los afrancesados*, Madrid 1976, pp.53–5.
3. Barbastro Gil, op. cit., pp.39, 52.
4. 'They borrowed little from France, their outlook was shaped by English philosophy and Prussian political theory': Artola, op. cit., p.51.
5. *Memorias de D. Antonio Galiano*, (on-line) chap. XI.
6. There is a brief study by Juan Rico Giménez, *De la Ilustración al Liberalismo (Juan Sempere y Guarinos)*, Alicante 1997.
7. Rinaldo Froldi, 'Carlos III y la Ilustración en Sempere y Guarinos', in the collective book *La literatura española de la Ilustración*, Madrid 1989, pp.21–38.
8. Llorens 1968, p.240.
9. On Flórez Estrada, see the articles in the journal *Historia constitucional*, no.5, 2004.
10. Antoni Puigblanch, *La Inquisición sin Máscara*, Barcelona 1988, with a preface by Joan Abelló, p.488.
11. Now in the Bowes Museum, Barnard Castle, County Durham.
12. Joël Saugnieux, *Le Jansénisme espagnol du XVIIIe siècle*, Oviedo 1975, p.119.
13. In a traditional Catholic society such as Spain, respect for the Host – the wafer representing the body of Christ – was such that people stepped back when it was carried through the street by priests, and fell to their knees in worship.
14. For the last years of the Inquisition, see the documented study by Luis Alonso Tejada, *Ocaso de la Inquisición en los últimos años del reinado de Fernando VII*, Madrid 1969.
15. Llorente, p.114.
16. See the introduction by Gerard Dufour to his edition of the *Memoria histórica*, Paris 1977.
17. Llorente, p.124.
18. Dufour, pp.141–2.
19. Ibid., p.351.
20. Ibid., pp.318–28.
21. Llorente, p.134.
22. Menéndez Pelayo, VI, pp.18–19.
23. My impression is that there is not a single textual reference to Lea in any of the books published on the Inquisition in Spain before 1983, when a Spanish translation of his work was finally brought out in Madrid.

24. Jacques Fauque and Ramón Villanueva, *Goya y Burdeos 1824-1828*, Saragossa 1982, p.71.

25. From February to May 2006 the Frick Collection in New York put on an unprecedented exhibition of 'Goya's Last Works', showing approximately fifty works by the artist related to his period of exile.

26. Fauque and Villanueva, op. cit., p.132.

27. Cf. Robert Hughes, *Goya*, New York 2003, p.395.

28. Sánchez Mantero, p.15.

29. Radomski, p.2, sheds new light on his origins and early life.

30. Ibid., p.194.

31. Ibid., p.197.

32. Ibid., p.xiii.

33. Quoted in Pierre L. Ullman, *Mariano de Larra and Spanish Political Rhetoric*, Madison, Wisc. 1971, p.25.

34. Quoted in Torrecilla, p.56.

35. Llorens 1968, p.215.

36. And also from Scott's novel *The Pirate* (1821).

37. Tinterow and Lacambre, p.358.

38. Ibid., p.11.

39. Ibid., p.38.

40. Llorens 1989, p.71.

41. Nino Rodríguez, p.14.

42. A wonderful book could be done on the life of the exiles in Paris.

43. Peers, I, p.105.

44. Philip W. Silver, *Ruin and Restitution. Reinterpreting Romanticism in Spain*, Nashville 1997, p.25.

45. Quoted in Llorens 1989, p.144.

46. Samuel A. Dunham, *The History of Spain and Portugal*, 5 vols., Philadelphia 1832.

47. J. S. Pérez-Garzón, *Modesto Lafuente, artífice de la Historia de España*, Pamplona 2002, p.70.

48. Ibid., p.79.

49. Quoted in Llorens 1968, p.410.

50. For much that follows, I rely on Murphy.

51. *Autobiography* (1845).

52. Vicente Llorens, ed., *José María Blanco White, Antología de obras en español*, Barcelona 1971, p.320.

53. Tony Cross, *Joseph Blanco White. Stranger and pilgrim*, Liverpool 1984, p.37.

54. Llorens 1968, p.23.

55. Murphy, p.123.

56. Ibid., p.205.

57. The following year Newman left the Anglican Church and joined the Catholic.

58. Apart from Llorens 1968, see Llorens, *Antología*, op. cit., and Juan Goytisolo, *Obra inglesa de Blanco White*, Barcelona 1972, revised 1998.

59. Daniel Rivadulla et al., eds., *El Exilio español en América en el siglo XIX*, Madrid 1992, p.328.

60. Rafael Rodríguez-Moñino, *El exilio carlista en la España del XIX*, Madrid 1984, p.67.

61. Carr, p.188.

6. SEARCHING FOR A NATIONAL IDENTITY

1. Hess 1991, p.35.

2. Cited by J. M. Díez Borque, *La Sociedad española y los viajeros del siglo XVII*, Madrid 1975.

3. Townsend, I, p.230.

4. Fusi, p.172.

5. Valera 1984, p.153.

6. A listing of Spanish artists who went to Paris is given in the volume by Carlos González and Montse Martí, *Pintores españoles en Paris (1850–1900)*, Barcelona 1989.

7. Christophe Charle, *Paris fin de siècle: Culture et politique*, Paris 1998, p.44.

8. Carr, p.265.

9. Ortega y Gasset, *España invertebrada*, Madrid 1964, p.64.

10. Ironically, the first modern Spanish scholar to make a profound study of the Krausist movement was an exile, Juan López-Morillas (d.1997), who spent all his working life at Brown University. His book *El krausismo español*, 1956, is still the best approach to the subject (English edition, *The Krausist Movement and Ideological Change in Spain, 1854–1874*, Cambridge 1981).

11. Carr, p.470; I have retouched the quotation.

12. Gayana Jurkevich, 'Defining Castile in literature and art: institucionalismo, the Generation of 98, and the origins of modern Spanish landscape', *Revista Hispánica Moderna*, 67, 1994.

13. Laín Entralgo, p.48.

14. Carr, p.472.

15. E. Inman Fox, 'Unamuno, Ganivet y la identidad nacional', in David T. Gies, ed., *Negotiating Past and Present*, Charlottesville, Va. 1997.

16. Cf. J. L. Marfany, 'Minority languages and literary revivals', *Past and Present*, 184, 2004.

17. Vicente Cacho Viu, 'Catalonian modernism and cultural nationalism', in Godzich and Spadaccini, p.233.

18. Daniel-Henry Kahnweiler, *Juan Gris. His life and work*, New York 1968, p.46.

19. Emmanuel Bréon, *Juan Gris à Boulogne*, Paris 1992, p.85.

20. James Thrall, *Juan Gris*, New York 1958, is the excellent catalogue of the exhibition.

21. Juan Antonio Gaya-Nuno, *Juan Gris*, Barcelona and Boston 1975, p.7.

22. Quoted in *Angel Ganivet, 1898–1998*, Granada 1998, p.75.

23. Angel Ganivet, *Idearium español*, Madrid 1964, pp.132, 45, 116, 54.

24. Ganivet and Unamuno.

25. Valera, 1984, p.14.

26. Ibid., pp.55, 72.

27. Valera 1946, p.197.

28. Ibid., p.265.

29. The best short study of the Disaster and Spanish politics is Balfour.

30. Cited in Pike, p.39.

31. Antonio Ramos-Gascón, 'Spanish literature as a historiographic invention: the case of the Generation of 1898', in Godzich and Spadaccini.

32. Azorín, *Clasicos y Modernos*, 6th edn, Buenos Aires 1939, p.177.

33. The best short guides are Balfour, chap. 3 and Carr, chap. 12.

34. The first Spaniard to win the Nobel Prize (in 1904) was the dramatist José Echegaray.

35. See J. M. Sánchez Ron, 'Más allá del laboratorio: Cajal y el regeneracionismo a través de la ciencia', in Molas, pp.350, 353.

36. 'Reglas y Consejos', in *Obras literarias completas*, Madrid 1947, pp.625–6.

37. I take the quote from Balfour, p.94.

38. Christophe Charle, *Les Intellectuels en Europe au XIXe siècle*, Paris 1996, in particular p.256. Cf. Eric Storm, 'The rise of the Intellectual around 1900: Spain and France', *European Historical Quarterly*, 32, 2, 2002. Storm gives references to recent French and Spanish essays on this theme. A valuable analysis is given by José Alvarez Junco, 'Los intelectuales: anticlericalismo y republicanismo', in *Los Orígenes culturales de la II República*, Madrid 1993. A recent detailed discussion is that by Santos Juliá, *Historia de las dos Españas*, Madrid 2004.

39. Charle, *Les Intellectuels*, op. cit., p.255.

40. Quoted in Ouimette, I, p.10.

41. Valverde 1975, p.213.

42. *Azorín–Unamuno. Cartas y Escritos complementarios*, Valencia 1990, p.182.

43. Ouimette, I, p.201.

44. Ibid., I, p.210.

45. Ibid., I, p.269.

46. Defourneaux, p.85.

47. Julio Caro Baroja, *Razas, pueblos y linajes*, Madrid 1957, pp.263–92.

48. Only passing reference is made in this book to the notion of 'empire', which would take us well beyond the main argument.

49. Gómez-Santos 1971, p.23.

50. Morán, p.41.

51. The most thorough analysis of Spanish attention to the novel is Anthony Close, *The Romantic Approach to Don Quixote*, Cambridge 1978. For a comment and clarifications, see Carlos M. Gutiérrez, 'Cervantes, un proyecto de modernidad para el Fin de Siglo (1880–1905)', *Cervantes: Bulletin of the Cervantes Society of America*, 19, 1999.

52. Ganivet and Unamuno.

53. E. Storm, 'El tercer centenario del *Don Quijote* en 1905 y el nacionalismo español', *Hispania*, 199, 1998.

54. Cited in Pike, p.57.

55. Ramón y Cajal, pp.1292–5.

56. Lucas Mallada, *La futura revolución española*, Madrid 1998, p.104.

57. Cited in *Cervantes: Bulletin of the Cervantes Society of America*, 22, 2002, p.207.

58. Tess Knighton, 'Northern influence on cultural developments in the Iberian peninsula during the fifteenth century', *Renaissance Studies*, I, i, 1987.

59. Spain today has official state music but no national anthem. At one event in the Olympic Games in Australia in 2000, the organizers could find no anthem to play for a winning Spanish team, and by mistake ordered the band to play the nineteenth-century Liberal *Hymn of Riego*.

60. *The New Grove Dictionary of Music and Musicians*, vol.24, p.130.

61. Cf. Marco, p.90.

62. J. Parakilas, 'What to do about Carmen?', *International Hispanic Music Study Group Newsletter*, vol.4, no.2, 1998.

63. Cited in Hess 2001, p.170.

64. Iberni, p.29.

65. Ibid., p.81.

66. J. Lloyd Webber, *Song of the Birds. Sayings, stories and impressions of Pablo Casals*, London 1985, p.25.

67. Cf. L. Charnon-Deutsch, *The Spanish Gypsy: The history of a European obsession*, University Park, Pa. 2004

68. Quoted in Walter Aaron Clark, *Isaac Albéniz. Portrait of a Romantic*, Oxford 1999, p.65.

69. Quoted ibid., p.112.

70. Ibid., p.81.

71. Romero, p.45.

72. Ibid., p.43.

73. Ibid., p.49.

74. Clark, p.290.

75. Quoted in Hess 1991, p.10.

76. Ibid., p.35.

77. Marco, p.8.

7. THE ELITE DIASPORA OF 1936–9

1. Quoted in Gómez-Santos 1971, p.23.

2. Quoted in Ouimette, I, p.47.

3. Payne, 1993, p.59.

4. Ibid., pp.274–5, citing studies by Javier Tusell.

5. Casanova, pp.150–1, outlines the role of the anarchists during these crucial months.

6. Stanley G. Payne, *El Colapso de la República. Los orígenes de la Guerra Civil (1933–1936)*, Madrid 2005.

7. Cf. Juliá, p.98. There are several versions of what happened on this occasion.

8. Fraser, p.208.

9. Gómez-Santos 1983, p.214.

10 Pio Baroja, *La Guerra Civil en la Frontera*, Madrid 2005. I take my quotes from the useful extracts published in *El País*, 26 June 2005.

11. Ouimette, I, p.66.

12. Quoted in Ouimette, I, p.65.

13. Because of subsequent events, the play was first staged only in 1945, in Buenos Aires.

14. In Russian, 'special commission', with the initials 'Ch. K.' (*chrezvichainii komitet*).

15. Juliá, p.133.

16. José Luis Alfaya, *Como un río de fuego. Madrid, 1936*, Barcelona 1998, p.83.

17. Ronald Radosh, Mary Radosh Habeck and Grigory Sevostianov, *Spain*

Betrayed: The Soviet Union in the Spanish Civil War, New Haven, Conn. 2001, p.223, document 46.

18. The book edited by Juliá is the most rounded, though not necessarily reliable, summary of the question.

19. Juliá, chap. IV.

20. Quoted in Payne 2004, p.117.

21. Quoted in Martín, p.65.

22. Quoted in Payne 1993, p.347.

23. Alberti, p.302.

24. Gómez-Santos 1983, p.122.

25. Cited in Morán, p.59.

26. Ibid., p.70.

27. Cited ibid., p.80.

28. Cf. Gómez-Santos 1983, p.13.

29. The date 1939 figures prominently in virtually all studies, beginning with the highly unsatisfactory work edited by J. L. Abellán, *El Exilio español de 1939*, 6 vols., Madrid 1976–78.

30. Jiménez 1985, p.320.

31. Camprubí, I, p.12.

32. Jiménez 1985, p.160.

33. Ibid., p.161.

34. Cf. Kathleen M. Glenn, *Azorín*, Boston 1981, pp.76–82.

35. Valverde 1971, p.361.

36. Quoted in Ouimette, I, p.459.

37. Gómez-Santos 1983, pp.81–2.

38. I follow the scheme given in Rubio, I, chap. 2.

39. Ralph Fox, *Portugal Now*, London 1937, cited by Douglas L. Wheeler, 'La invasión española: los españoles en Portugal (1931–1939)', in an offprint of 1988 kindly presented to me by Mr Wheeler.

40. David Wingate Pike, *Spaniards in the Holocaust*, London 2000.

41. Cf. Fraser, pp.433, 437.

42. Paul Tabori, *The Anatomy of Exile*, London 1972, p.383. In another source, the number of children sent to the Soviet Union is given as 2,895, with some 225 still alive in Russia in the year 2004.

43. Marañón 1984, p.130.

44. Bosch-Gimpera's role in the executions carried out by the Republic in Barcelona during the Civil War, has provoked critical commentaries.

45. We shall refer to the theme of 'consequences' in Chapter 10.

46. An excellent anthology of his work is *The Selected Poems of Miguel Hernández*, ed. Ted Genoways, Chicago 2001.

47. Machado, p.78.

48. Cited Valverde 1975, p.270.

49. Quoted in Jiménez 1999, p.6.

50. *Poetry of Cernuda*, New York 1971, p.169.

51. Casals, p.230.

52. Payne 2004, p.337.

53. All the quotations here come from *Cartes de Carles Riba*, 3 vols., Barcelona 1991, vol. II, 1939–52. I give no page numbers, to save excessive citation.

54. *Historia General de la Emigración*, I, p.541.

55. F. Vilanova, 'Exiliats catalans sota Vichy', *L'Avenç*, no.293, July–Aug. 2004.

56. *Memorias (1921–1936)*, Madrid 1974, p.566.

57. Salvador de Madariaga, *Spain. A modern history*, New York 1958, p.692.

58. Arturo Barea, *The Forging of a Rebel*, London 2001, p.ix.

59. Cited in Luis Monferrer, 'La colaboración de Arturo Barea en la BBC', in Aznar, I, p.163.

60. Ugarte, p.12.

61. Vicente Aleixandre, *Epistolario*, Madrid 1986, p.19. Letter of September 1939.

62. Ibid., p.128.

63. He was baptized 'Pablo', but later in life reverted to the Catalan form 'Pau'.

64. The quotes that follow are from his *Joys and Sorrows*.

65. Kirk, p.401.

66. Ibid., p.398.

67. *The New Grove*, vol. 9, pp.690, 695.

68. E. F. Granell, *Picasso's Guernica. The end of a Spanish era*, Ann Arbor, Mich. 1981, p.7.

69. Among the many studies on *Guernica*, see Hensbergen. Some of the material in my discussion is derived from a review by J. Hoberman in *The Nation*, 24 Nov. 2004.

70. For minotaur symbolism, the stages of the painting and imagery, see Herschel B. Chipp, *Picasso's Guernica*, Berkeley 1988.

71. Hensbergen, p.266.

72. Quoted ibid., p.303.

73. I follow the perceptive presentation of Faber, pp.130–5.

74. Caudet, p.26.

75. Dreyfus-Armand, pp.273–4.

76. Faber, p.45.

77. Francisco Caudet, 'Dialogizar el exilio', in Aznar, I, p.46.

78. Faber, p.137.

79. *Cuadernos americanos*, 8, vol.43, Jan.–Feb. 1949, pp.36, 49.

80. *España Peregrina*, no.7, in Caudet, p.101.

81. Cited in Faber, p.197.

82. Keller, pp.12, 212.

83. Quoted in Ouimette, II, p.431.

84. Notably the study by J. H. Elliott, *The Count Duke of Olivares*, New Haven, Conn. and London 1986.

85. Ouimette, II, pp.394, 397.

86. Quoted in Gómez-Santos 1971, p.346.

87. Quoted in Keller, p.207. The work in question was Miguel Artola's *Los Afrancesados*.

88. Américo Castro, *The Spaniards. An introduction to their history*, Berkeley 1971, p.4.

89. Gómez-Santos 1971, p.348.

90. Gregorio Marañón, *Liberalisme et Communisme. En marge de la guerre civile espagnole*, Paris 1938, p.25.

91. Lee Catterall, *The Great Dali Art Fraud*, New Jersey 1992, p.35.

92. Alberti, p.164.

93. For Alberti's poetry of this period, see Judith Nantell, *Rafael Alberti's Poetry of the Thirties*, Athens, Ga. 1986.

94. Quoted in Manuel Bayo, *Sobre Alberti*, Madrid 1974, p.53.

95. *Poesías Completas*, Buenos Aires 1961, p.982.

96. 'Poemas de Punta del Este' (1945–56), no.11, in *The Other Shore. 100 Poems by Rafael Alberti*, San Francisco 1981.

97. Alberti, *Roma, peligro para caminantes*, Barcelona 1976, p.17.

98. Holguin, p.223.

99. Cited in ibid., p.131.

100. Victor Fuentes, 'El exilio creador de Buñuel: su periplo norteamericano', in Naharro-Calderón.

101. Quoted by Bryan M. Papciak, in *Sync: The Regent Journal of Film and Video* (1993).

102. *El País*, 5 June 1994.

8. THE SEARCH FOR ATLANTIS

1. Jiménez 1988, p.47.

2. Jacint Verdaguer, *Atlántida*, Barcelona 1955, p.177.

3. Diana de Armas Wilson, 'The matter of America', in Marina S. Brownlee

and Hans Ulrich Gumbrecht, eds., *Cultural Authority in Golden Age Spain*, Baltimore 1995.

4. Ida Altman and James Horn, *'To Make America'. European emigration in the early modern period*, Berkeley 1992, p.3.

5. Auke P. Jacobs gives a good summary of a convincing argument in 'Las migraciones españolas a América dentro de una perspectiva europea, 1500–1700', in Jan Lechner, ed., *España y Holanda*, Amsterdam and Atlanta, Ga. 1995.

6. The authoritative survey of Spanish emigration is the *Historia General de la Emigración*. A short survey is Germán Rueda Hernanz, *Españoles emigrantes en América (siglos XVI–XX)*, Madrid 2000.

7. Otte, p.526.

8. Tamar Herzog, 'Private organizations as global networks in early modern Spain and Spanish America', in L. Roniger and T. Herzog, *The Collective and the Public in Latin America. Cultural identities and political order*, Brighton 2000, p.121.

9. Otte, p.307.

10. Ibid., p.124.

11. Isabela Macías and Francisco Morales Padrón, *Cartas desde América 1700–1800*, Seville 1991, p.187.

12. *Historia General de la Emigración*, I, pp.180, 183.

13. Walter Nugent, *Crossings. The great transatlantic migrations, 1870–1914*, Bloomington, Ind. 1992, p.104.

14. Blanca Sanchez Alonso, *Las causas de la emigración española 1880–1930*, Madrid 1995, p.83.

15. *Historia General de la Emigración*, I, p.447.

16. Dreyfus-Armand, p.20.

17. Andrés Sorel, *40 Mundo. Emigración Española en Europa*, Madrid 1974. The relevant term here is 'active'. In terms of the overall labour force, the proportion of guest workers was probably nearer 10 per cent.

18. Blanco White, *Autobiografía*.

19. Ganivet and Unamuno.

20. Isabel Santaolalla, 'Ethnic and racial configurations in contemporary Spanish culture', in Jo Labanyi, *Constructing Identity in Contemporary Spain*, Oxford 2002, p.67.

21. Valera 1946, p.265.

22. Cf. Ucelay-Da Cal, *passim*.

23. The great success of the popular historical novels of the writer Pérez Reverte is due in part to his fictionalized – and national-imperialist – rendering of Spain's imperial role.

24. The exceptions, naturally, were those who found themselves in the United States during the Civil War, and chose to stay there.

25. John T. Reid, *Spanish American Images of the United States*, Gainesville 1977, p.59.

26. Ibid., p.124.

27. Ramiro Reig, *Vicente Blasco Ibáñez*, Madrid 2002, p.194.

28. Vicente Ribelles, *Vicente Blasco Ibáñez*, Madrid 1967, p.24.

29. Cf. Pike, p.6.

30. A useful summary of his career is Alistair Hennessy, 'Ramiro de Maeztu: *hispanidad* and the search for a surrogate imperialism', in Harrison and Hoyle.

31. Ricardo Landeira, *Ramiro de Maeztu*, Boston 1978, p.36.

32. Madariaga, pp.140, 151.

33. I rely in part here on the very balanced study by Landeira, op. cit.

34. See Ucelay-Da Cal.

35. Pérez Villanueva, p.342.

36. Ugarte, p.56.

37. An excellent, albeit officially sponsored, survey of the Spanish exiles from the Mexican viewpoint is given in *El Exilio Español*.

38. Cf. *Historia General de la Emigración*, I, p.458.

39. Clara E. Lida, in *Historia General de la Emigración*, I, p.726.

40. Pérez Villanueva, p.348.

41. *España Peregrina*, no.5, p.229, cited in Caudet, p.96.

42. *España Peregrina*, in various issues, cited in Caudet, pp.26, 33, 58, 109.

43. Sebastiaan Faber, 'Between Cernuda's Paradise and Buñuel's Hell: Mexico through Spanish eyes', *Bulletin of Spanish Studies*, vol.80, 2, 2003, p.223.

44. Faber, p.xi.

45. http://dieumsnh.qfb.umich.mx/madridmexico/espa%C3%B1a_en_el_imaginario.htm

46. Robert Surroca, *Premsa catalana de l'exili i de l'emigració*, Barcelona 2004.

47. Albert Manent, *La literature catalana a l'exili*, Barcelona 1989.

48. Mitchell A. Codding, 'Archer Milton Huntington, champion of Spain in the United States', in Kagan, p.145.

49. Ibid., p.147.

50. *Sorolla*, p.380.

51. Coll, pp.127, 481.

52. Federico Onís, *España en América*, Madrid 1955, p.20.

53. In Kornberg et al., p.1.

54. Arthur Kornberg, *For the Love of Enzymes. The odyssey of a biochemist*, Boston 1989, p.50.

55. Strictly speaking, Ochoa belongs to the USA not Spain, which explains why in a recent *Diccionario biográfico sobre científicos españoles* his name is not included, since he was not a Spanish national.

56. Jiménez 2004, p.21.

57. Alberti, p.206

58. Cited in Casanova, p.97 n.35.

59. Vived, p.326.

60. Ibid., p.357.

61. Ibid., p.527.

62. *José María Sert 1874–1945*, Madrid 1987, p.200.

63. Madariaga, p.161.

64. Cf. Jaume Freixa, *Josep Lluís Sert*, Barcelona 1991, p.161 for a quick perspective.

65. Quoted in Küster, p.31.

66. Cited in Hess 2001, p.69.

67. Hess 2005, p.121. 'The Black Legend', the title of a Castilian nationalist book published in 1914, became a phrase applied to any opinion that was deemed to be critical of Spain.

68. Ibid., pp.138–46.

69. Ibid., p.218.

70. Starkie, II, p.128.

71. This is the suggestion of Tomás Marco, p.27.

72. Madariaga, p.178.

73. Cf. Crichton, pp.79–80.

74. Jiménez 1973, p.212.

75. Jiménez 1999.

9. HISPANIC IDENTITY AND THE PERMANENCE OF EXILE

1. Eugenio Hostos, *La Peregrinación de Bayoán*, Río Piedras 1970, p.86.

2. Roger P. Davis, 'The Odyssey of Identity: Culture and Politics in the Evolution of Latin American Nationalism', *Platte Valley Review*, 15, 1, 1987.

3. The first Spanish leader openly to support the USA, to the bewilderment of his nation, was the recent prime minister, Aznar. The voters got rid of him at the polls and opted for an anti-American policy under the Socialists.

4. I am grateful to Luce López-Baralt for calling my attention to the importance of Betances.

5. Hostos, op. cit., p.86.

6. Ibid., p.176.

7. Eugenio Hostos, *Obras Completas*, 2 vols. San Juan 1990, II, pp.39–46.

8. Quoted in John D. Perivolaris, 'Popular and intellectual responses to 1898 in Puerto Rico', in Harrison and Hoyle, p.270.

9. Joseph P. Fitzpatrick, *Puerto Rican Americans. The meaning of migration to the mainland*, 2nd edn, New Jersey 1987, p.4.

10. Duany, pp.33, 234.

11. Lillian Guerra, *Popular Expression and National Identity in Puerto Rico. The struggle for self, community and nation*, Gainesville, Fla. 1998.

12. Quoted in Stavans, p.10.

13. Ibid., p.43.

14. Duany, p.186.

15. Glasser, pp.156, 163.

16. Ibid., p.202.

17. Quoted in Teresa Justicia, 'Exile as permanent pain', in Alegria and Ruffinell.

18. The central figure in the Café is Miguel Algarín (b.1941 in Santurce in Puerto Rico). The Café functions at 236 East 3rd St.

19. Cf. the interview with Miguel Algarín in Carmen Dolores Hernández, *Puerto Rican Voices in English*, Westport, Conn. 1997.

20. Quoted in Eugene V. Mohr, *The Nuyorican Experience*, Westport, Conn. 1982, p.96.

21. Pedro Salinas and Jorge Guillén, *Correspondencia 1923–1951*, Barcelona 1992, p.171.

22. Newman, pp.158, 210.

23. The initials Afda stood for 'Asociación Fraternal de Amigos'.

24. Pedro Salinas, *Poesía*, Madrid 1971.

25. Quoted in Newman, p.229.

26. K. M. Sibbald, ed., *Guillén at McGill*, Ottawa 1996, p.28.

27. Jiménez 1973, pp.133, 134.

28. Graciela Palau de Nemes, 'El fondo del exilio de Juan Ramón Jiménez', in Naharro-Calderón, p.244.

29. Cited in Antonio Portero, *Zenobia Camprubí*, Moguer 2000, p.60.

30. Quoted in Jiménez 1988, p.46.

31. Baldock, p.219.

32. Marta Casals later moved to New York and pursued a distinguished career directing musical foundations until her retirement in 2005. She remarried (1975), her husband was the pianist Eugene Istomin (d.2003).

33. Dr Diego Cisteller, cited in Kamen 1993[b], p.365.

34. Enrique Otero Lana, *Los corsarios españoles durante la decadencia de los Austrias*, Madrid 1992, p.109.

35. My wife remembers how her grandmother, in the days when television first arrived in Catalonia, used to watch the screen happily for hours even though she did not understand a word of the language (Castilian) being spoken.

36. Holden Furber, *Rival Empires of Trade in the Orient 1600–1800*, Minneapolis 1976, p.298.

37. Andrew B. Gonzalez, 'Studies on language and society in the Philippines: state of the art', *International Journal of the Sociology of Language*, 88, 1991, pp.5–18.

38. Quoted in Anthony Pagden, *Spanish Imperialism and the Political Imagination*, New Haven, Conn. and London 1990, p.58.

39. Cf. Miguel Angel Ochoa Brun, *Historia de la diplomacia española*, 6 vols., Madrid 1999, IV, p.502.

40. Didier Ozanam, 'La diplomacia de los primeros Borbones (1714–1759)', *Cuadernos de Investigación Histórica*, no.6, p.182.

41. When I began my historical studies in Spain at the Residencia de Estudiantes in Madrid, I spoke no Spanish and the only language in which I could communicate was French. I was gratified to find that several Spanish scholars in the Residencia had no problem speaking French with me. Nobody, however, spoke English.

42. M. J. Martínez Alcalde, *Las ideas lingüísticas de Gregorio Mayáns*, Valencia 1992, pp.243–4.

43. Quoted in Küster, p.29 n.59.

44. Camprubí, II, p.25.

45. Cited in Urpi Montoya Uriarte, 'Hispanismo e Indigenismo: o dualismo cultural no pensamento social peruano (1900–1930)', *Revista de Antropología*, vol.41, no.1, 1998.

46. Valle and Gabriel-Stheeman, p.113.

47. Ibid., p.6.

48. *El Mundo*, Madrid, 18 Nov. 2004.

49. Cited in Pike, pp.32, 34.

50. Cited ibid., p.135.

51. Cited ibid., p.144.

52. There is an active debate about the acceptability of Spanglish in public life. A viewpoint favourable to it is that of Ilan Stavans, *Spanglish: The making of a new American language*, New York 2003.

53. A short survey of the multiple issues raised by Spanglish can be found in the detached survey by Joaquín Garrido, 'Spanglish, Spanish and English', in

a lecture given at Amherst College, April 2004, http://www.amherst.edu/
~spanglish/garrido.htm

10. THE RETURN OF THE EXILES

1. Max Aub, *Teatro Completo*, Mexico 1968, p.1006.
2. A different aspect of social reality, namely 'discrimination' rather than
'expulsion', is discussed for the pre-industrial period in Augustin Redondo,
ed., *Les problèmes de l'exclusion en Espagne (XVe–XVIIe siècles)*, Paris
1983.
3. Quoted in Menéndez Pidal, p.204.
4. Ramón y Cajal, p.647; Marañón 1947, p.20.
5. Menéndez Pidal, p.132.
6. José Antonio Maravall, *Estado moderno y mentalidad social, siglos XV a
XVII*, 2 vols., Madrid 1972, I, pp.472, 478.
7. A. Rodríguez Moñino, 'Viaje a oriente de Fr. Diego de Mérida', *Analecta
Sacra Tarraconensa*, XVIII, 1945, p.138.
8. Cited in Teresa de Castro, 'L'émergence d'une identité alimentaire: musul-
mans et chrétiens dans le royaume de Grenade', in M. Bruegel and B.
Laurioux, *Histoire et Identités alimentaires en Europe*, Paris 2002.
9. Vives, p.356.
10. J. L. Vives, *Obras Completas*, 2 vols., Madrid 1948, I, pp.931, 959. The
dialogues referred to come from Vives' popular textbook *Exercitatis linguae
latinae*, of 1539.
11. Cited in Fernand Braudel, *The Identity of France*, vol.I, London 1988,
p.89.
12. Sarrailh, p.358.
13. Casas actually refers to 'terrapin' or tortoise, but I assume he was being
humorous about meat in general.
14. Coll, p.482.
15. Newman, p.34.
16. Anne J. Kershen, ed., *Food in the Migrant Experience*, Aldershot 2002.
17. Llorens 1968, p.59.
18. Cited in Duany, p.201.
19. Cf. Américo Castro, *El epistolario. Cartas a Juan Goytisolo 1968–1972*,
Valencia 1997, p.90.
20. Marañón 1947, p.30.
21. Gómez-Santos 1971, p.23.
22. Expressly not identified here.
23. Quoted in Clark, p.110.

24. Pérez Villanueva, p.469. Pidal's reference was to the half of Spain, the Falangists, who had split up yet further, with a new, more liberal half.

25. Ibid., p.349.

26. Work on the linguistic atlas was resumed in the 1950s and a first volume was published in 1962. Then the project was consigned to oblivion, and not resumed until in 1999 a Canadian professor, David Heap, located the dispersed materials and began cataloguing them.

27. Machado, p.163.

28. Menéndez Pidal, pp.204–45.

29. Juan Valera, *Disertaciones y Juicios literarios*, Madrid 1878, p.107, 'Del influjo de la Inquisición en la decadencia de la literatura española'.

30. Américo Castro, *España en su Historia*, Barcelona 1983, p.597.

31. John Elliott, *Imperial Spain*, Harmondsworth 1963, p.110.

32. Earl J. Hamilton, 'The Decline of Spain', *Economic History Review*, 8, 1938.

33. L. E. Otero Carvajal, 'La ciencia en España. Un balance del siglo XX', *Cuadernos de Historia Contemporánea*, 22, 2000.

34. Francisco Giral, *La ciencia española en el exilio. El exilio de los científicos españoles (1939–1989)*, Barcelona 1994. A recent analysis, by Magdalena Ortiz, suggests that 'for Spain the Republican emigration represented in qualitative terms a notable blood-letting' ('Los científicos del exilio español en México: un perfil', unpublished on-line article), but is unable to give any details of the scientific qualifications of the émigrés.

35. A columnist in the Barcelona daily *La Vanguardia*, commenting on an official European survey showing that among Europeans the Spaniards had the highest level (82 per cent) of ignorance of the English language, claimed (26 February 2005) that it was 'a legacy of the Franco regime'.

36. In the supplement *El Cultural* of the leading Spanish daily *El Mundo*, 20 January 2005, a writer maintained that the failure of Spain between 1940 and 2005 to produce historians of the calibre of foreigners like Gerald Brenan, Hugh Thomas and Raymond Carr was the fault of Franco.

37. There are, for example, no Spanish names for the period after the year 1500 in Bertrand Russell's *History of Western Philosophy*, London 1955.

38. J. L. Abellán, *Panorama de la filosofía española actual*, Madrid 1978.

39. J. M. López Piñero et al., *Materiales para la Historia de las Ciencias en España, s.XVI–XVII*, Valencia 1976, p.4.

40. Ganivet and Unamuno, letter to Unamuno, published in a Granada newspaper, 1898.

41. In Laín Entralgo, p.224.

42. Quoted in Keller, p.153.

43. Castro 1954, p.616.

44. Cf. the excellent studies of the Valencian scholar J. M. López Piñero, and his colleagues, on this theme.

45. Faustino Cordón, 'Estado actual de la ciencia española', in *La Cultura bajo el franquismo*, Barcelona 1977, p.263; Santesmases, p.15.

46. Quoted in Peers, II, p.269.

47. José Zorrilla, *Obras Completas*, 2 vols., Valladolid 1943, II, p.620.

48. Hess 2005, p.264.

49. Cf. Robin Cohen, 'Diasporas and the nation state: from victims to challengers', in Steven Vertovec and Robin Cohen, *Migration, Diasporas and Transnationalism*, Cheltenham 1999.

50. Cited in Llorens 1968, p.46.

51. Yosef Kaplan, 'The travels of Portuguese Jews from Amsterdam to the "lands of idolatry", 1644–1724', in Kaplan, ed., *Jews and Conversos. Studies in society and the Inquisition*, Jerusalem 1985.

52. This is the main argument of David Graizbord, *Souls in Dispute. Converso identities in Iberia and the Jewish Diaspora, 1580–1700*, Philadelphia 2004, pp.6–7.

53. Sachar, pp.398, 400.

54. Yosef Hayim Yerushalmi, 'Exile and Expulsion in Jewish history', in Gampel, pp.11–12.

55. Quoted in Al-Da'mi, p.167.

56. Batllori, p.61.

57. Ibid., p.79.

58. Quoted by Geneviève Dreyfus-Armand, 'Les cultures de l'exil espagnol en France', in Alted and Aznar, p.44.

59. Ebtehal Younes, 'La noción del exilio: el ejemplo de Jorge Semprun', in Alted and Aznar, p.256.

60. Cited in Soledad Fox, 'Exile and return: the many Madrids of Jorge Semprun', *Ciberletras: Revista de Crítica Literaria y de Cultura*, December 2003.

61. Figes, p.569.

62. Max Aub, *Diarios (1939–1972)*, Barcelona 1998, p.192.

63. *Antología de Relatos y Prosas Breves de Max Aub*, Mexico 1993, *El Remate*, p.261.

64. *El Exilio Español*, p.383.

65. 'Peregrino', in Barnette, p.66.

66. 'Díptico español', ibid., p.107.

67. Jorge Semprun, *Literature or Life*, New York 1996, p.150.

68. Quoted in Morán, p.33.

69. Cf. Morán, p.174 and following.

70. Cf. Peter Linehan, 'The court historiographer of Francoism?: *la leyenda oscura* of Ramón Menéndez Pidal', *Bulletin of Hispanic Studies*, 73, 1996.

71. Quoted ibid., p.442.

72. Valverde 1971, pp.393–4.

73. Victoria Kamhi, *Hand in Hand with Joaquín Rodrigo*, Pittsburgh, Pa. 1992, p.102.

74. Ibid., p.109.

75. Ibid., p.110.

76. Quoted in Gómez-Santos 1971, p.379.

77. Quoted in Pérez Villanueva, p.351.

78. Gómez-Santos 1983, p.100.

79. Madariaga, p.405.

80. The word 'prisoner' belongs to Joseph H. Silverman, in Rubia, p.162; the reference to the Widener is Castro's own.

81. Quoted in Faber, p.152.

82. I attended in Paris in 1963 a public meeting he addressed on the subject of democratic reforms in Spain.

83. Rubio, II, pp.768–9.

84. Aub, *Diarios*, op. cit., p.25.

85. Max Aub, *La gallina ciega*, Mexico 1971, p.197.

86. Aub, *Diarios*, p.520. Cela was the writer Camilo José Cela, who later gained a Nobel Prize.

87. Cited in J. L. de la Granja, 'Max Aub y Manuel Tuñón de Lara', in Aznar, I, p.496.

88. Cited by José Angel Saínz, 'El retorno de Max Aub o la poética de un imposible' (on-line article).

89. Quoted in Ilie, p.12.

90. Nigel Dennis, *José Bergamín. A critical introduction 1920–1936*, Toronto 1986, p.19.

91. In Saínz, op. cit.

92. Kilduff and Corley, p.6.

93. Santesmases, p.163.

94. Quoted in Kornberg et al., p.419.

95. I take these quotations from the article by J. M. Sánchez Ron in *Babelia*, 8 Oct. 2005.

96. Cited in Laín Entralgo, p.127.

97. Llorens 1968, p.42.

98. Cited in Saínz, op. cit.

99. Newman, p.209.

100. Cf. Michael Kenny, '"Which Spain?" The conservation of regionalism among Spanish emigrants and exiles', *Iberian Studies*, V, 2, 1976.

101. Cf. Figes, p.539.

102. Vives, p.298.

103. Ibid., p.480.

104. Valera, 1946, p.76.

105. Valera, 1984, pp.153, 162.

106. Ibid., p.120.

107. Riba, II, p.65.

108. Duany, p.167.

109. Derek Harris, ed., *Changing Times in Hispanic Culture*, Aberdeen 1996, p.2.

110. Cf. the diagram of Castilian books published abroad, in Kamen 1993[b], p.404.

111. Henry Thomas, 'The output of Spanish books in the sixteenth century', *The Library*, 1, 1920, p.30.

112. Jaime Moll, 'Problemas bibliográficas del libro del Siglo de Oro', *Boletín de la Real Academia Española*, 59, 1979; also his 'Valoración de la industria editorial española del siglo XVI', in *Livre et lecture en Espagne et en France sous l'Ancien Régime*, Paris 1981.

113. Jan Lechner, *Repertorio de obras de autores españoles en bibliotecas holandesas hasta comienzos del siglo XVIII*, Utrecht 2001.

114. Though London might also be mentioned, its role was considerably lessened by the barrier of the English language. By contrast, elite exiles communicated in French in Paris and in Spanish in the United States.

115. Cf. Eugen Weber, *France, fin de siècle*, Cambridge, Mass. 1986.

116. Quoted in Marcy E. Schwartz, 'Cultural Exile and the Canon', in Alegría and Ruffinelli, pp.195–6.

117. Ernesto Giménez Caballero, *Retratos españoles*, Madrid 1985, p.142.

118. Alfred Giner-Sorolla, 'Diaspora y conexión: el impacto de los científicos españoles en los Estados Unidos', in *Impacto y Futuro de la Civilización Española en el Nuevo Mundo*, Madrid 1991.

119. Kirk, p.542.

120. C. Grant MacCurdy, *Jorge Guillén*, Boston 1982, p.26.

121. The rendering of Boethius given here is mine.

122. This is a fascinating subject that will evidently not be discussed here at length. Among recent discussions, see Joseph Brodsky, 'The Condition we call Exile', *New York Review of Books*, 21 Jan. 1988; and John Glad, ed., *Literature in Exile*, Durham, NC 1990.

123. Madariaga, p.171.

124. Carol Hess suggests that the *Harpsichord Concerto* 'came to epitomize universalism in Spanish music' (Hess 2001, p.232), but the music critic Gilbert Chase considers it 'the most Spanish of all Falla's musical utterances'.

Index

Items that recur frequently (e.g. Madrid, Italy) are not indexed.